W9-BUH-862

Stephen A. Wynalda is a journalist, civil war buff, and freelance writer. His fiction has been nominated for the Pushcart Prize. He lives in Camby, Indiana.

Harry Turtledove has a doctorate in history from UCLA. He is the author of several scholarly articles and the translator of a Byzantine chronicle. He has taught at UCLA, Cal State Fullerton, and Cal State Los Angeles. He has been a fulltime writer since 1991. His work includes science fiction, fantasy, alternate history, and historical fiction. Among his novels are *The Guns of the South*, *How Few Remain*, *Fort Pillow*, and *Sentry Peak*, all of which deal in one way or another with the American Civil War and its aftermath. A lifelong Californian, he lives in Los Angeles. He is married to fellow author Laura Frankos. They have three daughters and the mandatory writers' cat.

366 DAYS IN

ABRAHAM LINCOLN'S PRESIDENCY

The Private, Political, and Military Decisions of America's Greatest President

STEPHEN A. WYNALDA

A Herman Graf Book
SKYHORSE PUBLISHING

Skyhorse Publishing books may be purchased in bulk at special discounts for sales promotion, corporate gifts, fund-raising, or educational purposes. Special editions can also be created to specifications. For details, contact the Special Sales Department, Skyhorse Publishing, 555 Eighth Avenue, Suite 903, New York, NY 10018 or info@skyhorsepublishing.com.

www.skyhorsepublishing.com

10 9 8 7 6 5 4 3 2

Library of Congress Cataloging-in-Publication Data

Wynalda, Stephen A.
366 days in Abraham Lincoln's presidency : the private, political, and military decisions of America's greatest president / Stephen A. Wynalda.
p. cm.
"A Herman Graf Book."
ISBN 978-1-60239-994-5
1. Lincoln, Abraham, 1809-1865—Chronology. 2. United States—Politics and government—1861-1865—Chronology. I. Title. II. Title: Three hundred and sixty-six days in Abraham Lincoln's Presidency.
E457.45.W96 2010
973.7092—dc22
[B]
2009037876

Printed in the United States of America

Contents

1862

1865

Introduction

The Civil War is the great choke point in American history. We are what we are today—for better *and* for worse—because of what did and didn't happen during those four crowded years from 1861 to 1865. As a writer and a historian, I've looked at things that did happen and at things that might have happened in books like *The Guns of the South*, *How Few Remain*, and *Fort Pillow*, and in shorter pieces such as "Must and Shall" and "The Last Reunion."

However, I was academically trained in the history of the Byzantine Empire. We know a surprising amount about the history of the Roman Empire's eastern half which eclipsed the western half after the western half suffered political collapse. But there's even more that we don't know and probably never will. The historical process when working with material like that is to find a fact here and another fact there, and then infer how the two isolated pieces of data fit together.

When I started conducting research for *The Guns of the South*, I discovered that American Civil War history isn't like that. You aren't starved for material; you're drowning in it. Even ephemera—like letters, cartoons, and newspaper articles—survive and can be compared and analyzed. Most prominent Civil War figures—and plenty of obscure ones, too—wrote their memoirs after the fighting stopped. The historical process here involves pulling a drop from the ocean of information in which you're drowning and demonstrating that it's a representative drop.

As I write this, the beginning of the Civil War sesquicentennial is only a year away. Interest in the war and what it means to American history will surely grow, as it did during the observance of the Civil War centennial in the early 1960s. You would think that, in the century and a half since the guns fell silent, every possible thing to be said about the Civil War would have been said, and in every possible way, too. But you would be wrong.

In *366 Days in Abraham Lincoln's Presidency*, Stephen A. Wynalda has found a new perspective from which to examine the events of 1861–1865. Rather than chronicle President Lincoln's actions over the course of a year, Wynalda discusses important moments within the context of Lincoln's entire presidency.

Wynalda's first entry for 1863, for example, talks about January 1st, the day the Emancipation Proclamation went into effect, and therefore the day the whole moral nature of the Civil War changed. His first entry for 1865 looks at January 2nd and deals with the New Year's Ball (January 1st was a Sunday, so the ball was held the following day). He describes how Washington, D.C.'s black inhabitants went to the White House anxious about how they would be received, how Lincoln in turn welcomed them, and how overwhelmed they were by this. It reflects and comments on what had happened two years and a day before.

Moving chronologically in time as Wynalda does allows him to note something in one entry and, sometimes, comment upon its consequences later on. He is not simply a chronicler or an annalist like you find in Byzantine historiography; he is a historian and an analyst. A chronicler just writes things down: "This happened, and then that happened, and then, over in this other place, that third thing happened." A historian puts things together and shows what they mean: "This happened, and because it happened, two years later that other thing happened, a thing that would have been inconceivable unless the previous event had laid the groundwork for it."

So we get not only a year (including 1864's leap day) in the presidency of Abraham Lincoln, but a year taken from all of his presidency. And, thanks to Stephen Wynalda's extensive research and sympathetic understanding of his subject, we see Lincoln from an angle we never have seen before. Wynalda shows us how results spring from events, and does so in a novel way. My hat's off to him in unabashed admiration.

Harry Turtledove, 2010

Foreword

According to recent scholarship, the only historical figure more written about than Abraham Lincoln is Jesus Christ. In just the last quarter century, Lincoln's political career, his marriage, his writing ability, his mental health, his friendships, and even his sexual orientation have been examined ad nauseam in books and articles. And yet many of these scholars and writers would admit that no one has a full grasp of exactly who Lincoln was. This is a difficult task, particularly because Lincoln left behind no diary or journal. Lincoln is an especially tough nut to crack. As Pulitzer Prize–winning author David Donald noted in *We Are Lincoln Men*, the sixteenth president had many acquaintances but few intimate friends, and none that saw every aspect of this complicated man. Moreover, one of Lincoln's primary intimates—Mary Lincoln—did not write anything of length about the man she loved, and took her private knowledge of him to her grave.

I've decided to address this problem from a new angle. The eighteenth-century Scottish literary theorist Hugh Blair wrote, "It is from private life, from familiar, domestic, and seemingly trivial occurrences, that we most often receive light into the real character." If Blair was right, we might reveal more about Lincoln not just by chronicling how he steadied a wearied hand to sign the Emancipation Proclamation, but how his face brightened when he saw that a contingent of black Washingtonians—heretofore unwelcome in the White House—had come there simply to shake the hand of "Marse Linkum." Perhaps it is just as revealing to see the father who wrote out a pretend pardon for his son Tad's errant doll as it is the commander in chief who scoured thousands of courts-martial documents to find reasons to commute executions. We can see Lincoln weep not only at the death of his friend Edward Baker, but at the death of his son Willie's pony.

To do this, I reveal Lincoln's activities during 366 days (a year, counting leap day) out of the over 1,600 days he was president and president-elect. I hope that this slice, representing a quarter of Lincoln's life as chief executive, will illuminate what his life was like during those four and a half pivotal years in American history. Some of the selected days are historically important, such as the days he signed the Homestead Act (May 20, 1862) and the legislation enacting the first federal income tax (the Revenue Act on August 5, 1861). Others were important to Lincoln personally, such as the day Willie died (February 20, 1862) and, of course, the day he was shot (April 14, 1865). However, the majority of these days are marked by occurrences that are mundane and noted by historians only in passing. I use them to illuminate some aspect of Lincoln's life, whether as president, commander in chief, father, husband, or friend.

These daily logs are arranged chronologically and, to keep them interesting, I made them brief narratives. If a log needed further illustration or explanation, I provide sidebars of equal brevity. Each log usually has one focus, but many share a focus with other daily entries, representing an ongoing series of events, such as the progression of decisions that led to the shelling of Fort Sumter. Related entries are referenced in the index.

This technique highlights how things evolved for Lincoln during his tenure as president. We can see Lincoln's frustrating search for a general to lead the Army of the Potomac; the progression of Lincoln's thoughts on emancipation; his efforts to get himself reelected; the evolution of Lincoln's fight not just with political rivals, but with fellow Republicans. With this comes a new appreciation of Lincoln not just as the "Great Emancipator" but as a man who virtually willed the Union back together.

Here, too, the contrasts and ironies in his life are illustrated. While he was adroit in reading the public and his political opponents, he greatly underestimated Southern secession fever, could not comprehend why African Americans refused to emigrate to Africa, and found his eldest son, Robert, incomprehensible. While the black activist Frederick Douglass raved about how Lincoln treated him like a "gentlemen" and felt as if he could put his "hand on his shoulder," Lincoln also told racist jokes, used racial epithets, and enjoyed racially degrading minstrel shows. And while he made much of his "oath registered in heaven" to defend the Constitution, he abridged its protections more than any other president in history.

Chronicling selected days reveals aspects of Lincoln that are perhaps not as well known. Lincoln was among the least educated of our presidents but is still the only one who owned a patent for an invention. He hated to hunt but loved to test-fire guns in the open field that surrounded the unfinished Washington Monument. He wrote poetry and, to relieve tension, recited an obscure Scottish poem so often that people thought he had written it. And, while his features were generally considered to be unattractive, he was one of the most photographed Americans of the nineteenth century.

Following a discussion of what this book does provide comes a discussion of what it does not. This book is strictly biographical, focusing on Lincoln and the people important to him personally or politically. It is therefore not a history of the Civil War and does not provide detailed accounts of battles.

Along those same lines, when this book does touch on military actions, they will disproportionally focus on events that happened in the eastern theater. Any Civil War scholar will tell you that the war was won in the western theater and the actions in Virginia, Maryland, and Pennsylvania were a costly stalemate at best. The reason the East receives more attention here is because it received more attention from Lincoln. This is partly due to his own obsession with capturing Richmond. It is also because the time it took for events to be relayed by telegraph between Washington and the western theater prohibited his involvement.

In the political realm, Lincoln came to Washington with just two years of experience working in the federal government and zero executive experience. He relied heavily on his more experienced cabinet secretaries to manage the day-to-day workings of the various departments. Matters of foreign policy, the Navy, and Native American affairs receive little attention in this book because they received little from Lincoln.

This book is also written for the general reader. There is nothing here that will surprise Lincoln or Civil War scholars. While I do include a few minor discussions about our sixteenth president (such as whether he was homosexual and whether he manipulated the rebels into firing on Fort Sumter), these are not meant to be comprehensive or detailed and are certainly not intended to be an entry into the ongoing scholarly debates.

I'd like to thank Kathleen Schuckel-Andrews, Teri Barnett, Pete Cava, Bob Chenoweth, June McCarty-Clair, John Clair, Nancy Frenzel, Pat Watson-Grande, Andrew Horning, Joyce Jensen, Kathy Nappier, Tony Perona, and Lucy Schilling, all members of the illustrious Indiana Writer's Workshop who gave generously of their time and considerable talent to polish this manuscript. And I'd like to give a special thank-you to my wife, Melody, who believed in me and my project, and my son Nicolas, whose boundless excitement over everything makes me dream big.

Stephen A. Wynalda, 2010

Ed. Note: *Lincoln's letters and papers contain a number of irregular spellings and misspellings. For ease of reading we have included these as they originally appeared, without notation.*

366 DAYS IN

ABRAHAM LINCOLN'S PRESIDENCY

The Private, Political, and Military Decisions of America's Greatest President

1860

"WE ARE NOT ENEMIES, BUT FRIENDS. WE MUST NOT BE ENEMIES. THOUGH PASSION MAY HAVE STRAINED, IT MUST NOT BREAK OUR BONDS OF AFFECTION."

—ABRAHAM LINCOLN

NOVEMBER 6

The Sixteenth President

Lincoln, on this Tuesday in 1860, waited for the election returns in the vote that would put him in the White House.

With the Illinois legislature out of session, Lincoln acquired a temporary office at the State Capitol where he stayed most of the day, rarely mentioning the election. His law partner, William Herndon, convinced him to vote in the state elections and, before Lincoln walked to the polls, he cut off the top of the ballot listing the presidential candidates so that he couldn't vote for himself.

That evening he waited with a crowd as a courier delivered election returns from the telegraph. First came news that Lincoln carried Illinois, then Indiana. He also carried the Northwest and New England, but there was no word from the critical eastern states. At nine o'clock, Lincoln walked to the telegraph office to read the results as soon as they arrived. At ten came word that Lincoln took Pennsylvania. He decided to take a break and had coffee and sandwiches with his wife, Mary, at Watson's Saloon, where he was greeted at the door with "How do you do, Mr. President!"

When Lincoln returned to the telegraph office, returns from the South were coming in. "Now we shall get a few licks back," Lincoln said. Indeed the news was ominous. Ten Southern states had not even carried Lincoln on the ballot. At two in the morning, Lincoln was told that he carried New York and he decided to go home. The final tallies showed that Lincoln received less than 40 percent of the popular vote, with the other 60 percent split between three Democrats. Lincoln carried all the Northern states except New Jersey, garnering 180 electoral votes, 28 more than he needed.

#1

How Did Lincoln Get Elected?

How did an uneducated Midwesterner with only two years of experience in national politics become the chief magistrate of the land? For one thing, Lincoln was not an unknown. Americans had watched for years the growing sectional tensions over slavery, emphasized by a race war in Kansas, the Dred Scott Supreme Court decision, and John Brown's attempt to spark a slave insurrection in Virginia. When Lincoln took on Stephen Douglas for his seat in the Senate in 1858, the public read with relish their heated debates over slavery. While Lincoln lost this election, he became nationally known, particularly after the debates were published. The popularity of the debates led to an invitation in early 1860 to speak in New York at Cooper Union—a speech that was reprinted nationwide.

When the Republican convention was held in Chicago—Lincoln's backyard—Lincoln's managers worked hard to present him as a moderate second choice to the more radical favorites—William Seward and Salmon Chase. Unlike Seward and Chase, Lincoln's lack of experience in national politics meant he had fewer enemies. When neither Chase nor Seward could garner the Republican nomination, the convention turned to Lincoln.

By then the Democratic Party was imploding. The party had dominated politics for forty years and was itself dominated by Southerners who forced Northern Democrats to swallow compromise after compromise over slavery just to keep the South from seceding. At the Democratic convention in Charleston, South Carolina, the Northerners could not stomach another compromise. The convention collapsed and a total of three Democrats—Stephen Douglas, John Breckinridge and John Bell—found themselves on the presidential ticket, bleeding votes from each other. None of the Democrats could match Lincoln's 40 percent of the popular vote.

NOVEMBER 10

The Gravest Apprehensions

Lincoln, on this Saturday in 1860, responded in writing to former Connecticut congressman Truman Smith's plea that Lincoln assuage Southern fears about his policies as president—fears that fueled secession fervor.

Shortly after the election, a letter from Smith was delivered to Lincoln, warning the president-elect of a circular that was handed out at the Connecticut polls on Election Day. The circular used inaccuracies and misquotes to claim that Lincoln was "an undisguised enemy of the peace and safety of the Union." Smith wrote that "the most strenuous exertions have been made to fill the minds of the people of the South with the gravest apprehensions as to what would be your purposes and policy." Smith advised that Lincoln "speak out . . . to disarm mischief makers, to allay causeless anxiety, to compose the public mind." Indeed, newspapers were already predicting a secession crisis. That night in Charleston, South Carolina, a mob carried an effigy of Lincoln with a placard that read, ABE LINCOLN, FIRST PRESIDENT NORTHERN CONFEDERACY. A pair of slaves hoisted the effigy onto a scaffold and set it alight.

Lincoln, on this Saturday, rebuffed Smith's urgings, saying that he felt "constrained . . . to make no declaration for the public." He added, "I could say nothing which I have not already said, and which is in print, and open for inspection of all. To press a repetition of this upon those who have listened, is useless; to press it upon those who have refused to listen, and still refuse, would be wanting in self-respect, and would have an appearance of sycophancy and timidity, which would excite the contempt of good men, and encourage bad ones to clamor the more loudly."

A week and a half later, the clamor became so great that Lincoln finally spoke out for the first time.

NOVEMBER 20

A Public Statement

During the 1860 presidential campaign, Lincoln made no speeches and issued no public statements—referring all inquiries to his party's platform and his public statements before his nomination. It was not unusual for presidential candidates in those days to eschew campaigning, but Lincoln also wanted to avoid rhetoric that could be used to fan the flames of sectionalism.

Once Lincoln was elected, Southerners began calling for secession because they were told Lincoln was planning to emancipate their slaves. Letters poured in to Lincoln, begging him to make a public statement to mollify the fears of Southerners. "I could say nothing which I have not already said," Lincoln responded. Lincoln was concerned about those who were "eager for something new upon which to base new misrepresentations."

Bending to political pressure, Lincoln, on this Tuesday in 1860, inserted a response to the secession crisis into his friend Lyman Trumbull's Republican victory speech.

On this day, Springfield was holding a celebration of Lincoln's election with a speech from Trumbull, into which Lincoln inserted a few paragraphs he considered to be his stance on the crisis. "Each and all States will be left in as complete control of their own affairs respectively, and at as perfect liberty to choose, and employ, their means of protecting property, and preserving peace . . . as they have ever been under any administration," Lincoln wrote. To this Trumbull naively added, "When this is shown, a re-action will assuredly take place in favor of Republicanism, the Southern mind even will be satisfied . . . and the fraternal feeling existing in olden times . . . will be restored."

Just as Lincoln expected, the speech was used against him, particularly in the press. "The *Boston Courier* . . . endeavor[s] to inflame the North with the belief that [the speech] foreshadows an abandonment of Republican ground," the president-elect lamented.

#2

Why Did the South Fear Lincoln?

Why did Lincoln's election prompt Southern states to secede from the Union? A look at those states' articles of secession, which included declarations of the causes of their decision, is instructive. For example, Mississippi's "Immediate Causes" of secession originated as far back as the 1787 Northwest Ordinance, the first of a handful of instances where the North refused "the admission of new slave States into the Union." As Texas's "causes" stated, the absence of any entry of new slave states, and thus no new senators or congressmen, "placed the slave-holding States in a hopeless minority in the federal congress, and rendered representation of no avail in protecting Southern rights against their [Northern] exactions and encroachments." Some of the other causes included the lack of enforcement of fugitive slave laws, inflammatory rhetoric from abolitionists, the Republican Party's advocacy of "Negro equality," and Republican support of John Brown's 1859 attempt to spark a slave uprising in Virginia. The final straw, as South Carolina's "causes" stated, was "the election of a man to the high office of President . . . whose opinions and purposes are hostile to slavery."

Any thorough and fair reading of Lincoln's opinions and speeches reveals that he was not "hostile" to slavery. While he was, indeed, against the expansion of slavery into the territories, he openly supported fugitive slave laws. He was critical of abolitionists and their inflammatory demands, and vehemently eschewed John Brown's methods. Time after time during the 1858 Lincoln–Douglas debates, Lincoln declared himself against black social and political equality. Lincoln's 1858 Springfield speech, in which he declared that "this government cannot endure, permanently half slave and half free," was often cited as a threat against the South. A closer look reveals that it was instead a prediction. But the truth was hidden from most Southerners behind sectional rhetoric, outright lies, and emotional appeals to the universal fear of change.

NOVEMBER 30

Alexander Stephens

Lincoln and the future vice president of the Confederacy, Alexander Stephens, became friends in the late 1840s when they were both Whigs in Congress; Lincoln for Illinois, Stephens for Georgia. After Lincoln's election as president in 1860, Georgia governor Joe Brown called the state legislature into session to consider secession. On November 14, Stephens delivered a passionate plea urging Georgians to show "good judgment" and not depart the Union.

On this Friday in 1860, Lincoln—the future president of the Union—sent a letter to Stephens, touching off an exchange of letters.

Lincoln wrote Stephens for a copy of his November 14 speech. Stephens responded two weeks later admitting that "the Country is certainly in great peril and no man ever had heavier or greater responsibilities resting upon him than you." Lincoln wrote, "Do the people of the South really entertain fears that a Republican administration would directly, or indirectly, interfere with their slaves . . . ? If they do, I wish to assure you, as a friend and still, I hope, not an enemy, that there is no cause for such fears. The South would be in no more danger in this respect, than it was in the days of [George] Washington." Stephen wrote back, "When men come under the influence of fanaticism, there is no telling where their impulses or passions may drive them . . . In addressing you thus, I would have you understand me as being not a personal enemy, but as one who would have you do what you can to save our common country."

Lincoln briefly considered offering a cabinet post to Stephens, but once he was made the vice president of the new Confederate Republic that, of course, was impossible.

DECEMBER 5

The Buchanan Perspective

Lincoln, on this Wednesday in 1860, was angry after reading a synopsis of President James Buchanan's last annual message to Congress, in which he blamed the North for the secession crisis.

While Buchanan was a Pennsylvanian—a state known for its abolitionist movements—he was pro-South and pro-slavery virtually all his political career. After Lincoln was elected and the Deep South scheduled secession conventions, Buchanan looked for a way to deflect the crisis. He tried to appeal to reason in his annual message on December 3. "The immediate peril arises . . . [from] the incessant and violent agitation on the slavery question throughout the North," he said, ignoring the "agitation" of slavery proponents. "Hence a sense of security no longer exists around the family altar. This feeling of peace at home has given place to apprehensions of servile insurrections." According to Buchanan, this, and not Lincoln's election, was the source of secessionist fervor.

Then, in an appeal to the North, Buchanan wrote an argument against secession. "In order to justify secession as a constitutional remedy, it must be on the principle that the Federal Government is a mere voluntary association of States, to be dissolved at pleasure by any one of the contracting parties. If this be so, the Confederacy is a rope of sand, to be penetrated and dissolved by the adverse wave of public opinion in any of the States. . . . [Our] Union might be entirely broken into fragments in a few weeks which cost our forefathers many years of toil, privation and blood to establish." He also believed, however, that the federal government had no recourse should a state decide to break away from the Union.

Lincoln's anger was mollified when he read the president's entire message. Yet despite Buchanan's plea, on December 8, South Carolina would elect delegates to its secession convention.

DECEMBER 18

"No Sign Will Be Given Them"

As secessionist fever grew, Lincoln grew weary of misrepresentations of his words, as demonstrated by an angry letter he penned on this day in 1860.

Distortions of Lincoln's words were not new to him, but they were particularly irksome when used to inflame secessionists. During and after his election, Lincoln avoided any public statements for just that reason. As one friend warned, Lincoln "must keep his feet out of all such wolfe traps." The one time Lincoln made a statement through his friend Lyman Trumbull (November 20), the press trumpeted it as a declaration of war on the South. "These political fiends are not half sick enough yet," Lincoln said. "They seek a sign, and no sign will be given them."

To Henry Raymond, editor of the *New York Times*, Lincoln became caustic. Raymond had forwarded a letter from William Smedes, one of his reporters in Vicksburg, Mississippi. Smedes claimed that Lincoln's presidency was "disastrous" to the South because "he is pledged to ultimate extinction of slavery, holds the black man to be the equal of the white & stigmatizes our whole people as immoral & unchristian." Smedes adds "that it makes every particle of blood in me boil with suppressed indignation that I have to submit my country to the rule of such a man . . . . I would regard death by a stroke of lightning to Mr. Lincoln as but just punishment from an offended Deity for his infamous & unpatriotic avowals."

"What a very mad-man your correspondent, Smedes is," Lincoln responded on this day. "Mr. S[medes] can not prove one of his assertions true. Mr. S[medes] seems sensitive on the question of morals and Christianity. What does he think of a man who makes charges against another which he does not know to be true, and could easily learn to be false?"

DECEMBER 24

Forts

On this day in 1860 Lincoln wrote his friend Lyman Trumbull of his concern that secessionists would seize federal forts in Charleston, South Carolina.

Shortly after Lincoln's election as president in November 1860, Major Robert Anderson—who was in charge of the Charleston forts—asked Washington for reinforcements. He also asked that his troops be moved from the less-defensible Fort Moultrie to one of the other forts—Castle Pinckney or Fort Sumter. Despite assurances from state authorities that they would not attack him, Anderson could see a growing army of militia and batteries of cannon around him. The Carolinians thought they had an agreement with President James Buchanan that Anderson would not move from Moultrie, but Buchanan sent an order that the major misunderstood as giving him permission to move his men to Sumter. Meanwhile, South Carolina seceded from the Union on December 20.

In Springfield, Lincoln received word that General in Chief Winfield Scott had told Buchanan that Anderson needed to be reinforced. Lincoln sent a message to Scott to be "prepared . . . to either hold, or retake, the forts, as the case may require, at, and after the inaugeration." Then on this Christmas Eve, Lincoln wrote Trumbull, "Despaches have come here two days in secession, that the Forts in South Carolina, will be surrendered by the order, or consent at least, of the President. I can scarely believe this; but if it prove true, I will . . . announce publicly at once that they are to be retaken after the inaugeration."

During the night of December 26, Anderson moved his men to Sumter. When the Charleston authorities sent emissaries to direct Anderson to return to Moultrie, Anderson responded, "I decline to accede to his request; I cannot and will not go back."

DECEMBER 27

Lincoln in Stone

Lincoln, on this Thursday in 1860, sat for sculptor Thomas Jones in his effort to make a bust of the president-elect.

The proliferation of Lincoln statues since his death has arguably made him the most sculpted American in history. But the sculpting of Lincoln actually began in the last five years of his life. The first was by Leonard Volk who, in March 1860, made a cast of Lincoln's face to use for a model. Two months later he came to Springfield, Illinois, to make casts of Lincoln's hands. While Volk's subsequent bust never attained the fame of his casts, Daniel French used Volk's hand casts when he sculpted the seated statue for Washington's Lincoln Memorial.

Jones came to Springfield to sculpt a bust of Lincoln. On this day, Lincoln began daily sessions at the St. Nicolas Hotel posing for Jones, using the time to write or read. During one session, Lincoln had been reading his mail when he discovered a suspicious package that Jones feared contained "an infernal machine or torpedo [bomb]." After carefully unwrapping it, they found a gift—a homemade pigtail whistle—which Lincoln practiced with for the rest of the session. Jones's sculpture was unusual in that it was the first to show Lincoln's new beard and it sported a smile—a rare feature on Lincoln sculptures.

Sculptors William Swayne, Sarah Fisher Ames, and Vinnie Ream had Lincoln pose for them in the White House. Clark Mills acquired another face cast of Lincoln in February 1865. When comparing Volk's and Mills's masks, Lincoln's secretary John Hay thought the difference profound, the latter with features so weathered that at least one sculptor mistook it for a death mask. Hay added that the Mills's mask had "a look as one on whom sorrow and care had done their worst . . . the whole expression is of unspeakable sadness. . . . Yet the peace is not the dreadful peace of death; it is the peace that passeth understanding."

1861

"YOU ARE GREEN, IT IS TRUE, BUT THEY [THE CONFEDERATES] ARE GREEN TOO; YOU ARE ALL GREEN ALIKE."
—ABRAHAM LINCOLN

JANUARY 3

Lincoln Vacillates

Lincoln rarely changed his mind after he made a carefully considered decision, but his inexperience in national politics made him indecisive during the months before and after his first inauguration. An excellent example of this occurred on this Thursday in 1861, when he struggled to fill a cabinet position.

At the 1860 Republican presidential convention in Chicago, powerful Pennsylvania Senator Simon Cameron threw his support to Lincoln's nomination, allegedly because he had been promised a cabinet post. And, when Pennsylvania proved pivotal to Lincoln's election, the president-elect decided the state should be represented in his cabinet. On New Year's Eve 1860, Lincoln offered Cameron a cabinet seat as either the Secretary of War or Treasury.

Lincoln's choice caused a furor among fellow Republicans. Cameron's own party detested him, largely because of his ineptitude and corruption. The "Great Winnebago Chief"—a nickname acquired after he bilked Native Americans—had a reputation that was "shockingly bad." By mid-January, twenty Republican Congressmen had signed a petition protesting Cameron's appointment.

Under this pressure, Lincoln, on this day, rescinded his offer. "Things have developed which make it impossible for me to take you into the cabinet," he wrote. Mindful of how this might be perceived, he added, "And now, I suggest that you write me declining the appointment, in which case I do not object to its being known that it was tendered [to] you. Better do this at once, before things so change, that you can not honorably decline, and I be compelled to openly recall the tender."

Cameron refused to respond and his supporters applied their own pressure on Lincoln. A few days before his inauguration, Lincoln reversed himself again and named Cameron his Secretary of War. Afterward, Cameron repeatedly embarrassed Lincoln with his mismanagement of the critical War Department.

#3

A Divisive Cabinet

In Lincoln's day, candidates did not attend presidential conventions. Despite a persistent legend, in his absence Lincoln's political managers at the Chicago convention did not promise cabinet posts to competing candidates in exchange for his nomination. Lincoln wired his managers, "Make no contracts that will bind me." And they obeyed him.

Lincoln, however, was interested in unifying the Republican Party. The party was only a few years old and Lincoln had become a Republican after he watched his old Whig party fracture into ideological pieces. When he was elected, it was largely because the Democrats had fractured as well. After his election, he decided to make his cabinet representative of all the varied Republican factions.

To do this, Lincoln made political history by filling critical cabinet posts with the four most prominent Republicans who had competed with him for the presidential nomination in Chicago. Lincoln named Edward Bates his Attorney General, Simon Cameron his Secretary of War, Salmon Chase his Secretary of Treasury, and the man everyone expected to win the Chicago nomination—William Seward—became Secretary of State.

Unfortunately this also meant that more than half of his cabinet advisors (there were seven at that time) were men who believed they deserved the presidency more than Lincoln. It made for volatile relationships. Chase in particular tried to undermine Lincoln and ultimately would resign because of his ambition. Seward, too, attempted to usurp the presidential power in the first month of Lincoln's administration but, once thwarted, Seward came to respect Lincoln and even became a close friend.

JANUARY 11

Lincoln Stands Firm

On this Friday in 1861, Alabama became the fourth state to secede from the Union as a direct result of Lincoln's election to the presidency. Many worried that there wouldn't be a country for Lincoln to preside over and there were several congressional efforts to mollify the Southern states with a compromise.

The most serious compromise was submitted by Kentucky Senator John Crittenden, proposing several amendments to the Constitution. These amendments, among other things, would reestablish the old Missouri Compromise line (latitude 36°30'), ban slavery north of it, protect slavery south of it, and prohibit any future amendment from reversing these amendments. This

Crittenden Compromise would effectively allow slavery to spread westward—something Lincoln had promised not to allow in the election he had just won. It would also make slavery a permanent institution—something Lincoln personally could not stomach.

Fearing secession and war, Republicans were tempted to accept this compromise, but Lincoln refused, saying it "would lose us everything we have gained in the election." He added, "The tug has got to come and better now, than any time hereafter." Following his wishes, Republicans defeated the measure.

Afterward, colleagues tried to persuade Lincoln to reconsider. To one of these compromisers—Rep. James T. Hale of Pennsylvania—Lincoln, on this day in 1861, wrote, "What is our present condition? We have just carried an election on principles fairly stated to the people. Now we are told . . . the government shall be broken up, unless we surrender to those we have beaten, before we take office . . . if we surrender, it is the end of us, and of the government." As he later wrote to his future Secretary of State William Seward, any such compromise would "put us again on the high road to a slave empire."

#4

The Other Thirteenth Amendment

There were several efforts in late 1860 and early 1861 to placate secessionist states in order to bring them back into the Union. One was the Crittenden Compromise and another was the Corwin Amendment to the Constitution, which would have forbidden the federal government from ever interfering with slavery, and no future amendment could be passed to abolish it.

Lincoln's response to such amendments was cautious: "I do not desire any amendment to the Constitution. Recognizing, however, that questions of such [an] amendment rightfully belongs to the American people, I should not feel justified nor inclined to withhold from them, if I could, a fair opportunity of expressing their will."

The Corwin Amendment passed in the House on February 27, 1861, and in the Senate just before the inauguration on March 4. As one of his last acts as president, James Buchanan signed the amendment, although his signature was not required. It was then sent to the states for ratification. While a few states actually ratified it, the shelling of Fort Sumter and the ensuing war killed the amendment before it ever got the needed ratification by two-thirds of the states.

It is an irony of history that by seceding from the Union to protect their way of life, particularly their "peculiar institution" of slavery, the Southern states abandoned what may have been their best chance to preserve that way of life. Had they not seceded and had the Thirteenth Amendment been ratified, slavery would have indeed been permanently protected. Instead the Thirteenth Amendment that was eventually ratified, more than four years later (in December 1865), permanently abolished slavery.

JANUARY 12

Visitors

After Lincoln was elected president in November 1860, well-wishers and office-seekers thronged to Springfield to see the new president-elect. One of the former came to see Lincoln on this Saturday in 1861. He was an old Hoosier farmer named Jones, and Lincoln had worked for him more than thirty years before at a wage of a dollar a day.

Lincoln saw him in the Governor's Room of the State Capitol. Many other visitors that day, like every day, were office-seekers looking for a place in his administration. "Lincoln told us he felt like a surveyor in the wild woods of the West," noted one reporter, "who, while looking for a corner, kept an eye over his shoulder for an Indian."

By December, he was holding daily receptions from nine until noon, where visitors could speak to him without invitation. From noon until two he would go home for lunch, then return to see people by invitation only. A news reporter, Henry Villard, from the *New York Herald*, observed these daily visitations and remarked,

> As a rule he showed remarkable tact in dealing with each of them [visitors], whether they were rough-looking Sagamon County farmers still addressing him familiarly as "Abe," sleek and pert commercial travelers, staid merchants, sharp politicians, or preachers, lawyers, or other professional men. He showed a very quick and shrewd perception of and adaptation to individual characteristics and peculiarities. . . . He was ever ready for an argument, which always had an original flavor, and as a rule, he got the better in the discussions. There was, however, one limitation to the freedom of his talks with his visitors. A great many of them naturally tried to draw him out as to his future policy as President regarding the secession movement in the South, but he would not commit himself.

JANUARY 24

"Diamond in the Rough"

On this Thursday in 1861, President-elect Lincoln waited for the second night in a row at the Springfield train station in vain for his wife, Mary, and their eldest son, Robert, to return from an excursion to the East. Mary had been on a two-week shopping spree, buying a new wardrobe. She was determined not to appear in Washington with dowdy small-town clothes. She was overwhelmed with the variety of fashions and jewels in New York, where she was fussed over and extended exorbitant credit simply because she was the future first lady. This would be the first of many such splurges in New York.

Lincoln, himself, was unaffected by his elevated stature. Even in the White House, he would continue to greet visitors in slippers and was sometimes seen late at night without pants, his long stork-like legs bared below his shirttails. One Southern governor claimed Lincoln received him in bare feet. "He probably had as little taste about dress and attire as anybody that was ever born; he simply wore clothes because it was needful and customary; whether they fitted or looked well was entirely above or beneath his comprehension," recalled an acquaintance. "If ever there was a diamond in the rough, or good fruit enclosed in a shabby husk, it was Abraham Lincoln," said Erasmus Keyes.

Lincoln trudged home alone, this night, and the next day Mary and Robert finally returned from their trip, Mary glowing from "the winter gaieties of New York," said a reporter. With the help of her sisters, Mary subsequently threw an open house to show off her new wardrobe.

#5

Informal Wear

Lincoln's size-14 feet were so unusually large that his boots had to be specially made for him. But his feet were not just large, they were flat-footed, slightly pigeon-toed, and afflicted with corns and bunions. So painful were Lincoln's boots that he would frequently shuck them, preferring to walk around his office and the White House in backless slippers that made *flip-flop* sounds as he walked, to the consternation of those who thought he should be more formal.

Yet Lincoln was oblivious to criticism. One of his two personal secretaries, John Hay, relates an event that occurred on April 30, 1864:

> A little after midnight . . . the President came in the office laughing, with a volume of [English Comic Writer Thomas] Hood's works in his hand, to show Nico [another secretary, John Nicolay] and me the little caricature . . . seemingly utterly unconscious that he with short shirt hanging above his long legs & setting out behind like the tail feathers of an enormous ostrich was infinitely funnier than anything in the book he was laughing at. What a man it is! Occupied all day with matters of vast moment, deeply anxious about the fate of the greatest army of the world, with his own fame & future hanging on events of the passing hour, he yet has such a wealth of simple bonhomie & good fellowship that he gets out of bed & perambulates the house in his shirt to find us that we may share with him the fun of one of poor Hood's queer little conceits.

JANUARY 28

Inaugural Preparations

By late January, the president-elect was gathering material and secluding himself in order to write his inaugural address. But on this Monday in 1861 he had to put aside his speech to attend to business.

In order to write his address, Lincoln borrowed from his law partner, William Herndon, speeches by Henry Clay and Noah Webster, Andrew Jackson's proclamation against nullification, and a copy of the Constitution. For privacy, Lincoln accepted an offer from his brother-in-law, Clark Moulton Smith, to use a third-floor room above Smith's stores, just across the street from the State House. Lincoln even advertised his need for seclusion in papers as far away as New York. "The first draft of the Inaugural Message is now being made by the President-elect. . . . No further invitations will be issued," he advertised in the *New York Tribune* on January 29.

Nevertheless, Lincoln, on this day, welcomed a committee from Indianapolis inviting him to visit their city en route from Springfield, Illinois to Washington. Lincoln then accepted their invitation and indicated February 12 as the day he would arrive in the Hoosier capital, his first overnight stop on his inaugural trip. He was already solidifying plans for his other stops: Cincinnati, Columbus, Pittsburgh, Cleveland, Buffalo, Albany, New York City, Philadelphia, Harrisburg, and Baltimore. In total, Lincoln's inaugural trip would wind through 1,900 miles of the country he would soon preside over.

Four years later, Lincoln's funeral train would take the opposite route (with the omission of Cincinnati and Pittsburgh and the addition of Chicago) back home to Springfield.

JANUARY 31

A Tearful Goodbye

On January 30, 1861, Lincoln took a train from Springfield to Charleston, Illinois and, with a shawl over his shoulders, trudged through the ice and mud to a buggy. The buggy delivered him to State Senator Thomas A. Marshall's house, where he stayed the night. The next morning, on this Thursday in 1861, Lincoln rode eight miles to Coles County where he visited with his stepmother, Sarah "Sally" Lincoln.

Sarah had been as much of a mother to Lincoln as his mother Nancy had been. His relationship with his father was far more problematic. Thomas Lincoln was a harsh man, and no one could ever recall Lincoln saying a kind word about him. They were so estranged that Lincoln refused to visit his father on Thomas's deathbed in 1851 and did not attend his funeral. Nevertheless, on this day, he did visit his father's grave, at Shiloh Cemetery and gave instructions for a grave marker, perhaps recalling that his mother was buried in Indiana without one.

The next day, February 1, Lincoln rode out to Coles County one last time to see Sarah. They held hands for quite awhile and between her tearful kisses, Sarah told her boy that she would never see him again. Lincoln muttered a response and said they would meet "up yonder."

Sarah's prophecy would prove true and more than four years later, when Sarah was told of her stepson's assassination, she said, "I know'd they'd kill him. I've been waitin' fer it."

#6

Sally

Just two years after Thomas and Nancy Lincoln brought their daughter, Sarah, and son, Abe, to Little Pigeon Creek in southern Indiana, Nancy died. The cause of death was probably "milk sickness," an illness contracted from drinking the milk of a cow that had consumed the deadly white snakeroot. Lincoln was nine years old when he helped his father cobble together his mother's coffin and bury her in an unmarked grave.

A year later, Thomas approached an old Kentucky girlfriend who was now a thirty-one-year-old widow named Sarah "Sally" Johnston. "I have no wife and you no husband, Thomas said. "I came a-purpose to marry you." Sally, upon her arrival at the Lincoln log cabin, replaced little Abe's cornhusk bed with a feather mattress, thus winning his affection. She also encouraged—unlike his father—the young Lincoln's inquisitive mind. She would later relate,

> Abe read the Bible some, though not as much as said; he sought more congenial books suitable for his age. . . . Abe had no particular religion, didn't think of that question at that time, if he ever did. . . . Abe read all the books he could lay his hands on, and when he came across a passage that struck him, he would write it down on boards if he had no paper and keep it there till he did get paper. . . . He never told me a lie in his life, never evaded, never quarreled, never dodged nor turned a corner to avoid a chastisement or other responsibility. He never swore or used profane language in my presence. . . . Abe didn't care much for crowds of people; he chose his own company, which was always good. He was not very fond of girls, as he seemed to me.

FEBRUARY 6

A Last Springfield Reception

On this evening in 1861, from 7:00 PM until midnight, the Lincolns hosted a reception at their house to say goodbye to Springfield.

The Lincolns were in the middle of their final week before heading to Washington when they hosted a reception, inviting not only their neighbors but, as one newspaper noted, "the political elite of this State, and the beauty and fashion of this vicinity." Over seven hundred people filed into the Lincolns small house on Eighth and Jackson, with Lincoln standing at the front door shaking the hands of every one of them.

Many of the visitors noted the hair sprouting from the president-elect's jaw, already nearly three months old. The previous October, just before the election, eleven-year-old Grace Bedell of Westfell,

New York wrote Lincoln, promising that her brothers would vote for him if he grew whiskers. "You would look a great deal better for your face is so thin," she wrote. "All the ladies like whiskers and they would tease their husbands to vote for you and then you would be President." So pleased was Lincoln with Bedell's letter that he not only took her advice, but carried her letter in his hat for years afterward. A few weeks later when Lincoln was sworn in, he became the first president to sport a beard.

Many noted the new dress Mary was wearing. "Mrs. Lincoln's splendid toilette," one reporter wrote, "gave satisfactory evidence of extensive purchases during her late visit to New York."

#7

What the Lincolns Left Behind

In the weeks prior to their inaugural trip to Washington, the Lincolns packed up their belongings, rented their house, and sold their furniture. Lincoln appeared one evening at the home of Mary's cousin Lizzy carrying a satchel filled with his letters and writings. He told his favorite cousin that if he did not come back, she could do with them what she wanted. Mary, already worried about public sentiment toward her and her husband, burned her old letters in the alley behind the house. She would continue to destroy letters written to her for the rest of her life.

To his law partner, William Herndon, owner of one of the largest private libraries in the area, Lincoln gave his small collection of books, which included Edward Gibbon's *The Decline and Fall of the Roman Empire*, Edward Hitchcock's *Religious Truth Illustrated from Science* and a *Dictionary of Congress*. He also insisted that Herndon keep the LINCOLN

AND HERNDON sign hanging above their law firm. "Let it hang there undisturbed," Lincoln told him, "Give our clients to understand that the election of a President makes no change in the firm. . . . If I live I'm coming back some time, and then we'll go right on practicing law as if nothing had ever happened."

The Lincolns had a yellow dog, named Fido, who was routinely given table scraps and loved to chase his own tail. Despite the protests of his youngest son, Tad, Lincoln gave Fido to a neighbor, Johnny Roll. Lincoln's faithful horse Old Bob (to differentiate him from Young Bob) had taken him on many a circuit through the Illinois wilderness, and was retired to pasture. Four years later, when Lincoln's body would return to Springfield, Old Bob would be given a position of honor, paraded through the streets behind the president's hearse. Besides Robert Lincoln, Bob would be the only member of the president's immediate family to attend his burial.

FEBRUARY 8

The Lincolns Move Out

On this Friday in 1861, Lincoln packed up and left the only home he ever owned. The Lincolns had lived in the two-story wood-frame home on the corner of Eighth and Jackson streets (homes in Springfield didn't have numbered addresses until 1873) for seventeen years. Three of their four sons (Willie, Eddie, and Tad) were born in this house and one—Eddie—died in it. It was in its parlor that Lincoln received delegates from the 1860 Republican Convention to officially inform him that he was nominated for president.

Abraham and Mary had purchased the house from the pastor who had married them—Rev. Charles Dresser—for $1,200 cash and a little shop Lincoln owned in downtown Springfield. Originally the house was one and a half stories and only six rooms. But once their family had blossomed to five, the Lincolns expanded the home, doubling its size. Out back, a wood-planked walkway led to the privy and the barn where Lincoln kept his buggy, Old Bob the horse, and a cow that Lincoln milked daily. At the time of their departure, Lincoln had the siding of the house painted chocolate, the shutters a deep green.

In anticipation of leaving for Washington, the Lincolns had rented their home and, on this day, moved into a hotel, the Chenery House. Also on this day, Lincoln took out fire insurance policies on the house ($3,000), the carriage house ($75), woodhouse and privy ($125) for a premium of $24 a year.

Lincoln never returned to his Springfield home and, although Mary went back to Springfield after his death, she refused to live in the house. Their only surviving son, Robert, donated the home to the state of Illinois in 1887.

FEBRUARY 11

Lincoln Leaves Springfield

Lincoln lived in Springfield longer than he did anywhere else. On this Monday, 1861, he left his home of twenty-four years for the last time.

It was raining when Lincoln arrived at the Great Northern Depot without his wife (Mary was shopping in St. Louis and joined him in Indianapolis). Idling at the depot was a Hinkley locomotive—the L. M. Wiley—pulling two coaches. Lincoln had requested there be no public demonstration and had prepared nothing to say, but when he saw the hundreds of friends and neighbors at the station to see him off, he decided to deliver a farewell. At 7:55 AM, Lincoln stepped onto the platform of the rear coach and took off his hat. As he spoke, his voice was husky with emotion:

> My Friends—No one, not in my situation, can appreciate my feeling of sadness at this parting. To this place, and the kindness of these people, I owe everything. Here I have lived a quarter century, and have passed from a young to an old man. Here my children have been born, and one is buried. I leave, not knowing when, or whether ever, I may return, with a task before me greater than that which rested upon [George] Washington. Without the assistance of that Divine Being, who ever attended him, I cannot succeed. With that assistance I cannot fail. . . . To His care commending you, as I hope in your prayers you will commend me, I bid you an affectionate farewell.

A few minutes later, Engineer Elias H. Fralick rolled the Hinkley out of the station and began Lincoln's journey to Washington.

FEBRUARY 14

Whistle-stops

Despite a cold rain falling on western Ohio, thousands turned out to greet Lincoln's train on this Thursday in 1861, as the president-elect made his way to Washington.

Between leaving Columbus, Ohio, at 8:00 AM and reaching Pittsburgh twelve hours later, the inaugural train stopped at nearly a dozen small Ohio and Pennsylvania towns. Usually these "whistle-stops" were just long enough for Lincoln to step out on the rear platform of the train to see the crowds and for them to see him. "I certainly think I have the best of the bargain," he joked more than once.

Some of the small towns had prepared elaborate celebrations, but Lincoln said he couldn't stay because he had an appointment in Washington (his inauguration). Three days earlier he had tried to illustrate this in Thorntown, Indiana with one of his famous anecdotes about a county politician and his horse. The horse, on the way to the nominating convention, decided to stop at every bush to eat, and made his master so late that he lost the nomination. Unfortunately, the train pulled out of the station before he finished the story. Lincoln was delighted to find that several Thorntown residents ran all the way to Lebanon—his next stop some ten miles away—to hear the rest of the story.

On this day in Wellsville, Ohio, a drunk rushed up to Lincoln saying he was a Democrat and had voted for Stephen Douglas. Lincoln shook the man's hand and said that if Douglas helped keep the "ship of state" afloat, he might be elected to pilot it in the future. Two days later at still another whistle-stop (Westfield, New York), Lincoln met Grace Bedell, the little girl he credited with inducing him to grow a beard.

FEBRUARY 15

"There Is No Crisis"

By the middle of February 1861, seven states—South Carolina, Mississippi, Florida, Alabama, Georgia, Louisiana, and Texas—had seceded from the Union, six of which had met in Montgomery, Alabama to form the Confederate States of America. This new government adopted a constitution and elected a president—Jefferson Davis. Nevertheless, Lincoln delivered two speeches on this day in 1861, the fifth day of his inaugural journey to Washington, claiming that the country wasn't facing a crisis at all.

In Pittsburgh he said, "There is no crisis, excepting such a one as may be gotten up at anytime by designing politicians. . . . If the American people will only keep their temper, on both sides of the [Mason-Dixon] line, the troubles will come to an end." Later that day, in Cleveland, he said, "I think there is no occasion for any excitement. The crisis, as it is called, is altogether an artificial crisis." He then oversimplified the problems as a mere difference of opinions, and that it had "no foundation in facts." He added, "Let it [the secession crisis] alone and it will go down of itself."

Over and over again throughout his journey east, Lincoln delivered speeches that picked apart Southern arguments for seceding (in a democracy, the majority ruled, not the minority; the election of another president in four years was a more legitimate recourse than secession). He challenged Southerners to "point us to anything in which they are being injured, or about to be injured."

Lincoln clearly believed that cooler heads—convinced by his logical arguments—would prevail over the emotional ones. He earnestly believed that Union sentiment in the South was strong enough to overcome the secessionists. It was a naive belief he clung to until war finally came.

FEBRUARY 21

The Baltimore Plot

On this eleventh day of Lincoln's journey to Washington and his inauguration, Lincoln left New York City at 8:00 AM via the Cortlandt Street ferry, boarded his train, and rode through New Jersey. At four that afternoon, the Lincolns arrived in Philadelphia, where they took a carriage to the Continental Hotel. Late in the evening, a Chicago detective named Allan Pinkerton, hired to watch secessionists in Baltimore, met with Lincoln to deliver an ominous warning.

Pinkerton told Lincoln of a specific plot to assassinate him during his visit to Baltimore—a hotbed of pro-secessionist sentiment—on February 23. Pinkerton recommended that Lincoln leave that very night for Washington, rolling secretly through Baltimore. Lincoln refused. "I could not believe there was a plot to murder me," Lincoln would later write. Besides, he already had engagements for the next day in Philadelphia and Harrisburg that he felt compelled to honor.

After leaving Pinkerton, Lincoln was introduced to Frederick Seward, son of New York Senator (and soon to be Lincoln's Secretary of State) William Seward. Seward had a letter from Colonel Charles Stone, who had the job of watching pro-secessionists in Washington. He had information of a Baltimore plot as well. "I now believed such a plot existed," Lincoln wrote. Still, he refused to change his plans.

The next day, Lincoln attended a ceremony at Independence Hall, where the first American flag with thirty-four stars (Kansas had been admitted to the Union on January 29) was raised. During his dedication speech, Lincoln revealed what was much on his mind, "But if this country cannot be saved without giving up that principle [freedom]—I was about to say I would rather be assassinated on the spot than surrender it."

#8

Should Lincoln Have Been Worried?

Long before he left for Washington, the president-elect had heard rumors of people who intended "mischief," Lincoln later admitted. "I never attached much importance to them." But on February 21, Lincoln received word from two separate sources of a Baltimore plot. One of those sources—Allan Pinkerton—revealed that a barber named Cypriano Ferrandini and his associates planned to kill Lincoln as he emerged from the narrow vestibule at the Baltimore Calvert Street Station. But Pinkerton was uncertain that the conspirators had the guts to carry out their plot.

There were, however, others who tried to convince Lincoln of the danger. General in Chief Winfield Scott was worried. And Captain George Hazzard, who had lived in the tough, pro-South city of Baltimore, also warned Lincoln that the risk was genuine. Hazzard recommended that Lincoln take an unannounced late night train through Baltimore (the only direct rail connection to Washington), wearing "an old slouched hat, and long cloak or overcoat for concealment." That is eventually what Lincoln did.

As it turned out, there was a disturbance at the Calvert Station. On the day Lincoln was to appear there, a New York train was mistaken for his and a crowd swarmed over it, mounting the cars and "shouting, hallooing and making all manner of noises," a local newspaper reported. But a rambunctious crowd is not the same as a group of assassins.

Lincoln himself was dubious of the plot. "I did not then, nor do I now believe I should have been assassinated had I gone through Baltimore," he said later. "But I thought it wise to run no risk where no risk was necessary."

FEBRUARY 23

Lincoln's Secret Train Ride

By the morning of February 22, 1861, Lincoln was finally convinced that the plot to assassinate him in Baltimore the next day was legitimate. He agreed to sneak in and out of Baltimore and on this night in 1861 he did just that.

On the evening of February 22, one of Detective Allan Pinkerton's operatives—Andrew Wynné—cut Harrisburg, Pennsylvania's telegraph wires to prevent leaks to the would-be conspirators. Lincoln left his hotel wearing a soft felt "Kossuth" hat and an overcoat thrown over his shoulders. He took a train from Harrisburg to Philadelphia, and there Pinkerton took Lincoln on a carriage ride around the city until the train to Baltimore was about to leave the station. Another operative created an elaborate hoax to distract the conductor while the secret party slipped into the rear sleeping car, Lincoln stooping to disguise his height.

The sleeping berth was so short that Lincoln had to double up his legs to lie on it and spent an uncomfortable, sleepless night telling jokes. The presidential party passed quietly through Baltimore at 3:00 AM and arrived in Washington three hours later. Emerging from the station, Lincoln remained unrecognized until someone yelled, "Abe, you can't play that on me!" Pinkerton whirled around to meet the attacker, only to find Lincoln's friend and Illinois Congressman Elihu Washburne hailing them.

The press severely criticized Lincoln for the episode, questioning his courage. A supporter, George Templeton Strong, wrote, "this surreptitious nocturnal dodging and sneaking of the president-elect into his capital city . . . will be used to damage his moral position and throw ridicule on his administration." Lincoln's family went through Baltimore separately.

#9

Lincoln's First Day in Washington

Upon reaching Washington, Lincoln checked into the Willard Hotel at Pennsylvania Avenue and Fourteenth Street. There, in suite six, where he would remain for the next ten days until his inauguration, Lincoln found a letter waiting for him. "If you don't Resign we are going to put a spider in your dumpling and play the Devil with you," it read. What followed were nine lines of obscenities.

Lincoln wired Mary to tell her of his safe arrival and then had breakfast with Secretary of State–designate William Seward. Lincoln and Seward walked to the White House, where President James Buchanan greeted his successor exuberantly and took him on a brief tour of the executive mansion.

Late that afternoon the rest of the Lincolns finally arrived in Washington. Mary was shaken and had a severe headache. As her train passed through Baltimore, a crowd, unaware that the president-elect had already slipped through the city, greeted the presidential coaches. The clamoring for Lincoln, the menacing faces, and the abusive cat-calls were something Mary would never forget.

At Willard's, Lincoln received visitors all day, including delegates from a peace conference organized to stem the secession crisis. After nine that night, Lincoln held an informal reception for members of Congress and guests. One of the guests was William Dodge, a rich New York merchant who told Lincoln that he must make concessions to the South or the nation would go bankrupt and "grass shall grow in the streets of our commercial cities." Lincoln frowned and said he preferred that grass grow in meadows but that he'd defend the Constitution and "let the grass grow where it may."

FEBRUARY 27

The Old Nemesis

On this Wednesday in 1861, Lincoln met with his old nemesis Stephen Douglas and forged a working partnership based on their mutual patriotism.

Lincoln owed his presidency to his public animosity with Douglas. In 1854, Lincoln was all but retired from political life when Illinois Senator Douglas introduced the Kansas–Nebraska Act, allowing a Northern territory to vote to be a slave state (Douglas's popular sovereignty policy). Lincoln began to heavily campaign against this "great wrong and injustice."

When Douglas was up for reelection in 1858, Lincoln carried the argument onto the campaign trail. The ensuing debates launched the relatively unknown Lincoln into the national spotlight, even though he didn't win the Senate seat. Afterwards, Lincoln rebutted Douglas's arguments one more time in a speech at Cooper Union in Manhattan, a speech that made Lincoln the Republican darling of the East as well the Midwest. Together with his first Matthew Brady portrait (reproduced in mass quantities for the election), Cooper Union made Lincoln a contender for the White House, a prize he eventually took out of Douglas's grasp. "Brady and Cooper Institute made me President," Lincoln told a friend.

On this day—the one-year anniversary of Cooper Union and just a week before Lincoln's inauguration—Douglas visited him at Willard's Hotel to urge conciliation and compromise with the South. Douglas also promised that he and his fellow Democrats would not use the crisis for their own political purposes. "Our Union must be preserved," Douglas said. "Partisan feeling must yield to patriotism. I am with you, Mr. President, and God bless you." After Douglas left, Lincoln, visibly touched, said, "What a noble man Douglas is!"

Four months later, Douglas would die while actively campaigning for Lincoln's war effort.

MARCH 5

Anderson's Warning

On this Tuesday in 1861—his first morning as president—Lincoln found on his desk a letter with some unexpected bad news. It was from Major Robert Anderson, the commander of Fort Sumter, a bastion that sat on a granite island four miles from downtown

Charleston, South Carolina. It represented the only federal authority remaining in all of South Carolina and—along with Fort Pickens in Florida—was nearly the only federal presence in all of the Confederate Deep South. A ring of cannon and thousands of South Carolina militiamen had surrounded Anderson and his 127 men for three months, itching to start a war. In his letter, Anderson warned that provisions for his garrison would be exhausted in six weeks and he would be forced to surrender. Worse, Anderson estimated that he would need 20,000 reinforcements for him to hold the fort. Lincoln, at the time, had a total of only 16,000 men in the entire army.

Lincoln turned to Winfield Scott, the seventy-five-year-old general in chief who was so enfeebled and corpulent that he could neither ride a horse nor climb the White House steps. And yet the hero of the Mexican War was perhaps the most experienced and most respected military mind in America. That evening Scott wrote Lincoln that it was too late to save Fort Sumter. "We cannot send a third of the men . . . necessary to give them [Sumter] relief," said Scott, and felt that surrender was the only alternative.

Lincoln had a dilemma, in his inaugural speech, he pledged not only to "hold . . . places belonging to the government," but to avoid "bloodshed or violence . . . unless it be forced upon the national authority." Now, just a day later, he was faced with the possibility of breaking one or both of his promises.

MARCH 10

Lincoln Goes to Church

This Sunday in 1861 was Lincoln's first as president, and he attended—with his family—services at the New York Avenue Presbyterian Church on the corner of New York Avenue and Thirteenth Street. While Lincoln would never join any church, he did become a regular attendee at this one and, on June 1 of that year, he reserved a pew eight rows from the front at $50 a year. It was church custom to remain seated during prayer, but Lincoln always stood. When he attended Wednesday night prayer services, Lincoln would sit in the pastor's private study where he could listen and not be seen.

The pastor, Dr. Phineas Gurley, was a frequent visitor to the White House, often to petition the president on behalf of clergymen who had been arrested, usually because of their sympathies toward the South. He warned that the War Department's removal of pastors from Northern churches would be more "injurious than beneficial to the Government."

For a year after Willie's death, Mary rarely appeared in public except to attend church where—as one observer noted—she "was so hid behind an immense black veil—and very deep black flounces—that one could scarcely tell she was there." Nine months after Willie's death, journalist Noah Brooks attended a Sunday service at Lincoln's church, and observed Lincoln's sad charisma:

> As he moves down the church aisle, recognizing, with a cheerful nod, his friends on either side, his homely face lighted with a smile, there is an involuntary expression of respect on every face, and men, who would scorn to "toady" to any President, look with commiserating admiration on that tall, mourning figure.

#10

Praying for the President

It was the custom of many churches during the nineteenth century to say a prayer for the president during Sunday services. When the South seceded from the Union, however, this practice became contentious. Dr. J. C. Smith, pastor of the Fourth Presbyterian Church in Washington, refused to give up the practice, to the consternation of secessionists in his church. Willie and Tad Lincoln occasionally attended the Fourth Presbyterian, the regular church of their best friends, Bud and Holly Taft. Their older sister Julia recorded one such visit:

> Many in our church were in sympathy with the secessionists, and when Doctor Smith prayed for the President . . . they would express their disapproval by rising and leaving the church, banging the pew doors . . . on their way out. This went on for several weeks until one Sunday a slim young lieutenant appeared with a file of soldiers . . . [and announced] "it is the order of the Provost Marshal that any one disturbing this service or leaving it before it is out will be arrested and taken to the guardhouse." It seemed to me that the Doctor Smith prayed rather longer and more fervently than usual that day for the President but there was no disturbance on the part of the secessionists. Tad Lincoln was frankly disappointed. The indignant exodus of the secessionists with their banging of pew doors had been a welcome respite in the long prayer.

Later, when Willie told his father the story, Tad asked why preachers insist on praying "so long for you, Pa?" The president's smile left his face and he replied, "Well, Tad, I supposed it's because the preachers think I need it, and I guess I do."

MARCH 12

Surrendering Sumter?

On this day in 1861, Lincoln struggled over whether he should abandon or send provisions to beseiged Fort Sumter off Charleston, South Carolina.

Lincoln was not a man who reached conclusions quickly or acted impetuously. After he was informed of Major Robert Anderson's dire situation at Fort Sumter (the fort would run out of supplies soon), he made no public pronouncements or promises that he might later regret. For four days he didn't even discuss it with his cabinet, to allow, he said, "the Administration to get in working order." Then on March 9 he broke the news during an evening cabinet meeting, with Lincoln adding that General in Chief Winfield Scott recommended surrendering Sumter. The majority of the shocked department heads quickly concurred.

Lincoln, unwilling to make a decision yet, on that same day went back to Scott for more information. He asked the general how long Sumter's supplies could last, and if Scott could reinforce or resupply the fort in time. On this day, Scott responded that Major Anderson's men could "hold out some forty days without much suffering from hunger" but reinforcement or resupply couldn't be attempted in less than "six to eight months." Either surrender of the fort or starvation of Anderson's men was, Scott maintained, "merely a question of time."

"It is, therefore, my opinion and advice," Scott wrote, "that Major Anderson be instructed to evacuate the Fort . . . immediately on procuring suitable water transportation."

Lincoln, still not satisfied, gathered around him less pessimistic military minds. One optimist in particular—former Navy lieutenant Gustavus Fox—was knowledgeable of coastal defenses and had for months been advocating a plan to use powerful light-draft tugboats to quickly run past the Charleston shallows and gun batteries to take men and supplies to the fort at night. Scott, with the usual scorn the army had for navy planners, thought the plan impractical. But Lincoln began to consider it.

MARCH 16

Lincoln Polls His Cabinet

Lincoln was still undecided about what to do with Fort Sumter and was considering Lieutenant Gustavus Fox's plans to replenish and/or reinforce the fort using shallow-draft tugs. On March 15,

1861, Lincoln decided to poll his cabinet, sending each of them a note: "Assuming it to be possible to now provision Fort-Sumpter, under all the circumstances, is it wise to attempt it?" The next day, this Saturday in 1861, all seven department heads submitted a written opinion.

Secretary of State William Seward believed that any attempt to send provisions to the fort would "provoke combat, and probably initiate a civil war." Seward believed that Union sentiment was still prevalent in the South and that a policy of conciliation would buy time for rebellious sentiment to subside. Attorney General Edward Bates concurred, believing that the South would reunite with the North "if encouraged by wise, moderate, and firm measures . . . without the effusion of blood." Three other department heads agreed that reinforcing Fort Sumter shouldn't be attempted.

Postmaster General Montgomery Blair took the opposite view, believing that a strengthened and resupplied Fort Sumter stubbornly maintained in the heart of South Carolina would "demoralize the Rebellion" and leave its instigators to stew in an "impotent rage." Such a symbol would stir an "outburst of patriotic feeling which . . . would speedily overwhelm the traitors." Salmon Chase, secretary of the treasury, also believed that the fort should be provisioned, but only because he did not believe it would spark armed conflict.

Lincoln was not happy with his advisors' opinions. He felt that surrendering the fort "would be utterly ruinous" politically. As he explained to Congress later, such actions "would discourage friends of the Union, [and] embolden its adversaries . . . in fact, it would be our national destruction consummated." Despite the advice of his general in chief and most of his cabinet, Lincoln began to lean toward resupplying and reinforcing the fort.

#11

The Surrounded Fortress

Traditionally the first shots of the Civil War are said to have been fired at Fort Sumter at 4:30 AM on April 12, 1861. Technically, however, they were fired more than three months earlier when James Buchanan, not Abraham Lincoln, was president.

In the days after South Carolina seceded from the Union, on December 20, 1860, it was clear that the state government meant to confiscate all federal property in Charleston, including Forts Sumter, Moultrie, Johnson, and Castle Pickney. And, if necessary, the state militia meant to forcibly remove the troops from those forts. On the day after Christmas, Major Robert Anderson secretly moved his seventy-five soldiers from the indefensible Fort Moultrie on Sullivan's Island to the highly defensible Fort Sumter in the middle of Charleston Harbor. The Carolinians, led by General P. G. T. Beauregard, responded by isolating the Sumter garrison, forming a ring of cannon and mortar batteries around it.

In January 1861, Buchanan's administration attempted to slip an unarmed passenger liner named *Star of the West* into Charleston harbor and deliver 200 soldiers to the besieged garrison. The *Star of the West* arrived outside the ship channel during the night of January 9 but, because the rebels had destroyed the lighthouse and pulled out the channel buoys, she couldn't make her run until first light. By then the federal troops could plainly be seen crowding her decks.

At 7:15 AM, a young military cadet named G. W. Haynesworth fired a twenty-four-pound shot across the *Star of the*

West's bow. Two shots from his battery actually struck the liner before she turned around and left without reaching Sumter. The ship's American flag was clearly visible and firing upon it was an act of war. Had President Buchanan been so inclined, the Civil War could have started two months before Lincoln was inaugurated.

MARCH 18

The Green President

When Lincoln took office, he had only two years of experience in national politics and zero experience within the executive branch. He would later admit that he was "entirely ignorant not only of the duties, but of the manner of doing business" in the office of the president. Inevitably, he made mistakes. For one, he placed the corrupt, incompetent Simon Cameron at the helm of the critical War Department, despite Cameron's reputation. For another, Lincoln tried to issue orders directly to naval officers, completely circumventing the chain of command. And on this Monday in 1861, Lincoln attempted to establish a militia bureau without congressional approval.

Each individual state equipped its own militia and this led to a rather eclectic variety within the ranks. For instance, some of the militias wore gray or butternut uniforms similar to some Confederate units. This would lead to instances where Union soldiers fired on fellow Union soldiers. The bureau Lincoln wanted was to be attached to the War Department and given the task of "promoting a uniform system of organization, drill, [and] equipment" of the militias. Lincoln sent his proposal to Attorney General Edward Bates for his opinion on its legality.

A month later (April 18), Bates responded to this March 18 initiative, noting that Article I, Section 8 of the Constitution conferred on Congress the power to organize militias and "reserving to the

States respectively, the appointment of officers and the authority of training the militia." In short, Lincoln's bureau would infringe on the rights of Congress and the states. Congress would have to approve the bureau and its appropriations. The bureau was never formed, but uniformity of the militias was eventually established.

Lincoln continued to fumble through. "The difficulty with Mr. Lincoln," Massachusetts Senator Charles Sumner said, "is that he has no conception of his situation."

MARCH 19

Patronage

In Lincoln's time—long before civil service reform—the president was responsible for filling more than 1,500 federal positions. Since Lincoln was the first Republican president, it's not surprising that he found most of those 1,500 positions filled with Democrats. Lincoln removed 1,100 of them and replaced the majority of them with either Republicans or War Democrats sympathetic to the war effort. It was the most sweeping change in federal personnel up to that time. One such position was the office of surveyor general for the Utah Territory. On this Tuesday in 1861, Lincoln met with Ohio Congressman James Ashley to discuss who should fill that position.

With so many offices opening for presidential patronage, office-seekers flocked to the White House. And Lincoln agreed to see them all. He saw them from nine in the morning until late at night, and sometimes they were so numerous that the line stretched from his office on the second floor down the stairs to the front entrance. "Even members of his [Lincoln's] cabinet had to force their way through the crowd . . . before they could impart to him grave matters of state," said a deputy secretary.

Lincoln rarely rejected applicants outright, usually using one of his stories to deflect the request. Reporter Henry Villard wrote that

Lincoln had "a humorous remark for nearly everyone that seeks his presence, and that but few, if any, emerge from his reception room without being strongly and favorably impressed with his general disposition." He added that Lincoln's stories "helped many times to heal wounded feelings and mitigate disappointments."

The numbers of office-seekers were so great, Lincoln's secretary John Nicolay wrote, that "we have scarcely had time to eat sleep or even breathe." But Lincoln refused to turn anyone away. They "don't want much and don't get but little, and I must see them," Lincoln said.

MARCH 29

The Commander in Chief Decides

On this Friday in 1861, Lincoln finally decided what to do with Fort Sumter.

By late March, Lincoln was receiving pressure from all sides over the Sumter crisis. He could neither reinforce nor resupply the Charleston garrison without the secessionists firing on the fort, thus precipitating a war. Most of Lincoln's cabinet and General in Chief Winfield Scott felt Major Robert Anderson should surrender his Sumter garrison. But to do so without a fight would mean political suicide. "If he [Anderson] goes out of Fort Sumter, I shall have to go out of the White House," Lincoln said. "It is the duty of the President to use all means in his power to hold and protect the public property of the United States," a Senate resolution demanded. Republican Congressmen warned Lincoln that surrendering the fort would destroy his own party. Lincoln struggled to decide. Then, on March 28, he received advice that crystallized his decision.

The Lincolns were, on that day, preparing for their first state dinner when Scott visited the White House. Scott advised his president that not only should Sumter be evacuated, but Fort Pickens in

Florida should be surrendered as well, even though it could be reinforced without interference. Until then, Lincoln had assumed that Scott's recommendations were derived from military necessity. But Scott's reason for surrendering Pickens was political, to keep the eight remaining slave states—including his home state of Virginia—from joining the Confederacy. Lincoln now questioned the motives behind Scott's advice on Sumter and, after the state dinner, Lincoln expressed his outrage to his cabinet. That night Lincoln couldn't sleep.

At noon on this day, Lincoln once more polled his cabinet on Forts Sumter and Pickens. Now the cabinet favored reinforcing or resupplying them. Attorney General Francis Blair even threatened to resign if Lincoln accepted Scott's advice. Lincoln concurred and immediately began making plans. Lincoln later confided that "all the troubles and anxieties of my life" could not equal the apprehension he felt during the Sumter crisis.

MARCH 30

A Share in the Patronage Pie

Lincoln spent much of this Saturday in 1861 addressing friends about patronage jobs.

Amid the stress of the Sumter crisis, Lincoln also had to oil the cogs of nineteenth-century politics, handing out jobs to retain political support. The tide of office-seekers was overwhelming and constant. He felt "like a man letting lodgings at one end of his house, while the other end is on fire." But when the office-seekers were friends and family, the pressure was greater still.

On this day in 1861, Lincoln wrote Jesse K. Dubois, a friend and fellow Illinois lawyer, that he regretted not giving Dubois's son-in-law, John Luse, the position of superintendent of Indian affairs in Minnesota. Republicans from Minnesota had blocked Luse's appointment. "My heart was set on this application for him, as in his appointment I could have transferred my dying daughter from the Wabash Valley to the healthy climate of Minnessotta and perhaps prolonged her life," Dubois wrote Lincoln. Dubois, afterward, felt that Lincoln had turned his back on his friends: "The moment [he] was elevated to his proud position he seemed all at once to have entirely changed his whole nature."

Lincoln also wrote John Stuart, his first law-partner and one of Mary Lincoln's cousins, about his desire to name another of Mary's cousins—Elizabeth Grimsley—postmistress of Springfield. Lincoln wondered at the propriety of naming a relative to office. Ultimately, Grimsley did not receive the position.

Still another friend of Lincoln's—Oregon Senator Edward Baker—met this day with Lincoln and a California delegation to discuss their recommendations for appointments in their state. When one of the delegates disparaged Baker and offended the president, Lincoln angrily tossed the delegation's written recommendations into his fireplace.

APRIL 1

The American Prime Minister

Lincoln received a memorandum on this afternoon in 1861 that was so extraordinary, he could have characterized it as an April Fool's joke. Unfortunately, it wasn't funny.

The previous February, William Seward—soon to be the Secretary of State—told a German diplomat "that there was no great difference between an elected president . . . and an hereditary monarch." Both were figureheads and the government was directed by "the leader of the ruling party." Seward thought he was that leader. When Lincoln refused to be a figurehead, particularly in deciding to reinforce Sumter instead of surrendering it, Seward sent Lincoln, on this day, a memorandum titled "some thoughts for the President's consideration."

"We are at the end of a month's administration and yet without a policy either domestic or foreign," Seward wrote. He believed that Sumter should be evacuated and that public attention should be shifted to foreign policy, declaring war on Spain (for Santo Domingo rebel support) and France (for its intervention in Mexican affairs). He added that Lincoln was too distracted with filling offices and declared that a policy must be adopted and "either the President must do it himself . . . or devolve it on some member of his Cabinet." In effect, Seward was recommending that Lincoln appoint a prime minister. Seward wanted the position.

"Had Mr. Lincoln been an envious or resentful man, he could not have wished for a better occasion to put a rival under his feet," wrote Lincoln's secretary John Nicolay. Instead, Lincoln responded that he had already set domestic policy in his inaugural address, promising to "hold" all federal property—including Sumter. As to who would run the administration, "I remark that if this must be done, I must do it." To save Seward's reputation, Lincoln never told anyone about the memorandum.

#12

Seward's Ambition

On the day the Republican Party nominated its candidate to run for president (May 18, 1860), people were so certain that William Seward would be the nominee that neighbors drove miles to Seward's Auburn, New York, home to stand outside it and cheer at his victory. Auburn restaurants were fully stocked, banners made. Seward himself had already begun writing his speech resigning as senator from New York. When word arrived that Lincoln had been nominated instead, Seward turned "as pale as ashes." Months later the hurt was still fresh when, in response to a complaint, Seward snapped, "Disappointment! You speak to me of disappointment. To me, who was justly entitled to the Republican nomination for the presidency, and who had to stand aside and see it given to a little Illinois lawyer!"

Seward was sure that the wrong man had been nominated. When Lincoln gave Seward the most powerful cabinet position—Secretary of State—Seward began to see himself as a premier or prime minister, guiding this Western rube through a national crisis. This first manifested itself when Seward wanted to choose Lincoln's cabinet. When Lincoln rebuffed his attempts to interfere, Seward submitted his resignation as secretary-designate two days before the inauguration (March 2, 1861). "I can't afford to let Seward take the first trick," Lincoln said. He told Seward, through mutual acquaintances, that he already had a replacement for Seward in mind. Seward quickly withdrew his resignation.

Still believing he could manipulate Lincoln, Seward promised Confederate representatives, without consulting the president, that Fort Sumter would be surrendered. When it was clear that it would not be, Seward, in desperation, submitted the infamous April Fool's Day memorandum. After Lincoln rebuffed him, Seward stopped challenging Lincoln's authority and eventually became a close friend.

APRIL 5

The Presidential Paycheck

On this Friday in 1861, Lincoln received his first presidential paycheck—called a salary warrant—for $2,083.33 and deposited it into a new account at the bank Riggs & Co.

A prevalent legend about Lincoln is that he was born in abject poverty and spent the rest of his life poor. While the one-room cabin where Lincoln was born seems pathetic to modern eyes, the Lincoln family's standard of living was actually above the average household at that time and place (1809, Sinking Springs, Kentucky).

By the time Lincoln was elected president, he was worth about $15,000. One legend has it that Lincoln had to borrow $400 to make the trip to Washington, but the money actually came from his savings account. The Lincolns spent their first ten days in Washington at the Willard Hotel, accumulating a bill for $773.75. He paid that bill on this day after he received his paycheck.

Lincoln would receive forty-eight more warrants, all on or around the fifth of each month. He deposited nineteen of them into Washington banks (all but one at Riggs & Co.) and used twenty-six of them to purchase government obligations such as treasury notes or bonds. The final four warrants were found in a desk drawer after his death. Lincoln wrote 222 checks against his Riggs & Co. account, at least two of which have survived, one five-dollar check to "Tad when he is well enough to present"; the other a five-dollar check to a "colored man, with one leg."

Through his government obligations and warrant savings, Lincoln's estate at his death was worth $90,000—six times his estate's worth four years earlier. Because Lincoln died intestate (he, a lawyer, had written no will) the sum was divided between Mary and the two surviving sons, Tad and Robert.

APRIL 6

To Avoid War

On this Saturday in 1861, Lincoln sent an emissary to South Carolina Governor Francis Pickens, warning him that "an attempt will be made to supply Fort-Sumpter with provisions only; and that, if such attempt be not resisted, no effort to throw in men, arms or ammunition, will be made."

The plan to resupply Fort Sumter had changed since Gustavus Fox had first presented it to Lincoln in March. Instead of the shallow-draft tugs entering Charleston Harbor with an escort blazing away at the harbor defenses, the escorts would remain outside the harbor along with two hundred reinforcements for the garrison while the unarmed tugs made the journey. The escorts would wait there as long as the Confederate batteries did not fire upon the tugs. If they didn't fire, Lincoln would have a much-needed symbolic victory. If they did fire, the South would stand convicted of starting the war.

To avoid that war, Lincoln, on April 4, met with a Virginia representative and, according to some sources, offered to surrender Sumter in exchange for assurances that Virginia would not secede. "If you will guarantee to me the State of Virginia I shall remove the troops. A State for a fort is no bad business," he allegedly said. Nothing came of the offer and, on that same day, Lincoln ordered the Sumter expedition to proceed.

Lincoln sent his warning to Pickens because he wanted the secessionists to know that the tugs were carrying only food for a hungry garrison. Not only did he not want the tugs fired upon, he wanted a record of his efforts to resolve the crisis peacefully.

APRIL 13

Sumter Falls

Lincoln, on this Saturday in 1861, waited with the rest of country for official news from Charleston, South Carolina while he read newspaper accounts of the bombardment of Fort Sumter.

At the beginning of April 1861, Lincoln sent a courier to South Carolina's governor Francis Pickens to inform him that an expedition was en route to peacefully supply the Sumter garrison. When the new Confederate president, Jefferson Davis, was apprised of Lincoln's message, he ordered (on April 10) the South Carolina forces to deliver an ultimatum to Major Robert Anderson: surrender the fort or be fired upon. Anderson refused to surrender and at 4:30 on the morning of April 12 the bombardment of Sumter commenced. The Civil War had begun.

"The ball has opened," read a Charleston dispatch printed in the *New York Times* on this day. "With the very first boom of the guns thousands rushed from their beds to the harbor front." Lincoln's only sources of information were newspapers on this second day of bombardment. While waiting for official news, Lincoln took time to reply in writing to Virginia delegates as to what his policy would be toward them. He still wanted peace. "But if, as now appears to be true . . . an unprovoked assault, has been made upon Fort-Sumpter . . . I shall . . . repel force with force."

After thirty-four hours of bombardment, Anderson surrendered. More than 4,341 shots had been fired at or from Fort Sumter and yet not a single combatant on either side had been killed. The surrender became official the next day—April 14—when Anderson gave his flag a cannon salute as he hauled it down. One of the cannons misfired, killing Private Daniel Hough—the first casualty of the war.

APRIL 17

Virginia Secedes from the Union

On this Wednesday in 1861, Lincoln conferred with his General in Chief Winfield Scott on the secession of Virginia from the Union.

The day after Fort Sumter was surrendered (April 15), Lincoln issued a proclamation declaring that the Confederacy had obstructed federal laws "by combinations too powerful to be suppressed by the ordinary course of judicial proceedings." He called for the states to supply 75,000 militiamen "to suppress said combinations" and summoned Congress to special session on July 4. Lincoln was criticized for summoning too few men. "I would make it 200,000," said Lincoln's old nemesis, Stephen Douglas. But the government did not yet have the logistics to support hundreds of thousands of men. And a larger army might give secessionists in the border slave states the leverage to force their states to secede.

That fear turned out to be well founded. Border states Missouri and Tennessee refused to furnish militiamen. "You can get no troops from North Carolina," Governor John Ellis declared. And on this day Virginia, citing Lincoln's call for militia as the reason, seceded from the Union. Although it did not immediately join the rebels, Virginia's eventual membership would give the Confederacy a strategic and financial boost and a new national capitol (Richmond). Its prestige would spur three more states—North Carolina, Tennessee, and Arkansas—to join the Confederacy.

On this day Lincoln conferred with Scott over the federal installations in Virginia, specifically the armory at Harpers Ferry and the Gosport Naval Yard in Norfolk. Within days, both facilities would be in rebel hands. On April 18, Lincoln offered Robert E. Lee the command of the federal army. The Virginian admitted he opposed secession, but he declined the offer, saying he could not "raise my hand against my relatives, my children, my home." Lee would join the Confederacy, providing it what both sides badly needed—a great military mind.

#13

The Anguished Decision

A short time after Robert E. Lee resigned his commission in the U.S. Army (April 20, 1861), Lee reportedly bumped into Benjamin Hardin Helm, Lincoln's brother-in-law. "Are you feeling well, Colonel Lee?" Helm asked when he saw

Lee's anxious face. "Well in body but not in mind," Lee responded, according to Helm's wife Emilie (Mary Lincoln's half sister). "In the prime of life I quit the service in which were all my hopes and expectations in this world."

Helm then showed Lee a letter handed to him by Lincoln that very morning, offering a commission as major and a position as army paymaster. But Helm was a Kentuckian and a rabid "Southern-Rights" Democrat. On the other hand, he had formed a friendship with Lincoln that Emilie characterized as "more like the affection of brothers than the ordinary liking of men." When Helm asked Lee for advice, Lee was "too much disturbed" to say anything but to "do as your conscience and your honor bid."

That night Helm was unable to sleep and when he returned to the White House the next day, he said, "I am going home. I will answer you from there. The position you offer me is beyond what I had expected, even in my most hopeful dreams. You have been very generous to me, Mr. Lincoln. . . . I had no claim upon you, for I opposed your candidacy, and did what I could to prevent your election. . . . Don't let this offer be made public yet. I will send you my answer in a few days."

Back in Kentucky, Helm decided "to cast his destinies with his native southland." Helm wrote Lincoln an anguished letter declining the offer and afterward accepted a commission in the Confederate Army. He died a brigadier general at the battle of Chickamauga.

APRIL 19

The Blockade

On this day in 1861, Lincoln issued a proclamation that the federal government would blockade the seaports of the initial seven members of the Confederacy: South Carolina, Georgia, Alabama, Florida, Mississippi, Louisiana, and Texas. On April 27, Lincoln added Virginia and North Carolina to the blockade list (Arkansas and Tennessee did not have seaports).

The task of blockading 3,549 miles of Confederate coastline was daunting, especially since the navy had only fourteen ships for immediate use. Of its ninety commissioned warships, forty-eight were either not seaworthy or under repair (eleven of which were lost when the Gosport Naval Yard was abandoned on April 20) and twenty-eight were patrolling overseas. Almost immediately the navy called for 18,000 more men—many from the merchant marine—and purchased or chartered dozens of merchant ships and armed them. Within a year three hundred new ships had either been purchased or built and, by war's end, more than six hundred new ships had been added to the navy.

Lincoln's blockade presented a legal quandary. He insisted that the rebel states were still part of the Union. But since blockades were acts of war used against foreign belligerents, not domestic ports, Lincoln's proclamation essentially recognized the Confederacy as an independent nation. Lincoln could have simply closed Southern ports, but this would not allow U.S. ships to search ships from neutral countries. When Pennsylvania congressman Thaddeus Stevens confronted Lincoln on this "great blunder and absurdity," Lincoln pretended ignorance. "As a lawyer, Mr. Lincoln, I should have supposed you would have seen the difficulty at once," Stevens snapped. "Oh, well, I'm a good enough lawyer in Western law court, I suppose, but we don't practice the law of nations up there," Lincoln responded. "But it's done now and can't be helped, so we must get along as well as we can."

#14

Was Lincoln's Blockade Effective?

Some historians have criticized Lincoln's blockade as ineffective, "scarcely a respectable paper blockade." They cite the fact that during the war five out of every six blockade runners successfully made it through (this is an average; nine out of ten were successful in 1861, but only one out of two in 1865). Indeed, during the war Southerners exported half a million bales of cotton and imported a million pairs of shoes, half a million rifles, and a thousand tons of gunpowder.

This, however, is deceptive. The successful blockade runners had to use small boats built for speed rather than freighters built for capacity, greatly reducing the amount of material shipped. The half million bales of cotton exported in the three years of the war (the Confederacy voluntarily embargoed cotton the first year) does not compare well with the ten million exported in the three years prior to the war. Nor did the port traffic remain the same; there were twenty thousand ships cleared to arrive or leave Southern ports in the four years before the war, but there were only one thousand successful blockade-running sorties. All told, the blockade reduced Southern trade by two-thirds.

Because the South had little industry, it had to import virtually all its war material. Combined with a deteriorating railroad system that couldn't be fixed (no pig iron) and speculators who hoarded, the blockade created shortages that drove up prices until even non-imported items such as food became unaffordable. Confederate soldiers began to starve. "Short rations are having a bad effect upon the men, both morally and physically," wrote Confederate general Robert E. Lee. "Unless there is a change, I fear the army cannot be kept together." While their families starved, it was hard for soldiers to justify staying in the field. A Mississippi private wrote in 1862, "There is already a heap of men gone home and a heap says if their familys get to suffering that they will go [too]."

APRIL 21

Washington is Isolated

In response to deadly anti-Union riots in Baltimore on April 19, 1861, the city's mayor, George Brown, with the blessing of Maryland's governor, Thomas Hicks, ordered the rail bridges to Baltimore from Philadelphia and Harrisburg burned. As a major Maryland railhead, nearly all trains to Washington had to go through Baltimore and thus Brown's actions cut all rail connections between the capitol and the rest of the North. For the next few days a string of Maryland representatives—including Hicks and Brown—came to Washington to speak to Lincoln. A Baltimore delegation, which Lincoln's secretary John Hay described as a "penitent and suppliant crowd of conditional Secessionists . . . who having sowed the wind seem to have no particular desire to reap the whirlwind," arrived at the White House on this Sunday in 1861. They begged Lincoln to not send any more troops through their city, which might spark another riot. Hoping to keep Maryland from seceding, Lincoln agreed.

With no other direct rail routes to Washington, troops on their way to protect Washington would have to march rather than ride to the capital. For a very long week Lincoln waited for the troops to make the trek, while he watched the Confederates across the Potomac, building up their army, preparing to attack a virtually unprotected Washington. What was worse, secessionists cut Washington's telegraph wires and stopped its mail. Journalist Henry Villard said, "Literally, it was as though the government of a great nation had been suddenly removed to an island in mid-ocean in a state of entire isolation."

"The whining traitors from Baltimore were here again this morning," Hay noted the next day (April 22). Yet another Baltimore delegation arrived that day, who also insisted that troops not be allowed to march through Maryland. "I must have troops to defend this Capital," Lincoln replied. "Geographically it lies surrounded by the soil of Maryland. . . . Our men are not moles, and can't dig under the earth; they are not birds, and can't fly through the air. There is no way but to march across, and that they must do."

APRIL 24

The Wait

Lincoln, on this Wednesday in 1861, lamented that Washington seemed to stand alone against the Confederacy.

With the Washington telegraphs cut, its railroad bridges burned and the capital isolated by secessionists, Northerners wondered at the fate of the federal government. George Templeton Strong of New York wrote in his diary, "No despatches from Washington. People talked darkly of its being attacked before our reinforcements come to the rescue, and everyone said we must not be surprised by news that Lincoln . . . and all the Administration are prisoners." The anxiety outside of Washington, however, was nothing compared to that inside. "The town is full tonight of feverish rumors about a mediated assault upon this town," Lincoln's secretary, John Hay, wrote in his diary. Government employees were organized into militias. Stores were closed, hotels emptied, and food prices skyrocketed.

Every day Washingtonians heard that regiments from New York and Rhode Island were attempting to make it to the capital and every day they failed to arrive. "A large and disappointed throng gathered at the [rail] depot this morning hoping to get deliverance. But the hope was futile," Hay wrote on April 23. On that same day Hay discovered Lincoln standing at a window, saying, "Why don't they come! Why don't they come!" On this day, soldiers from the Sixth Massachusetts Regiment, who had been pummeled by Baltimore rioters on April 19, walked to the White House to see their president. While talking to a soldier, Lincoln said, "I don't believe there is any North. The Seventh [New York] Regiment is a myth. Rhode Island is not known in our geography any longer. You are the only Northern realities."

At noon the next day the Seventh New York finally arrived. When Hay delivered the news, he "gladdened the heart of the Ancient [Hay's nickname for Lincoln]."

APRIL 25

Maryland and Secession

On this day in 1861, Lincoln decided not to arrest or detain Maryland legislators who threatened their state's secession.

Under intense pressure from secessionists, the governor of Maryland, Thomas Hicks, called the state legislature into special session on April 26 to consider seceding from the Union. If Maryland did so and joined the rebels, Washington would be untenable, as it would be surrounded by the Confederacy. Lincoln and his administration would be forced to flee—a political and logistical disaster.

Lincoln had considered whether— "upon the ground of necessary defense"—to have the army "arrest or disperse" the legislators. On this day, Lincoln wrote General in Chief Winfield Scott that such a move would not be "justifiable." He acknowledged that the legislature "clearly [had the] legal right to assemble; and we can not know in advance, that their action will not be lawful, and peaceful." He also believed that arresting them would only delay them: "we can not long hold them as prisoners . . . [and] they will immediately re-assemble in some other place." Lincoln concluded that they should "watch, and await their action."

It was a wise move. The legislature, despite some heated debate, refused to consider an ordinance of secession. Just to be sure, Lincoln ordered General Benjamin Butler to hold Annapolis and keep the legislators from voting to secede even if it meant "bombardment of their cities." Butler went a step further and confiscated the state seal. If Maryland did attempt to secede, they could not make it legal.

However, secessionist sentiment died hard in Maryland and later that summer Lincoln did arrest anti-Union legislators.

APRIL 27

The First Suspension of Habeas Corpus

For the first time in American history, a president—on this Saturday in 1861—suspended the writ of habeas corpus in an area of the country. Writs (written order) of habeas corpus—Latin for "right of the body"—were issued by judges to demand that a prisoner appear before the court. They assured the prisoner's rights under due process and required the prisoner to be formally charged for a crime. This check against arbitrary arrest was among the most cherished of legal rights and was incorporated into the Constitution (Article I, Section 9). Its suspension meant that suspected rebel agents operating in the North could be held in jail indefinitely without a trial.

The spark for Lincoln's action occured on April 19 when the Sixth Massachusetts found itself in the middle of a riot in Baltimore. When General Benjamin Butler—head of the Eighth Massachusetts—heard of the riot, he commandeered a boat, and sailed his men across the Chesapeake Bay to Annapolis. Finding that secessionists had torn up the track between Annapolis and Washington, Butler's men (along with the Seventh New York) laid the track and repaired an old derelict locomotive. The Seventh New York and Eighth Massachusetts finally arrived in Washington on April 25.

Still, Lincoln had only about 1,600 men while there were reports that the Confederates had 8,000 at Harpers Ferry. Butler's tentative rail line had to be kept open for more troops. When word reached Lincoln that secessionists intended to cut the line between Philadelphia and Annapolis, he sent troops to protect it and authorized General in Chief Winfield Scott to suspend habeas corpus along the entire rail route from Philadelphia to Washington. Scott was allowed to "arrest, and detain, without resort to the ordinary processes and forms of law, such individuals as he might deem dangerous to the public safety." It was among Lincoln's most controversial decisions.

APRIL 29

The Irregulars

Lincoln spent part of this Monday in 1861 with volunteers who had come to Washington to protect it.

During the tense week in mid-April following the Baltimore riots, Washington waited for troops to arrive and expected the Confederates to seize the capital at any moment. Some unusual characters came to the rescue. One was Senator-elect James Lane of Kansas, a fiery abolitionist. Lane recruited senators, congressmen and office-seeking Kansans for his Frontier Guard. The guards, during the crisis, were quartered in the East Room of the White House, ready to whisk the first family to the formidable Treasury Building across the street should the rebels attack. John Hay, one of Lincoln's secretaries, described Lane as he appeared one night at the White House dinner table: "He wore a rough rusty overcoat, a torn shirt, and suspenderless breeches. His neck was innocent of collar, guiltless of necktie. His thin hair stood fretful—porcupine-quill-wise upon his crown." When Lane, on this day, noted that from a White House window a Confederate flag could be seen impudently flying over a roof across the Potomac in Alexandria, Virginia, he swore loudly, "We have got to whip these scoundrels like hell."

Cassius Clay was an abolitionist as well and hailed not only from a slave state—Kentucky—but from a slave-owning family. Clay formed the Clay Guards to protect Washington. Hay recorded that Clay one day appeared in the Presidential Reception Room, wearing, "with a sublimely unconscious air, three pistols and an Arkansas toothpick [large knife], and looked like an admirable vignette to twenty-five-cents-worth of yellow-covered romance." Lincoln, on this day, had his picture taken with Clay's citizen soldiers.

MAY 1

The Powhatan Fiasco

On this Wednesday in 1861, Lincoln wrote to Captain Gustavus Fox, attempting to soothe the captain's bitterness over his failed Sumter expedition.

Fox had been told that he would have for his expedition the navy's most powerful ship—the *Powhatan*. Secretary of State William Seward, who was sponsoring an expedition to Fort Pickens in Florida, either accidentally or deliberately inserted, among other papers Lincoln was signing, an order reassigning the *Powhatan* to the Pickens expedition. Lincoln signed it without reading it. When the switch was discovered, Seward attempted to reassign the warship to its original mission, but his message was ignored.

In his report on April 19, Fox cited a storm (which delayed the tugs he needed) and his expectation of using the *Powhatan* as the reasons he failed to supply or reinforce Sumter. "I learned on the 13th instant that the *Powhatan* was withdrawn from duty off Charleston on the 7th instant, yet I was permitted to sail on the 9th . . . without intimation that the main portion—the fighting portion of our expedition was taken away." With neither the *Powhatan* nor the tugs, Fox's expedition sat outside Charleston Harbor impotently watching the rebels reduce Sumter.

Lincoln took responsibility for the mix-up and wrote Fox that he still had the president's confidence. "For a daring and dangerous enterprize" Lincoln wrote, "you would, to-day, be the man . . . whom I would select." Then Lincoln wrote a comment that still has some wondering how much Lincoln manipulated the Sumter events: "You and I both anticipated that the cause of the country would be advanced by making the attempt to provision Fort-Sumpter, even if it should fail; and it is no small consolation now to feel that our anticipation is justified by the result."

#15

Did Lincoln Provoke the War?

One controversy about the war that still rages is whether Lincoln provoked the Confederates to fire on Sumter. Some argue that Lincoln suspected his Sumter expedition would spark a military response. There's much to support this view. For one, the South Carolinians had already fired on an expedition in January 1861. For another, there is the May 1, 1861 letter to Gustavus Fox. Then there is the statement Lincoln made to his friend Orville Browning. On February 17, just weeks before the inauguration, Browning wrote Lincoln, "In any conflict which may ensue . . . it is very important that the traitors shall be the aggressors, and that they be kept constantly and palpably in the wrong. The first attempt that is made to furnish supplies or reinforcements to Sumter will induce aggression by South Carolina, and then the [federal] government will stand justified, before the entire country, in repelling that aggression." When Browning met with Lincoln after Sumter, the president reminded his friend of the letter. "The plan succeeded," Lincoln said. "They attacked

Sumter—it fell, and thus, did more service than it otherwise could."

Lincoln's expectation of an aggressive act should not be mistaken for a wish for one. During the month before, Lincoln consulted experts, spoke with negotiators, sent emissaries south, and agonized over the situation. When starvation became imminent for the Sumter garrison, Lincoln decided to send supplies to the fort and made sure Charleston could not mistake an act of mercy for an act of war.

It was Confederate president Jefferson Davis that gave the order to open fire on a understaffed, starving garrison which posed no danger to Charleston or the Confederacy but, admittedly, plenty of danger to Davis's reputation. The better question is, why couldn't Davis allow the garrison to be provisioned so that peace negotiations could continue? Davis's own secretary of state, Robert Toombs, warned of the result of firing on Sumter: "Mr. President, at this time it is suicide, murder, and you will lose every friend you have at the North. . . . It is unnecessary. It puts us in the wrong. It is fatal."

MAY 4

The Committee

The possibility that Maryland—a slave state—might secede from the Union and join the Confederacy was of deep concern for Lincoln and his administration because it would require moving the federal government from Washington. A concerned Lincoln even considered arresting the Maryland Legislature, which was meeting in late April 1861 to debate secession. Lincoln decided to wait and see what they would do. On May 2 the Marylanders appointed a three-man committee to meet with Lincoln to ascertain the government's military intentions regarding their state. Lincoln agreed to meet with the committee—along with Secretary of State William Seward—on this Saturday in 1861.

"The Maryland Disunionists . . . called today upon the President," Lincoln's secretary, John Hay, wrote in his diary. "Their roaring was exquisitely modulated. It had lost the ferocious timbre of the April days. They roared as gently as twere any nightingale. The only point they particularly desired to press was that there was no particular necessity at present existing for the armed occupation of Maryland." In a reference to the Baltimore riots where Union troops were attacked by secessionists resulting in the death of four soldiers and twelve civilians, the committee begged the president "not to act in any spirit of revenge." Hay wrote, "The President coolly replied that he never acted from any such impulse." He added that public interest and not vengeance would direct his actions.

MAY 21

A Letter to London

Lincoln had virtually no experience in foreign relations and diplomacy and had few if any personal or political acquaintances living abroad. Lincoln relied heavily on Secretary of State William Seward to handle foreign affairs. But Lincoln knew a lot about human nature and it was for that reason that on this Tuesday in 1861 Lincoln toned down a provocative letter written by Seward threatening the government of Great Britain.

Britain's textile industry was deeply dependent on cotton from Southern plantations, which were now behind Lincoln's blockade. Without that cotton, England's textile mills would shut down. When Seward learned British Foreign Secretary Lord John Russell had agreed to talk unofficially with Confederate emissaries about recognizing the Confederacy as a new sovereign government and possibly breaking Lincoln's blockade, he exploded.

Seward responded with a bellicose letter ordering Charles Adams, America's minister to England, to break off relations with Britain should those informal talks occur. When he read it, Lincoln knew immediately that the letter was too abrasive. He had no desire for a war with England. Lincoln rewrote the letter, changing Seward's claim that the president was "surprised and grieved" at the news from London to "regrets." Lincoln replaced Seward's threat that England's interference would not "be borne" to "will [not] pass unnoticed" (later changed to "unquestioned"). In referring to the Revolutionary War, Seward wrote that Britain committed a "crime" in "provoking that contest" and Lincoln changed it to an "error." But Lincoln allowed Seward's threat to stand that if London "decided to fraternize with our domestic enemy," war could ensue.

#16

Thorny Relations

Lincoln's blockade and England's neutrality strained the two countries' relations throughout the war. When Queen Victoria proclaimed Britain's neutrality in the conflict on May 13, 1861, she also declared the Confederacy a belligerent, giving them far more diplomatic status than normally given to an insurrectionist. Britain also had an agreement with France that it would do the same. As belligerents, Confederate raiders and privateers would not be treated as pirates, as the Union treated them. Confederate agents would also be able to purchase supplies in neutral ports and obtain loans from neutral banks. These agents commissioned English shipbuilders—among the best in the world—to build commerce raiders, rams, and ironclads. Overall, two hundred Union merchant vessels were sunk by commerce raiders at an estimated cost of $15.5 million.

When England declared herself neutral, she also invoked the Foreign Enlistment Act (1815), which barred its citizens from participating in the war. Many Western states, however, allowed foreigners to vote if they declared their intention to become U.S. citizens. These states argued that if foreigners accepted the rights of Americans, they should also fight with their intended countrymen and proceeded to draft them. Britain complained and, in May 1863, Lincoln proclaimed that any foreigners who intended to be Americans but refused to fight must leave the country in sixty-five days or face conscription.

Lincoln's blockade was also a source of contention. While the Union tried to avoid provoking the English, in November 1861 an unarmed mail steamer—the *Trent*—was stopped by a Union warship and two Confederate commissioners bound for England and France were arrested. The incident almost sparked a war between the Union and England. And because blockade running was so lucrative, the "*Trent* affair" was not the only instance where an English vessel was stopped by Union picket ships, requiring Lincoln and Secretary of State William Seward to delicately handle the situation.

MAY 24

Elmer Ellsworth

Early on this Friday morning in 1861, visitors arrived at Lincoln's office to find him standing at the window, staring out on the Potomac. He choked as he extended his hand in greeting. "Excuse me, I cannot talk," he managed. He then burst into tears. He had just found out that his friend, young Elmer Ellsworth, had become one of the first casualties of the war.

Elmer Ellsworth had apprenticed—called "reading" law—in Lincoln's Springfield law office. Ellsworth became so close to the Lincoln family that he often romped and wrestled with Willie and Tad and even caught the measles from the Lincoln boys. After Sumter fell, Ellsworth organized New York firemen into a Zouave unit (officially, the Eleventh New York Regiment). Young Tad was so taken with their baggy pants and tasseled fezzes that he had his picture taken in his own child-size Zouave uniform.

On May 23, 1861 Virginia officially seceded from the Union and Lincoln ordered the town of Alexandria—just across the Potomac—to be taken that night in a moonlit raid. One of the buildings to be secured was the Marshall House hotel, above which flew a Confederate flag that had taunted Lincoln for a month (he could see it from the White House). "We must have that thing down," Ellsworth told his men as they climbed to the roof to cut down the flag. On the way back downstairs the hotel owner, James Jackson, shot Ellsworth and was subsequently shot and killed himself.

Ellsworth was given a full military funeral in the East Room of the White House. Mary Lincoln was given the Confederate flag that had cost Ellsworth his life, but Mary couldn't bear to see the bloodstained reminder and had it stored away.

MAY 27

The Quartermaster General

Only about a third (313) of the pre-war army's 1,098 officers resigned their commissions so they could serve the Confederacy. A disproportionate number of these defectors were, however, experienced and/or talented officers. One who was both and yet remained loyal to the Union was a Georgia captain named Montgomery Meigs. On May 14, 1861, Lincoln promoted Meigs to colonel, likely because of his help in the Fort Pickens expedition in April. Lincoln, however, wanted Meigs appointed Quartermaster General of the Army, a position responsible for supplying the army with everything except food and ammunition. Even as Lincoln met with Meigs on this Monday in 1861 to discuss his promotion, the president knew he'd have to fight to get Meigs appointed.

For one thing, there were officers in the Quartermaster Bureau with more seniority, such as Colonel Charles Thomas—Secretary of War Simon Cameron's personal choice for the position. But Cameron's refusal to appoint Meigs had more to do with how close Meigs was to William Seward, Secretary of State. Meigs had worked with Seward on the Pickens expedition and Cameron resented Seward's meddling in War Department affairs. For weeks Lincoln campaigned to convince Cameron to name Meigs, but it wasn't until Lincoln enlisted General in Chief Winfield Scott's help that Cameron changed his mind, in June. Meigs' nomination for Brigadier General was submitted on July 13.

Meigs served with distinction as Quartermaster General, reversing some of Cameron's dishonest and chaotic purchasing practices for army supplies. Meigs oversaw the spending of $1.5 billion. His most enduring act was to take control of Robert E. Lee's property after Alexandria, Virginia, was taken on May 24 and to oversee the burial of Union dead in the new Arlington Cemetery. When he died in 1892, he too was buried there.

MAY 30

Taney vs. Lincoln

On this Friday in 1861, Lincoln asked Attorney General Edward Bates for help to counter an attack from none other than Roger Taney, the chief justice of the Supreme Court.

On April 27, 1861, Lincoln had suspended habeas corpus along the rail lines between Washington and Philadelphia. A month later, on May 25, John Merryman, an alleged Maryland secessionist, was roused out of his bed, arrested, and taken to Fort Henry in Baltimore. In those days Supreme Court justices also sat on circuit courts. When Merryman applied for a hearing to either be charged or released, Taney was on the bench to issue a writ of habeas corpus to appear in his court. The commander of Fort Henry refused to release Merryman, citing Lincoln's suspension.

On May 28, Taney delivered a scathing opinion in *Ex parte Merryman*. "[Merryman] appears to have been arrested upon general charges of treason and rebellion, without proof . . . or specifying the . . . crimes," Taney wrote. Taney claimed that under Article I, Section 9 of the Constitution, habeas corpus could be suspended only by Congress in "cases of rebellion or invasion," not by the president. In an oblique threat, Taney reminded his readers that the president could be "made personally responsible, by impeachment, for malfeasance in office."

Taney's opinion was sent to Lincoln, but he refused to respond without legal ammunition and so asked his attorney general to write a defense. Bates wrote that the Constitution never explicitly awarded the power to suspend habeas corpus to either the president or Congress but that logically that power belonged to the commander in chief.

Merryman was eventually released without a trial and Taney was still angry with Lincoln seven months later when he refused to attend the usual New Year's reception at the White House.

JUNE 3

"His Name Fills the Nation"

One of the things Lincoln did very well, particularly at the beginning of the war, was to build a coalition of support for the war effort that crossed party lines. War Democrats—such as Andrew Johnson and soon-to-be-named generals George McClellan, John Dix, Benjamin Butler, John McClernand, and Daniel Sickles—worked with Republicans to mobilize the Union's war effort. On this Monday in 1861, however, Lincoln lost an important ally when his old Democratic opponent, Stephen Douglas, died at the age of forty-eight.

The day after Fort Sumter (April 14), Lincoln had met with Douglas and allowed him to read his proclamation calling for the states to supply 75,000 men to fight. Douglas concurred with his proclamation, "except that . . . I would make it two hundred thousand." The next day Douglas issued a public statement supporting Lincoln's proclamation. Douglas declared that he supported Lincoln in "all his constitutional functions to preserve the Union." On his way home to Illinois, Douglas delivered speeches avowing patriotism over party. "There can be no neutrals in this war," he said in Chicago, "only patriots and traitors." During that same trip he became ill and his body, ravaged by years of alcohol abuse, could not recover. He died early on this morning.

When word reached Lincoln, he directed that all government offices be closed for the funeral and that the White House and the State Department be draped in mourning for thirty days. In a memo Lincoln wrote to himself (sometime in the mid-1850s) that was discovered after his own death, he wrote of Douglas, "With me the race of ambition has been a failure—a flat failure; with him it has been one of splendid success. His name fills the nation, and it is not unknown, even in foreign lands."

JUNE 13

The Sharpshooters

Lincoln, on this Thursday morning in 1861, met with a mechanical engineer and inventor named Hiram Berdan about organizing a regiment of the best marksmen in the nation to act as snipers and skirmishers. Lincoln then sent Berdan to see Secretary of War Simon Cameron.

Berdan had been the top marksman in America for fifteen years, and he used his clout to pique the War Department's interest in a regiment of green-clad sharpshooters. But despite Lincoln's and General in Chief Winfield Scott's support, the head of the Ordinance Department—General James Ripley—refused to purchase Sharps rifles for the men. The Sharps was accurate to five hundred yards and could fire eight rounds a minute. When used during the Kansas guerrilla war a few years before, one participant claimed the Sharps had "more moral power . . . than a hundred Bibles." Ripley told Berdan's men they'd have to settle for muskets. It would not be until January 1862 that Cameron pushed through the order for the Sharps.

Dubbed the First and Second U.S. Sharpshooters, Berdan's men saw action in the Peninsula Campaign and the battles of Second Bull Run, Antietam, Fredericksburg, Chancellorsville, and Gettysburg. Berdan, who had quite an ego, quit the army and his men in early 1864 largely because he was disappointed with the lack of fame his unit garnered him. He returned to engineering while his men served throughout the rest of the war.

The Confederates effectively utilized sharpshooters as well. Their preferred gun was the British Whitworth Sharpshooter with a range of better than a thousand yards, particularly when fitted with a Davidson telescopic sight. They liked to target Union signalmen, pickets, artillerymen, and particularly officers. The most senior Union casualty happened at the hand of a Confederate sharpshooter. "Don't worry, boys. They couldn't hit an elephant at this range,"

General John Sedgwick, head of the Sixth Corps, told his men at Spotsylvania Court House on May 9, 1864. A few moments later he was shot dead.

JUNE 17

Executive Decor

When the Lincolns first entered the White House in March 1861, they found its furnishings, tapestries, wallpaper, and carpeting shockingly neglected. Still smarting from the public's characterization of her as a Midwestern rube, Mary took it upon herself to restore the White House to semi-opulence. In mid-May, Mary went shopping and on this day in 1861 her husband approved the first of what eventually became exorbitant expenditures.

After Mary discovered that each president was allocated $20,000 to maintain the White House, she took her cousin Elizabeth Grimsley and William Wood, commissioner of public buildings and responsible for White House spending, to Philadelphia and New York to shop. To replace the threadbare carpet in the East room, Mary purchased a $2,500 carpet from the famous shopping emporium Alexander T. Stewart. From Haughwout & Company she bought a gold-and-red-trimmed china set. She also purchased a new $900 carriage, vases and mantle ornaments for the Green and Blue rooms, a seven-hundred-piece Bohemian cut glass set and $6,800 worth of French wallpaper. It was during this trip that Mary purchased an eight-foot-long rosewood bedstead with birds and grapevines carved into the headboard. This bed was placed in the state bedroom, the Prince of Wales Room, and her son Willie died on it eight months later. The bed is still in the White House, and is now known as the "Lincoln bed."

On May 29, Lincoln received a bill from William Carryl and Brother of Philadelphia for $7,500 worth of drapes and trimmings. Lincoln asked Secretary of the Treasury Salmon Chase to issue a check for the bill, and on this Monday approved it. While Lincoln was obviously aware of this bill, as more came in, Mary began to hide them from her husband and look for creative ways to pay them.

#17

How Bad Was the White House?

By the time the Lincolns moved in, the White House had been home to chief executives for sixty-one years. For each four-year term, the president was given a one-time stipend of $20,000 to maintain the building. This was inadequate—even in 1861 dollars—for such a large, overused building. Worse, few presidents used the entire stipend and many of the furnishings were old and worn. "The family apartments were in a deplorably shabby condition as to furniture (which looked as if it had been brought by the first President)," Mary's cousin Elizabeth Grimsley observed. One of Lincoln's secretaries, William Stoddard, thought the East Room had "a faded, worn, untidy look. . . . Its paint and furniture require renewal; but so does almost everything else about the house, within and without." Another visitor called the White House "miserable . . . gloomy . . . like an old unsuccessful hotel."

What's worse, the White House was an unguarded tourist attraction. Visitors had virtually unrestricted access to the main floor rooms and some would snip off or take mementos. Lincoln's secretary William Stoddard said that "one relic-worshipping vandal . . . cut nearly two feet in length out of a nearly new silk window curtain." He added that everything "from buttons deftly cloven off from Mrs. Lincoln's dress, or flowers from the vases, to strips rudely severed from the curtains or carpet" were up for grabs. And, during the first weeks of the war, soldiers were bivouacked in the East Room, their boots and stacked guns ruining the carpet.

Mary's efforts to renovate the White House would have been applauded in peacetime, but during the war her actions drew considerable hostility. Lincoln recognized this and once angrily declared it "would stink in the land" should the public hear of the expensive renovations "when poor freezing soldiers could not have blankets."

JUNE 18

Aerial Reconnaissance

On this Tuesday in 1861, Lincoln received an unusual telegram, sent to him not from the field but from above it.

One evening in June 1861, Joseph Henry, director of the Smithsonian Institute, introduced Lincoln to Thaddeus Sobieski Coulincourt Lowe. Lowe was a balloonist who had been preparing for a transatlantic flight when the war broke out. During a trial run in April 1861, the wind drove his balloon into South Carolina, where he saw Confederate preparations for war firsthand. He was arrested and, when released, he went to Washington to offer his services. He told Lincoln he could provide aerial reconnaissance to the army, transmitting his observations via a telegraph wire trailing to the ground. To demonstrate its potential, Lowe took his balloon up above Washington on this day, and transmitted to Lincoln, "This point observation commands an area near fifty miles in diameter—The city with its girdle of encampments presents a superb scene—I have [the] pleasure in sending you this first dispatch ever telegraphed from an aerial station." Impressed, Lincoln gave Lowe a letter of introduction to General in Chief Winfield Scott, but Scott refused to meet with Lowe. Lincoln then personally took Lowe over to the Ordinance Department to inaugurate Lowe's "Balloon Corps."

By 1862, Lowe had four balloons traveling with the Army of the Potomac. Often these balloons drew Confederate fire and eventually the rebels inaugurated their own balloon reconnaissance. Lowe and his corps saw plenty of action during General George McClellan's Peninsula Campaign, particularly at the Battle of Seven Pines. It was he who discovered that the Confederates had evacuated Yorktown. But after a squabble over pay, Lowe quit the army in May of 1863. His corps was disbanded shortly afterward.

JUNE 22

The Daunting Task

In the early weeks of the war, Secretary of War Simon Cameron found the job of putting together a massive army impossible. The War Department in 1861 had only two hundred personnel to handle mustering tens of thousands of troops, and to provide uniforms, guns, ammunition, blankets, tents, horses, food, water, medical treatment, and pay to those troops. "We were entirely unprepared for such a conflict," Cameron later recounted. "We had no guns . . . we had no ammunition to put in them—no powder, no saltpeter, no bullets, no anything." Lincoln tried to lend a hand, as he did on this Saturday in 1861.

When, on April 15, 1861, Lincoln called for 75,000 ninety-day state volunteers, nearly 92,000 ultimately answered the call. From April to year's end the Union army swelled from 16,000 to 575,000 soldiers. Traditionally, the state governments provided uniforms for the men they sent and chose its officers. This made for an eclectic variety in uniforms (some of which were so similar to Confederate uniforms that they were fired upon by fellow Union soldiers). It also meant many officers were commissioned with zero military qualifications. To help Cameron sort through the mess, Lincoln put Secretary of the Treasury Salmon Chase in charge of deciding when regiments were to be mustered into service. Chase also advised governors on officer's commissions.

Lincoln, himself, tried to help by communicating directly with the governors. This became confusing when he informed the War Department of new regiments after he'd already authorized them. Sometimes regiments appeared out of nowhere without Chase or Cameron expecting them. On this day, Lincoln forwarded a request from the governor of Indiana, Oliver Morton, to change an Indiana regiment to cavalry. "If agreeable to the Secretary of the War, I approve," Lincoln wrote on the back of Morton's request. Cameron accepted the request.

JUNE 29

Two Plans

On this Saturday in 1861, Lincoln met with his cabinet and top generals in the White House library, where they could spread out their maps to discuss plans for the war.

General in Chief Winfield Scott and General Irvin McDowell each submitted a plan to Lincoln. Scott's plan was the more complicated of the two. "If you will maintain a strict blockade on the seacoast . . . and send a force down the Mississippi strong enough to open it and keep it free along the course to its mouth, you will thus cut off the luxuries to which people are accustomed," Scott said. He added that these deprived Southerners would pressure their leaders "and I will guarantee that in one year . . . all difficulties will be settled." Scott wanted four and a half months to train Western troops. Then, starting from Cairo, Illinois or Xenia, Ohio, he wanted to float down the Mississippi in ironclads and take New Orleans by spring. Scott admitted that the unpopular aspect of his plan was that the eastern theater armies would remain on the defensive. "I would march to Richmond with ten thousand men armed only with lathes," said Postmaster General Montgomery Blair disdainfully. "Yes, as prisoners of war," Scott countered.

McDowell's plan was to march his 30,000 troops twenty-six miles southwest of Washington to take the railhead at Manassas Junction, where Confederate general P. G. T. Beauregard was amassing 35,000 soldiers. He had no idea what to do after that.

Lincoln decided to implement McDowell's plan. Ultimately much of Scott's plan would be implemented as well, with the critical exception of keeping the eastern army in a static, defensive posture. Such a plan would be extremely unpopular to an impatient public. Instead, Lincoln was stubbornly focused on Richmond and authorized seven offensives to take the Confederate capital; all but the last one would fail.

JULY 20

"You Are All Green Alike"

On this Saturday in 1861, Lincoln listened to Secretary of War Simon Cameron's report on General Irvin McDowell's preparations for an impending battle with the Confederates at what would be called the First Battle of Bull Run (Manassas).

McDowell's plan to attack Confederate general P. G. T. Beauregard's 20,000 men at Manassas, Virginia was sound. The problem was that most of McDowell's 30,000 men were militia, nominally trained and inexperienced. "You are green," Lincoln admitted to McDowell. "But they [the Confederates] are green, too. You are all green alike." Another flaw was that a rebel army of 11,000 under Confederate general Joe Johnston was in the nearby Shenandoah Valley and could reinforce Beauregard. To keep Johnston in place, General Robert Patterson's 15,000 men were sent to the Shenandoah.

McDowell's campaign began to unravel when his jump-off date of July 8 was delayed a week because he had no horses or mules to transport equipment. Washington's Southern sympathizers fed McDowell's plans to the Confederates, and during that critical week Johnston began sending his men to Beauregard while Patterson remained oblivious. "General Johnston is a very able soldier and he has a railroad at his command with which to move his troops," General in Chief Winfield Scott told McDowell. "If your plan . . . depends upon General Patterson holding Johnston in check, it is not worth the paper it is written on."

McDowell pressed on to Manassas without a reliable map and without sufficient cavalry to reconnoiter the area or cannon to support the infantry; the militia supposedly could not handle horses or artillery. What was worse, McDowell's plan for the July 21 battle was to march his "green" troops fourteen miles to slam into Beauregard's left flank, something difficult even for seasoned troops. The result was the first major Confederate victory.

JULY 21

Distant Guns

As Union and Confederate troops grappled with each other in the war's first major engagement, Lincoln would receive news, on this day in 1861, that went from good to very bad.

Sunday, July 21, 1861 was beautiful but hot, with temperatures rising to nearly a hundred degrees. Confident in General in Chief Winfield Scott's assurances of success, Lincoln and his family went to church, passing dozens of Washingtonians in their carriages heading south to watch the battle. After church, as Lincoln headed for the War Department's telegraph office, he could hear faint rumblings of artillery in the distance. "Rapid firing from heavy Guns & small arms," read an 11:25 AM dispatch from a short distance from the battle. By the afternoon the dispatcher wired, "Firing more in the distance & greatly slackened." Later, "Still fainter and less guns. You can draw your own inference." Lincoln showed the telegram to Scott, asking him what inference could be drawn. Scott shrugged it off, saying that little could be concluded from distant sounds of battle. Finally at 5:20 PM a *New York Herald* reporter wired, "We have carried the day—Rebels accepted battle in their strength but are totally routed." Relieved, Lincoln decided to take a carriage ride with his family until a courier with bad news interrupted it.

Union forces had initially made progress against the Confederate's left flank, but the rebels were steadied by the steely Confederate general Thomas Jackson and his men long enough for reinforcements to arrive. Jackson's stubborn stand in this battle earned him the sobriquet "Stonewall." The Union's right flank collapsed, sending the whole Union army in retreat all the way to Washington. "The day is lost," the telegraph now proclaimed. "Save Washington and the remnants of the Army."

JULY 23

A Grim Reevaluation

In the wake of the Union defeat at Bull Run (Manassas), Lincoln, on this day in 1861, tried to make the best of the situation by drawing up a new military policy.

Lincoln didn't sleep after the battle, the night of July 21–22, and instead talked to witnesses while he watched demoralized soldiers trudge through the darkened streets. "Some had neither great coats nor shoes, others were covered in blankets," one observer wrote. The greatest concern was that the Confederates would attack the federal capital. "The capture of Washington seems now inevitable," wrote the future Secretary of War Edwin Stanton. "Even now I doubt whether any serious opposition to the entrance of the Confederate forces could be offered." Lincoln's wife Mary was asked to flee with their children but she refused. And the Confederates, inexplicably, never came.

That same day, July 22, Lincoln ordered General George McClellan to come to Washington to take over the city's defenses. Congress authorized the enlistment of 500,000 more men and another $500 million for the war. It was clear to everyone now that the war would not be short-lived nor would it pass without plenty of spilled blood.

On the night of July 22, Lincoln spent another sleepless night and in the wee hours of this day composed a list of policy changes. Lincoln recommended that the soldiers be trained ("constantly drilled, disciplined and instructed") and the armies reorganized after the ninety-day militias were cashiered out. Afterward, he added to the list that he wanted a three-pronged advance of armies in both the eastern and western theaters. Later in the day he took a carriage ride across the Potomac to see some of his troops and to get a feel for their morale. He was pleasantly surprised to find that his defeated army's spirit was higher than his own.

#18

"I Believe He Would Do It"

Colonel William Sherman did not have a good first impression of Lincoln when, in March 1861, his brother—Senator John Sherman of Ohio—introduced him to the new president. Sherman, who had just returned from a Southern assignment, warned Lincoln that the Confederates were preparing for war. Lincoln's glib response angered Sherman and, upon leaving, he turned to his brother and said, "You have things in a hell of a fix."

Lincoln and Sherman met again on July 23, when the president visited Sherman's camp near Fort Cocoran. Sherman's men had just returned from fighting at the Battle of Bull Run (Manassas). Lincoln greeted Sherman and said, "Yes, we heard that you had got over the big scare and we thought we would come over to see the boys." Sherman had one stipulation: "No hurrahing, no humbug. We had enough of it before Bull Run to spoil any set of men." After Lincoln delivered to the troops what Sherman described as the "neatest, best and most feeling" address he had ever heard, the soldiers tried to hurrah but Lincoln "promptly checked them, saying 'Don't cheer, boys. I confess I rather like it myself, but Colonel Sherman here says it is not military.'"

Afterward, one of Sherman's officers approached Lincoln. The officer explained that he was a ninety-day volunteer whose enlistment had expired, but Sherman refused to let him go home, threatening to shoot him if he tried. Sherman interjected, "And I repeat it, sir, that if I remain in command here, and he or any other man refuses to obey my orders, I'll shoot him on the spot." Lincoln turned to the officer, "My lad, if I were you, and he threatened to shoot, I would not trust him, for I believe he would do it!"

JULY 27

McClellan Comes to Washington

Amid fears that the Confederates would attack Washington after the Union defeat at Bull Run (Manassas), Lincoln, on this day in 1861, tapped an up-and-coming general named George McClellan to head the capital defenses.

General in Chief Winfield Scott had recommended the retired General Ethan Allen Hitchcock for the position. Hitchcock was an experienced, able general who was indispensable to Scott during the Mexican War. Hitchcock, however, had made an enemy of Secretary of War Simon Cameron some twenty-two years earlier when Hitchcock called Cameron—then an Indian agent—"corrupt." Cameron refused to summon Hitchcock out of retirement. It is likely that Hitchcock would have refused the summons anyway, as he did three times in 1862 after Cameron was replaced. Scott's second choice was General Henry Halleck, whose intelligence earned him the nickname "Old Brains." But Halleck was a virtual unknown.

Not so with McClellan, who had touted his handful of successful skirmishes as if they were major battles. The public, starved for success, swallowed his accounts with relish. One small action at Corrick's Ford, Virginia—resulting in the war's first death of a general (Confederate Robert Garnett)—made McClellan a hero despite the fact that his subordinate—General William Rosecrans—was responsible for the victory. "We have annihilated the enemy in western Virginia," McClellan wrote. "Our success is complete, and secession is killed in this country."

Instead of following the chain of command, Lincoln had Cameron, not Scott, summon McClellan to Washington. It would not be the last time the president would circumvent the command chain. This was the beginning of a rift between McClellan and Scott, one that would widen over the coming months.

AUGUST 2

The Picnic

Lincoln, on this day in 1861, responded to a congressional resolution asking about "loyal citizens" held by the Confederacy in the aftermath of the First Battle of Bull Run (Manassas).

When the Union and Confederate armies met near Manassas, Virginia, on July 21, 1861, many believed it would be the first and only large-scale engagement of the war. Hundreds of Washingtonians prepared picnic baskets and rode out to the battle to witness the expected Union victory. Six senators and ten representatives were among them. During the battle, British journalist William Russell heard one female gawker exclaim after a heavy cannon barrage, "This is splendid. Oh my! Is not this first-rate? I guess we will be in Richmond this time tomorrow."

When the Union army fled the field in panic, these spectators impeded their escape. "Every moment the crowd increased; drivers and men cried out with the most vehement gestures, 'Turn back! Turn back! We are whipped!'" one witness recounted. Among the chaos was New York congressman Alfred Ely, who had accompanied the Thirteenth New York Infantry to the battle. In the rush to escape, Ely's carriage broke down and he hid in the woods until the Confederates captured him. Among the 460 Union dead was Colonel James Cameron, brother of Secretary of War Simon Cameron. Two friends—Arnold Harris and Henry Magraw—headed to Manassas to retrieve the colonel's body and were taken prisoner as well. Along with Ely, they were sent to Richmond's Liggons Tobacco Warehouse, soon to be known as Libby Prison.

Lincoln, on this day, forwarded to Congress a telegram from the prisoners in Richmond pleading for help. However, it would be months before they were released and sent home.

AUGUST 3

Prince Napoleon

On this Saturday in 1861, Lincoln hosted royalty as Prince Napoleon Joseph Charles Paul Bonaparte—cousin of Napoleon III of France—visited the White House.

At noon Prince Napoleon and his entourage appeared at the White House door, but neither Lincoln nor even a doorman was there to greet his highness. Lincoln's son Willie answered the door. "One goes right in [to the White House] as if entering a café," the Prince wrote in his diary. In retaliation for this informality, Napoleon snubbed Lincoln's greeting, taking a "cruel pleasure in remaining silent," said a witness.

Things improved at seven that evening when the Lincolns hosted a state dinner for the Prince. While Mary was officially the hostess, Lincoln felt that his wife was too inexperienced for such dinners and assigned his secretary John Nicolay to head the affair. Mary was unhappy at this slight from her husband, particularly after Nicolay removed some of her choices from the guest list. Nevertheless, she made the most of it. Because the prince's wife—Marie Clothilde, daughter of Sardinia's Victor Emanuel II—had chosen to remain in New York on their personal yacht instead of braving the Maryland heat, Mary entered the party on the prince's arm. Paired with Napoleon at dinner, Mary exercised her fluent French. Mary's cousin Elizabeth Grimsley—the only other woman at the dinner—was paired with Lincoln. At the end of the evening, the Marine Band struck up "La Marseillaise"—the French Republican anthem—instead of the appropriate imperial anthem "Partant pour la Syrie." The prince afterward wrote that the President resembled a "bootmaker."

AUGUST 5

Income Tax

Lincoln, on this Monday in 1861, signed the Revenue Act, implementing an income tax for the first time in U.S. history.

For much of U.S. history, individuals have not been subjected to a personal income tax. Before the Civil War, the federal government's fiscal needs were small enough to be funded by excise taxes (tax on purchases), tariffs (tax on imports), and sales of federal land. The Revolutionary War and the War of 1812 were funded by excise taxes and, in the case of the latter, treasury notes. In 1817 Congress repealed the excise tax and the federal government for the next forty-four years supported itself with custom duties and property sales.

When the Civil War began, Secretary of the Treasury Salmon Chase tried to sell bonds and treasury notes, but the public was slow to purchase them. To spark sales by proving the government could pay the interest on the bonds and notes, Chase recommended to Congress an income tax. Congress passed the Revenue Act, imposing a 3 percent tax on incomes over $800 annually. It would take another year and another law—the Internal Revenue Act—to establish an Internal Revenue Bureau and a two-tiered income tax (3 percent on annual incomes up to $10,000 and 5 percent on incomes above $10,000). It also imposed an excise tax on almost everything: liquor, tobacco, playing cards, carriages, yachts, jewelry, medicines, newspaper advertisements, and licenses for nearly every profession.

While the income tax and most of the excise taxes expired a few years after the war, the Internal Revenue Bureau remained a permanent fixture. It would not be until the Sixteenth Amendment was ratified in 1913 that a federal income tax was imposed again.

AUGUST 6

Lincoln vs. Congress

On this Tuesday in 1861—the last day in a month-long congressional special session called in response to the war—Lincoln signed two last-minute bills, one on the confiscation of rebel slaves and another that retroactively acquiesced to all of the president's proclamations to date.

When Congress finally opened on July 5, it found itself shorn of Southern Democrats and heavily lopsided politically (32 out of 48 senators and 106 out of 176 representatives were Republican). But if the Republican president thought he could control Congress, he was wrong; the relationship was strained almost from the beginning.

An early rift was over the Confiscation Act, which upset the border slave states because it allowed for the confiscation of slaves who labored for the Confederate Army. The president reluctantly signed it. Then there was the resolution introduced early in the session that retroactively approved all of Lincoln's war proclamations since April 1. But passage was delayed as Congress debated Lincoln's suspension of habeas corpus (protection against indefinite imprisonment without charges). Lincoln's July 5 message to Congress left many unconvinced: "The whole of the laws . . . were being resisted, and failing of execution, in nearly one-third of the States. . . . Are all the laws, *but one* [habeas corpus], to go unexecuted, and the government itself go to pieces, lest that one be violated?" Senator John Sherman of Ohio responded, "I approve of the action of the President . . . but I cannot . . . declare what he did was . . . strictly legal, and in consonance with the provisions of the Constitution." Congress waited until the session's last day to pass the measure.

AUGUST 15

Missouri's Woes

In the aftermath of the Union debacle at Wilson's Creek, Missouri, General John Fremont began to panic and on this day in 1861 Lincoln tried to calm the general's nerves.

At the outbreak of war, Missouri was deeply divided on whether to stay in or out of the Union. There was enough pro-Union sentiment, however, to defeat efforts to secede. But Governor Claiborne Fox Jackson favored secession and refused Lincoln's call to provide troops. Instead he mobilized the militia for the Confederates to use. In June, Union general Nathaniel Lyons deposed Jackson after retaking the state capital of Jefferson City.

In July, Lincoln named Fremont to take charge of the new Department of the West. But once in St. Louis, Fremont found the governmental chaos beyond his abilities. What was worse, a Confederate force was threatening to march into Missouri. Lyons decided to attack first, but he was outnumbered almost two-to-one (Fremont had dispersed rather than concentrated his forces). Not only did General Lyons lose the Battle of Wilson's Creek on August 10, he lost his life. The Confederates would move forward deep into Missouri.

Fremont began frantically calling for more troops, and on August 14 wrote, "Will the Pres't read my urgent dispatch to the Sec'y of War?" On this day Lincoln fired back, "Been answering your messages ever since day before yesterday," adding that troops were on the way. On this same day Lincoln sent a Cincinnati, Ohio regiment to Missouri. Lincoln also ordered Indiana governor Oliver Morton to send four regiments and three artillery battalions westward. But things did not improve and Missouri descended into a brutal four-year-long guerrilla war.

AUGUST 16

Trade Across the Lines

Lincoln, on this day in 1861, issued a proclamation outlawing "all commercial intercourse between . . . [the Confederate States] and citizens of other [Union] States."

Despite the proclamation and a similar one issued by the Confederate government, trade continued throughout the war. In the war's first year, illicit trade usually came across the Kentucky and Maryland borders. As the Union armies in the west moved southward, Memphis, Nashville, and New Orleans became centers of trade. "Every colonel, captain, or quartermaster is in secret partnership with some operator in cotton; every soldier dreams of adding a bale of cotton to his monthly pay," wrote Assistant Secretary of War Charles Dana.

Southern cotton was perhaps the most lucrative item smuggled across the lines. Because of shortages and inflation (6,000 percent), Southerners were forced to sell or barter cotton bales for food or necessities. The irony is that cotton smuggling exacerbated the food shortages, particularly for Confederate civilians. Planters would crowd out acreage for foodstuffs to grow cotton. Georgia, for one, tried to stem this practice by limiting the acreage farmers could devote to cotton, but the law was largely ignored. When a Georgia neighbor complained that Confederate general Robert Toombs (who was at one time the Confederate secretary of state) was growing too much cotton, Toombs scoffed at the law.

The Union also turned a blind eye to the trade. Lincoln believed that every bale sold across state lines was one less bale that was smuggled through the blockade to European markets for considerable more trade value. "Better to give him guns for it, than let him, as now, get both guns and ammunition for it," the president said. By some estimates, 900,000 bales of cotton were traded across lines, double the cotton smuggled through the blockade.

AUGUST 17

The "Coffee-mill Gun"

Near the stump that was the unfinished Washington Monument, Lincoln, on this Saturday in 1861, watched a demonstration of a rapid-fire gun he dubbed the "coffee-mill gun."

Himself an inventor, Lincoln was fascinated with inventions and inventors of new weapons invariably got a favorable hearing from the president. On this day, inventor J. D. Mills showed Lincoln what he called a "Union repeating gun." His invention was a container mounted atop a gun barrel and fed fifty to sixty rounds into the breech per minute. Similar to the famous Gatling gun, Mills's repeater was mounted on an artillery carriage, used .58 caliber bullets, and was operated by a hand crank (reminding Lincoln of a coffee mill or grinder). But the Gatling gun had six gun barrels—not one—revolving around a central axis.

While Lincoln was impressed, his chief of ordinance, General James Ripley, was not. The sixty-five-year-old general was unimaginative and overly cautious, earning him the derogatory nickname of "Ripley Van Winkle." Ripley viewed inventions with suspicion, even contempt. "I saw this gun myself," Lincoln wrote Ripley of Mills's invention, "and witnessed some experiments with it, and I really think it worth the attention of the Government." Ripley refused to consider it.

Lincoln then turned to General George McClellan, who was no more imaginative than Ripley. When McClellan attended a demonstration, Lincoln pressured him into buying fifty. No doubt to placate the president, McClellan agreed. While a few were purchased by officers, none were issued to Union troops. Ripley stonewalled Gatling guns as well, mainly because of the stringent cleaning procedures they required. General Benjamin Butler reportedly did use Gatlings during his retreat from Drewry's Bluff in May 1864.

#19

The Father of Invention

With the start of the war, inventors streamed to Washington to demonstrate how their new contraption would help the war effort. A few of these inventions Lincoln endorsed. While several flamethrowers were demonstrated for Lincoln—most of which nearly incinerated the operators—one incendiary caught his eye. Inventor Levi Short developed a thirteen-inch incendiary shell that would blanket a radius of fifty yards with what Lincoln called "Greek fire." These shells were used at Vicksburg, Mississippi, and when Lincoln ordered them to be lobbed into Charleston, South Carolina, the Confederate commander complained that "a number of the most destructive missiles ever used in war [were shot] into the midst of the city . . . filled with sleeping women and children." Lincoln was also involved in distributing explosive bullets which burst inside the victim after entering him. Lincoln ordered 100,000 of the bullets and they were used at Gettysburg. While European nations outlawed such bullets and General Ulysses Grant called them "barbarous," Lincoln obviously did not agree.

Lincoln did not endorse several other inventions. One inventor sent a bulletproof "cuirass" or breastplate made of steel. "So that's a cuirass!" Lincoln said. "Well, the inventor must be a queer ass to think a man could lug that thing on a march in a hot sun or on the double-quick [run]." He was sent all kinds of grenades, one of which he used as a paperweight. He was once peppered with shrapnel as he watched a rocket blow up on its launch pad. Perhaps the most unusual weapon he saw was the "cross-eyed gun," a rifle with two diverging barrels. "I know enough cross-eyed men to fill up a regiment," said the inventor, "and, by Thunder! Mr. Lincoln, I'm cross-eyed enough to be colonel of it."

AUGUST 24

Neutral Kentucky

On this day in 1861, Lincoln refused a request from Kentucky's governor, Beriah Magoffin, to remove the small military force in his state that was armed and commanded by the Union and threatened to tip Kentucky toward secession.

Kentucky was important to the Union because it controlled the southern bank of the Ohio River, a major tributary to the Mississippi. Any serious military advance into Confederate Tennessee would almost certainly have to come through Kentucky. Despite commercial ties to the South, Kentucky had a large pro-Union population and a pro-Union general assembly but a pro-secession governor. Blocked from seceeding the state, Magoffin declared Kentucky a neutral, something Lincoln considered no more constitutional than secession. Lincoln told a Kentucky representative that he reserved "the unquestioned right at all times to march . . . troops into and over any and every State," but "if Kentucky made no demonstration of force . . . he would not molest her."

A guerrilla war broke out within the state and in May Lincoln authorized the smuggling of 5,000 guns into the state for Unionists. Magoffin countered by shipping guns in for secessionists. Pro-Union militias began forming and Lincoln agreed to provide officers for them. "In a word," wrote Magoffin on August 19, "an Army is now being organized and quartered . . . without the advice or consent of the Authorities of this state." Lincoln countered that no one but the governor had asked Lincoln to remove such forces. "I do not believe it is the popular wish of Kentucky that this force shall be removed . . . [and] I must respectfully decline to so remove it." Despite Lincoln's assertion, these regiments could be construed as a break in his promise to leave Kentucky unmolested. Fortunately for him, the Confederates would invade Kentucky in early September, making the argument moot.

AUGUST 31

"Our First Naval Victory"

Lincoln was not feeling well on this day in 1861, but two things would lift his spirits: kittens and a victory.

Hatteras Inlet was the only deepwater passage from the Atlantic to North Carolina's Pamlico Sound, allowing access to the islands and inlets of the Outer Banks. Hatteras was essential to the Confederates' efforts to run the Union blockade, and to protect it the rebels had constructed Forts Hatteras and Clark from wood and sand. On August 27 a small Union fleet transporting nine hundred troops under General Benjamin Butler dropped anchor off the inlet. The next morning the fleet attacked Fort Clark using European naval tactics; the ships fired not from anchored positions but while in constant motion. The cannon fire forced the rebels to flee and Butler's men took the fort without a shot. The next day, August 29, the fleet used plunging fire (shots fired over the fort's walls instead of against them) that threatened Fort Hatteras's magazines and the Confederates surrendered after three hours. The war's first amphibious assault had captured two forts and 700 Confederates without a single Union fatality.

Back in Washington, Lincoln was ill on this day. "[The President] looks sick, and is I fear threatened with intermitting fever," wrote Frances Seward. Her husband William, the Secretary of State, found Lincoln playing with the kittens Seward had given the first family. "Mr. L. seems quite fond of them. They climb all over him," Seward wrote. That night, Butler awakened Lincoln in his bed with news of the Hatteras victory. After more than four months of war without a major Union victory, the news was elating. "This was our first naval victory," wrote Commodore David Porter, "indeed our first victory of any kind, and should not be forgotten."

SEPTEMBER 2

Fremont's Proclamation

Lincoln, on this Monday in 1861, wrote General John Fremont asking him to modify his August 30 proclamation that freed the slaves of rebellious Missourians.

The president may have regretted his wording when he named Fremont to head the Department of the West and gave him "carte blanche" in dealing with tumultuous Missouri. With the state deeply divided over Union and Confederate sentiments, guerrilla warfare was rampant. Desperate, Fremont proclaimed martial law throughout the state without consulting Washington. He drew a line from the state's southeast corner to its northwest and declared that any civilian north of the line who bore arms would be tried and shot. Last of all, Fremont declared that any Missourian aiding the rebellion would have his property confiscated, including slaves, proclaiming that "their slaves, if they have any, are hereby declared freemen."

While Fremont claimed he told Lincoln of his edict, Lincoln actually found out about it from the press. Fremont's proclamation exceeded the First Confiscation Act that Congress passed in August, which allowed emancipation of slaves working for the Confederate army—not slaves owned by civilians who were Confederate sympathizers. Lincoln feared that the border slave states might join the Confederacy because of the edict. Weary of infuriating Radical Republicans who were already applauding Fremont's proclamation, Lincoln asked but did not order the general to modify his order: "Allow me therefore to ask, that you will as of your own motion, modify . . . [it] to conform" to the Confiscation Act, Lincoln wrote Fremont on this day. He did order Fremont not to invoke capital punishment: "It is therefore my order that you allow no man to be shot . . . without first having my approbation or consent." He added, "should you shoot a man . . . the Confederates would very certainly shoot our best man in their hands in retaliation; and so man for man, indefinitely."

SEPTEMBER 9

Lincoln Sends Fremont Help

Chaos in Missouri as well as in General John Fremont's command prompted Lincoln, on this day in 1861, to write to his friend General David Hunter to act as consultant to Fremont.

In July Lincoln named Fremont to head the new Department of the West, which encompassed Missouri. Soon after arriving in St. Louis, Fremont and his wife Jesse took over a $6,000 mansion and isolated themselves, refusing unwanted visitors, including Missouri's former governor, Hamilton Gamble. Unmonitored, Fremont's subordinates mishandled and misappropriated military funds. The general had given his friends "stupendous contracts" to supply army equipment, horses, and railroad cars without competitive bidding. Lincoln wanted something done.

On September 5, Lincoln visited his general in chief, Winfield Scott, asking if Hunter could be assigned "chief of staff to act as Adjutant & Inspector General" in Fremont's army. Scott agreed that "rash measures might be staved off" with Hunter's presence, but his rank was "too high, by one degree" for the position. Lincoln decided to ask Hunter anyway, writing that "[Fremont's] cardinal mistake is that he isolates himself & allows nobody to see him; and by which he does not know what is going on in the very matter he is dealing with. He needs to have, by his side, a man of large experience. Will you not, for me, take that place?" The letter was given to Montgomery Blair and General Montgomery Meigs, the Army Quartermaster whom Lincoln was sending to Missouri to scout the situation. Upon receiving the letter, Hunter went straight to St. Louis.

SEPTEMBER 10

Ironclads

One of many lasting legacies of Lincoln's administration was the evolution of wooden warships to metal. On this Tuesday in 1861, Lincoln attended a naval committee on ironclads.

As reports came in during the summer of 1861 about the Confederate's first ironclad—the *Virginia*—Secretary of the Navy Gideon Welles decided the Union needed ironclads as well. A board was formed and on August 3 Welles took out newspaper ads calling for designs. One of the responses was from Cornelius Bushnell, a Connecticut shipbuilder who was unsure his vessel design was seaworthy. Bushnell went to New York City to show his design to Swedish engineering genius John Ericsson. "She will easily carry the load you propose," Ericsson assured Bushnell of his design. Ericsson then showed Bushnell his own design for "a floating battery absolutely impregnable to the heaviest shot or shell." Ericsson's ship was small and flat with a rotating turret.

Excited, Bushnell showed Ericsson's design to Welles, but when Welles showed it to the Ironclad Board, they thought the design too radical. Knowing of Lincoln's love for innovation, Welles arranged for the president to meet with the board on this day. During the discussion, Lincoln was asked what he thought of the design. "All I have to say is what the girl said when she stuck her foot into the stocking, 'It strikes me there's something in it.'" With the board still not convinced, Bushnell had Ericsson speak to the board himself later that September. The Ironclad Board was so impressed that it awarded Ericcson the contract immediately. Named to be a monitor or beacon of Union strength, the *Monitor*—the Union's first ironclad—slipped into New York's East River 118 days later, on January 30, 1862.

SEPTEMBER 11

"He Knows What I Want Done"

A feud between Lincoln and General John Fremont and his wife Jesse came to a head this Wednesday in 1861, when the president ordered Fremont to alter his emancipation edict.

Fremont, as the head of the Department of the West, had ordered the slaves of all rebellious Missouri owners freed. Lincoln wrote Fremont asking—not ordering—him to alter his proclamation. Lincoln awaited response until the evening of September 10, when he received a card from Fremont's wife Jesse, just arrived from St. Louis and asking for an interview. "Now, at once," Lincoln ordered. Jesse was shown to the Red Room at nine in her still-wrinkled traveling clothes. Without offering her a seat, Lincoln read the letters she carried from her husband. The president was furious. Fremont refused to modify his edict unless he was ordered. "If I were to retract of my own accord it would imply that I myself thought it wrong," Fremont wrote. Even more galling, Fremont asked that his department be expanded to include Kentucky and Tennessee.

"I have written to the general and he knows what I want done," Lincoln told Jesse. But emancipation would enlist Europe in the Union's cause, she responded. "You are quite the female politician," Lincoln said coldly. Jesse countered with a threat to defy the president. "She more than once intimated that if General Fremont should conclude to try conclusions with me, he could set up for himself," Lincoln later related. Lincoln dismissed her and the next day—this day—he "cheerfully" ordered Fremont to alter his proclamation. Lincoln later said that Jesse "taxed me so violently with many things that I had to exercise all the awkward tact I have to avoid quarreling with her."

SEPTEMBER 16

The Fremonts vs. the Blairs

General John Fremont's self-destruction continued on this Monday in 1861, as General in Chief Winfield Scott informed Lincoln that Fremont had arrested a member of the powerful Blair family.

It was the Blairs who urged Lincoln to name Fremont as the head of the Department of the West in July. The Blairs quickly became disillusioned with Fremont when he ineptly handled the factions vying for control of Missouri. Things came to a head when Fremont proclaimed all Missouri slaves free of their rebellious owners. Then, when Lincoln asked Fremont to alter his proclamation, Fremont's wife Jesse came to Washington on September 11 to deliver Fremont's refusal.

During her stay in Washington, Blair family patriarch Frank Senior visited Jesse in her room at the Willard Hotel. The old man had long been friends with the Fremonts and had been influential in getting Fremont the Republican nomination for president in 1856. The Fremonts had even named their son Frank after the old man. "I had been like a child in their family," Jesse recalled. But Frank Senior was so angry that he foolishly told Jesse of a letter Frank Junior had sent to his other son—Postmaster General Montgomery Blair. Frank Junior, a congressman in Missouri and an army officer, had urged that Fremont—his superior—be replaced. Jesse demanded a copy of the letter. She even told the old man that he would lose his son should her husband challenge Frank Junior to a duel. When Frank Senior stonewalled Jesse, she turned to the president and demanded that the he turn over his copy of Frank Junior's letter. Lincoln refused and Jesse returned to St. Louis to urge her husband to arrest Frank Junior for insubordination. When Lincoln heard of Frank's arrest on this day, he moved to have the congressman released and squashed any military trial.

SEPTEMBER 30

Political Arrests

Lincoln, on this Monday in 1861, met with Baltimore representatives to discuss the arrest of Baltimore mayor George Brown for "complicity with those in armed rebellion against the Government."

Maryland was deeply divided at the beginning of the war and many of its state legislators vacated their seats, either because of their Unionist or secessionist beliefs. During the summer, secessionists worked to fill these seats and the administration's heavy hand on Marylanders—censoring the press and arresting civilians—only made them more determined. In late summer, Lincoln had reason to believe that when the state legislature met on September 17 in special session, it would vote to secede from the Union. According to General George McClellan, "this action was to be supported by an advance of the Southern army across the Potomac." The administration decided to take action.

On September 11, Secretary of War Simon Cameron wrote General Nathaniel Banks at Darnestown, Maryland: "The passage of any act of secession by the Legislature of Maryland must be prevented. If necessary all or any part of the members must be arrested." On that same day, Cameron ordered General John Dix, military head at Baltimore, to arrest several Baltimore residents, including three congressmen and the editor of the secessionist newspaper *The South*. Dix added names to the list, including Mayor Brown, who appears to have had a dispute with Dix and was arrested with at least ten others during the night of September 12. Still more legislators were arrested in the next few days, so that on September 17 only eleven answered the roll call in Frederick. Oddly, McClellan (a Democrat), Maryland governor Thomas Hicks, and many newspapers applauded the action. These political prisoners were eventually released, the last of them in November 1862.

#20

Maryland and Civil Liberties

While abridgments of civil liberties occurred throughout the war virtually everywhere, North and South, what happened during the summer of 1861 in Maryland represented the low tide. This was due in a large degree to Maryland's proximity and importance to the federal government. It was also due to early conflicts with the Lincoln administration. On his way to his inauguration in February, Lincoln had to steal into and out of Baltimore because of a plot to assassinate him. In April, Baltimore secessionists attacked soldiers marching through their city, resulting in a riot and twenty-six deaths. Afterward, secessionists burned bridges, tore up railroad tracks, and terrorized Unionists.

The military occupied Annapolis and Baltimore and instituted martial law. The presence of thousands of Union troops cooled secessionists' ardor so much that there was not enough support for secession when the legislature met on April 26. But the federal government was petrified of a renewal of secessionist sentiment and had hundreds arrested without the protection of habeas corpus. On July 1 the Baltimore police board was arrested, including the police chief. Secessionist newspapers were closed. Even churches were forced to fly the Union flag. "No secession flag has to the knowledge of the police been exhibited in Baltimore for many weeks, except a small paper flag displayed by a child from an upper window," wrote General John Dix. The child's flag was removed. Dix added, "I have prohibited the exhibition in shop windows of rebel envelopes and music."

> While secession sentiment declined after the first year, abridgement of civil liberties did not. In November and in every election afterward, the military were present at the voting booths, cooling dissension. Over 2,000 Marylanders were arrested during the war, including twenty-nine legislators and seventeen newspaper owners.

OCTOBER 8

Troop Reviews

The Lincolns, on this day in 1861, rode out to a plain some three miles east of the Capitol to review General George McClellan's cavalry and artillery units.

Lincoln knew the value to troop morale in seeing their commander in chief. While the actual number is unknown, there are at least sixty-two separate recorded instances when Lincoln reviewed troops. He reviewed everything from single regiments to whole armies. Lincoln reviewed sharpshooters, sailors, the Invalid Corps (made up of wounded soldiers), and black regiments. In the heady three months between Fort Sumter and the first battle of Manassas, there were twenty-four recorded reviews by Lincoln, all of them in Washington. After that, Lincoln's reviews tapered off, with only sixteen in the rest of 1861 and twenty-two in the next three years. After May 1862, almost all of his reviews were conducted in the field.

What the soldiers saw and admired in Lincoln during these reviews was his earthiness. Lincoln's ugliness and awkwardness on a horse only reinforced his ordinariness, his lack of affectation. General Ulysses Grant's aid, Horace Porter, thought Lincoln's appearance on a horse "bordered upon the grotesque," but as he reviewed the troops, the soldiers "were so lost in admiration of the man that the humorous aspect did not seem to strike them . . .

enthusiastic shouts and even words of familiar greeting met him on all sides." A soldier admitted that he laughed at the "ludicrous sight" of Lincoln reviewing the troops, but added that "his benignant smile as he passed on was a real reflection of this honest, kindly heart. . . . His popularity in the army is and has been universal." As one sergeant wrote, "He is the soldier's friend and the man above all men in the right place. . . . [He] take[s] nobody's word or reports got up for effect. He came and saw for himself. Talk of McClellan's popularity among the soldiers—it will never measure 100th part of Honest Abe's. Such cheers as greeted him never tickled the ears of Napoleon in his palmiest days."

OCTOBER 19

The Navy Yard

After a cabinet meeting on this day in 1861, Lincoln and his cabinet adjourned to the Navy Yard for a trip to Alexandria, Virginia, where they inspected the steamer *Pensacola*. From there they took a diverting trip on the Potomac to Fort Washington, Maryland.

Lincoln was a frequent visitor to the Navy Yard. On May 9, 1861, Lincoln took his family there to watch a demonstration of the eleven-inch cannon developed by the Yard's commander, John Dahlgren, aboard the very same *Pensacola*. Lincoln was so thrilled with the experiment that he returned to the Yard at least nine times for ordnance tests during the war. The president also found his trips to the Yard diverting and relaxing. The Yard was usually closed to the public, insulating Lincoln from his usual glut of visitors. "Well, there has been a pleasant day," Lincoln said once, after a short cruise at the Yard. "Such a relief from politicians."

The Navy Yard was the scene of at least two mishaps that nearly injured Lincoln. On November 15, 1863, the president was watching a demonstration of the "Hyde" rocket when it exploded on launch, raining shrapnel everywhere but leaving Lincoln unscathed. Seven months earlier, on April 26, 1863, after inspecting the French frigate the *Gassendi*, Lincoln asked Dahlgren if he could inspect the ship at the waterline. As the presidential launch rounded the bow, the French officers—believing Lincoln had headed for the docks—decided to fire a twenty-one-gun salute. The first shot went off just above Lincoln's head. "Pull like the devil, boys!" Dahlgren yelled at the oarsmen as they rowed the launch to safety.

It was at the Navy Yard that Lincoln inspected the damage to the *Monitor* after its historic battle with the *Merrimack*. And, on the last day of his life, Lincoln inspected the ironclad *Montauk* at the Yard. By coincidence, John Wilkes Booth's autopsy was performed on the *Montauk* and many of Booth's co-conspirators were initially imprisoned aboard her.

OCTOBER 20

Wires that Spanned a Continent

On this Sunday in 1861, Lincoln received a telegram from Utah's secretary of state, Frank Fuller, reporting that the eastern leg of the first transcontinental telegraph had reached Salt Lake City. "Utah . . . congratulates the President upon the completion of an enterprise which spans the continent, unites two oceans and connects remote extremities of the body politic with the great government heart," Fuller wrote. Lincoln reciprocated his congratulations.

The Civil War was the first American conflict to use the telegraph. Its greatest use was in the ability of commanders to communicate with different segments of their armies. This led to efforts to tap and intercept the messages by the opposing side. Confederate general Robert E. Lee tapped General Ulysses Grant's line for six weeks during the Petersburg, Virginia siege. Both sides developed codes—called arbitraries—for specific people. Lincoln was "Adam,"

Confederate president Jefferson Davis was "Husband," General George McClellan was "Egypt," and Lee was "Hunter." About 6.5 million telegrams were sent in code during the war.

While telegraphs had been in use since the 1840s, it wasn't until 1860 that Congress appropriated $40,000 to build a transcontinental telegraph. A year later, the western leg of the transcontinental line stretched from Carson City, Nevada to Salt Lake City, Utah, and the eastern leg met it in Salt Lake City from Omaha, Nebraska. The eastern leg was completed on October 18, prompting Fuller's telegram. The western leg was connected to the eastern on October 24. That evening Lincoln received a telegram from California chief justice Stephen Field, "[I] send you the first message which will be transmitted over the wires . . . which connects the Pacific with the Atlantic States."

OCTOBER 21

Edward Baker

Lincoln, on this Monday in 1861, received news that his good friend Edward Baker had been killed in battle.

By October 1861 the public's love for General George McClellan had waned, particularly after his army sat inactive for months. Radical Benjamin Wade raged that McClellan was camped in Washington so "that Mr. Lincoln and cabinet may breathe freely and eat their dinners in peace, and that Mrs. Lincoln may, without interruption, pursue her French and dancing." Finally, McClellan decided to attack the Confederates near Leesburg, Virginia, forty miles north of Washington. Leesburg overlooked two key Potomac crossings and between them was a steep slope known as Ball's Bluff. McClellan ordered a "slight demonstration" against the town and Baker led the attack.

Lincoln and Baker had been friends for decades, dating from when they had both been Illinois legislators and Lincoln had named his second son after Baker. Baker spent his final day on earth visiting with the president on the White House lawn. "Mr. Lincoln sat on the ground, leaning against a tree," wrote an observer, "Colonel Baker was lying prone on the ground his head supported by his clasped hands." Nearby, Willie Lincoln "was tossing the fallen leaves about in childish grace and abandon."

The next day—this day—Baker and his men were surprised to find Ball's Bluff swarming with Confederates. The rebels charged, killing Baker and forcing his men to retreat down the bluff and cross the Potomac with snipers at their back. The Union troops suffered nearly nine hundred casualties, compared to less than one hundred and fifty Confederates.

Lincoln received the news at the telegraph office that afternoon. A reporter observed Lincoln's "bowed head and tears rolling down his furrowed cheeks, his face pale and wan, his heart heaving with emotion" as he stumbled out into the street.

OCTOBER 27

Fremont Is Dismissed

With Lincoln about to remove General John Fremont from command, the president, on this Sunday in 1861, received reports from Fremont of his own heroic military exploits.

In the three months since Fremont took command of the Department of the West, he had nearly handed Missouri to the Confederates. Fremont's mismanagement of his department and attempt to emancipate Missouri slaves quickly led to calls for his dismissal. Fremont's failure to reinforce the popular General Nathaniel Lyon at Wilson's Creek resulted in a loss and Lyon's death. In September the Confederates drove deep into the state, took Lexington and a month later, despite Lincoln's orders to retake the city, it was still in rebel hands.

That same month, Lincoln dispatched Quartermaster General Montgomery Meigs to St. Louis to assess the situation. "The rebels are killing and ravaging Union men throughout the state," Meigs reported, and recommended Fremont's removal. Secretary of War Simon Cameron and Adjutant General Lorenzo Thomas were next dispatched, and Cameron carried a letter relieving Fremont of command. Fremont convinced Cameron to hold the order because, he promised, he was about to attack the Confederates. Thomas, however, told Lincoln that Fremont should be fired. Fremont's own subordinates told Lincoln they had no confidence in their superior. Finally, on October 24, Lincoln sent his friend Leonard Swett to Missouri, carrying Fremont's dismissal.

In Missouri, Fremont was aware his career was in jeopardy and began sending Washington glowing reports of his efforts to retake the pro-Confederate town of Lexington. On this day, Lincoln received a telegram from Fremont about a small but valiant cavalry charge by Fremont's men which cleared Springfield, Missouri, of Confederates on October 25. It was to no avail; the battle was too insignificant to save Fremont's job and he was relieved on November 2.

#21

Handling Fremont

Lincoln's delay in firing General John Fremont was viewed by his contemporaries as an example of his inexperience, even weakness. "He has no will, no power to command," wrote Attorney General Edward Bates. "He makes nobody afraid of him. And hence discipline is relaxed, & stupid inanity takes place of action." But there was calculation in Lincoln's actions.

Fremont was extremely popular. Fremont's highly publicized expeditions to California, Oregon, and Utah ignited national interest in western migration. Fremont was the Republican Party's first presidential nominee and, during the war, was the darling of Radical Republicans, particularly after his emancipation order of August 1861. When Lincoln forced Fremont to rescind the order, many major Northern newspapers roasted the president. Radical Republican Benjamin Wade claimed that Lincoln's action were expected "of one, born of 'poor white trash.'"

Anticipating the fallout from firing Fremont, Lincoln collected the reports of two senior generals and two cabinet secretaries who inspected Fremont's command personally and all but one of who recommended his dismissal. After he sent Leonard Swett to Missouri to remove Fremont, Lincoln leaked Adjutant General Lorenzo Thomas's report on the general's command to the *New York Times*. Thomas reported on the command's "defective equipment . . . its confusion and imbecility, its lack of transportation." He added that Fremont was "incompetent and unsafe to be instructed with its [the army's] management." It worked; Fremont's removal was seen as justified. "Slowly and reluctantly we are forced to the conviction that General Fremont is unequal to command," wrote the *Philadelphia Inquirer*.

In Missouri, Swett realized that Fremont would deny him entry to his headquarters, so he donned a farmer's outfit. On November 2 Swett walked right up to Fremont to deliver Lincoln's dismissal. The general was livid, "Sir, how did you get admission into my lines?"

NOVEMBER 1

Scott's Out, McClellan's In

On this Friday in 1861, Lincoln accepted the resignation of his general in chief, Winfield Scott.

While the seventy-five-year-old Scott still had a sharp, brilliant mind, physically he could no longer take the field. What was more, Scott had grown weary of McClellan's machinations to take his position and Scott told Lincoln he was willing to retire. After the Union failure at the Battle of Ball's Bluff on October 21, the public outcry against the army's inaction and incompetence mounted. On the evening of October 26 Radical Republicans met with McClellan, and the general claimed Scott was the source of the army's troubles.

When Lincoln entered his office on this morning he found Scott's resignation on his desk. At four in the afternoon Lincoln and his cabinet met with Scott at his headquarters, the general so ill that he had to lie on the couch during the meeting. Lincoln read a proclamation announcing Scott's retirement and extolling his "faithful devotion to the Constitution, the Union and the flag." An aide helped Scott to his feet so that he could shake the president's hand. Afterward, Lincoln visited McClellan to officially tell him he was now general in chief. "In addition to the present command [of the Army of the Potomac], the supreme command of the Army will entail a vast labor on you," Lincoln warned. "I can do it all," McClellan responded.

The next morning, McClellan accompanied Scott to the train station. Afterward, McClellan couldn't resist a parting shot. He wrote his wife that all he saw "was a feeble old man scarce able to walk—hardly any one there to see him off." The truth was that a large crowd of officers and civilians came to say goodbye to Scott.

#22

SCOTT VS. MCCLELLAN

Scott, known as "Old Fuss and Feathers" because of his proclivity for protocol and ornate uniforms, was the most experienced general in the army. His 1847 campaign to take Mexico City during the Mexican War was brilliant and more than a hundred future Civil War generals—including Robert E. Lee, Thomas "Stonewall" Jackson, Ulysses Grant, and George McClellan—received much of their combat experience during that operation. But by 1861 Scott weighed over three hundred pounds and suffered from rheumatism, gout, and dropsy. He could neither climb stairs nor mount a horse. Still, Lincoln thought that Scott and McClellan would make a great team—Scott as the tactician, McClellan as a field commander.

Both generals thought otherwise. McClellan believed thought Scott was an "imbecile" and "dotard" and saw his superior as "the great obstacle" on his own road to greatness. "God has placed a great work in my hands," said McClellan. "[If] the people call upon me to save the country—I must save it & cannot respect anything that is in the way." Scott found McClellan insubordinate. In August 1861, McClellan submitted a letter to Lincoln questioning Scott's assessment that Washington was secure from Confederate invasion. Scott was furious and asked to retire. Lincoln temporarily smoothed over the situation. When Scott asked McClellan for a report on the readiness of the Army of the Potomac, McClellan ignored him for more than three weeks. "[McClellan] has now long prided himself in treating me with uniform neglect—running into disobedience of orders," Scott said. He told Secretary of War Simon Cameron, "The remedy by arrest and trial before a court-martial would probably, soon cure the evil." But, he added, such a move "would be encouraging the enemy and depressing to the friends of the Union." In the end, Scott decided what was best for the country was his retirement.

NOVEMBER 13

Dodging the President

On this Wednesday in 1861, General George McClellan received an unwanted visitor—Lincoln—and decided to teach him a lesson.

McClellan's headquarters on Fifteenth and H streets was just a short walk from the White House and Lincoln visited it almost daily. "I have just been interrupted here by the Presdt. & Secty. [of State William] Seward who had nothing very particular to say except some stories to tell," McClellan wrote in October.

McClellan's annoyance gave way to angst and the general began to stay at his friend Edwin Stanton's house in order "to dodge all enemies in shape of [the] browsing Presdt." McClellan called Lincoln "the original gorilla" and wrote one day, "I went to Seward's where I found the 'Gorilla' again, & was of course much edified by his anecdotes—ever apropos, & ever unworthy of one holding his high position." Many noted that McClellan made the president wait; Lincoln responded to this slight by saying he would hold McClellan's horse if he'd only bring a victory.

Then on this night, McClellan had had enough. Lincoln's secretary John Hay described the incident:

> The President, Governor Seward, and I, went over to McClellan's house tonight. The servant at the door said the General was

> [out] . . . and would soon return . . . after we had waited about an hour, McC[lellan] came in and without paying any particular attention of the porter, who told him the President was waiting to see him, went up stairs, passing the door of the room where the President and Secretary of State were seated. They waited about half-an-hour, and sent once more a servant to tell the General they were there, and the answer cooly came that the General had gone to bed.

Lincoln rarely visited McClellan after that.

NOVEMBER 15

The Trent Affair

On this Friday in 1861, Lincoln received word that a Union sloop-of-war had intercepted a British mail steamer and arrested two Confederate envoys bound for Europe.

In March 1861, the Confederacy sought European recognition—particularly from Britain—that they were a new country, not a collection of states in rebellion. Instead, in May, Britain declared itself neutral and the Confederacy a belligerent, a status that allowed the rebels to purchase goods from England but was not a recognition of nationhood. Frustrated, the Confederates appointed two more commissioners—former Senators James Mason and John Slidell—to go to London and Paris. On the night of October 12 Mason and Slidell boarded a steamer in Charleston and evaded the Union blockade to reach Havana, Cuba.

By then, the Mason–Slidell mission was reported in newspapers North and South, and Secretary of the Navy Gideon Welles encouraged his ships to intercept the commissioners. While the captain of the *San Jacinto*—Charles Wilkes—did not get Welles's message, he was aware of the Confederate mission and parked his ship just off Havana. At noon on November 8 he sighted the steamer the

Trent and fired a shot across its bow. When the *Trent* heaved to, Wilkes arrested the envoys. Wilkes then took the envoys to Fortress Monroe, Virginia, from where he wired Washington, on this day.

Lincoln—along with most of the North—was elated at the news, but asked his attorney general, Edward Bates, if the seizure was legal. "I can't at the moment refer to cases," Bates replied, but assured the president the action was legal. It, however, was not and Lincoln's elation turned to angst as Britain rattled its sabers over what it perceived as an act of war.

#23

Why Was Recognition of the Confederacy Important?

When the South decided to secede from the Union and form the Confederacy, its leaders were confident that both Britain and France would intervene on their behalf. And if they did, the huge British and French navies could easily brush aside Lincoln's blockade and could change the course of the war. It is almost certain the Union could not handle both the Confederacy and Europe. The first step to intervention—indeed before any treaties could be signed—was official recognition of the Confederacy as a sovereign nation.

Europe—specifically Britain—had a good reason to intervene. Seventy-five percent of the cotton supplied to Britain's textile industry came from the American South. The rebels even imposed their own embargo of cotton early in the war to pressure England. Unfortunately for them, Britain had a surplus of cotton that lasted until the end of 1862. By then the British were buying cotton from India and Egypt.

Nevertheless, it's clear there was some European support for recognition and even intervention. Late in 1862, France's Napoleon III tried to mediate an end to the war, but Lincoln rebuffed his efforts. "I expect to maintain this contest until successful, or till I die," Lincoln said. In July 1862 and again in June 1863, Britain's House of Commons had serious debates over officially recognizing the Confederacy.

Hopes for recognition rested squarely on the success the Confederacy had on the battlefield. After the Union victories at Gettysburg and Vicksburg, the European powers never again seriously considered intervention. In desperation, the Confederacy, in 1865, offered to emancipate its slaves in exchange for England's recognition. Britain refused.

NOVEMBER 16

The Gardener

Lincoln, on this Saturday in 1861, wrote Adjutant General Lorenzo Thomas that the White House gardener—Lieutenant John Watt—was no longer "needed" and asked that he be assigned "to his proper place in [his] Regiment."

In 1861, the congressional Potter Investigating Committee—named for Wisconsin Congressman John Potter—had been tasked to unearth Confederate-sympathizers within the government. The committee claimed to have evidence of treason on hundreds of federal employees, including Watt and other White House employees. When Lincoln asked Benjamin French, Commissioner of Public Buildings, what he should do, French responded that "it might be expedient to try to get rid of the clamor by the removal or resignation of some of them."

There was another reason for Watt's removal: Lincoln may have been aware of Watt's efforts to pad White House expenditures to help the first lady hide her overspending. By that fall, Mary had overspent her allowance of $20,000 to furnish the Executive Mansion by $7,000. To cover the deficit, Watt showed Mary how to submit inflated bills or vouchers for purchases never made. Watt, for instance, submitted bills for flowers ($700) for the Executive Mansion grounds, 215 loads of manure evidently to fertilize them ($107) and a horse and cart to haul it ($47), none of which was provided. Worse, Watt convinced Mary to fire the White House steward, hire Watt's wife, Jane, as cover, then keep the steward's salary while Mary performed the duties herself. In exchange, Watt somehow garnered a commission as a first lieutenant, was protected from the Potter Committee's accusations, and, despite Lincoln's order made on this day, was not sent to his regiment.

In February 1862, Watt was finally dismissed from White House service, allegedly after he unsuccessfully tried to blackmail the Lincolns. In exchange for three letters he had from Mary revealing her illicit activities, Watt wanted $20,000. He was given $1,500 hush money before he was fired. The Senate revoked his commission and in August 1863 he enlisted as a private.

#24

Mary's Bills

In the waning months of 1861, bills began pouring in from Philadelphia and New York, where Mary had spent exorbitantly for furnishings for the White House. Hoping to pay the bills without her husband's knowledge, Mary sold old White House furniture, but made too little to make a difference. Even the ten cents per wagonload that was paid for manure from the White House stables was inadequate. She asked Lincoln's secretary John Hay to give her the executive stationary fund and when Hay refused, she tried to have him fired. "I told her to kiss mine," Hay told another secretary, John Nicolay.

Desperate, Mary—with the help of White House gardener John Watt—began bilking the government by padding household bills. Still, it wasn't enough, and in late December Mary knew she would have to tell her husband. The first lady enlisted the help of the Commissioner of Public Buildings Benjamin French to ask Lincoln to request money from Congress. "He said it would stink in the land to have it said that an appropriation of $20,000 for furnishing the house had been overrun by the President when the poor freezing soldiers could not have blankets," French recalled, after he spoke to Lincoln, "and he swore he would never approve the bills for flub dubs for that damned old house." Lincoln added that the Executive Mansion was "furnished well enough when they came—better than any house they had ever lived in—& rather than put his name to such a bill he would pay it out of his own pocket."

In the end, French resolved the issue when he convinced Congress to appropriate the needed amount and hid it within a military spending bill. Mary's spending problems, however, were never resolved.

NOVEMBER 28

Thanksgiving

Lincoln spent this Wednesday in 1861—his first Thanksgiving in the White House—having dinner with his best friend, Joshua Speed, and his wife.

Thanksgiving is a North American tradition (it's celebrated in both America and Canada) that dates from 1621, when the Plymouth colonists invited Native Americans—the Wampanoug people—to a feast. Many states instituted annual Thanksgiving holidays but celebrated them on different days of the year. For instance, Lincoln celebrated the holiday on this Wednesday in Washington while the year before, in Illinois, he had celebrated it on Thursday, November 29. But until the Civil War, there was not a national thanksgiving holiday unless the president declared one for a special reason. George Washington, for instance, declared a day of thanksgiving in 1789 after the Constitution was ratified.

Then a woman named Sarah Josepha Hale changed that. Hale was an accomplished writer and author of the nursery rhyme "Mary Had a Little Lamb." She was credited as one of America's first female magazine editors (*Lady's Magazine* from 1827–36 and *Godey's Lady's Book* from 1836–77). As editor of *Godey's*, Hale began a campaign for a national holiday on the last Thursday in November. Lincoln, on October 3, 1863, proclaimed an annual holiday. By then the war had turned in the Union's favor and Lincoln had issued his Emancipation Proclamation. "It has seemed fit and proper that they [God's blessings] should be solemnly, reverently, and gratefully acknowledged, as one heart and one voice, by the whole American people," Lincoln wrote. The first annual national Thanksgiving was on November 25, 1863.

Thanksgiving was usually celebrated on the last Thursday in November, until 1941, when it was permanently designated to be the fourth (not necessarily the last) Thursday of the month.

NOVEMBER 29

"Chevalier" Wikoff

Lincoln, on this day in 1861, read to his cabinet part of his first annual message to Congress. Subsequently the message—to be delivered on December 3—was, however, prematurely leaked to the press, prompting an investigation of Henry Wikoff and the first lady.

In her first year in the White House, Mary Lincoln held evening soirees in the downstairs Blue Room. Her guests were mostly men who doted on her and, as journalist Henry Villard noted, Mary was vulnerable to "a common set of men and women whose bare-faced flattery easily gained controlling influence over her."

One such flatterer was Wikoff, a European adventurer who was an intimate of the French emperor, Napoleon. The *New York Herald* sent Wikoff to Washington as a secret correspondent for them. Wikoff charmed his way into Mary's salon to become, as Villard claimed, a "guide in matters of social etiquette, domestic arrangements, and personal requirements, including her toilette." The "Chevalier" Wikoff escorted Mary on her shopping sprees as an advisor, and repaid the first lady with stories in the *Herald* about her lavish spending.

When the *Herald* published excerpts of Lincoln's annual message, it was alleged that Wikoff was the leak and Mary his source. A House judiciary committee investigated and Wikoff claimed that it was not Mary but the White House gardener, John Watt, who was his source, and Watt confirmed Wikoff's claim. As reporter Ben Poore wrote, "Mr. Lincoln had visited the Capitol and urged the Republicans on the Committee to spare him disgrace, so Watt's improbable story was received and Wikoff liberated." In February 1862, a reporter named Matthew Hale Smith of the *Boston Journal* showed Lincoln proof that Wikoff was working for the *Herald*. "Give me those papers and sit here till I return," said the president on his way to confront Wikoff. He returned to tell Smith that the "chevalier" had been "driven from the Mansion [White House] that night."

DECEMBER 3

Chaplains

On this Tuesday in 1861, Lincoln delivered his first annual message to Congress and he recommended a "general provision be made for chaplains to serve at hospitals as well as regiments."

At the start of the war, Congress had made provisions for only thirty chaplains to cover the nineteen regiments in the pre-war army. By the fall of 1861 the army had 650 regiments. On May 4, 1861, the army issued orders that mandated that commanders appoint chaplains and confirm them by regimental elections. But in the growing number of military hospitals, chaplains were not appointed. Sometime in late September, Lincoln drew up a form letter to give to any chaplain wishing to work in the hospitals. "Feeling the intrinsic propriety of having such person to so act, and yet believing there is no law conferring power upon me to appoint them . . . if you will voluntarily enter upon and perform the appropriate duties of such position, I will recommend that Congress make compensation therefore at the same rate as chaplains in the army are compensated," Lincoln wrote to applicants. Keeping his promise, Lincoln forwarded the names of seven hospital chaplains to Congress this day along with a recommendation for legislation on the subject. On May 20, 1862, Congress finally followed Lincoln's suggestion.

About 2,300 chaplains served the Union Army (never more than 600 at one time). Almost all of them were Protestant Christian, despite the fact that 7,000 Jews and 200,000 Catholics served in the Union forces. Oddly, the Confederacy had the war's first African American chaplain. But at least fourteen black chaplains also served the Union. One woman—Rev. Ella Gibson—briefly served the First Wisconsin Heavy Artillery. Despite the president saying he had "no objection to her appointment," Secretary of War Edwin Stanton refused to let her serve.

DECEMBER 26

Seward's Argument

Lincoln, along with his cabinet, on this Friday in 1862, decided what to do with the Confederate commissioners—James Mason and John Slidell—who had been forcibly removed from a British ship in November.

Mason and Slidell had been en route to Europe to seek recognition for the Confederacy as a sovereign nation when they were intercepted. Then came word that England considered the arrest aboard one of their ships as an act of war. Eleven thousand British soldiers and fifteen ships were dispatched to Canada. Despite the threat, Secretary of State William Seward refused to believe Britain would start a war. "You know the bulldog will not bite," Lincoln told Seward, "but does the bulldog know he will not bite?"

On December 19, an official response from London finally arrived, declaring the incident an "affront" and demanding an apology and the release of the commissioners. Informally, Britain gave Lincoln seven days to respond. Seward wrote out a reply "cheerfully" returning the commissioners without an apology. But the president was not ready to concede defeat when they discussed it in a Christmas Day cabinet meeting. After they adjourned, Lincoln asked Seward to write a list of reasons for letting the commissioners leave and he would write out a list of reasons for holding them. When they met on this day, Lincoln did not have his list. "I found I could not make an argument that would satisfy my own mind, and that proved to me your ground was the right one," Lincoln told Seward. The commissioners were released in January, but they never succeeded in garnering recognition for the Confederacy.

1862

"I PASS MY LIFE IN PREVENTING THE STORM FROM BLOWING DOWN THE TENT, AND I DRIVE IN THE PEGS AS FAST AS THEY ARE PULLED UP."
—ABRAHAM LINCOLN

JANUARY 6

Lincoln Defends McClellan

On this Monday morning in 1862, Lincoln met with his general in chief, George McClellan, at his Washington headquarters at Nineteenth Street and Pennsylvania Avenue. It was there that the general had been convalescing from typhoid fever for more than a week. Lincoln had come to warn the general that Congress's Joint Committee on the Conduct of the War was demanding that McClellan be fired.

The previous month, Congress had authorized the creation of the Joint Committee to investigate military incompetence. The committee cast a wide net, investigating the Union routs at Bull Run (Manassas) in July and at Ball's Bluff in October. The committee also investigated why the Army of the Potomac had been idle since McClellan had been named its chief five months earlier.

There is little doubt that the investigation of McClellan was partly political; he was a Democrat and definitely not an abolitionist. The Radical Republicans who chaired and dominated the

Committee were staunch abolitionists. But McClellan was also a victim of his own ego. While he was particularly adept at training and equipping his men, he was not adept at military planning and refused to admit it. His ego also meant that he had no second in command, and thus no subordinates privy to McClellan's plans who could testify before the Committee while he was ill. Nor did McClellan divulge his plans to his superior—Lincoln—on this or any other day.

The Committee was astonished to hear this when they met with the president on this evening. Lincoln told them he "did not think he had any right to know [the plans], but that, as he was not a military man, it was his duty to defer to General McClellan." When the head of the committee, Senator Benjamin Wade of Ohio, demanded McClellan's removal, Lincoln refused.

JANUARY 10

"The Bottom Is Out of the Tub"

On this Friday in 1862, Lincoln was depressed because of the lack of activity with his armies and looked for solutions to the impasse.

During the first month of 1862, Lincoln drew considerable criticism from the press and the public over the idleness of the Union armies. Washingtonians could look across the Potomac and see the Confederate army thumbing its collective nose at them. What was worse, the Army of the Potomac had gone into winter quarters without any effort to dislodge the rebels. It didn't help that the army's general in chief, George McClellan, had been ill and indisposed since late December. Lincoln began, for the first time, to speak "of the bare possibility of our being two nations."

On this day, Lincoln quipped that if McClellan did not want to use the army, he would like to borrow it for a while. Lincoln also received news that two other generals—Henry Halleck, head of the army in Missouri, and Don Carlos Buell, head of the army in Kentucky—both felt an immediate offensive was impossible. "It is exceedingly discouraging," Lincoln wrote.

Later this day, Lincoln met with General Montgomery Meigs, the Quartermaster General of the Army. Distraught, Lincoln said, "The people are impatient; [Secretary of the Treasury Salmon] Chase has no money, and he tells me he can raise no money; the General of the Army has typhoid fever. The bottom is out of the tub. What shall I do?" That evening, he summoned Generals Irvin McDowell and William Franklin, and Secretaries Chase and William Seward for a "Council of War" and began forming plans for a concerted push against the Confederacy.

JANUARY 13

Lincoln Removes Cameron

Finally, after ten months of corruption in his War Department, Lincoln, on this day in 1862, removed Simon Cameron as his Secretary of War and named him minister to Russia—a virtual exile to Siberia.

Cameron was corrupt, inept, and insensible to the profligacy and waste in his own department. Cameron was "incapable of either organizing details or conceiving and advising general plans," Lincoln admitted. But even after a congressional committee investigated allegations of fraud and mismanagement, Lincoln was reluctant to fire him. The president dropped hints hoping Cameron would quit, but the secretary stubbornly refused.

The final straw was not malfeasance but an attempt to change government policy. Within an annual report, Cameron inserted, "It's clearly a right of the Government to arm slaves when it may become necessary, it is to take gunpowder from the enemy." He then forwarded the report to major newspapers. Still trying to keep the border slave states—who were petrified of armed slaves—loyal to the Union, Lincoln was furious and recalled the report.

When Lincoln, on January 11, 1862, informed Cameron that he would be named minister to Russia, the secretary broke into tears. To save Cameron's feelings, Lincoln allowed him to resign before he was formally named, on this day, to his new post.

Lincoln then appointed Edwin Stanton as his new War Secretary. Stanton had once professionally embarrassed Lincoln and had even characterized the president as a "giraffe" and the "original gorilla." As usual, Lincoln did not hold a grudge. He considered Stanton's attention to detail and indisputable honesty to be what the War Department needed. Stanton, indeed, threw himself into his work, vowing, "This army has got to fight. The champagne and oysters on the Potomac must be stopped."

#25

Cameron's "Shoddy" Department

During Secretary Simon Cameron's tenure, the War Department was wracked with embarrassing controversies and scandals. For one, a suspiciously large portion of the contracts Cameron assigned for war materiel went to companies in his home state of Pennsylvania. Many of these contracts were assigned without competitive bidding, leading to profiteering and price gouging. Likewise, military traffic was routed over the Northern Central Railroad and Pennsylvania Railroad in which Cameron and his assistant secretary had a financial stake.

The War Department spent $21,000 earmarked for military expenses on straw hats and linen pantaloons. The department also purchased such "army supplies" as barreled pickles and Scotch ale. In another instance, Hall carbines were sold by the department for a small sum, then bought back for $15 apiece, resold for $3.50, then repurchased for $22. Literally hundreds of diseased and dying horses were purchased for the cavalry at inflated prices. For the navy, the War Department spent $200,000 to purchase warships the navy itself declared unsafe. One of the ships sank on its first voyage. The army received tainted pork, knapsacks that came unglued in the rain, antiquated Austrian muskets, and overpriced shoes. Half-wool blankets—weighing only five pounds—were sold to soldiers for the same price as regulation ten-pound all-wool blankets. Textile contractors compressed woolen fibers into a material called "shoddy" and used them to make uniforms and blankets that disintegrated after only a few weeks in the field. Subsequently, "shoddy" became a part of the American lexicon, used to describe anything of inferior quality.

JANUARY 26

The Not-So-Tenderhearted Lincoln

Historians familiar with Lincoln's tenderness and words of reconciliation for his enemies are often surprised when they read his letter to Flag Officer Andrew Foote ordering him to "rain the rebels out" with mortars and "treat them to a refreshing shower of sulphur and brimstone." Foote was heading the naval leg of the Mississippi River Campaign and, with the Confederates manning forts along the river, mortars were essential for lobbing explosives over walls. The manufacture of mortars, however, had been slow. On this day in 1862, an irritated Lincoln vowed, "to take matters into his own hands" and met with a construction engineer on increasing production. Later Lincoln wrote, "Now I am going to devote a part of every day to these mortars and I won't leave off until it fairly rains bombs."

The mortar was, indeed, an effective killing machine. In July 1864, a Confederate in the trenches around Petersburg wrote, "They [the Union army] kill and wound more men with Morter Shell than any other way for the last few weeks. They throw them up and Drop them Right into the trenches." Lincoln was enthusiastic about many weapons that would inflict horrific casualties: explosive bullets, incendiary shells, and machine guns. This ran counter to his altruistic image.

Much of this apparent conflict in the president's personality can be explained by his total commitment to a Union victory. But Lincoln's former law partner, William Herndon, gave a more interesting explanation, "Mr. Lincoln was tenderhearted when in the presence of suffering or when it was enthusiastically or poetically described to him . . . [but] he had no imagination to invoke, through the distances, suffering, nor fancy to paint it. The subject of mercy must be presented to him."

JANUARY 27

Lincoln Demands His Armies Move

Still waiting for military action from his armies, Lincoln's patience finally ended. On this Monday in 1862, Lincoln issued the unprecedented President's General War Order No. 1, which ordered the armies in both the east and the west to move against Confederate forces on or before February 22 (Washington's birthday). This remarkable document was issued to spur the idle armies into a concerted action and realize Lincoln's strategy.

With the help of military experts and books, Lincoln formed a strategy that maximized the Union's greater numbers and infrastructure. He believed that the Union armies could menace the enemy "with superior forces at different points, at the same time; so that we safely attack, one, or both, if he makes no change; and if he weakens one to strengthen the other, forbear to attack the strengthened one, but seize, and hold the weakened one." This military precept—known as strategic concentration in time—would ultimately be used two years later to win the war.

Unfortunately, the current general in chief, George McClellan, believed in a strategic concentration of space, one army against the other, in a single massive battle. And McClellan was egotistical enough to believe he would and should lead his army—the Army of the Potomac—in that single battle. He just didn't know where it should be fought. In response to McClellan's indecisiveness, Lincoln issued another command—"Special War Order No. 1"—on January 31, specifically ordering McClellan to march his army south through the Virginia heartland. The general then sullenly submitted a counterplan, an amphibious landing east of Richmond.

Within a week the armies to the west began their offensives, less because of Lincoln's General War Order and more because the time was ripe. From those offensives would rise a star that eventually eclipsed McClellan: Ulysses S. Grant.

FEBRUARY 2

Lincoln Meets Ralph Waldo Emerson

At the White House on this Sunday in 1862, Massachusetts Senator Charles Sumner introduced Lincoln to one of his illustrious constituents—poet and philosopher Ralph Waldo Emerson. Lincoln pointed out he had met Emerson already, more than nine years before at the Springfield State House, where Emerson delivered a trio of his lectures on three successive nights (January 10–12, 1853). After delivering his lecture titled "Power" on the second night, Mary Lincoln and the ladies of the First Presbyterian Church—the church the Lincolns attended—held a reception in his honor.

During the 1850s, Emerson, an ardent abolitionist, became involved with the growing political turmoil over slavery. He was also a pacifist, describing war as "an epidemic insanity, breaking out here and there like the cholera or influenza, infecting men's brains instead of their bowels." And yet he supported the Union war effort. That same war cut deeply into Emerson's book sales and lecture income.

Yet Emerson's reputation as a man of letters still brought him speaking opportunities. He was in Washington that February of 1862 to deliver his lecture on "American Civilization" at the Smithsonian Institute. As he sat in the White House, conversing about the slave trade and abolition, he found the president a "frank, sincere, well-meaning man . . . not vulgar, as described; but with a sort of boyish cheerfulness."

#26

Emerson on Lincoln

Emerson, on two occasions, voiced his growing appreciation of Lincoln. The first was in a speech in Boston in September 1862, shortly after Lincoln announced his preliminary Emancipation Proclamation:

> He has been permitted to do more for America than any other American man . . . Forget all that we thought [were his] shortcomings, every mistake, every delay. In the extreme embarrassments of his part, call these endurance, wisdom, magnanimity, illuminated, as they are now, by this dazzling success.

On April 19, 1865—just four days after Lincoln died—Emerson delivered a eulogy for the fallen president at the Unitarian Church in his hometown of Concord:

> Then, what an occasion was the whirlwind of the war. Here was place for no holiday magistrate, no fair-weather sailor;

> the new pilot was hurried to the helm in a tornado. In four years—four years of battle-days—his endurance, his fertility of resources, his magnanimity, were sorely tried and never found wanting. There, by his courage, his justice, his even temper, his fertile counsel, his humanity, he stood a heroic figure in the center of a heroic epoch. He is the true history of the American people of his time . . . father of his country, the pulse of twenty million throbbing in his heart, the thought of their minds articulated by his tongue.

FEBRUARY 4

Lincoln Refuses a Pardon

On this Tuesday in 1862, Lincoln, who had pardoned so many men condemned to death, refused to pardon Nathaniel Gordon.

While the United States outlawed the importation of slaves in 1808, for fifty-two years the government did not aggressively stop the trade. Some 250,000 more slaves came into America between 1808 and 1860. New York City became the hub of the illegal trade, with an estimated 20,000 slaves smuggled through in the peak years of 1859 and 1860. Slave ship captains were virtually immune from prosecution. When a federal judge released one such captain on bail to sail to Rio de Janeiro to gather evidence, he never returned. The captain afterward boasted, "You don't have to worry about facing trial in New York City. . . . I can get a man off in New York for a thousand dollars."

In 1820, the United States made it possible for any American working on a slave ship to be charged with piracy, punishable by death. But it would not be until 1861 that any seafarer was successfully prosecuted under the law. That year the *Erie*—a ship built in Massachusetts and originating from New York—was captured off the mouth of the Congo River in August 1860. On board were nine hundred Africans, half of them children. The Africans were released in Liberia and Captain Nathaniel Gordon was indicted in New York City for piracy. The case floundered until Lincoln named Edward Delafield Smith New York's new district attorney. Smith won a conviction of Gordon on November 8, 1861, and he was sentenced to hang.

Gordon appealed to the president for clemency but Lincoln refused. He did grant Gordon a two-week reprieve. Lincoln wrote on this day, "In granting this respite, it becomes my painful duty to admonish the prisoner that, relinquishing all expectation of pardon by Human Authority, he refer himself alone to the mercy of the Common God and Father of all men." Gordon attempted suicide by smoking cigars laced with strychnine, but he survived to be executed on February 21, the only American ever so punished for slave trading.

FEBRUARY 5

A White House Ball

In the first year the Lincolns occupied the White House, Mary had taken to redecorating it lavishly, especially the East Room. To show off the new decor, she invited more than eight hundred people to a major ball in the East Room—the first ever in the White House—followed by a late dinner in the State Dining Room, set for this Wednesday night in 1862. "Are the President and Mrs. Lincoln aware that there is a civil war?" replied Senator Benjamin Wade to his invitation. "If they are not, Mr. and Mrs. Wade are, and for that reason decline to participate in feasting and dancing."

During the week before the party, eleven-year-old Willie Lincoln became ill (probably of typhoid fever from the White House's polluted drinking water) and the Lincolns considered canceling the festivities. However, they, were urged to proceed and the Lincolns left their boy's bedside to greet their guests. "He [Lincoln] was receiving at the large door of the East Room, speaking to the people as they came, but feeling so deeply that he spoke of what he felt and thought, instead of welcoming the guests," wrote one visitor. "To Gen. Fremont he at once said that his son was very ill and that he feared for the result. . . . The ball was becoming a ghastly failure."

Mary left the party several times to sit at her son's bedside and watch his labored breathing. Because of Willie's condition, dancing was prohibited, but Willie could hear the Marine Band play at the foot of the stairs. Dinner wasn't served until midnight and included a miniature of Fort Sumter sculpted in sugar. The cost for the affair was paid out of Lincoln's own pocket.

FEBRUARY 12

Lincoln's Sick Child

Lincoln spent much of this Wednesday in 1862—his fifty-third birthday—in the Prince of Wales room attending to his son Willie, stroking the boy's hair.

South of the White House was a canal that was so polluted by raw sewage and filth that its odor sometimes reached the White House Executive Mansion. "The ghosts of twenty thousand drowned cats come in nights through the South Windows," John Hay, secretary to the president, complained. Water from this canal was pumped through the White House sinks and it's believed that both of Lincoln's youngest sons—Willie and Tad—contracted either typhoid fever or an acute malarial infection from this putrid water in late January or early February of 1862. Willie, in particular, fought the fever for more than two weeks.

In addition to their family doctor, Robert Stone, the Lincolns hired a widowed army nurse by the name of Rebecca Pomroy to look after the boys. After Dorothea Dix, Superintendent of Women

Nurses, recommended Pomroy, Lincoln took Dix's hand and said "Well, all I want to say is, let her turn right in."

Willie had been moved to the large, canopied, rosewood bed in the Prince of Wales room, so-called because the prince had slept there during a 1860 visit. Mary was constantly at the boy's bedside, while Willie's friend, Horatio Nelson (Bud) Taft, kept watch, holding Willie's hand, sometimes falling asleep at his side.

The president, too, spent long hours at Willie's side, comforting him. "The President is nearly worn out, with grief and watching," observed Attorney General Edward Bates. Social occasions were canceled and affairs of state were delayed while Lincoln kept vigil over his eleven-year-old.

#27

Willie

William Wallace Lincoln was born ten months after his older brother Edward died, and Abraham and Mary looked to Willie to be a balm for their grief. He, in fact, was named after Mary's brother-in-law, Dr. William Wallace, who had treated Edward in his final days. While the Lincolns' grief was never fully assuaged, Willie became a favorite, and was especially doted on by his father.

Like his brother Robert, Willie attended private school in Springfield but was far more studious. Willie had a natural ability with math and, like his father, had an exceptional memory. Willie memorized the railroad stations from New York to Chicago, and could recite the train table as he conducted an imaginary train between the two cities. Also like his father, Willie took to writing poetry and had an exceptional sensitivity to other people's feelings. Lincoln felt that, of all his children, Willie's mind was closest to his own. As he watched Willie work out a problem, Lincoln once said, "I know every step of the process by which that boy arrived at his satisfactory solution of the question before him, as it is by just such slow methods I attain results."

Julia Taft, occasional babysitter for the Lincoln boys in the White House, described Willie as "the most lovable boy I ever knew, bright, sensible, sweet-tempered and gentle-mannered." Willie was the most handsome of the Lincoln sons. Mary's cousin, Elizabeth Todd Grimsley wrote, "[Willie was] a noble, beautiful boy . . . of great mental activity, unusual intelligence, wonderful memory, methodical, frank and loving, a counterpart of his father, save that he was handsome."

FEBRUARY 16

Fort Donelson Surrenders

Even as General Ulysses S. Grant was completing the first major Union victory in the West, Lincoln, on this Sunday in 1862, micromanaged and fretted over the Confederates.

At daybreak on this frigid morning in northern Tennessee, Union general Ulysses S. Grant received a note from Confederate general Simon Buckner, who had been a good friend before the war. The note asked for terms of the surrender of Fort Donelson. "No terms except unconditional surrender can be accepted," Grant shot back. Buckner reluctantly accepted these "ungenerous and unchivalrous terms."

The result was the surrender of more than 11,000 Confederate soldiers. What was worse, the loss of Donelson, on the Cumberland River, combined with the loss of Fort Henry on the Tennessee River the week before, represented a huge penetration into Confederate

Tennessee. The Confederates were forced to abandon Nashville. "If we yield this state with its important railroads and tributaries to the Ohio River," a Confederate chaplain lamented, "we have . . . surrendered the best avenues to the heart of the Confederacy."

In Washington, Lincoln was micromanaging, sending Grant's superior, General Henry Halleck, several suggestions about cutting rail lines through Tennessee. But when he received word on this day of the victory, he was exultant. "If the Southerners think that man for man they are better than our Illinois men, or Western men generally, they will discover themselves in a grievous mistake."

The next day, Lincoln promoted Grant to major-general of volunteers. The press awarded the general a new sobriquet, using his unusual initials. He was now "Unconditional Surrender" Grant. The irony is that Grant would, during the war, accept two more surrenders of large Confederate forces—at Vicksburg in July 1863 and at Appomattox in April 1865—and in both cases there would be conditions to the surrender.

FEBRUARY 20

"My Boy is Gone!"

At five in the afternoon of this Thursday in 1862, eleven-year-old Willie Lincoln drew his last labored breath. His mother, Mary, collapsed, sobbing, until her friend and dressmaker, Elizabeth Keckley, led her away. Mary would be inconsolable with grief for the next three weeks, unable even to attend Willie's funeral.

Keckley returned to the room to assist in washing and dressing the body when Lincoln came in. "My poor boy," he murmured. "He was too good for this earth . . . but then we loved him so. It is hard, hard to have him die." Keckley described the president at that moment:

> Great sobs choked his utterance. He buried his head in his hands, his tall frame was convulsed with emotion. I stood at the foot of the bed, my eyes full of tears, looking at the man in silent, awe-stricken wonder. His grief unnerved him, and made him a weak, passive child. I did not dream that his rugged nature could be so moved.

Lincoln then staggered down the hall to his office where he found one of his private secretaries, John Nicolay, and said in a voice choked with emotion, "Well, Nicolay, my boy is gone—he is actually gone!" At that, the president burst into sobs and left to console Willie's younger brother, Tad.

Tad, who was also suffering a fever, was in his room down the hall. Lincoln lay down beside Tad in his bed, weeping. The eight-year-old was too incredulous to respond until it began to dawn on him that he would no longer be able to play with his brother. Then he, too, began to cry.

FEBRUARY 24

Willie's Funeral

At noon on this Monday in 1862, Lincoln, his wife, Mary, and son Robert came down to the Green Room to visit Willie one last time as he lay in his metal, imitation rosewood coffin. Willie was dressed in a military uniform he liked to play in, his brown hair neatly parted and a bouquet of flowers clasped in his little hands. During the half hour they wept over Willie's body, one of the heaviest wind and rainstorms ever to plague Washington began to knock at the windows. The gales were so strong that roofs were ripped off, trees were knocked down, and chimneys were toppled. In the midst of it, Lincoln took his wife back upstairs to their still-ailing son, Tad, where Mary stayed, so prostrate from grief that she could not attend the funeral services.

The solemn ceremony took place in the East Room—which adjoined the Green Room—and its windows and chandeliers were festooned—like the rest of the White House—in black crepe. Lincoln and Robert sat in front, surrounded by much of official Washington. It was the first funeral for a child held in the White House.

Afterwards the pallbearers and a group of children—Willie's Sunday school class—placed the coffin in a hearse. Lincoln led the procession to Oak Hill Cemetery, hardly noticing the devastation wrought by the storm. Willie was placed in a borrowed crypt, provided by Lincoln's friend William Carroll, a clerk in the Supreme Court. In the days that followed, Lincoln twice returned to the crypt, to lift the coffin lid and see the face of his dead son.

Three years later, after the president was assassinated, Willie's casket would travel with that of his father's back home to Springfield.

FEBRUARY 25

The National Bank

A crisis sometimes creates opportunities that would be nearly impossible in peaceful times. For three decades Lincoln and his Whig party (and later the Republicans) had clamored for a federal bank that issued a national currency. Because of the war, Lincoln finally realized that dream on this day in 1862.

Before the war, Democrats, especially Southern Democrats, were suspicious of a national bank, correctly believing that it catered to Northeastern merchants and ignored Southern planters. When Andrew Jackson dismantled the national bank in 1832, he ushered in thirty years of deregulated banking. During that time, each state chartered banks to issue paper money in "specie," redeemable by gold or silver held in the bank's vaults. With hundreds of different shapes and sizes of money, counterfeiters were rampant. And, without regulations, by 1860 some 8,000 state banks circulated unredeemable "wildcat" notes—so-called because they could be redeemed only by remote banks more accessible to wildcats than humans—or "broken" notes from bankrupt banks.

By the end of 1861, with the Union's war efforts stalled, a financial panic set in and Northerners streamed to their banks to redeem notes. The banks refused. In response, Congress (with Southern Democrats absent) passed the Legal Tender Act, empowering the Treasury to issue paper money that was not backed by gold but by the promise of a Union victory. The money would be inked on one side in green (thus garnering the name "greenbacks"). They became the first national legal tender used for private and public debt.

Lincoln signed the Act on this Tuesday in 1862. One year later to the day, Lincoln signed the National Currency Act (later named the National Banking Act), setting up a federally chartered system of banks.

FEBRUARY 28

McClellan's Mistake

For better than six months, General in Chief George McClellan refused to move his Army of the Potomac south to attack the Confederates in Virginia. The country was furious over this inactivity. To his discredit, McClellan answered not with action but with ineptitude, and on this Friday in 1862 he was called before Lincoln to explain himself.

McClellan had submitted a battle plan to Lincoln in late January. His plan was to hold the Confederate forces at Manassas in check while he sent most of his army down the Chesapeake to the Rappahannock River, eighty miles southeast of Manassas. He could then reach Richmond ahead of the Confederate army, led by General Joseph Johnston and take the lightly defended Confederate capital. But Lincoln was dubious; with McClellan south of Johnston, what would stop the Confederates from marching north to take Washington? The president nevertheless acquiesced.

A month went by and McClellan still hadn't moved. To placate critics with some kind of operation, McClellan was ordered to cross the Potomac, retake Harpers Ferry, Virginia, and reopen the B&O Railroad. But the operation was scrapped at the last minute when it was discovered that the canal boats used to bridge the Potomac were six inches too wide for the Harpers Ferry lift-locks.

On this day McClellan held a conference with Lincoln, explaining why the operation failed. "Why in tarnation . . . couldn't the General have known whether a boat would go through the lock, before he spent a million of dollars getting them there?" Lincoln exploded. "I am no engineer; but it seems to me that if I wished to know whether a boat would go through a . . . lock, common sense would teach me to go and measure it. . . . The general impression is daily gaining ground that the General does not intend to do anything."

That "general impression" would lead to McClellan's removal as general in chief.

MARCH 6

Compensated Emancipation

Early on this morning in 1862, Massachusetts Senator Charles Sumner was invited to the White House to read a proposal Lincoln planned to submit to Congress. Sumner, an avowed abolitionist, had been critical of the president's reticence to emancipate slaves. Sumner was astonished as Lincoln read his proposal. He then took the document and was reluctant to part with it. Afterward, Lincoln became the first U.S. president to submit an emancipation proposal to Congress.

In his message, Lincoln urged Congress to declare that the federal government "ought to co-operate with any state which may adopt gradual abolishment of slavery, giving to such state pecuniary aid . . . to compensate for the inconveniences public and private, produced by such a change of system." In effect, federal money would be available to states that gradually emancipated their slaves, to compensate slave owners for their losses. Lincoln argued that this was constitutional since the states would "initiate" emancipation, not the federal government.

This gradual compensated emancipation was directed at the border slave states still loyal to the Union (Delaware, Maryland, Missouri, and Kentucky). Lincoln reasoned that if these states became free states, there was no longer any threat that they would join the Confederacy. And Lincoln delivered a veiled warning that if they did not accept compensated emancipation, these states may have to swallow emancipation without compensation in the near future.

There was considerable approval for Lincoln's proposal. "This Message constitutes of itself an epoch in the history of our country," said Horace Greeley's *New York Tribune*, often critical of the president. The next day, the *Tribune* added that it was "thankful that we have at such a time so wise a ruler."

Congress did endorse the proposal, but not one border state ever accepted the invitation or the money.

#28

Why Compensated Emancipation Failed

Why did the border states reject Lincoln's gradual compensated emancipation proposal in 1862, while—in some cases grudgingly—accepting immediate *un*compensated emancipation three years later with the Thirteenth Amendment?

The border states' main objection to compensated emancipation was its cost to the government. Lincoln quickly attacked this objection. In a letter to Senator James McDougall on March 14, 1862, Lincoln estimated that it would cost the government $173 million to compensate slave owners for the loss of their slaves (432,622 slaves at $400 a head). Lincoln demonstrated that the cost of prosecuting the war for eighty-seven days was about $174 million. "Do you doubt that . . . [emancipating the slaves] of those states and this District, would shorten the war more than eighty-seven days, and thus be an actual saving of expense?" Lincoln asked.

The more likely reason that they rejected Lincoln's proposal was because it was still only the first year of the war, and the border states believed the war would change nothing, that slavery would remain untouched. "You prefer that the constitutional relations of the states to the nation shall be practically restored, without disturbance of the institution [of slavery]," Lincoln wrote border state representatives. But the war would change everything.

Gradually, the border states began to realize this. West Virginia, the newest border state, approved gradual emancipation on March 26, 1863. Maryland adopted a new state constitution abolishing slavery on October 13, 1864, and Missouri did the same on June 6, 1865. These three border states would be among the first states to ratify the Thirteenth Amendment, which abolished slavery nationwide.

MARCH 9

The CSS Virginia

At 2:00 PM on Saturday, March 8, 1862, an ironclad vessel, described as "a terrapin with a chimney on its back," steamed into Hampton Roads and attacked the blockading Union fleet stationed there. It sank the frigate *Cumberland*, burned the *Congress*, and forced the *Minnesota* to run aground. The vessel was the CSS *Virginia*, formerly the USS *Merrimack*, and in three hours she had made the world's navies—all of them wooden—obsolete. When Lincoln received word of the engagement, he scheduled an emergency cabinet meeting for early this morning.

During the meeting, Secretary of War Edwin Stanton declared that the *Virginia* would sink "every naval vessel" in the Union fleet and could attack any harbor on the eastern seaboard. Lincoln was visibly shaken when he was told that the *Virginia* couldn't even be stopped from entering the Chesapeake Bay, steaming up the Potomac, and shelling Washington. Stanton said it was "not unlikely, we shall have a shell or a cannonball from one of her guns in the White House before we leave this room."

Naval Secretary Gideon Welles doubted the *Virginia* could pass the Potomac's Kettle Bottom Shoals to get to Washington. He also reminded the cabinet that the Union had an ironclad as well—the USS *Monitor*—and it was already en route to Hampton Roads from New York. Indeed, before the meeting broke up, the *Monitor* had engaged the *Virginia*.

The *Monitor*, described as "a tin can on a shingle," fought the *Virginia* for four and a half hours before the Confederate vessel withdrew. The next day Lincoln visited the *Monitor*'s wounded captain—Lieutenant Commander John Worden—and, partly out of relief and partly because he was still emotional over his son Willie's death, Lincoln began to weep uncontrollably.

MARCH 11

Lincoln Demotes McClellan

On this day in 1862, Lincoln had finally had enough of General in Chief George McClellan. For seven months, Lincoln had defended the general's inaction. McClellan had organized the Army of the Potomac, but was petrified to move it. On those rare times when he did move—his attempt to take Harpers Ferry and in the battle of Ball's Bluff—he embarrassed himself. But by March 1862, McClellan was ready to transport the army to Urbana, Virginia and strike at the rear of Joe Johnston's army entrenched at Manassas.

On March 9, however, word reached Washington that Johnston had moved his army to the Rappahannock River. It was a mortal blow to McClellan's plan; if he landed at Urbana, Johnston would be at McClellan's rear instead of the other way around. There was a loud public outcry that McClellan had let the Confederates slip away. "It had been a contest of inertia," one news reporter wrote, "our side outsat the other." Worse, when the abandoned Confederate camps were analyzed, it was discovered that Johnston had only 45,000 men, half of what McClellan maintained Johnston fielded. And some of his entrenchments were protected not by real cannons but "Quaker" guns—logs painted to look like cannons.

On this day, Lincoln demoted McClellan to head only the Army of the Potomac. Lincoln would—for the next few months—act as his own general in chief, directing all theaters of operations. Lincoln said that he was doing McClellan "a very great kindness in permitting him to retain command of the Army of the Potomac, and giving him an opportunity to retrieve his errors."

McClellan wrote the president, "I shall work just as cheerfully as ever before." Privately, however, McClellan was bitter.

MARCH 13

The Peninsula Campaign Begins

Lincoln had never been fond of General George McClellan's plan to ship the Army of the Potomac south, down the Potomac to Urbana, Virginia, and slip behind Joe Johnston's Confederates at

Manassas. With McClellan at Urbana, there would be little to stop Johnston from heading north and taking Washington. Then Johnston foiled McClellan's plan by moving his army south of Urbana. Lincoln wasn't thrilled when McClellan sent the president a new plan, on this Thursday in 1862, to move the army even farther south.

McClellan wanted to ferry 146,000 men to the beaches near Fortress Monroe on the tip of the Virginia Peninsula, then brush aside General John Magruder's Confederates on his way to Richmond in the northwest. This meant McClellan's flanks could be protected by the navy (from positions on the York and James rivers), their big guns used against Confederate entrenchments.

Lincoln didn't exactly approve of the plan, but he made "no objection" as long as McClellan adhered to two conditions: McClellan would leave a force at Manassas to keep Johnston from retaking it and another force would be left to protect Washington. Once these conditions were met, McClellan would be free to "move the remainder of the force down the Potomac, choosing a new base at Fortress Monroe, or anywhere between here and there."

McClellan was already assembling his transports in Alexandria—188 schooners, 113 steamers, and 88 barges. It would be the largest amphibious expedition in the western hemisphere to that time. They would depart in ten-thousand-men echelons for three solid weeks, and on March 17 McClellan saw the first echelon off.

He wired Secretary of War Edwin Stanton: "The worst is over. Rely upon it that I will carry this thing through handsomely." In this, like so many other things, McClellan was wrong.

MARCH 14

Seizing Neutral Ships

Lincoln, on this day in 1862, resolved a naval dispute between the United States and the owners of a Danish merchant ship.

On the day after the first Christmas of the war, the USS *Morning Light*, part of the Gulf Blockading Group (later the West Gulf Blockading Group) sighted the Danish barque (or bark) *Jorgen Lorentzen* in the Gulf of Mexico just a few days out, which originated in from Rio de Janeiro, Brazil and now churned through the Gulf of Mexico. The commander of the *Morning Light*, Lieutenant Henry Moore, believed the barque was trying to run the blockade into New Orleans. He forced the ship to heave-to, then seized it and its cargo as a "prize" of war. While the *Jorgen Lorentzen* was bound for Havana, Cuba— a neutral port—the United States had invoked the maritime policy of "continuous voyage." First implemented during the French Revolution, the doctrine stated that cargo—even if carried by a neutral ship bound for a neutral port—was on a "continuous voyage" if ultimately bound for a blockaded port and could be seized. In this case, it was later determined that neither the barque nor its cargo was bound for the Confederacy and it was released.

When the war began, the Confederacy had virtually no industrial infrastructure to wage a war. Guns, cannon, gunpowder, and clothing all had to be imported. When Lincoln declared a blockade of Confederate ports on April 19, 1861, the prices for imports skyrocketed and lucrative profits tempted many foreign merchants to risk running the Union blockade. What was more, many countries considered the blockade and the policy of "continuous voyage" illegal.

There were several instances during the war when the United States seized the cargo of neutral ships, the most famous of which was the *Trent* affair that nearly sparked a war with Britain. In the case of the *Jorgen Lorentzen*, Lincoln decided to smooth things over and, on this day, he accepted the recommendation of U.S. referees and asked Congress to award $1,850 in damages to the ship's owners for the incident. Congress approved the appropriation on April 25.

APRIL 9

"But You Must Act"

General George McClellan's army had finally reached the tip of the Virginia Peninsula and on Peninsula Campaign began April 4, 1862 as his army moved he began to move north, toward Richmond up the Virginia Peninsula. A day later he discovered two obstacles to his progress. First, Confederate general John Magruder had constructed entrenchments in front of Yorktown that stretched ten miles, across the entire width of the peninsula. Then McClellan was notified that General Irvin McDowell's army would not join him for the offensive, thus cutting McClellan's intended force by a third. As a result, McClellan froze and nothing Lincoln could do—not even a surly letter sent on this Wednesday in 1862—could budge him.

Before McClellan left for Virginia, Lincoln explicitly ordered him to leave a sufficient number of troops behind to protect Washington. It was recommended that at least 40,000 men were needed. McClellan left 26,000, an inadequate force, especially after Confederate general Thomas "Stonewall" Jackson and his army began lurking in the Shenandoah Valley, threatening Washington. When Lincoln found out, he ordered McDowell—bivouacked in northern Virginia—to remain near Washington.

At Yorktown, Magruder, with a mere 13,000 troops, was shifting them from one front line to another, to give the impression that he had a much larger force. The ploy unnerved McClellan and he immediately began preparing for an unnecessary siege. McClellan's 53,000 men could have easily overwhelmed Magruder.

On April 6, Lincoln warned McClellan that his delay in attacking Magruder would just give the Confederates time to reinforce. In fact, Richmond was already sending reinforcements to Magruder, although they wouldn't reach Yorktown until April 10. A frustrated president praised McClellan as an excellent engineer—the general's previous position in the army—but, Lincoln quipped, "he seems to have a special talent for developing a 'stationary' engine." McClellan still didn't move, and Lincoln, on this day, ordered him to "strike a blow." He added, "I have never written you . . . in greater kindness of feeling than now . . . but you must act."

For the next month, McClellan refused to move his army.

APRIL 10

"Place of Peace"

Lincoln, on this Thursday in 1862, issued a proclamation asking Americans to "render thanks to our Heavenly Father" for "signal victories to the land and naval forces." One of these victories was a battle in a place few had heard of—Pittsburg Landing, or Shiloh, Tennessee.

By early April, General Ulysses Grant's army was waiting at Pittsburg Landing—a small depot on the Tennessee River—for General Don Carlos Buell's army to join him from Nashville. The area around the depot was called Shiloh (Hebrew for "Place of Peace"), named after a local church. When Buell arrived, they would march twenty miles south to Corinth, Mississippi, where a Confederate army under Albert Sidney Johnston was massing. Johnston, however, planned to attack Grant before Buell arrived.

Grant decided not to entrench his men in defensive positions. "I do not apprehend anything like an attack on our position," General William Sherman wrote on April 5. Sherman's breakfast was interrupted the next morning when 44,000 Confederates swarmed out of the woods, attaining a complete surprise. During the day's desperate fighting, only the death of Johnston, darkness, and the timely arrival of Buell kept Grant's army from being driven into the river. The next day, Grant and Buell forced the Confederates to retreat.

Total casualties for this one battle exceeded the combined casualties of America's three previous wars—the Revolutionary War, the War of 1812, and the Mexican War. "I saw an open field . . . so covered with dead," said Grant, "that it would have been possible to walk across the clearing, in any direction, stepping on bodies, without a foot touching the ground." The general was criticized for being surprised and there were fallacious rumors that he was drunk during the battle. Lincoln shrugged off the criticism, "I can't spare this man; he fights."

APRIL 16

Slaves Freed in the District of Columbia

As early as 1837 Lincoln had affirmed that Congress had "no power, under the constitution, to interfere with the institution of slavery within the different States." He added, however, that Congress did have "the power, under the constitution, to abolish slavery in the [federal] District of Columbia," as long as it had the consent of its voters. Twenty-five years later, on this day in 1862, Lincoln signed a bill that realized that dream.

As a congressman in 1848, Lincoln was troubled by the presence of 2,000 slaves in the capital of a country espousing freedom. Even more troubling was the slave trade within the district. The warehouse of the nation's largest slave traders—Franklin and Armfield—stood just seven blocks from the Capitol. Lincoln called the warehouse a "sort of Negro livery-stable" where slaves were housed on their way south. In 1849, Lincoln introduced a proposal in Congress calling for a referendum to abolish slavery in the District. Support for the measure quickly dwindled and Lincoln never submitted the proposed bill.

In March 1862, President Lincoln submitted to Congress a proposal to extend compensation to any border slave states that emancipated their slaves. Congress overwhelmingly adopted the resolution but no border state ever took the offer. Disappointed, Lincoln took some consolation when Congress passed a bill to abolish slavery in the district, paying slave owners $300 for every slave. It was to be the only compensated emancipation adopted anywhere in the country.

MAY 5

On the March to Richmond

At dusk on this Monday in 1862, Lincoln, Secretary of War Edwin Stanton, and Secretary of the Treasury Salmon Chase boarded the new Treasury revenue cutter *Miami* to sail to the Virginia Peninsula in hopes of conferring with General George McClellan about his campaign there.

During almost the entire month of April 1862, General George McClellan prepared to lay siege to Yorktown, Virginia and the Warwick Creek entrenchments that stood between his army and Richmond. This despite the fact that his army greatly outnumbered the Confederate defenders. "I think you better break the enemies' line . . . at once," Lincoln urged. "I was much tempted to reply that he had better come and do it himself," McClellan wrote his wife. The general spent the month begging Washington for reinforcements, siege guns, and naval support. The Confederates used the time to reinforce and watch McClellan's unnecessary preparations. "No one but McClellan could have hesitated to attack," wrote Confederate General Joseph Johnston. On May 3 when the Union troops were ready to start the siege, Johnston pulled his troops out, falling back toward Richmond.

"Yorktown is in our possession," McClellan wired Washington as his troops entered the empty entrenchments on May 4. He later telegraphed that he had "thrown all my cavalry and horse artillery in pursuit" of the Confederates. "I shall push the enemy to the wall." Even as Lincoln headed for the peninsula on this day to spur McClellan forward, the general was already on his way to Richmond.

MAY 7

A Trip to Fortress Monroe

After a two-day trip to Fortress Monroe, Virginia, where Lincoln hoped to talk to General George McClellan, Lincoln, on this Wednesday in 1862, toured the famous ironclad the USS *Monitor*, which had fought the Confederate ironclad the *Virginia* (formerly the *Merrimack*) to a draw almost exactly two months before.

After the fall of Yorktown, Virginia (May 4), Lincoln and his Secretary of War Edwin Stanton and Secretary of the Treasury Salmon Chase embarked for Fortress Monroe. During the twenty-seven hour journey to the Virginia Peninsula, Lincoln entertained everyone on board the *Miami* by reciting Shakespeare and "page after page of Browning and whole cantos of Byron," recalled an accompanying general.

He, of course, regaled his listeners with jokes. One was about a teacher who, in order to discipline one of her students, demanded, "Hold out your hand!" When the boy extended a filthy hand, the teacher said, "Now if there were such another dirty thing in the room, I would let you off." The boy brightened. "There it is," he said as he drew his other hand from behind his back.

Lincoln also demonstrated for his audience his extraordinary arm strength. He picked up an ax and "held it at arms length at the extremity of the [handle] with his thumb and forefinger, continuing to hold it there for a number of minutes," recalled a witness. "The most powerful sailors on board tried in vain to imitate him."

The *Miami* anchored off of Fortress Monroe at 10:00 PM on May 6 and, after a 9:00 AM breakfast on this day, Lincoln toured the

Monitor. In the afternoon, Lincoln rode a horse to see the town of Hampton, Virginia, which the Confederates had burned. McClellan, however, would not be able to meet with Lincoln as he was busy chasing the Confederates northward.

MAY 9

A Private Little War

On this Friday in 1862, Lincoln scouted a landing point for Union troops to take Norfolk, Virginia.

By mid-winter of 1862, Lincoln had had more than a belly full of timidity—not only from his general in chief, George McClellan, but from other senior officers. When Lincoln demoted McClellan in March, the president acted as his own general in chief for the next several months. And for a week in May, Lincoln even acted as a general.

When Lincoln arrived at Fortress Monroe on May 6, he was dismayed to find that McClellan had made no plans to take Norfolk after it was exposed in the wake of the Confederate withdrawal from Yorktown. Not only was it strategically important (it had one of the South's few naval yards), it also protected the Confederacy's first ironclad, the *Virginia*. Lincoln ordered an immediate attack but General John Wool, head of Fort Monroe's garrison, was afraid of what the *Virginia* might do to his troop transports. Lincoln and Wool devised a trap using the frigate *Minnesota* as bait while a yacht, packed with explosives, was to ram the *Virginia*. Because of the *Minnesota*'s timidity, the *Virginia* never ventured far enough out of its lair for the yacht to strike.

Disappointed, Lincoln pressed Wool to take Norfolk anyway. Wool selected Willoughby Point to land his troops, giving his 5,000 men some ten miles to march to their objective. Lincoln was sure a closer beachhead could be found, and, on this Friday in 1862, he scouted the Virginia coastline, finding a beach just three miles from Norfolk. Lincoln even risked going ashore. Wool was unimpressed with Lincoln's find, however, and insisted on using Willoughby Point.

The next day (May 10), Wool made his move against Norfolk, while Lincoln wisely stayed behind.

#29

Commander in Chief

Before Lincoln, the role of the president as commander in chief was limited and ambiguous. The Constitution granted Congress—not the president—almost all war powers, such as declaring war and ratifying peace treaties, maintaining navies, and raising and regulating armies. The commander in chief was viewed as little more than an administrator. This was largely due to a fear of monarchical power where kings led their countries into war. "The Provision of the Constitution giving war-making power to Congress, was dictated . . . [because] kings had always been involving and impoverishing their people in wars," Lincoln acknowledged in a 1848 letter. "This, our [Constitutional] Convention understood to be the most oppressive of all Kingly oppressions."

So pervasive was the fear of this "Kingly" power that American presidents rarely led troops in the field as European kings often had. Only two sitting presidents—George Washington during the Whiskey Rebellion of 1794 and James Madison during the British invasion of Washington in 1814—had strapped on their swords and personally led armies. On both occasions the president's leadership was temporary, and limited to the men directly under him.

By the time Lincoln had briefly led military operations in the capture of Norfolk, he had already done things as president that would have made Washington and Madison shudder. He had declared war, raised an army, declared a blockade, enlarged the navy, and suspended habeas corpus—essentially jailing citizens without due process—all without Congressional approval. While Congress afterward approved all of these acts, Lincoln continued to expand his role. He interfered with his generals' military operations and pardoned their court-martialed solders. And in the name of a national emergency, Lincoln did things that no president ever dreamed of doing: emancipating slaves and imposing conscription.

MAY 11

"Norfolk Is Ours"

Early on this Sunday in 1862, Lincoln celebrated the capture of Norfolk, Virginia.

When Lincoln arrived at Fortress Monroe in early May, to consult with General George McClellan, he was surprised to find that McClellan had not captured the shipyards at Norfolk, Virginia. The president prodded General John Wool to take Norfolk and destroy the Confederacy's formidable ironclad *Virginia* harbored there.

On May 10, Wool marched from Willoughby Point to Norfolk, and found the city abandoned by the rebels. He took the city without a fight. Waiting back at Monroe, Lincoln was shocked when two officers, whose troops were supposed to reinforce Wool, walked in. "Why are you not on the other side at Norfolk?" Lincoln asked. "I'm waiting for orders," one retorted. Lincoln snatched his stovepipe hat and flung it down in anger before writing orders dispatching them to Wool.

About midnight on this day, Lincoln had already undressed and was ready for bed when Wool walked into his room unannounced. "No time for ceremony, Mr. President," Wool said, "Norfolk is ours!" Secretary of War Edwin Stanton, who followed Wool into the room and was also in his nightgown, hugged the aged general so exuberantly that he lifted him off the floor.

Five hours later, a plume of smoke testified to the fact that the rebels had scuttled the *Virginia* to keep it out of Union hands. On his way back to Washington, Lincoln's ship took a detour to Norfolk so that the president could spend an hour in the captured city. "So has ended a brilliant week's campaign of the President," wrote Secretary of the Treasury Salmon Chase. "For I think it quite certain that if he had not come down, [Norfolk] would still have been in possession of the enemy and the *Merrimack* as grim and defiant . . . as ever." McClellan wouldn't credit Lincoln for the victory. "Norfolk is in our possession," McClellan wrote his wife, "the result of my movements."

MAY 15

The Department of Agriculture

Lincoln, the son of a farmer, had no love for working the land. His father Thomas had worked the young Abe hard and even hired him out to neighbors. The work bored Lincoln and he would often feed his fertile mind with other pursuits during his breaks in the work, giving the false impression that he was indolent. "Lincoln was a lazy—very lazy man," remembered a distant relative, Dennis Hanks. "He was always reading—scribbling—writing—ciphering—writing poetry." When Lincoln moved out of his father's house, he turned his back on farming forever. "I have no farm, nor ever expect to have;

and, consequently, have not studied the subject enough to be much interested in it," Lincoln wrote his friend Joshua Speed. In a time when most Americans were farmers, politicians often tried to connect themselves to their agrarian constituents. But Lincoln rarely referred to his years working a farm. It's ironic then that Lincoln, as president, not only solicited Congress to create the Department of Agriculture but signed—on this Thursday in 1862—the bill establishing it.

In Lincoln's time, America was still an agrarian society with 58 percent of its population working as farmers. In his December 1861 annual message to Congress, Lincoln wrote, "Agriculture, confessedly the largest interest of the nation, has, not a department, nor a bureau, but a clerkship only, assigned to it in the government." He was referring to the small Agricultural Division which was established in 1839 as a part of the Patent Office, itself—since 1849—a part of the Department of the Interior. "I respectfully ask Congress to consider whether more cannot be given," Lincoln added.

Congress followed Lincoln's suggestion and on this day Lincoln signed the act providing for the Department of Agriculture (USDA). Isaac Newton, the head of the Agriculture Division, became the new department's first commissioner. His staff included a chemist and was quickly supplemented with an entomologist and a statistician. It would not be until 1889 that USDA commissioners would be replaced with secretaries authorized to sit in the president's cabinet.

MAY 16

The General's Pet

In the middle of his drive for Richmond, General George McClellan still found time to bicker with Washington over the reinstatement of one of his generals. On this day in 1862, Lincoln met with that general—Charles Hamilton—to sort out the problem.

On March 8, 1862, Lincoln reorganized McClellan's Army of the Potomac from twelve divisions to four corps, believing that McClellan could better attend to four direct subordinates than twelve. McClellan opposed the move partly, some in Washington said, because McClellan wanted to "pamper" his favorite generals. After the Battle of Williamsburg, McClellan wired Washington on May 9 claiming that his army's reorganization had cost the lives of a thousand soldiers. He asked if he could "relieve from duty . . . commanders of corps or divisions who prove themselves incompetent." He neglected to mention that he had already relieved a division commander—Hamilton—three days before the battle. According to Hamilton, he was sacked for complaining of the "inhuman overworking" of his men while the troops of General Fitz John Porter's division—one of McClellan's pets—sat idly by.

Lincoln allowed McClellan to suspend the corps organization but warned that Hamilton was politically well connected. Indeed, after Lincoln met with Hamilton, Lincoln received a petition signed by twenty-three Senators and eighty-four Congressmen demanding Hamilton's reinstatement. On May 21, Lincoln asked McClellan to return Hamilton to his command. The next day McClellan wired back, "You cannot do anything better calculated to injure my army . . . than to restore Gen[eral] Hamilton to his Division." McClellan then boldly stated to his commander in chief, "I trust that after that statement you will not think of sending General Hamilton back to this Army." Hamilton was sent to the western theater and Porter was given command of a corps.

#30

McClellan's Ego

George McClellan knew very few disappointments in his life. Born to a prominent Philadelphia physician, he was so brilliant that by fifteen he had already completed two years of college and West Point waived the age requirement to allow the young prodigy to attend. He distinguished himself as an engineer during the Mexican War and, when he left the army, became president of the Ohio and Mississippi Railroad.

It was for all these reasons that, when McClellan was called to protect Washington after the fiasco of Bull Run in July 1861, he was greeted with such hope. All that adulation, however, fed an already gargantuan ego. When the public deference faded, he compensated by belittling his superiors. McClellan called Lincoln "nothing more than a well meaning baboon." He was particularly critical of General in Chief Winfield Scott. "I do not know whether he is a dotard or a traitor," he wrote his wife. "If he cannot be taken out of my path, I . . . will resign and let the admin[istration] take care of itself. . . . The people call upon me to save the country—I must save it and cannot respect anything that is in the way."

But Scott had something that McClellan didn't; he had failed enough that he was not afraid of failure. McClellan was so paralyzed by his fear of it that his inaction had to be covered by excuses, usually by blaming others. There were always too many Confederates to fight and too little support from Lincoln. He once wrote, "The enemy have from 3 to 4 times my force [McClellan actually outnumbered the Confederates two to one at the time]—the Presdt. is an idiot, the old General [Scott] is in his dotage—they cannot or will not see the true state of affairs."

MAY 17

Reinforcements

As General George McClellan's army moved up the Virginia Peninsula toward Richmond, he clamored for additional men. On May 14, he wired Lincoln claiming that the Richmond defenses had "perhaps double my number" in men (in actuality it was McClellan who had nearly double the Confederate's strength) and begging for reinforcements. "If he [McClellan] had a million men he would swear the enemy had two million," complained Secretary of War Edwin Stanton. "And he would sit down in the mud and yell for three [million]." Lincoln, too, was exasperated, "He's been hollering for help ever since he went south [to the peninsula]—wants somebody to come to his deliverance and get him out of the place he's got himself into." Nevertheless, Lincoln, on this Saturday in 1862, made arrangements to reinforce McClellan.

Lincoln ordered General Irvin McDowell—located near the Shenandoah Valley—to march part of his army south to attack Richmond from the north while McClellan attacked from the southeast. Lincoln's order—perhaps the most confusing he ever wrote—revealed his lack of experience, "You will retain the separated command of the forces taken with you; but while co-operating with Gen[eral] McClellan you will obey, his orders, except that you are to Judge."

McDowell's movements were just what Robert E. Lee—then the head of the Confederate forces—had been waiting for. Lee sent General Thomas "Stonewall" Jackson's army to threaten Washington and stop McDowell from linking with McClellan. Lincoln inadvertently helped Jackson with his mission; he transferred a cavalry unit—Blenker's Division, which was guarding the mouth of the Shenandoah—to western Virginia, leaving the Valley exposed. It was a profound strategic error.

MAY 19

Hunter's Emancipation

After Union forces captured stretches of Georgia's, Florida's, and South Carolina's coasts, a military command was created—called the Department of the South—encompassing those three Southern states. Lincoln's good friend General David Hunter headed the department from Hilton Head, South Carolina. On this day in 1862, Lincoln had to revoke an order his friend issued.

Hunter—an abolitionist—issued on May 9 his General Order No. 11 stating that since the three states under his command had "declared themselves no longer under the protection of the United States . . . and having taken up arms against" the Union, martial law was in effect. "Slavery and martial law in a free country are altogether incompatible," Hunter wrote. "Persons in these three States . . . held as slaves, are therefore declared forever free." The order was reminiscent of General John Fremont's August 30, 1861 edict declaring martial law in Missouri and freeing its slaves. Hunter was familiar with Fremont's edict; after Lincoln modified Fremont's order, he had sent Hunter to relieve Fremont as head of the Department of the West.

As for Hunter's order, Salmon Chase, secretary of the treasury and himself an abolitionist, exalted it. "It will be cordially approved, I am sure, by more than nine tenths of the people on whom you must rely for support of your Administration," Chase wrote Lincoln. The president bluntly replied, "No commanding general shall do such a thing upon my responsibility." Lincoln declared Hunter's order "void." But in his proclamation, Lincoln, for the first time, acknowledged that he, as commander in chief, might have the right to "declare Slaves of any state or states free" if it became "indispensable to the maintenance of the government." The decision as to when it would become "indispensable" he reserved for himself.

#31

WHY LINCOLN HAD TO BE THE EMANCIPATOR

Just over a month after Lincoln revoked General David Hunter's emancipation proclamation, Lincoln was reportedly working on a rough draft of his own proclamation. Since emancipating the slaves was a war measure (depriving the Confederates of slave labor), why couldn't Hunter—a military department head—be the one to issue the emancipation proclamation?

The reason, in part, was because neither the nation nor Lincoln was ready for emancipation. Lincoln said as much in an April 4, 1864 letter to reporter Albert Hodges,

> When, early in the war, Gen. Fremont attempted military emancipation, I forbade it, because I did not then think it an indispensable necessity. . . . When, still later, Gen. Hunter attempted military emancipation, I again forbade it, because I did not yet think the indispensable necessity had come. When, in March, and May, and July 1862 I made earnest, successive appeals to the border states to favor compensated emancipation, . . . they declined the proposition; and I was, in my best judgment, driven to the alternative of either surrendering the Union . . . or laying a strong hand upon the colored element.

Lincoln also did not consider emancipation wholly a military issue. After General John Fremont's emancipation (in August 1861) Lincoln told his friend Orville Browning, "Fremont's proclamation, as to . . . the liberation of slaves, is purely political and not within the range of military law." He reiterated this during Hunter's debacle when he said, "No commanding general shall do such a thing upon my responsibility." Lincoln's claim was supported by what happened after he issued his own Emancipation Proclamation. There was some military backlash (some soldiers, disgruntled about fighting for emancipation, either deserted or refused to reenlist), but there was considerably more political backlash. Emancipation nearly cost Lincoln his reelection in 1864.

MAY 20

The Homestead Act

Shorn of Southern congressmen, the Thirty-seventh Congress began to enact the Republican political platform, involving some of the most important legislation of Lincoln's administration. Congress created the Department of Agriculture; enacted the Morrill Act (public land for land-grant colleges) and the Pacific Railroad Act (construction of a Transcontinental Railroad); established the Internal Revenue Bureau (levying the first federal income tax); and passed the Legal Tender Bill (creating paper money). On this Tuesday in 1862, Lincoln signed what is arguably among the most important legislation in American history: the Homestead Act.

In America's early days, the sale of federal lands was a revenue generator and not used to settle land. To buy public property, individuals were required to purchase a minimum of one square mile (640 acres) at a dollar per acre. Few could afford such an investment, even when the minimum was halved in 1800. Sales were stagnant, and by the mid-1800s Congress was pushing for legislation allowing land parcels to be sold more cheaply. Northern industrialists opposed it, afraid their cheap labor base would be drained. Southern planters opposed it, afraid to compete with small-yield farmers. In 1860 Congress finally passed a Homestead Act, but the Southern-leaning

President James Buchanan vetoed it. Many voters in the west voted for Lincoln because his platform promised such an act.

The Act that Lincoln signed on this day allowed people to purchase a quarter of a square mile (160 acres) of land for an $18 filing fee and five years of work to improve the lot. The Act remained in effect for 113 years (1863–1976) with 270 million acres—10 percent of all U.S. acreage—sold to individuals. The first plot sold was near Beatrice, Nebraska, in 1863 and the last sold was on Stony River, Alaska in the mid-1980s.

MAY 23

A Day at Fredericksburg

After Lincoln ordered General Irvin McDowell to cooperate with General George McClellan in attacking Richmond, Lincoln decided to visit McDowell at Fredericksburg, Virginia before he left, arriving there on this Friday in 1862.

As Lincoln relaxed aboard the steamboat that transported them south, he entertained the party by reading poetry from the American poet Fitz-Greene Halleck. Halleck, hailed as the "American Byron," was famous for his poetic social commentaries, but it was Halleck's "Marco Bozzaris"—an overly romanticized poem on how heroes are immortalized—that Lincoln preferred. Lincoln, who had long dreamed of doing something that would be remembered, was drawn to the poem's imagery.

McDowell greeted the president at Aquia Creek on this day and Lincoln rode back to McDowell's Fredericksburg camp in what was described as "a common baggage car, with camp-stools" to sit on. Once at camp, McDowell eagerly showed Lincoln how they had rebuilt bridges around the area, and he took him to a nearby trestle that spanned a hundred-foot ravine. When Lincoln asked to cross the trestle, which had a single plank to walk on, McDowell followed the president, with Secretary of War Edwin Stanton and Captain John Dahlgren taking up the rear. "About half-way the Secretary [Stanton] said he was dizzy and feared he would fall," wrote Dahlgren. "So he stopped, unable to proceed. I managed to step by him, and took his hand, thus leading him over, when in fact my own head was somewhat confused by the giddy height." Lincoln spent the rest of the day reviewing troops. He left for Aquia Creek and the voyage home late that night.

On this same day Thomas "Stonewall" Jackson attacked Front Royal, Virginia, kicking off the most relevant portion of his Shenandoah Campaign. Within days, McDowell's march to Richmond was canceled.

MAY 25

McDowell Is Recalled

Lincoln had been without a general in chief since he relieved General George McClellan in late March 1862. Lincoln would spend much of this Saturday in 1862 acting as his own general in chief, directing armies in an effort to stop Confederate general Thomas "Stonewall" Jackson and his forces in the Shenandoah Valley.

Lincoln had ordered General Irvin McDowell's forces at Fredericksburg, Virginia to head for Richmond in order to help McClellan take the Confederate capital. Lincoln had just returned from visiting McDowell when news reached him that Jackson had attacked and routed General Nathaniel Banks's army at Front Royal on May 23. Banks had barely retreated to Winchester before Jackson again attacked him—on this day—and pushed him out of Winchester. On the road outside Winchester, Banks called to a group of retreating soldiers, "Stop, men! Don't you love your country?" "Yes, by God," one replied, "and I'm trying to get back to it just as fast as I can."

Back in Washington, Lincoln began furiously sending telegrams. On consecutive days—May 24 and 25—Lincoln sent a spatches to his generals. He wired McClellan, "I have been ed to suspend Gen. McDowell's movement to join you. The are making a push upon Harpers Ferry, and we are trying w [General John] Fremont's force & part of McDowell's in ar." Lincoln was also concerned about Washington's safety. wired McClellan again: "Stripped bare, as we are here, it l that we can do to prevent [Jackson] crossing the Potomac ers Ferry . . . If McDowell's force was now beyond our ve should be utterly helpless." Still later, Lincoln believed h Jackson in the Shenandoah, Richmond's defenses were well, "I think the time is near when you must either mond or give up the job and come to the defence of "

of General McDowell was exactly what Jackson and Robert E. Lee, had hoped Lincoln would do.

MAY 26

incoln Protects Cameron's Reputation

the ten months that Simon Cameron had been Secretary of ar, he had politically and publicly humiliated Lincoln and his administration. But instead of firing Cameron in January 1862, Lincoln chose to name him minister to Russia. Lincoln even took a step further on this day in 1862 by taking part of the blame for Cameron's transgressions.

Lincoln had been reluctant to name Cameron to his cabinet after he heard of Senator Cameron's reputation for avarice. Lincoln would regret bending to pressure by naming Cameron to head the War Department just as the country was on the brink of war. By July 1861—just three months into the war—the accusations of corruption and inefficiency were so great that Congress appointed a committee to investigate Cameron and the War Department. In February 1862, the House Committee on Contracts published a report detailing extensive corruption in the War Department. Although C was not charged personally, the House censured him, claimi he had "adopted a policy highly injurious to public service."

On this day Lincoln responded with an extensive explana what happened after Sumter. Washington had been cut off f rest of the country, Congress was adjourned, and he needed a growing army (from March to early 1862 it swelled from 700,000). Snap decisions and unusual avenues of purchasing were used, all endorsed by Lincoln. "Not only the Presiden the other heads of departments were at least equally respons him for whatever error, wrong, or fault was committed," From the Russian capital of St. Petersburg, Cameron thar for the endorsement. Filled with gratitude, Cameron, Lincoln's secretaries, became "one of most intimate a Lincoln's personal friends."

#32

Lincoln's Magnanimity

One trait of Lincoln's that people would remember long after he was gone was his magnanimity—his willingness to forgive the most difficult people and their deeds. This stemmed from Lincoln's mature and stable self-confidence and a belief that his own ego came second to political and even military objectives. As Lincoln's friend Leonard Swett wrote, "He was certainly a very poor hater. He never judged men by his like, or dislike for them. If any given act was to be performed, he could understand that his enemy could do just as well as any one. If a man maligned him, or been guilty of personal ill-treatment and abuse, and was the fittest man for the place, he would put him in his Cabinet just as soon as he would his friend."

Lincoln's first secretary of war—Simon Cameron—embarrassed Lincoln and yet the president gave him a plum position as minister to Russia. Lincoln's secretary of the treasury—Salmon Chase—spent three years undermining Lincoln's policies and even attempted to wrest the 1864 Republican nomination for president from him. But after Chase resigned, Lincoln named him Chief Justice of the Supreme Court, a position Chase coveted almost as much as that of the presidency.

Then there was Edwin Stanton. In June 1855, Lincoln had been hired to aid the defense in a patent infringement case—*McCormick vs. Manny*—because he was familiar with the Chicago judge. When the case was moved to Cincinnati, an Ohio lawyer—Stanton—was hired instead. Lincoln, however, was not informed of the change and when he appeared in Cincinnati, Stanton snubbed Lincoln. "Where did that long-armed creature come from and what can he expect to do in this case?" Lincoln overheard Stanton say. Lincoln was so hurt by the snub that he vowed never to return to Cincinnati. Yet six years later Lincoln named Stanton as Cameron's replacement as secretary of war. Stanton, Cameron, and Chase subsequently became among Lincoln's closest political and personal allies.

MAY 28

Three Generals

This Wednesday in 1862 did not start well for Lincoln. He received word that General John Fremont had not marched to Harrisonburg, Virginia at the southern end of the Shenandoah Valley, as Lincoln had ordered. Instead, Fremont had gone forty miles north to Moorefield. This allowed Confederate general Thomas "Stonewall" Jackson's army to slip down the valley with no Union army to the south to cut him off. Fremont, in his telegram, claimed it took him eight days to cover seventy miles because his men were hungry and tired (while Jackson's tired and hungry men marched fifty miles in two days) and felt compelled to disobey Lincoln's orders. "If . . . literal obedience to orders is required please say so," Fremont wrote Lincoln.

Unhappy, Lincoln wired General Irvin McDowell, who was marching to the valley as well. "It is, for you a question of legs," Lincoln prodded. "I beg to assure you that I am doing everything which legs and steam [trains] are capable of to hurry forward," McDowell responded.

Late in the afternoon Lincoln received news that General George McClellan had failed to cut the rail line between the Shenandoah and Richmond, giving Jackson an avenue of escape. McClellan, as usual, was focused only on his own interests. McClellan wired, "It is the policy and duty of the Government to send me by water all the well-trained troops available. I am confident that Washington is no longer in danger [from Jackson]. . . . The real issue is the battle about to be fought in front of Richmond."

"That the whole force of the enemy is concentrating in Richmond, I think can not be certainly known to you or me," Lincoln responded, adding, "I must be the judge as to the duty of the Government." Then he thought the final line too harsh and crossed it out.

JUNE 1

"Hold All Your Ground"

By the end of May 1862, General George McClellan's Army of the Potomac had advanced to within four miles of Richmond, so close that its church bells could be heard. Arrayed east and southeast of the city, McClellan made the mistake of positioning his army astride the Chickahominy River with three corps north of it and two corps—General Samuel Heintzelman's Third Corps and General Erasmus Keyes's Fourth Corps—south of it numbering just 31,000 men. With rains swelling the Chickahominy and muddying roads, neither wing of the army could easily support the other. It was an opportunity Confederate general Joseph Johnston—head of the Richmond defenses—couldn't resist. On May 31, Johnston attacked the Third and Fourth Corps with his 75,000 men. As news reached Washington of the Confederate offensive, Lincoln, on this Sunday in 1862, sent McClellan both encouragement and reinforcements.

"Stand well on your guard," Lincoln wired. "Hold all your ground, or yield any only, inch by inch." Lincoln ordered the troops at Fortress Monroe, commanded by General John Dix, to reinforce McClellan. Lincoln also sent one of General Irvin McDowell's divisions near Manassas to Richmond.

Had Johnston's May 31 attack not been piecemeal, he might have won the Battle of Fair Oaks (Seven Pines). McClellan, however, stood his ground and, on June 1, he pushed the Confederates back into their Richmond entrenchments. The most noteworthy effect of the battle was that Johnston was wounded and he was replaced by the soon-to-be-legendary Robert E. Lee, who would take over as head of the army later designated the Army of Northern Virginia.

JUNE 7

"Quiet is Very Necessary to Us"

It had been a lengthy tradition to hold weekly Marine Band concerts on the White House lawn during the summer, attended by Washington's social and political elite. On this Saturday in 1862, Lincoln publicly announced that the concerts would be suspended because the first family was still mourning their son Willie's death the previous February.

For three weeks after Willie's passing, Mary took to her bed, unable to attend her son's funeral or care for her other son, Tad. She herself had to be cared for by a nurse. For a year she wore nothing but a mourning dress weighted with layers and layers of ebony veils and crepes. Willie's toys were either sold or stored out of sight and Mary never again entered the Prince of Wales Room, where Willie succumbed, nor the Green Room, where he was embalmed.

The annual spring receptions had already been canceled when Lincoln's secretary John Hay sent a note to the first lady, asking if the summer Marine Band concerts might be held. "We are in sorrow, quiet is very necessary to us," she responded. "It is our especial desire that the Band, does not play in these grounds, this summer." She added testily, "We expect our wishes to be complied with." Hay then sent another note asking if the concerts could be performed in Lafayette Park across the street. "It is hard that in this time of our sorrow we should be harassed," she wrote back. Lincoln cancelled the concerts.

That summer when journalist Laura Redden visited the White House, Redden recalled that she had barely shaken Mary's hand when she "burst into a passion of tears" and, when Redden tried to console her, Mary "could neither think nor talk of anything but Willie."

JUNE 14

A Twenty-dollar Fine

Lincoln, on this Saturday in 1862, found himself briefly pushing aside weighty matters of state to address a simple $20 fine charged against a Washington restaurateur.

own force amounts to." By the end of the month, both Fremont and Shields were relieved of their commands.

#33

The Shenandoah or Richmond?

Historians have long debated whether Lincoln made a mistake in sending General Irvin McDowell's army after Confederate general Thomas "Stonewall" Jackson in the Shenandoah Valley rather than to Richmond to reinforce General George McClellan. The pivotal question, however, is, where was McDowell needed most?

Lincoln claimed to have two reasons to send McDowell to the Shenandoah: to protect Washington from Jackson and to capture or destroy Jackson's army. The former could not have been of much concern. Forces in and around Washington greatly outnumbered Jackson and stood behind a ring of forty-six forts (eventually there would be sixty-eight forts). What Lincoln really wanted most was to catch Jackson in a pincer formed by Fremont and McDowell. Because the Confederacy was starved for men, the capture of 17,000 soldiers—especially if one of those soldiers was the legendary Jackson—would be a worthy prize.

Richmond, too, would have been worthy if McDowell could have aided McClellan in capturing it. But McDowell would travel through hostile Virginia territory to reach Richmond and Confederate general Joe Johnston would have ample warning and time to attack McClellan at Seven Pines before McDowell arrived. Therefore, the results of the Seven Pines battle would have been the same, the casualties of the battle would unnerve McClellan into inactivity, and both McClellan and McDowell would face Johnston's replacement—the formidable Robert E. Lee.

Through experience, Lincoln certainly suspected that McClellan would be slow to attack Richmond. He probably hoped McDowell could bag Jackson with sufficient time to march to Richmond and capture it, too. Even though the plan failed (through no fault of Lincoln's), it was a solid plan.

JUNE 19

The Extension of Slavery

On the face of it, the law Lincoln signed on this Thursday in 1862 seemed insignificant, but it actually was the culmination of his political efforts since 1854, an act emancipating slaves throughout the western territories.

Almost from the beginning of the Republic the issue of carrying slaves into newly acquired territories ignited sectional controversies. In 1787 it was over the Northwest Territories; in 1820, over lands acquired by the Louisiana Purchase; in 1850, over lands acquired from the Mexican War; and in 1854, it was over the impending statehood of each Kansas and Nebraska.

While Lincoln hated slavery and looked forward to its extinction, he was not an abolitionist advocating immediate nationwide prohibition. In 1854, when the Kansas–Nebraska issue pulled him out of semi-retirement from politics, Lincoln answered critics who called him an abolitionist by saying, "I now do no more than oppose the extension of slavery [into the territories]." Six years later he elaborated in his famous Cooper Union address: "This is all Republicans ask—all Republicans desire—in relation to slavery. . . . [It is] an evil not to be extended, but to be tolerated and protected only because of and so far as its actual presence among us makes that toleration and protection a necessity." Lincoln believed that as long as slavery was contained to the South, it would slowly, inevitably die. If allowed to be extended, its demise could be delayed indefinitely.

When Lincoln signed the document on this day emancipating territorial slaves, there were, according to the 1860 census, less than 50 slaves in all of the Colorado, Dakota, Nevada, New Mexico, Utah, and Washington territories. As insignificant as this seems, it must have given Lincoln satisfaction to sign it.

JUNE 20

"Public Opinion Baths"

Despite a busy schedule, Lincoln rarely turned away White House visitors, calling such meetings his "public opinion baths," giving him a feel for what Americans thought and helping him hone his arguments to persuade them. A likely example of this happened on this day in 1862, when a Quaker delegation—the "Religious Society of Progressive Friends"—met with him.

In early June, the Society drafted a memorial stating that the cause of the war was slavery and therefore "the nation . . . should lose no time in proclaiming immediate and universal emancipation; so that the present frightful effusion of blood may cease." As the *New York Tribune* reported, when the delegation presented the memorial on this Friday in 1862, Lincoln "agreed that Slavery was wrong, but in regard to the ways and means of its removal, his views probably differed from theirs." Since Lincoln was already considering an emancipation proclamation, his next comment was interesting. Referring to the abolitionist John Brown, who led an 1859 slave insurrection at Harpers Ferry, Virginia, Lincoln said, "If a decree of emancipation could abolish Slavery, John Brown would have done the work effectually. Such a decree surely could not be more binding upon the South than the Constitution, and that cannot be enforced in that part of the country now. Would a proclamation of freedom be any more effective?" One delegate cunningly responded that ineffectual enforcement of the Constitution in the South had not stopped Lincoln from trying to do so by force of arms.

Lincoln's question was probably directed as much to the press as to the delegation, gauging how the public would react to an emancipation "decree" with its limitations in enforcement. Lincoln would continue to test public opinion, even as he wrote and finally issued the Emancipation Proclamation.

#34

His Changing Mind

One of the more challenging debates surrounding Lincoln is just when he changed from believing he, as president, could not constitutionally prohibit slavery to believing he could. From the beginning of his tenure, Lincoln felt pressure to emancipate the slaves. Lincoln remained adamantly opposed to it, afraid emancipation would drive critical border slave states into the Confederacy's welcoming arms.

Then in early May 1862, when he revoked General David Hunter's emancipation of slaves within his department, Lincoln hinted for the first time that he might emancipate slaves if it were a "necessity." Almost a month later (June 18), Vice President Hannibal Hamlin met with the president and Lincoln supposedly showed Hamlin an early draft of his emancipation proclamation. Many historians believe this story is a myth. Nevertheless, according to a telegraph operator named Major Thomas Eckert, in late June Lincoln began working in his cipher room. The president felt he could work "more quietly and command his thoughts better than at the White House where he was frequently interrupted." Sitting at Eckert's desk, where a window faced Pennsylvania Avenue, "he would look out the window a while and then put pen to paper," Eckert said, "but he did not write much at once. He would study between times and when he had made up his mind he would put down a line or two." After a few weeks, Lincoln told Eckert that he was writing a proclamation "giving freedom to slaves in the South."

Lincoln almost never made abrupt decisions, so it is doubtful that historians can point to one day or one event that changed Lincoln's mind. But it's probable that by mid-May he had reached a tentative conclusion and by late June he had decided to act on it.

JUNE 23

Advice From an Old War Horse

With General George McClellan still sitting on the outskirts of Richmond (he'd been there since late May) shrilly calling for reinforcements, and with Confederate general Thomas "Stonewall" Jackson's forces just south of the Shenandoah, Lincoln met, on this Monday in 1862, with retired General Winfield Scott for military advice.

Scott had been Lincoln's general in chief at the beginning of the war and was still among the best military minds in the North. When Lincoln boarded a special train bound for New York City at four in the afternoon on this day, he had two questions to pose to Scott: Was Washington safe from Jackson? And should Lincoln support McClellan's drive for Richmond? Eleven hours later, Lincoln checked into the Cozzens' Hotel at West Point. At 7:30, Lincoln breakfasted with Scott and General John Pope.

Scott was convinced the Shenandoah Union forces—although they had been soundly beaten by the Confederates—were still strong enough to keep Jackson in check. As for Richmond, Scott's written response was, "the defeat of the rebels at Richmond or their forced retreat thence, combined with our previous victories, would be a virtual end of the rebellion." Scott recommended that General Irvin McDowell—commander of one of the forces in the Shenandoah—be sent to reinforce McClellan.

Lincoln disagreed and headed home on June 25, disappointed. It was clear to the president that as long as the Confederacy fielded armies, the Richmond government could always be moved elsewhere. Nor did Lincoln believe McClellan would ever take Richmond with or without reinforcements. As soon as Lincoln returned to Washington, he began to consolidate all the forces in the Shenandoah—including McDowell's—into the new Army of Virginia, naming Pope its commander.

JUNE 25

"I Owe No Thanks to You"

Lincoln, on this Wednesday in 1862, received the first of two telegrams from General George McClellan accusing Lincoln's administration of not supporting his army.

After McClellan's army sat idle for three weeks just four miles outside Richmond, Confederate general Robert E. Lee correctly surmised that while he was outnumbered by McClellan, Lee could unnerve his opponent enough to force him to retreat. On this day, Lee struck McClellan's right flank in the first of several battles in the coming week, to be known as the Seven Days Campaign. That evening, McClellan warned Washington that he was facing "vastly superior odds"—he estimated the Confederate strength at 200,000 while in reality it was 90,000—and if he were not reinforced and a "disaster" occurred, "the responsibility cannot be thrown on my shoulders." Lincoln wired back that McClellan's message "pains me very much. I give you all I can . . . while you continue . . . to assume that I could give you more if I could."

The next day, Lincoln combined all available troops in the Shenandoah and around Washington into the new Army of Virginia with General John Pope to head it. But it was too late for Pope to help McClellan. Lee attacked McClellan again on June 26 (at Mechanicsville) and 27 (at Gaines' Mill). As McClellan began his retreat, he wired Stanton, "I have lost this battle because my force is too small." He added, "The Gov[ernment] has not sustained this Army. If I save this Army now, I tell you plainly that I owe no thanks to you or to any other person in Washington—you have done your best to sacrifice this army." The supervisor of the Washington telegraph office, appalled at McClellan's insubordinate tone, deleted the last two sentences before sending it to Lincoln.

JULY 2

The Peninsula Campaign Ends

After a week of constant fighting, General George McClellan's confidence had been shattered. Nowhere was this more evident than in his continual pleading for troops that were not available, as pointed out on this Wednesday in 1862 by Lincoln.

For seven consecutive days (June 25 to July 1), McClellan's Army of the Potomac had fought seven straight battles (Oak Grove; Mechanicsville; Gaines' Mill; Garrett's Farm; Savage's Station; White Oak Swamp; and Malvern Hill). After his prickly telegram of June 28 to Washington ("If I save this Army now . . . I owe no thanks to you"), McClellan withdrew his army westward toward the James River. His corps commanders performed superbly, completing the most difficult tactical maneuver an army can make—a fighting withdrawal.

Despite this, McClellan still could have taken the offensive, particularly after Malvern Hill where Confederate general Robert E. Lee foolishly made a frontal attack in the face of McClellan's 250 cannons. Lee's army was badly mauled and some historians believe that had McClellan moved north, he might well have captured Richmond and Lee's army.

Instead McClellan called for "50,000 more men" to "retrieve our fortunes." Lincoln exploded when he read McClellan's telegram and, on this day, wired back, "I have not, outside your Army, seventy-five thousand men East of the [Allegheny] mountains. Thus the idea of sending you fifty thousand . . . is simply absurd." Nevertheless, Lincoln did send reinforcements and called for 300,000 more enlistments. All of this left McClellan literally unmoved as his army sat idle for over a month before evacuating the Virginia Peninsula. It would take two years and hundreds of thousands of lives to get as close to Richmond again.

JULY 9

The "Harrison Bar Letter"

On this Wednesday in 1862 (the second day of Lincoln's visit to the Army of the Potomac bivouacked on the James River) the president ignored—much to General George McClellan's consternation—the general's political advice.

In the aftermath of McClellan's failed Peninsula Campaign, Lincoln was depressed. Lincoln was neither eating nor sleeping and decided that a visit with his soldiers might not only lift their morale, but his as well. Lincoln arrived at Harrison's Landing (or Harrison Bar) the evening of July 8 and, as soon as McClellan stepped aboard Lincoln's ship, the general handed the president a letter that was a virtual tirade against Lincoln's policies. In particular, McClellan insisted that the "forcible abolition of slavery should [not] be contemplated." Although most of McClellan's suggestions involved the political rather than the military realm, McClellan believed Lincoln needed to be shepherded by a new general in chief (McClellan made a Freudian slip here, calling for a new "Commander-in-Chief," which was Lincoln's title) and McClellan clearly believed that should be him. Lincoln finished the letter, removed his glasses, and said nothing.

Lincoln reviewed the troops for three hours that evening, receiving—according to the press—boisterous acclamation from the soldiers. McClellan claimed that he "had to order the men to cheer and they did it very feebly." On this day, Lincoln toured the camps with McClellan but refused to even mention the letter. Returning to Washington invigorated, Lincoln showed just what he thought of the letter; in less than two weeks he would reveal his preliminary Emancipation Proclamation and name Henry Halleck—not McClellan—as the new general in chief.

JULY 12

Medal of Honor

Special awards to soldiers and sailors for service had long been shunned in America, associating such medals with European aristocrats. Even when George Washington created the Purple Heart in August 1782, few were actually awarded it. Before the Civil War, then General in Chief Winfield Scott blocked attempts by Congress to introduce a special award. After Scott retired, Iowa Senator James Grimes introduced a bill that distributed "medals of honor" to enlisted naval and marine personnel. The Medal of Honor, the most prestigious American military award, was born on December 21, 1861 with Lincoln's signature. On this Saturday in 1862, Lincoln signed a second bill that did the same for army enlisted men. On March 3, 1863, Congress extended the award to army officers (naval officers would wait until World War I).

On March 25, 1863, six ex-prisoners of war were the first to receive the Medal of Honor. They were survivors of the ill-fated "Andrews' Raiders" who, eleven months before, perpetrated the "Great Locomotive Chase." Union spy James Andrews led a handful of Union soldiers south to hijack an engine—the General—intending to tear up tracks and burn bridges for the 100 miles between Big Shanty, Georgia, and Chattanooga, Tennessee. They were, however, chased down, captured, and many of them executed.

More than 1,500 Medals of Honor were awarded during the Civil War, considerably more than any other war. Twenty-three black soldiers were recipients. The first black recipient was Sergeant William Carney of the Fifty-fourth Massachusetts for valor during his regiment's famous assault on Fort Wagner, Charleston. The most contentious Medal of Honor was the only one awarded to a woman, Dr. Mary Edwards Walker. Walker, a field surgeon for three years, during which she was a prisoner of war, was given the award in 1866. In 1917, her medal was rescinded—officially because she was a civilian, but allegedly because she was a suffragette. In 1977, President Jimmy Carter reinstated her medal.

JULY 17

Congress and Slavery

Lincoln surprised nearly everyone on this day in 1862 when he approved a bill titled "An Act to suppress insurrection, to punish treason and rebellion, to seize and confiscate the property of rebels and for other purposes," later to be known as the Second Confiscation Act.

In the final days of the congressional session, Radical Republicans passed a measure that defined Confederates as traitors and allowed their slaves to be emancipated. An earlier Confiscation Act (passed in August 1861) freed slaves only if they were directly employed in aiding the rebel army. This second act made no such distinction.

The bill provided no means to legally determine if a slave belonged to a rebellious owner and it was virtually unenforceable. Nor did Lincoln think the bill was constitutional. "Congress has no power over slavery in the states . . . [and slavery] must be left to the exclusive control of the states where it may exist," Lincoln told his friend Orville Browning.

Lincoln planned to veto the bill and asked Congress to remain in session long enough to give him time to write a message to accompany his veto. "It is startling to say that Congress can free a slave within a state," Lincoln's message read. Maine Senator William Fessenden worked with Lincoln to soften the bill's stringent provisions and, after Congress provided a joint resolution that made the bill more constitutionally palatable, Lincoln signed the bill but took the unusual step of submitting his veto message anyway. He thus went on record as having misgivings for the bill.

Privately, Lincoln decided that he needed to head off any further congressional attempts at emancipation which would extend freedom to slaves only to have the courts cruelly strip it away on constitutional grounds. He felt that to pass constitutional muster, the federal government must emancipate slaves as a war power exercised by the president as commander in chief. Less than a week later, Lincoln revealed his preliminary Emancipation Proclamation.

JULY 22

The Preliminary Emancipation

This day in 1862 was an important day in American history as Lincoln officially revealed for the first time his intention to issue an Emancipation Proclamation.

With his generals (John Fremont in August 1861 and David Hunter in May 1862) and Congress (via the Second Confiscation Act in July 1862) attempting to free slaves, Lincoln was faced with the need to make a decision about emancipation. Lincoln felt that for emancipation to pass constitutional muster, it must be a war measure from the commander in chief's pen. On July 13, Lincoln, while riding in a carriage with Secretary of State William Seward and Secretary of the Navy Gideon Welles to a funeral, said that "he had about come to the conclusion that we must free the slaves or be ourselves subdued." As shocked as Seward and Welles were, they were unprepared for what Lincoln, on this day, read to the entire cabinet. The document he read was devoid of his usual literary flourish, it was purely a legal document. But he ended it with perhaps the most important sentence he ever wrote: "I, as Commander-in-Chief . . . do order and declare that on the first day of January in the year of Our Lord one thousand, eight hundred and sixty-three, all persons held as slaves within any state or states, wherein the constitutional authority of the United States shall not be practically recognized, submitted to, and maintained, shall then, thenceforward, and forever, be free."

While this preliminary proclamation would not free the 425,000 slaves in loyal border states still in the Union, it did promise to free 3.5 million slaves that were, admittedly, still not yet under his jurisdiction. Seward advised waiting to issue the proclamation for a Union victory so that the measure would not be "viewed as the last measure of an exhausted government." Lincoln agreed.

JULY 28

"Friends Who Would Hold My Hands"

The capture of the Confederacy's largest city, New Orleans, in April 1862 was the greatest Union prize in the first year of the war. After General Benjamin Butler took control of the city, his harshness became legendary. But it was not the rebels' response to such harshness that frustrated Lincoln, it was that of the loyalists, as shown in a letter Lincoln sent this Monday in 1862.

Not long after Butler arrived, he allowed a subordinate—General John Phelps—to not only protect fugitive slaves that escaped into his lines, but to arm them as well. George Shepley—military governor of Louisiana—rushed to Washington to protest, bringing the written complaints from two Unionists. "If the agitations about slavery is not silenced, every man, woman and child capable of using the knife or pistol will rush into the fight," wrote one loyalist. Lincoln, irritated over their complaints, wrote a response on July 26, saying that "the people of Louisiana" rebelled, prompting such harsh measures. He added, "I distrust the wisdom if not sincerity of friends, who would hold my hands while enemies stab me."

In response to another Unionist's complaint, Lincoln on this day wrote yet another harsh letter. Referring to Unionists who would do nothing but complain, he wrote, "This class of men will do nothing for the government, nothing for themselves, except demanding that the government shall not strike its open enemies, lest they be struck by accident!" He added, "What would you do in my position? . . . would you prosecute it [the war] in [the] future with elder-stalk squirts, charged with rose-water? Would you deal lighter blows rather than heavier ones? Would you give up the contest, leaving any available means unapplied?"

Despite Lincoln's protestations, the issue of arming blacks was too politically charged and in August, Phelps was forced to stop. In response, Phelps resigned.

AUGUST 4

"Gentlemen, You Have My Decision"

On this Monday in 1862, Lincoln turned down an offer of two black regiments from Indiana to serve in the army.

Two weeks before, Lincoln had presented to his cabinet his preliminary Emancipation Proclamation to free Confederate slaves.

The document did not include a provision to allow blacks to fight. The final proclamation—just five months later—did provide for fully armed blacks to "garrison forts, positions, stations and other places." This marked a significant change in Lincoln's thoughts for he was, at first, stubbornly against blacks in uniform. Such an action "would produce dangerous and fatal dissatisfactions in our army, and do more injury than good," he insisted.

When Lincoln met with a small "deputation of Western gentlemen" on this day, it was clear his mind still had not changed. The deputation appeared at the White House to offer two Hoosier black regiments. According to the *New York Tribune*, Lincoln said he "would employ all colored men offered as laborers but would not promise to make soldiers of them." The *Tribune* added, "The President argued that the nation could not afford to lose Kentucky at this crisis, and gave it as his opinion that to arm the Negroes would turn 50,000 bayonets from loyal Border States against us that were for us." When the men persisted, according to one witness, Lincoln became angry: "Gentlemen, you have my decision . . . if the people are dissatisfied, I will resign and let Mr. [Vice President Hannibal] Hamlin try it."

#35

What Changed His Mind

Historians have long recognized that a defining feature of Lincoln was his willingness to learn, to allow his opinions to evolve. This happened with the issue of arming blacks. Lincoln, like most Northerners, had little exposure to black Americans and was skeptical that they would fight. He thought this despite how gallantly blacks had served in both the Revolutionary War and the War of 1812, and despite their service on the navy's combat ships since the beginning of the Civil War.

Lincoln later claimed that his change in policy followed a change in public sentiment. "A man watches his pear-tree day after day, impatient for the ripening fruit," Lincoln told the artist Francis Carpenter. "Let him attempt to force the process, and he may spoil both fruit and tree. But let him patiently wait, and the ripe pear at length falls in his lap!" Lincoln saw "public sentiment slowly but surely progressing." During the late summer and fall of 1862, black regiments were formed—mostly without Lincoln's knowledge or consent—in Louisiana, Kansas, South Carolina, and Indiana. By October blacks had seen combat in Missouri and during 1863 the exploits of black regiments became highly publicized. "It is no longer possible to doubt the bravery and steadiness of the colored race, when rightly led," wrote the *New York Times*. By March 1863 Lincoln's conversion was complete. "The bare sight of fifty thousand armed, and drilled black soldiers on the banks of the Mississippi, would end the rebellion at once," Lincoln wrote Andrew Johnson, Tennessee's military governor.

AUGUST 14

An Unpopular Policy

Lincoln made history on this Thursday in 1862, when he invited a black delegation to the White House for the first time. Unfortunately, the subject of the meeting was the voluntary emigration of free blacks to colonies in Latin America.

Lincoln believed that cultural differences between the races could not be overcome by peaceful coexistence. Like most of his fellow Northerners, however, Lincoln had little exposure to either black Americans or those supposed differences. In Springfield, perhaps his closest black friend was his barber, a Haitian named Billy de

Fleurville. Unlike Billy, most blacks were American-born and had no interest in emigrating. Lincoln also worried that pervasive racism could be a political impediment to emancipation. "If the colored people instead of having been stolen and forcibly brought to the United States had come as free immigrants," former slave Frederick Douglass responded, "they never would have become objects of aversion."

Colonizationists endorsed a colony of blacks funded and protected by the United States in either Haiti, Honduras, or the Chiriqui Lagoon in New Granada (Panama).

On this day, Lincoln invited a delegation of freed blacks headed by Edward Thomas, president of the Anglo-African Institute for the Encouragement of Industry and Art, to the White House. "We have between us a broader difference than exists between almost any other two races," Lincoln said. "The aspirations of men is to enjoy equality . . . but on this broad continent, not a single man of your race is made the equal of single man of ours." After he lectured the delegates on sacrifice, he offered to support a black colony in the Chiriqui Lagoon.

Free blacks responded almost universally with hostility and contempt for Lincoln's offer. The reason, as the newspaper *Liberator* put it, was that blacks "are as much the natives of the country as any of their oppressors." It added, "[one might] as well attempt to roll back the Niagara to its source . . . as to think of driving or enticing them out of the country."

#36

Lincoln and Colonization

As early as 1852, Lincoln advocated colonization as a solution to racial problems. "Coming generations of our countrymen shall by any means, succeed in freeing our land from the dangerous presence of slavery; and at the same time in restoring a captive people to their long-lost fatherland," Lincoln said in his eulogy of Kentucky Senator Henry Clay. But he acknowledged that it was impractical to transport four and a half million ex-slaves to another country and provide for them. He was also aware that free blacks almost universally opposed colonization and he did not advocate forced colonization. Frederick Douglass wrote that the black man's "attachment to the place of his birth is stronger than iron."

Interest in colonization resurged during the Civil War. As Lincoln considered emancipation, he felt such a move would be more easily swallowed if it were lubricated with colonization. Congress appropriated a total of $600,000 (in April and July 1862) to start a colony and Lincoln planned to start one at Chiriqui Lagoon. But when Honduras, Nicaragua, and Costa Rica objected to an American colony and even threatened armed resistance, Lincoln turned to an isle south of Haiti—Île à Vache. This failed, too, when disease ravaged the few blacks who migrated there and Lincoln had to send a ship to rescue them.

By the winter of 1863, it was clear to Lincoln that colonization was impractical and had little support. In March 1863, Lincoln started a refugee program headed by Adjutant General Lorenzo Thomas. Ex-slaves were enrolled in the army, hired as military laborers, or hired to work plantations for wages. The program provided integration into white society. After May 1863, Lincoln never again publicly advocated colonization and ever afterward promoted assimilation.

AUGUST 22

"The Prayer of Twenty Millions"

Lincoln's draft of his preliminary Emancipation Proclamation was locked up in his desk drawer and he took it out occasionally, "touching it up here and there, anxiously watching the progress of events." He was waiting for a military victory to issue it. Meanwhile, Lincoln looked for an opportunity to soften what he was sure would be a shock. He found it in a *New York Tribune* editorial on August 20 titled "The Prayer of Twenty Millions" and on this day in 1862, he responded to it.

In South Carolina, Union general David Hunter, head of the Department of the South, freed and armed slaves, enlisting them into the First South Carolina Regiment. The War Department, however, ordered him to disband the regiment. In response, Horace Greeley, editor of the *Tribune*, published an editorial lambasting Lincoln. "We complain that the Union cause has suffered . . . from the mistaken deference to Rebel Slavery," Greeley wrote. The reason: "We think you are unduly influenced by the counsels . . . of certain fossil politicians hailing from the Border Slave States."

On this day, Lincoln sent his response not to Greeley's paper, but to a Democratic organ, the *National Intelligencer*. Lincoln agreed with most of Greeley's assertions, except the charge that he was influenced by anything but his patriotism. "My paramount object in this struggle is to save the Union, and is not either to save or destroy slavery. If I could save the Union without freeing any slave I would do it; and if I could save it by freeing all the slaves I would do it; and if I could save it by freeing some and leaving others alone I would also do that," he wrote.

AUGUST 29

Waiting on a Victory

Lincoln spent much of this Friday in 1862 listening to the boom of cannon and wondering if he might finally be able to issue his preliminary Emancipation Proclamation.

After he decided in July to await a military victory to issue his proclamation, Lincoln pinned his hopes on the new Army of Virginia, headed by General John Pope. In early August, General George McClellan's Army of the Potomac, sitting idle southwest of Richmond, was ordered to board transports and head to Aquia Creek and Alexandria in Virginia to reinforce Pope. Together they would again move on Richmond from the north.

Confederate general Robert E. Lee had other ideas. Aware that Pope and McClellan's combined force would significantly outnumber his own, Lee decided to attack Pope before he was reinforced. Lee sent Thomas "Stonewall" Jackson north to check Pope's advance at Cedar Mountain on August 9. When, on August 14, Lee learned that McClellan was boarding his transports, he rushed north to join Jackson. Four days later Jackson and elements of Lee's army faced Pope across the Rappahannock River. Lee took a huge risk and divided his forces, sending Jackson around and behind Pope's army. As anticipated, Pope turned to strike at Jackson, exposing his own flank to Lee. Meanwhile, Jackson took up a strong defensive position near the old Manassas battlefield.

On this day, as Pope attacked Jackson, Lincoln stood on the White House lawn listening to the roar of cannon. According to a Washington newspaper, "the smell of gunpowder was quite perceptible" when the wind blew from the west. Lincoln spent almost all day and night at the telegraph office, sending out dispatches begging for information. "What news from the direction of Masassas?" he asked. By the next evening Lincoln knew that Pope had been beaten and his proclamation would have to wait.

AUGUST 30

"Leave Pope to Get Out of His Scrape"

Even as Lincoln was informed that General John Pope had been beaten at the Battle of Second Manassas, it was clear, on this day, that much of the fault lay with General George McClellan.

When McClellan was ordered to withdraw his army from the Virginia Peninsula on August 3, 1862, and send it north to reinforce Pope, he stalled. He complained that the withdrawal would demoralize his troops. When that failed, he said he had insufficient transports. Afraid that Pope would be given command of the merged armies, McClellan told his wife that he was looking for ways to "induce the enemy to attack" him before he left the peninsula, apparently to give him another excuse to stay. "I am almost broken down," Lincoln said. "I can't get General McClellan to do what I wish." Finally, on August 14, McClellan boarded his transports.

Even as McClellan's boats arrived at Aquia Creek on August 24, he delayed. That same day McClellan wrote his wife that he was tempted to submit "a leave of absence" in order to forestall the merger. He added that his fortunes would change if "Pope is beaten, in which case they may want me to save Wash[ingto]n again." Lincoln wired McClellan for information and, instead, the general sent advice: "leave Pope to get out of his scrape & at once use all our means to make the capitol safe."

The next morning—on this day—Lincoln lamented "McClellan's present conduct" and believed McClellan wanted Pope to lose. McClellan got his wish. "Well, John," Lincoln told his secretary John Hay that evening, "we are whipped again." Within days McClellan was given command of both his own and Pope's army in order to protect Washington from the victorious Confederates.

SEPTEMBER 1

"I Must Have McClellan"

For the second time in thirteen months, a rout of Union forces at Manassas and fears that the Confederates would attack Washington spurred Lincoln, on this day in 1862, to put General George McClellan in charge of protecting the capital, despite protestations from his cabinet.

General in Chief Henry Halleck reported that McClellan had not obeyed his order to reinforce General John Pope at the Second Battle of Bull Run (Manassas) "with the promptness I expected and the national safety, in my opinion, required." Secretary of War Edwin Stanton blamed McClellan for Pope's loss in the battle. Stanton drafted a remonstrance to be signed by Lincoln's cabinet stating that its members were "unwilling to be accessory to the . . . protraction of the war, the destruction of our armies, and the imperiling of the Union which we believe must result from the continuance of George B. McClellan in command." Stanton wanted McClellan removed. Secretary of the Treasury Salmon Chase wanted more: "McClellan ought to be shot."

Lincoln agreed: "Unquestionably he acted badly toward Pope. He wanted him to fail. That is unpardonable." But there were rumors that the Confederates were crossing the Potomac at Georgetown. Washingtonians were fleeing the capital. While there were enough troops to beat back the Confederates, they were demoralized. There was one man who could change that. "I must have McClellan to reorganize the army and bring it out of chaos," Lincoln said. Lincoln met with McClellan, on this day, to offer command not only of the Army of the Potomac, but of Pope's Army of Virginia. "I only consent to take it for my country's sake," McClellan maintained. The next day when Lincoln told his cabinet of McClellan's reinstatement, he faced almost unanimous dissent. But Lincoln stuck to his decision. "We must use what tools we have," he said.

#37

"Almost Ready to Hang Himself"

Lincoln's September 2, 1862, cabinet meeting was among the most contentious of his presidency. Four of the seven cabinet members—Secretary of War Edwin Stanton; Secretary of the Treasury Salmon Chase; Secretary of the Interior Caleb Smith; and Attorney General Edward Bates—had come to the meeting with a petition declaring a "want of Confidence in Gen. McClellan" and essentially demanded his removal.

After Lincoln opened the meeting, he told his cabinet that he had named McClellan as head of Washington's defenses because "McClellan knows this whole ground" and could "be trusted to act on the defensive." They were stunned. McClellan's command orders had not come from the War Department, Stanton complained. "No, Mr. Secretary, the order is mine, and I will be responsible for it to the country," Lincoln replied. Stanton handed Lincoln their petition and after the president read it, he tried to convince them of the peril Washington was in: "the city will be overrun by the enemy in forty-eight hours!" General in Chief Henry Halleck could lead the troops, Bates said. But, Lincoln argued, the army was demoralized. "He [McClellan] has the slows, is worth little for onward movement," Lincoln admitted, "but beyond any other officer he has the confidence of the army." Secretary of the Navy Gideon Welles characterized the discussion as filled with "more disturbed and desponding feeling" than he had ever witnessed in a cabinet meeting. But Lincoln persisted, saying he would "gladly resign his place, but he could not see who could do the work wanted as well as McClellan."

Lincoln was depressed that he did not have the support of his cabinet. Welles said he "seemed wrung by bitterest anguish—said he felt almost ready to hang himself."

SEPTEMBER 5

Bucktails

With Confederate general Robert E. Lee moving his army into Maryland, General George McClellan, concerned for the president's safety when he stayed at the Old Soldiers' Home cottage, decided to post guards there. On this day in 1862, McClellan sent a note to Lincoln informing him of the new security detail.

In response to Lincoln's July call for 300,000 more troops, Pennsylvania governor Andrew Curtin authorized financial incentives for new enlistees ($25 on enlistment and $75 at war's end). He also formed two new "Bucktail Brigades," a title made famous by the First Pennsylvania Rifles and represented by hats with flaps of deer skin attached. The 150th Pennsylvania was assigned to a Bucktail Brigade. The 150th reached Washington on September 5 and the next evening two companies—Companies D and K—were dispatched to the Soldiers' Home.

Still unaware whom they were to protect, the next morning the men sat down for breakfast. "When the soldiers were seated, they noticed that a chair had been reserved at the head of the table for someone," Private John Nichols recalled, "and pretty soon the president, Abraham Lincoln, entered and said, 'Good morning, boys, I am informed that your company has been detailed to act as my bodyguard.'" Afterward, Lincoln rode into Washington with Company K's captain, David Derickson of Meadville, Pennsylvania. During the ride, Derickson revealed that a member of General in Chief Henry Halleck's staff was from Meadville, and Lincoln took a detour to Halleck's office so that Derickson could be introduced to

Halleck. The general had "a kind of quizzical look" that Derickson interpreted as saying "isn't this rather a joke to ask the Commander-in-Chief [*sic*] . . . to be introduced to a country captain?" While Company D would be reassigned, Company K would remain on Lincoln's security detail for the remainder of his presidency.

#38

Company K

Almost from the moment Company K had been assigned to protect Lincoln at the Old Soldiers' Home on September 6, 1862, it was clear they were needed. According to Private Willard Cutter, on September 9 an alleged spy was caught using a telescope from the top of Scott's Hall, near the president's cottage, apparently reconnoitering Washington's forts. Cutter also claimed that seventeen more rebels were "captured half a mile" from the retreat. Private Albert See recalled that in July 1864, Confederate general John Mosby was rumored to be in the area with five hundred partisans intent on kidnapping Lincoln. The president was one day conversing on the cottage's porch when they heard the sound of a horseman riding at a full gallop. "President, step into the house, and shut the door," See shouted. Lincoln obeyed and only came out when the horseman was identified as a Union messenger. "I presume I am the only private soldier that ever gave a command to the President," See said.

Lincoln's youngest son, Tad, became a favorite of Company K. They gave him a uniform and a commission (third lieutenant). See recalled that Tad appeared in their ranks "almost daily" and when dinner was called, would "get in line and draw his rations the same as the rest of us."

Lincoln himself en ed one of the companies' amuse-
ments called the "t ed elephant." Two men would cover
themselves in an ny blanket, then dance and swing a
trunk made ou a plank of wood wrapped in another
blanket. Linc ne day witnessed the elephant's routine
and was so d that he returned later that day with a
friend and the men to perform the elephant's antics
again.

SEPTEMBER 12

aryland, My Maryland"

e clear that Confederate general Robert E. Lee was my into Maryland, Lincoln, on this Friday in 1862, the nerves of governors and mayors alike.

th victory after he successfully beat General George away from Richmond, then routed General John Pope at of Second Manassas; Lee wanted to carry his momentum rd into enemy territory. "We cannot afford to be idle," Lee onfederate president Jefferson Davis, "and though weaker our opponents in men and military equipment, [we] must deavor to harass, if we cannot destroy them." Lee believed that a victory on Northern soil would garner European recognition for the Confederacy and his army could forage from the North's breadbasket instead of Virginia's. As Lee's army rolled across the Potomac in early September, they sang "Maryland, My Maryland" as they marched, hoping sympathizers in Maryland would fly to their flag. That didn't happen, probably because of what the Confederate army looked like. "Posterity will scarcely believe that the wonderful campaign . . . was made by men, one-fourth of whom were entirely barefooted and one-half of whom were as ragged as scarecrows," wrote the *Richmond Dispatch*.

Lincoln saw the invasion as an opportunity to destroy Lee. "We could end the war by allowing the enemy to go to Harrisburg and Philadelphia," he said. Pennsylvania governor Andrew Curtin did not agree, pleading for 80,000 troops to protect his state. "We have not . . . eighty thousand disciplined troops, properly so called, this side of the [Allegheny] Mountains," Lincoln responded. "The emergency demands the assignment of a competent general to take command of this city," Philadelphia mayor Alexander Henry wired Lincoln on this day. The president responded that Philadelphia was not in danger.

SEPTEMBER 13

A Bull Against a Comet

While Lincoln still held onto his preliminary Emancipation Proclamation, he continued, on this day in 1862, to debate visitors over the prudence of issuing such a document.

The visitors were a delegation of "Chicago Christians" who presented to Lincoln a memorial or petition arguing that God willed a national emancipation. According to Rev. William Patton and Rev. John Dempster, Lincoln responded, "If it is probable that God would reveal his will to others, on a point so connected with my duty, it might be supposed he would reveal it directly to me." He added that he had not received a "direct revelation" and that "religious men, who are equally certain that they represent the Divine will" have opposite views on slavery. The delegates answered "that good men, indeed, differed in their opinions on this subject; nevertheless the truth was somewhere, and it was a matter of solemn moment for him to ascertain it." They added that Lincoln needed no direct revelation since the "Bible denounced oppression as one of the highest crimes."

\s for issuing a proclamation, Lincoln argued, "I do not want to a document that . . . must necessarily be inoperative, like the ; bull against the comet [a reference to the myth that Pope ıs III tried to excommunicate Halley's Comet in 1456]. Would ·d free the slaves, when I cannot enforce the Constitution ·bel States?" The delegates countered that Lincoln would ɔose to abandon the Constitution [simply] because of the fficulty of enforcing it." Why should he abandon eman-

/ith answers to arguments he would soon hear, Lincoln iscussion with, "Whatever shall appear to be God's will wo weeks later Lincoln would cite God's will as the n he was issuing his preliminary Emancipation Proc-

SEPTEMBER 15

The Cigar Wrapper

te general Robert E. Lee in the second week of rdinate made a mistake that might have proved been General George McClellan who needed . Despite himself, McClellan did beat elements tember 14 for which Lincoln, on this day in m.

the Battle of Second Manassas, Lincoln, in McClellan to make battle-ready the demor- ıshington. "Again I have been called upon Clellan wrote his wife. "It makes my heart tered remnants of my noble Army of the d to see how they love me even now." As did get his army ready within days.

Then came an incredible stroke of luck. On September 13, a corporal in the Twenty-seventh Indiana Infantry—bivouacked in the same camp the Confederates had occupied the day before—found three cigars wrapped in an order from Lee outlining his campaign strategy. The order indicated that Lee's army was dangerously dispersed. "Here is a paper with which if I cannot whip Bobbie Lee I will be willing to go home," said McClellan. And yet McClella did nothing for half a day. What was worse, McClellan's jubilatio over the discovered papers was observed by civilians, one of who w a Confederate sympathizer. That sympathizer informed Lee that plan had been exposed and Lee began to gather in his dispers divisions. But not before McClellan slammed into Lee at key pas through South Mountain in the Shenandoah Valley range, bea back the rebel forces. Lincoln wired McClellan on this day, " bless you, and all with you. Destroy the rebel army, if possible."

SEPTEMBER 17

Antietam

As Union and Confederate armies bloodied each other a etam Creek, Maryland, Lincoln, on this day in 1862, put the fi touches to his preliminary Emancipation Proclamation.

The battle that came to be known as Antietam evolve Confederate general Robert E. Lee was told that his plan northern offensive had fallen into Union hands. Lee began g his dangerously dispersed army together to move back into But when word arrived that his men had taken Harpe Virginia on September 15, Lee decided to make a stand be Potomac and Antietam Creek near Sharpsburg, Marylanc

Almost immediately, McClellan's timidity lost him a opportunity; many of McClellan's 75,000 men were ava on September 16 and almost certainly would have ov

Lee's 11,000 men. Instead McClellan waited a day, allowing Lee to reinforce. And, when he did attack on this day, it was piecemeal, allowing Lee to shift his forces to plug holes or blunt offensives. Nor did McClellan he use the 30,000 men he held in reserve. Lincoln was elated when initial reports indicated Lee's army was destroyed. "Our victory is complete," wrote McClellan. "I feel some little pride in having with a beaten and demoralized army defeated Lee utterly & saved the North so completely." On September 18, Lee and his army remained on the battlefield to prove he wasn't beaten. The next day Lee withdrew across the Potomac unmolested. It wasn't until September 21 that Lincoln was informed that the Confederates had escaped. Nevertheless, Lee's offensive had been stopped and it was close enough to a victory for Lincoln to issue his preliminary Emancipation Proclamation. On this day he finished it at his Old Soldiers' Home cottage, then immediately began to edit and revise it.

SEPTEMBER 22

The Promise of Freedom

Lincoln spent the weekend following the Battle of Antietam revising his preliminary Emancipation Proclamation and, on this Monday in 1862, he convened a cabinet meeting to announce that he was going to issue it.

"September 17, 1862 [day of the Antietam battle] will, we predict, hereafter be looked upon as an epoch in the history of the rebellion from which will date the inauguration of its downfall," wrote the *New York Times*. Lincoln, on this day, fulfilled their prediction as he opened perhaps his most important cabinet meeting. Wishing to relieve tension, Lincoln read from Charles Farrar Browne's *Artemus Ward, His Book*, an autobiographical spoof about a fictional showman who traveled with historical wax figures.

After he closed the book, he told his cabinet that when Confederate general Robert E. Lee's army invaded Maryland, he decided "as soon as it should be driven out" he would issue the proclamation. "I said nothing to any one, but I made the promise to myself and to my Maker," he said. Unused to Lincoln making political decisions based on religious convictions, Secretary of the Treasury Salmon Chase asked, "Did I understand you correctly, Mr. President?" Lincoln explained, "I have . . . thought a great deal about the relation of this war to slavery. . .. I wish it were a better time . . . the action of the army against the rebels has not been quite what I should have best liked. But they have been driven out of Maryland." He then read the proclamation. Secretary of War Edwin Stanton "made a very emphatic speech sustaining the measure." Postmaster General Montgomery Blair feared the proclamation might alienate the border slave states (it didn't) and affect the fall elections (it did). The next day, Lincoln's opus was made public.

#39

"Queer Little Conceits"

It may seem odd that Lincoln would choose to open the September 22, 1862 cabinet meeting by reading humor but Lincoln frequently did this, often to relieve his own stress. He kept his favorites in his pocket or in a nearby desk drawer. He preferred literary writers who had turned their sharp wit toward the social or political realm, often writing under pseudonyms. These writers—the most famous of whom was Samuel Clemens (Mark Twain)—included such Lincoln favorites as Charles Browne (Artemus Ward), David Locke (Petoleum V. Nasby), and Robert Newell (Orpheus C. Kerr). His secretary John Hay called them his "queer little conceits." Lincoln would read them while waiting for news at the telegraph office or ply visitors to his office with a few lines. This sometimes caused angst among his visitors. In response to one complaint, Lincoln said, "If I couldn't tell these stories, I would die."

While humor could be a great stress reliever, Lincoln also read poetry—particularly morbid, "gloomy" poetry—to lift him out of depression. In the early 1840s, Lincoln carried around a copy of Edgar Allen Poe's "The Raven." Lincoln's friend Orville Browning found Lincoln melancholy one day at the White House. Lincoln procured a copy of Thomas Hood's poetry "and he read to me several of those sad pathetic pieces—I suppose because they were accurate pictures of his own experiences and feelings. I remained with [him] about an hour & a half and left [him] in high spirits, and a very genial mood."

SEPTEMBER 24

Habeas Corpus Suspended Nationally

Two days after Lincoln issued his groundbreaking preliminary Emancipation Proclamation, Lincoln issued on this Wednesday in 1862 a proclamation far more dubious, the first nationwide suspension of the writ of habeas corpus in U.S. history.

The Militia Act of July 17, 1862 allowed Secretary of War Edwin Stanton to draft soldiers already in the ranks who had not been replaced by enlistees. This attempt to disguise an unpopular conscription fooled nobody, and the act was dubbed the Militia Draft of 1862. To enforce the draft, Stanton, on August 8, issued orders to arrest enlistees attempting to dodge the draft and suspended the writ of habeas corpus on such cases. Additionally, anyone "engaged, by act, speech or writing, in discouraging volunteer enlistments, in any way giving aid and comfort to the enemy" would be treated the same. Almost immediately the orders caused chaos, particularly after Judge Advocate Levi Turner authorized local sheriffs and constables to make the arrests. Many arrests were made to satisfy personal vendettas. Between 354 and 643 civilians were arrested (records are incomplete) in the first month and less than half of them were draft dodgers.

It was clear that an organized system needed to be in place, and on September 8 Stanton's orders were rescinded. On this day Lincoln issued his own proclamation, declaring that "all Rebels and Insurgents, the aiders and abettors . . . and all persons discouraging volunteer enlistments, resisting militia drafts, or guilty of any disloyal practice" anywhere in the country would be arrested, and their writ suspended. Later this day when serenaders came to the White House to celebrate Lincoln's Emancipation Proclamation, Lincoln told them, "I can only trust in God I have made no mistake." Lincoln voiced no such qualms over a far more contentious issue of suspending a cherished protection against imprisonment without trial.

#40

Multiple Suspensions

Lincoln suspended or authorized his military subordinates to suspend the writ of habeas corpus nine times. On October 24, 1861, Lincoln also barred the delivery of writs to military commanders, but while this effectively suspended the writ, it was not officially ordered. Why did Lincoln suspend it so many times?

The first six suspensions were made in the critical first six months of the war. In response to sabotage of Maryland railways, Lincoln on April 27, 1861 suspended the writ for arrests made between Philadelphia and Washington. On May 10, Lincoln authorized it for Union holdings off the Florida coast after the state joined the Confederacy. When Maryland arrests touched off criticism in late May, Lincoln waited a month before ordering it again, this time for a single person. As criticism waned, Lincoln in July expanded his earlier suspension in Maryland to cover any point on a "military line" between New York and Washington. On October 14, he expanded it still farther north to Bangor, Maine. Finally, on December 2, he suspended it in Missouri as well.

While these six suspensions were limited geographically and in response to partisan activities, during the second year of the war Lincoln's concern was that his army ranks were thinning. Lincoln's September 24, 1862 nationwide suspension was an effort to enforce a draft and stifle efforts to induce men to not enlist or desert from the army. He may have also wanted to quell opposition to his Emancipation Proclamation. Not coincidentally, on the same day (March 3, 1863) Congress passed the Enrollment Act that officially instituted the draft, they also passed the Habeas Corpus Act that officially granted Lincoln the power to suspend the writ. Lincoln twice more suspended the writ and both suspensions were essentially unnecessary and redundant (again nationwide on September 15, 1863, and in Kentucky on July 4, 1864).

SEPTEMBER 26

"That Is Not the Game"

Lincoln, on this Friday in 1862, wrote to Major John Key, an acting judge advocate on General George McClellan's staff, demanding that he answer for a statement he supposedly made.

A week after the Battle of Antietam, Lincoln sent Key a letter on this day regarding a conversation that was recounted to him. "I am informed that in answer to the question 'Why was not the rebel army bagged immediately after the battle near Sharpsburg [Antietam]?' propounded to you by Major Levi C. Turner," Lincoln wrote, "You answered 'That is not the game. The object is that neither Army [Union or Confederate] shall get much advantage of the other, that both shall be kept in the field till they are exhausted, when we will make a compromise [sue for peace] & save slavery.'" Lincoln was already angry because of McClellan's lack of aggressiveness after Antietam, during the Peninsula Campaign, and in aiding General John Pope at the Battle of Second Manassas. Lincoln was also sensitive to the public reaction to his preliminary Emancipation Proclamation he had announced just a few days before.

The next day both Key and Turner appeared in Lincoln's office. When Turner repeated what Key allegedly said, Key tried to defend it. As Lincoln later wrote to Key, "You did not deny or attempt to deny it, but confirmed it in my mind, by attempting to sustain the position of the argument." Lincoln then dismissed Key from service in order to send a message. "I had been brought to fear that there was a class of officers in the army, not very inconsiderable in numbers who were playing a game to not beat the enemy when they could, on some peculiar notion as to the proper way of saving the Union," Lincoln wrote Key. "I dismissed you as an example and warning to that supposed class." It didn't help that Key's brother Thomas, a Cincinnati judge, was considered a Southern sympathizer.

SEPTEMBER 28

"Breath Alone Kills No Rebels"

Lincoln, on this Sunday in 1862, wrote Vice President Hannibal Hamlin expressing how discouraged he was over the response to his preliminary Emancipation Proclamation.

Much of the response had been positive. “God bless you for the word you have spoken,” wrote three men from the Keystone State. “All good men upon the earth will glorify you and all the angels in Heaven will hold a jubilee.” The great orator Frederick Douglass wrote, “We shout for the joy that we live to record this righteous decree.”

Criticism for the proclamation came from expected quarters. The Democratic *New York Evening Express* declared that the proclamation would make “the restoration of the Old Constitution and the Union impossible.” The *Richmond Enquirer* claimed that Lincoln was inciting slaves to rebel, in turn forcing their owners to kill them. “Cheerful and happy now, he [Lincoln] plots their death,” the *Enquirer* wrote. Radical Republicans who could no longer complain of Lincoln’s tardiness in emancipating slaves looked for other fodder. One radical—Count Adam Gurowski—complained that the proclamation was written “in the meanest and the most dry routine style; not a word to evoke a generous thrill.”

After Lincoln received Hamlin’s accolades for his proclamation, Lincoln, on this day, responded by venting his frustration. Lincoln felt that a positive response to the proclamation in the North should be “instantaneous.” And yet “it was six days old, and while commendation in newspapers and by distinguished individuals is all that a vain man could wish, the stocks have declined, and troops come forward [enlist] more slowly than ever. This looked soberly in the face, is not very satisfactory. . . . The North responds to the proclamation sufficiently in breath; but breath alone kills no rebels.” It would get worse. In the November midterm elections, the Republicans would take a beating.

OCTOBER 2

How the Troops Felt

On this second day of Lincoln’s visit to General George McClellan’s Army of the Potomac, the president found himself among his soldiers, gauging their reaction to him now that he had he issued his preliminary Emancipation Proclamation.

Lincoln had long feared disaffection in the ranks due to emancipation and there was indeed some. "The boys think it their duty to put down the rebellion and nothing more," wrote Private Wilbur Fisk of the Second Vermont Infantry, "and they view the abolition of slavery as saddling so much additional labor upon them before the present great work is accomplished." Admiral Andrew Foote claimed the proclamation was "damping their zeal and ardor and producing discontent at the idea of fighting only for the negro." Lincoln's friend Orville Browning reported second-hand accounts in which soldiers complained that "they had been deceived—that the[y] volunteered to fight for the Country, and had they known it was be converted into a war for the negro they would not have enlisted." McClellan thought the proclamation an "accursed doctrine" meant to spark a slave insurrection in the South.

But when Lincoln reviewed the troops on this day at Loudoun and Maryland Heights, the president was enthusiastically cheered. "The troops . . . presented a fine appearance for which they were highly complimented. The president indulged in a number of humorous anecdotes, which greatly amused the company," wrote a reporter. The obvious reverence the soldiers had for their commander in chief lifted his spirits. "I am stronger with the Army of the Potomac than McClellan," Lincoln said. He added, "The supremacy of the civil power has been restored and the Executive is again the master of the situation."

OCTOBER 3

"McClellan's Bodyguard"

After the Battle of Antietam (September 17), General George McClellan not only allowed the Confederates to sit on the battlefield unmolested for a day, but also allowed them to recross the Potomac. Nor did he pursue them in the weeks afterward. Lincoln decided to visit McClellan at Harpers Ferry and on this day in 1862 Lincoln despaired of reversing McClellan's inertia.

On the same day that Lincoln issued his preliminary Emancipation Proclamation (September 22), Lincoln interviewed McClellan's intelligence operative Allan Pinkerton. Asked about McClellan's reticence to attack, Pinkerton ticked off one excuse after another. Lincoln decided he needed to talk to McClellan himself. On October 1, Lincoln took a train to Harpers Ferry, arriving at noon. Lincoln rode to McClellan's headquarters from the depot in "a common ambulance," said one observer, "with his long legs doubled up so that his knees almost struck his chin and grinning out of the windows like a baboon."

In conference, Lincoln told McClellan to drop his "over-cautiousness" and move against the enemy. McClellan admitted to his wife that Lincoln was "affable" but the "real purpose of his visit is to push me into a premature advance in Virginia." Early on this day, Lincoln asked Ozias Hatch, the Illinois Secretary of State, to take a stroll that led them to a hill overlooking the army. "Hatch—Hatch, what is all this?" Lincoln asked, indicating the view. "Why, Mr. Lincoln, this is the Army of the Potomac," Hatch responded. "No, Hatch, no, this is General McClellan's bodyguard."

When Lincoln returned to Washington, he had an order sent to McClellan, "The President directs that you cross the Potomac and give battle to the enemy or drive him south. Your army must move now while the roads are good."

#41

"Ditties"

An incident while inspecting the Army of the Potomac on October 3, 1862 would come to haunt Lincoln. That morning Lincoln reviewed General Ambrose Burnside's troops. Afterward, Lincoln and his friend Ward Lamon, Marshal of the District of Columbia, climbed into an ambulance to ride to yet another review. The trip brought them across the Antietam battlefield, where Lamon sang a few songs that were later characterized as bawdy and inappropriate. The press latched onto the story as proof that Lincoln was an unsophisticated rube, and two years later the story still had legs.

On September 9, 1864—two months before the presidential elections—the *New York World* printed a retelling of the story.

> While the President was driving over the field in an ambulance, accompanied by Marshal Lamon, General [George] McClellan, and another officer, heavy details of men were engaged in the task of burying the dead. The ambulance had just reached the neighborhood of the old stone bridge, where the dead were piled highest, when Mr. Lincoln, suddenly slapping Marshal Lamon on the knee, exclaimed, "Come, Lamon, give us that song about Picayune Butler, McClellan has never heard it." "Not now, if you please" said General McClellan, with a shudder; "I would prefer to hear it some other place and time."

In response, Lamon wrote out an account of the incident and had it signed by Lincoln. Lamon denied that there were burial details during their visit, nor were the dead "piled" anywhere. The battle had been fought sixteen days before, the dead already buried. While Lamon admitted he sang the "comic" song "Picayune Butler," that wasn't the song Lincoln requested. Instead, Lincoln asked for a "little sad song" which Lamon followed up with lighter "ditties." Lamon added that "neither Gen. McClellan or any one else made any objection to the singing."

OCTOBER 4

"No Enemies Here"

On this Saturday in 1862—the last day of Lincoln's inspection of General George McClellan's army near Antietam—the president visited not only wounded Union soldiers, but Confederates as well.

By October 1862, there were nearly eighty hospitals in Georgetown, Washington, and Alexandria, Virginia, five miles to the south. Lincoln visited many of them, sometimes by himself, sometimes with Mary. While visiting armies out in the field, he frequented hospitals as well. On this morning, Lincoln visited General Israel "Fighting Dick" Richardson, wounded at Antietam and dying at a nearby farmhouse. Afterward, Lincoln visited the wounded. As one reporter wrote,

> Passing through one of the hospitals devoted exclusively to Confederate sick and wounded, President Lincoln's attention was drawn to a young Georgian . . . stretched upon a humble cot. He was pale, emaciated and anxious, far from kindred and home. . . . President Lincoln . . . approached and spoke, asking him if he suffered much pain. "I do," was the reply. "I have lost a leg, and I feel I am sinking from exhaustion." "Would you," said Lincoln, "shake hands with me if I were to tell you who I am?" . . . "There should," remarked the young Georgian, "be no enemies in this place." Then said the distinguished visitor, "I am Abraham Lincoln, President of the United States." The young sufferer raised his hand, looking amazed, and freely extended his hand."

Nor was this an isolated incident. On April 8, 1865, at City Point, days before the end of the war, Lincoln asked to shake hands with as many wounded soldiers as he could. "I will probably never see the boys again," he said, "and I want them to know that I appreciate what they have done for their country." For five hours Lincoln shook hands of both Union and Confederate wounded.

#42

Mary and the Wounded

Six years after the war, author Mary Clemmer Ames derided Mary Lincoln: "While her sister-women scraped lint, sewed bandages, and put on nurse's caps, the wife of the President spent her time rolling to and fro between Washington and New York, intent on extravagant purchases for herself and the White House." Both Ms. Ames and history might have been kinder to Mary had her frequent visits to hospitals been better publicized. "If she [Mary] were worldly wise, she would carry newspaper correspondents, from two to five, of both sexes, every time she went [to the hospitals] and she would have them take shorthand notes," wrote Lincoln's secretary William Stoddard. "By keeping up such a process . . . she could sweeten the contents of many journals." There may be another explanation for her silence: Victorian sensibilities were prohibitive of women visiting nude and mangled men.

Mary took with her food to distribute among the wounded men and from the White House conservatory she brought fresh flowers to lie on the soldiers' pillows to counter the hospital stench. She read to the wounded and wrote letters for them. Often Lincoln joined his wife and once, while visiting the hospital housed in the Patent Office, the Lincolns were following a woman who was handing out religious tracts. One soldier laughed at the tract handed to him. "My good fellow," said the president, "the lady doubtless means you well, and it is hardly fair for you to laugh at her gift." The soldier responded, "Well, Mr. President, how can I help laughing? She has given me a tract on 'The Sin of Dancing' and both of my legs are shot off."

OCTOBER 7

"To Hurt the Enemy"

On October 6, Lincoln had his general in chief, Henry Halleck, wire General George McClellan to "give battle to the enemy or drive him south." On this Tuesday in 1862, Lincoln parried the first of McClellan's excuses against a movement.

With midterm elections in November and public support for his administration bruised by his preliminary Emancipation Proclamation, Lincoln could ill afford criticism for McClellan's idleness. Lincoln decided to give McClellan one more chance. "I began to fear he was playing false—that he did not want to hurt the enemy," Lincoln later explained. "I saw how he could intercept the enemy on the way to Richmond. I determined to let that be the test. If he let them get away I would remove him."

Lincoln was indeed concerned that McClellan was contriving not to "hurt the enemy." A McClellan subordinate—Major John Key—had, during a discussion, claimed that leadership in the Army of the Potomac had no intention of destroying the rebel army but that "both shall be kept in the field till they are exhausted . . . [then] we will make a compromise and save slavery." Lincoln cashiered Key out of the army as a message to McClellan. The general responded with General Order No. 163, issued on this day, which read that "discussions" about the government which exceeded "temperate and respectfull Expressions of opinion" were prohibited.

As for moving his army, McClellan wired Lincoln that first he wanted a furlough. "You wish to see your family, and I wish to oblige you," Lincoln wired back today. "It might be left to your own discretion—certainly so, if Mrs. M[cClellan] could meet you here at Washington."

OCTOBER 12

Buell

In the wake of the Battle of Perryville, Kentucky, Lincoln, on this day in 1862, tried to ascertain whether General Don Carlos Buell was pursuing the Confederates.

In August, the Confederates launched an audacious plan to wrest Kentucky from the Union. Together with slashing cavalry raids and in conjunction with Confederate general Robert E. Lee's Maryland offensive, Confederate generals Braxton Bragg and Edmund Kirby-Smith drove a two-pronged offensive deep into Kentucky. Initially they had success taking the Cumberland Gap, then Lexington. Lincoln was deluged with pleas for help. On September 6, a delegation of Midwestern legislators appeared at the White House, making demands. After Lincoln answered that he would agree to none of their demands, he told them a story about farmers who moved so much that, whenever their chickens saw the furniture coverings, "they laid themselves on their back and crossed their legs, ready to be tied. If I were to be guided by every committee that comes in that door, I might just as well cross my hands and let you tie me."

Lincoln dispatched Buell, head of the Army of the Ohio, to meet the threat. In mid-September, Buell sent word that he, despite outnumbering the Confederates two to one, was retreating a hundred miles north, ceding central Tennessee and half of Kentucky to the rebels without a fight. Lincoln was about to fire Buell when, on October 8, Buell reluctantly fought the Confederates at Perryville—the largest battle fought in Kentucky. The battle was indecisive but the rebels retreated. Lincoln on this day tried to find where Buell was and what he was doing. "We are very anxious to hear from Gen. Buell's Army," Lincoln wrote a general in Louisville, Kentucky. "We have nothing since day-before yesterday. Have you anything?" Buell was content to merely follow the Confederates south unmolested for over three hundred miles.

OCTOBER 14

Tad and the Military

Lincoln, on this Tuesday in 1862, wrote Captain John Dahlgren, giving him permission to provide Tad Lincoln with "a little gun that he can not hurt himself with."

With the war starting just weeks after his eighth birthday, it's not surprising Tad was fascinated with all things military. He owned several uniforms and guns stripped of their ability to function, and put his friends through military drills. Together with his late brother Willie, Tad had converted the White House's roof into a fort and the attic into a prison. The Sanitary Commission sent Tad a doll he named Jack and dressed in a colorful Zouave uniform. Jack was frequently court-martialed and sentenced to death, executed with Tad's play cannon and interred "with honors" in the executive garden. One day, babysitter Julia Taft reported that a dirge played on a "broken fiddle, a banged-up horn, paper over a comb and Tad's drum" caught the attention of the gardener who "looked at the yawning grave amid his rose bushes in helpless anger. He made a sort of helpless gesture and said, 'Boys, why don't you get Jack pardoned?'" Tad liked the idea and acquired a written pardon from his father.

Nothing obsessed Tad more than getting his hands on a gun. Once, while visiting Julia's home, where her father stored muskets in the bathroom, Tad fired one out the bathroom window. "It nicked the corner of Mr. Bartle's house, next door, the bullet whistling over the head of their old mammy who was washing some clothes in a tub," wrote Julia. "She looked up anxiously and said 'Pears like dose boys'll kill somebody's nigger yet.'" Tad pestered his father so relentlessly for a gun that Lincoln, on this day, had Dahlgren provide him with a brass miniature cannon.

#43

"Cussed Old Abe Himself"

Tad Lincoln's love of firearms probably came from his father. The president loved to shoot guns and often test-fired new rifles and muskets in the empty lots adjoining the White House. "The Mall is that great slope of grass and weeds and rubbish between the White House grounds and the Potomac," wrote Lincoln's secretary, William Stoddard. "Away out in the middle of it there is a pile of old lumber as large as a small house. It is just the thing to set up a target against."

Early one morning, Lincoln took Stoddard out to the Mall to test-fire two rifles. Stoddard—who wrote his memoirs in present tense—explained what happened:

> Down he crouches, to hold his piece across his knee, but he has entirely forgotten one thing. There are stringent orders out forbidding all firing within the camp limits of this frontier post called Washington City. . . . There they come! There is a short sergeant . . . and four or five men of the regiment on guard duty, and they are on a clean run from the avenue. . . . The short sergeant. . . is beginning to make remarks, and he has forgotten all he learned in Sunday-school. "Stop that firing! Stop that firing!" . . . Bang goes the rifle, just as the sergeant . . . arrives within a few paces and is putting out an eager, angry hand, as if he had an arrest to make . . .. His [Lincoln's] tall, gaunt form shoots up, up, up, uncoiling to its full height. . . . Their faces . . . look up at his, and all their jaws seem to drop in unison. . . .

> Now it is a double-quick, quicker, quicker, as they race back toward the avenue, leaving behind them only a confused, suppressed breath about having "cussed Old Abe himself." . . . [Then Lincoln said] "Well, they might have stayed to see the shooting."

OCTOBER 17

Lincoln Meets Commodore Nutt

On this Friday in 1862, Lincoln met a twenty-nine-inch dwarf whom the famous showman Phineas T. Barnum dubbed "Commodore" Nutt.

Barnum had made a career as a promoter of the exotic. One of his first attractions was Joice Heth, a blind, toothless black woman he claimed to be the 161-year-old slave and nurse of an infant George Washington. He traveled the country looking for "industrious fleas, automatons, jugglers, ventriloquists, living statuary, tableaux gypsies, albinos, fat boys, giants, dwarfs, rope-dancers . . . [and] American Indians." None of his attractions were as popular as that of Charles Sherwood Stratton, dubbed General Tom Thumb. When Barnum met the boy at age five, Stratton was twenty-five inches tall. Beginning in 1843, Barnum toured America and Europe with Stratton, who was taught to sing, dance, and impersonate historical figures.

Then, in December 1861, Barnum signed a contract with seventeen-year-old George Nutt. Stratton returned from a tour to find competition not only for his audience but for the affections of another newly-signed dwarf named Lavinia Warren.

On this day, Barnum took Nutt to the White House. When Lincoln bent over to take Nutt's hand, he said, "Commodore, permit me to give you a parting word of advice. When you are in command of your fleet, if you find yourself in danger of being taken prisoner, I advise you to wade ashore." As Barnum recalled, "The Commodore found the laugh was against him, but placing himself at the side of the President, and gradually raising his eyes up the whole length of Mr. Lincoln's long legs, he replied, 'I guess, Mr. President, you could do that better than I could.'" In February 1863, Stratton married Warren, with Nutt as the best man. All three came to the White House afterward where Nutt, Stratton, and Lincoln participated in a contest of puns.

OCTOBER 24

Lincoln Removes Buell

On this day in 1862, Lincoln relieved General Don Carlos Buell as head of the Department of the Ohio.

Buell was a career military man, graduating from West Point in 1837, and had been wounded at the Battle of Churubusco during the Mexican–American War. Buell had an adequate career early in the Civil War, taking Nashville, Tennessee after General Ulysses Grant took Forts Henry and Donelson, making central Tennessee untenable for the Confederates. Buell also rescued Grant's army from near annihilation at Shiloh and was involved in the painfully slow but successful campaign to take Corinth, Tennessee.

Unfortunately for Buell, he was also adept at making political enemies. His refusal to march into eastern Tennessee—an area rich with Unionist sentiment—cost him political currency. And he was strongly opposed to fighting for emancipation. When Confederate general Braxton Bragg marched into Kentucky in August 1862, Buell withdrew to Louisville without orders, ceding central Tennessee and much of Kentucky to the Confederates. Lincoln decided to fire Buell, replacing him with General George Thomas. But Buell was already preparing to fight Bragg and the indecisive battle of Perryville on October 8 temporarily saved Buell's job.

But to Lincoln's disappointment, Buell did not attack the retreating Bragg and was satisfied merely to follow him. And with elections just weeks away and General George McClellan demonstrating dilatory conduct as well, Lincoln needed to act. "If we are beaten in this State two weeks hence, it will be because McClellan & Buell won't fight," an Illinois Republican friend wrote Lincoln. Ohio congressman Samuel Shellabarger was up for reelection and wrote Lincoln that he prayed, "as your country does, [for] the removal of Buell." On this day Lincoln removed Buell from command and on October 30 General William Rosecrans took over. Buell was never given a command again.

OCTOBER 25

The Couchant Lion

On this day in 1862, Lincoln sent General George McClellan what became a famous rebuke.

It had been a month since the battle of Antietam and three weeks since Lincoln had ordered McClellan to attack the enemy. McClellan began making excuses for his inaction. "Are you not over-cautious when you assume that you can not do what the enemy is constantly doing?" Lincoln wrote McClellan on October 13. "[You claim] you can not subsist your army at Winchester unless the Railroad from Harpers Ferry to that point be put in working order. But the enemy does now subsist his army at Winchester. . . . He now wagons from Culpeper C[ourt] H[ouse] which is just about twice as far as you would have to do from Harpers Ferry."

Still McClellan did not attack. "Our war on rebellion languishes," wrote George Templeton Strong. "McClellan's repose is doubtless majestic, but if couchant lion postpones his spring too long, people will begin wondering whether he is not a stuffed specimen after all." Lincoln's secretary John Hay wrote that Lincoln's promptings amounted to "poking sharp sticks under little Mac's ribs."

Then, in mid-October, Confederate general J. E. B. Stuart rode around McClellan's army, destroying property in Maryland and Pennsylvania and returned unscathed. Early on this day McClellan passed on a report that half his cavalry horses were "broken down from fatigue." Lincoln exploded, "Will you pardon me for asking what the horses of your army have done since the battle of Antietam that fatigue anything?" Lincoln later pointed out that Stuart's cavalry, far more deprived than McClellan's, had run a literal circle around McClellan's army. "To be told after more than five weeks of total inaction of the Army . . . that the cavalry were too much fatigued to move, presented a very cheerless, almost hopeless prospect for the future," Lincoln wrote.

OCTOBER 26

Lincoln's Purpose

On this Sunday in 1862, Lincoln met with noted Quaker Eliza Gurney and revealed to her his growing belief that God was using him for a purpose.

Pinpointing what Lincoln believed about his Creator has always been problematic for historians. As a young man he went from skeptic to a more mechanistic belief in the "Doctrine of Necessity," basically a "power" which impels the "human mind" into action, but over "which the mind itself has no power." Later in life he considered that "power" to be God. One of Lincoln's favorite Shakespearean quotes was from *Hamlet:* "There's a divinity that shapes our ends, rough-hew them how we will."

As president, Lincoln referred to himself as an "instrument of Providence." But what purpose did God intend? Sometime while musing this—probably in the fall of 1862—Lincoln wrote to himself:

> In great contests each party claims to act in accordance with the will of God. Both may be, and one must be wrong. God can not be for, and against the same thing at the same time. In the present civil war it is possible that God's purpose is something different from the purpose of either party.

When Gurney visited Lincoln on this day, the president admitted, "If I had been allowed my way this war would have been ended before this, but we find it still continues; and we must believe that He [God] permits it for some wise purpose of his own, mysterious and unknown to us." Toward the end of his life, Lincoln began to see God's purpose as retribution. In his elegant Second Inaugural Address, he believed that God permitted the war to continue until "every drop of blood drawn by the lash shall be paid by another drawn with the sword."

NOVEMBER 5

"Hard, Tough Fighting"

After months of excuses for inactivity of the army; after a failed Peninsula Campaign; after failing to follow up a marginal victory at Antietam, Lincoln finally fired McClellan on this day in 1862.

Just a few days before, a small delegation of women from the Sanitary Commission visited the president asking for a word of encouragement. "I have no encouragement to give," Lincoln said. After a pause, he added, "General McClellan thinks he is going to whip the rebels by strategy, and the army has got the same notion. They have no idea that the war is to be carried on and put through by hard, tough fighting." The press, Radical Republicans, and a majority of Lincoln's cabinet were pressuring him to fire McClellan. Lincoln told a friend that with McClellan "he had tried long enough to bore with auger too dull to take hold." Lincoln, however, wanted to wait until after the November midterm elections.

A day after the elections, Lincoln wrote on this Wednesday, "By direction of the President, it is ordered that Major General McClellan be relieved from the command of the Army of the Potomac; and that Major General [Ambrose] Burnside take command of that Army." Burnside had twice before refused to take McClellan's command. Burnside firmly believed he was not equipped to lead an entire army. But Burnside also may have felt some loyalty to McClellan, who had rescued Burnside from bankruptcy in 1857. In the event Burnside refused again, Lincoln instructed the courier to tell Burnside that General Joe Hooker would be given the command. Burnside detested Hooker. Burnside personally took the orders of dismissal to McClellan. "Poor Burn[side] feels dreadfully, almost crazy," McClellan wrote his wife. "Of course I was much surprised . . . [but] not a muscle quivered nor was the slightest expression of feeling visible on my face."

NOVEMBER 7

Ellet's Rams

While the Navy Department initially disdained the idea of rams, Lincoln gave overall command of the ram fleet to it on this Friday in 1862.

Charles Ellet, a civil engineer, had been enthralled with the concept of rams. Rams were boats with reinforced bows used to ram enemy ships and had been around for centuries, primarily with oared vessels. Sailing ships were too slow to be effective rams, but steam-powered ships revived their use. Ellet, however, could not convince the Navy Department of their usefulness. It was the War Department that became Ellet's patron after the March 9, 1862 battle between the ironclads *Monitor* and the *Merrimack* (*Virginia*), when the Confederate craft dealt the *Monitor* considerable damage with a reinforced prow. Ellet was commissioned an army colonel and assigned to build a ram fleet to augment the Western Gunboat Flotilla.

Using side-wheel "palace" boats and stern-wheelers, Ellet reinforced the bows of nine ships. Initially they were unarmed to keep their weight down and their speed up (ten to twelve knots). They were first used in the June 6, 1862 attack on Memphis, Tennessee. Eight makeshift Confederate boats faced off with five Union gunboats and four of Ellet's rams. By the end of the battle, three rebel ships were destroyed and four captured, with only minor damage to one of Ellet's rams. Ellet, however, was wounded and died two weeks later.

Charles's brother Alfred took over the fleet and was commissioned a general. That fall Congress ordered all river war vessels transferred to the Navy Department, but Lincoln met with General Ellet, Secretary of War Edwin Stanton, Secretary of the Navy Gideon Welles, and General in Chief Henry Halleck on this day to decide if Ellet's rams were included in that order. Welles wrote that the congressional order "greatly disturbed Stanton, who, supported by Halleck and Ellet, opposes a transfer of the ram fleet." Lincoln ruled that the rams would, indeed, join the navy. They were effectively used during the operations at Vicksburg, Mississippi.

NOVEMBER 14

A "Soldier" or a "Housekeeper"

On this Friday in 1862, Lincoln gave his approval of General Ambrose Burnside's plans to attack the Confederates.

Lincoln claimed he had chosen Burnside to replace General George McClellan at the helm of the Army of the Potomac because "he is a better housekeeper." Pennsylvania Congressman William Kelley was astonished at this statement. "You are not in search of a housekeeper or a hospital stewart, but a soldier who will fight, and fight to win," Kelley said. Within days of Burnside taking over the army on November 9, Lincoln was pressuring the general for a plan to attack Confederate general Robert E. Lee's army. Lee was spread out over the Virginia countryside with Confederate general Thomas "Stonewall" Jackson in the Shenandoah Valley and Confederate general James Longstreet at Culpeper Court House directly between Burnside and Richmond. Burnside's plan was to fool Lee into thinking he was heading straight at Longstreet, as he shifted to Falmouth to the southwest where he would cross the Rappahannock River and take the lightly defended Fredericksburg and its railhead. From there he'd attack Longstreet's 45,000 men with his 120,000 before Jackson could arrive. Once Longstreet's army was shattered, Burnside could either deal with Jackson or attack Richmond fifty miles away.

On this day, Lincoln had his general in chief, Henry Halleck, wire Burnside, "The President has just assented to your plan. He thinks it will succeed if you move rapidly; otherwise not." It was not to be. Halleck forgot to order pontoons to cross the Rappahannock and while Burnside did fool Lee and sprinted to Falmouth, he sat on the north side of the river watching Longstreet occupy Fredericksburg. A more audacious general would have improvised but Burnside decided to wait. By the time the pontoons arrived at the end of the month, Jackson was in Fredericksburg as well.

NOVEMBER 22

"*Impedimenta*"

On this day in 1862, Lincoln revealed the stress he experienced because of his generals when he uncharacteristically blasted General Nathaniel Banks for a supply requisition.

The fall of 1862 had been particularly painful for the president. He drew considerable criticism both in the East for general George McClellan's reticence to fight and in the West for general

Don Carlos Buell's delays. It cost the Republicans dearly in the November midterm elections and Lincoln replaced Buell and McClellan. Another general—Benjamin Butler—was embarrassing Lincoln with his heavy-handed administration of New Orleans. He became so hated that chamber pots appeared throughout the city with Butler's face painted at the bottom of them.

On November 9, Lincoln replaced Butler with Banks and sent Banks to Fortress Monroe for embarkation. Lincoln knew Butler's removal would draw criticism, particularly from Radical Republicans. Lincoln hoped the fact that Banks was an abolitionist and a Republican (Butler was a Democrat) would mollify them. Nevertheless he kept the change of command secret, even from his cabinet, and asked Banks to set sail for New Orleans before Congress returned from their holiday break. Then Lincoln received a requisition by Banks for supplies. "I have just been overwhelmed and confounded with the sight of a requisition . . . which . . . can not be filled and got off within an hour short of two months," he wired Banks. Lincoln insisted that Banks could not wait for supplies. Referring to other generals and their shortcomings, Lincoln added, "My dear General, this expanding, and piling up of impedimenta, has been, so far, almost our ruin, and will be our final ruin if it is not abandoned."

Banks replied that the requisition was sent in error and that he would soon be underway. On December 14, Banks took over command from Butler.

NOVEMBER 26

Missed Opportunities

On this Wednesday in 1862, Lincoln left Washington for Aquia Creek, Virginia where he consulted with General Ambrose Burnside about attacking the Confederates.

An opportunity had already been squandered when in mid-November Burnside surprised Confederate general Robert E. Lee by moving the Army of the Potomac from Manassas to Falmouth, Virginia, just across the Rappahannock River from Fredericksburg. Only a few thousand Confederates held the river crossing but Burnside was delayed because General in Chief Henry Halleck had neglected to order pontoons. By the time they arrived a week later, half of Lee's army held Fredericksburg, with the other half on its way from the Shenandoah Valley.

Worried about the situation, Lincoln made an unscheduled trip on this evening, meeting Burnside at Aquia Landing. The next morning, the general told the president that he had 110,000 men and wanted to cross the Rappahannock for a frontal assault on Lee. Lincoln proposed a counterplan where Burnside attacked in a three-pronged offensive. The north and south prongs of 25,000 men each would strike from Pamunkey and Port Royal (north and south of Fredericksburg, respectively), driving into Lee's flanks while the rest of the army attacked frontally at Fredericksburg. Burnside said that such a maneuver would delay the assault and Halleck had insisted Burnside attack immediately. Lincoln shrugged that off saying that Halleck answered to him. But when Lincoln returned to Washington, Halleck still insisted on an immediate assault and Lincoln dropped a promising plan.

Weather delayed the assault even further and it wasn't until December 10 before it began. By then, Lee was at full strength, fully entrenched, and ready for Burnside.

DECEMBER 1

The Minnesota Sioux Uprising

Lincoln, on this Monday in 1862, asked Judge Advocate General Joseph Holt for legal advice in pardoning Native Americans involved in the so-called Minnesota Sioux Indian Uprising.

The Santee Dakota, popularly called the Sioux, signed two treaties in 1851, trading twenty-four million acres of their land in exchange for yearly payments in food and annuities and a reservation on the Minnesota River. But the money and food rarely arrived on time, and the food was often spoiled. After Minnesota became a state in 1858, the government took from the Dakota over half their reservation, promising compensation. But the money never came. Wedged in among competing white settlements, the Dakota found that buffalo and other game became scarce.

By 1862, many Dakotas were starving, forced to eat their horses and dogs. In July, they were told that their yearly annuity and food would again be delayed. "If they are hungry," wrote Andrew Myrick, a white settler, "let them eat grass." On August 17, Dakota youths returning from a disappointing hunt murdered five settlers out of frustration. Dakota warriors, convinced that the whites would retaliate, decided take the offensive. On August 18 the Dakotas attacked the settlements and among the dead was Myrick, his mouth stuffed with grass. In six weeks, 150 Dakotas and more than 500 white soldiers and civilians were dead.

In October, 303 participants in the uprising were tried and sentenced to hang. Lincoln had the trial transcripts sent to him. On this day, Lincoln wrote Holt: "I wish your legal opinion if I should conclude to execute only a part of them, I must myself designate which, or could I leave the designation to some officer on the ground?" Holt recommended Lincoln grant any pardons himself. Lincoln did so on December 6.

DECEMBER 6

Mercy

Lincoln, on this Saturday in 1862, granted a reprieve to nearly three hundred Native Americans scheduled to be executed on December 19.

For three weeks the previous fall, the Santee Dakota rebelled against the government, resulting in the death of 650 people. Some three hundred Dakotas were tried and sentenced to hang. After Henry Whipple, Episcopal Bishop of Minnesota, appealed to the president for mercy, Lincoln asked for the trial transcripts. He found that many of the prisoners were convicted merely for being present at one of the four battles between the Dakota and the army. Over the objections of the Minnesota governor, Alexander Ramsey, Lincoln reduced the number of condemned to thirty-nine prisoners convicted of murder and/or rape. To avoid mistakes, Lincoln, on this day, carefully wrote out the names ("Te-he-hdo-ne-cha" and "Hin-han-shoon-ko-yag") of those to remain condemned and provided their case numbers to the general—Henry Sibley—in charge of the prisoners. He added, "The other condemned prisoners you will hold subject to further orders, taking care that they neither escape, nor are subjected to any unlawful violence."

Despite precautions, Lincoln still worried about mistakes and on December 9 had his secretary John Hay write Sibley to warn of the similarities in names of Chaskay-tay—one of the men to be executed—and Chas-Kay-don (a.k.a. Robert Hopkins) who had protected a white family from harm. There were several instances of Dakotas shielding white civilians during the uprising. A Dakota chief named Anpetu-Tokeca (a.k.a John Otherday) rescued sixty-two missionaries and traders.

Thirty-eight prisoners (one had his death sentence commuted because he testified against the others) were hanged simultaneously at Mankato, Minnesota on December 26. It was the largest mass execution in U.S. history.

#44

Lincoln and Native Americans

Some 20,000 American Indians served in the Civil War, roughly 10,000 on each side. The Confederacy was first to enlist their help, sending Albert Pike to the Indian Territory (west of Arkansas and north of the Red River) to negotiate treaties in 1861 with Cherokees, Creeks, Seminoles, Chickasaws, and Choctaws. One Cherokee—Stand Watie—became a Confederate general, the only Native American on either side to attain that rank. The Union was initially reluctant to arm Indians, but that changed by 1862. Colonel Ely Parker, a Tonawanda Seneca chief, served on General Ulysses Grant's staff and handwrote the official surrender that Confederate general Robert E. Lee signed at Appomattox Court House in Virginia.

During the war, Lincoln left Indian affairs to his secretaries of the interior: Caleb Smith and, after January 1863, John Usher. Nor did Lincoln have much pre-war contact with Native Americans. At age twenty-three, Lincoln enlisted to fight in the Black Hawk War, an Indian uprising. The uprising was over before he and his men arrived at the scene. He did, however, protect an elderly Native American who had stumbled into his camp. Lincoln's men thought the old man was a spy and Lincoln intervened before they could kill him.

In the first year of his presidency, he was visited at the White House by a handful of chiefs. Lincoln used "Indian talk" to communicate: "Where live now?" and "When go back Iowa?" Two years later, in March 1863, Lincoln spoke a little plainer to a group of chiefs, although still with naivete. When asked how the two races differed, Lincoln said, "although we are now engaged in a great war betw[...] one another, we are not, as a race, so m[uc]h dispo[...] fight and kill one another as our red brethre[n.]"

DECEMBER 11

Resolution

On this Thursday in 1861, Li[...] from the Senate asking for det[...]

Starvation prompted hu[...] to attack nearby white s[...] 650 were dead and o[...]

During Lincol[...] basically reque[...] to joint res[...] from report[...] between foreig[...] at hand, asked the [...] December 5, the Sena[...] in his possession touching[...] Minnesota."

On this day, Lincoln forwar[...] outlined why he had pardoned so m[...] with so much clemency as to encourag[...] hand, nor with so much severity as to be [...] caused a careful examination of the records o[...] He found two of the accused had been "prove[...] females." Forty more—which included the previous[...] been involved in "massacres as distinguished from p[...] battles." One of the forty—O-Ta-kla—supplied informa[...] court and was rewarded with commutation of his sentence[...] years imprisonment." The other thirty-nine were hanged.

Nothing came of the supposed peace effort. Nor would it be the last time Wood called for a negotiated peace. In late 1863, he met with Lincoln, asking that he lead a committee to Richmond to parlay a cease-fire. Again, nothing came of the effort.

DECEMBER 14

Fredericksburg

On this Sunday in 1862, Lincoln received word that Ambrose Burnside was beaten at the Battle of Frede[...] Virginia.

Before the battle, Burnside divided up his army into Divisions, headed by Generals William Franklin, E[...] and Joe Hooker. Franklin's division would be the ma[...] of Fredericksburg against Confederate general T[...] wall" Jackson's corps. Once Franklin pushed Jacks[...] head north, rolling up the flank of the strong def[...] Marye's Heights, just west of town. Supported [...] had the unenviable job of keeping the Confed[...] marched through Fredericksburg and uphi[...] under Confederate fire.

It was a foggy morning on December 13[...] delaying Franklin's assault. Franklin's di[...] budged Jackson's forces, much less ro[...] Sumner's and Hooker's forces were ma[...] erate defenses. The Union suffered ov[...] to 4,200 for the rebels. Confederate[...] watching the carnage, said "it is we[...] [...]ould grow too fond of it." [...] full day Lincoln heard li[...] Herman Haup[...] [...]d his

order Burnside to withdraw. "If such orders are issued, you must issue them yourself," Halleck responded. "I hold that a general in command of an army in the field is the best judge of existing conditions." Lincoln reluctantly agreed.

The next day, Lincoln interviewed Pennsylvania governor Andrew Curtin, who had just returned from Fredericksburg. "Well, Governor, so you have been down to the battlefield?" Lincoln asked. "Battlefied? Slaughter-pen! It was a terrible slaughter, Mr. Lincoln," Curtin responded.

DECEMBER 17

"Lincoln's Evil Genius"

On this Wednesday in 1862, Lincoln arranged a meeting for the next evening with members of a Republican caucus looking to remove Secretary of State William Seward.

In the aftermath of the November midterm elections—in which Republicans lost key congressional seats—and the debacle at the battle of Fredericksburg, Lincoln's party looked for a scapegoat. On December 16, Republican senators met and formed an informal caucus. They knew they could not directly attack a president with more than half his term in front of him, so they focused on his cabinet. Iowa Senator James Grimes claimed Lincoln was a "tow string of a President" whose backbone needed to be shored up "with strong, sturdy rods in the shape of cabinet ministers."

The senators perceived friction within the cabinet and focused on Seward as the source. Citing Lincoln's and Seward's close friendship, the Republicans saw the secretary as a "paralyzing influence" on the president. Josh Medill of the *Chicago Tribune* called Seward "Lincoln's evil genius. He [Seward] has been President *de facto*, and has kept a sponge saturated with chloroform to Uncle Abe's nose."

The caucus reached an impasse and a unanimous vote of "a want of confidence" in Seward was stymied. The meeting was adjourned. That night New York senator Preston King told Seward of the caucus. "They may do as they please about me, but they shall not put the President in a false position on my account," the secretary said, and immediately wrote out his resignation. When Lincoln received it, he was surprised: "What does this mean?"

When the caucus met again on this day, they decided they'd force Lincoln to remove Seward. When Lincoln heard, he scheduled a meeting for the next evening, December 18. It would be a showdown between the executive and congressional branches of government.

#45

The Cabinet Crisis

What came to be known as the cabinet crisis of 1862 was largely instigated by the ambitions of Salmon Chase, Lincoln's secretary of the treasury. Chase had been feeding fellow Radical Republicans reports of how disorganized Lincoln's cabinet meetings were. He claimed that "no reports are made; no regular discussions held; no ascertained conclusions reached" and said there was "no cabinet except in name." Chase claimed that the conservative William Seward, secretary of state, "overruled all the decisions of the cabinet."

Just before meeting the caucus on the evening of December 18, 1862, Lincoln pondered what they might want. "They wish to get rid of me, and I am sometimes half disposed to gratify them," Lincoln said. When the caucus arrived, they complained that the problems with the war were the result of Seward's interference in other departments. Lincoln scheduled another meeting for the next evening.

Much to the consternation of Chase and the caucus, Lincoln had his cabinet present when they met again. The president opened the meeting by reading the caucus's complaints and admitted he was not "very regular in consulting the cabinet as a whole" but "was not aware of any divisions or want of unity." He then asked each of the cabinet secretaries if they felt different. All agreed until they came to Chase. The treasury secretary was caught in a trap: If he were the lone dissenter, he would be revealed as the source of the caucus's complaints; if he agreed with the cabinet, he would appear duplicitous to the caucus. In the end he sided with the rest of the cabinet. The caucus left the meeting embarrassed and angry with Chase. Seward would remain in the cabinet.

DECEMBER 20

Cutting the Gordian Knot

Lincoln, on this Saturday in 1862, denied not one but three resignations from his department chiefs.

The cabinet crisis of 1862 began on December 16 when a caucus of Republican senators—fed information by Secretary of the Treasury Salmon Chase—looked for a scapegoat for the dismal war effort and fixed their sights on the conservative secretary of state, William Seward. When Seward heard of the caucus that evening, he submitted his resignation immediately. Lincoln held on to it.

Though the Republican caucus was outmaneuvered by Lincoln, its members were aware that Seward had submitted his resignation. In order to placate them, Lincoln might have been forced to accept it. On this day, the treasury secretary admitted that out of his embarrassment, he had prepared his resignation. "Let me have it," Lincoln snapped and Chase reluctantly handed it over. "This cuts the Gordian knot . . . I can dispose of this subject now," Lincoln said, aware that the caucus could not now force Seward out without losing Chase as well. Secretary of War Edwin Stanton, who was also present, offered his own resignation. "I don't want yours," Lincoln said. He also refused to accept Seward's and Chase's resignations. Recalling how he learned to carry pumpkins while riding horseback, he said, "I can ride on now. I've got a pumpkin in each end of my [saddle]bag."

DECEMBER 29

Cabinet Meetings

In the aftermath of the cabinet crisis ten days before, when Lincoln drew criticism for not consulting his department heads, he, on this Monday in 1862, took pains to discuss his Emancipation Proclamation with his cabinet.

In their effort to oust William Seward, the more conservative secretary of state, Republican senators had accused Lincoln of neglecting to hold regular meetings or organized discussions with his cabinet. It was a blatant effort by the legislative branch to interfere with the executive. Nevertheless, their claims of Lincoln's lack of formality in cabinet meetings had a ring of truth.

Supposedly the cabinet was to meet twice a week, but, as Secretary of the Navy Gideon Welles complained, meetings were "infrequent" and "irregular." Secretary of the Treasury Salmon Chase complained there were no agendas and usually no discussions among the department heads when they did meet. Lincoln was observed to sit with his feet on the table and Secretary of War Edwin Stanton complained that Lincoln sometimes opened meetings by reading a humorous anecdote. Secretary of the Interior Caleb Smith complained that

Lincoln sometimes made decisions without seeking their counsel, as he did when he decided to issue his preliminary Emancipation Proclamation.

On this day, Lincoln read his Emancipation Proclamation to his cabinet and the next day asked his department heads to submit in writing suggestions for altering the wording of the proclamation. When he received them on New Year's Eve, he made a point of using some of their suggestions.

DECEMBER 30

"You Fail Me"

Lincoln, on this Tuesday in 1862, wired General Ambrose Burnside, "I have good reason for saying you must not make a general movement of the army without letting me know."

After the Battle of Fredericksburg, Virginia, Burnside lost the confidence of his subordinate generals. Two of those generals appeared unexpectedly in Lincoln's office on this day. Generals John Cochrane and John Newton had come to warn Lincoln that Burnside was attempting to attack the Confederates again at Fredericksburg and they believed this time he would destroy the Army of the Potomac. Lincoln suspected their real intent was to reinstate General George McClellan, Burnside's predecessor, but he wired Burnside to stop his movement anyway.

Burnside cancelled the offensive and on New Year's Eve appeared in Lincoln's office to defend his plan. Lincoln warned Burnside that his subordinates did not trust him. On New Year's Day, Burnside handed Lincoln his resignation. Lincoln tried to show Burnside's plan to his general in chief, Henry Halleck, and asked for an opinion. Halleck refused to look at it, saying "that a General in command of an army in the field is the best judge of existing condition." Lincoln then ordered Halleck to go to Falmouth—Burnside's headquarters—and examine the field, then provide an opinion. "If in such difficulty as this you do not help, you fail me precisely in the point for which I sought your assistance," Lincoln wrote Halleck. "Your military skill is useless to me, if you will not do this." Halleck offered his resignation and Lincoln was forced to rescind his order, writing on it "withdrawn, because considered harsh by Gen. Halleck."

In the weeks ahead, Burnside would try to court-martial Cochran and Newton and would twice more offer to resign. The second time it would be accepted. General Ulysses Grant would replace Halleck just over a year later.

DECEMBER 31

The Evolving Proclamation

Lincoln, on this New Year's Eve 1862, received written recommendations from his department heads on the final version of his Emancipation Proclamation.

When Lincoln first showed his cabinet his preliminary proclamation on July 22, the document freed all slaves of masters still in rebellion. Secretary of the Treasury Salmon Chase recorded in his diary, "The question of arming slaves was then brought up and I advocated it warmly. The President was unwilling to adopt this measure." While Lincoln said he did not seek advice from his secretaries, he did agree to Secretary of State William Seward's suggestion that they wait to issue the proclamation until after the Union had a military victory.

For two full months Lincoln waited until the Battle of Antietam (September 17) gave him that victory. The proclamation had grown in length by then, specifying what was meant by a rebellious state. Before issuing it on September 22, Lincoln made syntax changes to his draft as suggested by Seward and Chase.

The final proclamation—issued on January 1, 1863—differed from the September 22 document in significant ways. First, it explicitly listed the states considered in rebellion. The greatest difference, however, was the clause that read, "such persons [ex-slaves] . . . will be received into the armed service." Again he accepted syntax suggestions from Seward but he also accepted the addition of an invocation from Chase: "And upon this act, sincerely believed to be an act of justice warranted by the Constitution . . . I invoke the considerate judgment of Mankind and the gracious favor of Almighty God."

1863

"THAT WE ARE HIGHLY RESOLVED THAT THESE DEAD SHALL NOT HAVE DIED IN VAIN—THAT THIS NATION, UNDER GOD, SHALL HAVE A NEW BIRTH OF FREEDOM—AND THAT GOVERNMENT OF THE PEOPLE, BY THE PEOPLE, FOR THE PEOPLE, SHALL NOT PERISH FROM THE EARTH."
—ABRAHAM LINCOLN

JANUARY 1

The Emancipation Proclamation

The first day of the year was a dark anniversary for Lincoln. "That fatal first," he called it. It wasn't until this day in 1863 that Lincoln gave New Year's a happier significance when he signed his Emancipation Proclamation, freeing slaves owned by rebels.

It was in or around New Year's 1841 that Lincoln broke off his engagement to Mary Todd, and afterward his best friend, Joshua Speed, moved back home to Kentucky. As a result Lincoln fell into a depression—he called it his "hypo"—that lasted nearly a year. According to Speed, Lincoln even considered suicide and lamented to his friend that he'd "done nothing to make any human being remember that he had lived." He and Mary eventually reconciled and Speed remained a lifelong friend.

Twenty-two years later, Lincoln rose early this brisk Thursday and sent the proclamation to the State Department for its official calligraphy. The rest of the morning he attended a New Year's Day reception. That afternoon, Secretary of State William Seward presented Lincoln with the proclamation rolled into a scroll. "I never in my life felt more certain that I was doing right, than I do in signing this paper," Lincoln said. "If my name ever goes into history it will be for this act, and my whole soul is in it." He observed his hand was stiff and trembling from shaking hands all morning. "Now this signature is one that will be closely examined, and if they find my hand trembled, they will say 'he had some compunctions.'" He then signed it firmly.

In a conversation with Speed around this time, Lincoln was reminded of his desire to be remembered all those years before. He said, "I believe that in this measure [the proclamation] my fondest hope will be realized."

JANUARY 4

Anti-Semitism

On this day in 1863, Lincoln ordered his general in chief, Henry Halleck, to revoke General Ulysses S. Grant's controversial General Order No. 11 expelling Jews from his entire Department of the Tennessee (which included what the Union held of that state).

Trading between the Union and the Confederacy was, of course, illegal. But cotton trading and speculation were particularly lucrative in Memphis and western Tennessee. "I will venture that no honest man has made money in West Tennessee in the last year, whilst many fortunes have been made during that time," Grant said. What infuriated him more was that the Confederates would use the gold they traded for their cotton to purchase guns—guns his men would eventually face. Grant issued a number of regulations to stem the tide, but to no avail. And when Grant found that a few of the speculators were Jews, anti-Semitism raised its ugly head. In December 1862, he issued an order to expel "Jews, as a class" from Tennessee. Though the order was never fully implemented before it was revoked, it haunted Grant politically for years, even as he made his own bid for the White House.

Halleck, in a January 21 letter endorsed by Lincoln, explained, "The President has no objection to your expelling traitors and Jew peddlers," but the president did object to an indictment of "an entire religious class, some of whom are fighting in our ranks."

JANUARY 5

A Bright Moment in a Dark Year

Militarily, 1862 had been a disappointment for the Union, General George B. McClellan's reversals in his Peninsula Campaign; John Pope's rout at Second Manassas; Ambrose Burnside's debacle at Fredericksburg. Even Union victories such as Shiloh and Antietam were tempered by extremely heavy casualties and lost opportunities. On this Monday in 1863, Lincoln, however, received some welcome news; General William Rosecrans reported that his Army of the Cumberland had beaten Braxton Bragg's Confederate army at Murfreesboro (Stones River), Tennessee. Lincoln responded to Rosecrans's dispatch with a gush of congratulations: "God bless you, and all with you! Please tender to all and accept for yourself, the Nation's gratitude for yours, and their, skill, endurance, and dauntless courage."

The battle had begun the previous Christmas when Rosecrans's 47,000 men moved on Bragg's 38,000 men, entrenched northwest of town. On December 29, Rosecrans encamped so close to the Confederates that both armies jointly sang "Home Sweet Home" during the cold, lonely night. On the last day of the year, Bragg took the offensive, nearly bending Rosecrans's army in two. As the two armies rested for a day, Rosecrans fortified his positions so that when Bragg renewed his attack on January 2, he was beaten back. While the Union victory was marginal and Union casualties were greater than the Confederates', Bragg did surrender the field, giving Rosecrans a strategic victory.

Ever afterward, Lincoln was grateful to Rosecrans. More than eight months later, Lincoln wrote Rosecrans, "I can never forget, whilst I remember anything, that about the end of last year, and beginning of this, you gave us a hard earned victory which, had there been a defeat instead, the nation could scarcely have lived over."

JANUARY 8

Lincoln Refuses a Resignation

On this Thursday in 1863, Lincoln responded to the resignation submitted by General Ambrose Burnside, "I do not yet see how I could profit by changing the command of the AP [Army of the Potomac] and if I did, I should not wish to do it by accepting the resignation of your commission."

Just two weeks before Christmas 1862, Burnside sent his Army of the Potomac in a frontal attack against Confederate general Robert E. Lee's well-entrenched Army of Northern Virginia at Fredericksburg, Virginia. Burnside's men never came close to dislodging the Confederates from their lines, and suffered more than 12,600 casualties while the Confederates had barely 5,000. It was the most lopsided major battle of the war and Burnside was still stinging from it in January when he planned another attack, this one against Lee's left flank. When the plan was loudly criticized by his subordinate generals, among them General Joseph Hooker, Burnside tendered his resignation not once but twice in a week.

More than a week later Burnside attempted his flanking movement but it was foiled by rain. "The whole country is an ocean of mud," one soldier wrote. "The roads were a deep mire, and the heavy rain had made the ground a vast mortar bed." Eventually Burnside gave up trudging his men through the sticky Virginia mire without ever engaging the enemy. The pathetic enterprise was dubbed the "Mud March" and ultimately would lead to Burnside's removal. Burnside would be replaced by Hooker, who would himself use a similar plan—the very plan he criticized—at another Union rout known as the Battle of Chancellorsville.

#46

Resignations

In the turmoil of war, disagreements abound, but Lincoln spent an inordinate amount of time accepting or denying resignations because of those conflicts. During the first week of January 1863, Army of the Potomac general Ambrose Burnside twice tendered his resignation over criticism by his subordinates. General in Chief Henry Halleck offered to resign as well. Later in the year, Burnside offered to quit a third time as head of the Department of the Ohio. Burnside's successor, General Joe Hooker, offered to resign at least once, as did his successor General George Meade. Hooker's was accepted; Meade's was not. General John Fremont asked to be relieved of command after his assignment came under a commander he detested, and George McClellan would have had their resignations accepted because of political and ideological conflicts with the president.

Lincoln had problems with his cabinet as well. Secretary of State William Seward tried to withdraw from the cabinet two days before Lincoln's first inauguration and tendered his resignation again less than two years later. Secretary of the Treasury Salmon Chase offered his resignation no less than four times in eighteen months and the final time it was accepted. Montgomery Blair offered to relinquish his position as Postmaster General and, while it was refused, he was later asked to resign. Secretary of War Edwin Stanton offered to resign at least once and his predecessor Simon Cameron was asked to resign.

Three more cabinet members would quit their posts for various reasons: Secretary of the Treasury William Fessenden (reelected to Senate); Attorney General Edward Bates (poor health); and Secretary of the Interior Caleb Blood Smith (poor health).

JANUARY 14

Arming Black Soldiers

Two weeks after his Emancipation Proclamation made it legal to arm blacks, Lincoln, on this Wednesday in 1863, wrote John A. Dix, commander of Yorktown and Fortress Monroe, and asked if "colored troops" could be garrisoned under his command. The next day Lincoln discovered how much racism and resistance to black soldiers he'd find in the army, for Dix replied that he did not think that such an important post should "be confided to any other class than the white population." Dix added, "Prudence would, at least, dictate that the inferior element in the Military organization should be incorporated in very small proportion, and employed in Services of secondary importance."

Lincoln, himself, had been slow to convert to the idea of arming blacks. He insisted that enlisting them "would produce dangerous and fatal dissatisfactions in our army" and "half the Army would lay down their arms and three other States would join the rebellion." At another time he said, "There are now twenty thousand of our muskets on the shoulders of Kentuckians, who are bravely fighting our battles. Every one of them will be thrown down or carried over to the rebels."

Even after Lincoln wrote his preliminary Emancipation Proclamation in the summer of 1862, he resisted the notion of enlisting blacks. Yet the horrific casualties the Union suffered in 1862 not only depleted its fighting force but stifled enlistments. Lincoln needed more men. Under intense pressure from his party, Lincoln relented. The final proclamation allowed emancipated slaves to enlist, although their roles would be only "to garrison and defend forts, positions, stations and other places, and to man vessels of all sorts."

Undeterred by Dix's refusal, Lincoln continued looking for ways black soldiers could contribute to the war. By war's end 186,000 blacks served in the Army and Navy, a large portion of whom would see combat.

JANUARY 18

Churches

On this Sunday, in 1863, Lincoln visited the Foundry United Methodist Church (on G and Fourteenth streets) where he contributed $150 and was named "Life Director of the Parent Society."

Early in life, Lincoln became disillusioned with organized religion. Even after they married and bore two sons, the Lincolns did not regularly attend a church. After their son Eddie's death in 1850, the grieving parents were so touched by the counsel of Dr. James Smith, pastor of Springfield's First Presbyterian Church, that they rented a pew at his church. According to friends, however, Lincoln was an infrequent attendee, preferring to spend Sundays at home.

As president, Lincoln rented a pew at the New York Avenue Presbyterian Church (the "Lincoln Pew" is still there, though in a completely new building). It was here, during the Peninsula Campaign, that the church's pastor—Dr. Phineas Gurley—announced that "religious services would be suspended until further notice as the church was needed as a [military] hospital." Lincoln stood up and said, "Dr. Gurley, this action was taken without my consent, and I hereby countermand the order. The churches are needed as never before for divine services." Apparently Lincoln's countermand did not pertain to other churches because that same month the Epiphany Church just a block away was converted into a hospital.

Lincoln never joined any church. When asked why, he said, "Because I have found difficulty, without mental reservation, in giving my assent to their long and complicated confessions of faith. When any church will inscribe over its altar the Savior's condensed statement of law and gospel, 'Thou shalt love the Lord thy God with all thy heart and with all thy soul and with all thy mind, and love thy neighbor as thyself,' that church will I join with all my heart."

JANUARY 19

"*The Sleeping Sentinel*"

On this Monday afternoon in 1863, orator J. E. Murdoch held a private reading of patriotic poetry for the Lincolns at the White House, in which one poem was about the president.

Lincoln loved poetry and would often spontaneously recite one to himself quietly or loudly to his friends. In fact, he recited his favorite poem—"Mortality," or "Oh Why Should the Spirit of Mortal be Proud?" by Scottish poet William Knox—so often that many thought he wrote it. Lincoln was drawn to morbid verse. When he wrote poetry, it was often about death and fleeting mortality.

One of the poems Murdoch read on this day was a poem by Francis De Haes Janvier called "The Sleeping Sentinel," inspired by actual events. William Scott was a private in Company H of the Third Vermont Volunteers, stationed near the Chain Bridge, just outside Washington, in the fall of 1861. Scott fell asleep on guard duty and was convicted and sentenced to execution. According to a popular legend, Lincoln was so touched by the boy's story that he rode out to Camp Advance and pardoned him on the spot. Janiver's poetic version reads:

The pardoned soldier understood
The tones of jubilee,
And, bounding from his fetters,
Blessed the hand that made him free!

The young man promised the president that he'd prove worthy of his pardon, rejoined his Vermont unit, and in the midst of battle he was mortally wounded,

While yet his voice grew tremulous,
And death bedimmed his eye—
He called his comrades to attest
He had not feared to die!
And, in his last expiring breath,
A prayer to heaven was sent,
That God, with his unfailing grace,
Would bless our President!

Whether Lincoln actually rode out to Camp Advance is still debated, but Lincoln did, indeed, pardon Scott and Scott subsequently died on April 16, 1862 at the Battle of Lee's Mills.

#47

Childhood Home

We know of only one time—in the fall of 1844—that Lincoln returned to his old southern Indiana home, where he was raised and where his mother and sister were buried. Lincoln rarely spoke of his childhood in Little Pigeon Creek, preferring to forget his crude log cabin existence there, detesting every minute he had spent working its fields, chopping down its trees, and splitting its fence rails.

But when he returned after a decade and a half, nostalgia softened his memories. He described Little Pigeon Creek "as unpoetical as any spot of the earth; but still, seeing it and its objects and inhabitants aroused feelings in me which were certainly poetry." He penned a poem titled "My Childhood-Home I see Again":

My childhood-home I see again,
And gladden with the view;
And still as memories crowd my brain,
There's sadness in it too.

O Memory! thou midway world
'Twixt earth and paradise,
Where things decayed and loved ones lost
in dreamy shadows rise.

The poem ends:

Near twenty years have passed away
since here I bid farewell
To woods and fields, and scenes of play,
and playmates loved so well . . . .

The friends I left that parting day,
how changed, as time has sped!
Young childhood grown, strong manhood gray,
and half of all are dead.

I hear the loved survivors tell
how naught from death could save,
Till every sound appears a knell,
and every spot a grave.

I range the fields with pensive tread,
and pace the hollow rooms,
And feel (companion of the dead)
I'm living in the tombs.

JANUARY 21

Too Close to McClellan

On this day in 1863, a great miscarriage of justice was perpetrated when Lincoln—never a good judge of military character—cashiered out of the army one of his best corps commanders, General Fitz John Porter.

Porter, part of a fine military family, was an excellent general himself. During the Peninsula Campaign, Porter's Corps performed some of the war's finest defensive fighting at Mechanicsville, Gaines' Mill, and Malvern Hill. When the campaign was judged a failure in Washington, Porter's Fifth Corps was transferred from General George McClellan's Army of the Potomac to General John Pope's Army of Virginia, despite Porter's vocal admiration of McClellan and loathing of Pope.

Porter reported to Pope for duty just as Confederate general Robert E. Lee attacked Pope's army. Pope gave Porter conflicting and confusing orders during the battle, impossible to follow. He even gave Porter some ambiguous latitude when he ended one command with, "If any considerable advantages are to be gained by departing from this order it will not be strictly carried out."

When Pope was ultimately humiliated at Second Bull Run, Porter became the scapegoat. Porter was charged with disloyalty, disobedience, and misconduct in the face of the enemy and was relieved of duty the same day as McClellan. Porter was tried on flimsy evidence that included defective maps, perjured testimony, and his unwise statements about Pope. When he was found guilty, Lincoln signed his expulsion from the Army on this day. "The most magnificent soldier in the Army of the Potomac, ruined by his devotion to McClellan," John Hay, Lincoln's secretary, lamented.

It would take sixteen years for Porter to be exonerated and twenty-three years before he was reinstated in the army as a colonel.

JANUARY 22

Political Generals

On this Thursday in 1863, Lincoln advised one of his troublesome generals to keep his mouth shut.

The Union army had more than its share of political generals whose ranks were given not for experience or military prowess, but political expediency. Too often they became a liability. "It seems but little better than murder to give important commands to such men," General in Chief Henry Halleck wrote. One such man was John McClernand.

In many ways, McClernand's history paralleled Lincoln's. He was born in Kentucky, moved to Illinois, was mostly self-educated, was admitted to the bar, served in the brief Black Hawk War, and then as a Congressman. Though he had virtually no military experience,

Lincoln named McClernand a brigadier general, because he needed the loyalty of southern Illinois Democrats.

In the fall of 1862, while Generals Ulysses Grant and William Sherman were moving on Vicksburg, Mississippi, McClernand convinced Lincoln that he could recruit his own army. He sent recruits to Memphis, Tennessee to build his so-called Mississippi River Expedition and when Grant heard of it, he, with Halleck's permission, sent them south to be commanded by Sherman instead. McClernand complained of a West Point conspiracy (Grant, Halleck, and Sherman were West Pointers) and accused Halleck, his superior, of gross "incompetency." "Let me beseech you to dismiss him," McClernand wrote Lincoln, "and take upon yourself the exercise of his functions."

Lincoln, however, upheld Halleck and Grant, and, on this day, wrote McClernand, "I have too many family controversies, (so to speak) already on my hands . . . [to] take up another. You are now doing well . . . Allow me to beg, that for your sake, for my sake, and for the country's sake, you give up your whole attention to the better work." Less than five months later, Grant would relieve McClernand from command.

JANUARY 25

Hooker Replaces Burnside

General Ambrose Burnside, head of the Army of the Potomac, at 10:00 AM this Sunday in 1863, conferred with Lincoln over the insubordination of Burnside's corps commanders. Burnside's disaster at Fredericksburg in December and ill-advised "Mud March" the week before had drawn considerable criticism from many of his generals, and he asked Lincoln if he could fire them. Instead, Lincoln sacked Burnside and replaced him with one of Burnside's most vocal critics. General Joseph "Fighting Joe"

Hooker became the third general to head the Army of the Potomac in its seventeen months of existence.

Mindful of Hooker's acidic insubordination, Lincoln sent for him and the next day handed Hooker a letter, which read: "You are ambitious, which, within reasonable bounds, does good rather than harm. But I think that during Gen. Burnside's command . . . you have taken counsel of your ambition, and thwarted him as much as you could, in which you did a great wrong to the country, and to a most meritorious and honorable brother officer."

Lincoln was also aware of Hooker's insubordination to his commander in chief, "I have heard . . . of your recently saying that both the Army and the Government needed a Dictator. Of course it was not for this, but in spite of it, that I have given you the command. Only those generals who gain successes, can set up dictators. What I now ask of you is military success, and I will risk the dictatorship." Lincoln ended the letter with, "go forward, and give us victories." In this, Hooker would be just as disappointing as Burnside.

FEBRUARY 13

Lincoln Meets Tom Thumb

Nearly a year after Willie's death, Mary finally put away her black mourning clothes on this Friday in 1863. She put on a pink silk gown with a low neckline to host a reception for the midget Charles Sherwood Stratton—better known as General Tom Thumb—and his bride Lavinia.

Stratton was five years old, twenty-five inches tall, and weighed fifteen pounds when Phineas T. Barnum came to his Bridgeport, Connecticut home to enlist him as the world's newest sensation. It was 1842 and Barnum had just opened his American Museum in New York City, where he exhibited oddities such as the Fiji Mermaid (a fish tail and the torso of a dead monkey sewn together) and the original Siamese Twins, Chang and Eng. Barnum renamed Stratton "Tom Thumb" (after the hero of English folklore) and toured with him. By the time Stratton was ten, he had entertained queens Victoria (England) and Isabella (Spain), and kings Louis Phillippe (France) and Leopold (Belgium). At age twenty-three, he met and fell in love with another midget, Lavinia Warren. On February 10, 1863, Stratton married Warren in New York's Grace Church.

The newlyweds came to the White House reception in their bridal suit and gown and a guest recalled their first introduction to Lincoln,

> I well remember the "pigeon-like stateliness" with which they advanced, almost to the feet of the President, and the profound respect with which they looked up, up to his kindly face. It was pleasant to see their tall host bend, and bend, to take their hands in his great palm, holding Madame's with especial chariness, as though it were a robin's egg, and he were fearful of breaking it.

FEBRUARY 18

The African Slave Trade

For fifty-five years America had outlawed the African slave trade but had never been seriously committed to its extinction. On this Wednesday in 1863, Lincoln demonstrated that he and his administration were committed.

The U.S. Congress and the British Parliament passed legislation outlawing the African slave trade at virtually the same time (Britain in 1807 and the United States in 1808). But from the start, America—unlike Great Britain—was unenthusiastic about stopping it. For one thing, cotton prices made free African labor lucrative and a string of pro-slavery administrations refused to aggressively stem the tide. For another, America's small navy made it imperative that she cooperate with Britain's huge Royal Navy. But the two nations had a history of animosity and suspicion and the U.S. refused the right of British ships to search American merchant vessels, even to look for slave traders. Inevitably, slave ships began registering themselves as American to avoid arrest by British and European squadrons. This lack of cooperation made American efforts extremely ineffective. In the two decades before the Civil War, the United States captured only two ships transporting slaves.

When the Civil War broke out, Lincoln was forced to pull all ships home for blockade duty. But he refused to forget about the slave trade. In April of 1862 he quietly signed a treaty with Britain, effectively granting them the right to search American ships off Africa and Cuba. On this day, Lincoln sent to the Senate an addendum to the treaty that expanded the patrolled area to include Madagascar, Puerto Rico, and San Domingo.

MARCH 3

Two Notorious Acts

Lincoln stayed at the President's Room in the Capitol until nearly eleven this night in 1863, signing last-minute bills on the final day of the congressional session. Among those approved were two pieces of legislation that would soon become notorious: the Enrollment Act and the Habeas Corpus Act.

By spring of that year, it was clear that a crisis was imminent. Within a few months, thirty-eight Union regiments (a regiment was ideally—but rarely—1,000 men strong) who had volunteered for state militias at the beginning of the war were about to have their two-year enlistments expire. And ninety-two nine-month regiments unofficially drafted under the July 1862 Militia Act were also about to have their enlistments expire. And, after the Union reversals of 1861 and 1862, with their copiously long casualty lists, reenlistments and volunteers for new regiments had all but dried up. Thus

Congress passed the Enrollment Act—the first official draft—to keep the Union army at fighting strength.

But state and local judges hated the draft so much that they were willing to file writs of habeas corpus—demands that a person appear before their courts—of men arrested for dodging the draft and essentially released them. To combat this, Lincoln suspended habeas corpus in certain areas of the country. But there was a question as to whether that right belonged to the president or Congress. The Habeas Corpus Act surrendered that right to the president.

The Enrollment Act would result in the terrible July 1863 draft riots in New York City, a dark moment in U.S. history. Because of the Habeas Corpus Act, Lincoln suspended habeas corpus nationally in September 1863, an equally dark moment in Lincoln's presidential career.

MARCH 15

Raiders

On this Sunday in 1863, Lincoln met with a delegation from New York that was concerned that warships under construction in English naval yards and supposedly commissioned by the Emperor of China were actually under contract to join the Confederate Navy.

The Confederacy entered the war with virtually no navy and no naval yards to build them. Faced with a small but growing Union Navy who declared a blockade on all southern ports, Confederate president Jefferson Davis initially turned to southern privateers. Davis offered to sanction any private ship owners who used their boats to capture Union merchant ships. But only thirty letters of marque were issued, partly because Lincoln threatened to hang privateers as pirates. As the war progressed, privateers also had trouble taking their confiscated prizes through the blockade to be compensated, [illegible]ost neutral foreign ports were closed to privateers (the practice was outlawed by the 1856 Treaty of Paris). In the first summer of the war, only fifty Union merchant ships were captured.

By the summer of 1861, the Confederates had turned to commerce raiders—ships manned by naval personnel and built to sink rather than capture merchant ships. Many of these raiders were cruisers built in English naval yards, purchased as unarmed merchant ships bound for somewhere other than the Confederacy (such as China), then armed and manned by Confederate sailors once they were out to sea. Some of these raiders became legendary. The *Alabama* captured sixty-seven Union ships, destroying fifty-one. The *Florida* and the *Shenandoah* captured thirty-eight and thirty-seven "prizes," respectively.

These raiders represented the most serious diplomatic tension between the Union and Great Britain, and Lincoln repeatedly pressured London to stop building them. England even built blockade runners, rams, and ironclads for the Confederacy (although the latter two were never delivered).

MARCH 20

The Banished Reporter

Lincoln, on this day in 1863, revoked the banishment of a reporter for the *New York Herald*—Thomas Knox—who had run afoul of General William Sherman.

Sherman had an antagonistic relationship with the press. He often accused reporters of spying and they reciprocated by calling him insane. When Sherman set out in December 1862 for the Chickasaw Bayou—an effort to attack Vicksburg from the north—he forbade any reporters to accompany his army. Knox not only disobeyed this order but when he reported on Sherman's ill-fated assault on the Chickasaw Bluffs (he lost 1,800 men to the Confederate's 200), Knox disparaged the general's sanity and sensitivity to his men. Sherman had the reporter arrested as a spy, for revealing troop streng his article and for disobeying an order. During Knox's February 5, 1863 court-martial, he was found not guilty of the first two counts but guilty of disobeying an order. He was banished from Sherman's theater of operations.

Lincoln, realizing that he needed the support of the powerful *Herald*, revoked Knox's court-martial and allowed him to return to Sherman's army, provided that his superior, General Ulysses Grant, gave his consent.

On April 6, Knox appeared at Grant's headquarters with Lincoln's letter, but Grant refused to honor Lincoln's wishes "unless General Sherman first gives his consent to your remaining." Sherman was even more blunt: "Come with a sword or musket in your hand . . . and I will welcome you . . . but come as you now do . . . as the representative of the press . . . and my answer is, Never." Knox left the theater for good.

APRIL 7

Princess Salm-Salm

On this Tuesday in 1863, Lincoln was kissed by a princess.

It was quiet in Washington during the early spring of 1863 with Congress adjourned and Lincoln, in April, decided to take Mary and Tad on a trip to northern Virginia to visit the new head of the Army of the Potomac, Joseph Hooker. The Lincolns left for Hooker's headquarters on April 4—Tad's tenth birthday—aboard the steamer *Carrie Martin*.

After arriving, the president reviewed the troops for five straight days (April 6–10). During one review, someone remarked that the soldiers, who were supposed to be standing at attention, "almost invariably turned their heads to get a glimpse of" Lincoln. The president defended his men: "I don't care how much my soldiers turn their heads, if they don't turn their backs [in battle]."

The head of Hooker's Third Corps was General Daniel Sickles who had on his staff a colonel—Felix de Salm-Salm—who was also an Austrian prince. While Lincoln visited Third Corps Headquarters, several women, headed by Prince Salm-Salm's wife Agnes, approached him. The princess asked Sickles if she could kiss the president. The general acquiesced and added, "I am only sorry not to be in his place." The president blushed as the princess stood on her tiptoes to kiss him. The journalist Noah Brooks witnessed the scene and reported, "As soon as he [Lincoln] could collect himself and recover from his astonishment, the President thanked the lady, but with evident discomposure; whereupon some of the party made haste to explain that the Princess Salm-Salm had laid wager with one of the officers that she would kiss the President."

APRIL 20

West Virginia Becomes a State

For years, citizens of western Virginia had yearned to be independent of Tidewater (eastern) Virginia. On this day in 1863, that dream was realized as Lincoln issued a proclamation granting statehood to West Virginia.

Despite the fact that the thirty-five counties between the Shenandoah Valley and the Ohio River, north of the Kanawha River, were home to a quarter of Virginia's population, they were underrepresented in the state legislature. Few in those counties owned slaves and the "Tidewater aristocrats" could count some of their slaves as citizen to be represented in the Virginia General Assembly (even though slaves didn't vote). Tidewater Virginia, therefore, received more money for internal improvements (railroads, bridges, etc.) and their slaves were taxed at a third of their value while the farms in western Virginia were taxed at full value. A Clarksburg newspaper lamented, "Western Virginia has suffered more from . . . her eastern

the Cotton States all put together have suffered

seceded, western Unionists met in Wheeling to secessionists. Article IV, Section 3 of the Constitu- required the state legislature's consent to carve out within its territory. Richmond, of course, would not e Wheeling convention erected its own government and ne Richmond legislature illegal. Claiming to speak for all ns, the new regime held a constitutional convention to set ries for the new state of "Kanawha" and on May 23, 1862, pplied for statehood.

incoln was dubious about the legality of the new government. vertheless, he officially recognized it and after it instituted gradual emancipation (freeing slaves born after July 4, 1863 and all others on their twenty-fifth birthday), he welcomed West Virginia into the Union.

APRIL 23

Séances in the White House

During the 1860s spiritualism enjoyed a boost in interest as families who had lost loved ones in the war ones sought to reconnect with them. Its two million adherents in 1850 grew to seven million in 1863 and ten million after the war. Elizabeth Keckley, Mary Lincoln's dressmaker, lost her son in battle and became a convert. After Willie's death, Keckley encouraged Mary to communicate with her boy through a medium. Mary hosted as many as eight séances in the White House (although she attended other séances elsewhere) and on this Thursday in 1863 her husband allegedly attended one with her, probably in the White House library. Cabinet secretaries Edwin Stanton and Gideon Welles also attended and the "spirits" allegedly pinched the former's ears and pulled the latter's beard.

Lincoln's involvement in these séances app rs to have been more to support his wife than because of a belie spiritualism. These "circles" also seemed to have piqued his curi He asked his friend Joseph Henry, superintendent of the Smiths to find out how mediums produced clicking sounds that they cl vere vocal manifestations of the dead. Henry later reported tha was strapped to the medium's biceps, which clicked when the stretched his/her muscles. Famous medium Lord Colcheste booted out of Lincoln's Old Soldier's Home cottage when he discovered to be using a mechanical device during a séance.

There was another alleged séance held in the White House that Lincoln is said to have attended. In December of 1862, Mary Lincoln invited two mediums to the White House—Nettie Colburn and Belle Miller. According to Colburn, Miller played a march on the Red Room's double grand piano and the "heavy end of the piano began rising and falling in perfect time to the music." Nettie fell into a trance, and, in the voice of Daniel Webster, warned Lincoln not to delay issuing the Emancipation Proclamation.

#48

"Long Brave" Joins a Séance

Nettie Colburn told of another séance Lincoln attended on February 5, 1863, this time at the home of Colburn's Georgetown friends. Colburn's recollections were written decades after Lincoln's death, and are unreliable in some particulars (her quotes of Lincoln are long and very un-Lincolnian). Her story is supported, however, by the reminiscences of S. P. Kase, who was also present at the séance. Lincoln surprised his wife that February evening when he, at the last minute, asked to accompany her. Meanwhile, Colburn's "familiar" spirit told her that "Long

”—the spirit’s name for Lincoln—would attend with

Miller treated the guests to tunes on her piano. Miller demonstrated her power to make the te to the rhythm of the music. Lincoln tried how Miller was performing this “miracle,” at, declared, “I think we can hold down this incoln then sat on the piano and, when joined him, the piano began to levitate

led a favorite spirit of Lincoln’s—Dr. icted that Lincoln would be reelected miled at that. According to Colburn, ained that no one would believe piano, the president responded, erson here, and when the piano his foot under the leg and be e weight of evidence resting

8

resident

ctions was evident, on this himself.

otomac under General nps across the Rappa- They headed north- ncellorsville, where flank. Despite the ln wired Hooker,

Lincoln had reason to be concerned. The Army of the Potoma had had a string of lost campaigns: First Manassas, the Peninsu Campaign, and Fredericksburg. "I can perceive he [Lincoln] h doubts and misgivings, though he does not express them," wr Secretary of the Navy Gideon Welles.

Hooker wired back to Lincoln that the Confederates didn't w him. "The only element which gives me apprehension with r to the success of this plan is the weather," Hooker wrote.

Lincoln was worried about the weather as well. Rain had a swelled the Rappahannock so that Hooker had to use pont cross it. Lincoln turned to "practical meteorologist" Francis who claimed he could predict the weather. On this day, wrote himself a memorandum: "It seems to me Mr. Cape nothing about the weather, in advance. He told me three that it would not rain again till the 30th of April or 1st o raining now and has been for ten hours. I can not spare time to Mr. Capen."

MAY 3

Telegrams

Lincoln spent this Sunday in 1863 apprehensi news from Chancellorsville, Virginia, where a battle for two days. General Joseph Hooker had crossed t River at Chancellorsville to strike at Robert E. Le

When Lincoln received a telegram from Gene field, Hooker's chief of staff, informing the pres is in progress," Lincoln fired back a telegram of Gen. Hooker? Where is Sedgwick? Where is S John Sedgwick was given the task of occupyi attacking Fredericksburg southeast of Chance Sedgwick didn't seriously move against his ob day of the battle, Lee was able to throw most of his men against Hooker while keeping a small screen of men in front of Sedgwick. General George Stoneman headed Hooker's cavalry and participated in small raids instead of acting as Hooker's eyes. And he failed to detect Lee's counteroffensive. Late this afternoon, Butterfield responded to Lincoln's query, saying, "General Hooker is at Chancellorsville. General Sedgwick, with 15,000 to 20,000 men . . . [is] on the road to Chancellorsville. Lee is between. Stoneman has not been heard from."

Butterfield had worse news in another telegram: "Genl Hooker [is] slightly but not at all severely wounded." Shortly after nine that morning, Hooker had been peppered with shrapnel. When Hooker wired his president later that day, he didn't mention his injuries but declared, "We have had a desperate fight yesterday and today which has resulted in no success to us."

Lincoln spent this evening (until eleven) at the telegraph office at the War Department, anxious for information. "We have been in a terrible suspense here for two days as the result of the battle," wrote John Nicolay, one of Lincoln's secretaries.

MAY 6

"What Will the Country Say?"

In the days following the battle of Chancellorsville, Lincoln spent almost all his time at the telegraph office at the War Department where, according to Secretary of the Navy Gideon Welles, he had "a feverish anxiety to get facts." The "facts" were that the Army of the Potomac—this time under Joseph Hooker—had sustained yet another loss at the hands of Robert E. Lee, and on this Tuesday in 1863 Lincoln finally received the news.

When Hooker crossed the Rappahannock River in late April, planning to strike at Lee's left flank, he caught Lee shorthanded.

Lee had sent General James Longstreet's two divisions to Suffolk, Virginia, leaving Lee with 61,000 men to Hooker's 134,000. Lee, however, boldly turned and struck Hooker so hard that Hooker stopped at Chancellorsville on May 1. Lee then broke a fundamental rule of warfare and split his smaller army in the face of a larger one by sending Thomas "Stonewall" Jackson around Hooker's right flank to attack it. When Lee struck again on May 3, Hooker blundered by relinquishing the high ground, allowing Lee to pummel him with cannon fire (Hooker was wounded by one of those cannonballs), forcing the Union troops back against the Rappahannock.

On this day Hooker's chief of staff, Daniel Butterfield, sent Lincoln a telegram with word that the army was retreating. When Lincoln received the dispatch this afternoon, he handed it to his friend Noah Brooks and said in a shaky voice, "Read it—news from the Army." Brooks couldn't remember a time when Lincoln was "so broken, so dispirited, and so ghostlike." As Brooks read the wire, Lincoln paced the room saying, "My God! My God! What will the country say! What will the country say!" Within the hour, Lincoln was on his way to confer with Hooker.

#49

"*I Am Down to Raisins*"

Lincoln went almost daily to the War Department's telegraph office, just a short walk west of the White House. He was known to spend the night at the telegraph office waiting for news from the front and it is alleged that he spent more time there than anywhere else besides the White House (although this may not take into account his time spent at the Old Soldiers' Home cottage). His routine was to fish war dispatches out of the daily stack of them, reading them one by one. According to David

Homer Bates, one of the telegraph operators, when Lincoln reached the end of the stack, he would typically say, "Well, boys, I am down to raisins." When asked what the phrase meant, Lincoln explained. Bates recounted Lincoln's explanation:

> He thereupon told us the story of the little girl who celebrated her birthday by eating very freely of many good things, topping off with raisins for desert. During the night she was taken ill, and when the doctor arrived she was busy casting up her accounts. The genial doctor, scrutinizing the contents of the vessel . . . remarked to the anxious parent that all danger was past, as the child was "down to raisins." "So," Lincoln said, "when I reach the message in this pile which I saw on my last visit, I know that I need go no further."

Lincoln felt more at ease with the telegraph operators, often reading Shakespeare to them or cracking endless jokes. He also read official correspondence to the War Department and once noted large, sweeping flourishes of an operator's signature. "It reminds me of a short-legged man in a big overcoat, the tail of which was so long that it wiped out his footprints in the snow," he quipped.

MAY 12

Death of a Legend

On this Thursday in 1863, Lincoln received word that the legendary Confederate general Thomas "Stonewall" Jackson was dead.

At Chancellorsville, the Army of the Potomac—this time under General Joseph Hooker—had once again sustained a heartbreaking loss. On hearing the news on May 6, Lincoln immediately took a steamer to Falmouth, Virginia to meet with Hooker. Lincoln found

Hooker, who had been injured by a cannonball's near miss, to be "cool, clear and satisfied" that the loss was not his fault. Lincoln, however, thought otherwise. "If Hooker had been killed by the shot which . . . stunned him, we should have been successful," Lincoln said bitterly. Three other generals were among the 1,600 Union dead. On the Confederate side, however, it would be one general—Jackson—who would be missed more than any other.

Jackson, a graduate of West Point and a veteran of the Mexican War, was a teacher at the Virginia Military Institute when war broke out. It was while making a stand at First Manassas that a fellow officer gave Jackson the sobriquet "Stonewall." His Shenandoah Valley campaign in the late spring of 1862 is arguably the most brilliant military operation in American history. But it was at Chancellorsville that Jackson delivered Robert E. Lee's daring left hook to Hooker's right flank.

That evening (May 2), Jackson was reconnoitering when fellow rebel soldiers mistook him for Union cavalry. Jackson was shot twice in his left arm, which had to be amputated. Jackson developed pneumonia and on the afternoon of May 10 he was in a delirium, calling out orders to his men, when he suddenly fell silent and smiled. "Let us cross over the river and rest under the shade of the trees," he said before dying.

MAY 13

Copperheads

Lincoln had in the first two years of the war suspended the writ of habeas corpus in areas of the country and even nationwide but, in May 1863, he was considering suspending it for one individual. On this Wednesday in 1863 he received news that convinced him to shelve the suspension.

In the conservative southern counties of Ohio, Indiana, and Illinois, a movement for the immediate cessation of the war—fueled by anger over the Emancipation Proclamation and conscription—began to grow. Leaders of this movement—called Peace Democrats or Copperheads (named for the venomous snake)—incited a string of violent anti-draft and anti-black demonstrations across the country. General Ambrose Burnside, head of the Department of the Ohio, responded on April 13 with General Order No. 38, which stated that anyone "declaring sympathy for the enemy" would be tried for treason.

A leading Copperhead was former Ohio congressman Clement Vallandigham. On May 1, Vallandigham held a rally at which he railed against Lincoln's "war of freedom of the blacks and enslavement of the whites." Vallandigham declared that the war would end only if soldiers deserted en masse and acted to "hurl King Lincoln from his throne." On May 5, Burnside had Vallandigham arrested, and within twenty-four hours a military tribunal had convicted and sentenced him to imprisonment for the war's duration.

Lincoln was unhappy with Burnside's action; imprisoning a former congressman was a political nightmare. But Lincoln felt compelled to support the general. When Vallandigham applied for a writ to be released to federal court, Lincoln supported Secretary of War Edwin Stanton's move for a special suspension of the writ. On this day Stanton's order was lying on Lincoln's desk when he received word that the federal judge—Humphrey Leavitt—would likely deny the writ anyway. Lincoln shelved the suspension and Leavitt did deny Vallandigham's application. On May 19, Lincoln commuted Vallandigham's imprisonment to banishment to the Confederacy, ridding himself—temporarily—of a thorn in his side.

MAY 14

"I Would Be Very Glad of Another Movement"

General Joseph Hooker had been given command of the Army of the Potomac after he had plotted against his predecessor—General Ambrose Burnside. Lincoln even admonished Hooker for this in January 1863: "You have taken counsel of your ambition and thwarted him [Burnside] as much as you could in which you did a great wrong to the country, and to a most meritorious and honorable brother officer." In an ironic twist, Lincoln, on this day in 1863, warned Hooker that his subordinates were intriguing against him.

The loss at the battle of Chancellorsville had been a huge political blow to Lincoln. There was a clamor to replace Hooker with a man who had already cost Lincoln considerable political capital—General George McClellan. Even Lincoln's general in chief, Henry Halleck, wanted Fighting Joe sacked. But Lincoln did not want to discard a gun after just one misfire, and "would pick the lock and try it again." The president declared, "I will give to Hooker one chance more."

Meanwhile, Lincoln was trying to spur Hooker into taking that chance. "What next?" Lincoln wrote Hooker on May 7. "If possible I would be very glad of another movement." But Hooker's confidence was shaken. When he refused to move, on May 13 Lincoln summoned him to Washington, where Hooker complained that Lee's forces "are much my superiors" in numbers. In Lincoln's written response on this day in 1863, he was obviously disappointed at a missed opportunity. "I . . . shall not complain if you do no more, for a time, than to keep the enemy at bay, and out of mischief." Lincoln, however, warned, "I have some painful intimations that some of your corps and Division Commanders are not giving you their entire confidence. This would be ruinous, if true." Six weeks later Hooker would himself be replaced by one of his subordinates.

MAY 22

The Vicksburg Siege Begins

On this Friday in 1863, Lincoln received some much-needed good news from the west; Vicksburg, Mississippi, was under siege.

For more than seven months, General Ulysses Grant had been attempting to take Vicksburg. Along with Port Hudson, Mississippi, Vicksburg was the last Confederate crossing of the Mississippi River, linking Texas, Arkansas, and Louisiana with the rest of the Confederacy. But Vicksburg, with its impenetrable bayous to the north and commanding bluffs to the west, was difficult to reach, much less attack. As time passed without success, Lincoln began to lose faith in the general. Word reached Washington that Grant was "a poor drunk imbecile" incapable of leading an army. The president sent emissaries to Grant to check up on him. He suggested that Grant head south and link up with General Nathaniel Banks, who was marching on Port Hudson.

Instead, Grant, telling no one, marched his men along the western side of the Mississippi to rendezvous with transports that had run Vicksburg's gauntlet. His men crossed the river and disappeared into the bayous. Lincoln anxiously waited for news. Then, on this day, good news came over the telegraph. After crossing the Mississippi River, Grant had cut loose from his supply train and his line of communication and drove deep into Mississippi. He took Jackson—the state capital—first, then advanced on Vicksburg. In a three-day period, Grant fought two separate armies, beating both. After two attempts to break Vicksburg's entrenchments—the last of which was on May 22—Grant settled into a siege. It was Grant's most audacious operation. "His [Grant's] campaign from beginning of this month up to the twenty second day of it," Lincoln wrote, "is one of the most brilliant in the world."

MAY 29

Burnside Offers to Resign Again

On this day in 1863, General Ambrose Burnside, head of the Department of the Ohio, wired Lincoln that he had heard that his actions in arresting and convicting former Congressman Clement Vallandigham had "been a source of embarrassment" to the president. He offered to submit his resignation "if the interest of public service requires it."

Burnside's actions had, indeed, embarrassed Lincoln. On May 1, 1863, Vallandigham, who was running for governor of Ohio, delivered a speech at Mount Vernon, Ohio, entreating soldiers to desert and civilians not to enlist. It was a deliberate violation of Burnside's General Order No. 38, which prohibited anyone from "declaring sympathy for the enemy." Burnside's order was in line with Lincoln's September 24, 1862 proclamation suspending the writ of habeas corpus across the nation to anyone who impeded the draft or enlistments or coaxed soldiers to desert. Lincoln never objected to Burnside's order and, after Vallandigham's arrest and conviction, Lincoln even sent Burnside his "assurance of support."

But when Lincoln consulted with his cabinet, every one of whom objected to Burnside's actions, Lincoln began to have second thoughts. Against Burnside's advice, Lincoln, on May 19, commuted Vallandigham's sentence (imprisonment) to banishment to the Confederacy. While this mollified some critics, others—particularly Democrats—were incensed. One New York commentator said that "the man who occupied the Presidential chair at Washington was tenfold a greater traitor to the country than was any Southern rebel." Hearing of the political pressure on Lincoln, Burnside sent his offer to resign. Lincoln wired back that he did not wish his resignation. He did, however, admit that his cabinet objected to Vallandigham's arrest, "some perhaps, doubting, that there was a real necessity for it—but, being done, all were for seeing you through with it."

JUNE 2

Grant Worries Lincoln

Lincoln rarely interfered with operations in the western theater because communications lagged behind events by a few days. On this Tuesday in 1863, however, Lincoln was so worried about General Ulysses Grant's Vicksburg Campaign that he felt compelled to get involved.

For weeks Lincoln had fretted over Grant's efforts to attack Vicksburg, Mississippi. After seven months of failures to even reach Vicksburg, much less attack it, Lincoln felt his confidence in Grant wane. He wanted Grant to give up on Vicksburg and join with General Nathaniel Banks as he moved on Port Hudson, the only other Confederate stronghold on the Mississippi River. Instead, Grant and his army disappeared in May, crossing the Mississippi. "Have you anything from Grant?" Lincoln asked a general in Tennessee. To another general Lincoln queried, "Do the Richmond papers have anything about . . . Vicksburg?" Then Grant reappeared, driving Confederate forces into Vicksburg and laying a siege.

On this day Lincoln met with his cabinet to discuss the campaign, and while his advisors expressed "confidence . . . in Grant" they felt more could be done to break the siege. If Grant wouldn't go to Banks, maybe Banks could join Grant. Lincoln fired off a telegram: "Are you in communication with Gen. Banks? Is he coming towards you, or going further off? Is there been anything to hinder his coming to you . . . ?" A week later, Grant forwarded a telegram from Banks, who had started his own siege of Port Hudson. It was too late to extract himself, Banks said, so he would come to Vicksburg after Port Hudson had fallen. "This I hope to accomplish in a few days," he added. It would, however, be more than a month before Banks would take Port Hudson and by then Vicksburg had already surrendered.

JUNE 4

Lincoln Reopens the Chicago Times

On this Thursday in 1863, Lincoln intervened in the closing of a large metropolitan newspaper.

When General Ambrose Burnside, head of the Department of the Ohio, arrested, tried, and convicted former congressman Clement Vallandigham for supposedly treasonous remarks at a May 1, 1863, rally, Burnside struck a match to what became a firestorm of criticism for both himself and the Lincoln administration. Republicans joined Democrats in their outrage and newspapers across the country were shrill in their protests. The *New York Atlas* called this act an example of "military despotism" and "the weakness, folly, oppression, mismanagement and general wickedness of the administration in Washington." The *New York Herald* declared that Lincoln was on a path that "must terminate at last in bloody anarchy." Lincoln ignored this journalistic vitriol but Burnside did not. On June 1, Burnside suspended the publication of the *Chicago Times*, perhaps the most influential Democratic newspaper in the Midwest, for its criticism of his actions.

The Illinois legislature in Lincoln's hometown of Springfield was, on this day, censoring Burnside's action. "Such an order is in direct violation of the constitution of the United States and this State," their resolution read, "and destructive of those God-given principles . . . [that are] as much part of our rights as the air we breathe or the life which sustains us." What convinced Lincoln, however, was a telegram from his friends Isaac Arnold and Senator Lyman Trumball with a petition against Burnside's order. On this day Lincoln revoked the order. Burnside had also apparently prohibited the circulation of the bitterly critical *New York World* within his jurisdiction and Lincoln also lifted that ban. Lincoln later wrote of the incident, "I can only say I was embarrassed with the question between what was due to the military service on one hand, and the Liberty of the Press on the other."

#50

Lincoln and Freedom of the Press

Lincoln and his administration did restrict the press. One of the most prevalent ways it did so was for the Postmaster to deny mail service to newspapers which were critical of the war and the administration. In an era when the mail was a newspaper's primary means of delivery, this caused several newspapers to either close their doors or promise that there would be no more negative editorials. When the *New York Daily News* was denied postal service, editor Ben Wood (brother of New York City mayor Fernando Wood) hired private couriers to deliver his newspaper. Federal marshals subsequently confiscated the paper in several cities. The *Daily News* went bankrupt.

Another tactic was for the military to shut down the newspapers, as General Ambrose Burnside did on June 1, 1863, to the *Chicago Times*. Often this happened without the consent of the president but he was ultimately responsible for what his military did. And Lincoln clearly believed that the government had the right to do this when he himself closed down the *New York World* and the *Journal of Commerce* on May 18, 1864, after they printed a declaration falsely attributed to the president.

The military also sometimes arrested editors and publishers or banished reporters because of their critical views. Again, this was often done without Lincoln's consent and sometimes he ordered the release of the prisoner. On July 13, 1863, Lincoln wrote General John Schofield about the arrest of St. Louis newspaper editor William McKee for refusing to reveal a source. "Please spare me the trouble this is likely to bring," Lincoln implored Schofield. Clearly this would have stopped had Lincoln so ordered it. The fact that he didn't shows at least an ambivalence toward a free press.

JUNE 5

Lee Moves North

Lincoln was still disappointed that General Joe Hooker had done little more than lick his wounds after his defeat at Chancellorsville when Hooker sent word, on this Friday in 1863, that Confederate general Robert E. Lee was not going to sit at all.

In the wake of General Ulysses Grant's siege of Vicksburg, Lee was pressured to transport his Army of Northern Virginia west—possibly to Tennessee—to draw Grant away from the siege. Lee, who had always been a little myopic about operations outside the Virginia theater, refused but countered with a plan to strike north into Pennsylvania.

By early June, Lee was moving northwest to the Shenandoah Valley. Hooker's cavalry misinterpreted the movement, believing Lee was heading east around Hooker's left flank toward Washington. "[Lee will] probably be headed towards the Potomac via Gordonsville or Culpeper," Hooker wired Lincoln on this Friday morning. Hooker then recommended that he "pitch into his [Lee's] rear" located across the Rappahannock River at Fredericksburg.

Lincoln advised against crossing the river (to the south side) while most of Lee's army was north of it, able to "pitch into" Hooker's rear. "I would not take any risk of being entangled upon the river, like an ox jumped half over a fence, and liable to be torn by dogs, front and rear, without a fair chance to gore one way or kick the other," Lincoln wrote. A week later Hooker recommended that he dash southward to take Richmond. Lincoln reminded Hooker—as he had reminded so many other commanders, that "Lee's Army, and not Richmond, is your true objective point." Thus began what would become known as the Gettysburg Campaign, culminating in the most important battle of the war.

JUNE 9

Nightmares

Lincoln was plagued much of his life with vivid dreams and nightmares and, to some extent, he believed them to be prophetic either symbolically or literally. His wife, Mary, shared this belief. In late March 1865, while visiting City Point, Virginia, Lincoln dreamed that the White House was on fire and Mary sent not one but two telegrams to Washington to make sure the White House was still there. On this Monday in 1863, Lincoln was disconcerted enough by a nightmare to wire his wife.

At three in the afternoon on June 8, Lincoln accompanied Mary and their son Tad to the train station. Mother and son were departing for a two-week shopping vacation in Philadelphia. Prior to leaving, Lincoln had allowed Tad to take with him a pistol "big enough to snap caps—but no cartridges or powder." After Lincoln returned to his office, Secretary of the Navy Gideon Welles approached the president about the weekly summer concerts of the Marine Band on the White House lawn. The previous summer, concerts had been canceled because the Lincolns were mourning Willie, who died in

February 1862. Willie had loved the Marine Band concerts and they reminded Mary of him. Welles warned Lincoln that the public's "grumbling and discontent" would increase if another concert season were canceled. Lincoln was initially reluctant to allow the concerts but finally relented.

All the talk about Willie likely spurred Lincoln to have a nightmare that night about Tad and death. Lincoln on this day wired Mary, "Think you better put 'Tad's' pistol away. I had an ugly dream about him."

#51

Lincoln's Dreams

There are several recorded accounts of Lincoln's rather vivid dreams and nightmares. In the mid-1850s, a fellow lawyer witnessed Lincoln "sitting up in bed. . . . talking the wildest and most incoherent nonsense all to himself." When Lincoln awoke, he "put some wood on the fire, and then sat in front of it . . . in the most somber and gloomy spell, till the breakfast bell rang."

As president, Lincoln had a recurring dream just before a number of battles. Lincoln said the dream involved "water—that he seemed to be in some singular indescribable vessel, and that he was moving with great rapidity toward an indefinite shore." He had the dream again the night before his assassination. The night before he signed the Emancipation Proclamation (January 1, 1863) he had a nightmare about death and war.

The most famous story of Lincoln's dreams came from his friend Ward Lamon. The dream, as he related it to Lamon, started with a "death-like stillness." Lincoln continued:

> Then I heard subdued sobs as if a number of people were weeping. . . . I went from room to room; no living person was in sight, but the same mournful sounds of distress met me as I passed along. . . . I kept on until I arrived at the East Room [of the White House], which I entered. There I met with a sickening surprise. Before me was a catafalque, on which rested a corpse wrapped in funeral vestments. Around it were stationed soldiers who were acting as guards; and there was a throng of people, some gazing mournfully upon the corpse, whose face was covered. . . . "Who is dead in the White House?" I demanded of one of the soldiers. "The President," was his answer, "he was killed by an assassin!"

He told Lamon that the dream "has haunted me ever since."

JUNE 12

The Corning Letter

The arrest and conviction of former Ohio congressman Clement Vallandigham for "treasonous" utterances had become a political nightmare for Lincoln. On May 16, Democrats met in Albany, New York and issued resolutions that condemned the military trial of a civilian "for no other reason than words addressed to a public meeting." A member of the group, wealthy iron manufacturer Erastus Corning, forwarded the resolutions to Lincoln, who, on this Friday in 1863, used his response to speak to the public.

In his lengthy response, Lincoln wrote, "Their [the Confederacy's] sympathizers pervaded all departments of the government, nearly all communities. . . . [and] under cover of 'Liberty of speech,' 'Liberty of the press' and 'Habeas corpus' they hoped to keep . . . amongst us a most efficient corps of spies, informers, supplyers and aiders and abettors." Lincoln argued that the actions of such "traitors" were not necessarily unlawful but were still harmful to a government fighting for its survival. In such cases, these "traitors" would be released to continue their activities by civil courts and therefore had to be held in military prisons without trial or tried by military courts. Vallandigham's speech, for example, dissuaded its listeners from enlisting in the service and persuaded troops to desert. "Must I shoot a simple-minded soldier boy who deserts, while I must not touch a hair of a wily agitator who induces him to desert?" Lincoln asked. "To silence the agitator, and save the boy, is . . . a great mercy."

Lincoln not only sent his letter to Corning letter on this day, but released it to the public. On June 30, Corning fired back that the administration's "absolute sovereignty, wielded by one man; so that liberty perishes, or is depended on his will, his discretion or his caprice" was wrong.

JUNE 16

Hooker and Halleck

By mid-June 1863, Confederate general Robert E. Lee's Gettysburg campaign was gaining momentum, his army strung out from Virginia to Pennsylvania. And while Lincoln nervously watched this, on this Sunday in 1863 he had to mediate a dispute between General Joe Hooker and General in Chief Henry Halleck.

Lincoln knew he was not competent at drafting proper military orders and usually couched his messages to generals as suggestions. "If the head of Lee's army is at Martinsburg [Pennsylvania] and the tail of it on the Plank Road between Fredericksburg and Chancellorsville, the animal must be very slim somewhere. Could you not break him?" Lincoln wired Hooker on June 14. Earlier that same day, Lincoln forwarded word that Union forces at Winchester, Virginia were surrounded and asked, "could you help them?" Hooker responded, "I do not feel like making a move for an Enemy until I be satisfied as to his whereabouts." Then, "To proceed to Winchester and have him [the enemy] make his appearance elsewhere would subject me to ridicule." Hooker declared that "unless otherwise directed," he would continue as before.

Lincoln preferred that Halleck, Hooker's superior, issue orders. But Halleck and Hooker detested each other because of an unpaid debt, and neither would correspond with the other. "If you and he [Halleck] would use the same frankness to one another, and to me, that I use to both of you, there would be no difficulty," Lincoln wrote to Hooker. By this day, Lincoln had had enough. "To remove all misunderstanding, I now place you in strict military relation to Gen. Halleck, of a commander of one of the armies, to the General-in-Chief of all the armies," Lincoln wired Hooker. "I shall direct him to give you orders, and you to obey them."

JUNE 26

Late-Night Visitors

On this Friday in 1863, Lincoln had three late-evening visitors to his retreat at the old Soldiers' Home, one of whom would insult his commander in chief.

In late June Washington was anxious about the Confederate Army's new offensive into Pennsylvania. The bartender at the Willard Hotel was laying bets that Confederate general Robert E. Lee would "eat his Fourth of July dinner" at the hotel. Two Union officers from New York, Silas T. Burt and John Van Buren, had come to Washington to assure Lincoln that New York governor Horatio Seymour, despite criticism of the administration, still supported the Union. Lincoln, busy watching Lee's offensive, repeatedly refused to see the emissaries. They then enlisted the help of Seymour's cousin, who was a major in the army. Despite his obvious inebriation, the major claimed he could get an audience with Lincoln at his Old Soldiers' Home cottage. At 9:00 PM on this evening, they arrived at the cottage to find, "gleaming amid the shrubbery," the bayonets of Lincoln's security contingent. The emissaries were shown into the cottage.

"At length we heard slow, shuffling steps come down the uncarpeted stairs. . . . His [Lincoln's] form was bowed, his hair disheveled; he wore no necktie or collar, and his large feet were partly encased in very loose, heelless slippers," Burt remembered. After delivering Seymour's assurances of continued loyalty, they spoke of Lee's offensive. As they talked, Burt noticed Lincoln's "long legs stretched out in front, the loose slippers half-fallen from his feet, while the drowsy eyelids had almost closed." Then the drunken major slapped Lincoln's knee, "Mr. President, tell us one of your good stories." Lincoln stood up, obviously angry, and told them that his stories were used to illustrate his thoughts, not for amusement. He then left for bed.

JUNE 27

"His Own Dunghill"

On this day in 1863, Lincoln removed the third commander of the Army of the Potomac in its twenty-two months of existence.

During the month of June, Confederate general Robert E. Lee slowly moved his army north to Pennsylvania and Hooker followed. As Lincoln began to pressure Hooker to attack Lee and take "the best opportunity we have have had since the war began," Hooker complained of Lee's supposedly superior numbers. Lincoln's confidence in Hooker had been deteriorating for weeks and Hooker was also feuding with his superior, General in Chief Henry Halleck. The feud came to a head over Harpers Ferry. Halleck wanted its garrison to remain in place to threaten Lee's rear elements, forcing him to divide his forces as Lee had done during his 1862 offensive in the Antietam Campaign. Harpers Ferry, however, with its surrounding hills, was virtually indefensible. Hooker feared the garrison would be captured, as happened during the same Antietam Campaign, resulting in the largest single Union surrender (14,000 soldiers) of the war.

On June 27, Hooker wired Washington, "My original instructions require me to cover Harpers Ferry and Washington. I have now imposed on me, in addition, an enemy in my front of more than my number. . . . I am unable to comply . . . with the means at my disposal, and earnestly request that I may at once be relieved." It is likely that Hooker—with a battle imminent—believed his request would be denied. But Lincoln quickly accepted it. The next day Lincoln named General George Meade as Hooker's replacement. With Lee racing into Meade's home state of Pennsylvania, Lincoln told Stanton, "He will fight well on his own dunghill."

JULY 3

A Carriage Accident

On this Friday in 1863, Lincoln sent a short telegram to his son Robert, who was studying at Harvard, which read, "Don't be uneasy. Your mother very slightly hurt by her fall." But the injuries that Mary sustained in an accident were not slight. Lincoln was just inattentive.

On the morning of July 2, Mary had been riding in the family carriage on Rock Creek Road, north of Washington. She was nearing Mount Pleasant Hospital when her coachman's seat detached, throwing the coachman and leaving Mary alone in the carriage with runaway horses. According to a newspaper account, the horses "dashed along with fearful velocity." Mary either fell or jumped out, sustaining—among other injuries—a head laceration that required stitches. When the carriage was examined, it was discovered that the screws securing the coachmen's seat had been loosened in an apparent attempt to assassinate the first family. Despite this, Lincoln never ordered an investigation and blamed the incident on Rock Creek Road. "The place on the road near Mt. Pleasant Hospital ought to be repaired," Lincoln wrote a subordinate.

Instead of attending to Mary, Lincoln had a nurse look after her while he spent nearly all day, for several days, at the telegraph office, awaiting news of the battle at Gettysburg. It wasn't until Mary's head wound began seeping that anyone realized it was infected. In an era when infection killed more troops than bullets, Mary was in legitimate danger. On July 11 Lincoln wired Robert to "come to Washington" and, when Robert did not appear in three days, wired again, "Why do I hear no more of you?" Robert appeared the next day. It took Mary three weeks to recover and her chronic migraines became more intense. Robert would, afterward, maintain that his mother's accident contributed to her emotional instability.

#52

Threats

Historians will never know how many serious attempts were made on Lincoln's life. Neither can many of the reported attempts be substantiated. For instance, there was a rumor that Lincoln's castor oil had been poisoned, but because of the odd taste the president never took enough of it. There's another story of a trunk full of clothes worn by Cuban yellow-fever victims that was sent to the White House in hopes that they would infect Lincoln with the deadly disease. (Not until 1881 would it be discovered that yellow fever was transmitted by mosquitoes, not contaminated clothing.) There supposedly was a plot to attach a bomb to the crossbars under the Lincolns' carriage. A more credible story is from one of Lincoln's guards, Private

John Nichols, who claimed that in mid-August 1864 he was on guard duty at the Old Soldiers' Home cottage when a rifle shot rang out. A moment later Lincoln appeared on the road "bareheaded," his horse galloping. Lincoln told Nichols that "somebody had fired a gun off at the foot of the hill," spooking his horse and causing him to lose his hat. When Nichols retrieved Lincoln's silk plug hat, he found a bullet hole through the crown. Lincoln shrugged it off as "some foolish gunner" and asked Nichols to keep the matter quiet.

Lincoln, throughout his presidency, received death threats through the mail. Many threats were in the form of photographs or drawings of Lincoln with a rope sketched around his neck or red spots on his shirt. Lincoln saw enough of them to become apathetic. When artist Francis Carpenter voiced surprise that such letters did not make him apprehensive, Lincoln replied, "Oh, there is nothing like getting used to things!"

JULY 4

Gettysburg

At a tiny crossroads town in Pennsylvania, two huge armies grappled with each other for three sultry July days. On this Saturday in 1863, Lincoln received word that the largest and most important battle of the war was over.

Confederate general Robert E. Lee's offensive into Pennsylvania was designed to wreck the Army of the Potomac, the only significant army that stood between Lee and the North. His opponent was General George Meade, who was an experienced corps commander but untried as an army commander (he had replaced Joseph Hooker three days earlier). When lead elements of Lee's army collided with

Meade's cavalry at Gettysburg on July 1, a battle developed. On July 2, Lee tried to turn Meade's left flank, which was anchored at a hill called Little Round Top. If Lee could have taken the hill, he could have poured men into Meade's rear, thus forcing Meade to retreat with large chunks of his army captured or killed. The desperate fight over Little Round Top became the stuff of legends. When Lee failed, the next day he attempted a Napoleonic strategy: soften up Meade's center with his cannon, then drive a wedge into it with a frontal attack (which became known as Pickett's Charge after the assault) headed by Confederate general George Pickett. Pickett's Charge was Lee's biggest error of the war.

For all three days, Lincoln stayed at the War Department's telegraph office, sleeping on the office couch. One observer later remembered the "painful anxiety" of those days and the "restless solicitude of Mr. Lincoln, as he paced up and down the room, reading dispatches, soliloquizing, and often stopping to trace the map which hung on the wall." Shortly after sunrise on this day, Meade wired that the battle was concluded. Lee had lost nearly a third of his army and for the remainder of the war, he would be unable to mount another major offensive.

JULY 5

"The Pretended Confederate States"

Lincoln, on this Sunday in 1863, conferred with his cabinet over a very unusual situation. The Confederate vice president, Alexander Stephens, was at Fortress Monroe, waiting for permission to speak with Lincoln.

Stephens appeared at Fortress Monroe aboard the steamer *Torpedo* on July 4 with a message: "As military Commissioner, I am bearer of a communication in writing from [Confederate president] Jefferson Davis . . . to Abraham Lincoln." Stephens asked if the

Torpedo could proceed through the blockade to Washington where Stephens ostensibly wanted to discuss prisoner exchanges. Lincoln curtly ordered the head of Fortress Monroe, "You will not permit Mr. Stephens to proceed to Washington, or to pass the blockade." He added, "Of course nothing else will be received by the President . . . in terms assuming the independence of the so-called Confederate States."

Stephens had been isolated from his own Confederate government because of political differences with President Davis. So when Stephens, in June 1863, recommended he negotiate with Washington to reestablish the prisoner exchange cartel (and perhaps open a dialogue for peace negotiations) he was unaware of Confederate general Robert E. Lee's planned offensive into the North. Such an offensive would make amicable dialogue between the governments unlikely, particularly if Lee failed. Davis gave him permission to go. But when Lincoln met with his cabinet on this day—two days after Lee's failure at Gettysburg—no one wanted a dialogue with the rebels, especially if it could be viewed as a tacit acknowledgment of the Confederacy's right to exist. The next day Lincoln had Secretary of State William Seward draft a message to Stephens: "The President will not . . . receive any communication emanating from Mr. Jefferson Davis as President of the pretended Confederate States." Lincoln's political enemies would use this snub as evidence that Lincoln had no wish to end the war.

JULY 6

"The Whole Country Is Our Soil"

In the aftermath of Gettysburg, Confederate general Robert E. Lee retreated southward in a downpour that swelled the Potomac River until it could not be forded (Lee did not have pontoon boats to carry his men across). Lee was trapped and expected General

George Meade to attack him. Lincoln expected it, too, but on this day in 1863 Lincoln saw this opportunity begin to slip away.

On July 4, Meade issued General Order No. 68, which thanked his men for their success at Gettysburg (and made the tiresome mistake of pronouncing the Confederates "superior in numbers"), then added "the commanding general looks to the army . . . to drive from our soil . . . the invader." When Lincoln read the order he spat, "The whole country is our soil." Then, late on this day, came word that until Lee's intentions were "ascertained," Meade did not want to pursue him.

Citing Meade's General Order No. 68, Lincoln wrote his general in chief, Henry Halleck, that evening, saying, "I left the telegraph office a good deal dissatisfied." Lincoln's anger suppressed his usually sympathetic nature when he complained of a report that the Confederates were "crossing his wounded over the [Potomac] river in flats." He added, "These things appear to me to be connected with a purpose . . . to get the enemy across the river again without a further collision, and . . . [not] to prevent his crossing and destroy him. . . . If you are satisfied the latter purpose is entertained and judiciously pursued, I am content. If you are not so satisfied, please look to it."

The next day, when news came that Vicksburg, Mississippi had finally fallen, Lincoln wrote Halleck again: "Now, if General Meade can complete his work, so gloriously prosecuted thus far, by the literal or substantial destruction of Lee's army, the rebellion will be over."

JULY 7

"Caught the Rabbit"

On top of the victory at Gettysburg, Lincoln, on this Tuesday in 1863, received welcome news that the siege of Vicksburg, Mississippi was finally over.

For forty-six days General Ulysses Grant laid siege to the city that overlooked the Mississippi River. Starving Vicksburg civilians and soldiers alike were forced to eat pets, rats, and mules. As Grant continually bombarded the city, the inhabitants sought shelter in bunkers, bombproof shelters, and the city's natural caves. One disgruntled resident posted a FOR RENT sign in front of a vacated house that directed inquiries to Confederate president Jefferson Davis. After a shell smashed into the house the sign was replaced with RENTED, BY [generals] GRANT AND MCPHERSON.

Word spread that Grant wished to end the siege by July 4 and the *Vicksburg Daily Citizen* editorialized that "the Yankee Generalissimo, surnamed Grant—has expressed his intention of dining in Vicksburg . . . and celebrating the 4th of July by a grand dinner." It added, "Ulysses must fight to get into the city before he dines in it. The way to cook a rabbit is 'first catch the rabbit.'" When the Confederates capitulated on July 4 (they believed they would receive better terms on the national holiday), Union soldiers printed the message, "Gen. Grant has 'caught the rabbit.'" Independence Day would not be celebrated in Vicksburg for another eighty-six years.

Word of the surrender reached Washington on this day and when the shy, dour secretary of the navy, Gideon Welles, handed the telegram to Lincoln, Welles "executed a double shuffle and threw up his hat." A week later Lincoln sent Grant a letter in which he admitted that he had harbored misgivings about Grant's plan to take Vicksburg. "I feared it was a mistake," Lincoln wrote. "I now wish to make the personal acknowledgment that you were right and I was wrong."

JULY 13

Draft Riots

On this Monday in 1863, Lincoln received word that New York City was in chaos as fury over the draft sparked the worst riot in American history.

Shortages of men prompted Congress, in March 1863, to pass the Enrollment Act, instituting the first official U.S. draft. Male citizens between the ages of twenty and forty-five had to register, beginning in May, and were eligible for the draft in July. Opponents of conscription—particularly Democrats—were quick to point out that not only were blacks exempt from the draft, but so was anyone who could pay $300 for a substitute. While Lincoln objected to the exemptions, he was made the scapegoat for the provision, with some taking up the slogan "a rich man's war and a poor man's fight."

The first day of the New York draft (July 12, 1863) passed without incident but on the second day a mob stormed the draft headquarters. The mob, composed mostly of poor Irish immigrants who competed with free blacks for jobs, then took to the streets, looting, killing police officers, and burning down an orphanage for black children. The *New York Times* reported, "It seemed to be an understood thing that the Negroes should be attacked wherever found, whether they offered any provocation or not." *Harper's Weekly* described a mob that beat a black man into "insensibility," then hung him from a tree. Not satisfied, the mob lit torches and "danced around their victim, setting fire to him and his clothes, and burning him almost to a cinder."

Troops straight from the Gettysburg battlefield were dispatched to New York. After five days of rioting, $1.5 million in damages were inflicted on the city and casualty estimates reached as high as one thousand.

JULY 14

"Your Golden Opportunity is Gone"

Lincoln was depressed on this day in 1863, in part because of the massive draft riots in New York City. But Lincoln was far more distressed over news that Confederate general Robert E. Lee's army had escaped across the Potomac.

After Lee's loss at Gettysburg, his Army of Northern Virginia had been trapped on the north side of the Potomac, swollen by rain. Lincoln had ordered General George Meade to attack immediately. Instead, Meade moved sluggishly.

On this day came news that Lee had escaped. "On only one or two occasions have I ever seen the President so troubled, so dejected and discouraged," wrote Secretary of the Navy Gideon Welles. Later, Lincoln said, "We had gone through all the labor of tilling and planting an enormous crop and when it was ripe we did not harvest it."

That afternoon Halleck wired Meade, "I need hardly say to you that the escape of Lee's army without another battle has created great dissatisfaction in the mind of the President."

Meade responded by tendering his resignation. When Lincoln heard of the exchange, he sat down to compose a letter to Meade. "I am sorry now to be the author of the slightest pain to you," Lincoln wrote. "But I was in such deep distress myself that I could not restrain some expression of it." He added, "My dear general, I do not believe you appreciate the magnitude of the misfortune involved in Lee's escape. He was within your easy grasp, and to have closed upon him would, in connection with our other late successes, have ended the war. As it is, the war will be prolonged indefinitely. . . . Your golden opportunity is gone." Lincoln never sent the letter to Meade. Nor did he accept Meade's resignation.

#53

Could Meade Have Ended the War?

One ongoing debate regarding the Civil War is whether General George Meade could have ended the war if he had attacked and decimated Confederate general Robert E. Lee's trapped army. Lincoln certainly thought so. Lincoln once claimed that Meade's lost opportunity was one of three occasions when "better management . . . of the commanding general might have terminated the war." (The other two occasions were during General George McClellan's Peninsula Campaign and General Joseph Hooker's Chancellorsville Campaign.) He admitted that he wasn't sure how he'd react in Meade's place: "I do not know that I could have given any different orders. . . . I might run away."

But was it even possible for Meade to decimate Lee's army if he had attacked? By the time Gettysburg was over, Meade had been in command for only a week. While one out of every three soldiers in Lee's army were Gettysburg casualties, a quarter of Meade's men were casualties as well, among them his most aggressive commanders. What's more, pursuing Lee had exhausted an already tired army. Gettysburg had also nearly depleted Meade's ammunition. Could an army in such a state realistically defeat an army led by Lee, who would demonstrate his prowess at defensive warfare against both Meade and General Ulysses Grant in the Overland Campaign of 1864?

But even if Meade decimated Lee's army, would it end the war? Historians have long maintained that the war was won in the western theater, not the east. One significant

Confederate army—the Army of the Tennessee—and a few smaller armies were still in the field. If Lee's army were destroyed and Richmond taken, the indefatigable Confederate president Jefferson Davis would have moved his administration south and west to continue the war, as he tried to do in April 1865.

JULY 15

From Anger to Laughter

The news that Confederate general Robert E. Lee's army had escaped across the Potomac River had infuriated Lincoln. He even wrote an uncharacteristically sharp letter on July 14 to General George Meade, the commander who allowed Lee to escape. But, on this Wednesday in 1863, Lincoln swallowed his angst and named a day of Thanksgiving celebrating Meade and his Gettysburg victory (as well as General Ulysses Grant's taking of Vicksburg, Mississippi).

Lincoln began the day still angry. He and his eldest son, Robert, were not close during the White House years and Lincoln almost never confided in his son about matters of state. "I scarcely had ten minutes quiet talk during his Presidency, on account of his constant devotion to business," Robert later wrote. Lincoln was so distraught on this morning that he told Robert—who had just come home to see his injured mother after her July 2 carriage accident—about Lee's escape. "If I had gone up there I could have licked them myself," Lincoln said.

As the week wore on, Lincoln's vitriol subsided and he began referring to Meade "as a brave and skillful officer, and a true man." And on Sunday Lincoln was sanguine enough to pen a doggerel titled "Gen. Lees invasion of the North."

In eighteen sixty three, with pomp and mighty swell,

Me and Jeff's Confederacy, went forth to sack Phil-del [Philadelphia],
The Yankees they got arter us, and give us particular hell,
And we skedaddled back again, and didn't sack Phil-del.

#54

Robert

Lincoln's oldest son, even as a child, was something of an outsider in his own family. Robert's disposition and chubby face was more reminiscent of the in-laws (the Todds) than the Lincolns. What's more, Lincoln spent Robert's early childhood away from the family for three months out of every year, riding through central Illinois as a circuit attorney. Robert's earliest memory of his father was of Lincoln packing his saddlebags. While the Lincolns did discipline their oldest son, after the younger boys were born—and particularly after Eddie, the second son, died—the parents became extremely indulgent of the children. "It is my pleasure that my children are free, happy and unrestrained by parental tyranny," Lincoln said. Robert took this disparity personally.

The father–son relationship did not improve during Lincoln's tenure in the White House, as they also coincided with Robert's four years at Harvard. Their busy schedules often conflicted. Mary was not so constrained and used Robert as an escort for her shopping excursions. Mary was present (while Lincoln was not) at Robert's college graduation and was unabashedly proud of him.

Robert was the only son of the Lincolns to reach adulthood. He was successful as a Chicago lawyer, president and chairman of the Pullman Corporation (manufacturers of

Cover illustration for 1860 presidential campaign sheet music titled "Lincoln Quick Step" by an unnamed composer (not to be mistaken for the "Lincoln Quick-step" by Jesse Brinley or the "Campaign Quick Step" by M. B. Cross). As was the case in the campaign, the motifs and vignettes that surround Lincoln's portrait emphasize Lincoln's humble beginnings splitting rails and piloting a flatboat down the Mississippi. Some of the song's words read, "He has guided his flat boat thro many a strait, and watchful he'll prove at the Helm of the State." (Courtesy of the Library of Congress)

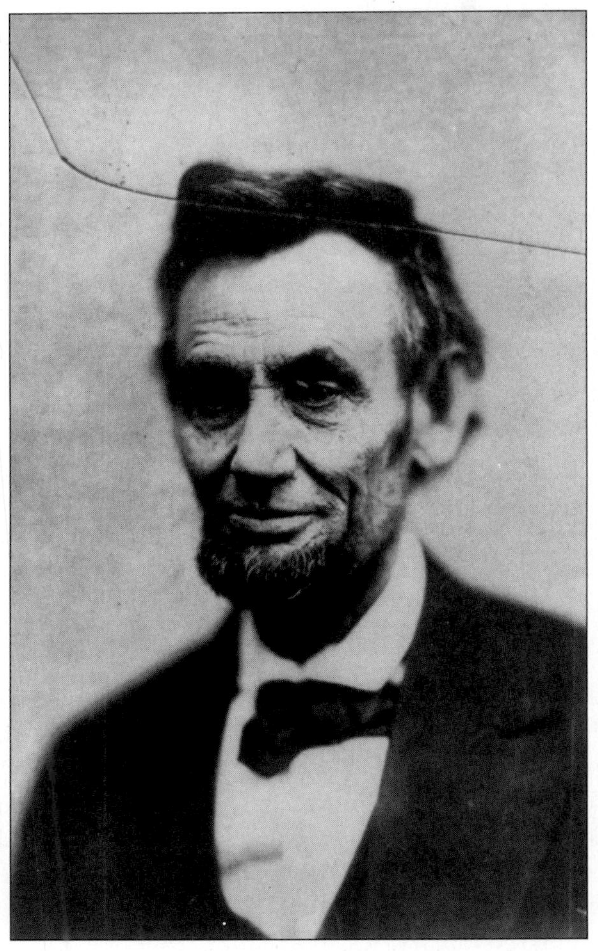

Four years later the lines in Lincoln's face are deeper, the circles under the eyes more pronounced, and the face itself more haggard. By the time this photograph was taken on February 5, 1865, the burdens of war were clearly evident on his countenance. (Courtesy of Wikimedia Commons)

Mary Todd in the March 1861 gown she wore to her husband's first inaugural ball. (Courtesy of the Library of Congress)

Mary Todd in 1846 or 1847 around the time of the birth of the Lincolns' second child, Eddie. The Lincolns were in their fourth or fifth year of marriage, and they already had a toddler, Robert, at home. (Courtesy of the Library of Congress)

The eldest son, Robert, in 1865 near the time of his graduation from Harvard. (Courtesy of the Library of Congress)

The two younger Lincoln boys, Tad (right) and Willie (standing), as they pose with their mother's nephew, Lockwood Todd, in 1861. (Courtesy of the Library of Congress)

Eddie was the Lincoln boy who never made it to the White House as he died just before his fourth birthday in 1850. (Courtesy of Wikimedia Commons)

The president poses with his two private secretaries, John Nicolay (left) and John Hay, in a November 8, 1863 sitting at Alexander Gardner's Studio. Hay wrote in his diary that day: "We had a great many pictures taken . . . some of the Prest, the best I have seen. . . . Nico & I immortalized ourselves by having ourselves done in a group with the Prest." (Courtesy of the Library of Congress)

During Lincoln's highly documented trip to the Antietam battlefield, Lincoln stopped to pose with his bodyguard, Major Allan Pinkerton (left), and General John McClernand on October 3, 1862. (Courtesy of Wikimedia Commons)

On that same day, Lincoln posed with several officers of General George McClellan's Army of the Potomac at Antietam. McClellan stands facing Lincoln while one of his officers, Captain George Armstrong Custer, stands at far right. Lincoln was not at Antietam just to see the field of the worst single-day battle of the war; he was there to goad McClellan into moving against the enemy. After another month of excuses from McClellan, Lincoln finally sacked the general. (Courtesy of Wikimedia Commons).

The famous Francis Bicknell Carpenter painting depicting the "First Reading of the Emancipation Proclamation of President Lincoln." Portrayed from left are Secretary of War Edwin Stanton (seated); Secretary of the Treasury Salmon Chase (standing); Lincoln (seated); Secretary of the Navy Gideon Welles (seated); Secretary of the Interior Caleb Smith (standing); Secretary of State William Seward (seated); Postmaster General Montgomery Blair (standing); and Attorney General Edward Bates (seated). (Courtesy of Wikimedia Commons)

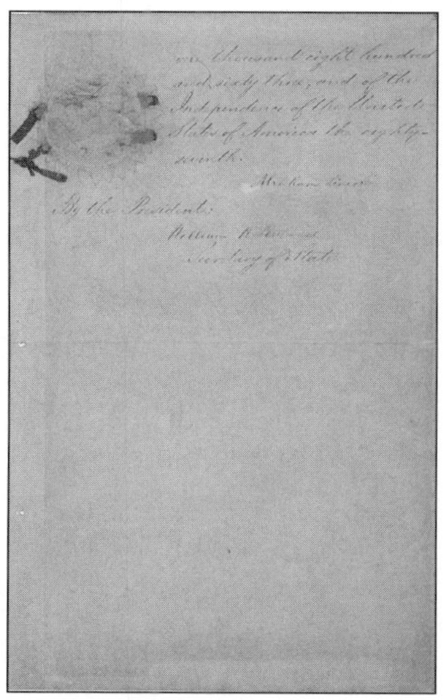

one thousand eight hundred and sixty three, and of the Independence of the United States of America the eighty-seventh.

Abraham Lincoln

By the President:

William H. Seward

Secretary of State

After shaking hands all New Year's morning that January 1, 1863, Lincoln had to concentrate to steady his hand before signing this page—page five of the Emancipation Proclamation—below the Great Seal of the United States. (Courtesy of the National Archives)

Four score and seven years ago our fathers brought forth, upon this continent, a new nation, conceived in Liberty, and dedicated to the proposition that all men are created equal.

Now we are engaged in a great civil war, testing whether that nation, or any nation, so conceived, and so dedicated, can long endure. We are met here on a great battle field of that war. We have come to dedicate a portion of it as a final resting place for those who here gave their lives, that that nation might live. It is altogether fitting and proper that we should do this.

But in a larger sense we can not dedicate—we can not consecrate—we can not hallow this ground. The brave men, living and dead, who struggled here, have consecrated it far above our poor power to add or detract. The world will little note, nor long remember, what we say here, but can never forget what they did here. It is for us, the living, rather to be dedicated here to the unfinished work which they have, thus far, so nobly carried on. It is rather

There are five known surviving copies of the Gettysburg Address, each given to a different person. This draft was given to Lincoln's secretary, John Hay, and is considered the second draft of the speech. Many believe that this draft was written on the day of the speech (November 19, 1863) and may have been the draft he read from at the Gettysburg ceremony. If it is the draft he read from, it does not include the words "under God," which lends credence to the theory that the words were impulsive and impromptu when Lincoln finished the speech with: "we here highly resolve that these dead shall not have died in vain—that this nation, under God, shall have a new birth of freedom—and that government of the people, by the people, for the people, shall not perish from the earth." (Courtesy of Wikimedia Commons)

This photograph of Lincoln at the Gettysburg National Cemetery ceremony on November 19, 1863 was not identified until 1952. It is estimated that this picture was taken at noon, just after Lincoln arrived at the ceremony and about three hours before he would deliver his famous Gettysburg Address. To Lincoln's right is his bodyguard, Ward Hill Lamon.

February 9, 1864 was an unusually busy day for Lincoln at Mathew Brady's Studio in Washington. Photographer Anthony Berger took three photographs of Lincoln that eventually became iconic to Americans. The first is a profile of Lincoln that was later used as a guide for the penny (below). (Courtesy of the Library of Congress)

Anthony Berger also took this photograph of Lincoln on February 9, 1864 that was adapted for the five dollar bill (below). (Courtesy of the Library of Congress)

A third photograph of Lincoln by Anthony Berger became the only known photograph that he shared with a family member. Here, the president is looking at a photo album with his son Tad. It is also the only close-up of Lincoln with his glasses on. It became one of the most popular photos of Lincoln.

An example of how Democrats in the 1864 campaign tried to paint Lincoln's Republicans as espousing racial equality and intermingling (or "miscegenation," as they called it). On the left, a black woman is introduced to Lincoln and says, "Don't do nuffin now but gallevant 'round widde white gemmen!" On the right, a white woman embraces a black man asking him to seek her father's permission for her hand in marriage. In the center, a black family rides in a carriage with a white driver and white footmen. (Courtesy of the Library of Congress)

Democrats believed that General George McClellan's popularity among the soldiers would translate into a victory for them in the 1864 presidential election. Soldiers, however, did not care for the Democratic platform to negotiate with the Confederacy for peace, and the majority of their votes went for Lincoln. (Courtesy of Wikimedia Commons)

THE ASSASSINATION OF PRESIDENT LINCOLN,
AT FORD'S THEATRE WASHINGTON, D.C. APRIL 14TH 1865.

With the war all but over, a desperate John Wilkes Booth shot Lincoln in the head on April 14, 1865 at Ford's Theatre. From the left is Henry Rathbone, Clara Harris, Mary Todd Lincoln, the president, and Booth. (Courtesy of Wikimedia Commons)

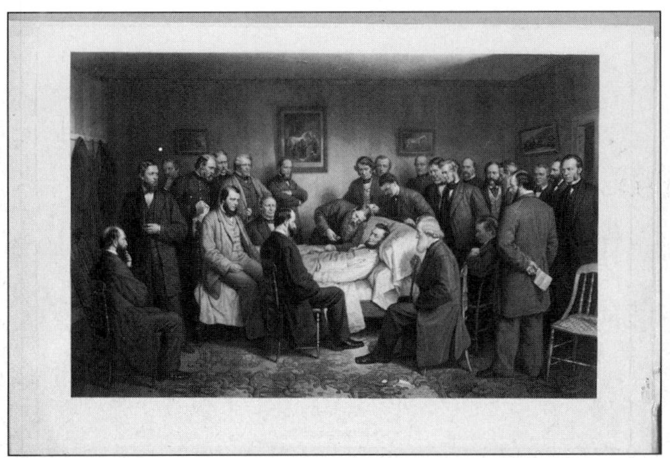

Lincoln's eventful life came to an end at 7:22 on the morning of April 15, 1865 as he lay diagonally on a walnut cottage bed in a boarding house owned by William Petersen. The painting depicts Dr. Charles Leale checking Lincoln's pulse, which, along with his breathing, had stopped. After Lincoln's pastor, Phineas Gurley, said a prayer, Secretary of War Edwin Stanton, probably depicted standing with his back to the viewer on the right, said, "Now he belongs to the ages." Mary was in the front parlor of the house at the time, too distraught to watch her husband die. (Courtesy of the Library of Congress)

train sleeping cars), and served as Secretary of War and minister to London. While not present when his father was shot, he was present when two other presidents—James Garfield in 1881 and William McKinley in 1901—were shot. When Robert's grandson, Robert Todd Lincoln Beckwith, died in 1985, Lincoln's direct lineage died with him.

JULY 18

Reviewing Courts-martial

Lincoln's sour mood over the New York draft riots was dramatically lifted on this day in 1863 after he reviewed a hundred courts-martial cases.

No matter how pressing Lincoln's schedule was, he usually spent at least a few hours every week reviewing courts-martial. For six straight hours on this day, Lincoln, his secretary John Hay, and Judge Advocate Joseph Holt went over the cases. "I was amused at the eagerness with which the President caught at any fact which could justify him in saving the life of a condemned soldier," Hay wrote in his diary. "He said it would frighten the poor devils too terribly to shoot them."

Private Michael Delany of the First Colorado Calvary had been convicted of desertion but had reenlisted. "Let him fight instead of being shot," Lincoln wrote. "He [Lincoln] was only merciless in cases where meanness or cruelty were shown," Hay noted. Apparently this also included inebriation, because Lincoln upheld the dismissal from service of a lieutenant in the Sixth Iowa Calvary for drunkenness. When Lincoln reviewed the case of a captain convicted of "looking thro keyholes & over transoms at a lady undressing," the president quipped that the officer should "be elevated to peerage so he could receive the proper title of 'Count Peeper.'"

While Hay was "in a state of entire collapse" after the six-hour marathon, Lincoln's mood had improved. "The Tycoon was in a very good humor," Hay wrote the next day. Lincoln derived great satisfaction from granting pardons. "It rests me after a hard day's work," Lincoln once told Indiana congressman Schuyler Colfax, "that I can find some excuse for saving some poor fellow's life, and I shall go to bed happy tonight."

#55

"Leg Cases"

During the war, more than 250,000 Union desertions were reported. If all alleged deserters were executed according to military regulations, that would require an execution of 1,200 men per week during the 200 weeks of the Civil War. In November 1862, Lincoln told a Sanitary Commission delegation that desertions were hurting the army. When a delegate asked why Lincoln didn't enforce the death penalty on desertions, Lincoln replied, "You can't order men shot by dozens or twenties. People won't stand it, and they ought not to stand it." The fact that a total of only 276 soldiers were executed during the war (for reasons including but not limited to desertion) can be attributed in part to Lincoln's prolific pardons.

In July 1863, Lincoln was meeting with General John Eaton when they were interrupted by gunshots. "This is the day they shoot deserters," Lincoln said forlornly. He told Eaton that he tried to understand the situation from the young soldier's perspective, the boy so "overcome by a physical fear greater than his will." Lincoln often told the story of the soldier who, when asked why he deserted, responded, "Well, Captain, it was not my fault. I have . . . [a] brave heart . . . but these legs of mine will always run away with me when the battle begins."

One evening, while discussing with Judge Advocate Joseph Holt a soldier's desertion during a battle, Lincoln said, "Well, Judge, I think I must put this with my leg cases." Lincoln pointed to a pigeonhole in his desk stuffed with files. "They are the cases that you call 'cowardice in the face of the enemy' but I call them leg cases. . . . If Almighty God gives a man a pair of cowardly legs, how can he help their running away with him?"

JULY 24

War Widows

On this day in 1863, Lincoln sent a note to Postmaster General Montgomery Blair recommending that disabled soldiers and war widows be given preference in filling government jobs.

By the 1850s, America's Industrial Revolution had pulled many Northern women into the labor force. While women continued to work as domestic housekeepers, a quarter of the workforce in manufacturing was composed of women, particularly in textiles. Still, only 25 percent of single women in the north worked, with less than 5 percent continuing to work after marriage. But as the war pulled men out of the workforce, there were 100,000 jobs opened. This doesn't include the thousands of acres of farmland that had to be tended. Women filled teaching and nursing positions, in particular. In Washington, they filled jobs as clerks and copyists at the Treasury, War, and Interior departments. The Post Office employed postmistresses all over the country and Lincoln even considered recommending Mary's cousin—Elizabeth Todd Grimsley—as Springfield, Illinois's postmistress. Unfortunately, women civil servants were paid half of what men were paid and their salaries would not be raised for another twenty years.

On July 23, 1863, Lincoln sent Blair endorsements for two war widows to receive postmistress positions and on this day Lincoln sent another note to Blair, saying that "These [two] cases occurring on the same day brought me to reflect more attentively . . . in dispensing patronage [jobs], towards men who, by fighting our battles bear the chief burden of saving our country. My conclusion is that . . . they have the better right; and this is especially applicable to the disabled soldier, and the deceased soldier's family." Lincoln's endorsements are lost but one of them was probably for the widow of Colonel Melancthon Smith, who had died at Vicksburg, Mississippi. Mrs. Smith had been Rockford, Illinois's acting deputy postmistress in her husband's absence and Blair awarded her a permanent position.

JULY 25

Routes

On this Saturday in 1863, Lincoln's secretary John Hay logged in his diary, "I rode out to the Soldiers' Home with the Tycoon [his nickname for Lincoln] tonight . . . Rode home in the dark amid a party of drunken gamblers & harlots." Such fellow travelers were just a few of many that Lincoln encountered on his trips to and from the Soldiers' Home cottage during the summers of 1862, 1863, and 1864.

One of Lincoln's routes to the cottage was via Fourteenth Street, which the President probably reached via Pennsylvania Avenue, where he'd pass "Hooker's Division" (located where the Departments of Commerce and Internal Revenue presently sit), Washington's largest center for gambling and prostitution. Hay's "party of drunken gamblers & harlots" could have taken this route out to the military camps and forts north of town. The area north of town also featured military hospitals and Lincoln was known to talk to wounded soldiers en route to them. "The President on the Fourth [of July, 1863], while on his way to his summer residence at Soldiers' Home, meeting a train of ambulances conveying wounded men . . . rode beside them for a considerable distance, conversing freely with the men," the *New York Tribune* reported.

Another of Lincoln's routes was to take the Seventh Street Turnpike (Seventh Street) then Rhode Island and Vermont avenues to the White House. In the summer of 1862, the poet Walt Whitman lived on Vermont and saw Lincoln so frequently that they had a habit of bowing to each other. "Mr. Lincoln on the saddle generally rides a good-sized easy going gray horse, is dress'd in plain black, somewhat rusty and dusty, wears a black, stiff hat, and looks about as ordinary in attire, etc. as the commonest man," Whitman wrote. "None of the artists or pictures has caught the deep, though subtle and indirect expression of this man's face. . . . One of the great portrait painters of two or three centuries ago is needed."

JULY 29

Caution

On this day in 1863, Lincoln, after pressing General George Meade to attack Confederate general Robert E. Lee for weeks, grew cautious about a "general engagement" with Lee.

Meade's Army of the Potomac had, in mid-July, failed to attack Lee's army when it was trapped by a flooded Potomac. Meade submitted his resignation in response to Lincoln's disappointment, but Lincoln could not afford to fire the hero of Gettysburg. Still, Lincoln felt the missed opportunity was the "greatest disaster of the war." In response, Meade pursued Lee when the aggressive Confederate general maneuvered toward the Shenandoah Valley in late July. Meade decided to strike at Lee's flank, and on the afternoon of July 28 Meade wired Washington, "I am in hopes to commence the movement to-morrow." Meade added that a scout had reported that Lee had been reinforced with 10,000 men.

After reading Meade's telegram, Lincoln was concerned. Not only had Gettysburg depleted Meade's army, but Meade had also sent some of his troops to New York City to quell its riots. On this day Lincoln wrote General in Chief Henry Halleck to deny that "the government here is demanding of him [Meade] to bring on a general engagement with Lee." Lincoln thought that with Meade depleted and Lee reinforced it would be "absurd" to take the offensive. "True, I desired Gen. Meade to pursue Lee across the Potomac," Lincoln admitted, but he did not want to pressure Meade into a disaster. Halleck passed Lincoln's message to Meade, who did not attack and remained inactive the rest of the summer and most of the fall.

JULY 30

Order of Retaliation

On this Thursday in 1863, Lincoln wrote General Order No. 252, which promised retaliation if the Confederacy fulfilled its promise to enslave or execute captured black soldiers.

The South was infuriated by the Emancipation Proclamation, particularly its stipulation on arming black soldiers. Confederate secretary of war James Seddon vowed that "we ought never to be inconvenienced with such [black] prisoners . . . summary execution must therefore be inflicted on those taken." In his January 12, 1863 speech, Confederate president Jefferson Davis promised to try Union officers leading black troops "as criminals engaged in inciting insurrection." Less than five months later the Confederate Congress approved a resolution calling for the execution of captured officers of black regiments and for black soldiers to be either executed or sold into bondage. While the Confederate government never enforced that resolution, in the field there were recorded instances when surrendering or wounded black soldiers were summarily executed.

Lincoln did not initially respond to the Confederate edicts. "What has Mr. Lincoln to say about this slavery and murder?" said the famous black orator, Frederick Douglass. "In the hearing of the nation he is as silent as an oyster." Lincoln later explained to Douglass that he waited for battles "in which Negroes had distinguished themselves for bravery and good conduct," which would thus turn public sentiment favorably toward the black soldier. Finally, on this day, Lincoln wrote out a retaliatory edict: "It is therefore ordered that for every soldier . . . killed in violation of the laws of war, a rebel soldier shall be executed; and for every one enslaved by the enemy or sold into slavery, a rebel soldier shall be placed at hard labor" in a prison camp. Lincoln, however, had misgivings, declaring that "blood can not restore blood, and government should not act for revenge." Lincoln's order was never officially enforced.

#56

The "Black Flag"

Unofficially, Confederate soldiers gave black soldiers what was called the "black flag," which meant they were given no quarter and not allowed to surrender. The most famous example of this was on April 12, 1864 at a Tennessee garrison named Fort Pillow, where Confederate general Nathan Bedford Forrest attacked and surrounded the fort with its 580 men. When the garrison commander refused to surrender, Forrest's men assaulted and took the fort. The rebels chased down black soldiers specifically, killing many after they had surrendered. Sixty-four percent of its nearly 300 black soldiers were murdered.

The public outrage this elicited, especially after another massacre at Poison Springs, Arkansas six days later, prompted a congressional investigation. Lincoln devoted two cabinet meetings to determining a recourse. The cabinet decided to retaliate only against Forrest's command and set aside Confederate prisoners as hostages against future occurrences. Neither Forrest nor his men were ever brought to justice nor were Confederate prisoners executed. Many black units, however, took up the cry "Remember Fort Pillow" and vowed to never take prisoners.

There were other instances of racial atrocities. At Petersburg, Virginia, during the Battle of the Crater (July 30, 1864), wounded black soldiers were reportedly bayoneted. In April 1864, after Confederates retook Plymouth, North Carolina, a Union sergeant reported,

> All the Negroes found in blue uniform . . . was killed—I saw some taken into the woods and hung—Others I saw stripped of all their clothing, and they stood upon the bank of the river with their faces riverwards and then they were shot—Still others were killed by having their brains beaten out by the butt end of the muskets in the hands of the Rebels.

AUGUST 1

To "Live in History"

While Lincoln dealt with many timid generals, he also had a few that had more ambition than common sense. One such case was General Robert Milroy, who had lost his division during the Second Battle of Winchester, Virginia in June 1863. Lincoln, on this Saturday in 1863, forwarded a petition supporting Milroy to the Adjutant General investigating the incident.

Winchester, which sat at the northern end of the strategically important Shenandoah Valley, was the hub of the area's roads. By some accounts it changed hands seventy times during the war, and four major battles occurred around the town. None of its Union occupiers were as hated as Milroy during his six months there. Milroy was painfully ambitious, looking for battlefield honors "that would live in history." Milroy emancipated the town's slaves and hired detectives to sniff out Confederate sympathizers, banishing them when found. He was so despised that the Confederate government put a $100,000 bounty on his head.

When Confederate general Robert E. Lee began his June 1863 offensive, Milroy found an army of 25,000 advancing on him. Orders for him to retreat never reached Winchester—the telegraph wires were severed—and Milroy foolishly decided to pit his 6,000 troops against the Confederates. Nearly his entire command was captured. Milroy was subsequently arrested for disobeying orders.

During the investigation, Milroy wrote Lincoln several times pleading his case and had petitions signed by soldiers and civilians sent to Lincoln (who forwarded one on this day to the board of inquiry). Even after Milroy was vindicated, no one would trust him with another command. "I was deprived of the privilege of participating in the glorious battle of Gettysburg," Milroy complained. "You have just lost a Division," Lincoln responded, "and prima facie the fault is upon you."

AUGUST 7

"Bullocks into a Slaughter Pen"

In the wake of the huge draft riot in New York City, Governor Horatio Seymour requested that conscription be suspended in New York State. On this Friday in 1863, Lincoln refused Seymour's request.

Seymour, almost from the moment he took office, was critical of Lincoln's policies. On July 4, 1863, Seymour scoffed at the "military necessity" of emancipation and conscription: "Remember this—that the bloody treasonable doctrine of public necessity can be proclaimed by a mob as well as by a government." A week later mobs took to the streets in New York because of the draft and Seymour was criticized for his "incitement of the people to resist the government."

When the New York draft was scheduled to recommence on August 19, Seymour wrote Lincoln a lengthy appeal for its suspension. "The harsh measure of raising troops by compulsion has heretofore been avoided by this Government and is now resorted to from the belief . . . that it is necessary for the support of our arms," Seymour wrote, blaming the riot on public sentiment against the draft. Seymour also claimed that Democratic districts in New York and Brooklyn were asked to conscript more men than Republican districts. Seymour asked Lincoln to suspend the draft until the discrepancies were investigated.

Lincoln, on this day, responded that the quota disparity would be investigated but "time was too important" to suspend the draft. "We are contending with an enemy who . . . drives every able bodied man he can reach, into his ranks, very much as a butcher drives bullocks into a slaughter pen. . . . This produces an army which will soon turn upon our now victorious soldiers already in the field."

AUGUST 9

"The Tycoon Is in a Fine Whack"

Lincoln and his secretary John Hay went, on this day in 1863, to Alexander Gardner's new photography studio on the corner of Seventh and D streets to have the president's picture taken.

The summer of 1863 in Washington was incredibly hot. One Washingtonian wrote, "The garments cling to the skin, shirt collars are laid low, moisture oozes from every object, standing in clammy erudition upon iron, marble, wood and human flesh." In July, Mary, Robert, and Tad escaped to the cool mountains of New Hampshire and Vermont while Lincoln stayed, both busy and productive. On August 7, Hay wrote in his diary, "The Tycoon [his nickname for Lincoln] is in a fine whack. I have rarely seen him more serene and busy. He is managing this war, the draft, foreign relations and planning reconstruction of the Union, all at once. . . . I am growing more and more firmly convinced that the good of the country absolutely demands that he should be kept where he is till this thing is over."

Hay accompanied the "Tycoon" everywhere: to the Observatory to view the moon; to target practice with a new repeating rifle; on a ride out to the Capitol to look at the new dome. On this day, they went to Gardner's studio to take a rare full-length photo of Lincoln's six-foot-four-inch frame. One huge hand rested on a stack of books and his somber expression belied Hay's assessment. "He [Lincoln] is in very good spirits," Hay wrote. "He thinks that the rebel power is at last beginning to disintegrate, that they will break to pieces if we only stand firm." Lincoln believed that if the Confederate army could be "crushed, the [Southern] people would be ready to swing back to their old bearings."

#57

The Physical Man

While Lincoln was campaigning for president in 1860, he described himself as "in height, six feet four inches, nearly; lean in flesh, weighing on an average one hundred and eighty pounds; dark complexion, with coarse black hair and gray eyes." Four years of war eventually trimmed off twenty pounds from his frame and his stooped stature shortened him by a quarter of an inch. His left shoulder was higher than his right, giving him a slightly off-balanced gait. He walked, said his pastor Dr. Phineas Gurley, as if "he was about to plunge forward, from his right shoulder, for he always walked, when he had anything in his hand, as if he was pushing something in front of him." Another described his walk as "a mariner who had found his sea legs but had to admit there was a rough sea running." His ex–law partner William Herndon said Lincoln lifted his size 14 feet all "at once—not lifting himself from the toes, and hence had no spring . . . to his walk."

Lincoln's back, chest, and shoulders were narrow and muscular. His long, pendulous arms ended in huge hands that had lost their sinewy strength and, by his presidency, had the long, delicate fingers of a writer. Most of his height was in his legs. "A marble placed on his knee thus sitting would roll hipward," Herndon wrote. "It was only when he stood up that he towered above other men."

"Mr. Lincoln's forehead was narrow but high. His hair . . . lay floating where the fingers or the winds left it, piled up at random," wrote Herndon. "His nose was large—long and blunt, having the tip glowing in red, and a little awry toward the right eye. . . . His face was long—sallow—cadaverous—shrunk—shrivelled—wrinkled and dry. . . . His cheeks were leathery and flabby . . . looking sorrowful and sad. Mr. Lincoln's ears were extremely large—and ran out almost at right angles from his head."

AUGUST 10

Lincoln Meets Frederick Douglass

On this Monday in 1863, Lincoln met for the first time a man he would come to respect and befriend—Frederick Douglass.

Douglass was a mulatto slave born in 1817 in Tuckahoe, Maryland, and given the name Frederick Augustus Washington Bailey. At age eight he was secretly taught to read and write. At twenty-one he escaped, changed his name to Douglass, and, because of his eloquence and firsthand knowledge of slavery, he became a spokesperson for abolition. During the war, he campaigned for emancipation and enlisting blacks in the army. “Once let the black man get upon his person the brass letters, U.S.; let him get an eagle on his button, and a musket on his shoulder,” Douglass said, “[and no one] can deny he has earned the right to citizenship.”

Concerned about discrimination in the army, Douglass went to the White House on this day to speak to the president. Douglass found Lincoln seated, his “legs extended in front of his chair. On my approach he slowly drew his feet in from the different parts of the room into which they strayed, and he began to rise.” Lincoln’s “transparent continence” put Douglass at ease and he later said he felt he could “put my hand on his shoulder.” Douglass spoke of equal pay for black soldiers and commissioning black officers. Lincoln promised the pay would eventually be equalized and “he would sign any commission to colored soldiers whom his Secretary of War would commend to him.” As Douglass was about to leave, Lincoln mentioned a recent speech where Douglass criticized the president for his “tardy, hesitating and vacillating policy.” Lincoln conceded that he took his time in deciding issues, but “I think it cannot be shown that when I have once taken a position, I have ever retreated from it.”

AUGUST 11

War Governors

With the New York City draft about to recommence on August 19, just over a month after the city’s horrific draft riots, a flurry of correspondence passed between Lincoln and Governor Horatio

Seymour in the first weeks of August. Seymour believed that Democratic districts in New York had to draft and enlist more men for the army than Republican districts. On this day in 1863, Lincoln refigured district quotas.

Lincoln's relationship with the twenty-two governors of the Union (there were twenty-four by the end of the war) was fairly acrimonious. This was, in part, because they were overwhelmingly Republican (seventeen of them). At the beginning of the war, the governors were enthusiastic recruiters of troops; for example, Connecticut governor William Buckingham raised 54,882 volunteers out of a population of 461,000 people) Once conscription was enacted, the governors, like Seymour, quarreled with Lincoln over state and district quotas—basically, over the number of draftees and volunteers they were required to supply. None were as publicly outspoken as Seymour, prompting some to unfairly question his patriotism.

In early August, Seymour asked Lincoln to suspend the New York City and Brooklyn drafts until disparities in quotas could be rectified; he also wanted time to test the constitutionality of conscription. Lincoln refused, citing time constraints in manning a depleted Union Army. Seymour fired back with more information that he thought demonstrated how the "law had been perverted." Lincoln's secretary John Hay wrote, "Seymour is in a terrible state of nervous excitement." Lincoln responded again by refusing to suspend the draft: "I consider time as being very important, both to the general cause of the country, and the soldiers already in the field." Lincoln then redistributed district quotas to make them fairer. He also sent troops to New York to squelch any possible draft riots. There were none, and the draft restarted without incident.

AUGUST 13

The Symbol

On this Thursday in 1863, Lincoln took a ride to the Capitol with his secretary John Hay to see the progress made on the Capitol's dome.

By 1850 it was clear that the Capitol Building—completed twenty-five years earlier—could no longer house the increasing number of senators and representatives. Expansion began in 1851, featuring new Senate and House wings. The new wings more than doubled the length of the Capitol, and it was decided that the wooden dome over the rotunda was disproportionately small. Work began on a new 287-foot cast-iron dome, capped by a 19-foot Statue of Freedom. More than 5 million pounds of masonry and nearly 9 million pounds of iron were lifted atop the rotunda using a steam-powered derrick fueled by the wood from the old dome. At the outbreak of the Civil War, it was recommended that work on the dome be stopped. Lincoln refused. "If the people see the Capitol [dome construction] is going on," he said, "it is a sign we intend this Union shall go on."

On this day, Hay wrote in his diary that he rode with Lincoln to see the Capitol construction. "Saw the statuary of the East Pediment. The Pres[iden]t objected to Power's statue of the Woodchopper, as he did not make a sufficiently clean cut," he wrote. He was probably referring to the sculpture *Progress of Civilization* located above the Senate (or North) wing of the Capitol sculpted not by "Power" but by Thomas Crawford. Near the center is a woodsman chopping a tree trunk. Crawford's eighty-foot marble sculpture was placed in the pediment above the Senate's east entrance earlier that year. The dome was completed in 1866.

AUGUST 20

The Telegraph Office

Early on this Thursday afternoon in 1863, Lincoln walked to the second-floor library of the War Department, where the telegraph office was kept. The room had alcoves where shelves of rare books were still kept, including an elephant folio of John Audubon's *Birds of America*. There were two telegrams waiting for him: one from a governor asking Lincoln not to remit the discharge of a disloyal soldier; the other was from a general passing on a rumor that Confederate general Robert E. Lee's army was about to retreat to Richmond.

It was in that same telegraph office, one operator recalled, that Lincoln, sometime in 1862 or 1863, read a dispatch about an insignificant skirmish resulting in the retreat of both parties. Lincoln was reminded of "two snappy dogs, separated by a rail fence and barking at each other like fury, until, as they ran along the fence, they came to an open gate, whereupon they suddenly stopped barking, and after looking at each other for a moment, turned tail."

Next to the telegraph room was the smaller cipher room where messages were decoded. Thomas Eckert, the chief of the telegraph staff, had a desk below one of the two windows and it was there that Lincoln typically sat, waiting for dispatches—sometimes all night—and, in July 1862, where he wrote the first draft of his preliminary Emancipation Proclamation. Lincoln was fascinated with codes and it is believed he wrote a coded message of his own at City Point, Virginia after the fall of Richmond and Petersburg on April 3, 1865:

> A. Lincoln its in fume a in hymn to start I army treating there possible if of cut too forward pushing is he so all Richmond aunt confide is Andy evacuated Petersburg reports Grant morning this Washington Sec'y War.

Read backwards with emphasis on phonetics rather than spelling, and the meaning emerges.

AUGUST 26

The Conklin Letter

On this Wednesday in 1863, Lincoln sent an old Springfield friend, James Conklin, a letter that would be widely quoted long after its reading at a Springfield rally.

The Republican rally had been organized as a show of loyalist unity against the growing Copperhead (Peace Democrats) influence in the Midwest. Conklin invited Lincoln to come to the September 3 rally and Lincoln was tempted to make a trip home. But Lincoln could not break away. He, however, decided to address his critics with a letter to be read at the rally in his stead.

"There are those who are dissatisfied with me," Lincoln wrote. "You desire peace; and you blame me that you do not have it." Lincoln then outlined the three ways to attain peace, "force of arms;" "give up the Union;" or "some imaginable compromise." The first Lincoln was pursuing, the second he could not accept, and the rebels would not accept a "peace compromise."

"But to be plain, you are dissatisfied with me about the negro," Lincoln continued. "You say you will not fight to free negroes. Some of them seem willing to fight for you." Lincoln explained that every slave taken from the rebels made them weaker and the Union stronger. Lincoln added that peace, once achieved, would prove that "there can be no successful appeal from the ballot to the bullet . . . . And then, there will be some black men who can remember that with silent tongue, and clenched teeth and steady eye, and well-poised bayonet, they have helped mankind on this great consummation."

AUGUST 27

Bounty-jumpers

On this Thursday in 1863, Lincoln sent General George Meade an uncharacteristic denial of clemency for five army deserters.

Despite prevalent volunteerism in the early months of the war, both the North and South implemented bounties—financial incentives to enlist. Union enlistees could receive bounties from local, state, and federal authorities, sometimes immediately upon enlisting, and sometimes after a period of service. As the war progressed and enlistments flagged, bounties grew larger. In May of 1861, federal bounties were up to $300 while in January of 1865 a county bounty (in New York) was $1,000. When the draft was instituted in 1863, Northern draftees were given five days to report for induction and many opted to volunteer during that grace period in order to receive a bounty. Because enlistees did not have to be residents of the county or state from which they received their bounty, many shopped around for the best rate. Brokers would even help them find the best bounty for a percentage of it. Inevitably, some of these volunteers became "bounty-jumpers," claiming bounties, deserting from their units, then under a false name reenlisting to receive another bounty.

On August 26, Lincoln received a telegram from five soldiers—Charles Walter (alias C. Zene); John Rainese (alias George Rionese); John Falene (or Faline/Folaney, alias Geacinto Lerchize); Emile Lae (or Lai, alias E. Duffie); and George Kuhne (or Kuhn, alias G. Weik)—asking the President to commute their death sentences for bounty-jumping. "We each have wives & children, depending on us," they wrote. Lincoln was unmoved. On this day, Lincoln wrote their superior, Meade, that "these are very flagrant cases" and "their appeal is denied." All five were executed on August 29.

SEPTEMBER 14

The Judiciary vs. the Executive

Lincoln, on this Monday in 1863, called a cabinet meeting to discuss an order that might have sparked a confrontation between the judiciary and executive branches of government.

Before the war, it was an accepted practice for judges to release soldiers from military service by issuing a writ of habeas corpus—a court order for authorities to produce the defendant in court. When conscription was instituted in 1863, state—and some federal—judges used writs to hinder the draft. State courts were "discharging the drafted men rapidly under habeas corpus," Lincoln said at this day's cabinet meeting. The judges, particularly in Pennsylvania, would also either "throw the officers of this [draft] bureau into custody, or keep them so constantly before the courts as to prevent their attendance upon . . . [their] duties," wrote the provost marshal general after the war. Sailors, too, were being "discharged" said Secretary of the Navy Gideon Welles, delaying his ships "on the eve of sailing."

Lincoln wanted to authorize the provost marshals to ignore writs by state judges and, if court officers persisted, the marshals could use force to resist. Secretary of the Treasury Salmon Chase said that such "collisions" were frightening. "If the President acted on Executive authority a civil war in the Free States would be inevitable," Chase wrote later. Chase suggested Lincoln suspend habeas corpus throughout the nation. Lincoln was dubious but, when he drew up an order to the provost marshals the next day, Chase still objected. The president relented and issued the second nationwide suspension of the writ (the first was on September 22, 1862) in American history. Then Lincoln quietly sent his order for marshals to ignore writs—with force if necessary—on September 17. Fortunately an armed confrontation never happened.

SEPTEMBER 18

Old Friends

Lincoln was a man who remembered his friends. On this Friday in 1863, Lincoln repaid the kindness Hannah Armstrong had shown him some thirty years before.

When a young Lincoln first moved to New Salem, Illinois, in August 1831, he found he shared it with a gang of bullies known as the "Clary Grove Boys." Jack Armstrong, a member of these roughs, was challenged to wrestle the wiry Lincoln. As friend James Short recalled, "They wrestled for a long time, withough either being able to throw the other, until Armstrong broke holds, caught L[incoln] by the leg & floored him. L[incoln] . . . laughed the matter off so pleasantly that he gained the good will of the roughs and was never disturbed by them." Lincoln became good friends with Jack and his wife, Hannah, trekking the four miles out to their home to visit while Hannah mended his clothes. "Abe would come out to our house, drink milk & mush, corn bread, butter, bring the Children Candy," Hannah recalled.

When, in 1857, Hannah became a widow and her son William "Duff" was arrested, she turned to Lincoln. Duff was accused of killing John Metzger in a drunken altercation and, in what became Lincoln's most famous trial, Lincoln successfully defended Duff by discrediting the prosecution's star witness.

Then in 1863 Hannah had need of Lincoln again. Duff had joined the Eighty-fifth Illinois Volunteers and was ill with rheumatism. Hannah asked Lincoln if he could secure a discharge. On this day, Lincoln wired Hannah, "I have just ordered the discharge of your boy William, as you say, now at Louisville, Ky." Eight months later, Hannah wrote Lincoln, saying that "Duff has got home and is now married and doing well at this present time."

#58

The Almanac Murder Trial

The trial that became Lincoln's most famous court case began with an altercation on the night of August 29, 1857 at a revival or camp meeting. William "Duff" Armstrong and James Norris had been accused of striking James Metzger in the head, Norris with a piece of wood and Duff with a slungshot (a lead weight encased in a leather pouch and swung from a cord). When Metzger died on September 1, Duff and Norris were charged with murder. On November 7, Norris was convicted of manslaughter. Shortly thereafter, Duff's father died and his final wish was that Duff be given the best defense possible. His widow Hannah turned to perhaps the best lawyer in Illinois, Abe Lincoln.

Lincoln, in the May 1858 trial, called the owner of the slungshot to the stand where he testified that on the night of the assault he—not Duff—possessed the weapon. Lincoln's masterstroke was in his cross-examination of the prosecution's star witness, Charles Allen. The witness claimed he was standing more than fifty to sixty feet from Duff under a full moon directly overhead when he saw the defendant strike Metzger in the face with the slungshot. A dozen times Lincoln had Allen meticulously repeat the details of his testimony. Then Lincoln pulled out an almanac, which showed the moon was not overhead as Allen claimed but had nearly set.

In his closing arguments, Lincoln told the jury, as one observer remembered, "of his once being a poor, friendless boy, that Armstrong's father took him into his house, fed and clothed him and gave him a home." There were tears in Lincoln's eyes and in many of the jurors. "I have never seen such mastery exhibited over the feelings and emotions of men, as on that occasion," said Lincoln's co-defense counsel, William Walker. Duff was acquitted.

SEPTEMBER 21

"River of Death"

As news that a horrific battle had taken place in northern Georgia, Lincoln, on this Monday in 1863, attempted to hurry reinforcements to a creek known as Chickamauga.

In early September, General William Rosecrans, at the head of the Army of the Cumberland, flanked Confederate general Braxton Bragg's Army of the Tennessee, hoping to force Bragg to evacuate Chattanooga, an important railway hub. The maneuver worked and Rosecrans marched into Chattanooga on September 9. But his army was spread over forty miles and separated by mountains. Bragg decided to set a trap for one of Rosecrans's isolated corps. Meanwhile, Richmond, upset over the loss of Chattanooga, sent some of Confederate general Robert E. Lee's men to Bragg. At the same time, Rosecrans realized his precarious position and began gathering his men together along the Chickamauga (a Cherokee word for "river of death").

What followed was the largest battle in the western theater, lasting two days (September 19 and 20). On the second day, Rosecrans moved a division, inadvertently opening a hole in the Union line. Bragg's men roared through the gap and much of Rosecrans's army panicked, running for Chattanooga. It was a stunning Confederate victory, but at a cost; out of 124,000 combatants, 28,000 were dead or wounded. Among the dead was Lincoln's brother-in-law, Confederate general Ben Helm.

On September 19, Rosecrans sent a telegram to Washington with news of the first day's action. "Be of good cheer. We have unabated confidence in you," Lincoln wired back on this day. "Save your army, by taking strong positions until [General Ambrose] Burnside joins you." Lincoln then wired General Ambrose Burnside at Knoxville, "Go to Rosecrans with your force, without a moment delay." By the next day news of the second day's disaster had reached the White House.

SEPTEMBER 25

The Rant

There were times when Lincoln wrote uncharacteristically angry telegrams and letters in order to vent some of the pressures of the presidency. Lincoln wrote one such telegram on this Friday in 1863, addressed to General Ambrose Burnside in Knoxville, Tennessee.

From the beginning of the war, Lincoln had wanted a Union army presence in eastern Tennessee, largely to protect its pro-Union populace. The problem was that the area—particularly in the Smokey Mountains—did not have adequate railroads to support an army. General after general ignored Lincoln's goadings to march into that logistical nightmare, until March 1863 when Burnside took command of the Army of the Ohio and was ordered to take Knoxville. Simultaneously, General William Rosecrans was to move on Chattanooga, Tennessee. In the first two weeks of September, Burnside and Rosecrans occupied their respective objectives, but Rosecrans was attacked at Chickamauga Creek on September 19. Lincoln tried to hurry Burnside southward to reinforce Rosecrans. On September 21, Burnside sent word that he was at Jonesboro which was farther away from Rosecrans. Before that day, the telegraph operators at the War Department had never heard Lincoln utter any stronger profanity than "by jings." When he was handed

Burnside's dispatch, he roared, "Damn Jonesboro!" Then Lincoln sent, "Go to Rosecrans with your force, without delay." Still Burnside did not move.

"Yours of 23rd is just received," Lincoln wrote Burnside on this day, "and it makes me doubt whether I am awake or dreaming. I have been struggling for ten days . . . to get you to assist Gen. Rosecrans in an extremity, and you have repeatedly declared you would do it, and yet you steadily move the contrary way." Once Lincoln finished his more than 250-word rant, he endorsed the back of the telegram with "Not sent" and filed it away. To be sure, Burnside needed to consolidate his position at Knoxville. But Burnside never went to Rosecrans, content to watch from afar the two-month siege of Chattanooga while Lincoln sent troops all the way from Virginia to Rosecrans's aid.

SEPTEMBER 27

Reinforcements for Rosecrans

On this Sunday, Lincoln spoke with General Joseph Hooker to ask him to lead the men who were en route to Chattanooga, Tennessee to relieve General William Rosecrans and his army under siege.

After Rosecrans's rout at Chicamauga, Lincoln did find some solace that Rosecrans still held Chattanooga. "It keeps all Tennessee clear of the enemy and also breaks one of his most important railroad lines," Lincoln said. But because Rosecrans gave up the high ground south of the city to the Confederates, he—with his back to the Tennessee River—was virtually trapped without an adequate route to supply himself.

Shortly after midnight on September 23, Secretary of War Edwin Stanton sent couriers to awaken Lincoln for a twilight meeting. As Lincoln got dressed, he later said, "he was considerably disturbed" because "it was the first time Stanton had sent for him." Once at the War Department, Stanton proposed sending two corps of the Army of the Potomac, numbering 23,000 men, and nine batteries of cannon to Tennessee in a week. "I bet you can't get them even to Washington in ten days," Lincoln said. "On such a subject I don't feel inclined to bet," Stanton countered, adding that it could be accomplished if the railroads were nationalized. Once a route was mapped out, Lincoln approved the movement.

On this day, Lincoln invited Hooker to the Old Soldiers' Home cottage to assign him overall command of the two corps heading west. The troops left on September 25 and arrived seven days later at Bridgeport, Alabama 1,159 miles away. It was a logistical miracle.

SEPTEMBER 29

Temperance

Lincoln, on this day in 1863, was visited by a temperance society—what Lincoln's secretary John Hay called "an assembly of cold-water men & cold-water women"—and was lectured on the evils of alcohol.

Lincoln was not an imbiber of alcohol. "He never drank whisky or other strong drink—was temperate in all things—too much so, I thought sometimes," Lincoln's stepmother Sarah said. Even on the day (May 19, 1860) when Republicans came to Springfield to formally tell Lincoln of his presidential nomination, he and Mary had a fight over celebrating with liquor. Ice water was instead served. Lincoln's temperance had less to do with moral constraints and more with an abhorrence of temporarily losing his faculties. In an 1842 temperance speech, Lincoln praised the "all conquering mind" and denounced moralists who shouted at drunkards "in the thundering tones of anathema and denunciation." The result, Lincoln said, was that the drunkard "will retreat within himself, close all avenues to his head and heart; and tho' your cause be naked truth itself, transformed to the heaviest lance . . . you shall no more be able to pierce him, than to penetrate the hard shell of a tortoise with a rye straw."

When the temperance society came to the White House on this day, Hay, who sometimes drank himself, viewed them with contempt. "They filed into the East Room looking blue & thin in the keen autumnal air," Hay wrote in his diary. "They made a long speech at the Tycoon [Lincoln] in which they called Intemperance the cause of our defeats. He [Lincoln] could not see it, as the rebels drink more & worse whisky than we do. They filed off drearily to a collation of cold water & green apples."

OCTOBER 5

"No Friends in Missouri"

Lincoln, on this day in 1863, tried to defuse political bickering in Missouri.

There were few places in the Union where the split between Radical and Conservative Republicans was more pronounced than in Missouri. Lincoln's Emancipation Proclamation did not cover border slave states like Missouri and Radicals—dubbed "Charcoals"—wanted a state constitutional amendment that immediately emancipated slaves while Conservatives—dubbed "Claybanks" (a pallid gray)—favored gradual emancipation or none at all. Lincoln tried not to take sides. "It is very painful to me that Missouri can not, or will not, settle your factional quarrel among yourselves. I have been tormented with it beyond endurance for months, by both sides," Lincoln wrote. Politically, Lincoln favored the Conservatives' gradual emancipation. Slavery in Missouri, Lincoln claimed, was like a man with "an excrescence on the back of his neck, the removal of which, in one operation, would result in the death of the patient, while 'tinkering it off by degrees' would preserve life." But in a state still in danger of secession, he knew the Radicals were more pro-Union than the Conservatives, many of whom still favored secession. "They [Radicals] are nearer to me than the other side, in thought and sentiment, though bitterly hostile personally," Lincoln said.

Then on August 21, 1863, William Quantrill and 450 Confederate guerrillas attacked Lawrence, Kansas—long a symbol of abolitionism—killing at least 150 civilians. When Missourians wanted to cross the border to hunt Quantrill down, General John Schofield, head of the Missouri District, refused. On September 30, several Missouri Radicals met with Lincoln and demanded Schofield's removal. "Though he [Lincoln] knows how immense the danger to himself from the unreasoning anger of that committee," Lincoln's secretary John Hay observed, "he never cringed to them for an instant." The president refused to start a war of vengeance. "Blood grows hot and blood is spilled," Lincoln wrote on this day to the delegation. "Revenge and retaliation follow." The Radicals left angry. Lincoln lamented afterward that he had "no friends in Missouri."

OCTOBER 6

Grover's National Theater

On this Tuesday in 1863, Lincoln attended a production of Shakespeare's *Othello* at Grover's "New" National Theater.

Grover's, located on E Street and now simply called the National Theater, was frequented by the Lincolns between two dozen and a hundred times. Lincoln saw everything from blackface minstrel shows to plays (*The Fool's Revenge*, *The Ticket of Leave Man*) to Shakespearean histories and tragedies (*Julius Caesar*, *Richard III*, *The Merchant of Venice*, *Hamlet*) to operas (*La Dame Blanche*, *Faust*, *Der Freischütz*). Operas were Lincoln's least favorite, and he often went simply to get away from the office. When Lincoln went to see

Mozart's *The Magic Flute* on March 15, 1865, he was accompanied by James Wilson, who said that the president "sat in the rear of the box leaning his head against the partition paying no attention to the play and looking . . . worn and weary." When Wilson asked if Lincoln liked the show, the president replied, "Oh, no, Colonel . . . I have not come for the play, but for the rest. I am hounded to death by office-seekers, who pursue me early and late, and it is simply to get two or three hours relief that I am here."

Tad sometimes accompanied Lincoln to Grover's, often going backstage during the performance to help move scenery, and he once took the stage as an extra. Tad was attending a performance of *Aladdin* at Grover's on April 14, 1865, when the news that the president was shot at Ford's Theater was announced. Before Tad was taken back to the White House, the twelve-year-old was seen running around "like a young deer, shrieking in agony."

OCTOBER 9

Prison Camps

Lincoln, on this Friday in 1863, wrote Secretary of War Edwin Stanton giving permission to a Southern woman to visit her imprisoned son.

Over 674,000 Americans, Union and Confederate, were taken prisoner during the war, over 409,000 of whom were incarcerated at the 150 prison camps nationwide (the rest—39 percent of them—were paroled while still on the battlefield). The first and nearly the largest Union prison camp was Johnson's Island, built just a mile offshore on Lake Erie, three miles from Sandusky, Ohio. In July 1862, the opposing sides formalized an exchange program known as the Dix–Hill Cartel (named after General John Dix and Confederate General Daniel Hill). Patterned after a similar system from the War of 1812, prisoners of one rank could be exchanged for prisoners of equal rank or for several prisoners of lower ranks. For instance, a lieutenant could be exchanged for four privates and a major general for forty privates.

The cartel emptied out the prison camps but, after blacks joined the fight in 1863, the Confederacy refused to exchange black soldiers, sending them instead into slavery. The Union refused exchanges as well, hoping to collapse the Confederate army by depriving them of men. By the summer of 1863 the cartel had broken down and prisoners began to overfill the prison camps. Conditions began to deteriorate and hunger and disease killed 56,000 prisoners of war on both sides (30,000 in Confederate prisons; 26,000 in those of the Union).

Mrs. Thomas Clemsin, daughter of the great Southern statesman John C. Calhoun, had a son—Calhoun Clemsin—imprisoned at Johnson's Island. "She asks the privilege merely of visiting him," Lincoln wrote Stanton on this day. "With your approbation, I consent for her to go."

OCTOBER 16

The Cracker Line

On this day in 1863, Lincoln named General Ulysses Grant commander of the departments of Ohio, Cumberland, and Tennessee—virtually all the armies in the western theater.

After the Battle of Chicamauga, General William Rosecrans's Army of the Cumberland retreated to Chattanooga, Tennessee, and the rebels put the town under siege and moved to cut off supplies to the beleaguered city. Secretary of War Edwin Stanton sent 23,000 reinforcements to Rosecrans and, while the new soldiers kept the Confederates in check, the extra mouths stressed Rosecrans's meager supplies. By the end of October, the men were starving. One witnessed observed that the men were "too weak to walk to the usual watering place." What was more, Rosecrans had lost confidence in himself. "Confused and stunned, like a duck hit on the head," was how Lincoln described the general. A change of command was needed and Stanton wired Grant and ordered him to head for Louisville, Kentucky, where he'd "meet an officer of the War Department" bearing new instructions.

That officer turned out to be Stanton, who intercepted Grant at Indianapolis. Stanton carried two orders for Grant to choose from, both signed by Lincoln and dated October 16 and both offering command of the "Military Division of the Mississippi" overseeing all Union troops between the Alleghenies and the Mississippi River (except troops in eastern Louisiana). The second order, however, had an added paragraph replacing Rosecrans with General George Thomas. "I chose the latter [order]," Grant later said, then headed for Chattanooga.

"The great thing about Grant," Lincoln said, "is his perfect coolness and persistency of purpose." Grant quickly opened Chattanooga's rail lines and Tennessee River crossings, the new route dubbed the "Cracker Line." In a week, food began pouring into the city. "The Cracker Line is open," a soldier shouted. "Full rations, boys!"

OCTOBER 18

The Chin-fly

After traveling for two weeks throughout the country, Lincoln's secretary John Hay returned to Washington on this Sunday in 1863 to tell the president that the head of the treasury, Salmon Chase, was campaigning against him.

The 1863 fall elections were important because of the trouncing the Republicans had received in 1862. The 1863 campaign held contests for the governor's seats in Maine, Kentucky, Iowa, Wisconsin, Minnesota, Ohio, Pennsylvania, and Massachusetts.

And Chase was campaigning not for the party but for himself. One Republican told Hay, during his travels, that "if Chase would pay a little attention to his damned old paper mill [Treasury Department] in Washington instead of running around the country electioneering, the finances of the country would be better off." Chase wrote hundreds of letters to potential supporters ticking off Lincoln's failures and flaws. "I should fear nothing," Chase wrote, "if we had an Administration . . . guided by a bold, resolute, farseeing & active mind, guided by an honest, earnest heart. But this we have not."

When Hay told Lincoln on this day of Chase's efforts, Lincoln shrugged it off. "I have all along seen his plan of strengthening himself. Whenever he sees that an important matter is troubling me, if I am compelled to decide it in a way to give offense to a man of some influence he always [ar]ranges himself in opposition to me and persuades the victim . . . that he would arrange it differently," Lincoln said. Lincoln told Hay at another time of when he was "plowing corn on a Kentucky farm" and his horse was bitten by a chin-fly, making the horse race to the end of the furrow. "Now if Mr. [Chase] has a presidential chin-fly biting him, I'm not going to knock him off, if it will only make his department go."

#59

"Pieces Upon a Chessboard"

The image of Lincoln as "Honest Abe" is often taken to mean that Lincoln was guileless and unmanipulative. Lincoln nurtured this image, once telling a Pennsylvania delegation, "You know I never was a contriver; I don't know how [such] things are done in politics." Lincoln's friend Leonard Swett, however, said the president "handled and moved man remotely as we do pieces upon a chessboard."

Few things illustrated this as well as Lincoln's relationship with Secretary of the Treasury Salmon Chase. When Lincoln became president, he filled four of seven cabinet seats with political rivals. Of the four, only Chase was unable to put aside his ambition, and for more than three years Chase worked to undermine Lincoln and advance his own political prospects. Lincoln was well aware of these machinations, once characterizing Chase as nothing but a "bluebottle fly" laying "his eggs in every rotten spot he could find." Why did Lincoln keep Chase in the cabinet for so long, particularly after denying Chase's resignation three times?

For one thing, Chase was, after the financial panic of 1862, reasonably competent as the head of the treasury. Chase was also useful politically, as he was in the fall of 1863 when Chase helped Republican John Brough beat the caustic Peace Democrat Clement Vallandigham in the Ohio governor's race. What was more, as long as Chase was in the cabinet, fellow Radical Republicans felt they were not completely isolated from Lincoln's administration. When Chase quit a final time in June 1864, Lincoln made a point of replacing him with another Radical, William Fessenden. Lincoln also knew that Chase would indulge his ambition whether he was in or out of the cabinet. If he was in, his machinations would be considered "disloyal" and fellow Republicans would feel obligated to keep the president apprised of them.

OCTOBER 23

Murder in Maryland

On this Friday in 1863, Lincoln conferred with General Robert Schenck, head of Maryland's Middle Department, about the murder of an officer by a Maryland civilian.

In August 1863, the army opened Camp Stanton near Benedict, Maryland to train black regiments and recruit escaped slaves. Aggressive recruiters, however, were known to encourage Maryland slaves—who, because they were slaves of loyal border state masters, were not freed by the Emancipation Proclamation—to escape their plantations and join the army. Allegedly some were even forced to enlist.

Not far from the camp was a plantation known as "The Plains," owned by one of southern Maryland's wealthiest and most prestigious men, Colonel John Sothoron. Lieutenant Eben White of the Seventh U.S. Colored Infantry, along with two black privates, went to "The Plains" on October 20, 1863 apparently to recruit Sothoron's slaves. A fight broke out and Sothoron reportedly killed White. Sothoron fled to Virginia and the government confiscated his plantation, forcing Elizabeth Sothoron and their children to leave.

The day after the murder, a delegation of Marylanders appeared at the White House, complaining. The next day—this day—Lincoln ordered Schenck to the White House to discuss the matter. After the meeting, Lincoln's secretary John Hay wrote, "The President is in favor of voluntary enlistment of negroes with the consent of their masters & on payment of the price. But Schenck's favorite way . . . is to take a file of soldiers into a neighborhood & carry off into the army all able bodied darkies they can find without asking master or slave to consent." Hay quoted Lincoln as saying, "Schenck is wider across the head in the region of the ears, & loves fight for its own sake."

In March 1864, Elizabeth Sothoron appealed to Lincoln to intervene in the loss of her home and slaves, and Lincoln brought the issue up with the War Department. Her husband was eventually acquitted for the murder and filed a $98,000 claim against the government for his plantation losses. The claim was rejected.

OCTOBER 28

Arming the Disloyal

On this Wednesday in 1863, Lincoln wrote General John Schofield, department head of Missouri, about reports that "Federal and State authorities are arming the disloyal."

Guerrilla warfare had virtually depopulated the southern and western counties of Missouri. Faced with manpower shortages, Schofield formed militias filled with men of questionable loyalty but with a personal stake in keeping the peace. In some cases these men had even served in the Confederate army. But men with military experience were indispensable to law enforcement. This practice led many Unionists in Missouri to question Schofield's loyalty.

The issue came to a head in the fall of 1863, when a Confederate guerrilla, William Quantrill, slaughtered nearly 150 people in Lawrence, Kansas, then escaped into western Missouri to hide out. Unionists wanted to launch a retaliatory raid into the western counties but Schofield refused to allow them. Unionists sent a delegation to Lincoln and demand Schofield's removal. When Lincoln refused, the Unionists sent a list of forty-two men, most of whom had "been in the rebel service," who were now being used by Schofield. "If it is the determination of His Excellency the President to surrender Missouri to the rule of the disloyalists," Missouri congressman Benjamin Loan wrote, "it would be an act of mercy to announce such a determination . . . that the loyal people might . . . remove beyond the borders of the state."

On this day, Lincoln forwarded the list of disloyalists to Schofield, and admitted that the use of such men was common. "I believe it could be shown that this government here have deliberately armed more than ten times as many, captured at Gettysburg, to say nothing of similar operations in East Tennessee," Lincoln wrote. Schofield responded on November 9 that after Quantrill's raid he organized militias in the western counties, their ranks filled with men who were formally disloyal but had a financial stake in keeping the peace. "I have yet to hear the first report of a murder, robbery, or arson in that whole region since the new organization was made," Schofield wrote.

OCTOBER 30

Ford's Theatre

On this Friday in 1863, the Lincolns attended a benefit performance at Ford's Theatre starring Maggie Mitchell in *Fanchon, the Cricket*.

Lincoln frequented Ford's considerably less than he did Grover's National Theater (there are ten recorded shows Lincoln saw at Ford's, compared to at least forty-eight at Grover's), but because Ford's was the site where Lincoln was shot, it is far more well known. One reason for Lincoln's infrequency was because Ford's did not open until 1862 and fire gutted it later that year. Another reason may have been that Grover's afforded Lincoln a certain amount of anonymity that Ford's could not. When Lincoln arrived at Ford's on April 14, 1865, to reach his box he had to cross behind the audience, and he was not only applauded, but the play was stopped and the orchestra struck up "Hail to the Chief." At Grover's he could reach his box unnoticed.

As he did at Grover's, Lincoln often went to Ford's to relax. "Mr. Lincoln liked the theatre not so much for itself as because of the rest it afforded him," wrote an observer. "I have seen him more than once looking at a play without seeming to know what was going on before him." And it was at Ford's that Lincoln was once heckled. At a December 1863 performance of *Henry IV*, a spectator interrupted the play by standing up and pointing at the president. "There he is! That's all he cares for his poor soldiers," the man shouted. Then a soldier stood up and in an accent said, "De President haf a right to his music! Put out dot feller! De President ees all right! Let him haf his music!" The heckler was expelled.

NOVEMBER 2

"I Am Used to It"

Lincoln, on this Monday in 1863, responded to an apology from the actor James Hackett for publishing a personal letter from the president.

Correspondence between the two began after the president attended Hackett's March 13, 1863 performance of Falstaff in Shakespeare's *Henry IV*. On March 20, Hackett sent Lincoln a copy of his recently published commentary on Shakespearean plays. Because of business, if took five months for Lincoln to thank him. Lincoln wrote:

> For one of my age, I have seen very little of drama. . . . Some of Shakespeare's plays I have never read; while others I have gone over perhaps as frequently as any unprofessional reader. Among the latter are *Lear*, *Richard Third*, *Henry Eighth*, *Hamlet*, and especially *Macbeth*. I think nothing equals *Macbeth*. It is wonderful.

Although Lincoln's letter was sent with the notice "Printed not for publication but for private distribution only, and its convenient perusal by personal friends," Hackett printed a broadside of the letter. Newspapers reprinted the letter with sarcastic comments about an uneducated rube critiquing classical literature.

On October 22, Hackett wrote the president to apologize for the media's barbs. The actor hoped that such an "experienced politician" as Lincoln would let such "squibs" affect him about as much as a "mustard seed" fired at an armored "Alligator." Lincoln responded on this day that he was not "shocked" at the press's comments, which "constitute a fair specimen of what has occurred to me through life. I have endured a great deal of ridicule without much malice; and have received a great deal of kindness, not quite free from ridicule. I am used to it."

NOVEMBER 9

Tyrannicide

On this Monday in 1863, Lincoln saw a production of *Marble Heart* starring John Wilkes Booth. One of his guests—Mary Clay—related an incident that occurred during the play: "The [presidential] box was right on the stage, with a railing around it. . . . Twice Booth in uttering disagreeable threats in the play came very near and put his finger close to Mr. Lincoln's face, when he came a third time I was impressed by it, and said, 'Mr. Lincoln, he looks as if he meant that for you.'"

It is telling that Lincoln's early exposure to Booth was through their shared love for the stage. For Lincoln, the stage was a distraction. For Booth, it was a way of life. One of the more prevalent dramatic themes he was exposed to was the romantic notion of tyrannicide—the assassination of tyrants for the cause of freedom. In such plays as *William Tell* and Shakespeare's *Hamlet*, *Richard III*, and *Julius Caesar*, assassins of tyrants were glorified. Booth's last stage performance was in a March 1865 production of *The Apostate*. Set in Granada during the Moor rebellion, the play climaxes with the assassination of the tyrant Pescara.

Booth saw Lincoln as a tyrant. Shortly after Lincoln's reelection in November 1864, Booth said, "He is . . . overturning this blind Republic and making himself king. This man's reelection . . . will be a reign." At about the same time, a Richmond newspaper cited historical examples of tyrannicide and wondered if there was anyone courageous enough to kill Lincoln. Even in the North, Copperheads were looking for a hero. "And if he is elected . . . for another four years, we trust some bold hand will pierce his heart with dagger point for the public good," wrote a Wisconsin paper. Booth romantically began to see himself as that "bold" hero. It was not coincidental that Booth killed Lincoln in front of an audience to whom he yelled, "Sic semper tyrannis" (Thus always to tyrants).

NOVEMBER 12

The Competition

Perhaps the biggest Washington social event of the war occurred on this Thursday in 1863 as Secretary of the Treasury Salmon Chase's daughter Kate married former Rhode Island governor William Sprague. Despite its social significance, the first lady refused to go and Lincoln went alone.

There was a popular myth at the time that Mary's animosity toward Kate stemmed from jealousy. During the Lincolns' inaugural journey, they stopped in Columbus, Ohio on February 13, 1861. Ohio was the Chase's home state and during an evening ball, it was alleged that the beautiful twenty-year-old Kate danced with the president-elect, drawing Mary's ire. According to Kate's later account, she wasn't at the ball, and not even in town. "Mrs. Lincoln was piqued that I did not remain in Columbus to see her," Kate wrote, "and I have always felt that this was the chief reason why she did not like me in Washington."

The real reason is probably more complex. For one thing, Kate's father made no secret that he was a competitor for Lincoln's presidency and Kate was his biggest promoter. Her greatest contribution was to compete with the White House for social prominence. She organized receptions on Mondays and dinners on Wednesdays. After Willie Lincoln's death, social events were cancelled at the White House while Kate's events continued unabated. "In reality there was no one in Washington to compare to Kate Chase," said a friend.

"She was the queen of society." But it was the first lady who aspired to be society's queen.

On this day, Mary refused to pay homage to the "Gods, Chase & daughter," so Lincoln went alone. "[He] stayed two and half hours to take the cuss off the meagerness of the presidential party," noted one observer.

NOVEMBER 17

A Cemetery in Gettysburg

On this Tuesday in 1863, Lincoln made last-minute preparations for his trip to commemorate the new cemetery at Gettysburg, Pennsylvania.

After the massive three-day Gettysburg battle, there were eight thousand Union and Confederate dead that needed to be buried. Crews quickly interred them in the July heat, often with little regard for the identity of the deceased. As weeks passed, families looking for their loved ones pulled bodies up, then inadequately reburied them. In late July, David Wills, a Gettysburg resident, wrote Governor Andrew Curtin, "In many instances arms and legs and sometimes heads protrude and my attention has been directed to several places where hogs were actually rooting out the bodies and devouring them."

Curtin put Wills in charge of building a proper cemetery for the honored dead. Wills hired architect William Saunders to design it and invited the famous speaker Edward Everett to dedicate it. Because it was a state rather than a federal function, inviting the president was an afterthought, made in late October, and only to make "a few appropriate remarks."

Secretary of War Edwin Stanton scheduled a 6:00 AM train to take Lincoln the eighty miles to Gettysburg the day of the event because of the president's busy schedule. "I do not like this arrangement," Lincoln wrote Stanton. "I do not wish to go so that by the slightest accident we fail entirely." The train was rescheduled for the day before the event. It was fortunate that he did, because locomotive traffic into the tiny town the day of the ceremony was so congested that Lincoln wouldn't have arrived on time, or delivered his famous address.

On this evening, Saunders showed Lincoln his plan for the cemetery, arranged on a graded incline in a semicircle so that no state's graves would get preferential status. The president was pleased.

NOVEMBER 18

Writing the Gettysburg Address

Of his 1,502 days as president, Lincoln was out of Washington less than fifty, most of them to visit the army in the field. One exception was on this day in 1863, when at noon Lincoln boarded a train bound for Gettysburg, Pennsylvania.

Lincoln was going to Gettysburg to dedicate a new cemetery for those who had perished in the July battle. Lincoln almost didn't go. His son Tad awoke that morning sick and unable to eat his breakfast and Mary had begged Lincoln not to leave. But Lincoln believed his message so important that he insisted on going.

A few witnesses claim that Lincoln worked on his address during the four-hour train ride. One man claimed he saw Lincoln, when the train stopped at a station, through the train car window working on the speech, "the top of his high hat serving as a makeshift desk." Lincoln's secretary John Nicolay, however, insisted that Lincoln wrote nothing during the trip, preferring to converse with fellow passengers. While it was out of character for Lincoln to wait to the last minute to write a speech, he admitted to a friend that he had only "found time to write about half of his speech."

The train arrived at dusk, and Lincoln's party walked to the mansion of David Wills, the ceremony's organizer. After dinner, Lincoln returned to his room to work on his speech, interrupted occasionally by serenaders. To one group that demanded a speech, he claimed it was important not to say "foolish things." "If you can help it!" yelled one serenader. "It very often happens that the only way to help it is to say nothing at all," Lincoln responded before returning to his address.

NOVEMBER 19

The Address

On this Thursday in 1863, Lincoln delivered his most famous speech, the Gettysburg Address.

Around eleven that morning, Lincoln mounted a horse and rode in a procession to the new cemetery about to be dedicated. The main speaker was the famous Edward Everett. Because he suffered from kidney disease, Everett insisted that a tent be erected near the speaker's stand so that he could relieve himself when needed. Everett delivered a two-hour description of the heroic battle. "He gave us plenty of words, but no heart," wrote a *Philadelphia Age* editor. "He talked like a historian, or an encyclopaedist . . . but not like an orator."

Then Lincoln rose to speak. A fifteen-year-old boy named George Gitt was hiding under the speaker's stand. "[The] flutter and motion of the crowd ceased the moment the President was on his feet," Gitt recalled. "Such was the quiet that his footfalls, I remember very distinctly, woke echoes, and with the creaking of the boards, it was as if some one were walking through the hallways of an empty house."

The speech was only ten sentences, 272 words, and took less than three minutes to deliver. He opened by declaring that America was "dedicated to the proposition that all men were created equal." At the end he delivered perhaps the most famous sentence in American history, "we here highly resolve that these dead shall not have died in vain—that this nation, under God, shall have a new birth of freedom—and that government of the people, by the people, for the people, shall not perish from the earth."

According to his friend Ward Lamon, Lincoln was not pleased with the speech. "Lamon, that speech won't scour!" he said, referring to wet soil that collects on a plow blade, refusing to fall or "scour" off. The public saw it different. "[The speech], though short, glittered with gems, evincing the gentleness and goodness of heart peculiar to him," wrote a *Washington Chronicle* reporter.

NOVEMBER 23

Siege at Knoxville

Lincoln and his cabinet were anxiously watching developments in eastern Tennessee as two cities—Knoxville and Chattanooga—were put simultaneously under siege. On this Monday in 1863, Lincoln passed word to his secretary of state, William Seward, that the general in charge at Knoxville, Ambrose Burnside, "thinks he can hold the place."

In March 1863, Burnside as the new head of the Army of the Ohio was ordered to take Knoxville. On September 2, Burnside took the eastern Tennessee city. To the south, General William Rosecrans also took Chattanooga but was repulsed at Chickamauga Creek and had to fall back. The rebels, headed by Confederate general Braxton Bragg, put Rosecrans's men under siege in Chattanooga. Despite the victory, bickering erupted between Bragg and his subordinates. "Nothing but the hand of God can save us or help us as long as we have our present commander," wrote Confederate general James Longstreet.

Partly because of this bickering, Longstreet was given the mission to head north and retake Knoxville. By November 15, the Confederates were to the south of the city. Burnside, however, had laid out a series of forts to protect him and Longstreet was forced into siege warfare.

For a week, both Knoxville and Chattanooga were under siege but Longstreet's absence at the latter city allowed General Ulysses Grant (who took over Rosecrans's command) to break the deadlock. And Longstreet never seriously threatened Knoxville and was forced to retire on December 4.

NOVEMBER 25

Missionary Ridge

Lincoln, on this Wednesday in 1863, sent a wire congratulating General Ulysses Grant for double victories the two previous days. Even as he sent this telegram, an even more spectacular victory was in progress.

Chattanooga sat cupped within a bend of the Tennessee River, with the Confederates holding Missionary Ridge overlooking the city from the east and southeast and Lookout Mountain guarding the southwest. Grant's plan to break the Confederates' stranglehold on the city was for Generals William Sherman and Joseph Hooker to attack the Confederate flanks while General George Thomas merely demonstrated against the center at Missionary Ridge.

But when the Confederate commander, General Braxton Bragg, weakened his army by sending troops to attack Knoxville, Tennessee, Grant decided to probe Bragg's center. On November 23, Thomas took a forward knoll called Orchard Knob. The next day it was Hooker's turn, as Bragg's depleted forces on Lookout Mountain allowed Hooker to roll up the mountain in what was romantically dubbed the "battle above the clouds."

With Sherman and Hooker on the flanks, Thomas's orders for this day was to take the Confederate rifle pits at the base of Missionary Ridge. But, partly out of courage and partly because of the galling fire from above, the soldiers began climbing the ridge without orders, driving the Confederates before them. Shocked, Grant asked Thomas who had ordered his men forward. Thomas replied, "When those fellows get started all hell can't stop them." Bragg's men fled, leaving Missionary Ridge to Thomas. "I believe I am not premature in announcing a complete victory over Bragg," Grant wired Washington. Chattanooga's siege was finally lifted.

NOVEMBER 27

Sickbed

On this Tuesday in 1863, Lincoln was bedridden all day, sequestered from seeing his cabinet secretaries or anyone on official business.

After delivering his famous speech at Gettysburg, Pennsylvania (November 19), Lincoln became ill. During the train ride back to Washington, he laid down in a drawing room with a cold compress on his forehead. Upon arrival, he immediately went to bed with a fever and a headache. First Lincoln's doctors diagnosed a cold, then scarlet fever. Two days later, the president developed red blisters all over his body and he was diagnosed with a mild form of smallpox known as varioloid, which is highly contagious. Later Lincoln remarked to several visitors, "Yes, it is a bad disease, but it has its advantages. For the first time since I have been in office, I have something now to give everybody that calls."

Lincoln was ill for at least three weeks and it may well have been the most serious illness Lincoln had as president. He was so sick that instead of waiting for important news from the battles in Tennessee (Lookout Mountain and Missionary Ridge) he went to bed early on November 25. His son Tad, who contracted what was diagnosed as scarlet fever (but was probably also smallpox) the day Lincoln left for Gettysburg (November 18), began to feel better by month's end.

Much of the time Lincoln was quarantined and on bed rest. He used the time to write his annual message to Congress, with a special emphasis on how to reconstruct Southern states who wished to return to the Union, a problem he considered "the greatest question ever presented to practical statesmanship."

#60

Lincoln's Health

Most of what is known about Lincoln's physical ailments come from contemporary testimony, photos, and the few surviving personal items we still have of him. Analysis of all but the latter can, at best, be speculative. For instance, from his reading glasses, it is known that Lincoln had presbyopia or was far-sighted, probably due to his age. It is estimated that his glasses were about three times stronger than he needed, which explains his headaches after reading for extended periods.

From testimony, it is known that Lincoln suffered from depression most of his adult life. For instance, one observer discovered Lincoln "wrapped in abstraction and gloom," sitting alone in the corner of the room. "It appeared as if he was pursuing in his mind some specific, sad subject, regularly and systematically through various sinuosities, and his sad face would assume, at times, deeper phases of grief." It was because of these depressive bouts that for years Lincoln took so-called blue mass pills. The mercury in blue mass medication was almost certainly slowly poisoning the president and may even have exacerbated rather than relieved his depression.

Some historians believe that Lincoln had a genetic connective tissue disorder known as Marfan syndrome. This comes from photos and descriptions that Lincoln was abnormally tall and had long limbs, an odd gait, and a "sunken chest." But all of these attributes could be ascribed to a number of other syndromes or disorders as well, and this theory has fallen into disfavor of late. The National Museum of Health and Medicine—which holds samples of Lincoln's hair and bones—has been petitioned to test the samples for Marfan but the museum refused, concerned about the destruction of the samples. Some experts, however, believe that if Lincoln did have Marfan—which can lead to fatal heart defects—he was dying of heart failure at the time of his assassination and they estimate that he had only six to twelve months to live.

DECEMBER 4

"Pipes"

On this Friday in 1863, Lincoln sent a thank-you to a comic named Stephen Massett for the gift of his book he sent to the White House. Massett himself came to the White House the following year, where he would not only meet Lincoln, but the soon-to-be-famous artist Francis Carpenter.

Carpenter would gain his fame by painting one of American history's most memorable portraits of that era: the *First Reading of the Emancipation Proclamation of President Lincoln*, which still hangs in the Senate. Carpenter stayed in the White House between February and July 1864, painting from life not only Lincoln but his cabinet secretaries as well. Carpenter also acquired what no one else thought to get while Lincoln was alive: accounts from Lincoln and his cabinet on how the Emancipation Proclamation came to fruition.

Carpenter also provided some of the more personal stories of Lincoln. One of them was about Massett's visit in early June. Massett toured the country reading from his comic autobiography, *Drifting About or What Jeems Pipes, of Pipesville, Saw-and-Did.* Massett performed one of his "lectures" in the White House Red Room. As Carpenter recounted:

> Comic imitations of various characters were given, among others that of a stammering man, which appeared greatly to amuse Mr. Lincoln. . . . When the "lecture" ceased, Mr. Lincoln said, "I want to offer a suggestion. I once knew a man who invariably whistled with his stammering," and he then gave an imitation. . . . "Pipes" [Massett] applauded the amendment, rehearsing it several times, until he had mastered it to the President's satisfaction; and I dare say the innovation became a part of all subsequent performances.

DECEMBER 8

Amnesty and Reconstruction

Lincoln, on this day in 1863, issued his Proclamation of Amnesty and Reconstruction.

By late 1863, there were already three separate plans advocated by legislators to bring rebellious states back into the Union. Democrats wanted the Emancipation Proclamation withdrawn, a general amnesty for the rebels, and since, according to some, the Southern states had never legally been out of the Union, they could simply elect new congressmen and send them to Washington. Conservative Republicans wanted emancipation as the sole condition for returning to the Union. Radical Republicans wanted dramatic changes in the Southern economy and social fabric before readmission. Some

Radicals wanted the South to be considered a territory, applying to Congress for statehood. Massachusetts senator Charles Sumner wanted Southern plantations "divided among patriot soldiers, poor whites and freedmen."

Lincoln took a more moderate approach. In the proclamation he issued this day, he wrote "all persons who have . . . participated in the existing rebellion" would be granted "a full pardon" with their property—except slaves—restored to them if they took an oath of allegiance to the Union. Exceptions to this amnesty would include Confederate government officials, anyone who mistreated white or black soldiers, and anyone who left "judicial stations," the U.S. Congress, or senior military commissions to aid the Confederacy. If the number of citizens in a former Confederate state who took the oath equaled one-tenth of the number who voted in that state during the 1860 election, that state could apply for statehood after they had passed a constitution that included emancipation. As to electing Congressmen, Lincoln said, that would be determined "exclusively" by Congress.

The proclamation was hailed from all sides. "I have never seen such an effect produced by a public document," Lincoln's secretary John Hay wrote, after he watched the proclamation's reading on the floor of the House of Representatives.

DECEMBER 9

Annual Message

Lincoln, on this Wednesday in 1863, sent his annual message to the Capitol to be read by Congress.

The Constitution requires that "the President shall from time to time give to Congress information of the State of the Union and recommend to their consideration such measures as he shall judge necessary and expedient" (Article II, Section 3). While George

Washington orally delivered his first message to Congress (in January 1790), Thomas Jefferson thought an oral presentation was too monarchical and, in 1801, sent copies to the Senate and the House. For the next 112 years (until Woodrow Wilson), the president did not orally deliver his annual message, and instead a proxy read it to Congress. In 1935, Franklin Roosevelt began calling it his "State of the Union" address.

The message delivered on this day was, as some newspapers noted, not "Lincolnian" at all. The president had been sick since mid-November and it was clear that the speech had been cobbled together using reports from the various departments. While Lincoln mentioned the 100,000 blacks that were now in uniform, he did not praise their heroics, virtually ignoring his administration's greatest political triumph that year.

It wasn't until the end of the speech, when he introduced his Proclamation of Amnesty and Reconstruction that Lincoln's voice appeared. The *New York Tribune* gushed that no presidential message since Washington had elicited "such general satisfaction." Everyone, for once, seemed happy with the president. "[Lincoln] is the great man of the century. There is none like him in the world," said Michigan congressman Francis Kellogg. Even Lincoln's cabinet "acquiesced" to the proclamation, the president said, adding, "the only member of the Cabinet who objected to it was Mr. [Secretary of the Treasury Salmon] Chase." The ambitious Chase no doubt objected to Lincoln uniting the Republican factions.

DECEMBER 13

Emilie's Visit

In mid-December of 1863, the Lincolns welcomed Mary's sister Emilie Todd Helm to the White House. But because Ms. Helm was the widow of Confederate general Ben Helm, the Lincolns kept her presence secret. It was so secret that there are few indications as to what days that December she was in the White House. One exception was in a diary entry made on this day by the president's secretary John Hay: "I visited Mrs. L[incoln]. Her sister Mrs. Gen. Helm, is with her, just arrived from Secessia [the Confederacy]."

After Ben Helm's death in September 1863 at the battle of Chickamauga, Emilie had a friend write to Lincoln asking for a pass to cross the front lines so she could "return to her mother and friends in Kentucky." The president obliged but when Emilie arrived at the front lines in mid-December the authorities demanded that she take an oath of allegiance to the Union. She refused. "Send her to me," Lincoln ordered.

The first night of Emilie's visit, Mary had the White House lit up while they toured the mansion. They stopped at the famous Gilbert Stuart portrait of George Washington that Dolly Madison had saved in 1814 when the White House was burned. Both women were proud that they were related to Dolly's first husband.

The most curious event that occurred during Emilie's visit happened when Mary told her sister of ghosts in the White House. Emilie was staying in the Prince of Wales Room, sleeping in the very bed that Willie Lincoln had died in nearly two years before. Late one night, Mary came in the room to tell her sister about how Willie still visited her. "He comes to me every night and stands at the foot of my bed with the same sweet, adorable smile he always had," Mary said. "He does not always come alone; [our son] little Eddie is sometimes with him, and twice he has come with our brother Alec[k]."

DECEMBER 16

A Rebel in the White House

On this Wednesday in 1863, New York congressman Fernando Wood met with Lincoln to discuss why the president's Proclamation of Amnesty and Reconstruction did not include amnesty for

Southern sympathizers living in the North. It was a sensitive subject for Lincoln, as he had just sent his Southern-sympathizing sister-in-law home to Kentucky.

The week before, Mary had been happy to have her younger sister at the White House. Others, however, were not. Lincoln tried to keep Emilie's presence a secret, but Mary, one evening, let it slip to two friends she thought were understanding: General Daniel Sickles and New York senator Ira Harris. Both were outraged that the widow of a Confederate general was staying at the White House. Harris directed a cutting remark at Emilie, "Well, we have whipped the rebels at Chattanooga and I hear, madam, that the scoundrels ran like scared rabbits." Emilie retorted, "It was an example, Senator Harris, that you set them, at Bull Run and Manassas."

As Mary's face turned "white as death," Harris turned his anger toward the first lady, asking why her son Robert was not in the army. Mary responded that she wanted Robert to "stay in college a little longer." Harris said, "I have only one son and he is fighting for his country." He turned to Emilie: "And, madam, if I had twenty sons, they should all be fighting the rebels." After Emilie left, Sickles shouted at the president, "You should not have that rebel in your house." Lincoln was indignant, "Excuse me, General Sickles, my wife and I are in the habit of choosing our own guests."

Emilie, upset over the incident, left within days. As for Lincoln's Amnesty Proclamation, it was never amended to cover Southern sympathizers in the North.

DECEMBER 19

The Imperial Navy

On this Saturday in 1863, the Lincolns hosted a reception for the officers of Russian warships that had dropped anchor in the Potomac earlier in the month.

During the Civil War, the Union and Imperial Russia formed an informal pact where America would help industrialize the motherland and the Imperial Navy would come to the Union's aid should England and France intervene on behalf of the Confederacy. Russia had just lost the Crimean War (1853–56), in part because of their lack of industrial infrastructure. While Russia had no love for American democracy, it, like most monarchies, feared rebellions even more. "All this I did because of love for my own dear Russia, rather than for love of the American Republic," Isar Alexander II wrote later. "I understood that Russia would have a more serious task to perform if the American Republic, with [its] advanced industrial development were broken up and Great Britain should be left in control of most branches of modern industrial development."

In the fall of 1862, Britain and France considered entering the war on the Confederacy's side and pressured Russia to withdraw its support of the Union. Russia refused. Then, in January 1863, Russia herself faced insurrections in Poland and France; Britain and Austria asked the United States to join them in intervening on behalf of the Poles. Secretary of State William Seward refused, cementing U.S.–Russian relations. In September 1863, the Russians sent its fleets to both New York City and San Francisco, probably to test them in the open seas and winter them in a warmer climate then the icy Baltic and Black seas. New York held parades and lavish parties for the Russian sailors. The public and the European powers saw the visit as a threat against British and French intervention, ending any discussion of recognizing the Confederacy. In early December the fleet sailed up the Potomac, anchoring off Washington. On this day, Lincoln and his wife Mary held a reception at the White House for the officers of the Russian fleet.

#61

DID RUSSIA SAVE THE UNION?

There is little doubt that had Britain and France militarily intervened in the war on the Confederacy side, the Union might well have lost the war. The two European powers sported the largest navies in the world. It is also clear that Europe seriously considered intervening. In first summer of the war, Cassius Clay, U.S. ambassador to St. Petersburg, wrote Lincoln, "I saw at a glance where the feeling of England was. They hoped for our ruin. . . . She [England] will now, if disaster comes upon our arms, join our enemies." After the Union's military disasters of 1862, the European powers made their move. Russian foreign minister Alexander Gorchakov warned Lincoln that fall that "England rejoices over what is happening to you. She longs and prays for your overthrow." Tsar Alexander II later wrote:

> In the autumn of 1862, the governments of France and Great Britain proposed to Russia, in a formal but not in an official way, the joint recognition of European powers of the independence of the Confederate States of America. My immediate answer was, "I will not cooperate in such action; and I will not acquiesce. On the contrary, I shall accept the recognition . . . by France and Great Britain as a *casus belli* [Latin for "case of" or act of "war"] for Russia. And in order that the governments of France and Great Britain may understand that this is no idle threat I will send a Pacific fleet to San Francisco and an Atlantic fleet to New York.

Many historians believe that Russia's support of the Union was pivotal in averting war with Britain and France. An October 1862 editorial in *Harper's Weekly* read, "An alliance between Russia and the United States . . . would probably be the best possible guarantee against war [with Western Europe]."

DECEMBER 22

Freedom of Religion

Lincoln, on this Tuesday in 1863, wrote that the government would not interfere with churches or their functions.

There were a few instances of government suppression of religious freedom. In at least one Washington church, the provost marshal forced Southern sympathizers to stay in their pews during the pastor's weekly prayer for the president. Rev. J. R. Stewart of Alexandria, Virginia, was arrested after he refused to pray for the president.

In December 1862, a Missouri pastor named Samuel McPheeters wrote Attorney General Edward Bates that in May he had objected to resolutions the General Assembly of the Presbyterian Church passed pertaining to the war. Afterwards, several of his parishioners questioned his loyalty and went to the provost marshal convincing him not only to remove McPheeters from the pulpit but banish him from the state.

Lincoln first suspended McPheeter's banishment, then met with him on December 29. Days later, Lincoln wrote General Samuel Curtis, head of the Missouri department. "After talking to him [McPheeters], I tell you frankly, I believe he does sympathize with the rebels, but the question remains whether such a man . . . who can be charged with no other specific act or omission, can, with safety to the government be exiled, upon the suspicion of his secret sympathies," Lincoln wrote. He added, "The U.S. government must not . . . undertake to run the churches."

A year went by and still McPheeters had not returned to his pulpit. When Lincoln received a petition to reinstate him, he wrote one of the signers on this day, “I have never interfered, nor thought of interfering as to who shall or shall not preach in any church; nor have I knowingly, or believingly, tolerated any one else to so interfere by my authority.” He added, “If, after all, the Dr. is kept out by the majority of his own parishioners, and my official power is sought to force him in over their heads, I decline that also.”

DECEMBER 23

The Storyteller

On this day in 1863, Lincoln had a dream in which he attended a party. “He is a very common-looking man,” one of the partygoers said of the president. “Common-looking people are the best in the world,” retorted Lincoln, “that is the reason the Lord makes so many of them.” The dream then became one of his many stories he recounted over and over.

“From his father came that knack of storytelling which has made him so delightful among acquaintances,” wrote a friend of Lincoln’s family. The president had an incredible memory, allowing him to recollect stories he had heard decades before. “He did not forget the good things that he heard and was never without a familiar story to illustrate his meaning,” Charles Sumner wrote. He had few equals in imitation and mimicry and his expressions were also tools. “His countenance and all his features seemed to take part in the performance,” said David Davis. “He provoked as much laughter by the grotesque expression of his homely face as by the abstract fun of his stories,” Henry Whitney wrote.

Few enjoyed his stories as much he did. “As he neared the pith or point of the joke or story every vestige of seriousness disappeared from his face,” Davis wrote. “His little gray eyes sparkled; a smile seemed to gather up curtain like the corners of his mouth; his frame quivered with suppressed excitement; and when the point—or 'nub' of the story, as he called it—came, no one's laugh was heartier than his." Sometimes he'd slap a thigh, but other times he'd wrap his arms around his shins, drawing his knees to his face and rock in his chair with laughter. The image was often funnier than the story. "His stories may be literally retold," wrote a friend, "every word, period and comma, but the real humor perished with Lincoln."

#62

The Uses of His Stories

Besides his intellect, storytelling was probably Lincoln's most useful asset. Often he used stories to illustrate his ideas. "Common people . . . are more easily influenced and informed through the medium of a story than in any other way," Lincoln said. To illustrate the illogic of something, Lincoln frequently told of a man who said of his new boots, "I shall never get 'em on, till I wear 'em a day or two, and stretch 'em a little."

Lincoln used his stories to deflect questions he didn't want to answer. Other times he used them to soften a rebuke or to deny a request. When a general asked Lincoln to pardon a Confederate friend, Lincoln told of a group of young people who came to a river. Each boy carried a girl across until all that remained was a small boy and "Gothic-built" girl. "You fellas are all getting your friends out of this scrape," Lincoln said, "and you will succeed in carrying off one after another until nobody but Jeff Davis and myself will be left. . . . How shall I look, lugging him over?"

By far, the best use Lincoln had for his stories was to raise his own spirits. "A funny story, if it has the element of wit, has the same effect on me that I suppose a good square drink of whisky has on an old roper. It puts new life in me," Lincoln said. One of his favorites was of the Revolutionary hero Ethan Allen when he traveled to England. In an effort to insult Allen, the Brits hung a picture of George Washington in Allen's outhouse. Allen thought it a great place to hang it because "there is nothing that will make an Englishman shit so quick as the sight of General Washington."

DECEMBER 28

Lincoln's Secretaries

Lincoln, on this Monday in 1863, discussed with his secretary John Hay two trips the president needed him to make.

While at the White House, Lincoln had three secretaries—John Nicolay, John Hay, and William Stoddard—but only Nicolay was officially a secretary. Hay and Stoddard were on loan from the Interior Department. Their duties included delivering presidential messages to Congress, screening visitors, and sorting through Lincoln's mail. They were also occasionally called to turn away cranks. According to Hay, a man once came to the White House claiming to be the "Son of God" and wanted to show Lincoln a plan to end the war. Hay told him to come back the following day with a letter of introduction from his Father.

Lincoln frequently sent his secretaries on working excursions, partly to give them vacations and partly because he couldn't go himself. On December 27, 1863, Lincoln visited a prison camp called Point Lookout in southern Maryland. On this day, the president recounted his trip to Hay and told him that many Confederate prisoners voiced a "strong feeling of attachment to the Union or rather a disgust for the rebellion." He added that "from one-third to one-half" of the prisoners did not want to return to the Confederacy "and about half of this number desire to enter our Army, having, poor devils, nowhere else to go & nothing else to do." Lincoln wanted Hay to go to the camp to see if any prisoners would take the oath of allegiance to the Union.

Hay left for Point Lookout in early January to deliver an "oath book" to log inmates who switched allegiances. Later that month, Hay took a second trip, this time to Florida carrying several logbooks for that state's rebels who wished to do the same.

1864

"DOESN'T IT STRIKE YOU AS QUEER THAT I, WHO COULDN'T CUT THE HEAD OFF OF A CHICKEN, AND WHO WAS SICK AT THE SIGHT OF BLOOD, SHOULD BE CAST INTO THE MIDDLE OF A GREAT WAR, WITH BLOOD FLOWING ALL ABOUT ME?"

—ABRAHAM LINCOLN

JANUARY 7

The Butchering Business

On this Thursday in 1864, Lincoln commuted the death sentence of a deserter named Henry Andrew, a private in Company I of the 124th Ohio Volunteers, to imprisonment at hard labor for the remainder of the war. He wrote, "I did this, not on any merit in this case, [but] because I am trying to evade the butchering business lately."

Military executions for everything from falling asleep on guard duty to desertions were usually carried out on Fridays. "Black Friday," Lincoln called it, and during his presidency he reviewed hundreds of courts-martial, commuting many executions to forfeiture of pay or hard labor. "No man on earth hated blood as Lincoln did, and he seized eagerly upon any excuse to pardon a man when the charge could possibly justify it," writer David Locke observed. "The generals always wanted an execution carried out before it could possibly be brought before the President." General William Sherman was once asked how he carried out the sentences of his courts-martial without Lincoln pardoning them. "I shot them first," he responded. One day during a conference, the sound of guns outside Lincoln's office window interrupted conversation. The president's eyes misted. "This is the day when they shoot deserters," he lamented.

Often a family member or the soldier himself would petition Lincoln for a pardon. Attorney General Edward Bates told artist F. B. Carpenter that Lincoln was a perfect wartime president, except for his pardons. "Why, if a man comes to him with a touching story, his judgment is almost certain to be affected by it," Bates said. "Should the applicant be a woman—a wife, or mother, or a sister—in nine cases out of ten, her tears, if nothing else, are sure to prevail."

#63

"Until Further Orders"

Speaker of the House Schuyler Colfax relates how an old man—whose son was in General Benjamin Butler's Army of the James—visited Lincoln to plead for his condemned son's life. As the old man spoke,

> A cloud of sorrow came over the President's face as he replied, "I am sorry to say I can do nothing for you. Listen to this telegram received from General Butler yesterday, 'President Lincoln, I pray you not to interfere with the courts-martial of the army. You will destroy all discipline among our soldiers. B. F. Butler.'" Every word of this dispatch seemed like the death-knell of despair to the old man's newly awakened hopes. Mr. Lincoln watched his grief for a minute, and then exclaimed, "by jingo, Butler or no Butler, here goes!" Writing a few words . . . [he handed a letter] to the old man. The confidence created by Mr. Lincoln's words broke down when

he read—"Job Smith is not to be shot until further orders from me.—Abraham Lincoln." "Why," said the old man, "I thought it was to be a pardon; but you say, 'not to be shot till further orders,' and you may order him to be shot next week." Mr. Lincoln smiled . . . "Well, my old friend, I see you are not very well acquainted with me. If your son never looks on death till further orders come from me to shoot him, he will live to be a great deal older than Methuselah."

JANUARY 16

Lincoln Meets Anna Dickinson

On this Saturday in 1864, Anna Elizabeth Dickinson, a well-known abolitionist and activist for women's rights, became the first woman to speak in the House of Representatives. Beforehand she attended a White House reception where she met Lincoln.

Called "America's Joan of Arc," Dickinson was born in 1842 to abolitionist Quaker parents. At the age of thirteen, Dickinson published an essay on slavery in William Lloyd Garrison's *The Liberator* and Garrison helped her launch a career as a lecturer. In 1860, she broadened her speaking repertoire to cover women's rights.

In 1861 she lost her job at the U.S. Mint after she publicly denounced General George McClellan as incompetent. Republicans, however, applauded her, partly because McClellan was a Democrat. Two years later New Hampshire and Connecticut Republicans asked Dickinson to campaign for them and, in recognition of her successful efforts, she was invited to speak in the House of Representatives.

While Dickinson was highly critical of the president—she called him a "scoundrel" and mimicked him in her speeches—the Lincolns held a reception for her and afterward attended her lecture in Congress, where she lambasted Lincoln for his reconstruction plan and its generosity to Confederates. But she also supported Lincoln's reelection. That would change.

Dickinson became more disillusioned with Lincoln as the election neared and she turned to abolitionist John Fremont as a Republican contender. But after Fremont withdrew from the campaign and McClellan became the Democratic nominee, Dickinson relented, returning her support to Lincoln.

After the war, Dickinson campaigned for women's suffrage and had close ties to other advocates such as Susan B. Anthony. Dickinson, however, broke ranks when she advocated black male suffrage and lost much of her prestige. Despite a successful theatrical career—she even played Hamlet on stage—she died in relative obscurity.

JANUARY 20

Reconstructing Arkansas

On this Wednesday in 1864, Lincoln ordered elections to be held in Arkansas in an important step to reconstruct the former Confederate state.

Lincoln believed that the surest way to undermine the Confederacy was to erect Union governments within their midst. So if a state wanted to reenter the Union, he wanted it to do so with little difficulty or penalty. There were many in the North who disagreed, however, expecting the South to make amends.

In December 1863, Lincoln issued his Proclamation of Amnesty and Reconstruction, which, with a few exceptions, allowed anyone who swore an oath of allegiance to the federal government to become a citizen again. The prospective citizen would swear to uphold the emancipation because any attempt to re-enslave newly freed blacks would be "a cruel and an astounding breach of faith." The proclamation also allowed states to reenter the Union with the consent of one-tenth of its citizens who had voted in the 1860 election and who swore the oath.

Among the first Confederate states to attempt to reenter the Union were Louisiana and Arkansas, both of which were already largely under federal control. In Little Rock on January 19, 1864, the Arkansas Constitutional Convention adopted a pro-Union constitution and elected Dr. Isaac Murphy as provisional governor. The problem was that the forty-five delegates to the convention represented less than half of Arkansas' fifty-three counties. Nor had the oath been widely administered throughout the state yet.

Lincoln, however, was willing to overlook these irregularities. On this day, he ordered General Frederick Steele, commander of Arkansas forces, to schedule elections as soon as possible, in order to ratify the new constitution and elect a pro-Union government. In March, Arkansas did both. But radicals in Congress blocked Arkansas's and Louisiana's readmission into the Union, largely because they wanted a less-forgiving reconstruction plan.

JANUARY 23

The "Voluntary Labor System"

Lincoln, on this day in 1864, embarked on a project to restart rebel economies and help former slaves make a living.

With the war turning in the North's favor, Lincoln worked on the problem of reconstructing the South. He was particularly concerned with the vacuum left after the South's slave labor was emancipated. The Southern economy could collapse and former slave owners and slaves could both starve.

Radical Republicans wanted to completely reorganize southern society, to exchange its agricultural economy for an industrial one. They wanted to confiscate southern plantations and divide them among freed black families.

On this day, Lincoln embarked on a test project he called the "voluntary labor system" which allowed Southern plantation owners to "fully recognize the freedom of those formerly slaves, and by fair contracts of hire with them, re-commence the cultivation of their plantations." Lincoln sent a representative, Alpheus Lewis, south to plantation owners in Mississippi and Arkansas. He gave them permission to cultivate their plantations and afforded them protection and supplies by the federal government, as long as the voluntary laborers were paid and the plantations did not aid the rebellion. "Such hiring and employment of the freed people, would be regarded by me with especial favor," Lincoln wrote.

This project never succeeded and Radical Republicans pushed to establish the Bureau of Refugees, Freedmen, and Abandoned Lands. After the war the Bureau was given 850,000 acres of confiscated land to distribute to former slaves. But President Andrew Johnson forced the Bureau to rescind the land grants and return the acreage to their former white owners. Ultimately, many black families were forced by poverty and entrenched social strata to work the very plantations they were freed from, for a wage so low that they were permanently indebted to their employers. Poverty enslaved them every bit as effectively as the law once did.

JANUARY 29

Lincoln Sends an Emissary South

The demands of war rarely allowed Lincoln to leave Washington. Out of his 1,500 nights in office, he spent less than 50 of them out of Washington and never traveled more than a few hundred miles from the capital. He did, however, send aides and friends to political trouble spots, and on this Friday in 1864 Lincoln asked his most colorful emissary to visit Arkansas.

General Daniel Sickles was famous for escorting a prostitute—Fanny White—into the chambers of the New York State Assembly. He then allegedly took White to London (leaving his pregnant wife at home), where he introduced her to Queen Victoria. He was best known before the war for ambushing and killing his wife's lover, Philip Barton Key, grandson of the writer of the "Star Spangled Banner." He won an acquittal after becoming the first person in American jurisprudence to claim he was not guilty by reason of temporary insanity. Afterward he publicly forgave Theresa, his wife.

As a Democrat, Sickles's offer of services was eagerly accepted by Lincoln's Republican administration and he was quickly named a brigadier general. He was a fearless division and corps commander, but, on the second day of Gettysburg, his poor decisions nearly cost the Union the battle.

At Gettysburg, Sickles had a leg amputated and, while recuperating in New York, he wrote Lincoln asking for an assignment. The former Confederate state of Arkansas, much of it now in Union hands, had just ratified a pro-Union, anti-slavery constitution and a pro-Union governor had been elected. On this day, Lincoln sent a telegram to Sickles asking him to look in on the new Arkansas government. Sickles agreed and by the time he left in mid-March, his trip had been expanded to a tour of the South: he watched General William Sherman's fight against the Confederates in Georgia, appeared in Memphis to investigate illegal trading, and, finally, visited Little Rock and New Orleans.

FEBRUARY 9

Two Photos That Became Icons

Lincoln was among the most photographed persons of the nineteenth century; more than a hundred different photos of him still exist today. Two, taken during the same studio sitting on this day in 1864, became the two most familiar images we have of him.

Lincoln was not handsome. In nearly every picture, his disheveled hair, huge ears, droopy right eyelid, leathery skin, and cavernous eye sockets are all prominent. And yet many contemporaries thought these photos never captured how he looked. *New York Herald* reporter Henry Villard wrote, "I have never seen a picture of him that does anything like justice to the original. He is a much better looking man than any of the pictures represent."

The reason is that the process of exposing images to wet-plate film was slow and tedious. Lincoln had to sit perfectly still and silent, his head held in place by a rack. Eventually, Lincoln would sink into a sad, distracted mood. Not one photo captured what he looked like when he told a joke, for when he did, according Horace White, editor of the *Chicago Tribune*, "the dull, listless features dropped like a mask." He added, "The eyes began to sparkle, the mouth to smile, the whole countenance was wreathed in animation, so that a stranger would have said, 'Why, this man, so angular and somber a moment ago, is really handsome.'"

Two photos were taken of Lincoln today in 1864, at Matthew Brady's Washington studio. One is a three-quarters face portrait that was later used for the five-dollar bill. The other is a profile used as a guide for the Lincoln penny. During this sitting, Lincoln also, for the first time, posed with his son Tad—the only member of his family he was ever photographed with.

FEBRUARY 10

Willie's Pony Dies

During this night in 1864, the White House stables caught fire, killing one of the few reminders the Lincolns had of their son Willie.

Young children were a novelty in the White House and the public doted on Tad and Willie Lincoln, sending them gifts. One such gift was a pony, given to Willie. The boy rode the pony nearly every day and often gave Tad a turn on it, even though his short legs stuck straight out to the sides. It was while riding this pony in the rain that Willie supposedly contracted "bilious fever" (more likely typhoid fever) during the winter of 1862.

The Lincolns were devastated when Willie died. Memories of him were so painful that Mary donated Willie's toys and books, everything that would remind her of him—everything except Willie's pony. Lincoln, too, found memories of his son painful, as he discovered on this night nearly two years after Willie died. That night Lincoln's personal stables just east of the White House caught fire. Security guard Smith Stimmel described the scene:

> We saw that, sure enough, the White House stable was on fire. . . . Mr. Lincoln hastily asked if the horses had been taken out, and when told they had not, he rushed through the crowd and began to break open one of the large doors with his own hands; but the building was full of fire, and none of the horses could be saved.

Among the animals within the inferno was little Willie's pony. Lincoln had to be restrained from entering the burning stable. Later, the president was found at a window in the East Room (which faced the stables), weeping bitterly and speaking sentimentally of Willie.

#64

The Lincolns' Pets

Lincoln loved animals. He was often seen in the White House caressing Tad's kittens or helping Tad train his dog Jip. Lincoln was particularly fond of two goats—Nanny and Nanko—given to his son Tad. According to Mary's seamstress, Elizabeth Keckley, the goats "knew the sound of his

[Lincoln's] voice, and when he called them they would come bounding to his side." In the warm bright days, he and Tad would sometimes play in the yard with these goats for an hour at a time. This pair of goats often helped themselves to the White House garden and slept in Tad's bed at night. One day Tad harnessed Nanko to a kitchen chair and drove his "sled" through the East Room where a reception was in progress, yelling, "Get out of the way there!"

Jack the Turkey was an unexpected addition to the family. "Jack was sent here to be killed and eaten," Lincoln told Tad near the 1863 holidays. Tad replied, "I can't help it. He's a good turkey, I don't want him killed." Jack was thus given a stay of execution. Noah Brooks relates a story about Jack:

> The soldiers were voting [on election day, November 8, 1864] . . . and Tad, bursting into his father's office, had besought the President to come to the window and see the soldiers who were "voting for Lincoln and Johnson." Noticing the turkey regarding the proceedings with evident interest, Lincoln asked. . . . "Does he vote?" "No," was the quick reply of the boy; "he is not of age."

FEBRUARY 19

The Booths and the Lincolns

On this Friday evening in 1864, the Lincolns attended a performance at Grover's Theater of Shakespeare's *Richard III*, starring Edwin Booth in the title role. For Booth, considered one of the first great American actors, the role of Richard was a sentimental one. His stage career began in Boston on September 10, 1849, playing Tressel in *Richard III*. His father—the brilliant but eccentric Junius Brutus Booth—played Richard that night.

Edwin honed his craft and, when Junius fell ill in 1851, he took his father's place as Richard. Edwin would go on to surpass his father's dramatic brilliance. Late in 1864, Edwin played his most famous role, Hamlet, in a record one-hundred-night run in New York. Edwin's career suffered only a temporary setback when his younger brother—John Wilkes—shot and killed President Lincoln (Edwin was back on stage nine months later playing Hamlet).

This was not the only night that the Booths' and Lincoln's paths crossed. Not only did they see Edwin in several productions, they were also entertained by John Wilkes, who inherited his father's oddness but not his acting ability. Nevertheless, Tad Lincoln once said of John Wilkes, "he makes me thrill."

Perhaps the strangest intersection of the two families happened on a Jersey City train station platform, sometime in 1863 or 1864. According to Robert Lincoln's account, he was waiting in line when he leaned against the side of a train. At that moment the train lurched and Robert fell from the platform and under the train. He might have been seriously injured, even killed, but his "coat collar was vigorously seized" and he was pulled back onto the platform. The rescuer was Edwin Booth.

FEBRUARY 22

The Pomeroy Circular

Lincoln's backwoods, uneducated background often caused people to underestimate him. Perhaps no one underestimated Lincoln more than Secretary of the Treasury Salmon Chase. But Lincoln, on this Monday in 1864, set in motion a political maneuver that would outfox the fox.

Until the 1864 election year, Lincoln had been noncommittal about running for reelection. After all, the eight previous presidents since Andrew Jackson had been limited to one term. But by

January of that year, Lincoln felt his reelection would vindicate his prosecution of the war, emancipation, and reconstruction policies. "A second term would be a great honor and a great labor, which together, perhaps I would not decline, if tendered," he said.

In February, it was not the Democrats but fellow Republicans that worried Lincoln. In virtually every Northern state, Republican factions opposed his reelection. Nearly every Republican senator and representative opposed it as well. Much of the disaffection crystallized around Kansas senator Samuel Pomeroy, who favored Chase as the new president.

In early February, Pomeroy's group sent to fellow Republicans a pamphlet, *The Next Presidential Election*, which declared that the "vascillation [sic] and indecision of the President," "the feebleness of his will," and his "want of intellectual grasp" were the reasons the war had not been won. A second pamphlet was sent out, this one dubbed the "Pomeroy Circular," which declared that Lincoln's reelection was "practically impossible" and openly endorsed Chase. Embarrassed to be seen as disloyal to the president, Chase, on this day in 1864, tendered his resignation.

Lincoln, who knew that if Chase resigned he'd be free to campaign without the stench of disloyalty, refused to either accept or deny the resignation, preferring to leave him dangling. "I will answer . . . more fully when I can find the leisure to do so," Lincoln wrote Chase.

FEBRUARY 29

Lincoln Outmaneuvers Chase

Lincoln, on this day in 1864, refused to accept Secretary of the Treasury Salmon Chase's third resignation.

Lincoln was very much aware of Chase's ambition. Chase wanted the presidency in 1860 and he coveted it even more in 1864. For the most part, Lincoln made light of these aspirations, but he couldn't ignore members of his own Republican Party who openly advocated

Chase's presidential nomination, not Lincoln's. Chase was embarrassed by the perception of disloyalty and on February 22, 1864, he tendered his resignation.

But Lincoln wasn't interested in just embarrassing Chase, and knew Chase could campaign more effectively if he were outside the cabinet than if he stayed in it. So Lincoln refused to answer Chase's resignation for a full week, while Lincoln's own political machinery began turning.

First, on February 22 the National Committee of the Republican Party—most of its members appointed by Lincoln—endorsed Lincoln's nomination. The committee also granted the president's request for an early nomination convention, to be held on June 7. This left Chase little time to garner support. Then, on February 25, the state Republican convention in Ohio—Chase's own state—endorsed Lincoln's nomination. Two days later, Lincoln's friend and congressman, Francis Blair, launched a savage attack on Chase from the floor of the House.

On this day Lincoln sent Chase a letter, saying he did not hold Chase responsible for what his political allies might do. "Whether you shall remain at the head of the Treasury Department is a question which I will not allow myself to consider from any stand-point other than my judgment of the public service; and, in that view, I do not perceive occasion for a change."

On March 5, Chase withdrew his candidacy. On June 29, after Lincoln secured his nomination, he finally accepted Chase's resignation after it was tendered a fourth time.

MARCH 1

Grant is Promoted

On this Tuesday in 1864, Lincoln sent to the Senate his recommendation to promote General Ulysses S. Grant to the rank of Lieutenant General. Previously no other American general had held that rank while still fighting in the field except George Washington. What was remarkable was that Lincoln had yet to even meet Grant, or to even discuss military strategy with him. Apparently Grant's successful record was all Lincoln needed.

Grant's record was indeed impressive, if less for its brilliance than for its tenacity. He had returned from his first ill-advised battle at Belmont, Missouri (which was a near disaster) to assault the center of the Confederate line that protected Nashville, Tennessee. The result was the capture of forts Henry and Donelson along with vast stretches of the Tennessee heartland, which forced the Confederates to evacuate Nashville. Then another near-disaster, this time at Shiloh, where Confederate general Albert Sidney Johnston surprised Grant and very nearly drove his army into the Tennessee River. At midnight that night, General William Sherman found Grant calmly puffing on a cigar. "Well, Grant, we've had the devil's own day, haven't we?" "Yes," Grant replied, "lick 'em in the morning, though." And he did.

Bouncing back from that setback, Grant spent more than a year attempting to split the Confederacy in two by closing its last major crossing of the Mississippi at Vicksburg. It took a bold dash across the river, forcing General John Pemberton's army into its Vicksburg entrenchments, and putting the town under siege. Starvation forced Pemberton to capitulate. Then it was back to Tennessee, this time to Chattanooga, where he drove the Confederates out of Tennessee for the first time in the war.

In the twenty-five months since Belmont, Grant had captured two entire Confederate armies, driven a third out of Tennessee, and closed the Mississippi. Grant would later write that Lincoln told him that "All he ever wanted . . . was some one who would take the responsibility and act."

Lincoln now had such a man.

MARCH 2

Lincoln's Memory

On this Wednesday in 1864, Lincoln demonstrated his exceptional memory.

Lincoln, as a boy, attended "blab" schools—so called because the lessons were recited over and over until they were memorized. It was a technique Lincoln would use all his life. He would later recall that whenever he tried to understand something, he would "hunt after an idea, until I had caught it; and when I thought I had caught it, I was not satisfied until I had repeated it over and over. . . . This was a kind of passion with me, and it has stuck by me."

It was the same with reading. His stepmother, Sarah Lincoln, recalled that Lincoln repeated passages of books over and over. Boyhood friend and relative Dennis Hanks agreed: "Abe'd lay on his stumick by the fire and read out loud to me'n Sairy [Lincoln's sister Sarah], an' we'd laugh when he did. I reakon Abe read the book a dozen times, and knowed those yarns by heart."

In one book, William Scott's *Lessons in Elocution*, Lincoln was first exposed to William Shakespeare's soliloquies and committed them to his remarkable memory. So remarkable was his memory that, decades later, he could still recite a lengthy soliloquy. Lincoln was posing for artist Francis Carpenter on this day as he painted the president's portrait. Lincoln was looking forward to attending a performance of *Hamlet* that evening. Lincoln believed that the best soliloquy in *Hamlet* was not the prince's anguished "To be or not to be," but King Claudius's lament in Act III, Scene III, which begins, "O, my offense is rank, it smells to heaven; it hath the primal eldest curse upon't,—a brother's murder!" and is nearly three hundred words long. Lincoln recited the entire passage from memory for Carpenter.

MARCH 7

The Dahlgren Conspiracy

On this Monday in 1864, Lincoln attempted to help his friend, Rear Admiral John Dahlgren, ascertain what had become of his son Ulric, who had participated in one of the most curious operations of the war, the Kilpatrick raid on Richmond.

In January, Brigadier General Judson Kilpatrick hatched a plan to drive 3,500 troopers behind Confederate general Robert E. Lee's army and liberate 5,000 federal prisoners in Richmond's Libby and Belle Isle prisons. Kilpatrick apparently only wanted to liberate the prisoners, but when Colonel Ulric Dahlgren joined the group, he carried orders to burn Richmond and kill Confederate president Jefferson Davis and his cabinet. No one knows whether Dahlgren wrote the orders on his own or if his superiors authorized them.

Once the raiders slipped deep behind enemy lines they split up, with Dahlgren taking five hundred men to attack Richmond from the southwest and Kilpatrick's three thousand attacking from the north. But Dahlgren had trouble crossing the James River, and when Dahlgren failed to reach Richmond, Kilpatrick retreated to leave Dahlgren's small force in the lurch. On March 2, Confederate cavalry general Custis Lee—Robert E. Lee's eldest son—attacked Dahlgren, killing him and capturing ninety-two of his men.

On March 6, Lincoln personally informed Admiral Dahlgren that he had information that Ulric was alive. To Lincoln's consternation and embarrassment, the next day—this day—he was informed that the *Richmond Sentinel* reported that Ulric was dead.

When Dahlgren's orders were found on his body, it created a sensation in the South. Newspapers declared that orders to burn Richmond and to assassinate heads of state had to have been authorized by Dahlgren's superiors, maybe even Lincoln. Dahlgren's commander denied it and Lincoln never addressed the accusations. The source of Dahlgren's orders remains a mystery.

MARCH 8

Lincoln Meets Grant

On this afternoon in 1864, a short, stocky man in a linen duster entered the Willard Hotel in Washington with a fourteen-year-old boy in tow. Unnoticed and unrecognized, the man signed the guest register, "U. S. Grant and son, Galena, Illinois." Grant was in Washington to receive his commission as lieutenant general, accept command of the Union armies, and finally meet Lincoln.

Lincoln had been initially reluctant to name Grant head of all armies. Both the Democrats and Republicans were courting Grant as a presidential candidate and with General George McClellan likely on the Democratic ticket, Lincoln wasn't going to appoint another general in chief with political aspirations. But Grant allayed Lincoln's fears with a letter denying any interest in the presidency. "You will never know how gratifying that is to me," Lincoln told J. Russell Jones, the deliverer of the letter. "No man knows, when the presidential grub gets to gnawing at him, just how deep it will get until he has tried it."

At 9:30 PM, Grant walked from his hotel in his rumpled traveling uniform to the White House, where the Lincolns were holding their weekly reception. "Why, here is General Grant! Well, this is a great pleasure, I assure you!" Lincoln said when he saw him. Lincoln led Grant into the East Room, where so many people crowded around to see Grant that he was obliged to stand on a sofa to shake hands. He stayed there an hour.

The next day, during a formal ceremony, Lincoln put Grant in command of 860,000 men. Grant wanted to command from his western headquarters but Lincoln refused. General William Sherman would command the western forces. Lincoln needed Grant nearby. Nevertheless, Grant wanted nothing to do with Washington and moved his command to Culpeper Court House in Virginia.

MARCH 21

Nevada to Become a State

On this Monday in 1864, Lincoln signed the congressional act allowing Nevada to become the nation's thirty-sixth state (counting the seceded states). Lincoln believed he needed Nevada's statehood so that it would cast its three electoral votes to reelect him as president. More importantly, Nevada would be the first western territory to become a state without Southerners clamoring for it to join as a slave state. The issue of slave expansion into the territories was finally dead. Lincoln also hoped that Nevada would vote for the Thirteenth Amendment to the Constitution, which would make emancipation absolute in the other thirty-five states.

One result of the Mexican War (1846–48) was that, under the Treaty of Guadalupe Hidalgo, the United States acquired vast stretches of land west of Texas to the Pacific Ocean. Then representative Lincoln opposed the war and was afraid the slave states would use the new territory to strengthen themselves politically. At the time, slave states held a slim majority in the Senate (there were fifteen slave states and fourteen free), but because of a larger population the North held a majority in the House. A Georgia newspaper boasted that the acquisition of more slave territories would "secure to the South the balance of power . . . [and] give to her the control in the operations of Government." For the next fifteen years, slavery in the territories would occupy national politics and culminate in Southern secession and the war. Some of this territory would eventually become Nevada.

As it turned out, Lincoln didn't need Nevada's electoral votes in the November elections because he took all the Northern states but three (Delaware, Kentucky, and New Jersey). Nevada did ratify the Thirteenth Amendment on February 16, 1865, just over two weeks after Congress sent it to the states for ratification.

#65

Words that Haunted Him

Then representative Lincoln's opposition to the Mexican War led him to make statements and take positions that would later be used against him and made for some interesting ironies.

For one thing, Lincoln argued that then president James Polk acted unconstitutionally when he—not Congress—ordered troops into the territory disputed with Mexico. Lincoln claimed that war was "the most oppressive of all Kingly oppressions" and that the Constitution had been worded so "that no one man should hold the power of bringing this oppression upon us." At the outbreak of the Civil War, Lincoln himself called up the militia while Congress was out of session and sent troops to areas disputed with the Confederacy. The difference, Lincoln argued, was that he was combating a rebellion, not a foreign power. His critics would use this as an example of Lincoln's "tyranny," a term reminiscent of "Kingly oppressions."

Lincoln's opposition to Polk spilled over into other areas. When Polk argued that internal improvements could not be funded by the federal government without a constitutional amendment, Lincoln opposed any amendment. "Better . . . to think of it [the Constitution], as unalterable," he said. "It can scarcely be made better than it is." Later, Lincoln vigorously worked for ratification of a constitutional amendment to end slavery.

Most embarrassing of all was Lincoln's argument that people have the right of revolution. In a speech attacking the Mexican War, Lincoln argued that the people in the disputed territory had revolted against the Mexican government. "Any people anywhere . . . have the right to rise up, and shake off the existing government, and form a new one that suits them better." He added, "This is a most valuable—a most sacred right." Those words would haunt him when he fought to deny the South its right to secede.

MARCH 24

Failure in Florida

Under Lincoln's Proclamation of Amnesty and Reconstruction of December 8, 1863, former Confederate states were eligible to reenter the Union if its citizens—equal to 10 percent of those who voted in the 1860 election—took the oath of allegiance to the Union and voted for readmission. Lincoln first turned to Louisiana and Arkansas to test his policy but the distractions of war and irregularities at the Arkansas constitutional convention delayed the process. In Tennessee, military governor Andrew Johnson had not built a pro-Union constituency. So Lincoln looked to Florida. After breakfast on this Thursday in 1864, Lincoln discussed with his secretary John Hay why his policy failed in Florida as well.

After news early in 1864 that "worthy gentlemen" were trying to restore a loyal government in Florida, Lincoln commissioned Hay a major and sent him southward. Acting as a provost marshal, Hay brought along blank logbooks to record the 1,400 loyal citizens (10 percent of the 13,301 Floridians who voted in 1860) needed to make Florida eligible for readmission.

In February, Hay wrote Lincoln that the rebels persecuted and killed loyalists and that "they will be very glad to see a government strong enough to protect them." He complained that most loyalists, however, were now refugees in the North. After the Union army was routed on February 20 at the Battle of Olustee (Ocean Pond)—the only major battle in Florida—it was clear that a loyal government was not possible. Hay returned to Washington, his logbooks unfilled.

Hay spoke to Lincoln, on this day, about the press and their claims that the Florida expedition was an effort to use the military to erect a government that would support Lincoln's reelection. Hay reported that the president was unconcerned about these "falsehoods."

MARCH 25

"Why Should the Spirit of Mortal Be Proud?"

Lincoln was deeply moved by poetry and he memorized his favorites to recite to friends. He considered the Scottish poet Robert Burns a "transcendent genius" and would recite the bawdy "Tam o' Shanter" with Burns's Scottish phrases in his Hoosier twang. He preferred more melancholy verse such as "The Last Leaf" by Oliver Wendell Holmes, Sr., the fourth verse of which Lincoln declared, "For pure pathos, in my judgment, there is nothing finer than those six lines in the English language." Another Scotsman, William Knox, wrote Lincoln's favorite poem. On this day in 1864, while Lincoln spent the evening in his study, posing for a portrait, he recited for the painter F. B. Carpenter "Why Should the Spirit of Mortal be Proud?"

Lincoln first read the poem in the 1830s and, afterward, repeated the poem so often that friends believed Lincoln himself wrote it. Lincoln didn't know the author, but stated, "I would give all I am worth, and go in debt, to be able to write so fine a piece as I think that is." The poem was a tension-reliever for Lincoln, who said of it, "I may say it is continually present with me, as it crosses my mind whenever I have relief from anxiety." His two favorite verses were:

Yea! Hope and despondency, pleasure and pain,
Are mingled together in sunshine and rain;
And the smile and the tear, and the song and the dirge,
Still follow each other, like surge upon surge.

'Tis the wink of an eye, 'tis the draught of a breath,
From the blossoms of health, to the paleness of death.
From the gilded saloon, to the bier and the shroud
Oh, why should the spirit of mortal be proud?

MARCH 28

White House Security

When Lincoln first took office, White House security consisted of a wrought-iron fence and a doorkeeper. The White House was easily accessible to anyone, particularly at night. "The President was frequently alone in his room evening after evening—the whole East Wing unoccupied except by himself and a sleepy messenger in the anteroom, and ingress and egress entirely unobstructed," said Lincoln's secretary William Stoddard. "Any assassin or maniac, seeking his life, could enter his presence without the interference of a single armed man to hold him back," wrote a staff officer. Eventually security personnel were instated but, as demonstrated by one Francis Xavier on this day in 1864, could easily be circumvented.

Lincoln took a fatalistic view toward his security. "I long ago made up my mind that if anybody wants to kill me, he will do it," Lincoln told Noah Brooks. "If I wore a shirt of mail, and kept myself surrounded by a body-guard, it would be all the same. There are a thousand ways of getting at a man if it is desired that he should be killed."

At another time, Lincoln told California senator Cornelius Cole, "One man's life is as sweet to him as another's and no man would take mine without losing his."

While such logical arguments might apply to most sane killers, it could hardly stop insane ones. "As to crazy folks, Major," Lincoln told Charles Halpine, "I must only take my chances." Early on this Monday morning, a man named Francis Xavier entered Lincoln's office and began a harangue about how he was the real president and tried to prove that he had been elected in 1856. Fortunately, Xavier did not have a weapon.

APRIL 3

The Hodges Letter

On March 26, 1864, Lincoln met with a Kentucky delegation. During the interview Albert Hodges, editor of the *Frankfort Commonwealth*, asked Lincoln why he had changed his policy from non-interference of slavery to emancipation. After the delegation left, Lincoln wrote out a response to Hodges's question, hoping Hodges would publish it. This letter—which Lincoln showed to his friend Orville Browning on this night in 1864—became one of his more famous correspondences.

"I am naturally anti-slavery. If slavery is not wrong, nothing is wrong," Lincoln wrote. He added that as president he was not allowed to "act officially upon this judgment and feeling." He had taken an oath to preserve both the nation and the Constitution. "Was it possible to lose the nation, and yet preserve the Constitution?" he asked. "By general law life *and* limb must be protected; yet often a limb must be amputated to save a life; but a life is never wisely given to save a limb."

He explained that he waited to emancipate the slaves until the war made it necessary. By the summer of 1862 he was "driven to the alternative of either surrendering the Union, and with it, the Constitution, or of laying strong hand upon the colored element. I chose the latter."

He ended his letter by avowing what he called the "Doctrine of Necessity," a belief that the actions and fate of individuals were predetermined and shaped by God. "I claim not to have controlled events, but confess plainly that events have controlled me," he said. "Now, at the end of three years struggle the nation's condition is not what either party, or any man devised, or expected. God alone can claim it."

#66

The Doctrine of Necessity

As a youth, Lincoln was probably exposed to Baptist predestination doctrines. After reading more rationalistic literature as a young man, he incorporated into his beliefs the doctrine of necessity—that people were not the captains of their fate, but rather their actions and lives were predetermined by a higher power. In later years, particularly during the war, Lincoln began to see this higher power as God.

The earliest example of Lincoln admitting to this fatalistic idea was in 1842. Lincoln had helped his best friend, Joshua Speed, and his fiancée, Fanny, get married. In response to a letter of thanks, Lincoln wrote, "I am not sure there was any merit, with me, in the part I took in your difficulty; I was drawn to it as by fate . . . I believe God made me one of the instruments of bringing your Fanny and you together, which union I have no doubt He had foreordained."

As president, Lincoln thought himself "an instrument of Providence." Lincoln was unsure just what his role was, however. "Doesn't it strike you as queer that I, who couldn't cut the head off of a chicken, and who was sick at the sight of blood, should be cast into the middle of a great war, with blood flowing all about me?" he asked Indiana congressman Daniel Voorhees.

He began to suspect that the purpose of the war was, in part, retribution. In his second inaugural he says, "If God wills that it [the war] continue, until all the wealth piled by the bond-man's two hundred and fifty years of unrequited toil shall be sunk, and until every drop of blood drawn with the lash, shall be paid by another with the sword, 'the judgments of the Lord, are true and righteous altogether.'"

APRIL 18

The Baltimore Riot

The U.S. Sanitary Commission was a national organization that coordinated the relief efforts of thousands of small, local aid societies or auxiliaries. Beginning in October of 1863, the Commission began holding Sanitary Fairs in various cities, featuring exhibits, food, entertainment, and merchandise for sale, all to raise funds to provide food, clothing, and medicine for Union troops. On this Monday in 1864, the Maryland Sanitary Fair opened in Baltimore and Lincoln delivered a fifteen-minute speech before a crowd of at least 6,000. Lincoln couldn't help but to note in his speech what had happened in Baltimore almost exactly three years before.

Nearly a third of Maryland's population lived in Baltimore at the beginning of the war, and its mayor, police chief, and much of the city was either marginally Unionist or openly secessionist. Confederate flags were everywhere, in windows and on flagpoles. On April 19, 1861, the Sixth Massachusetts Regiment entered Baltimore on its way to Washington in answer to Lincoln's call for troops. Since no rail line bisected the city, the regiment had to get off the train on the east side and march across town to board another train. While en route, mobs attacked the regiment with bricks, paving stones, and pistols, killing four soldiers. A few soldiers fired into the crowd, killing twelve. In response, the mayor destroyed the rail bridges leading to Harrisburg and Philadelphia, Pennsylvania, and refused to allow any more Union troops to enter his city.

In his Sanitary Fair address, Lincoln noted the change in sentiment. "Looking upon these many people, assembled here to serve, as they best may, the soldiers of the Union, it occurs at once that three years ago, the same soldiers could not so much as pass through Baltimore," he said. "The change from then till now, is both great, and gratifying."

APRIL 22

"In God We Trust"

Lincoln signed, on this Friday in 1864, the Mint Act, which authorized the U.S. Mint to imprint the words "In God We Trust" for the first time on American coins.

During the war, the country—North and South—experienced a religious revival. In the North this sparked several appeals to Secretary of the Treasury Salmon Chase for some recognition of God on American coins. The earliest known appeal came from Rev. M. R. Watkinson, a pastor from Ridleyville, Pennsylvania, on November 13, 1861. Watkinson recommended that the American flag be imprinted on the coins with the words "God, Liberty, Law" within the flag's bars. "This would place us openly under the Divine protection we have personally claimed," Watkinson wrote. A week later Chase wrote James Pollack, director of the Philadelphia mint, ordering him to write a motto declaring the "trust of our people in God."

On December 9, 1863, Pollack submitted the mottos "Our Country; Our God" and "God Our Trust." His final recommendations on December 9, 1863, also included "God and Our Country" and "In God We Trust." Chase picked the slogan "In God We Trust" and Pollack submitted the bill to Congress, which, after it passed, Lincoln signed. The two-cent coin was the first to display the motto.

Not all coins immediately carried the motto "In God We Trust". The penny didn't carry it until 1909 when, in celebration of the centennial of Lincoln's birth, his portrait became the first imprinted on a regular series coin. The dime followed in 1916, the nickel in 1938 (the quarter and other coins already had it inscribed). In 1956 Congress made the phrase the national motto and the next year it began to appear on all paper money as well.

APRIL 26

The Presidential Office

On this Tuesday in 1864, Anthony Berger, a photographer working for Mathew Brady's Washington studio, took two photographs of Lincoln in his office to help the artist Francis Carpenter paint the president's portrait. One is of Lincoln sitting at a table in front of the office fireplace; the other of him standing beside the table where his department heads sat during cabinet meetings. These are the only surviving photos of Lincoln in his office.

Lincoln's office was on the second floor in what is now called the Lincoln Bedroom. Its two windows faced south, giving the president a view of the unfinished Washington Monument and the Potomac River. On the north side of the office was a door opening to a hallway that was inevitably filled with visitors, office-seekers, and pardon petitioners. To the west was a door leading to a passageway that Lincoln had had built at the back of the Reception Room next door. Through this passage he could escape the crowds of visitors and enter the Family Library unseen, and from there his private quarters.

By 1864, Lincoln had moved a desk against this door, apparently no longer needing to escape the crush of petitioners.

Furniture in the room included an armchair, two horsehair sofas, a tall mahogany writing desk with pigeonholes, a smaller desk, and the large walnut table for meetings. The walls were covered with maps and a portrait of President Andrew Jackson hung over the fireplace. Behind it the wallpaper was green with gold star patterns. Gas lights provided illumination but were prone to leaks. Lincoln was nearly overcome by a gas leak in his office on the morning of September 9, 1864.

APRIL 30

Lincoln Meets Elizabeth Cady Stanton

On this Saturday in 1864 the artist Francis Carpenter, who was in the process of painting Lincoln's portrait, brought the women's rights activist Elizabeth Cady Stanton to the White House to meet the president.

Stanton was on her honeymoon in London when she attended the 1840 International Anti-Slavery Convention, where she met Quaker feminist Lucretia Mott. Together Stanton and Mott organized the first women's rights convention in America at Seneca Falls, New York, in 1848. Three years later Stanton met Susan B. Anthony, formed a lifelong friendship, and became the center of the feminist movement. "I am the better writer," Stanton said, "[and] she [Anthony] the better critic. She supplied the facts and statistics, I the philosophy and rhetoric, and together we have made arguments that have stood unshaken . . . arguments that no man has answered. Our speeches may be considered the united product of our two brains. So entirely one are we that . . . not one feeling of envy or jealousy has ever shadowed our lives."

Some of Stanton's sentiments, however, put her at odds with her supporters. She, for instance, was critical of Christianity and what she perceived as its sexist dogmas. When the Fourteenth and Fifteenth Amendments extended suffrage to black men but not women, both Anthony and Stanton broke from their abolitionist supporters and lobbied against the amendments.

Stanton did not think much of Lincoln when she met him. "Had a long talk with Abraham," she wrote afterward. She found him "a stronger and better man than I had from his official acts supposed him to be, but I am not in favor of his reelection."

MAY 2

An Annoyed General

Generals were never happy when Lincoln pardoned their court-martialed soldiers, but since the president was their superior their complaints were typically vented in their memoirs. One exception involved Alonzo Sheffield, whom Lincoln pardoned on this Monday in 1864.

According to his wife, Mary, Alonzo was inebriated and "not to be responsible for his acts," when he enlisted in Company G of the Fifty-first New York Regiment in August, 1861. After two months of service, Sheffield deserted and returned to his family in Brooklyn. The provost marshal finally found and arrested Sheffield on April 1, 1864. When Mary appealed to Lincoln, she claimed that her husband was disabled and the sole provider of the family. Lincoln pardoned Sheffield on the condition that he find a substitute to serve in the army.

Unbeknownst to Lincoln, Alonzo had deserted a second time (on April 29). Sheffield's friends—also unaware of his second desertion—paid Henry Vincent to be Sheffield's substitute. When Vincent reported for duty, the provost marshal decided to honor Lincoln's pardon rather than pursue a prosecution of the second desertion. But when the paperwork for Sheffield's pardon was forwarded to General John Dix's office, it was clear the general was unhappy. "[I] request that the attention of the President of the U.S. may be called to the [Sheffield] case for the purpose of suggesting that his interposition on ex parte representations of interested persons, in cases of military crime, is always hazardous," Dix wrote. "It is respectfully suggested that in all future cases, a reference may be made to the commanding general of the Department for a report before any final action is taken."

MAY 8

"There Will Be No Turning Back"

On this Sunday in 1864, Lincoln fretted about reports that General Ulysses Grant had lost his first major battle in the east—known as the Battle of the Wilderness—against Confederate general Robert E. Lee.

Grant's 1864 push for Richmond began at midnight on May 3, 1864. He planned to go around Lee's right flank, forcing the Confederates to retreat to protect their supply line. But Grant's army would have to march through the thick, mysterious forest near Chancellorsville known as the Wilderness. It was on that very ground that Lee had beaten General Joseph Hooker a year before.

The Battle of the Wilderness lasted two days (May 5–6) and resulted in horrific carnage. Casualties were over 25,000. Some of the wounded left lying in the forest were helpless against raging fires (probably ignited by cannon fire), and many were thus cremated.

So anxious was Lincoln for news from the front that he agreed to see Henry Wing, a reporter from the *New York Tribune*, at two in the morning on May 7 just to hear Wing's firsthand account of the battle. The next day—this day—Rep. Schuyler Colfax of Indiana observed how troubled Lincoln was as he paced "up and down the Executive Chamber." To another, Lincoln remarked, "Grant has gone into the Wilderness, crawled in, drawn up the ladder, and pulled in the hole after him."

"Whatever happens, there will be no turning back," Grant had promised Lincoln. Instead of retreating after the battle—as almost all his predecessors did—Grant moved his army south, again trying to turn Lee's flank. "If we were under any other General except Grant, I should expect a retreat," wrote one of his men, Elisha Hunt Rhodes, "but Grant is not that kind of soldier." Lincoln remarked, "It is the dogged pertinacity of Grant that wins."

MAY 10

Banishing Clergy

Lincoln, on this Tuesday in 1864, wired one of his generals about the banishment of a Baltimore pastor.

During the war, there were instances in which the army arrested or banished clergy who worked against the Union effort. Lincoln's official policy was to keep his hands off the clergy. "I have never interfered, nor thought of interfering as to who shall or shall not preach in any church," Lincoln wrote in December 1863, "nor have I knowingly, or believingly, tolerated any one else to so interfere by my authority." And yet less than five months later, in May 1864, Lincoln tolerated just that.

General Lew Wallace (the future writer of the best-selling *Ben Hur*) had received complaints about the secessionist opinions of Dr. Francis Hawks, Rector of St. Paul's Church of Baltimore. In April 1864, when Wallace "became satisfied and assured of his [Hawks's] dangerous character, abilities and operations," the general directed that Hawks either take the oath of allegiance to the Union or leave Baltimore and his church in twenty-four hours. Wallace admitted to Lincoln that Hawks had never said anything defamatory in public nor did he do anything "patently criminal." Wallace's only evidence was hearsay from witnesses he could not divulge—not even to Lincoln—about a secessionist pamphlet that Wallace had not read nor could prove that Hawks had written.

Hawks waited in New York as his friends appealed to the president and, on this day, Lincoln wired Wallace for an explanation. When Wallace explained his reasoning, Lincoln replied on May 13, "After reading, and considering your letter and inclosure, I have to say I leave you to act on your careful discretion in the matter."

MAY 18

The Ruse

By 1864, the three-year enlistments of many Union soldiers had expired and more than 100,000 decided not to reenlist. On May 17, Lincoln drafted a proclamation for conscripting 300,000 more men. The proclamation was never issued because on this Wednesday in 1864 two newspapers—the *New York World* and the *Journal of Commerce*—published a fake proclamation claiming to be authored by Lincoln and ordering the draft of 400,000 men.

The bogus proclamation was actually written by Joseph Howard, Jr., editor of the *Brooklyn Daily Eagle*, and Francis Mallison, one of Howard's reporters. Howard was a speculator who wanted to inflate gold prices, increasing the value of what gold he owned. He and Mallison wrote out a proclamation claiming that General Ulysses Grant's Virginia Campaign had failed and that 400,000 more men were needed. Howard then, pretending to be a messenger from the Associated Press, delivered the fake proclamation to several New York newspapers in the middle of the night just before press time, leaving editors little time to verify its authenticity. When the *New York World* and the *Journal of Commerce* printed the depressing news, the price of gold shot up 10 percent.

Lincoln responded harshly. He ordered General John Dix, the commander of the New York area, to close both papers and arrest the owners and editors for publishing spurious material of a "treasonable nature." The next day, after Howard's and Mallison's duplicity was discovered, the newspaper staffs were released and resumed publishing the day after. Despite protests that such action was tantamount to censorship, Lincoln refused to apologize. He was particularly angry at speculators such as Howard who profited by the war. "I wish every one of them had his devilish head shot!" Lincoln thundered as he banged his fist on a table.

MAY 31

"About Four Hundred Men"

As the 1864 Republican Convention approached (June 7), Lincoln found himself fighting fellow Republicans from all sides. Some thought his Emancipation Proclamation didn't go far enough and others thought his Reconstruction policies were too soft. "[Lincoln] looked like a man worn and harassed with petty faultfinding and criticisms," observed Ohio congressman Albert Riddle, "until he turned at bay, like an old stag pursued and hunted by a cowardly rabble of men and dogs." Then news came on this Tuesday in 1864 that disaffected Republicans had joined with Copperhead Democrats in Cleveland to nominate Republican John Fremont as a third-party nominee.

Fremont had never forgiven Lincoln for relieving him of command in 1861, and gathered around him those who hated the president almost as much. Radical Republicans, ultra-radical abolitionists, disappointed office-seekers, and Copperheads joined together to protest the "imbecile and vacillating policy of the present Administration." This new party—called the Radical Democracy—had a platform that called for a constitutional amendment ending slavery and a harsher Reconstruction policy.

Lincoln's agents who attended the Cleveland convention were not impressed with it. Attorney Solomon Pettis said the convention "has neither members nor talent to commend it to confidence, and it is destitute of enthusiasm." The *New York Times* called it "a congregation of malcontents, representing no constituencies and controlling no votes." When Lincoln heard that only four hundred people attended the convention, he pulled out his Bible and read a passage about David who was hiding from King Saul and gathering malcontents around him (1 Samuel 22:2): "And every one that was in distress, and every one that was in debt, and every one that was discontented, gathered themselves unto him; and he became a captain over them, and there were with him about four hundred men."

JUNE 6

The Baltimore Convention

On the eve of the Republican Party's third national convention (the party was only nine years old), Lincoln spent much of this day in 1864 greeting convention delegates on their way to Baltimore. While a few Radical Republicans wished to nominate General Ulysses Grant for president, Lincoln's nomination was virtually assured. Because Lincoln knew that a united party was necessary, he asked that the Radicals be welcomed and, in exchange, the Radicals agreed to switch their votes to Lincoln after the first ballot to make the nomination unanimous.

A non-contentious convention made for a quiet one. Lincoln's secretary John Nicolay attended the pre-convention preliminaries on this day. He reported that there was "little drinking—little quarreling . . . [the conventioneers] were intolerant of speeches—[they] remorselessly coughed down the crack orators of the party." Enthusiasm was further eroded with news that Grant had suffered some 7,000 casualties (compared to 1,500 Confederate casualties) in a frontal assault against Confederate general Robert E. Lee's entrenchments at Cold Harbor. The assault lasted less than an hour, becoming the bloodiest sixty minutes in U.S. history. "I regret this assault more than any one I ever ordered," Grant later said.

Many of the delegates wished to ascertain who Lincoln wanted to be his vice-presidential running mate. Lincoln initially favored nominating the current vice president, Hannibal Hamlin, but also favored undercutting his opponents by selecting a War Democrat such as New York's Daniel Dickinson, General Benjamin Butler, or Tennessee's military governor, Andrew Johnson. But Lincoln kept his choice to himself. "[The] convention must judge for itself," Hay wired Baltimore. The convention chose Johnson. It was a decision they would regret because Lincoln's assassination would place a Democrat in the White House, one who would constantly butt heads with a Republican administration.

JUNE 10

Vallindigham Returns

Before his secretary, John Hay, had even climbed out of bed on this Friday morning in 1864, Lincoln handed Hay a note he was to deliver to General William Rosecrans in St. Louis. For several days Lincoln had been trading telegrams with Rosecrans over a supposed conspiracy against the Union, but Rosecrans would not trust the particulars to a courier. Lincoln decided to send Hay to Rosecrans to hear the general's story.

When Hay arrived in St. Louis on June 13, Rosecrans said he was worried about a secret society called the Order of American Knights

(OAK for short), headed by former Ohio congressman Clement Vallandigham. Lincoln had exiled Vallandigham in May 1863 to the Confederacy, but Vallandigham reappeared in Canada from where he ran an unsuccessful bid for the Ohio governor's seat. Rosecrans told Hay that OAK boasted a membership throughout the Midwest. Their main endeavors were to protect rebel spies as they moved North, "some coming out of the bushes," Hay recalled, "with grass in their hair and the oath [of allegiance to the Union] in their pocket—to plunder, steal, persecute and kill and stand ready for insurrection and revolt." Rosecrans also warned that Vallandigham planned to have his old Ohio congressional district name him as delegate to the Democratic Convention in Chicago, hoping Lincoln's administration would embarrass itself by arresting him at the convention.

While Hay was returning to Washington, Vallandigham was, indeed, named a delegate to the Democratic Convention and slipped back into the country. But Lincoln had no intention of arresting the exile. According to Hay, Lincoln had long been considering revoking the exile order. Besides, Vallandigham's antics at Chicago were more of an embarrassment and disruption to the Democrats then a threat to the Republicans. As for OAK, Lincoln thought it "not especially worth regarding."

JUNE 11

Lincoln's Personal Finances

Many writers have claimed that Lincoln was careless with money, particularly as president. And yet, during those four years, his estate increased by $70,000, a substantial sum in those days. At least four times during his presidency (March 15, 1862; August 1 and 18, 1863; and January 12, 1864), Lincoln purchased government securities (bonds and temporary loans to the government). But by mid-1864 the stress of war and an upcoming election made it difficult for

Lincoln to concentrate on his investments and he asked Secretary of the Treasury Salmon Chase to handle his personal finances. On this Saturday in 1864, Lincoln pocketed his holdings and took them over to the Treasury Department. Assistant Secretary of the Treasury Maunsell Field recorded what happened:

> I happened once to be with the Secretary [Chase] when the President, without knocking, and unannounced, as was his habit, entered the room. His rusty black hat was on the back of his head, and he wore, as was his custom, an old gray shawl across his shoulders. . . . In less than five minutes I was summoned to return to the Secretary. . . . The President was gone, and there was lying upon one end of Mr. Chase's desk a confused mass of Treasury notes, Demand notes, Seven-thirty notes, and other representatives of value. Mr. Chase told us that this lot of money had just been brought by Mr. Lincoln, who desired to have it converted into bonds.

What was on Chase's desk was $54,515 worth of bonds, uncashed paychecks, cash, and even a bag of gold (worth $883). Chase gave all of it to another assistant treasury secretary, George Harrington, who reinvested it into government bonds. Harrington would handle Lincoln's personal finances for the next nine months (until Lincoln's death).

JUNE 21

"I Will Go In"

General Ulysses Grant's Overland Campaign had ended at the outskirts of Petersburg, Virginia, where Grant began the longest siege of the war. Worried about the campaign's staggering casualties, Lincoln, on this Tuesday in 1864, visited Grant at City Point.

It took Lincoln and his son Tad over sixteen hours to travel the 180 miles by steamer from Washington to City Point. When, at noon on this day, Lincoln stepped off the boat, he reached "out his long angular arm, [and] he wrung General Grant's hand vigorously," an aide observed. Despite an upset stomach, Lincoln sat down to lunch but refused champagne because, he quipped, many people get "seasick ashore from drinking that very stuff."

Afterward, Lincoln mounted Grant's horse—"Cincinnati"—and Grant climbed on another horse named "Jeff Davis" and together they rode the ten miles to the front. As he rode, one observer noted, Lincoln's "trousers gradually worked up above his ankles, and gave him the appearance of a country farmer riding into town wearing his Sunday clothes." Despite this, the troops along the route "were so lost in admiration of the man that the humorous aspect did not seem to strike them . . . [and instead] cheers broke forth from all commands." A black brigade shouted, "Hurrah for the Liberator! Hurray for the President!" Lincoln was moved to tears.

During an evening of storytelling, an aide observed that Lincoln "did not tell a story merely for the sake of an anecdote, but to point a moral or clench a fact." Before Lincoln left the next afternoon, Grant made a promise: "You will never hear of me further from Richmond than now, till I have taken it. . . . It may take a long summer day, but I will go in." It would take nine more months for Grant to "go in."

#67

Casualties of War

For seven weeks (May 4–June 12, 1864) General Ulysses Grant grappled with Confederate general Robert E. Lee through Virginia in what became known as the Overland Campaign. It was by far the most brutal and costly campaign of the war, with casualties reaching 100,000 (65,000 Union casualties; 35,000 Confederates). The Army of the Potomac's casualties for those two months were well over half of all casualties it sustained the previous three years. "The immense slaughter of our brave men chills and sickens us all," wrote Secretary of the Navy Gideon Welles.

Back in Washington, the papers carried long black-bordered columns listing Grant's dead. Washington area hospitals were filled to capacity. "He is a butcher," Mary Lincoln said of Grant. Lincoln told a friend, as they passed ambulances filled with wounded, "I cannot bear it. This suffering, this loss of life is dreadful." Lincoln was described during these weeks as "grave and anxious, and he looked like one who had lost the dearest member of his own family." Lincoln had difficulty sleeping and the artist Francis Carpenter bumped into the President one night "clad in a long morning wrapper, pacing . . . his hands behind him, great black rings under his eyes."

After Lincoln returned from City Point, however, he seemed revitalized, his faith in Grant unshaken. "Did I ever tell you the story of Grant at the circus?" Lincoln asked an associate at this time. Lincoln related the story of the boy Grant attending a circus where the ringmaster offered a dollar to anyone who could ride a particularly stubborn mule once around the ring. After several tried and failed, Grant tried and he too was thrown. On his second attempt, Grant sat backwards, holding the mule's tail and prodded it along until they both made the circuit. "Just so," Lincoln said, "Grant will hold on to Bobby Lee."

JUNE 24

Disparity

Nineteen months after the first black regiment saw combat (October 29, 1862), Congress finally made the pay of some black troops equal to that of white troops on June 15, 1864. On this Friday in 1864, Lincoln wrote Attorney General Edward Bates for clarification of the legislation.

During the first fifteen months of the war, blacks were allowed to participate in the war only as laborers or sailors. Then, on July 17, 1862, the Second Confiscation Act allowed the president to organize black regiments. Within a month, the War Department authorized five black regiments on the South Carolina Sea Islands, and they were to receive "the same pay and rations" as their white counterparts. Congress, however, had not authorized such equality in pay. And the Militia Act—which stipulated pay to black laborers, not soldiers—only allowed blacks to receive $10 per month, $3 of which was used for their uniforms. White soldiers were paid $13 a month with their clothing allowance paid by the government. Many black regiments refused to accept their pay. "As men who have families to feed, and clothe, and keep warm, we must say that the ten dollars by the greatest government in the world is an unjust distinction to men who have only a black skin to merit it," wrote Corporal James Gooding.

Despite the disparity, black soldiers fought bravely for the Union. Their well-publicized heroics changed public sentiment so that Congress finally granted equal pay to blacks who were free at the beginning of the war. This excluded tens of thousands of ex-slaves in the ranks, and Lincoln on this day asked for clarification. It would take another eight months (March 3, 1865) before equal pay would be granted to all black soldiers.

#68

Racial Discrimination

Many black soldiers enlisted into the Union army with the promise that they would receive the same pay as white soldiers. The black orator Frederick Douglass, in his March 14, 1863 recruitment appeal, called "Men of Color to Arms!" wrote, "I am authorized to assure you that you will receive the same wages, the same rations, the same equipments, the same protection, the same treatment, and the same bounty, secured by white soldiers." Less than three months later (June 4, 1863), the War Department decided to pay black troops considerably less than white soldiers. Nor were they allowed to receive bounties—monetary incentives to enlist—that white enlistees were given. Black soldiers protested and many soldiers refused to accept any pay.

Despite Douglass's promises, black soldiers were often given inferior weapons. And they were sent to the army's most unhealthy posts with inferior medical facilities. Some 29,000 black soldiers died of disease, nine times that of their combat deaths. For the rest of the army, death by disease was about two times that of combat deaths.

Black soldiers were also kept from becoming officers. When General Benjamin Butler, the military head of New Orleans, organized the Louisiana Native Guards in the fall of 1862, he commissioned seventy-six black officers to lead them. But his successor—General Nathaniel Banks—declared that the "appointment of colored officers is detrimental to the service" and had every black officer removed using false charges and humiliation. During the rest of the war, only thirty-two other blacks became officers. "We want black commissioned officers," a sergeant said, "and only because we want men we can understand and who can understand us."

JUNE 28

Fugitive Slave Laws

Lincoln, on this Tuesday in 1864, signed an act that repealed laws that before the war fanned the flames of sectional strife and were a key impetus of the war—the fugitive slave laws.

In 1793, Congress passed the first fugitive slave law, which allowed slave owners to pursue escaped slaves across state lines. As Northern states abolished slavery, they became a haven for escaping slaves. But when their owners caught up with them, they were not required to provide proof of ownership of the fugitive (whose own proof of freedom was inadmissible). Thus many free blacks were kidnapped from their homes and enslaved. This happened in 1837 when Marylander Edward Prigg seized a Pennsylvania woman—Margaret Morgan—and her children who had lived all their lives in freedom.

Between 1780 and 1859 fourteen states responded with "personal liberty laws" that provided legal protection to blacks and forbade state officials from aiding slave-catchers. It is an irony of history that Southerners, long advocates for individual state's rights, pressed for the repeal of their neighboring states' personal liberty laws. In 1850 they got their wish when Congress enacted the Fugitive Slave Act, requiring all citizens to aid in the apprehension of runaway slaves and depriving fugitives of a jury trial. Thousands of free blacks headed for Canada, and Northern apathy turned to anger. New personal liberty laws were enacted in defiance of the Act. When Southern states seceded from the Union, these personal liberty laws were among their chief grievances.

Before the war, Lincoln supported the South's right to apprehend slaves, citing the "fugitive slave clause" in the Constitution (Article IV, Section 2). In the early days of the war, escaped slaves were even returned to secessionist slave owners. But on this day the Fugitive Slave Act was forever repealed with Lincoln's signature.

JUNE 30

Chase Loses His Job

The long-standing love–hate relationship between Secretary of the Treasury Salmon Chase and Lincoln came to end this day in 1864 when Chase's fourth resignation was accepted.

Lincoln had, for months, been hearing complaints from New York Republicans—particularly from Senator Edwin Morgan—that Chase had been stocking New York custom houses with Radical Republicans who supported Chase's aspirations for the presidency. Now that Lincoln had secured the Republican presidential nomination (in early June), Lincoln felt secure enough to reassert leadership within his party. When John Cisco, assistant treasurer of New York, resigned, Chase nominated Maunsell Field, Cisco's assistant. Field had no experience in finances, but did have New York literary and social connections useful to Chase.

Chase was surprised to receive a note from Lincoln on June 28. "I cannot, without much embarrassment, make this appointment," Lincoln wrote, directing Chase to discuss a new nomination with Morgan. Chase penned a request for an immediate interview but Lincoln wrote back that such a meeting was not necessary since "the difficulty does not, in the main part, lie within the range of conversation between you and me." Referring to the need to consult New York Republicans about a New York position, Lincoln said, "As the proverb goes, no man knows so well where the shoe pinches, as he who wears it."

Meanwhile, Chase talked Cisco into remaining at his post another three months. That should have ended the issue, but Chase submitted his resignation, expecting it to be declined. But Lincoln had had enough and Chase was shocked on this day when his resignation was accepted. "You and I have reached a point of mutual embarrassment in our official relation which seems can not be overcome or longer sustained," Lincoln wrote.

#69

PARTING WAYS

Lincoln later related the events of the day that Secretary of the Treasury Salmon Chase submitted his resignation. Lincoln was at his desk when a courier delivered Chase's letter. "I opened it . . . read the first sentence, and inferred from its tenor that this matter was in the way of a satisfactory adjustment," Lincoln said. Chase had talked John Cisco, assistant treasurer of New York, into withdrawing his resignation, resolving the source of the rift between Lincoln and Chase. "I was truly glad of this, and laying the envelope with its enclosure down upon my desk, went on talking," Lincoln related. "People were coming and going all the time till 3 o'clock, and I forgot all about Chase's letter." Lincoln then decided to go downstairs to eat. As Mary and his son Tad were at Harvard for eldest son Robert's graduation (Lincoln said he was too busy to attend), the White House staff had forgotten to call Lincoln for lunch.

When Lincoln returned to his office, he decided to read the letter. "I took it out of the envelope . . . [and] another enclosure fell from it upon the floor. I picked it up, read it, and said to myself, 'Halloo, this is a horse of another color!' I put my pen into my mouth, and grit my teeth upon it," Lincoln stated. The president explained to his secretary, John Hay, how he interpreted Chase's resignation: "You have been acting very badly. Unless you say you are sorry, & ask me to stay & agree that I shall be absolute and that you shall have nothing, no matter how you beg for it, I will go." As Hay put it, "The President thought one or the other must resign. Mr. Chase elected to do so."

JULY 1

A New Treasury Secretary

Lincoln's acceptance of Secretary of the Treasury Salmon Chase's resignation created an uproar in Congress, particularly among Chase's fellow Radical Republicans. To mollify an already strained relationship, Lincoln nominated on this Friday in 1864 one of his Radical Republican critics for Chase's replacement.

Early on June 30, Chase was meeting with Senator William Fessenden of Maine, chairman of the Finance Committee, when a messenger arrived to inform Fessenden that Lincoln had nominated Chase's successor. "Have you resigned?" the Senator asked a stunned Chase. The Secretary admitted that he had, but was unaware it had been accepted (Lincoln's acceptance was waiting for Chase at his office).

Fessenden and the Finance Committee descended on Lincoln, vehemently protesting the loss of Chase and Lincoln's choice for a replacement—former Ohio governor David Tod—who, admittedly, had little financial experience. After listening, Lincoln pulled from a drawer Chase's other resignations, reading them along with Lincoln's gracious replies. "Mr. Chase had a full right to indulge in his ambition to be President," Lincoln said, but Chase's friends, in their enthusiasm to realize that ambition, had embarrassed the president and had become "unendurable." Their relationship had become so strained that Chase hadn't been to regular cabinet meetings in weeks. Later that day, Lincoln dropped a hint that he would, given the opportunity, name Chase Chief Justice to the Supreme Court, probably to silence Chase's protests. It worked.

When Tod declined the appointment, Lincoln spent a sleepless night considering another nominee. He settled on Fessenden and, without even consulting the Senator, submitted on this day his name to Congress (it took less than two minutes to confirm him). Fessenden wrote a letter declining the position but Lincoln refused to accept it. Fessenden finally accepted the post on July 4.

JULY 8

The Wade–Davis Bill

Lincoln, on this Friday in 1864, cleverly defused criticism of his pocket veto of the controversial Wade–Davis Bill with the issue of a proclamation to explain his action.

As the presidential election loomed, Radical Republicans, unhappy with Lincoln's Reconstruction policies, looked to a third-party candidate to unseat Lincoln. Conspirators in his own party hurt Lincoln deeply: "To be wounded in the house of one's friends is perhaps the most grievous affliction that can befall a man." Radicals looked to wrest party control from Lincoln by submitting the Wade–Davis Bill.

In December 1863, Lincoln's Proclamation of Amnesty and Reconstruction stipulated generous terms for former Confederate states to quickly be "reconstructed" back into the Union, thus eroding the morale of the still rebellious states. Arkansas and Louisiana already had made strides in rejoining the Union. The Wade–Davis Bill—sponsored by Senator Ben Wade and Representative. Henry Davis—aimed at asserting congressional (rather than executive) control over Reconstruction. First, the bill delayed Reconstruction, effectively precluding Lincoln from receiving electoral votes from Arkansas, Louisiana, or Tennessee in the election. It also mandated far more stringent terms for reentering the Union. Congress passed the bill on July 2, just hours before they adjourned for summer break.

Since Congress had already adjourned, Lincoln simply opted not to sign the bill—a pocket veto. He then submitted—on this day—a proclamation that claimed he had not really vetoed the bill but that it had been submitted too late for his thoughtful consideration. He cleverly stated that the Reconstruction policy in the bill was acceptable to him (it wasn't) and that any state that wished to be Reconstructed under its guidelines would receive his support (no state would voluntarily accept such strict guidelines).

JULY 10

"Keep Cool"

Washington's telegraph wires hummed on this day in 1864 as word arrived that Confederate general Jubal Early's army was marching on the capital.

With General Ulysses Grant's forces laying siege to Petersburg, Virginia, Confederate general Robert E. Lee hoped to draw some of Grant's men away by sending Early's Second Corps northward through the Shenandoah Valley. While Early's 15,000 men posed little danger to Washington—the most fortified city in the world at the time—the presence of Confederates at the capital might force Grant's hand and embarrass Lincoln in a volatile election year. Early's force remained largely undetected, until July 5 when he crossed the Potomac. Threats to destroy two Maryland towns garnered levies from the populace ($20,000 from Hagerstown; $200,000 from Frederick) for Early's coffers. On July 9, General Lew Wallace—future author of *Ben Hur*—fought a delaying action at Monocacy River before withdrawing.

On this day, Lincoln responded to a telegram from a Baltimore committee begging for troops to protect their city. "I have not a single soldier but whom is being disposed by the Military," Lincoln said. "By the latest account the enemy is moving on Washington. They can not fly to either place. Let us be vigilant but keep cool." Despite the fact that government clerks and ambulatory wounded soldiers manned the capital's defenses, Lincoln was less concerned for Washington's capture and more for the capture of Early's forces. "Retain your hold where you are," Lincoln wired Grant, "and bring the rest with you personally, and . . . destroy the enemy's force in this vicinity." That evening, Grant dispatched troops under General Horatio Wright to Washington. At ten that night, the Lincolns vacated the Soldiers' Home cottage for the far more secure White House.

JULY 11

Under Fire

The first of only two times in U.S. history that a sitting president has ever been under fire from enemy soldiers was on this Monday in 1864. The second time would be the next day.

Confederate general Jubal Early's forces stopped only briefly on their way to Washington to burn or ransack two mansions in Silver Spring—one owned by Postmaster General Montgomery Blair, the other owned by his father, Francis Blair. While looting Francis's home, the rebels were stopped and scolded by Confederate general John Breckinridge who, before the war, was a friend of the Blairs. A note was left on Francis's mantel, possibly from Breckinridge: "A Confederate officer, for himself & all his comrades, regrets exceedingly that damage & pilfering was committed in this house."

Even as the Confederates approached Washington at midday on this day, they could see dust in the distance kicked up by General Ulysses Grant's Sixth Corps as it arrived to reinforce the capital. But Early refused to retreat and ordered an attack on Fort Stevens, just off Seventh Street, five miles from the White House. Lincoln was on the fort's parapet when Early attacked, a field glass to his eye, one observer recounted, "making a very conspicuous figure." When a nearby soldier was shot, Lincoln was forced to vacate the parapet.

Lincoln left, only to return the next day with Mary. Lincoln again mounted the parapet to watch the fighting. When a nearby soldier was wounded, the commander, General Horatio Wright, tried to force Lincoln to leave. Lincoln instead sat behind the parapet but kept popping his head up. Legend has it that a captain—future Supreme Court Justice Oliver Wendell Holmes—shouted, "Get down, you fool!" Wright again tried to evict Lincoln, who allegedly asserted his right as commander in chief to be there. Wright insisted, and Lincoln finally departed.

JULY 16

The Niagara Falls Peace Efforts

On this Saturday in 1864, Lincoln wired his secretary John Hay at Niagara Falls, permitting him to issue "safe-conduct" papers to four Confederate commissioners so they could travel to Washington and negotiate an end to the war.

When, in July 1863, Lincoln rebuffed a Confederate effort to negotiate peace, Copperheads (or Peace Democrats) characterized Lincoln as uninterested in peace at any price. Lincoln's hawkish image in a war-weary country began to hurt his chances for reelection in November. On July 7, 1864, Horace Greeley, editor of the *New York Tribune*, wrote Lincoln that "ambassadors," supposedly given "full powers" to negotiate peace by Confederate president Jefferson Davis, were on the Canadian side of the Niagara Falls. Greeley urged Lincoln to meet them because "a widespread conviction that the Government . . . [is] not anxious for Peace . . . is doing great harm."

Lincoln knew that this was a Confederate–Copperhead ploy. If he rebuffed them, it would validate his hawkish image. But if he met with them, they would insist on a cease-fire before further negotiations. Once hostilities stopped, a war-weary country would never allow it to restart no matter what the Confederates demanded. "An armistice—a cessation of hostilities—is the end of the struggle, and the insurgents would be in peaceable possession of all that has been struggled for," Lincoln said. Lincoln's solution was to link emancipation—something the Confederates would never accept—to any peace negotiations. He knew the Confederates would do the rejecting and he insisted that Greeley deliver Lincoln's terms so that he'd witness their rejection. He then sent Hay to Niagara Falls as his representative. Lincoln, on this day, agreed to allow the Confederates safe-passage to Washington, again linking emancipation to negotiations. The commissioners never came to Washington, the peace efforts dead.

JULY 19

A Riot Close to Home

On this Tuesday in 1864, Lincoln discussed with his cabinet a riot in Coles County, Illinois—home of Lincoln's family—which may have involved relatives of the president.

Lincoln never lived in Coles County, but his father, Thomas, and stepmother, Sarah, lived there from 1831 until their deaths. Despite the presence of Lincoln's family, Coles County was evenly divided between Republicans and Democrats, and in the 1860 presidential election Lincoln (with 1,495 votes) barely beat Democrat Stephen Douglas (1,467 votes) there. During the war, the county was home to a large Peace Democrat (or Copperhead) population, who were anti-war and anti-Lincoln. In February 1864, the Fifty-fourth Illinois Infantry was bivouacked in the town of Mattoon and one unfortunate pastime of the soldiers was to harass Copperheads. Inevitably this led to fights, and on January 29 (in Mattoon) and February 16 and 22 (in nearby Paris), Copperheads were killed during altercations. On March 28, Charleston, Illinois hosted a Democratic rally and some of its attendees brought guns, expecting trouble. Several soldiers from the Fifty-fourth appeared at the rally, largely unarmed but drunk. When a fight broke out, guns appeared from everywhere. After it was over, nine were dead—six of them soldiers—and twelve wounded.

According to Lincoln's cousin Dennis Hanks, the president knew at least one of the dead (Major Shubal York) and one of the wounded (Young Winkler). In addition, at least three people involved—John Elsberry Hanks, Sheriff John O'Hair, and Stephen Greenville—may have been related by blood or marriage to Lincoln. In mid-July, Lincoln was petitioned for release of fifteen Copperhead suspects in military custody and Lincoln, on this day, discussed it with his cabinet. In November, Lincoln released the prisoners to civil authorities for trial. Only two were tried, both acquitted.

JULY 26

The Confederates Escape Again

On this Tuesday in 1864, Secretary of the Navy Gideon Welles and his wife, Mary Ann, visited the Lincolns at the Old Soldiers' cottage where the conversation centered on word that Confederate general Jubal Early was moving north of the Potomac for the second time in less than a month. Welles hoped that the Union army would, unlike Early's previous foray, get behind the Confederates, "cutting them off, and not permitting them to go back." Lincoln said he was urging his generals to do just that.

Early's previous excursion ended on July 11, 1864, when Early withdrew from Washington, heading for the Shenandoah Valley. General Horatio Wright pursued them sluggishly—"for fear he might come across the rebels and catch some of them," Lincoln quipped bitterly. Mary echoed this bitterness when Secretary of War Edwin Stanton praised her bravery for standing on the "ramparts of Fort Stevens, overlooking the fight." Mary replied, "If I had had a few more ladies with me the Rebels would not have been permitted to get away as they did!"

The press roasted the embarrassed military and Lincoln's administration. Even Postmaster General Montgomery Blair, after he saw what the rebels did to his Silver Springs home, called the military "poltroons." Army Chief of Staff Henry Halleck demanded that Blair be fired. "I do not consider what may have been hastily said in a moment of vexation . . . is sufficient ground for so grave a step," Lincoln said. "I propose continuing to be myself the judge as to when a member of the Cabinet shall be dismissed."

At the end of July, Early sent his cavalry across the Potomac to Pennsylvania. The rebels burned the town of Chambersburg when the citizens refused to pay a $500,000 tribute. Then they again escaped without molestation from Union troops.

JULY 31

"We Sleep at Night"

Lincoln, on this day in 1864, met General Ulysses Grant at Fortress Monroe, Virginia, to confer over the mess that came to be known as the Battle of the Crater.

After Grant failed to take Petersburg, Virginia on June 15, 1864, Grant's Army of the Potomac and Confederate general Robert E. Lee's Army of Northern Virginia settled into a siege. Colonel Henry Pleasants (who led the Forty-eighth Pennsylvania Infantry, partly made up of miners) came up with an innovative plan to dig a tunnel under the Confederate entrenchments, pack it with explosives, detonate it, then send hordes of troops through the breech. Grant approved the plan and Pleasants, beginning in late June, began digging. By late July, Pleasants's tunnel stretched five hundred feet and ended in a perpendicular seventy-five foot shaft under the Confederate works. Pleasants packed 320 kegs (about eight tons) of gunpowder into the shaft. On July 30, Pleasants's charges exploded, creating a 170-foot by 80-foot crater and killing some 208 Confederates immediately. The Union soldiers, however, instead of skirting the lip of the crater, went into it, and found themselves trapped. The Union suffered some 5,300 casualties compared to the Confederate's 1,000. "It was the saddest affair I have witnessed in this war," Grant wrote.

Secretary of the Navy Gideon Welles wrote that the battle depressed him, "less however from the result, bad as it is, than from an awakening apprehension that Grant is not equal to the position assigned him." Lincoln was on a steamer the same day as the battle, meeting Grant at Fortress Monroe the next morning. Grant's confident demeanor calmed Lincoln's anxiety and the president returned to Washington as confident as ever in Grant. "Since Grant assumed command," Lincoln said, "we sleep at night."

AUGUST 8

The Sister-in-Law

Lincoln, on this day in 1864, wrote to General Stephen Burbridge, commander of the District of Kentucky, and requested that he not treat his sister-in-law Emilie Todd Helm with favoritism.

The Lincolns had, before the war, been very close to Mary's half-sister Emilie and her husband, Benjamin. Lincoln thought so much of Ben that after Fort Sumter he offered him a commission in the Union Army. But Ben decided to "cast his destinies with his native Southland" and joined the Confederate Army. He was killed at the Battle of Chickamauga in September 1863. When a pregnant Emilie appeared at Fortress Monroe that December wishing to cross Union lines and return to Kentucky, Lincoln had her brought to the White House to stay, despite the uproar caused by hosting the widow of a rebel general. Emilie exacerbated the situation with her sharp, bitter tongue. When she decided to head home, Lincoln wrote out a pass and a letter offering amnesty on the condition that she swear a loyalty oath. Emilie refused the oath.

On this day, Lincoln wired Burbridge that he heard "a rumor to-day that you recently sought to arrest her [Emilie], but was prevented by her presenting the paper from me." Lincoln added, "I do not intend to protect her against the consequences of disloyal words or acts, spoken or done by her . . . and if the paper given by me can be construed to give her protection . . . it is hereby revoked *pro tanto*. Deal with her for current conduct, just as you would with any other." What Emilie did is lost to history but, thirty-one years later, when Emilie first read Lincoln's telegram, she wrote, "This dispatch is a surprise to me, since I was never arrested and never had any trouble with the United States authorities."

#70

Disloyal Kin

While the President's own family members were avid Democrats and may even have been Copperheads (anti-war, anti-Lincoln), there is no evidence they either aided or joined the Confederacy. Not so with his wife Mary's family.

Mary was the fourth child of seven born to Robert and Eliza Todd. After Eliza died in 1825, Robert married Elizabeth Humphreys and gave Mary nine half-siblings. Thirteen of Mary's brothers and sisters were still alive by the start of the Civil War and more than half were involved with the Confederacy. Her brother George served in the Confederate Army as a surgeon. Her half-brothers Samuel and David also joined the Confederate Army. Sam was killed at the Battle of Shiloh and David, a captain, was put in charge of the infamous Libby Prison in Richmond. Mary's favorite half-brother, Alexander ("Aleck"), was killed by "friendly-fire" at Baton Rouge, Louisiana, just a few months after Sam. When Mary heard the news, she exclaimed, "Oh, little Aleck, why did you have to die?" Later, however, she told her seamstress Elizabeth Keckley that Aleck "made his choices long ago. He decided against my husband, through him against me . . . since he chose to be our deadly enemy, I see no special reason why I should bitterly mourn his death." At another time she said of all her Confederate brothers, "[they'd] kill my husband if they could and destroy our government."

For all the rancor her brothers caused Mary, her sisters probably hurt her deeper. Her half-sister Emilie, whom Mary was extremely fond of, became estranged after her husband Ben joined the Confederacy and Emilie moved to

Selma, Alabama. Half-sister Elodie also married a Confederate officer and half-sister Martha married a Southern sympathizer, Clement White, and may have been involved in rebel smuggling.

AUGUST 12

"Let 'em Wriggle"

With the November elections less than three months away, Lincoln, on this day in 1864, had to deal with disaffection in his own Republican Party.

Two things happened during the first week in August to shake Lincoln's reelection chances. The first was the publication of Lincoln's "To Whom it May Concern" letter to Confederate envoys who had appeared at Niagara Falls in July to negotiate peace. In the letter, Lincoln linked emancipation to any negotiations. Democrats touted this as proof that the war was no longer fought to save the Union but to end slavery. It was a blow to conservative Republicans who did not favor emancipation. The second was the publication of the "Wade–Davis Manifesto"—a protest of Lincoln's pocket veto of the Wade–Davis Bill (the Radical Republicans' harsh Reconstruction plan). The manifesto claimed Lincoln's use of the rare pocket veto was a "grave Executive usurpation" of the Legislative Branch. "The authority of Congress is paramount. . . . He [Lincoln] must confine himself to his executive duties—to obey and execute, not make laws."

With Radical and conservative Republicans both unhappy, Thurlow Weed—a political advisor—told Lincoln on this day that "his reelection is an impossibility." What was more worrisome was word that some Republicans wanted to hold another convention and nominate another candidate. Most favored General Ulysses Grant and, on this day, Lincoln sent a friend to ask Grant about his political aspirations. Grant answered that he had none.

When asked about the dissension, Lincoln tried to mollify his hurt feelings with humor, "It reminds me of an old acquaintance, who, having a son of a scientific turn, bought him a microscope. . . . One day, at the dinner-table, his father took up a piece of cheese. 'Don't eat that, father,' said the boy, 'it is full of wrigglers.' 'My son,' replied the old gentleman, taking . . . a huge bite, 'let 'em wriggle; I can stand it if they can.'"

AUGUST 18

"I Fear He Is a Failure"

On this day in 1864, political advisor Leonard Swett visited the president to tell him his reelection was hopeless and asked him if he'd withdraw his nomination.

That summer was a disaster for Lincoln's administration. General Ulysses Grant's Overland Campaign had cost the Union some 65,000 casualties and ended in a stalemate before Petersburg, Virginia. Together with General William Sherman's as yet unsuccessful attempt to take Atlanta, the military situation was bleak. "He said we must be patient, all would come out right," said Commissioner Benjamin French, relating a "pleasant talk" he had with Lincoln. "He did not expect Sherman to take Atlanta in a day, nor that Grant could walk right into Richmond—but that we should have them both in time." Grant's horrendous casualties meant that Lincoln would have to institute another unpopular draft right on the eve of the election. And the treasury announced it needed yet another loan. Pessimism abounded. Even Lincoln's attorney general, Edward Bates, felt that the country did not have a "competent man at the head of affairs." Lincoln's close friend Orville Browning admitted, "I thought he [Lincoln] might get through, as many a boy through college, without disgrace . . . I fear he is a failure."

Swett, on this day, warned his friend that many in his own Republican Party wanted to "call another [nominating] convention and supplant him." They had even tentatively set the new convention for September 22 in Cincinnati. Swett asked if Lincoln would withdraw his nomination, but Lincoln refused. "I confess that I desire to be reelected," Lincoln told another visitor. "I have the common pride of humanity to wish my past four years administration endorsed; and besides I honestly believe that I can better serve the nation in its need and peril than any new man could possibly do."

AUGUST 19

The Robinson Letter

The famous orator Frederick Douglass, on this Friday in 1864, convinced Lincoln not to vacillate on the issue of emancipation.

On August 16, Lincoln received a letter from Wisconsin War Democrat Charles Robinson, editor of the *Green Bay Advocate*. Robinson said that he had supported Lincoln for the Union's sake, but felt betrayed when Lincoln linked not just reunification but emancipation with any peace negotiations in July (during the Niagara Falls peace efforts). "This puts the whole war question on a new basis, and takes us War Democrats clear off our feet," Robinson wrote. Believing that the support of War Democrats was essential in the coming election, Lincoln wrote a reply to be printed in Robinson's paper: "To me it seems plain that saying re-union and abandonment of slavery would be considered if offered is not saying that nothing else would be considered if offered." He admitted that if the Confederacy offered reunification without emancipation, Lincoln would be forced to accept it. This meant returning ex-slaves—some of who had fought for the Union—back to slavery. "But I could never be their [the public's] agent to do it," Lincoln added. "For such work, another would have to be found."

When Lincoln met with Douglass on this day, he read the Robinson letter aloud. Douglass urged Lincoln not to send it, "It would be taken as a complete surrender of your anti-slavery policy, and do you serious damage." Douglass's argument was effective enough to change Lincoln's mind. "No human power could subdue this rebellion without using the Emancipation lever," Lincoln told two other visitors. "Let them prove by the history of this war, that we can restore the Union without it."

Lincoln never sent the Robinson letter.

#71

"Damned in Time and Eternity"

The two meetings Lincoln had on August 19, 1864 illustrate how Lincoln's thoughts often evolved as he talked with others. Lincoln was about to send a letter to Charles Robinson which, if published, could have been perceived as a reconsideration of emancipation. Lincoln read his Robinson letter to black orator Frederick Douglass in a meeting that day, and listened to Douglass's plea not to send it. Then Lincoln changed the subject.

Douglass left the White House unsure of the effect of his words. It's clear, however, that Lincoln had adopted Douglass's arguments when he met that evening with Alexander Randall and Judge Joseph Mills. "[There are] between 1 & 200 thousand black men now in the service of the Union," Lincoln is recorded to have said. If emancipation were abandoned, these soldiers would throw down their arms and "surrender all these advantages to the enemy & we would be compelled to abandon the war in 3 weeks." He added, "There have been men who have proposed to me to return to slavery the black warriors of [the battles of] Port Hudson and Olustee to their masters to conciliate the South. I should be damned in time & eternity for so doing."

Mills observed that Lincoln was "free & animated" during this conversation. "As I heard a vindication of his policy from his own lips, I could not but feel that his mind grew in stature like his body & that I stood in the presence of the great guiding intellect of the age," Mills wrote. Lincoln was just as passionate when he rewrote his letter to Robinson, "If they [the black soldiers] stake their lives for us they must be prompted by the strongest motives—even the promise of freedom. And the promise, being made, must be kept." Lincoln never sent even the revised Robinson letter.

AUGUST 21

Wrought-iron

Not only was Lincoln involved in putting new weapons on the battlefield, but also improving weapons already there. On this Sunday in 1864, Lincoln gave the green light to test seven-inch wrought-iron cannon for "United States service."

Horatio Ames dwarfed even Lincoln, standing at six-foot-six-inches and tipping the scales at better than three hundred pounds. Ames's Connecticut ironworks produced wrought-iron cranks and axles for locomotives, but, at the outbreak of war, Ames tried to interest the government in rifled wrought-iron cannon. Ames was so confident in the superior strength of his wrought-iron guns over bronze or cast-iron cannon, he offered to sit on one of his guns as it was fired. But it wasn't until the spring of 1863 that Lincoln began to seriously look for stronger cannon.

That April a flotilla of ironclads churned into Charleston harbor, hoping to reduce Forts Sumter and Moultrie and thus close the

Confederate port. The ironclads' short-range cannon forced them to come in close to the forts and they took over 225 hits. Three ironclads were heavily damaged and one was sunk, without any serious damage to the forts. Afterward, Lincoln looked for naval and field cannon that could lob shells from a distance.

Lincoln met with Ames and Connecticut congressman Augustus Brandegee in the autumn of 1863. "I had prepared what I thought a neat little speech of introduction, but he at once put my rhetoric and embarrassment to flight," Brandegee said, "by taking my hand and saying, 'Well, what does little Connecticut want?' The tone, the familiar address . . . the gracious smile at once put me at ease, and I stated my case as to a friend." Lincoln agreed to purchase Ames's cannon as long as it passed ordinance tests. By August of 1864 Ames had guns ready to be tested and on this day Lincoln set up a three-man military panel to oversee the process.

Unfortunately for Ames, the war ended before his guns could see much action. A short time later steel processing made Ames's wrought-iron cannon obsolete and he lost both his foundry and fortune.

AUGUST 23

"The Tide Is Against Us"

Lincoln, on this Tuesday in 1864, wrote out a memorandum, folded it, sealed it, then had every member of his cabinet sign it without reading it.

The day before, Henry Raymond, editor of the *New York Times* and chairman of the National Union (the new, temporary name of the Republican Party) Executive Committee, wrote Lincoln, "The tide is against us." Raymond predicted that if the presidential election were held that day that Illinois, Pennsylvania, Indiana, and New York would go to the Democrats. Lincoln concurred with Raymond's dismal assessment. "Do you expect to be reelected?" Lincoln's friend Leonard Swett asked him. "Well, I don't think I have ever heard of any man being elected to an office unless someone was for him," Lincoln responded.

On this day, Lincoln wrote, "This morning, as for some days past, it seems exceedingly probable that this Administration will not be re-elected. Then it will be my duty to so co-operate with the President-elect, as to save the Union between the election and the inauguration; as he will have secured his election on such ground that he cannot possibly save it afterwards." He folded the note so as to hide its contents, then, at the scheduled cabinet meeting, had all his cabinet secretaries sign it unread and unexplained. Lincoln later claimed that he planned to meet with General George McClellan—the expected Democratic president-elect—and say, "General, the election has demonstrated that you are stronger, have more influence with the American people than I. Now let us together, you with your influence and I with all the executive power of the Government, try to save the country." Lincoln despaired of McClellan's cooperation but "at least . . . I should have done my duty and have stood clear before my own conscience."

AUGUST 25

"*Worse than Losing*"

Lincoln, on this Thursday in 1864, met with Henry Raymond, the editor of the *New York Times*, to persuade him that the his reelection was still possible.

Raymond was in Washington to chair a committee for organizing support for Lincoln in the November election. On August 22, Raymond delivered to the president a bleak assessment of his reelection chances, because of "the want of military successes" and because of Lincoln's Emancipation Proclamation. Raymond recommended that Lincoln send a commissioner to Richmond to offer reunification of North and South as the sole term for peace and allow the issue of slavery to be settled later. Raymond believed the Confederates would reject his peace offer, which "would plant seeds of disaffection in the South, dispel all the delusions about peace . . . in the North . . . [and] reconcile the public sentiment to the war, the draft & the [income] tax as inevitable necessities." In short, it could win the election for Lincoln.

Lincoln seriously considered Raymond's proposal, even drafting orders for Raymond to proceed to Richmond and offer peace terms on "restoration" of the Union, with slavery to be decided by "peaceful modes." In the end Lincoln decided that such a venture "would be utter ruination" and, as the president's secretary John Nicolay recounted, when Lincoln met Raymond on this day he told him "that to follow his plan . . . would be worse than losing the Presidential contest—it would be ignominiously surrendering it in advance." Raymond left impressed with Lincoln's iron will and two days later his paper declared, "Mr. Lincoln will be reelected." Lincoln, however, remained pessimistic and said privately, "You think I don't know I am going to be beaten, but I do and unless some great change takes place badly beaten." That great change was just over a week away.

AUGUST 28

"Am I to Have No Rest?"

At midnight on this day in 1864, a Baltimore lawyer named Charles Gwinn awakened Lincoln at the Old Soldiers' Home cottage. Gwinn was there to plead for the commutation of the death sentences of his four clients. They had been arrested in Baltimore as spies and were convicted and sentenced to hang. But Lincoln, after receiving other appeals, had already commuted their sentences to hard labor earlier that day.

During the warm summer months of 1862, 1863, and 1864 (usually from June until September), Lincoln spent nearly every night in the cooler cottage. Unfortunately, late night visitations there were not as rare as Lincoln liked. During the Peninsula Campaign of 1862, for instance, a general who was in a panic over reports that the Army of the Potomac was in danger awakened Lincoln. Lincoln said of the visit, "I who am not a specially brave man have had to sustain the sinking courage of these professional fighters in critical times."

On June 26, 1863, Lincoln had visitors who awakened him. During their conversation, Lincoln drifted off to sleep and one of the visitors—who was inebriated—slapped the president's knee. "Tell us one of your good stories," he said. Lincoln left angry. Two months later (August 23), a colonel visited Lincoln, finding him "reposed in a broad chair, one leg hanging over its arm." When the colonel spoke to him, Lincoln responded, "Am I to have no rest? Is there no hour or spot when or where I may escape this constant call? Why do you follow me out here with such business as this?" Lincoln apologized the next day.

#72

The Soldiers' Home

Lincoln spent thirteen of his fifty months as president (nearly a quarter of his presidency) living at the Old Soldiers' Home cottage, commuting the three miles to the White House. The cottage was originally built in 1842 by banker George Riggs in a Gothic Revival style with gabled roofs, a large porch, and stucco facade. In the early 1850s Riggs sold the cottage and its surrounding 256 acres to the government, which then named it the Military Asylum (and later the Old Soldiers' Home) and designated it as a refuge for impoverished, disabled veterans. Two more cottages were built—Quarters One and Two—and the main building, Scott Hall (after General in Chief Winfield Scott), was constructed to house 150 veterans.

When political support for the venture faded, the asylum's commissioners tried to drum up some by inviting presidents and secretaries of war to spend summers at the cottages. President James Buchanan stayed at Quarters One and probably recommended the retreat to Lincoln. The hilltop locale meant that it was several degrees cooler than Washington. The Riggs cottage, with its high ceilings and fourteen-inch-thick brick exterior, stayed pleasant in the summer, particularly if the front (north) door and south-facing windows were left open.

The first summer of the war was too hectic to move there but, after the death of their son Willie, the Lincolns needed a refuge in 1862. They displaced the asylum's governor to stay at the Riggs cottage in June. However, they never found solitude there. During the war, a total of two hundred disabled veterans shared the grounds with them and Lincoln received at least seventy recorded visitors to the cottage, usually in the evening. Nevertheless, Mary was fond of the retreat. "How dearly I loved the 'Soldiers' Home,'" she wrote after her husband's death.

SEPTEMBER 3

"Damn the Torpedoes"

Even as word arrived from the Chicago Democratic Convention that Lincoln's opponent in the coming presidential election would be General George McClellan, Lincoln received two pieces of news that greatly increased his chances of winning the coming presidential election. On this day in 1864, he celebrated.

The first news came from Mobile, Alabama's largest city and an important Confederate port. Admiral David Farragut put together a flotilla of fourteen ships and four ironclads to take Mobile Bay. The challenge was that the bay's main shipping lane was guarded by Forts Gaines and Morgan, and the Confederates had used piles to narrow the lane to a constricted passageway under Fort Morgan's guns. At the mouth of this passage the Confederates had anchored underwater mines called "torpedoes."

When, on August 5, Farragut filed his ships through the pass, the lead ship the *Tecumseh* struck a torpedo and sank with 90 of its 114-man crew. The flotilla stalled, unsure what to do. Farragut, who was lashed to the rigging of the *Brooklyn* so he could see the action, allegedly called down, "Damn the torpedoes—full speed ahead!" By August 23, Farragut secured Mobile Bay, closing the port (the city would fall the following April).

The second news came from Atlanta, where General William Sherman had finally maneuvered Confederate general John Bell Hood out of his entrenchments and had taken the city on September 2. Sherman fired off a telegram to Washington, "Atlanta is ours and fairly won."

Lincoln responded on this day by proclaiming a day of thanksgiving (set for September 11). He also ordered a one-hundred-gun salute and sent Farragut and Sherman his thanks. The twin victories were a stunning blow to the Democrats, who had just nominated McClellan on a platform that claimed the war had been "four years of failure."

#73

If Lincoln Was Not Reelected

Would the outcome of the war have been different if George McClellan, not Lincoln, had been elected in

November 1864? It's tempting to say that McClellan's election would have made no difference, since he would not take office until March 4, 1865, with the war all but over. By then Confederate general John Bell Hood's army had been all but destroyed at Nashville (December 1864). General William Sherman had not only taken Savannah, Georgia (December 1864), but had marched through Georgia, South Carolina, and North Carolina, destroying the Confederate infrastructure. General Ulysses Grant had stressed Confederate general Robert E. Lee's army so that less than a month after the inauguration it would collapse and two weeks later capitulate.

But there are other variables. First, it's possible that had there been some hope of a negotiated peace with McClellan, Hood may not have taken such a desperate measure as attacking Nashville. If he, instead, had dogged Sherman on his march to Savannah, or joined Lee at Petersburg, Virginia and broken Grant's stranglehold, the war might have dragged on past McClellan's inauguration, giving him the opportunity to negotiate a peace.

McClellan himself was another variable. He did not like the Democratic platform, which demanded a "cessation of hostilities" and reunification of North and South without stipulations (including emancipation). McClellan had no interest in ending slavery, but he could not tell his "gallant comrades of the army and navy" that the "labors and sacrifice of so many of our slain and wounded brethren had been in vain." After considering it, McClellan accepted the nomination but rejected the platform. Whether McClellan was strong enough personally or politically to reject efforts by his fellow Peace Democrats to end the war is, however, doubtful.

SEPTEMBER 4

Conscientious Objectors

A number of religious groups—the Shakers, Dunkards, Mennonites, and the Religious Society of Friends (Quakers)—were pacifists, opposed to war. On this Sunday in 1864, Lincoln wrote to Eliza Gurnery, a Quaker, to say that he would continue to help conscientious objectors.

Quakers were adamantly committed to nonviolence and against the shedding "of human blood." But it wasn't until February 1864 that the Conscription Act was amended to provide exemptions for conscientious objectors to work in hospitals or camps for ex-slaves instead of fighting. By then, many Quakers had volunteered to fight while still others were drafted or forced to enlist. Quaker Cyrus Pringle was drafted in July 1863 and in October, when he refused to drill with his weapon, two sergeants staked Pringle to the ground "in the form of an X" and left him "exposed to the heat of the sun." Pringle wrote, "I wept, not so much from my own suffering as from sorrow that such a thing should be in our own country."

In the fall of 1863, Gurney sent Lincoln a letter, thanking him for emancipating the slaves. "I do assuredly believe he [God] did . . . make thee instrumental in accomplishing [His will], when he appointed thee thy present post," she wrote. Another year passed before Lincoln, on this day, responded, acknowledging how difficult it is to be "opposed to both war and oppression" when war, in this instance, was God's instrument to remove oppression. He added, "For those appealing to me on conscientious grounds, I have done, and shall do, the best I could and can."

SEPTEMBER 6

Women in the Ranks

Lincoln, on this Tuesday in 1864, interviewed Mary Wise, a woman who disguised herself as a man and served with the Thirty-fourth Indiana Regiment until she was wounded.

During the war at least five hundred women disguised themselves and served as soldiers—women like Sarah Edmonds of New Brunswick, Canada, who grew up on a farm where she developed a "masculine" physique. At nineteen, she crossed into Michigan disguised as "Franklin Thompson" so she could earn a man's wages selling Bibles. When war broke out, she joined the Second Michigan Infantry and stayed with it for nearly two years before she deserted out of frustration (she had fallen in love with two of her fellow soldiers). Sarah Wakeman (a.k.a. Lyons Wakeman) served two years with the 153rd New York State Volunteers because she wanted to provide for her family by sending home her wages. Her sex remained undiscovered after a month in the hospital for severe diarrhea, from which she died. Many women couldn't part with their brothers, lovers, or husbands and enlisted with them. One witness recounted a scene where a disguised woman in the ranks was unmasked: "Clutching the [arresting] officer by the arm . . . she begged him not to expose her . . . Her husband had enlisted in his [the officer's] company, she said, and it would kill her if he marched without her."

Mary Wise was wounded in the shoulder during the Lookout Mountain battle (November 24, 1863), and her sex discovered in the hospital. She came to see Lincoln on this day because the army refused to pay her five months of back pay. Lincoln ordered the paymaster to pay her and if that could not be done legally, the president offered to pay Wise out of his own pocket.

SEPTEMBER 7

Lincoln and the Bible

On this Wednesday in 1864, Lincoln met with a delegation of blacks who presented a Bible to him. His response might have surprised a younger Lincoln.

Lincoln, in his youth, was a skeptic when it came to Christianity in general and the Bible in particular. In 1834 he allegedly wrote an essay that attempted to disprove the divine inspiration of the Bible and the divinity of Jesus. A friend burned the manuscript before it could be published. Lincoln's beliefs gradually changed, beginning in 1850 when his son Eddie died and culminating with the stresses and pain of the Civil War, particularly after another son, Willie, died and Lincoln turned to the Bible for solace. When his friend Joshua Speed visited Lincoln in the summer of 1864, he found the president "sitting near a window intensely reading his Bible. . . . 'Well,' said I, 'if you have recovered from your skepticism, I am sorry to say that I have not!' Looking me earnestly in the face . . . he [Lincoln] said, 'You are wrong, Speed; take all of this book upon reason that you can, and the balance on faith, and you will live and die a happier and better man.'"

The black delegation from Baltimore presented Lincoln with a pulpit-size Bible with a gold frontispiece embossed with Lincoln standing in a cotton field removing a slave's shackles. Though the occasion called for politeness, Lincoln's response was more effusive in his praise of the Bible than he had been before, "This Great Book . . . it is the best gift God has given to man. All the good the Savior gave to the world was communicated through this book. But for it we could not know right from wrong. All things most desirable for man's welfare, here and hereafter, are found portrayed in it."

#74

What Did Lincoln Believe?

Speculation as to what Lincoln's religious beliefs were started almost from the moment of his death. On one hand there's Lincoln's law partner, William Herndon, who claimed Lincoln was an "avowed and open infidel, and sometimes bordered on atheism," and Mary's assertion that her husband "had no faith and no hope in the usual acceptance of those words" and was "never a technical Christian." On the other hand there was Lincoln's friend Noah Brooks, who wrote that the president "talked always of Christ, his cross, his atonement." Dr. James Smith, pastor of Lincoln's Springfield church, insisted that Lincoln was a Christian.

Lincoln was a skeptic as a young man but after he lost an 1843 congressional race partly because his beliefs clashed with "church influence," Lincoln kept his tenets to himself. After Eddie's death in 1850—when Dr. Smith claims Lincoln was converted—it appears Lincoln sought consolation, not conversion. While he rented a pew at Dr. Smith's church, he never in his life joined Smith's or any church. But as president Lincoln's beliefs appeared to transform. "He first seemed to think about the subject [faith] when our boy Willie died," Mary admitted. But Lincoln himself said he began to think about it the year before, during the secession crisis. This disparity indicates Lincoln may have kept his beliefs even from his wife. Herndon never interacted with Lincoln as president and may not have known of his "change of heart," as Lincoln described it to Brooks. He told artist Francis Carpenter that his "change" did not happen all at once but was a "process of crystallization." We will never be sure what he believed but, as his friend

> Jesse Fell said, Lincoln's "principles and practices and the spirit of his whole life were of the very kind we universally agree to call Christian."

SEPTEMBER 8

Writing Mary

In August 1864, Mary and son Tad escaped Washington's sizzling heat for the cooler Manchester, Vermont. On this day in 1864, Lincoln sent Mary a telegram: "All well, including Tad's pony and the goats." While telegrams were typically short—they were paid for by their word count—Lincoln's thirty-one-word wire was notable for its lack of personal information. He even signed it "A. Lincoln" just as he did telegrams to total strangers.

Mary acknowledged that her husband, who could pen beautiful poetic prose and wrote hundreds of letters, was "not given to letter writing" to her. To some extent historians have to take her word for it because Mary burned much of the correspondence between them, as did their eldest son Robert after Lincoln's death. What little survives shows hints of playfulness. Once, while he was a U.S. representative, Mary asked if she and the boys could come to Washington. Lincoln responded on June 12, 1848, "Will you be a good girl in all things, if I consent? Then come along, and that as soon as possible. Having got the idea in my head, I shall be impatient till I see you." But he could be heavy-handed in his attempts to compliment his wife. "I am afraid you will get so well, and fat, and young as to be wanting to marry again," he wrote at another time.

As president, he missed his wife during her long excursions to shop or rest, but was not demonstrative in his expressions of it. During the summer of 1863, Mary had been gone two months when Lincoln wired simply, "I would be glad [to] see you and Tad." The next day (September 22) he was even briefer: "I really wish to see you."

SEPTEMBER 19

The Soldiers' Vote

Lincoln, on this Monday in 1864, wrote General William Sherman in Atlanta asking if he could send Hoosiers in his ranks home to Indiana to vote in the October 11 state elections.

Many thought the early state elections in Ohio, Pennsylvania, and Indiana would be a good indicator of how the November presidential election would go. With 850,000 Union soldiers in the field, it was clear that their vote would be pivotal to both elections. By then nineteen states allowed soldiers to vote in the field, while others—Indiana included—required voters to be physically present in their districts.

Democrats were confident of the soldiers' vote, recalling the devotion the troops held for their presidential candidate—General George McClellan—when he headed the army. "We are certain of two-thirds of the [soldiers'] vote for General McClellan as that the sun shines," wrote a Democrat. Lincoln, however, engendered plenty of devotion himself. "I would rather be defeated with the soldier vote behind me than to be elected without it," Lincoln said. What's more, McClellan's peace platform hurt his popularity among soldiers. "McClellan was our first commander, and, as such, he was worshipped by his soldiers," a private in the Twentieth Maine Infantry wrote. "It was cruel [of] General McClellan to ask us to vote that our campaigns had all been failures, and that our comrades had died in vain."

Lincoln, on this day, wrote Sherman that "the loss of it [the Indiana election] . . . would go far towards losing the whole Union cause." He asked Sherman to send as many soldiers as could safely go home to vote. As a result, the Republican governor Oliver Morton was reelected and Republicans took eight of the eleven congressional seats. In the November election, only one in three soldiers voted for McClellan.

SEPTEMBER 20

"Blows Upon a Dead Body"

On this day in 1864, Lincoln had reason to celebrate. "I have just heard of your great victory," he wired General Philip Sheridan. "God bless you all, officers and men."

Union victories at Atlanta and Mobile Bay in Alabama had greatly enhanced Lincoln's chances for reelection in November. But the public's (and Lincoln's) myopic obsession with the eastern theater made them hungry for a victory in Virginia. The strategically important Shenandoah Valley, which the Confederates had used numerous times to march into Maryland and Pennsylvania, was also a fertile breadbasket which Lee depended on to feed his troops. During his Overland Campaign, General Ulysses Grant had general Franz Sigel march into the valley. When Sigel was routed at New Market, Virginia, on May 15, he was replaced with General David Hunter. But after Confederate General Jubal Early slipped around Hunter in July to attack Washington, Grant put General Philip Sheridan in charge of shutting down the valley.

"Sheridan and Early are facing each other at a dead lock," Lincoln wrote Grant on September 12, and wanted Sheridan to "strike." A week later Sheridan attacked Early at Winchester (the town's seventh engagement and third battle) with 38,000 men. In the daylong battle, Early was forced to retreat with a third of his 11,000 men dead, wounded or captured. By the end of the week, Sheridan had driven Early a hundred miles south, denying Lee the coming Shenandoah harvest. Lincoln's reelection prospects jumped even further. "This will do much to encourage and stimulate all Union loving men," wrote Secretary of the Navy Gideon Welles. Confederate Mary Boykin Chestnut lamented, "These stories of our defeat in the Valley fall like blows upon a dead body. Since Atlanta, I have felt as if all were dead within me, forever."

SEPTEMBER 23

The Deal

On this Friday in 1864, Lincoln asked for and accepted the resignation of his postmaster general, Montgomery Blair.

The powerful Blair family had been a part of Washington politics for more than thirty years. The family patriarch—Francis Blair, Sr.—had helped form the Democratic Party into a national entity and later organized the Republican Party. Along with sons Frank, Jr. and Montgomery, Francis was instrumental in General John Fremont's presidential nomination in 1856 and Lincoln's in 1860. Typically, the postmaster general office had been filled with politicos who did little to modernize the post office. Montgomery, however, instituted free mail, a system for verifying delivery and money orders for soldiers.

The Blairs, however, infuriated the Radical Republicans, primarily because of their moderate stance on slavery. In May 1864, Radicals nominated as a third-party candidate the Blair's old friend Fremont (who now hated the Blairs over their role in his removal as head of the Department of the West in 1861). Weeks later at the Republican Convention, Radicals passed a resolution demanding Montgomery's removal. Lincoln refused, saying that "he did not think it good policy to sacrifice a true friend to an avowed enemy." But while Fremont's prospects of gaining the presidency were slight, his presence in the election could siphon off votes Lincoln needed. In August, Michigan senator Zachariah Chandler brokered a deal in which Radicals would support Lincoln and Fremont would withdraw from the race in exchange for Montgomery's resignation. On September 22, Fremont withdrew. "You have generously said to me more than once, that whenever your resignation could be a relief to me, it was at my disposal," Lincoln wrote Montgomery on this day. "The time has come." Montgomery resigned and Lincoln named former Ohio governor William Dennison to replace him.

OCTOBER 1

"The First Installment"

Lincoln, on this Saturday in 1864, met his representative recruit who would serve in the army in his stead for the remainder of the war.

On June 26, 1864, James Fry, provost marshal general, issued a circular that offered the opportunity for people either too old or ineligible for the draft to hire a representative recruit to serve in their place. It was meant as a publicity ploy to allow the wealthy to help in the war effort (the cost was $500—more than the average person made in a year) and was not the same as a substitute hired to replace draftees who could pay $300. In September, Lincoln decided he would fund a representative recruit credited to the District of Columbia's enlistment quota (the number of men the District was responsible for enlisting or drafting) and asked Fry to find a volunteer. A Pennsylvanian named John Summerfield Staples agreed to be Lincoln's representative.

Staples had already served in the army, joining in November 1862. He served as a private in Company C of the 176th Pennsylvania Militia until his discharge in May 1863 because of a "great disability and a broken down constitution" after a four-month bout with typhoid fever. Staples was still recuperating and working for his father as a carpenter in Washington when he was approached by Fry. In a special ceremony, Lincoln met with Staples on this day. When Staples—more than a foot shorter than the president—reported for duty, his sergeant allegedly asked, "Aren't you just the first installment?"

The representative recruitment program was not particularly successful—less than 1,300 men volunteered—but some of those who hired one included Edward Everett, James Russell Lowe, and Henry Wadsworth Longfellow.

OCTOBER 10

Cleaning Up a Piece of Ground

On this Monday in 1864, Lincoln sent his endorsement of Maryland's new state constitution that freed slaves.

Of all the border slave states that remained loyal to the Union (Delaware, Kentucky, Missouri, and Maryland), Maryland gave Lincoln the most headaches. Secessionism in Maryland was strong. Out of the nearly 92,000 votes Marylanders cast in the 1860 presidential election, only 2,200 were cast for Lincoln. Civilian arrests, the closing of disloyal newspapers, the arrests of Maryland legislators, and the influx of thousands of Union soldiers all weakened secessionist spirit in the state. After blacks began to join the army in 1863, slave valuations declined and the movement to free Maryland slaves began to grow. Since the Emancipation Proclamation did not cover Maryland, a Unionist convention was held in the summer of 1864 to ratify a new state constitution abolishing slavery. Lincoln was invited to an October 10 "Free Constitution" mass meeting on Baltimore's Monument Square and, while Lincoln could not attend, he did send a letter to be read at the meeting. "I wish all men to be free. . . . I wish to see in process of disappearing that only thing which ever could bring this nation to civil war," Lincoln wrote.

On October 12, Maryland, by a margin of only 375 votes, adopted the new constitution. "I had rather have Maryland upon that issue than have a State twice its size upon the Presidential issue; it cleans up a piece of ground," Lincoln told his friend Noah Brooks. Brooks later wrote, "Any one who has ever had to do with 'cleaning up' a piece of ground, digging out vicious roots and demolishing old stumps, can appreciate the homely simile applied to Maryland." Then in the November presidential election, Lincoln garnered 40,000 of Maryland's 73,000 votes.

OCTOBER 11

Reading "Balderdash"

This Tuesday in 1864 was election day for the so-called "October States"—Indiana, Ohio, and Pennsylvania—and Lincoln spent this evening at the telegraph office, watching the results.

"At eight o'clock the President went over to the War Department, to watch for despatches," wrote Lincoln's secretary John Hay. "We found the building in a state of preparation for siege." The October elections were expected to be indicative of how the Republicans would fare in the November presidential elections. And if Republican governors Oliver Morton (Indiana) and Andrew Curtin (Pennsylvania) lost their seats and Democrat David Tod (Ohio) retained his, the Democrats would have "a grand central rallying point" in those states.

According to Assistant Secretary of War Charles Dana, Lincoln, while waiting, pulled from a pocket "a thin yellow-covered pamphlet," and began reading from it aloud. "He would read a page or a story, pause to con[sider] a new election telegram, and then open the book again and go ahead with a new passage," Dana wrote. The book was *The Nasby Papers* by David Locke, with comical sketches about a Copperhead named Petroleum V. Nasby. Hay thought that stoic Secretary of War Edwin Stanton enjoyed the readings, but when Stanton pulled Dana into a nearby room, he blasted the president. Stanton couldn't fathom how Lincoln, "when the safety of the Republic was thus at issue . . . could turn aside to read such balderdash and to laugh at such frivolous jests."

The news was good from the Midwest. The Republicans now held both governor seats in Indiana and Ohio. And Republican Buckeyes had gained twelve congressional seats while Hoosier Republicans captured eight of the eleven seats. The race was too close to call in Pennsylvania until the soldier absentee ballots were counted and gave the Republicans only a slight edge.

OCTOBER 13

A Close Race

Lincoln, on this Thursday in 1864, calculated his chances for reelection.

With news that Pennsylvania barely went Republican in the October 11 state election, Lincoln believed that Pennsylvania would go to the Democrats along with its twenty-six electoral votes in the general election. On this evening, Lincoln appeared at the telegraph office looking "unusually weary." According to telegraph operator David Bates, Lincoln borrowed a piece of telegraph paper, sat down, and made two columns, one for the states he predicted would go to the Democratic candidate General George McClellan and the other for states that he would win. Lincoln wrote "slowly and deliberately, stopping at times in a thoughtful mood to look out of the window for a moment or two, and then resuming his writing."

Lincoln predicted the slave border states—Maryland, Delaware, Missouri and Kentucky—would give McClellan their 32 electoral votes. He felt the New England states would give him their 39 electoral votes. Most of the Midwest—Michigan, Indiana, Minnesota, Wisconsin, and Ohio—he expected to carry, garnering 54 votes. But his own state of Illinois with its 16 votes he thought would go to McClellan. Lincoln hoped that he'd carry the West, collecting another 19 votes. Together with West Virginia and the soon-to-be state of Nevada, he expected 120 electoral votes. But with Pennsylvania, New Jersey, and the monster state of New York (with 33 votes) going to the Democrats, Lincoln predicted that McClellan would have 114 electoral votes. Just one state could throw the outcome into a deadlock or give the presidency to McClellan. Even if Lincoln won, with such a close vote, he lamented that "the moral effect of his triumph would be broken and his power to prosecute the war and make peace would be greatly impaired."

OCTOBER 15

Citizen Taney

Lincoln, on this Saturday in 1864, attended the funeral and walked in the procession of Supreme Court Chief Justice Roger Taney.

Taney, whose twenty-eight years of careful decisions are still highly regarded, will forever be linked with the Dred Scott case, what Supreme Court Justice Felix Frankfurter dubbed "one of the court's great self-inflicted wounds." The case, incorrectly filed as *Scott vs. Sandford* (the defendant was John Sanford with no "d"), began in 1843 when a Missouri slave named Dred Scott sued for his freedom, claiming it was imparted to him by living in a free state (Illinois) and free territory (Wisconsin). The case was finally heard thirteen years later (after Scott was sold to Sanford) by the Supreme Court. "The question is simply this, can a negro whose ancestors were imported into this country become a citizen?" Taney asked in his majority opinion. Taney himself was descended from a white indentured servant who was "imported" around 1660. Ignoring the fact that in many states blacks voted in the ratification of the Constitution (five of the thirteen states), Taney wrote, "[blacks] are not included, and were not intended to be included, under the word 'citizen' in the Constitution, and can therefore claim none of [its] rights and privileges." He added that blacks were "so far inferior, that they had no rights which the white man was bound to respect." If that were not enough, Taney also ruled that Congress had no right to legislate slavery in the territories, nullifying decades of legislation.

The decision was a bigger blow to the Republican Party, whose fundamental platform was to curtail slavery in the territories. The decision inflamed such passion that it split the country and the Democratic Party, paving the way for Lincoln's election as president.

OCTOBER 22

Little Phil's Ride

On this Saturday in 1864, Lincoln wired General Philip Sheridan—known as "Little Phil"—his thanks for a victory in the Shenandoah Valley.

In late September, Sheridan's army drove Confederate general Jubal Early's army out of the Shenandoah. He then headed north again, destroying the Shenandoah's fall harvest. On October 7, Sheridan wired General Ulysses Grant that when he was finished "the Valley, from Winchester up to Staunton, ninety-two miles, will have little in it for man or beast." In the forty miles between Woodstock and Harrisonburg, Sheridan rounded up four thousand head of cattle, butchered three thousand sheep, and burned two thousand barns. "The people must be left nothing but their eyes to weep with over the war," Little Phil said.

General Early followed Sheridan through the valley, disgusted with what he found. Allegedly out of revenge, Early devised a surprise attack on Sheridan's left flank at Cedar Creek. Sheridan had left his command to meet with Secretary of War Edwin Stanton in Washington and was returning on October 18 when he stopped at Winchester for the night.

He awoke the next morning to news of Early's attack. At nine, Sheridan mounted his horse "Rienzi" and headed south, reaching Cedar Creek at 10:30 AM. On the way he encountered his men retreating northward. "The army is whipped!" shouted one of them. Sheridan answered, "You are but the army isn't." To others he shouted, "Come on back, boys," and "Men, by God, we'll whip them yet!" Sheridan rallied his men and led them to sweep the battlefield. Early would never again take the offensive in the Shenandoah.

"With great pleasure I tender to you and your brave army, the thanks of the Nation, and my own personal admiration and gratitude," Lincoln wrote on this day. Congress, too, thanked Little Phil with a promotion.

OCTOBER 29

Lincoln Meets Sojourner Truth

Lincoln, on this Saturday in 1864, met Sojourner Truth, the most famous African American woman of her time.

Truth was born Isabella Baumfree in 1797, a New York slave. She was sold three times and escaped once before she was emancipated by the state. When former owners illegally sold her son Peter to an Alabama slaveholder, Truth became the first black woman in history to successfully sue a white man in court and was reunited with Peter.

On June 1, 1843, she changed her name to Truth and became a preacher, abolitionist, and activist for women's rights. During the war, Truth was active in recruiting black regiments and moved to Washington to fight segregation on the city's streetcars.

When Truth met Lincoln on this day, the president took her hand and bowed. "I am pleased to see you," Lincoln said. Truth afterward declared that she "never was treated by any one with more kindness and cordiality." Truth asked the president to autograph a book she had brought and he took it with "the same hand that signed the death-warrant of slavery." He signed it, "For Aunty Sojourner Truth, Oct. 29, 1864. A. Lincoln." The old woman later said, "I felt that I was in the presence of a friend, and I now thank God from the bottom of my heart that I always advocated his cause."

#75

Was Lincoln a Racist?

Modern ears are shocked by some of the things Lincoln said about African Americans. During his 1858 debates with incumbent Senator Stephen Douglas, Lincoln said (at Ottawa, Illinois), "There is a physical difference between the two [races], which, in my judgment, will probably forever forbid their living together upon the footing of perfect equality." He added, "Inasmuch as it becomes a necessity that there be a difference, I . . . am in favor of the race to which I belong having the superior position." Lincoln supported sending blacks to other countries to form colonies and to keep them separated from whites. What was worse, Lincoln was known to use words like "nigger," "Sambo," and "Caffie" and told jokes with racial stereotypes. All this indicates that Lincoln was, indeed, a racist and any attempt to defend his behavior as a product of his time ignores many of Lincoln's contemporaries who were not racist.

But, just as all stereotypes are too simplistic, Lincoln was more complicated than the stereotypical racist. He was far more progressive. He was, for instance, the first president to invite a black man—Frederick Douglass—to the White House. Lincoln was the first president to welcome blacks to a White House reception and to meet with a black delegation. Douglass and Sojourner Truth, as well as many others, commented on how unusually fair Lincoln was to them. Lincoln considered Douglass his friend, a scandalous claim for any white man in a racist country. Lincoln's Springfield barber, William de Fleurville, was so close to Lincoln that he was invited to walk with the

Lincoln family in the president's final funeral procession (Fleurville declined, preferring to walk with other blacks at the end of the procession).

OCTOBER 31

Nevada Becomes a State

Lincoln, on this day in 1864, proclaimed Nevada as the thirty-sixth state.

Under the 1848 Treaty of Guadalupe Hidalgo, which ended the Mexican War, America acquired vast stretches of territory, which would be parceled into all, or part of, California, Utah, Nevada, Arizona, New Mexico, Colorado, and Wyoming. Nevada was still a territory in 1859 when silver ore was discovered on the eastern side of Mount Davidson under what is now Virginia City. There is a myth that Nevada was rushed to statehood because the yields from the Comstock Lode were needed to fill Lincoln's war coffers. But statehood reduced rather than heightened federal control of the mines. It is more likely that Lincoln wanted Nevada a state so that its three electoral votes might go to him in the 1864 presidential election. He also hoped the state would ratify a constitutional amendment to abolish slavery. It would do both.

On March 21, 1864, Congress passed an Enabling Act to allow Nevada's statehood. After ratifying a state constitution, Lincoln on this day welcomed the "Battle Born" state into the Union ("Battle Born" is actually a nickname, not the state motto; its motto is "All For Our Country"). A common misconception is that Nevada did not have a large enough population to enter the Union. The 1787 Northwest Ordinance required 60,000 inhabitants to reside in a territory before it could become a state and Nevada had about 35,000 at the time. But for states outside the Northwest (Nevada is in the Southwest), the ordinance allowed admission even if "there be less number of free inhabitants in the State than sixty thousand," as long as a "republican" government was formed. Nevada is nicknamed "Battle Born" state because it acquired statehood during the Civil War. It actually shares that distinction with West Virginia, which became a state on June 20, 1863.

NOVEMBER 3

Election Preparations

With the presidential election just a few days away on November 8, Lincoln was working behind the scenes for his reelection. On this Thursday in 1864, Lincoln met with a soldier who planned to use his furlough to vote for the Democratic nominee, General George McClellan. But the soldier had no way to get home for the election and Lincoln ordered transportation for him.

Presidential candidates in Lincoln's time did not publicly campaign for themselves. There were no debates and no campaign speeches. Just a week after his June 8 nomination, Lincoln attended a fair in Philadelphia and when asked to speak, he said, "I do not really think it is proper in my position for me to make a political speech." But Lincoln was not sitting on his hands. "The President is too busy looking after the election to think of any thing else," said Secretary of the Treasury William Fessenden.

Lincoln repeatedly intervened in Republican squabbles—particularly in Pennsylvania and New York—that threatened to fracture the party. Lincoln also worked hard to get furloughs for soldiers to return home to cast their ballot. "All the power and influence of the War Department . . . was employed to secure the re-election of Mr. Lincoln," Assistant Secretary of War Charles Dana wrote. Two out of every three soldiers rewarded his efforts with their vote.

Lincoln, however, did not try to rush the statehoods of Colorado and Nebraska to provide him with electoral votes. Nor did he delay the September draft call, despite its unpopularity. And he refused to postpone the election. "We can not have a free government without elections," he said, "and if the rebellion could force us to forego or postpone a national election, it might fairly claim to have already conquered and ruined us."

NOVEMBER 4

The Transcontinental Railroad

One of the crowning achievements of Lincoln's presidency was that he was involved in the early stages of building America's first transcontinental railroad. On this day in 1864, Lincoln approved the location of the first one hundred miles of the eastern leg of the railroad.

The transcontinental railroad had been discussed in Congress for more than a decade prior to the Civil War. The United States had even purchased a strip of land in what is now southern New Mexico and Arizona (the Gadsen Purchase) so that a southern route from Texas could cross to California without skirting Mexico. But a southern route versus a northern one became embroiled in sectional strife, and legislation for the railroad wasn't passed until after the Southern states vacated Congress. On July 1, 1862, Lincoln signed the Pacific Railroad Act to construct a railroad from the Missouri River to the Pacific Ocean. Two railroads—the Central Pacific from the west and the Union Pacific from the east—would lay the track, meeting in the middle.

The western terminus would be Sacramento, California, but the choice of the eastern terminus was given to Lincoln. Back in August 1859, Lincoln had reconnoitered a possible terminus at Council Bluffs, Iowa. Lincoln had gone there on business and met and discussed the advantages of terminus there with an engineer named Grenville Dodge. They discussed a railroad that would follow the fertile Platte River in Nebraska and go through the Continental Divide to Utah. "By his kindly ways," recalled Dodge, "[Lincoln] soon drew from me all I knew of the country west. . . . As the saying is, he completely 'shelled my woods,' getting all the secrets that were later to go to my employers." After another conference with Dodge in June 1863, Lincoln gave Council Bluffs the nod on this day.

Dodge would be present on May 10, 1869 when the Union and Central Pacific linked at Promontory Summit, Utah. Despite the hype, it wasn't until 1872 that a bridge would be built across the Missouri River at Council Bluffs and that east and west were actually connected by rail.

NOVEMBER 8

Reelection

On this Tuesday in 1864, Lincoln spent much of the evening at the telegraph office waiting for election results.

"The [White] house has been still and almost deserted today," Lincoln's secretary John Hay wrote. "Everybody in Washington, not at home voting, seems ashamed of it and stays away from the President." Lincoln himself couldn't vote because Illinois did not allow out-of-state voting.

At seven, Lincoln and Hay walked over to the War Department. "The night was rainy, steamy and dark," Hay wrote. "We splashed through the grounds to the side door of the War Department where a soaked and smoking sentinel was standing in his own vapor with his huddled-up frame covered with a cloak." Early returns were favorable and Lincoln forwarded optimistic telegrams—what Hay called the "first fruits"—to his wife. "She is more anxious than I," the president said. Unknown to Lincoln, Mary's anxiety stemmed from her fear that if her husband were not reelected, her mounting debts would be revealed.

By the time Lincoln left for bed at 2:00 AM, he knew he'd been reelected. In the popular vote, he beat George McClellan by only 400,000 votes. But in the electoral college he won all but three states—New Jersey, Delaware, and Kentucky.

The next day Lincoln told his friend Noah Brooks of a vision he had shortly before his first election as president. He was at home in Springfield, lying on a lounge next to a bureau with a mirror. In his reflection he was astonished to see a double image of his face and one of the two faces was pale, corpse-like. When he told Mary about it, she thought it was a sign that he would be elected twice as president. Lincoln, however, thought the vision ominous, and gave "me a pang, as though something uncomfortable had happened."

#76

Mary's Bad Habit

By election day in 1864, Mary had acquired a personal debt of more than $27,000 (about a quarter of million in today's dollars). "Mr. Lincoln has but little idea of the expense of a woman's wardrobe," she told her seamstress Elizabeth Keckley. "He glances at my rich dresses, and is happy in the belief that the few hundred dollars that I obtain from him supply my wants. I must dress in costly materials. . . . consequently I had, and still have, no alternative but to run in debt." Mary was petrified that if her husband was not reelected, her debts would come due and "he would know all."

"The people scrutinize every article that I wear with critical curiosity," Mary confided to Keckley. "The very fact of having grown up in the West, subjects me to more searching observation." It is true that after receptions, the newspapers carried detailed accounts of the first lady's attire. But the newspapers were even more detailed of her spending sprees in the midst of a national emergency. Despite her fears of exposure, just weeks after Lincoln reelection, Mary went to New York to purchase "300 pairs of kid gloves."

What was more, Mary's shopping sprees predated her White House years. The problem probably stemmed from her childhood, when she competed for attention among fifteen siblings. This was intensified when she married Lincoln, who could not provide her the comforts that she was accustomed to. While she purchased the most expensive clothes, she managed to limit her debts. That changed when Lincoln became president. Lincoln's greatly elevated income and visibility gave Mary sufficient excuse to indulge herself.

Her habit continued after Lincoln's death. Her irresponsible spending was part of the reason her son Robert had her committed to an insane asylum in 1875. When she died seven years later, she left behind sixty-four trunks filled with clothes.

NOVEMBER 11

To "Save the Union"

Lincoln, on this Friday in 1864, revealed to his department heads a memorandum they signed unread nearly three months before.

Lincoln was not the first president reelected during a war—James Madison was, during the War of 1812—but he was the first during a rebellion. "[The election] demonstrated that a people's government can sustain a national election, in the midst of a great civil war," Lincoln said. "Until now it has not been known to the world that this was a possibility." Lincoln wanted reconciliation, "Now that the election is over, may not all . . . reunite in a common effort to save our common country?" When a friend gloated that one of Lincoln's critics—Henry Davis—had lost his bid for Congress, Lincoln responded, "A man has not time to spend half his life in quarrels. If any man ceases to attack me, I never remember the past against him."

Lincoln's patriotism and magnanimity extended to working with George McClellan should he have won the presidency. Lincoln revealed this at a cabinet meeting on this day. According to Lincoln's secretary John Hay, the president said, "Gentlemen, do you remember last summer I asked you all to sign your names to the back of a paper of which I did not show you inside?" The president then produced the paper and opened it. "This morning, as for some days past," the paper read, "it seems exceedingly probable that this Administration will not be reelected. Then it will be my duty to so cooperate with the President elect, as to save the Union between the election and the inauguration; as he will have secured his election on such ground that he cannot save it afterwards." Fortunately, Lincoln won the presidency, not McClellan. Lincoln filed the paper away.

NOVEMBER 21

The Bixby Letter

On this Monday in 1864, Lincoln composed—or at least signed—one of the most famous letters of the war.

When a Boston widow named Lydia Bixby forwarded to Massachusetts adjutant general William Schouler "five different letters from five different company commanders" revealing the deaths of all five of her sons, Schouler wrote Governor Andrew Curtin, suggesting he contact the president. The result was a letter, dated this day, addressed to Bixby:

> I feel how weak and fruitless must be any words of mine which should attempt to beguile you from the grief of a loss so overwhelming. . . . I pray that our Heavenly Father may assuage the anguish of your bereavement and leave you only the cherished memory of the loved and lost, and the solemn pride that must be yours, to have laid so costly a sacrifice upon the altar of Freedom.

Bixby did not appreciate the letter, considered by many literary scholars as beautifully crafted literature. She was a Southern sympathizer and, as her granddaughter later recalled, she had "little good to say of President Lincoln." She destroyed the letter immediately.

There is some evidence that Bixby forged the notifications of her son's deaths that she sent to Schouler, in hopes of garnering money. Two of her sons—Charles and Oliver—had indeed died in battle but, their brother Henry was honorably discharged and brothers Arthur and George deserted the army; George died in prison. Unaware of this, Schouler appealed to the public on Bixby's behalf, then forwarded donations to the widow.

There is also a controversy surrounding whether Lincoln or his secretary John Hay wrote the letter. It was not unusual for Hay to write letters signed by Lincoln and Hay later claimed to be its author. But since the original letter was destroyed, the controversy remains unresolved.

NOVEMBER 24

Edward Bates

Lincoln, on this day in 1864, received the resignation of Attorney General Edward Bates.

Born of Virginia Quakers, Bates became a St. Louis lawyer at twenty-three and a congressman from Missouri at thirty-three. He became the state's most prominent Whig, known for opposing the extension of slavery into the territories but opposing federal intervention in slavery in the deep South. Because he was an influential border state voice, Lincoln offered him a seat in his cabinet.

Bates's influence began to wane in the first year of the war with his reluctance to confront Supreme Court Chief Justice Roger Taney over Lincoln's suspension of habeas corpus and his equivocation over the *Trent* affair. He began to alienate fellow Republicans when he opposed the admission of West Virginia as a state (he believed it unconstitutional) and the service of blacks in the army (he believed they might threaten their former masters). He did, however, believe those soldiers "of color" deserved "the same pay, bounty and clothing" as white soldiers.

The attorney general's appreciation of the president grew over the years. Early in the war, Bates was annoyed with Lincoln's "never-failing fund of anecdote," but learned to see how important Lincoln's storytelling was. "The character of the President's mind is such that his thought habitually takes on this form of illustration . . . [and the] point he wishes to enforce is invariably brought home with a strength and clearness impossible in hours of abstract argument," Bate wrote.

During the winter of 1864, Bates's declining health prompted him to consider retirement. However, he wanted to lend his influence to Lincoln's reelection. Just over two weeks after the election, he submitted his resignation on this day and Lincoln accepted it. A week later the president named James Speed, older brother of his best friend Joshua Speed, as Bates's replacement.

DECEMBER 2

Prison Overpopulation

Lincoln, on this Friday in 1864, met for the second time a pair of persistent women wishing to have their husbands, who were prisoners of war, released from Johnson's Island, Ohio.

The exchange of prisoners between the North and South broke down in 1863 and prisoner-of-war camps on both sides swelled, as did the death toll from disease and starvation. Lincoln, hoping to relieve some of the strain, wrote Secretary of War Edwin Stanton on March 18, 1864, about "prisoners of war in our custody, whose homes are within our lines, and who wish to not be exchanged, but to take the oath [of allegiance to the Union] and be discharged." Lincoln believed that "none of them will again go to the rebellion" and the discharge of them from camps "would give me some relief from an intolerable pressure." Stanton said he would "cheerfully and promptly" release any prisoners Lincoln recommended.

For three days in a row beginning on December 1, two women met with Lincoln, asking that their Confederate husbands be released from prison. As Lincoln later recounted, "at each of the interviews one of the ladies urged that her husband was a religious man." During the final interview, Lincoln pardoned the prisoners. Then he said, "You say your husband is a religious man; tell him when you meet him . . . that in my opinion, the religion that sets men to rebel and fight against their government, because, as they think, that government does not sufficiently help some men to eat their bread on the sweat of other men's faces, is not the sort of religion upon which people can get to heaven!" Lincoln liked the barb so much that he submitted it to the Washington *Daily Chronicle* under the headline "The President's Last, Shortest and Best Speech."

#77

Starving Prisoners

The Confederate military prison system—particularly at the Andersonville prison in Georgia—has been criticized as woefully inadequate in its treatment of Union prisoners. Out of 45,600 prisoners held at Andersonville in just over a year, 13,000 (about 35 percent) died of exposure, disease, and malnutrition. Overall, Union soldiers died at a rate of over 15 percent in Confederate prisons. But Confederate soldiers died in Union prisons at a rate of 12 percent and, at the New York Elmira Prison, the death rate was 24 percent. What was more, the Union with its vast resources had less of an excuse for mistreatment of prisoners than did the Confederacy, where soldiers and civilians were starving just as much as their prisoners.

Initially, captured Confederates were given the same amount of rations as Union soldiers. In July 1862, prisoner rations were cut under the pretext that men not in combat required less food. Then, in December 1863, Secretary of War Edwin Stanton prohibited prisoners to use their own money to buy food and their families from sending supplies. Five months later, in a special exchange of the sickest prisoners on both sides, the North was outraged when returning Union prisoners were pathetic "living skeletons." In retaliation, Stanton cut his prisoner's rations even more.

There are no documents that indicate Lincoln was aware that Stanton was starving prisoners, but he surely could not have missed the numerous newspaper accounts of conditions in Union prisons. In the spring of 1864, when a congressional committee was investigating conditions in Confederate prisons, Lincoln said, "I can never, never starve men like that!" Whether he was aware of it or not, the Union was, indeed, starving men.

DECEMBER 7

The Nominee

On this Wednesday in 1864, former secretary of the treasury Salmon Chase visited the White House to pay his respects to the man who had just nominated him as chief justice of the Supreme Court.

Lincoln had already named four justices to the Supreme Court, but his most important appointment was his replacement for Chief Justice Roger Taney. The president's initial choice was Chase. But when three members of his cabinet expressed interest, Lincoln decided to wait to consider his options.

Of the four possible nominees, Secretary of War Edwin Stanton seemed the most qualified. During his distinguished legal career, Stanton had argued several cases before the highest court. But Stanton was indispensable to Lincoln as the head of the War Department. Lincoln felt some obligation to Montgomery Blair, former Postmaster General. The conservative Blair had agreed to resign to placate Radical Republicans and avoid a party split in the presidential elections. But Lincoln knew that Blair's nomination to the court would incite the radicals once more. The same could be said of Attorney General Edward Bates.

In the end, Lincoln submitted Chase's name to Congress on December 6. After all the politicking Chase had done to thwart Lincoln's reelection, Lincoln's secretary John Nicolay was surprised. "Probably no other man than Lincoln would have had . . . the degree of magnanimity to thus forgive and exalt a rival who had so deeply and so unjustifiably intrigued against him," Nicolay wrote. Lincoln later confided that his decision was for the country's good and personally he "would have swallowed his buckhorn chair than nominated Chase." Chase wrote Lincoln, "Be assured that I prize your confidence & good will more than nomination or office." That was not entirely true because, while on the bench, Chase tried to secure a Democratic—not Republican—presidential nomination in 1868. Nor was Lincoln completely magnanimous. "His appointment will satisfy the Radicals," Lincoln said, "and after that they will not dare kick up against any appointment I make."

#78

Lincoln's Supreme Court

When Lincoln became president, the Supreme Court met once a year in the Capitol Building (it had just moved from the basement to the old Senate chamber). The court nervously watched as the incoming Republicans took power. The court's 1857 Dred Scott decision had been a thumb in the Republican Party's eye, undermining a central plank promising to limit the extension of slavery into the territories. Lincoln had vowed to have the decision overturned. There was already a vacant seat on the bench after the May 1860 death of Justice Peter Daniel. The remaining eight justices were all Democrats and half of them, including Chief Justice Roger Taney, hailed from slave states. Within seven weeks of Lincoln's inauguration, there were two more vacancies—Justice John McLean died on April 4 and Justice John Campbell resigned to join the Confederacy.

In 1862, Lincoln nominated three Republicans—Noah Swayne, Samuel Miller, and his good friend David Davis—to the court. The Constitution allows Congress to increase the number of justices to the court, which it did, in 1863, to ten. Lincoln named California Democrat Stephen Field to fill the seat. Lincoln's fifth nomination came after Taney died in 1864.

Lincoln knew how important his nominations were, as he expected the court to make decisions on the issuance of paper money. That was one of the reasons his former Secretary of the Treasury Salmon Chase, the man who issued that paper money, was his choice to replace Taney. He expected the court to hear cases on emancipation as well, and all five of his nominees were abolitionists. Indeed, the court heard arguments on several landmark cases testing Lincoln's policies including the *Prize Cases*, *Ex Parte Milligan*, *Ex Parte Garland*, *Cummings vs. Missouri* and *Hepburn vs. Griswold*.

DECEMBER 10

Lincoln and Friends

On this Saturday in 1864, Lincoln received the resignation of a good friend because the president wasn't careful enough.

There is little doubt of Lincoln's charisma. During his life and after his death, literally dozens claimed Lincoln as their friend and the president could inspire devotion like few could. "He always had influential and financial friends," wrote Lincoln's law partner William Herndon, "they almost fought each other for the privilege of assisting Lincoln." Few were as devoted as a stocky Danville, Illinois lawyer named Ward Hill Lamon. He appointed himself the president's personal bodyguard, sometimes sleeping outside Lincoln's bedroom door with guns and knives at his side. Lincoln appointed Lamon marshal of the District of Columbia.

Lamon thought himself close enough to Lincoln to later publish two biographies, but it is doubtful Lamon was as close as he thought. It's a phenomenon historians have noted that, while Lincoln had many friends, few if any knew him intimately. The early death (at age nine) of his mother and an emotionally distant father made it hard for Lincoln to develop close relationships. Herndon called his friend the most "shut-mouthed" man he ever knew. Another friend wrote, "I knew the man so well; he was the most reticent, secretive man I ever saw or expect to see." Leonard Swett said, "He always told only enough of his plans and purposes to induce the belief that he had communicated all; yet he reserved enough to have communicated nothing." Lincoln even kept some aspects of himself from his best friend, Joshua Speed—who some have speculated was Lincoln's homosexual partner—and his wife Mary.

Lamon submitted his resignation on this day because the president went to the theater without protection. Lincoln was escorted by a Prussian minister and a Massachusetts senator, "neither of whom could defend himself against an assault from any able-bodied woman in this city," Lamon chided. Ultimately, Lamon didn't resign, nor was he in Washington four months later when his fears were found to be justified when Lincoln went to Ford's Theatrer.

#79

Was Lincoln a Homosexual?

Speculation about whether Lincoln was "homoerotic"—the term used before the 1870s, when "homosexual" came into general use—has been based largely on the fact that he often shared a bed with other men. He did so as a young single man sharing a bed with Joshua Speed. He continued after his marriage, sharing beds with fellow lawyers while riding the Eighth Circuit and may have even shared a bed as president with Captain David Derickson, head of his security detail.

In the days before mega-hotels, it was not unusual for people to share beds. During the Gettysburg cemetery dedication (November 1863), accommodations were so crowded that it was recommended that Pennsylvania governor Andrew Curtin share a bed with the keynote speaker, Edward Everett. Everett's daughter shared a bed with two women.

Despite the fact that Lincoln was one of the most despised presidents in history while he lived, not one contemporary ever claimed Lincoln was "homoerotic." Lincoln's letters to Speed are bereft of any intimate or romantic innuendo (most of Speed's letters to Lincoln have not survived). Nor did he attempt to hide his sleeping arrangements. In 1864, when Lincoln was considering naming Speed's brother James as attorney general, he admitted James was "a man I know well, though not so well as his brother Joshua. That, however, is not strange, for I slept with Joshua for four years." Nor was he secretive about sharing a bed with Derickson in the summer of 1862. Derickson's superior Thomas Chamberlain wrote, "Captain Derickson, in particular, advanced so far in the President's confidence and esteem that, in Mrs. Lincoln's absence, he frequently spent the night at his [Old Soldiers' Home] cottage sleeping in the same bed with him, and—it is said—making use of his Excellency's night-shirts."

DECEMBER 15

George Thomas

Lincoln, on this Thursday in 1864, conferred with his senior staff about relieving General George Thomas, head of the Army of the Cumberland, on the very day Thomas was about to hand Lincoln one of the war's most decisive victories.

After General William Sherman occupied Atlanta in early September 1864, he decided to march his army three hundred miles to the Atlantic Ocean. Lincoln, however, was worried about Confederate general John Hood's forty-thousand-man army, which was headed into Tennessee. Sherman assigned Thomas the job of dealing with Hood and set out for Savannah, Georgia.

At the town of Franklin, Tennessee, Thomas checked the Confederate advance. Hood foolishly launched a frontal assault against Union entrenchments and sustained well over 6,000 casualties, including six senior generals. Hood had crippled his army. But he was not done yet; as the Union army withdrew to Nashville and even heavier entrenchments, Hood limped after them, too stubborn to quit.

Washington viewed Hood's deep penetration and Thomas falling back to Nashville with alarm. "The President feels solicitous about General Thomas to lay in fortifications for an indefinite period. . . . This looks like the [Generals George] McClellan and [William] Rosecrans strategy to do nothing and let the rebels raid the country," Secretary of War Edwin Stanton wrote Thomas's superior, General Ulysses Grant. What they didn't know was that Thomas was waiting for the weather to improve before he attacked Hood. On this day, Thomas slammed into the Confederate's flanks and virtually annihilated Hood's army.

Meanwhile Grant had orders drawn up relieving Thomas and discussed the situation on this day with Lincoln. Late this night, Lincoln, in his nightshirt, received news of Thomas's victory. The next day, instead of sending orders relieving Thomas of duty, Lincoln wired his thanks.

DECEMBER 21

War Democrats

Lincoln was less than diplomatic in a telegram he sent War Democrat General Benjamin Butler on this Wednesday in 1864.

War Democrats hailed from every state in the Union and had little in common except that they supported the war. Perhaps the most prominent early War Democrat was Lincoln's old rival Stephen Douglas. Until his death in June 1861, Douglas toured the country stirring up bipartisan support for the cause. Other War Democrats included former secretary of war Joseph Holt who helped keep

Kentucky from seceding; Edwin Stanton, who became Lincoln's second secretary of war; and Tennessee senator Andrew Johnson who became Lincoln's second vice president. Congressman John Henderson from Missouri—a slave state—would go on to pen the Thirteenth Amendment freeing slaves nationwide. Lincoln made generals of George McClellan, John McClernand, and Butler, all War Democrats.

Butler had a checkered record as a general. His thirst for military glory (without military prowess) cost him several battles and, when both Lincoln and McClellan approached him to be their running mate in the 1864 presidential elections, he refused, preferring to continue his hunt for glory.

As military administrator of parts of Virginia, Butler considered allowing civil elections on the Virginia coast. Lincoln felt the army had no jurisdiction over civil elections. On this day, Lincoln had his secretary John Hay write a letter ordering Butler to suspend any plans for elections. When Butler responded that the "President is incorrectly informed," Lincoln prickly shot back that he was not misinformed.

It was evidence of how the alliance between Republicans and War Democrats was diminishing. Many War Democrats had been marginalized by their own party because of their alliance with Republicans. Others could not stomach Lincoln's Emancipation Proclamation and abandoned that alliance. By war's end, McClellan, McClernand, and Butler no longer had commands in the field.

DECEMBER 25

The Christmas Gift

Lincoln, on this Christmas in 1864, received a telegram from General William Sherman: "I beg to present you as a Christmas gift the City of Savannah with 150 heavy guns & plenty of ammunition & also about 25,000 bales of cotton."

Sherman's "March to the Sea" began after he took Atlanta in early September and its defenders, Confederate general John Hood's army, moved north into Tennessee. Instead of pursuing him, Sherman severed his lines of supply and communication and began a 285-mile march to Savannah, Georgia on November 15. Later, Sherman recalled that day: "Behind us lay Atlanta, smoldering and in ruins, the black smoke rising high in the air. . . . Some band, by accident, struck up the anthem of 'John Brown's Soul Goes Marching On'; the men caught up the strain, and never before or since have I heard the chorus of 'Glory, Glory, hallelujah!' done with more spirit."

Before the march, Sherman told his troops they "will forage liberally on the country." He wrote, "In districts and neighborhoods where the army is unmolested, no destruction of property should be permitted." But if the Georgians "manifest local hostility, then army commanders should order and enforce a devastation more or less relentless." His 62,000 men cut a sixty-mile path of destruction, wrecking railroads and foraging or destroying 13,000 head of cattle and 90,000 bales of cotton. Sherman estimated that he inflicted $100 million worth of damage.

On December 20, Sherman took Savannah and two days later he sent his telegram to Lincoln. The message arrived on this day and Lincoln thanked him. "But what next?" he asked. Sherman was already looking north to South Carolina, the cradle of secession. "I almost tremble at her fate, but feel she deserves all that seems in store for her," Sherman wrote.

1865

"DIE WHEN I MAY, I WANT IT SAID BY THOSE WHO KNEW ME BEST THAT I ALWAYS PLUCKED A THISTLE AND PLANTED A FLOWER WHEN I THOUGHT A FLOWER WOULD GROW."
—ABRAHAM LINCOLN

JANUARY 2

"Marse Linkum"

Because New Year's Day fell on a Sunday in 1865, the usual White House reception was moved to this day at noon and Lincoln spent much of it meeting the public.

For the first hour the diplomatic corps, Supreme Court justices, and military officers greeted the Lincolns, wishing them a prosperous New Year. At one, the doors were opened to the public, among them members of Congress grumbling that they had to stand in line with their constituents. Some five thousand people formed that line, stretching all the way to Pennsylvania Avenue. Watching this crowd from behind the mansion gates were a group of Washingtonians who'd never before been welcome in the White House. Today, however, these black citizens were intent on shaking the hand of their president.

Many of these men and women were wealthy free blacks, wearing clothes indistinguishable from their white counterparts. Others were indigent, wearing the rags of poverty. All of them looked tentatively at the White House, uncertain of how their black skin would be received. After two hours of watching, they decided to go in.

A *New York Independent* reporter described the scene:

> For two long hours Mr. Lincoln had been shaking the hands of the "sovereigns," and had become excessively weary, and his grasp languid; but here his nerves rallied at the unwonted sight, and he welcomed this motley crowd with a heartiness that made them wild with exceeding joy. They laughed and wept . . . exclaiming, through their blinding tears, "God bless you!". . . "God bless Marse Linkum!" . . . For a long distance down the Avenue, on my way home, I heard fast young men cursing the President for this act; but all the way the refrain rang in my ears—"God bless Abraham Lincoln."

JANUARY 9

The Humblest Employee

The Lincolns held a reception or "levee" in the East Room on this Monday evening in 1865. Lincoln wore a black suit with white gloves while the first lady wore a white silk dress with flowers in her hair. After the traditional promenade to "Hail Columbia" at 11:00 PM, the Lincolns retired. The president, however, decided to walk to the War Department for news from the front. He wrapped himself in a gray shawl, put on his signature silk hat, and slipped out through the White House basement.

The War Department was a dingy two-story building just a short walk from the White House. Accompanying him this night was a young Washington policeman by the name of William Henry Crook. This was Crook's first night on Lincoln's security detail and the first time he'd met the President. "He looked just like his picture, but gentler," he later wrote. Crook was particularly struck by Lincoln's sensitivity:

> That night . . . I was a little nervous. The President noticed it. He seemed to know how I felt, too. I had fallen into line behind him, but he motioned me to walk by his side. He began to talk to me in a kindly way, as though I were a bashful boy whom he wanted to put at ease . . . his manner was due to the intuitive sympathy with every one, of which I afterward saw so many instances. It was shown particularly toward those who were subordinate to him. The statesmen who came to consult him, those who had it in their power to influence policy . . . never had the consideration from Mr. Lincoln that he gave the humblest of those who served him.

JANUARY 15

Lincoln Meets Jean Agassiz

On this Sunday in 1865, Lincoln was nervous because he was to meet Jean Louis Rodolphe Agassiz. Lincoln had always been self-conscious of his limited education and he was uncertain what to say to the famous scientist.

Lincoln had a passion for science, especially for inventions and new technologies. During the war 16,000 patents were issued, many of them tested by Lincoln himself. The president frequently watched demonstrations of new inventions at the Washington Navy Yard or test-fired new firearms in Treasury Park, just southeast of the White House. Lincoln himself had invented a boat that attached to vessels that ran aground, lifting them with buoyant chambers. While the invention was never built, Lincoln received Patent No. 6469 for it, becoming the only president in history to own a patent. Dr. Joseph Henry, who ran the Smithsonian Institute, remarked that "the most far-seeing head in this land is on the shoulders of that awkward rail-splitter from Illinois."

But inventions needed to be tested before the government used them. Thus Lincoln was convinced to establish the National Academy of Sciences (NAS), chartered to "investigate, examine, experiment, and report upon any subject of science or art" requested by a government department. One of the men who persuaded him was Agassiz, a Swiss geologist who, together with his friend Dr. Henry, created the NAS. Agassiz was best known for his glacier studies and was a vocal opponent of Charles Darwin's theory of evolution.

Instead of feeling intimidated, Lincoln, when he met Agassiz this day, relaxed and even surprised the scientist with his insights. Lincoln confided that he, at one time, had lectured on inventions. When asked later why he didn't ask Agassiz geological questions, Lincoln replied, "Why, what we got from him isn't printed in books, the other things are."

JANUARY 17

Fort Fisher

Lincoln, on this Tuesday in 1865, discussed the battle that would close the Confederacy's last remaining port.

One of the Union's earliest strategies—derogatorily dubbed the "Anaconda Plan"—was the brainchild of then General in Chief Winfield Scott. The plan called for an envelopment of most of the South, blockading her ports and controlling the Mississippi River, thus sealing off the Confederacy from imported provisions. But it would take time for the Union to build enough ships to blockade 3,500 miles of Southern coastline, with its ten major ports and 180 bays, inlets, and river mouths (the Union had a mere forty-two ships at the beginning of the war). It would also take time to train an army and build the gunboats in order to take the Mississippi.

It wasn't until January 15, 1865—less than three months before the end of the war—that the Confederacy was finally and fully blockaded. On that day, the Union took Fort Fisher, North Carolina and closed the Confederacy's last port in Wilmington, North Carolina. On this day Lincoln met with his cabinet and discussed the details of the fight.

There is still a debate as to how effective the blockade was, but there is little doubt how the loss of Fort Fisher devastated Southern morale. Confederate general Robert E. Lee's army, already starving in the trenches of Petersburg, looked forward to even fewer provisions. Desertion rose to frightening levels in February. Hopelessness in the Confederate Congress prompted attacks on President Jefferson Davis and his administration. Under the intense pressure, Secretary of War James Seddon resigned. Vice President Alexander Stephens called the loss of Fort Fisher "one of the greatest disasters that had befallen our Cause from the beginning of the war." Confederate admiral Raphael Semmes would later write, "Our ports were now all hermetically sealed. The anaconda had, at last, wound his fatal folds around us."

JANUARY 30

Peace Overtures

There were several attempts during the war to negotiate peace, but until this Monday in 1865, no serious talks were ever sanctioned by both the Confederate and Union governments.

This peace overture began in mid-December 1864, when Maryland Democrat Francis Preston Blair, Sr. wrote Confederate president Jefferson Davis that he wanted to negotiate a peace. Already weary of a peace movement in his own administration, Davis agreed. Davis gave Blair a letter, addressed to Lincoln, stating that he would name agents authorized to negotiate "with a view to secure peace to the two countries." When Lincoln read the letter on January 16, Blair also outlined a plan where the Union and the Confederacy might mend their wounds by cooperating in a joint conquest of

Mexico. Not only was Lincoln not interested in invading Mexico, he could not ignore Davis's stubborn insistence that the North and South were separate countries.

On January 18, Lincoln sent a letter to Davis via Blair stating that he would receive agents to negotiate the "peace to the people of our one common country." Davis ignored Lincoln's correction and, on January 28, named three commissioners: Vice President Alexander Stephens, Virginia senator Robert Hunter, and Assistant Secretary of War John A. Campbell. These commissioners left immediately, arriving at the front lines the next evening, asking to be taken to General Ulysses S. Grant's headquarters.

Early on this day, the president sent Major Thomas Eckert, superintendent of the War Department telegraph office, to deliver a letter from the president to the trio. Lincoln wrote the commissioners that peace negotiations could not proceed unless they were informal and Eckert was to acquire a signed agreement to that stipulation. Thus began peace talks soon to be known as the Hampton Roads Conference.

FEBRUARY 1

Lincoln Signs the Thirteenth Amendment

Lincoln had reason to forget the first day of February. His three-year-old son Eddie died on February 1, 1850 of either diphtheria or pulmonary tuberculosis. Lincoln brightened this anniversary when, in 1865, he signed the Thirteenth Amendment, which, when ratified by the states, would ban slavery throughout the country. This was a mild legal faux pas since a presidential signature was not necessary for an amendment to be sent to the states for ratification.

Lincoln had fought hard for the Thirteenth's passage. An amendment hadn't been ratified in sixty years and the amendment failed to pass the previous spring because it lacked Democratic support. In his December annual address, Lincoln pointed to Republican victories—including his own—in the November elections as a popular mandate for the amendment. He appealed to lame-duck Democrats and the legacy they would leave behind. When that failed, he hinted at patronage jobs as rewards. On January 31, 1865, thirteen House Democrats switched sides and voted to approve the measure.

The Thirteenth Amendment was far more important than the Emancipation Proclamation. While the proclamation freed slaves in areas in rebellion, it did not in loyal border states. The amendment freed slaves nationwide. The proclamation was also a war measure and might have been revoked after the war. "A question might be raised whether the proclamation was legally valid," Lincoln said. "It might be added that it only aided those who came into our lines . . . or that it would have no effect upon the children of the slaves born hereafter." A Constitutional amendment, however, would be "a King's cure for all the evils," he added. Lincoln was particularly pleased that his home state of Illinois was the first state to ratify it. More than ten months later the necessary twenty-seventh state—the former slave state of Georgia—ratified the amendment.

FEBRUARY 3

The Hampton Roads Conference

Lincoln, initially, had no intention of meeting with Confederate president Jefferson Davis's three commissioners, sent to negotiate a peace. He sent, instead, Secretary of State William Seward to Fortress Monroe to speak with them but, at the spur of the moment, changed his mind. He took a train to Annapolis and from there sailed on the steamer *Thomas Collyer* to Hampton Roads, the waterway adjacent to the fortress. There, he met for four hours on this Friday in 1865, aboard the steamer *River Queen*, with Confederates Vice President Alexander Stephens, President Pro Tempore of the Confederate Senate Robert Hunter, and Assistant Secretary of War John A. Campbell.

When the commissioners boarded the steamer, Lincoln watched Stephens, who stood barely five feet tall, take off an overcoat, hat, three scarves, two vestments, and a jacket. "Never have I seen so much shuck with such a little nubbin," Lincoln quipped.

The president was all serious, however, when it came to peace; it would come only with the reestablishment of the federal authority in the South, and emancipation would not be rescinded. Hunter proposed an armistice and a convention of states, but Lincoln was adamant that hostilities continue as long as Confederate armies were in the field. Hunter pointed out that during the English Civil War, Charles I had negotiated peace even as rebel armies still stood at arms. Lincoln countered, "I do not profess to be posted in history. . . . All I distinctly recollect about the case of Charles I is that he lost his head."

Sadly, the commissioners could not agree to Lincoln's terms and left empty-handed—all except Stephens, who had a personal request. His nephew, Lieutenant John Stephens, was a prisoner on Johnson Island, Ohio and Stephens asked Lincoln if he could be sent home. Lincoln had the young officer released the next day.

FEBRUARY 7

"*Waiting for the Hour*"

Lincoln received numerous gifts while president and president-elect. Many of the gifts were food, such as fruit, venison, a barrel of hominy, two cases of wine, and, of course, fruit cake. Others were homemade (slippers, quills, and socks), others expensive (ornamental swords, furniture, and a silver service), and some were even alive (eagles, sheep, cats, goats, and a pony). A few of the gifts the Lincolns kept but others were forwarded to Congress to be archived or donated to charities. On this Tuesday in 1865, Lincoln acknowledged a painting, a version of which can still be seen in the White House.

In early July 1864, William Lloyd Garrison, a leader in the abolitionist movement, sent Lincoln an oil painting, *Watch Meeting—Dec. 31st, 1862—Waiting for the Hour*. The painting depicted a large gathering of slaves around an elderly black man, waiting for midnight and the advent of the 1863 New Year, the moment when the Emancipation Proclamation would go into effect. Painted by William Tolman Carlton, Garrison thought Lincoln—as the author of the Proclamation—"the most fitting person in the world to receive it."

Typically when gifts were received, the president's secretaries sent an acknowledgment and thanks. "I directed my Secretary not to acknowledge its [the painting's] arrival at once, preferring to make my personal acknowledgment of the thoughtful kindness of the donors," Lincoln wrote Garrison, "and waiting for some leisure hour, I have committed the discourtesy of not replying at all." He added, "I hope you will believe that my thanks, though late, are most cordial . . . [for your] flattering and generous gift."

The *Watch Meeting* painting disappeared from the White House after Lincoln's assassination, but an earlier version of the painting was purchased and now hangs on the second floor of the White House in the so-called Lincoln Bedroom. The room was actually Lincoln's office, where he signed the Proclamation. Watch Meetings are now a tradition in many black churches, celebrated on every New Year's Eve with song and praise.

FEBRUARY 17

Robert Receives His Commission

Lincoln and his eldest son Robert rarely saw things the same way except when it came to his serving in the military. On this day in 1865, father and son got their wish and Robert finally went to war.

Lincoln was never very close to Robert. "During my childhood and early youth he [Lincoln] was almost constantly away from home, attending courts or making speeches," Robert later lamented. During Lincoln's presidency, it was Robert who was away, attending Harvard. Except for their dimples, father and son had little in common and little to talk about. What was more, Robert was not as brilliant as his father, despite the advantages of an education Lincoln never had. Lincoln called Robert a "rare-ripe type," smarter at age five than he would ever be again.

Once the war started, Robert wanted to join the army. It embarrassed and troubled Lincoln that Robert wasn't in uniform, especially when the press branded Robert a "shirker." But Mary had lost two sons and was distraught at the possibility that another son might be endangered. But after his graduation in 1864, Robert pressured his parents to allow him to volunteer. When Lincoln broached the subject, Mary exclaimed, "Of course, Mr. Lincoln, I know that Robert's plan to go into the Army is manly and noble and I want him to go, but oh! I am frightened he may never come back to us."

Mary finally relented and Lincoln wrote General Ulysses S. Grant, "My son . . . wishes to see something of the war before it ends . . . Could he . . . go into your military family, with some nominal rank?" Grant agreed to put Robert on his staff and promised to keep the boy safe. Then, on this day, Lincoln proudly signed Robert's commission as a captain.

FEBRUARY 26

"Lots of Wisdom in That Document"

Lincoln was never a good extemporaneous speaker. As a lawyer, his examinations of witnesses and arguments were better when he had time to prepare. As for speeches, he rarely delivered one that he had not composed, sometimes taking weeks to write it. Lincoln would jot down ideas as they came to him, slipping them into the lining of his stovepipe hat, using them later as the framework of his speech. Often he was pleased with the result and sometimes—as in the case of his Gettysburg Address—he was not. But on this Sunday in 1865, he proudly pulled his second inaugural address out and showed it to artist and friend F. B. Carpenter.

It was the shortest inaugural address (703 words) in U.S. history. It was also second only to his Gettysburg Address in fame. It was one of his most impersonal speeches, referring only to himself once and making no references to what he did or said in the previous four years. Despite the fact that he was the least educated of all American presidents, the speech's closing—which begins, "With malice toward none, with charity for all"—highlights an internal rhyme and iambic pentameter that is more poetry than public discourse. Even today, it is considered to be among the best speeches ever uttered by a statesman.

After he delivered the address on March 4, he beamed with appreciation when Frederick Douglass declared it "a sacred effort." Lincoln told politican Thurlow Weed he believed the speech would "wear as well as—perhaps better than—any thing I have produced." He added, "Lots of wisdom in that document, I suspect."

MARCH 4

Lincoln Is Inaugurated

Lincoln's first stop on this inaugural day in 1865 was the Senate chamber at the Capitol, where his new vice president was sworn in. Andrew Johnson, still recovering from typhoid fever, had asked for whisky to calm his nerves. He subsequently delivered a long, rambling acceptance speech. Afterward, Lincoln whispered to the parade marshal, "Do not let Johnson speak outside."

Lincoln moved out to the east portico of the Capitol, and as he stepped up to the podium (a thigh-high white table), the clouds suddenly parted and the sun fell on him like a spotlight. He began his address by reminding his audience that they had suffered a civil conflict with two parties: "one of them would make war rather than let the nation survive; and the other would accept war rather than let it perish." But the war wasn't just about the survival of the Union, as he claimed four years before in his first inaugural. Now he admitted that slavery was "the cause of the war." But the war's meaning wasn't just to emancipate slaves, but God's retribution on the nation—both North and South. If God willed that the war continue "until all the wealth piled by bond-man's two hundred and fifty years of unrequited toil shall be sunk, until every drop of blood drawn with the lash, shall be paid by another drawn with the sword . . . 'the judgments of the Lord, are true and righteous altogether.'"

He then softened his rhetoric: "With malice toward none; with charity for all; with firmness in the right, as God gives us to see the right, let us strive to finish the work we are in; to bind up the nation's wounds."

#80

Four Years Earlier

Until the Twentieth Amendment and the 1937 inauguration of Franklin D. Roosevelt, presidential inaugurations were constitutionally set for March 4. And so Lincoln's first inaugural was on the same day four years earlier. On that sunny, brisk Monday, Lincoln rode with the incumbent president James Buchanan in an open barouche in the noon parade down Pennsylvania Avenue to the Capitol as sharpshooters looked on from the roofs.

As he stepped up to the podium to deliver his speech, he was perplexed as to what to do with his ever-present stovepipe hat. Lincoln's old nemesis Stephen Douglas rescued him by offering to hold it. The president-elect then put on his steel-rimmed glasses and began to speak.

He first reassured Southerners that he would not interfere with slavery where it already existed. He argued, however, that the Union was perpetual, that secession was constitutionally illegal, and armed resistance against the federal government was "insurrectionary." He promised to "hold, occupy, and possess" federal forts not already confiscated by Southern states. But beyond that, the federal government would not shed blood unless attacked.

"In your hands, my dissatisfied fellow countrymen, and not mine, is the momentous issue of civil war," Lincoln said. "You have no oath registered in Heaven to destroy the government, while I shall have the most solemn one to 'preserve, protect and defend' it.

"I am loath to close. We are not enemies, but friends. . . . The mystic chords of memory, stretching from every battlefield and patriot grave, to every living heart and hearthstone all over this broad land, will yet swell the chorus of the Union, when again touched, as surely they will be, by the better angels of our nature."

He then turned to Chief Justice Roger Taney and took the oath as the sixteenth president.

MARCH 17

The Plot

On this Friday in 1865, Lincoln was scheduled to visit convalescing soldiers at Campbell Hospital on Seventh Street near the

Maryland border. The road leading to it was rural and isolated. It was on that road that John Wilkes Booth and his co-conspirators planned to kidnap the president and dash into southern Maryland on their way to Richmond.

Booth hated the president as much for his Emancipation Proclamation as he did for the president's "appearance, his pedigree, his coarse low jokes." In the fall of 1864, Booth hatched a plot to kidnap Lincoln and take him to Richmond, where he would be exchanged for thousands of Confederate soldiers in northern prisons. Booth recruited friends from Baltimore and Washington. When he heard that several of his fellow actors would put on a play called *Still Waters Run Deep* for the president at Campbell Hospital that afternoon, he gathered his crew together.

Using a rope stretched across the path to unseat Lincoln's cavalry escort, Booth and his men would overtake Lincoln's carriage, dispatch the driver, cross the Benning's Bridge (just four and half miles southeast of the hospital) over the Potomac, switch to horses, and head through Prince George's and Charles counties to Surrattsville in southern Maryland. From there they would ride hard for the Confederate capital.

Lincoln, however, changed his plans at the last minute because Indiana governor Oliver Morton invited the president to attend a flag presentation. By coincidence the presentation was performed at the National Hotel, where Booth was living at the time. The conspirators, fearing that the president changed his plans because their plot had been discovered, soon dispersed.

#81

Booth's Other Attempts

Investigations into Booth's and his conspirators' activities prior to the end of the war reveal that their first attempt to kidnap Lincoln was on January 18, 1865. Lincoln was supposed to attend a play at Ford's Theatre. The plan allegedly was for the theater gaslights to go out while Booth and small band of men would enter the presidential box. They would handcuff the president, then lower him to the stage, and carry him out to a waiting carriage and head for Richmond. On that Wednesday night, Booth waited at the theater, the carriage ready. But Lincoln never showed.

Booth waited two months—until March 15—when he and two other conspirators went to Ford's Theatre for a one-night performance of *Jane Shore*. During an intermission the trio inspected the presidential box, the very place that Booth would shoot Lincoln a month later.

Afterward, Booth met his co-conspirators at Gautier's Restaurant for an all-night drinking and planning session. Booth's men had a problem with their leader's unrealistic plans to abduct the president at a theater under the noses of an audience. A quarrel broke out and ultimately Booth agreed to a more practical abduction plan: to seize Lincoln during his many rides around Washington.

On March 17 the conspirators tried to kidnap Lincoln on his way to the Campbell Hospital. Booth and seven other men waited in ambush in a wooded area near the hospital, but the president had changed his plans. The conspirators scattered, some of them leaving town.

Booth, at this point, began drinking heavily and sometime in the coming weeks his plans to kidnap the president turned to plans for assassination.

MARCH 22

The Abduction

Inevitably the anarchy of war frequently clashes with the ordered nature of the military. On this day in 1865, Lincoln tried to untie a communication snarl and prevent General George Crook—who had already suffered much in the past month—from being arrested.

In February 1865, Crook, in command of the Department of West Virginia, made his headquarters at the Revere House, a hotel in Cumberland, Maryland. The owner of the hotel, unfortunately, had a son who was a member of Captain Jesse McNeill's Confederate "Partisan Rangers." On February 21, 1865, sixty of McNeill's rangers boldly stole in among ten thousand of Crook's men and abducted Crook and his subordinate, General Benjamin Kelly, then rode with them south all the way to Richmond and Libby Prison.

The generals were eventually released and, on March 20, Crook was officially exchanged as a prisoner, allowing him to return to duty. General in Chief Ulysses Grant ordered Crook back to his command and added, "As soon as he goes on duty I will have him relieved and ordered at once to command the cavalry of the Army of the Potomac." Apparently Crook was not informed of his new assignment and assumed he'd be given his old command back. Nor was General Winfield Hancock—his replacement after the abduction—informed of Grant's orders. After hearing that Crook had tried to reestablish his command, Hancock ordered him arrested.

The War Department quickly tried to intercede and Lincoln on this day sent a separate telegram to Hancock so as to avoid "something unpleasant," and forwarded copies of Grant's orders to "fully explain Gen. Crook's movements." Hancock promised to send Crook to General Grant. Crook commanded a division of cavalry in the final operations of the war.

The bold incident may well have given John Wilkes Booth and his co-conspirators the needed courage to go on with their plans to abduct Lincoln and take him to Richmond.

MARCH 23

The Lincolns Head for the Front

For the first three weeks of March, Lincoln had been sick part of the time and besieged by office-seekers the rest of the time. So when General in Chief Ulysses Grant—at the urging of his wife, Julia—invited the president to get away from Washington and visit him at his headquarters at City Point, Virginia, Lincoln jumped at the opportunity. He also decided to bring along Mary and his son Tad and wrote Robert—now on Grant's staff—to join them for a family reunion. At 1:00 PM on this Thursday in 1865, Lincoln and his family departed aboard the *River Queen* from the arsenal dock at the Sixth Street wharf for City Point.

The trip started out poorly as the *River Queen* churned through a raging rainstorm. What was worse, the polluted Potomac from which the ship drew its potable water made the entire family sick. By the next morning, however, everyone was feeling better and at noon the ship took on fresh water from Fortress Monroe on the Chesapeake Bay before heading up the James River.

Tad's curiosity took him to every corner of the side-wheel steamer. White House guard William Crook observed that Tad "studied every screw of the engine and knew and counted among his friends every man of the crew." Lincoln made the mistake of telling Mary that he had a dream the night before that the White House was on fire and Mary fretted about it the rest of the trip.

The ship anchored off City Point on March 24 and Lincoln directed that a telegram be sent to Secretary of War Edwin Stanton in Washington, informing him that "both he and the family are well, having entirely recovered." It was the start of an eventful eighteen-day vacation, the longest Lincoln had as president. And it would be his last.

MARCH 26

Hackles of the "Hellcat"

In his four years as Lincoln's secretary, John Hay had borne the brunt of many of Mary Lincoln's tantrums and had taken to calling her the "hellcat." On this Saturday in 1865, Mary lived up to the nickname.

Once the Lincolns arrived at City Point, Virginia to visit General Ulysses Grant's headquarters, Mary's disposition soured. On March 25, Lincoln made the mistake of reviewing troops riding beside an officer's wife. Mary flew into a rage at the news: "Do you mean to say that she saw the President alone? Do you know that I never allow the President to see any woman alone?"

A bigger explosion came on this day, when another troop review was scheduled. Lincoln left early, leaving Mary to ride to the review in a covered ambulance. Unfortunately the route was deeply rutted and a bump threw Mary's head against an iron rib of the canvas top, inaugurating an excruciating headache. When Mary got to the review, she found that General Edward Ord's wife, Mary, was already reviewing the troops, riding between the president and her husband.

"What does this woman mean by riding by the side of the president and ahead of me?" she shouted. When Julia Grant tried to intervene, Mary turned to her and said, "I suppose you think you'll get to the White House yourself, don't you?" When Lincoln tried to mollify his wife, she shouted at him.

At dinner that night, Mary attacked her husband for flirting with Mrs. Ord and demanded that Lincoln fire General Ord immediately. Lincoln tried to ignore her, but her tirade lasted well into the night. Mary spent the remainder of the trip claiming she was ill.

#82

Mary's Temper

Even before the White House, Mary's fits of temper were legendary. In Springfield, stories circulated about her tantrums over incompetent maids or workmen renovating their home. "Mrs. L. got the devil in her," a friend remembered. "Lincoln paid no attention—would pick up one of the children and walk off."

Recent historians have tried to explain her actions beyond the oversimplified view that she was mentally ill. She did have symptoms that suggest a manic-depressive disorder. One observer said Mary's "emotional temperament [was] much like an April day, sunning all over with laughter one moment, the next crying as though her heart would break." Headaches probably contributed to her tirades. Some of them were so severe that she stayed for days in a darkened room and, she said, sometimes felt as if wires were being pulled out of her eyes. They became worse after a July 1863 carriage accident where she hit her head on a rock. It is probably no coincidence that just prior to her famous City Point tirade, she hit her head again, probably reinjuring herself. Mary was also likely a long-term diabetic, resulting in mood swings.

Yet another contributing factor was Lincoln himself. He often, particularly during the White House years, was inattentive to Mary's needs. Even in Springfield, after a long day in the office, Lincoln would sit by the fire and read, not realizing that Mary, cooped up with her boys, needed adult conversation. On one occasion when Mary warned her husband that the fire was going out, he was so absorbed with his reading, he didn't respond. After he ignored her a third time, she struck him on the nose with a piece of firewood.

MARCH 27

The City Point Conference

On this Monday evening in 1865, General William Sherman arrived at City Point, Virginia from Goldsborough, North Carolina where his army was concentrated. He subsequently boarded the president's steamer—the *River Queen*—and sat down with Lincoln, General in Chief Ulysses Grant, and Admiral David Porter for an impromptu conference.

Lincoln first listened to Sherman's report on Confederate general Joseph Johnston's army in North Carolina, then voiced his concern that Johnston might slip away via the railroads. "Yes, he will get away if he can," Lincoln fretted. "And you will never catch him until after miles of travel and many bloody battles." Sherman assured him that would not happen.

The conversation then turned to the terms of surrender to be given Johnston. Sherman insisted that Johnston would accept any terms, even harsh ones. Lincoln, however, feared that heavy-handed peace terms would force rebel soldiers to take up guerrilla warfare against the federal government. The next day, when they continued the conversation, Lincoln said, "Let them . . . surrender and reach their homes, [and] they won't take up arms again. Let them all go, officers and all, I want submission, and no more bloodshed. . . . We want those people to return to their allegiance to the Union and submit to the laws." What about the Confederate president Jefferson Davis? Lincoln was asked. The president answered with a story: "A man once had taken the total-abstinence pledge. When visiting a friend he was invited to take a drink, but declined, on the score of his pledge; when his friend suggested lemonade, which was accepted. In preparing the lemonade the friend pointed to the brandy bottle, and said the lemonade, would be more palatable if he were to pour in a little brandy when the guest said, if he could do so 'unbeknown' to him, he would not object." Lincoln then said that, while he could not officially say so, he hoped Davis would leave the country, "escape, 'unbeknown' to him."

MARCH 31

The Beginning of the End

Lincoln, who spent so many hours in the Washington telegraph office waiting for news of military actions from afar, on this day in 1865 would himself send news from the front to Washington as he bore witness to the collapse of Robert E. Lee's mighty Army of Northern Virginia.

By March 1865, Lee knew that he would have to evacuate Petersburg and Richmond, Virginia when his depleted army finally collapsed. His plan was to load his men onto trains and, via the Southside Railroad in Petersburg, head south to join with Joseph Johnston's army in North Carolina. His opponent, General Ulysses S. Grant, planned to strike at Lee's right flank southwest of Petersburg in order to take the Southside Railroad, jeopardizing Lee's escape route. On March 29, Grant launched his attack and that night Lincoln could hear the cannonade and see the "flashes of the guns upon the clouds." The next evening Lincoln telegraphed Secretary of War Edwin Stanton: "I begin to feel that I ought to be at home, and yet I dislike to leave without seeing nearer to the end of General Grant's present movement."

On this morning in 1865, Lincoln knew that Grant would make a big push and expected a considerable loss of life. During the day, Grant sent Lincoln telegrams of the seesaw actions at White Oak Road and Dinwiddie Court House, which Lincoln forwarded to Washington. To meet Grant's onslaught, Lee stripped men from other parts of the front, severely weakening those areas. Within two days Lee's army collapsed, with Grant forcing him to escape westward, not south, and by foot, not rail.

Lincoln decided to stay and watch this momentous occasion, sending Mary and Tad home to Washington the next day.

APRIL 2

"This Is Victory"

On April 1, 1865, General Philip Sheridan attacked a little-known crossroads called Five Forks. With its acquisition his commander, General Ulysses Grant, had effectively encircled Petersburg, Virginia from the south. Grant sent a bundle of captured Confederate flags to Lincoln at City Point, Virginia on this Sunday in 1865, and, when the president unfurled them, he said, "Here is something material, something I can see, feel and understand. This means victory. This is victory."

Mary Lincoln had returned to Washington that day and Lincoln decided to sleep aboard Admiral David Porter's flagship *Malvern*. Declining to use the admiral's quarters, Lincoln was given a tiny cabin with a bunk four inches shorter than his six-foot-four-inch frame. When, on this day in 1865, he was asked how he slept, he said, "You can't put a long blade into a short scabbard."

Grant began his final push to take Petersburg at 4:30 that morning and Lincoln spent the day in the telegraph office, reading Grant's reports and forwarding them to Washington. Twelve hours later, Grant reported that Petersburg was surrounded and Robert E. Lee's army had all but collapsed. That evening Lincoln wired Mary that Grant "suggests that I shall go out [to Petersburg] and see him in the morning, which I think I will do."

A weary Lincoln returned to the *Malvern* to find that Porter had enlarged his cabin and installed a bunk that was twice as wide and a half-foot longer. The next morning Lincoln quipped that a miracle had happened during the night: "I shrunk six inches in length, and about a foot sideways." Lincoln received even better news that morning; Lee, during the night, had pulled his army out of Petersburg and Richmond, and Confederate president Jefferson Davis had evacuated his government. Both Lee and Davis were on the run.

APRIL 4

Lincoln Takes a Seat

Secretary of War Edwin Stanton was horrified to learn that Lincoln, on April 3, 1865, risked a train ride to Petersburg, Virginia to visit Ulysses Grant, just hours after the Confederate Army had pulled out of the city. When Lincoln returned he found a telegram from Stanton, asking "whether you ought to expose the nation to the consequences of any disaster to yourself?" Lincoln must have smiled when he wired back, "Thanks for your caution, but I have already been to Petersburg. . . . It is certain now that Richmond is in our hands, and I think I will go there tomorrow."

On this day in 1865, Lincoln celebrated his son Tad's twelfth birthday by taking him to the Confederate capital just thirty hours after Union soldiers entered it. Despite the hazards of an easily recognizable figure walking the streets of a city where nearly every inhabitant wished him ill, Lincoln insisted on going. "Thank God I have lived to see this," he said. "It seems to me that I have been dreaming a horrid dream for four years, and now the nightmare is gone. I want to see Richmond."

On his arrival, Lincoln was first recognized by a group of black workmen, one of whom exclaimed, "Bless the Lord, there is the great Messiah!" and fell on his knees trying to kiss the president's feet. "Don't kneel to me," Lincoln responded. "You must kneel to God only, and thank Him for the liberty you will hereafter enjoy."

The group walked two miles through the city with a relatively small escort until they reached the Confederate White House. Weary, Lincoln sat down in the office chair that Confederate president

Jefferson Davis had vacated less than two days before. Lincoln, however, didn't gloat, but instead simply asked for a glass of water.

APRIL 8

"Let the Thing Be Pressed"

While visiting General Ulysses Grant's headquarters at City Point, Virginia, Lincoln had toured the now-conquered cities of Petersburg and Richmond after both the Confederate army and government had collapsed. On this Monday in 1861, Lincoln reluctantly decided it was time to return to Washington.

By the time Confederate general Robert E. Lee's retreating divisions had rendezvoused at Amelia Court House west of Petersburg on April 4, the once mighty Army of Northern Virginia was reduced to a mere 33,000 men. During the battle of Sayler's (or Sailer's) Creek two days later, 8,000 more men were captured, killed, or wounded. Afterward, Lee exclaimed, "My God! Has the army been dissolved?"

On April 7, 1865, General Ulysses Grant sent Lee a note asking for his surrender. While Lee considered it, Lincoln, back at City Point, was thrilled when Grant forwarded a message from one of his generals, Philip Sheridan, which read: "If the thing be pressed I think that Lee will surrender." Lincoln wired back, "Let the thing be pressed."

On this day Lincoln decided it was time to return to Washington and that evening a military band gave Lincoln a farewell concert aboard the *River Queen* before it embarked.

For several hours on the voyage home, Lincoln read passages from Shakespeare to his fellow passengers. From *Macbeth*, Lincoln read the king's lament where the burden of guilt over the murder of his predecessor, Duncan, has made the monarch envious of his victim's peace:

Duncan is in his grave,
After life's fitful fever he sleeps well,
Treason has done his worst; not steel, nor poison,
Malice domestic, foreign levy, nothing
Can touch him further.

It was to be prophetic; Lincoln himself would be beyond "life's fitful fever" in one week's time. While Lincoln was still en route to Washington, Lee, on April 9, capitulated. The war was all but over.

APRIL 11

Lincoln's Last Speech

Washington was still celebrating, on this Tuesday evening, the surrender of Robert E. Lee's army. Lanterns and candles illuminated the windows of every government building, bonfires were lit, and, across the Potomac on the lawn of Lee's Arlington home, thousands of former slaves gathered to sing "The Year of Jubilee." Lincoln had promised to speak that night and a huge crowd gathered below the White House's north portico. He appeared at the second-story window with his speech in one hand and a candle in the other. After he fumbled with the candle, he handed it to his friend, Noah Brooks, and began reading.

"The speech was longer than most people had expected, and of a different character," said Brooks. Instead of delivering a celebratory oration, Lincoln talked about Reconstruction. Lincoln pointed out that Louisiana, in its attempt to reenter the Union, had ratified a remarkable new state constitution, emancipating its slaves and providing an education "equally to black and white." Lincoln admitted that Louisiana had not given the black man the right to vote. "I would myself prefer that it were now conferred on the very intelligent, and on those who serve our cause as soldiers," he said.

But to discard the new state government because of flaws would be disaster. "Shall [we] sooner have the fowl by hatching the egg than by smashing it?" he asked.

In the audience that night was John Wilkes Booth. During the speech, Booth turned to his companions and said, "That means nigger citizenship. That is the last speech he will ever make." He begged one of his friends to shoot Lincoln in the window and when the friend refused, Booth exclaimed, "By God, I'll put him through."

#83

Why Did Booth Kill Lincoln?

There are several theories as to why John Wilkes Booth assassinated Lincoln. There are claims that he was disgruntled over a failed oil speculation enterprise and a diminishing theatrical career (he developed throat problems during the winter of 1864). Another theory has it that the Confederate government funded Booth. In October 1864, Booth did travel to Montreal, Canada, where he allegedly met two Confederate agents to propose his plan to kidnap Lincoln. Booth returned from Montreal with a letter of introduction to key Confederate sympathizers in Maryland. It also appears he received $1,500 (about $16,000 in today's money). How much the Confederate government aided Booth, however, will never be known. But before his throat ailment and Montreal, Booth was obsessed with a romantic image of Southern life and with a belief that Lincoln would exterminate it.

While Booth was a Southerner (he was born in Maryland), he became particularly enamored with the Southern lifestyle while on stage at the Richmond Theatre in

1858, largely because Richmond—particularly Richmond women—was enamored with him. According to Booth, Lincoln was the antithesis of cultured Southern life, with his offensive "appearance, his pedigree, his coarse low jokes and anecdotes." He was sure that Lincoln would "crush out slavery, by robbery, rapine, slaughter and bought armies." He told his sister that "my soul, life and possession are for the South."

He promised his mother he would not fight in the war but when the war turned in favor of the North, Booth became desperate to help the South. He wrote after the assassination, "Our [the Confederacy's] cause being almost lost, something decisive and great must be done. . . . Our country owed all her troubles to him [Lincoln], and God simply made me the instrument of his punishment."

APRIL 12

"Giving Away the Scepter"

On this Wednesday in 1865, Lincoln walked over to the War Department and wrote out what would be his final telegram under his name as he withdrew permission for the Virginia legislature to meet under his authority.

After the withdrawal of Robert E. Lee's army and the Confederate government from Richmond in early April, Lincoln formulated a plan to spare both sides further bloodshed. On April 5, 1865, he met with Confederate assistant secretary of war John Campbell, where Lincoln offered to allow the Confederate Virginia legislature to meet in Richmond and vote "to withdraw the Virginia troops, and other support from resistance to the General Government." Thus Lee and much of his army would be asked to throw down their arms. It was an offer Lincoln would regret.

There were some problems with the plan. For one, allowing the state legislature to meet overturned Lincoln's own policy of refusing to recognize the legitimacy of the rebel government. For another, Lincoln's blessing of the disloyal legislature would infuriate the loyalist Virginia government that had ruled for four years in virtual exile in West Virginia. And the plan wasn't necessary once Lee's army surrendered on April 9.

Still, Lincoln presented the idea to his cabinet and was surprised at their vehement disagreement with it. Edwin Stanton, secretary of war, said "that to place such powers in the Virginia legislature would be giving away the scepter of the conqueror; that it would transfer the result of victory of our arms from the field to the very legislature which four years before had said 'give us war.'"

The final straw happened today when the president learned that Campbell was exceeding the terms they had negotiated. He then, on this day, wired Richmond that his offer to Campbell was "countermanded." He added, "do not now allow them [the Virginia legislature] to assemble."

APRIL 14

Lincoln's Final Day

This Good Friday in 1865 was perhaps the most enjoyable day Lincoln had as president. It was the fourth anniversary of the surrender of Fort Sumter and breakfast was spent with his eldest son, Robert, who had just returned to Washington. "Well, my son," Lincoln said, "you have returned safely from the front. The war is now closed." He then advised Robert to "lay aside" his uniform and continue his education.

General Ulysses Grant arrived at eleven for the usual Friday cabinet meeting. Cabinet members asked him for news from General William Sherman, still facing a rebel army in North Carolina.

Lincoln was optimistic that the rebels would surrender, "for he had last night the usual dream which he had preceding nearly every great and important event in the War." He explained that in the dream he was riding a boat "with great rapidity towards some indefinite shore." Lincoln had the dream just before the bombardment of Fort Sumter and the battles at Bull Run, Antietam, Gettysburg, Stones River, Vicksburg, and Wilmington. Grant pointed out, however, that not all these "events" were Union victories.

At three, Lincoln took a carriage ride with his wife. As they drove to the Navy Yard, they reminisced about home in Springfield and made plans to travel. Mary would later recollect, "During the drive he was so gay, that I said to him, laughingly, 'Dear Husband, you almost startle me by your great cheerfulness.' He replied, 'And well I may feel so, Mary, I consider this day, the war, has come to a close.'"

At the Navy Yard, the Lincolns, by coincidence, toured the ironclad *Montauk*, the very ship where, in the coming weeks, John Wilkes Booth's co-conspirators would be temporarily held and where Booth's autopsy would be performed.

#84

"Sic Semper Tyrannis"

It had been widely advertised on April 14 that the first family, along with General Ulysses Grant and his wife, Julia, would attend that evening's performance at Ford's Theatre of *Our American Cousin*. Ticket scalpers bought up many of the tickets, reselling $.75 and S1 tickets for $2.50. When the Grants declined to attend, the Lincolns invited a young couple—Clara Harris and her stepbrother (who was also her fiancé), Major Henry Rathbone.

When the presidential party arrived at 8:30 PM, the play, already in progress, was interrupted as the orchestra played

"Hail to the Chief." As the audience cheered, one witness recalled that "the President stepped to the box rail and acknowledged the applause with dignified bows and never-to-be-forgotten smiles." The play, a farce about an American bumpkin traveling in England, then resumed. Mary snuggled against her husband's side. "What will Miss Harris think of my hanging on to you so?" Mary asked. Smiling, Lincoln replied, "She won't think any thing about it."

At twelve after ten, Booth presented his calling card to Charles Forbes, Lincoln's footman. Forbes let him enter the box's anteroom, where Booth waited until a line in the play was delivered that was sure to evoke a raucous laughter. He then entered the box and shot Lincoln behind the left ear. When Booth jumped over the railing, he caught his spur on a flag and fell awkwardly on the stage, breaking his left leg. He then brandished a knife at the audience and shouted "*Sic semper tyrannis*" ("Thus always to tyrants"—the Virginia state motto) before limping from the stage.

Most of the audience believed the incident was part of the play until they heard Mary wail from the box, "They have shot the President! They have shot the President!"

APRIL 15

"*Now He Belongs to the Ages*"

Early on this Saturday in 1865, Lincoln died.

John Wilkes Booth's bullet—the size of a fingertip—entered Lincoln's skull behind his left ear and traveled forward to the center of his brain, the force cracking the bones behind both eyes. When Dr. Charles Leale entered the presidential box at Ford's Theatre that April 14 evening, he found Lincoln slumped in his rocker. "He appeared dead," he said. "His eyes were closed and his head fallen forward. He was being held upright in his chair by Mrs. Lincoln who was weeping bitterly." After Lincoln's condition was stabilized, he was moved across the street to the house of a German tailor named William Peterson. Lincoln was carried to a rear bedroom and laid diagonally across the short bed.

At eleven, Secretary of War Edwin Stanton and Secretary of the Navy Gideon Welles arrived at the Peterson House. Welles later wrote, "His [Lincoln's] features were calm and striking. I had never seen them appear to better advantage than for the first hour. . . . After that, his right eye began to swell and that part of his face became discolored."

Stanton moved to a rear parlor of the house and began sending out orders and interviewing eyewitnesses to the murder. Legend has it that Stanton was involved in Booth's conspiracy and that he delayed in closing Washington's bridges and disabled its telegraphs. The truth is that Booth was already across the Navy Bridge and racing across Maryland before Stanton even arrived at the scene. And while the commercial telegraph line was disrupted for two hours, the military telegraph—the one controlled by Stanton—was not.

At seven on this Saturday morning in 1865, Mary was brought from the front parlor to see her husband one last time. "Love," she exclaimed, "live but one moment to speak to me once." Twenty-two minutes later Lincoln expired.

"Now he belongs to the ages," Stanton said.

Afterword-I

After Lincoln's death, authorities found in his pockets two pairs of eyeglasses, one of which had been repaired with a piece of string. They also found a silver eyeglass case, an eyeglass lens polisher, a white Irish linen handkerchief with "A. Lincoln" embroidered on it, a quartz watch fob, an ivory pocketknife, a sleeve button with a gold initial "L" on it, and a leather wallet. In the wallet were nine newspaper clippings and a five-dollar Confederate note that Lincoln probably kept as a souvenir.

The things this great man carried with him on the night he met his fate are remarkable only in how mundane, how practical they are. Even the newspaper clippings are just what we would expect, complimentary articles on his policies and his presidency, most written during his campaign for reelection the previous fall. When Daniel J. Boorstin, the Librarian of the National Archives, first revealed what was in Lincoln's pockets to the world in 1976, he said, "This certainly shows he [Lincoln] was very much like the rest of us." The reason Boorstin revealed the collection was to show the human side of the sixteenth president. "Abraham Lincoln is mythologically engulfed," Boorstin said. "We should try to humanize him."

But because these were Lincolnian relics, we refused to allow them to remain insignificant. Speculation surrounded the historical coincidence that Lincoln appears on the five-dollar bill, the same denomination in Confederate currency he carried in his wallet. There was no chance that this was tribute to Lincoln by the Federal Reserve since Lincoln's face first appeared on a "fin" way back in 1914. According to Boorstin, no one outside the Lincoln family knew of Lincoln's Confederate note until Boorstin revealed it in 1976. So this coincidence became a part of the Lincoln mythology.

The effort to mythologize the man began while he was still living. During his 1860 bid for the presidency, Lincoln was the backwoods "rail-splitter" too innocuous to threaten either Southern or Northern interests. After 1863, he was to slaves the American "Moses," slipping the shackles from their wrists. To much of the South and, indeed, to much of the

North, Lincoln was a "tyrant," forcing his ideals on the nation. There was a nugget of truth in all of these monikers. But just a nugget.

After his death, Lincoln became the darling of the Republican Party. While many in the party—particularly Radicals—detested their party head in life, in death they paraded his body for three weeks in front of millions of Northerners and paired with it eulogies that described Lincoln as a martyr at the hands of the Democrats. One Democrat equated the spectacle with "Mark Anthony [Antony] . . . displaying to the Roman people the bloody mantle of Caesar." It's no wonder that for the next fifty years the Republicans—with the exception of the two terms of Grover Cleveland—had a lock on the presidency.

Democrats, too, eventually claimed Lincoln was a Democrat in GOP clothing. Franklin Roosevelt felt that Lincoln's public aid to the less fortunate and huge expansion of government meant that he was as much a father of the New Deal as Woodrow Wilson, Thomas Jefferson, and Andrew Jackson. Barack Obama was so unabashed in comparing himself to Lincoln that he registered his oath of office on the cover of the same Bible that Lincoln's palm rested on nearly 150 years before.

To others, Lincoln was a communist and the American Communist Party at one time held Lincoln–Lenin rallies in February. The fact that Lincoln rarely drank made him a prohibitionist. To others he was a socialist. Twisting Lincoln's words on equality and using his quest for colonization, Lincoln even became a hero for white supremacists like the Ku Klux Klan. But the fight over making the fallen president the figurehead of a political ideal was only the beginning.

After his death, pastors nationwide began to eulogize Lincoln as the "American Christ" and much was made of the fact that he was shot on Good Friday. "It is no blasphemy against the Son of God and the Saviour of men that we declare the fitness of the slaying of the second Father of our Republic on the anniversary of the day on which He was slain," said C. B. Crane from his Broadway Tabernacle pulpit. "Jesus Christ died for the world, Abraham Lincoln died for his country." Despite the insistence from his widow and close friend William Herndon that Lincoln was not a practicing Christian, dozens of stories circulated of Lincoln's ardor for Christ, the Bible, and salvation. There were claims that Lincoln was a Catholic, a Universalist, a Congregationalist, and even a Spiritualist.

For anyone who had a position or idea to legitimize, Lincoln was the perfect icon. Because Lincoln hated to hunt and kill animals, he was a vegetarian. Because Lincoln sometimes shared a bed with other men, he was a homosexual. Because he loved to shoot guns, he must have eschewed gun control.

Then there were the biographers. There was Josiah Holland's 1866 *The Life of Abraham Lincoln*, in which Lincoln was from his youth a perfect gentleman, Christian, and statesman. In William Herndon's biography, Lincoln was born in squalor to poor white trash and a mother who was illegitimate. To Herndon, beneath his friend's statesmanship was still that crude backwoodsman who told dirty jokes, could out-wrestle anyone, and darkened the doorways of churches only because of his domineering wife whom he did not love. Then there's Carl Sandburg, who blended Herndon's and Holland's Lincolns together. To Sandburg, Lincoln was the mythic Man of the People, overcoming his poor beginnings to attain the highest seat of government. He was a walking, talking image of democratic ideals.

Mixed in with all this was the folklore that surrounded Lincoln. After his death, pictures of Lincoln appeared above the mantles and walls of the sitting rooms of African Americans all over the nation, just as others hung pictures of Jesus and his mother Mary. In a sense, Lincoln became god-like to black Americans, and they created stories that infused him with the piety, wisdom, and honesty of a god. "I think Abe Lincoln was next to the Lord," one ex-slave explained. He then related a story:

> 'Fore the election he [Lincoln] traveled all over the South, and he come to our house and slept in Old Mistress's bed. Didn't nobody know who he was. . . . He come to our house and he watched close . . . . When he got back up North he writ Old Master a letter and told him that he was going to have to free his slaves, that everybody was going to have to. . . . He also told him that he had visited at his house and if he doubted it to go in the room he slept in and look at the bedstead at the head and he'd see where he'd writ his name. Sure enough, there was his name, A. Lincoln.

Another bit of Lincoln lore was recently debunked. In 1905, a watchmaker by the name of Jonathan Dillon told the *New York Times* that he had etched a secret message within Lincoln's personal pocket watch. Dillon was working in M. W. Galt & Company jewelry store on April 13, 1861 and was given the president's watch to repair. "I was in the act of screwing on the dial when Mr. Galt announced the news [that Confederate forces had fired on Fort Sumter]. I unscrewed the dial, and with a sharp instrument wrote on the metal beneath, 'The first gun is fired. Slavery is dead. Thank God we have a President who at least will try.'"

In 1905, the watch in question was owned by the Lincoln family and Dillon's claim was not verified. The sixteenth president's great-grandson Lincoln Isham gave the watch to the Smithsonian in 1958 but it wasn't until February of 2009 that Dillon's claim was brought to the attention of museum curator Harry Rubenstein. In March, Rubenstein allowed a master jeweler to open the watch. "It's sort of amazing," Rubenstein said, "when you think that two years before the Emancipation Proclamation, Abraham Lincoln is carrying this hopeful message in his pocket, and never knowing it."

When Lincoln's watch was opened, a message was indeed found. It read, "Jonathan Dillon April 13-1861 Fort Sumpter was attacked by the rebels on the above date. J Dillon April 13-1861 Washington thank God we have a government Jonth Dillon." While Dillon's claim to the etchings was verified, it bore little resemblance to what Dillon remembered he wrote. There was no mention of slavery. There was no mention of Lincoln as the man to end it. In fact it seemed more important to Dillon that he marked his name (as it was repeated twice) in the president's watch on that historic day than it was to mention slavery and its demise. It was a lesson in how time and pretension to be a part of history can color a person's memory.

The gold timepiece was cherished by Lincoln, who purchased it in the 1850s at home in Springfield. It may well have belonged to the watch fob found in Lincoln's pocket after his death. But while interesting, what was etched inside that watch reveals little about the man. Nor does the coincidence that he carried the same denomination in Confederate money that his face is now embossed on. What is more revealing is that Lincoln, who made nearly $2,100 a month, was frugal enough to hold onto a button that came off his jacket. Or that he was unpretentious enough to wear a pair of eyeglasses repaired with a piece of string. Or that he, with all that he had on his mind, was practical enough to bring a second pristine pair of glasses along with his lens cleaner to the theater.

This was the Lincoln I searched for while writing this book. Not the iconic Great Emancipator, not the savior of the Union, but the man revealed by the little things in his life. I wanted to prune out the icons, the legends, the mythology and see the man as he was, as he lived.

Abbreviations

ALP *Abraham Lincoln Papers at the Library of Congress*, Manuscript Division, Library of Congress (Washington D.C., American Memory Project: 2000-1]. Can be found on the Internet, http://memory.loc.gov/ammem/alhtml/malhome.html. Citation usually includes brief description provided by ALP editors to aid in locating document. Citation also includes notes and footnotes attached to document.

CW *Collected Works of Abraham Lincoln*. Roy P. Basler et al., eds., *The Collected Works of Abraham Lincoln* (New Brunswick, NJ: Rutgers University Press, 1953), and can be found on the Internet (Ann Arbor, MI: University of Michigan Digital Library Production Services, 2001) at http://name.umdl.umich.edu/lincoln6. Citation includes notes and footnotes attached to document.

CWRE *The Collected Works of Ralph Waldo Emerson*. Ralph Waldo Emerson, *The Collected Works of Ralph Waldo Emerson* (New York: Houghton Mifflin, 1903–04), and can be found on the Internet (Ann Arbor, MI: University of Michigan Digital Library Production Services, 2006) at http://name.umdl.umich.edu/4957107.0011.001.

GBS Book listed was found on Google Books, http://books.google.com/. To find entry, simply type title, author, or quote into "Search Books" box.

SB Sidebar

JAN January

FEB February

MAR March

APR April

JUN June

JUL July

AUG August

SEP September

OCT October

NOV November

DEC December

Notes

"The sixteenth president . . . friends," David Herbert Donald, "*We Are Lincoln Men*" (New York: Simon & Schuster, 2003), xiv, xvi.

"'It is from private life . . . character,'" Mark Salber Phillips, *Society and Sentiment: Genres of Historical Writing in Britain, 1740–1820* (Princeton, NJ: Princeton University Press, 2000), 44. As quoted in John Brewer, *A Sentimental Murder: Love and Madness in the Eighteenth Century* (New York: Farrar, Straus and Giroux, 2004), 60.

1860

NOV 6 "With the Illinois . . . vote for himself," Doris Kearns Goodwin, *Team of Rivals: The Political Genius of Abraham Lincoln* (New York: Simon & Schuster, 2005), 276.

"Rarely mentioning the election," Stephen B. Oates, *With Malice Toward None: The Life of Abraham Lincoln* (New York: Mentor Books, 1977), 205.

"That evening he . . . then Indiana," David Herbert Donald, *Lincoln* (London: Jonathan Cape Random House, 1995), 255.

"He also carried . . . as they arrived," Goodwin, 277.

"At ten came . . . 'Mr. President,'" Donald, *Lincoln*, 255.

"Returns from the South . . . Lincoln said," Oates, 206.

"Ten Southern states . . . on the ballot," David S. Heidler and Jeanne T. Heidler, ed., *Encyclopedia of the American Civil War: A Political, Social and Military History* (New York: W.W. Norton & Co., 2000), 638.

"At two in . . . electoral votes," Donald, *Lincoln*, 256.

SB1 "For one thing . . . turned to Lincoln," James M. McPherson, *Battle Cry of Freedom: The Civil War Era* (New York: Ballantine Books, 1988), 217–20.

"By then the . . . popular vote," Margaret E. Wagner, Gary W. Gallagher, and Paul Finkelman, eds., *Civil War Desk Reference* (New York: Simon & Schuster, 2002), 124–7.

NOV 10 "On November 7 . . . 'have just begun,'" Oates, 211.

"That night . . . set it alight," Goodwin, 293.

"Shortly after the election . . . 'the public mind,'" Truman Smith to Lincoln, November 7, 1860 (Wants Lincoln to clarify his positions publicly), in *ALP*.

"Lincoln, on this . . . 'the more loudly,'" Lincoln to Truman Smith, November 10, 1860, in *CW*, IV, 138–9.

NOV 20 "During the 1860 . . . of sectionalism," Donald, *Lincoln*, 260.

"Once Lincoln . . . fears of Southerners," see Alexander to Lincoln, November 7, 1860 (Lincoln should issue statement on slavery); Truman Smith to Lincoln, November 7, 1860; Truman Smith to Lincoln, November 8, 1860 (Statement of Lincoln's policies), all in *ALP*.

"'I could say' . . . Lincoln responded," Lincoln to Truman Smith, November 10, 1860, in *CW*, 138–9.

"Lincoln was concerned . . . 'misrepresentations,'" Lincoln to George D. Prentice, October 30, 1860, in *CW*, IV, 134–5.

"On this day . . . from Trumbull," Donald, *Lincoln*, 261.

"into which Lincoln. . . 'will be restored,'" passage written for Lyman Trumbull's speech at Springfield, Illinois, November 20, 1860, in *CW*, IV, 141–2.

"Just as Lincoln . . . president-elect lamented," Goodwin, 295.

SB2 "For example . . . 'hostile to slavery,'" see Digital History: http://www.digitalhistory.uh.edu/learning_history/south_secede_mississippi.cfm, http://www.digitalhistory.uh.edu/learning_history/south_secede_texas.cfm, http://www.digitalhistory.uh.edu/learning_history/south_secede/south_secede_southcarolina.cfm, http://www.digitalhistory.uh.edu/learning_history/south_secede/south_secede_georgia.cfm (December 18, 2007).

"Any thorough . . . instead a prediction," William Lee Miller, *Lincoln's Virtues: An Ethical Biography* (New York: Knopf, 2002), 121–2, 192–3, 234–7, 290, 353–65, 380, 434.

NOV 30 "Lincoln and the . . . for Georgia," Donald, *Lincoln*, 121–2.

"After Lincoln's . . . depart the Union," Heidler, 1859.

"On this . . . November 14 speech," Earl Schenck Miers, *Lincoln Day by Day: A Chronology 1809–1865*, Vol. II (Dayton, Ohio: Morningside, 1991), 299.

"Stephens responded . . . 'him than you,'" Alexander Stephens to Lincoln, December 14, 1860 (Sectional Crisis), in *ALP*.

"Lincoln wrote . . . 'our common country,'" Lincoln to Alexander Stephens, December 22, 1860, in *CW*, 160–1.

"Lincoln briefly . . . post to Stephens," John D. Defrees to Lincoln, December 15, 1860 (Suggest appointing Alexander Stephens to cabinet in order to avoid secession), in *ALP*.

DEC 5 "Lincoln, on . . . secession crisis," Miers, Vol. II, 300.

"While Buchanan . . . deflect the crisis," Heidler, 304.

"He tried to appeal. . . away from the Union," John B. Wooley and Gerhard Peters, *The American Presidency Project*, University of California at Santa Barbara, in a reprint of "James

Buchanan Fourth Annual Message, December 3rd, 1860," and on their website, http://www.presidency.ucsb.edu/ws/print.php?pid=29501 (January 9, 2008).

"Lincoln's anger . . . entire message," Miers, Vol. II, 300.

DEC 18 "During and after . . . 'given them,'" Donald, *Lincoln*, 259–61.

"Raymond had forwarded . . . 'unpatriotic avowals,'" William C. Smedes to Henry J. Raymond, December 8, 1860 (Secessionist sentiment in Mississippi), in *ALP*.

"'What a very . . . to be false?'" Lincoln to Henry J. Raymond, December 18, 1860, in *CW*, IV, 156.

DEC 24 "Shortly after Lincoln's . . . around him," David Detzer, *Allegiance: Fort Sumter, Charleston, and the Beginning of the Civil War* (New York: Harcourt Inc., 2001), 57–63.

"The Carolinians . . . men to Sumter," McPherson, 265.

"In Springfield . . . 'after the inaugeration,'" Lincoln to Elihu B. Washburne, December 21, 1860, in *CW*, IV.

"Then on this . . . 'retaken after the inaugeration,'" Lincoln to Lyman Trumbull, December 24, 1860, in *CW*, IV, 162.

"During the . . . 'not go back,'" Detzer, 113–20, 125–6.

DEC 27 "The first was by . . . Lincoln Memorial," Harold Holzer, "The Many Images of Lincoln," *Antique Trader*, April 1995, and reprinted on the Abraham Lincoln Art Gallery website, http://www/abrahamlincolnartgallery.com/referenceholzerpg1.html (February 29, 2008).

"Jones came to . . . write or read," Miers, Vol. II, 303.

"During one . . . February 1865," Holzer, see above.

"When comparing Volk's . . . 'passeth understanding,'" Ervin S. Chapman, *Latest Light on Abraham Lincoln and War-Time Memories: Including Many Heretofore Unpublished Incidents and Historical Facts Concerning His Ancestry, Boyhood, Family, Religion, Public Life, Trials and Triumphs* (New York: Fleming H. Revell Company, 1917), 78–9. In *GBS*.

1861

JAN 3 "At the 1860 . . . or Treasury," Goodwin, 290.

"Lincoln's . . . 'shockingly bad,'" Donald, *Lincoln*, 266.

"By mid-January . . . Cameron's appointment," House of Representatives Republicans to Abraham Lincoln, January 19, 1861(Petition protesting appointment of Cameron), in *ALP*.

"'Things have developed . . . tender,'" Abraham Lincoln to Simon Cameron, January 3, 1861(Lincoln will not appoint Cameron to cabinet), in *ALP*.

"Cameron refused . . . Secretary of War," Goodwin, 313.

SB3 "Despite a persistent... obeyed him," ibid., 246. There are accounts from participants of the 1860 Republican Convention that support both contentions that Lincoln's managers promised cabinet positions in exchange for support or did not. If they did not, they no doubt wished they could have, particularly after Lincoln ordered them not to "bind" him. The question will probably never be fully resolved.

"'Make no . . . me,'" endorsement on the margin of the *Missouri Democrat*, May 17, 1860, in *CW*, IV, 50.

JAN 11 "The most serious . . . reversing these amendments," Heidler, 520.

"'would lose. . . election,'" Lincoln to Thurlow Weed, December 17, 1860, in *CW*, IV, 154.

"'The tug . . . hereafter,'" Lincoln to Lyman Trumbull, December 10, 1860, in *CW*, IV, 149–50.

"'What is . . . government,'" Lincoln to James Hale, January 11, 1861, in *CW*, IV, 172.

"'put us . . . empire,'" Lincoln to William Seward, February 1, 1861, in *CW*, IV, 183.

SB4 "'I do not . . . will,'" Lincoln to Duff Green, December 28, 1860, in *CW*, IV, 162–3.

"The Crowin Amendment . . . states," Phillip Van Doren Stern, *Prologue to Sumter: The Beginnings of the Civil War from the John Brown Raid to the Surrender of Fort Sumter* (Greenwich, CT: Fawcett Publications, 1961), 296.

JAN 12 "One of the former . . . a day," Miers, Vol. III, 5. Unless otherwise noted, all further footnotes from Miers will be from Volume III.

"Many other . . . 'for an Indian,'" Carl Sandburg, *Abraham Lincoln: The Prairie Years and The War Years* (New York: Harcourt, Brace, & World, Inc., 1954), 186.

"So many . . . 'commit himself,'" Stern, 152–3.

JAN 24 "On this Thursday . . . East," Miers, 7.

"Mary had been . . . first lady," Donald, *Lincoln*, 271.

"Even in . . . shirttails," Phillip B. Kunhardt, Jr., Phillip B. Kunhardt III, Peter Kunhardt, *Lincoln: An Illustrated Biography* (New York: Alfred A. Knopf, 1992), 321.

"'He probably . . . comprehension,'" Henry C. Whitney, *Life on the Circuit with Lincoln: With Sketches of Generals Grant, Sherman, and McClellan, Judge Davis, Leonard Swett, and Other Contemporaries* (Boston: Estes and Lauriat, 1892), 32. In *GBS*.

"'If ever . . . Lincoln,'" Erasus Darwin Keyes, *Fifty Years' Observations of Men and Events, Civil and Military* (New York: Charles Scribner's Sons, 1884), 421. In *GBS*.

"Lincoln trudged . . . a reporter," Oates, 223.

"With the . . . wardrobe," Kunhardt, *Lincoln*, 136.

SB5 "Lincoln's size . . . formal," in ibid., 321.

"'A little . . . conceits.'" Tyler Dennett, ed., *Lincoln and the Civil War in the Diaries and Letters of John Hay* (New York: Da Capo Press, 1988), 179.

JAN 28 "In order . . . Constitution," Donald, *Lincoln*, 270.

"For privacy . . . House," Ralph Gary, *Following in Lincoln's Footsteps: A Complete Annotated Reference to Hundreds of Historical Sites Visited by Abraham Lincoln* (New York: Carroll & Graf Publishers, 2001), 138, 153.

"Lincoln even . . . Illinois to Washington," Miers, 8.

"Lincoln then . . . inuagural trip," Lincoln to James Sulgrove, Eric Locke, William Wallace, and John F. Wood, January 28, 1861, in *CW*, IV, 181–2.

"He was already . . . preside over," Donald, *Lincoln*, 273.

"Four years . . . Springfield," Dorothy Meserve Kunhardt and Philip B. Kunhardt Jr., *Twenty Days: A Narrative in Text and Pictures of the Assasination of Abraham Lincoln and the Twenty Days and Nights that followed—The Nation in Mourning, the Long Trip Home to Springfield* (Secaucus, NJ: Castle Books, 1965), 140.

JAN 31 "On January . . . 'Sally' Lincoln," Sandburg, 192–3.

"Senator Thomas A. Marshall's house," Miers, 8.

"Sarah had . . . fer it,'" Kunhardt, *Lincoln*, 137, 386.

SB6 "Just two years . . . 'to me,'" in ibid., 38, 42.

FEB 6 "On this . . . Springfield," Miers, 9.

"The Lincolns . . . one of them," Sandburg, 193.

"Many of the . . . afterward," Kunhardt, *Lincoln*, 13.

"Many noted . . . 'New York,'" Donald, *Lincoln*, 272.

SB7 "In the weeks . . . *of Congress*," Kunhardt, *Lincoln*, 134–6.

"He also . . . 'ever happened,'" Donald, *Lincoln*, 272.

"The Lincolns . . . burial," Kunhardt, *Lincoln*, 136, 385.

FEB 8 "Springfield didn't have . . . 1873)," National Park Service website of Lincoln Springfield Home, http://www.nps.gov/liho/home/home.html (May 23, 2008).

"Abraham and Mary . . . green," Kunhardt, *Lincoln*, 70, 98.

"In anticipation . . . a year," Miers, 10.

"Mary went . . . in 1887," in National Park Service website, http://www.nps.gov/liho/home/home.html (May 23, 2008).

FEB 11 "It was raining . . . Springfield," Kunhardt, *Lincoln*, 138.

"(Mary was . . . Indianapolis)," Donald, *Lincoln*, 273.

FEB 14 "Despite a cold . . . see him," Miers, 13.

"'I certainly' . . . than once," see Remarks at Painsville, Ohio, February 16, 1861; Remarks at Westfield, New York, February 16, 1861; Remarks at Little Falls, New York, February 18, 1861; Remarks at Jersey City, New Jersey, February 21, 1861 all in *CW*, all in Volume IV, 218, 219, 223, and 233–4, respectively.

"Some of the small towns . . . (his inauguration)," see Remarks from Balcony at Bates House, Indianapolis, Indiana, February 11, 1861; Remarks at Cadiz Junction, Ohio, February 14, 1861; Remarks at Alliance, Ohio, February 15, 1861, all in *CW*, all in Volume IV, 196, 206, and 215, respectively.

"Three days . . . of the story," Remarks at Thorntown and Lebanon Indiana, February 11, 1861, in *CW*, IV, 192–3.

"On this . . . the future," Remarks at Wellsville, Ohio, February 14, 1861, in *CW*, IV, 207–8.

"Two days later . . . a beard," Miers, 16.

FEB 15 "In Pittsburgh . . . 'an end,'" Speech at Pittsburgh, Pennsylvania, February 15, 1861, in *CW*, IV, 210–5.

"Later that . . . 'of itself,'" Speech at Cleveland, Ohio, February 15, 1861, in *CW*, IV, 215–6.

"Over and . . . than secession)," see Speech from the Balcony of the Bates House at Indianapolis, Indiana, February 11, 1861; Remarks at Lawrenceburg, Indiana, February 12, 1861; Fragment of Speech Intended for Kentuckians, February 12, 1861; Speech at Steubenville, Ohio, February 14, 1861, all in *CW*, all in Volume IV, 194–6, 197, 200–1, 206–7 respectively.

"He challenged . . . 'be injured,'" Reply to Mayor Alexander Henry at Philadelphia, Pennsylvania, February 21, 1861, in *CW*, IV, 238–9.

FEB 21 "On this eleventh . . . Hotel," Miers, 21.

"Late in the . . . 'surrender it,'" Stern, 381, 385–7.

SB8 "Long before . . . 'to them,'" in ibid., 383.

"One of those sources . . . was worried" Donald, *Lincoln*, 277.

"And Captain . . . newspaper reported," Stern, 379–80, 391.

"Lincoln himself . . . he said later," Donald, *Lincoln*, 279.

FEB 23 "On the evening . . . his height," Stern, 388–90.

"The sleeping . . . separately," Donald, *Lincoln*, 278–9.

SB9 "Upon reaching . . . obscenities," Oates, 230.

"Lincoln wired . . . to be meeting," Donald, *Lincoln*, 279.

"Late that afternoon . . . never forget," Stern, 391.

"At Willard's . . . 'it may'," Donald, *Lincoln*, 279–80.

FEB 27 "In 1854 . . . 'injustice,'" in ibid., 170.

"When Douglas . . . grasp," Kunhardt, *Lincoln*, 109–10, 115.

"'Brady and . . . a friend," Harold Holzer, *Lincoln at Cooper Union: The Speech That Made Abraham Lincoln President* (New York: Simon & Schuster, 2004), 5. Lincoln's quote here was recounted by Ward Hill Lamon, who is considered by many historians to be unreliable. But the sentiment embodied in the quote is held by historians—including Mr. Holzer—as consistent with history and Lincoln's beliefs.

"On this . . . the South," Miers, 23.

"Douglas also . . . 'Douglas is!'" Donald, *Lincoln*, 280.

MAR 5 "On this . . . start a war," Kunhardt, *Lincoln*, 146.

"In his letter . . . entire army," Geoffrey Perret, *Lincoln's War: The Untold Story of America's Greatest President as Commander in Chief* (New York: Random House, 2004), 4.

"That evening . . . alternative," Joseph Holt and Winfield Scott to Lincoln, March 5, 1861(Fort Sumter), in *ALP*.

MAR 10 "This Sunday . . . $50 a year," Miers, 27, 45.

"It was church custom . . . be seen," Gary, 352–3.

"The pastor . . . 'beneficial to the Government,'" see Phineas D. Gurley to Lincoln, August 10, 1863 (Introduces Alexander Hagner), October 12, 1864 (Case of Isaac Handy), and March 30, 1864 (Case of Dr. Armstong), all in *ALP*.

"For a year. . . 'was there,'" Goodwin, 454.

"Nine months . . . 'figure,'" Michael Burlingame, ed., *Lincoln Observed: Civil War Dispatches of Noah Brooks* (Baltimore: The Johns Hopkins University Press, 1998), 14.

SB10 "Dr. J. C. Smith . . . his office," Julia Taft Bayne, *Tad Lincoln's Father* (Lincoln, Nebraska: University of Nebraska Press, 2001), 12–4.

MAR 12 "Lincoln was not . . . 'working order,'" Donald, *Lincoln*, 285–6.

"Lincoln, unwillinging . . . in time," Lincoln to Winfield Scott, March 9, 1861, in *CW*, IV, 279.

"On this day . . . 'water transportation,'" Winfield Scott to Lincoln, March 12, 1861 (Report on Fort Sumter), in *ALP*.

"Lincoln, still not . . . plan impractical," Donald, *Lincoln*, 286.

MAR 16 "Lincoln was still . . . 'working order,'" Donald, *Lincoln*, 285–6.

SB11 "In the days after . . . act of war," Detzer, 91, 113, 153, 156–9.

MAR 18 "He would later . . . of command," Donald, *Lincoln*, 285.

"The bureau . . . its legality," Draft of a Proposed Order to Establish a Militia Bureau, March 18, 1861, in *CW*, IV, 291. Also Lincoln to Edward Bates, March 18, 1861, in *CW*, IV, 291–2.

"A month later . . . its appropriations," Edward Bates to Lincoln, April 18, 1861 (Opinion on establishing a militia bureau), in *ALP*.

"'The difficulty . . . situation,'" Donald, *Lincoln*, 285.

MAR 19 "In Lincoln's . . . to that time," William Lee Miller, 101.

"One such . . . that position," Miers, 29.

"He saw them . . . front entrance," Donald, *Lincoln*, 285.

"'Even members' . . . deputy secretary," Frederick Seward, *Reminiscences of a War-Time Statesman and Diplomat 1830–1915* (New York: G.P. Putnam's Sons, 1916), 147–8.

"Lincoln rarely . . . 'mitigate disappointments,'" Goodwin, 281.

"The numbers of . . . Lincoln said," Donald, *Lincoln*, 285.

MAR 29 "By late March . . . to his cabinet," Perrett, 17, 20–1.

"That night . . . making plans," Donald, *Lincoln*, 288–9.

"Lincoln later . . . Sumter crisis," Oates, 240.

MAR 30 "He felt . . . 'is on fire'," Oates, 241.

"On this day . . . wrote Lincoln," Jesse K. Dubois to Lincoln, March 30 1861, in *CW*, IV, 302.

"Dubois, afterward . . . 'whole nature,'" Douglas L. Wilson and Rodney O. Davis, ed., *Herndon's Informants: Letters, Interviews, and Statements about Abraham Lincoln* (Chicago: University of Illinois Press, 1998) in a letter from Jesse K. Dubois to Henry C. Whitney, April 6, 1865, 620.

"Lincoln also . . . the position," Lincoln to John T. Stuart, March 30, 1861, in *CW*, IV, 303.

"Still another . . . his fireplace," Kunhardt, *Lincoln*, 147.

APR 1 "The previous . . . 'ruling party,'" Goodwin, 342.

"Seward sent Lincoln . . . 'of his Cabinet,'" William Seward to Lincoln, April 1, 1861 (Memorandum, "Some thoughts for the President's consideration"), in *ALP*.

"In effect . . . John Nicolay," Goodwin, 342.

"Instead, Lincoln . . . 'must do it,'" Lincoln to William Seward, April 1, 1861, in *CW*, IV, 316–8.

"To save . . . memorandum," Goodwin, 342. There is speculation that Lincoln never gave his response to Seward, preferring to talk to the secretary instead. This is supported by the fact that no written response from Seward has been found and that the letter was found not in Seward's personal papers but in Lincoln's, long after his death. Even Lincoln's personal secretaries were unaware of the exchange.

SB12 "On the day . . . 'as ashes,'" in ibid., 11–2, 250.

"Months later . . . 'Illinois lawyer!'" Michael Knox Beran, *Forge of Empire 1861–1871: Three Revolutionary Statesmen and the World They Made* (New York: Free Press, 2007), 25.

"When Lincoln gave . . . April Fool's Day memorandum," Donald, *Lincoln*, 281–2, 289.

APR 5 "On this Friday . . . Riggs & Co.," Miers, 33.

"A prevalent . . . Tad and Robert," Harry E. Pratt, *The Personal Finances of Abraham Lincoln* (Springfield, IL: The Abraham Lincoln Association, 1943), vii–viii, 124–5, 133–4.

"The Lincolns spent . . . on this day," Miers, 36.

APR 6 "On this Saturday . . . 'will be made,'" Lincoln to Robert S. Chew, April 6, 1861, in *CW*, IV, 323.

"The plan to resupply . . . garrison," Detzer, 230–1.

"To avoid that . . . the offer," Donald, *Lincoln*, 290.

"Lincoln sent his . . . peacefully," Goodwin, 344.

APR 13 "At the beginning . . . commenced," Stern, 496–8, 502.

"'The ball . . . harbor front,'" Goodwin, 348.

"Lincoln's only . . . 'with force,'" Miers, 34–5.

"After thirty–four . . . of the war," Detzer, 304, 308–9.

APR 17 "The day after . . . July 4," Proclamation Calling Militia and Convening Congress, in *CW*, IV, 331–3.

"Lincoln was criticized . . . John Ellis declared," Donald, *Lincoln*, 296–7.

"On this day Virginia . . . the Confederacy," Goodwin, 349.

"On this day Lincoln . . . in Norfolk," Miers, 35–6.

"On April 18 . . . 'my home,'" Kunhardt, *Lincoln*, 148–9.

SB13 "A short time . . . anguished letter," Goodwin, 350–1.

APR 19 "On this day . . . have seaports," Proclamation of a Blockade, April 19, 1861, in *CW*, IV, 338–9.

"The task of . . . added to the navy," Wagner, 543, 547.

"Lincoln's blockade . . . 'as we can,'" Donald, *Lincoln*, 302–3.

SB14 "Some historians . . . by two–thirds," McPherson, 380–2.

"Because the South . . . unaffordable," Wagner, 548, 670.

"Confederate soldiers . . . 'kept together.'" David Eicher, *The Longest Night: A Military History of the Civil War* (New York: Simon & Schuster, 2001), 628.

"While their families . . . 'go [too],'" McPherson, 613.

APR 21 "In response . . . Harrisburg burned," McPherson, 285.

"For the next . . . to Lincoln," Miers, 36–7.

"A Baltimore . . . Lincoln agreed," Dennett, 6.

"There, however . . . 'of entire isolation,'" Goodwin, 353.

"'The whining . . . 'with them,'" Dennett, 7.

"yet another . . . 'they must do,'" Goodwin, 352–3.

APR 24 "With the Washington . . . 'are prisoners,'" in ibid., 353.

"'The town' . . . in his diary," Dennett, 5.

"Government employees . . . skyrocketed," Goodwin, 353.

"Every day there . . . on April 23," Dennett, 10.

"On that same . . . 'Northern realities,'" Goodwin, 354.

"At noon. . . for Lincoln]," Dennett, 11.

APR 25 "Under intense . . . from the Union," Mark E. Neely, Jr., *The Fate of Liberty: Abraham Lincoln and Civil Liberty* (New York: Oxford University Press, 1991), 6.

"If Maryland . . . logistical disaster," Oates, 255.

"Lincoln had considered . . . 'their action,'" Lincoln to Winfield Scott, April 25, 1861, in *CW*, IV, 344.

"It was a wise . . . it legal," Perret, 39.

APR 27 "Writs (written . . . before the court," Heidler, 906.

"This assured . . . without a trial," Neely, xiv, xvi.

"The spark . . . on April 25," Perret, 36, 39–40.

"Still, Lincoln had . . . to Washington," Neely, 8.

"Scott was allowed . . . 'public safety,'" Message to Congress in Special Session, July 4, 1861, in *CW*, IV, 421–41.

APR 29 "One was Senator–elect . . . rebels attack," Jerrold Packard, *The Lincolns in the White House: Four Years that Shattered a Family* (New York: St. Martin's Press, 2005), 45.

"John Hay, one . . . 'like hell,'" Dennett, 9, 13.

"Cassius Clay . . . protect Washington," Heidler, 449–50.

"Hay recorded . . . 'yellow–covered romance,'" Dennett, 8.

"Lincoln, on this . . . citizen soldiers," Miers, 38.

MAY 1 "Fox had been . . . was ignored," Donald, *Lincoln*, 291–2.

"In his report . . . 'justified by the result,'" Lincoln to Gustavus V. Fox, May 1, 1861, in *CW*, IV, 350–1.

SB15 "Some argue that . . . from the rebels," see Thomas J. DiLorenzo, *The Real Lincoln: A New Look at Abraham Lincoln, His Agenda, and an Unnecessary War* (New York: Three Rivers Press, 2003), 118–22. Professor DiLorenzo cites Shelby Foote's masterful *Civil War: A Narrative* to support his contention that Lincoln deliberately mislead the

Confederate government in order to spark the war. A closer look at Foote's text shows that he believed the opposite and that if Davis and his government were mislead, it was unintentional, "For though Lincoln himself had practiced no deception (at least not toward the Confederates) [Secretary of State William] Seward's well-meant misrepresentations had led exactly to that effect." (see Foote, Vol. I, 46–8 and for his full explanation of that statement found on page 47).

"Then there is . . . 'repelling that aggression,'" Orville H. Browning to Lincoln, February 17, 1861 (Inaugural address), in *ALP*.

"When Browning . . . 'otherwise could,'" Donald, *Lincoln*, 293.

"During the month . . . 'It is fatal,'" Shelby Foote, *The Civil War: A Narrative* (New York: Random House, Vol. 1–1958, Vol. II–1963, and Vol. III–1974) Vol. I, 44–8.

MAY 4 "On May 2 . . . Saturday in 1861," Lincoln to William H. Seward, May 4, 1861 (Meeting with Maryland commissioners), in *ALP*.

"'The Maryland Disunionists' . . . his actions," Dennett, 18.

MAY 21 "Lincoln had . . . foreign affairs," Donald, *Lincoln*, 320–1.

"Britain's textile . . . he exploded," McPherson, 383, 388.

"Seward responded . . . war could ensue," William Seward to Charles F. Adams, May 21, 1861 (Instructions on how to deal with the British; with revisions in Lincoln's hand), in *ALP*.

SB16 "When Queen . . . of $15.5 million," Wagner, 144, 202–3.

"When Britain . . . or face conscription," Heidler, 875.

"Lincoln's blockade . . . the situation," Wagner, 202–3.

MAY 24 "Early on this . . . Springfield law office," Perret, 50, 7.

"Ellsworth became . . . (New York Regiment)," Oates, 253.

"Young Tad . . . Zouave uniform," Kunhardt, *Lincoln*, 150.

"On May 23 . . . killed himself," Perret, 49–50.

"Ellsworth was . . . it stored away," Oates, 259.

MAY 27 "Only about . . . and/or talented officers," Perret, 51.

"On May 14 . . . to colonel," Warner, 318.

"likely because . . . food and ammunition," Perret, 51.

"Even as Lincoln . . . Meigs appointed," Miers, 44.

"For one thing . . . the position," see Simon Cameron to Lincoln, June 10, 1861 (Promotion of Col. Charles Thomas) and Charles Thomas to James Buchanan, June 19, 1861 (Printed Letter concerning U.S. Army Quartermaster) both in *ALP*.

"But Cameron's . . . Department affairs," Perret, 51.

"For weeks Lincoln . . . mind in June," Lincoln to Winfield Scott, June 5, 1861, in *CW*, IV, 394–5.

"Meigs served with . . . buried there," Warner, 319.

"His most enduring . . . Arlington Cemetery," Perret, 52.

MAY 30 "On this Friday . . . the Supreme Court," Lincoln to Edward Bates, May 30, 1861, in *CW*, IV, 390.

"On April 27 . . . Lincoln's suspension," Heidler, 668.

"On May 28 . . . 'malfeasance in office,'" Taney's opinion was reprinted under *The Merryman Case*, *New York Times*, June 4, 1861, 9 and can be found in the *Times*' archives online, http://query.nytimes.com/gst/abstract.html?res=9907E4DA103BE63BBC4C53DFB066838A679FDE (August 13, 2008).

"Taney's opinion . . . commander in chief," Edward Bates to Lincoln, July 5, 1861 (Opinion on suspension of writ of habeas corpus), in *ALP*.

"Taney was . . . still in 1862," David M. Silver, *Lincoln's Supreme Court* (Urbana, Illinois: University of Illinois Press, 1956), 33–4.

JUN 3 "One of the things . . . Union's war effort," Heidler, 2059–60; also Donald, *Lincoln*, 313–4.

"The day . . . 'preserve the Union,'" Donald, *Lincoln*, 296.

"On his way . . . 'and traitors,'" Heidler, 614.

"During that . . . could not recover," Goodwin, 348.

"When word reached . . . thirty days," Miers, 46.

"In a memo . . . 'in foreign lands,'" Fragment on Stephen A. Douglas, [December, 1856?], in *CW*, II, 382–3.

JUN 13 "Lincoln, on this . . . Simon Cameron," Miers, 48.

"Berdan had been . . . fifteen years," Heidler, 217.

"used his clout . . . for the Sharps," Perret, 150–1.

"Dubbed the First . . . rest of the war," Heidler, 217–8.

"The Confederates effectively utilized . . . shot dead," Wagner, 494.

JUN 17 "When the Lincolns . . . York to shop," Goodwin, 359.

"To replace . . . china set," Packard, 53.

"She also purchased a new $900 carriage," Goodwin, 359.

"vases and . . . French wallpaper," Packard, 53–4.

"It was during . . . 'Lincoln bed,'" Goodwin, 359.

"On May 29 . . . Monday approved it," Lincoln to Salmon P. Chase, June 15, 1861, in *CW*, IV, 407.

SB17 "For each four–year . . . old and worn," Packard, 50.

"'The family apartments' . . . Grimsely observed," Goodwin, 359.

"One of Lincoln's . . . 'and without,'" William Stoddard, *Inside the White House in War Times: Memoirs and Reports of Lincoln's Secretary* (Lincoln, NE: University of Nebraska Press, 2000), 5.

"Another visitor . . . 'hotel,'" Elizabeth Smith Brownstein, *Lincoln's Other White House: The Untold Story of the Man and His Presidency* (Hoboken, NJ: John Wiley and Sons, 2005), 37.

"What's worse . . . take mementos," Packard, 50–1.

"Lincoln's secretary . . . ruining the carpet," Stoddard, 5, 183.

"Mary's efforts . . . 'blankets,'" Donald, *Lincoln*, 313.

JUN 18 "One evening . . . Coulincourt Lowe," Perret, 148.

"Lowe was a balloonist . . . to the ground," Wagner, 362.

"To demonstrate . . . 'aerial station,'" Thaddeus S. C. Lowe to Lincoln, June 16, 1861 (Telegram from balloon), in *ALP*. The editors of Abraham Lincoln Papers date this telegram as June 16, but Miers dates it as June 18 (49) as does Heidler (1,228) and Perret (425). Wagner dates it as June 17 (362).

"Impressed, Lincoln . . . Army of the Potomac," Perret, 148.

"Often . . . own balloon reconnaissance," Wagner, 364–5.

"Lowe and his . . . shortly afterward," Heidler, 1228.

JUN 22 "In the early . . . 'no anything,'" Goodwin, 366.

"When, in April 15; 1861 Lincoln called . . . 575,000 soldiers," Eicher, 58.

"Traditionally . . . military qualifications," McPherson, 323, 326–7.

"To help Cameron . . . expecting them," Perret, 44–5.

"On this day . . . accepted the request," Lincoln to Simon Cameron, June 22, 1861, in *CW*, IV, 415.

JUN 29 "On this Saturday . . . one would fail," Perret, 54–60.

JUL 20 "On this Saturday . . . Run (Manassas)," Miers, 55.

"McDowell's plan . . . remained oblivious," McPherson, 335–6, 339–40.

"'General Johnston' . . . seasoned troops," Perret, 59, 64–5.

JUL 21 "Sunday, July 21 . . . watch the battle," in ibid., 65.

"After church . . . in the distance," Goodwin, 371.

"'Rapid firing . . . 'slackened,'" Manassas Virginia Telegraph, July 21, 1861 (Dispatches), in *ALP*.

"Later, 'Still' . . . interrupted it," Perret, 66–7.

"Union forces . . . 'of the Army,'" Goodwin, 371–2.

JUL 23 "Lincoln didn't sleep . . . never came," in ibid., 373–5.

"That same day . . . list of policy changes," Perret, 68–9, 71.

"Lincoln recommended . . . and western theaters," Memoranda of Military Policy Suggested by the Bull Run Defeat, July 23, 1861, in *CW*, IV, 457–8.

"Later in the day . . . than his own," Miers, 56.

SB18 "Colonel William . . . 'hell of a fix,'" Perret, 16

"Lincoln and Sherman . . . Fort Cocoran," Miers, 56.

"Sherman's men . . . 'spoil any set of men,'" Perret, 72–3.

"After Lincoln delivered . . . 'not military,'" Goodwin, 375

'Afterward, one . . . 'would do it!'" Perret, 73.

JUL 27 "Lincoln, on this . . . capital defenses," Miers, 57

"General in Chief . . . virtual unknown," Perret, 70–2, 129–30.

"Not so with . . . 'this country,'" Eicher, 86–7.

"Instead of following . . . coming months," Perret, 72.

AUG 2 "When the Union . . . among them," Donald, *Lincoln*, 307.

"During the battle . . . 'time tomorrow,'" Goodwin, 371.

"When the Union army . . . captured him," Eicher, 98–9.

"Colonel James Cameron . . . exhanged and sent home," Lincoln to House of Representatives, August 2, 1861, in *CW*, IV, 469.

"Along with Ely . . . Libby Prison," Eicher, 99.

AUG 3 "On this Saturday . . . a 'bootmaker,'" Packard, 71–2.

AUG 5 "Lincoln, on this . . . income tax," Wagner, 10.

"For much of . . . and property sales," from Department of Treasury Fact Sheet on the Web, http://www.treas.gov/education/fact-sheets/taxes/ustax.shtml (June 11, 2007).

"When the Civil . . . $800 annually," McPherson, 443.

"The law was . . . uncollected . . . every profession," Fact sheet from Department of Treasury (see above).

"While the income . . . permanent fixture," Wagner, 20.

"It would not . . . imposed again," Fact sheet from Department of Treasury (see above).

AUG 6 "On this Tuesday . . . to date," Miers, 59.

"When Congress . . . "'provisions of the Constitution,'" Donald, *Lincoln*, 304–5, 313–4.

"Lincoln's July 5 . . . 'one be violated?'" Message to Congress in Special Session, July 4, 1861, in *CW*, IV, 422–41.

AUG 15 "At the outbreak . . . lost his life," McPherson, 290–2, 350–2.

"Lincoln also gave . . . Lincoln told Fremont," Perret, 82.

"Fremont began . . . Sec'y of War," see telegrams John C. Fremont to Lincoln on August 5 (Situation in Missouri), August 6 (Military affairs in Missouri), August 11 (Sends messenger), August 13 (Telegram reporting battle of Wilson's Creek), and August 14 (Telegram requesting Lincoln to read his dispatch), all in 1861, all in *ALP*.

"On this day . . . on the way," Lincoln to John C. Fremont, August 15, 1861, in *CW*, IV, 484–5.

"On this same . . . battalions westward," see Lincoln to John A. Gurley and Lincoln to Oliver P. Morton, both August 15, 1861, in *CW*, IV, 485.

AUG 16 "Lincoln, on this . . . 'other [union] States,'" Proclamation Forbidding Intercourse with Rebel States, August 16, 1861, in *CW*, IV, 487–8.

"Despite the . . . or necessities," McPherson, 620–1.

"The irony is . . . at the law," Heidler, 820.

"The Union also . . . smuggled illegally," McPherson, 624–5.

AUG 17 "Near the stump . . . 'coffee-mill gun,'" Miers, 61.

"On this day . . . coffee grinder)," Perret, 153.

"But the Gatling . . . central axis," Heidler, 817.

"While Lincoln . . . McClellan agreed," Perret, 147, 153.

"While a few . . . issued to Union troops," Wagner, 488.

"Ripley stonewalled . . . May 1864," Heidler, 817–8.

SB19 "While several flame throwers . . . 'Greek fire,'" Perret, 153–4.

"These shells . . . did not agree," Current, 179–81.

"One inventor . . . 'colonel of it,'" Perret, 145–6, 154.

AUG 24 "Kentucky was . . . through Kentucky," in ibid., 299–300.

"Despite commercial . . . officers for them," McPherson, 293–5.

"'In a word . . . of this state,'" Beriah Magoffin to Lincoln, August 19, 1861 (Situation in Kentucky), in *ALP*.

"Lincoln countered . . . 'so remove it,'" Lincoln to Beriah Magoffin, August 24, 1861, in *CW*, IV, 497.

AUG 31 "Hatteras Inlet . . . Union fatality," Heidler, 946–7.

"Back in Washigton . . . Hatteras victory," Miers, 63.

"'This was our first . . . be forgotten,'" Eicher, 109.

SEP 2 "The president may . . . 'declared freemen,'" Perret, 82, 84.

"While Fremont . . . in the press," Goodwin, 390.

"Fremont's proclamation . . . not civilians," Donald, *Lincoln*, 314.

"Weary of . . . 'for man, indefinitely,'" Lincoln to John C. Fremont, September 2, 1861 (Fremont's August 30 Proclamation), in *ALP*.

SEP 9 "In July . . . Hamilton Gamble," Goodwin, 389.

"Unmonitored . . . competitive bidding," Oates, 283.

"On September 5 . . . Winfield Scott," Miers, 64.

"asking if Hunter . . . for the position," Winfield Scott to Lincoln, September 5, 1861 (Fremont and situation in Missouri), in *ALP*.

"Lincoln decided . . . given Fremont's command," Lincoln to David Hunter, September 9, 1861, in *CW*, IV, 513.

SEP 10 "As reports came . . . January 30, 1862," James L. Nelson, *Reign of Iron: The Story of the First Battling Ironclads, the Monitor and the Merrimack* (New York: HarperCollins Publishers, 2004), 83, 85–9, 101–5, 130–6, 189.

SEP 11 "Fremont, as the . . . Lincoln said coldly," Perret, 87–8.

"Jesse countered . . . later related," Goodwin, 392.

"Lincoln dismissed . . . his proclamation," Donald, *Lincoln*, 315.

"Lincoln later . . . 'with her,'" Goodwin, 392.

SEP 16 "General John . . . Blair family," Miers, 67.

"It was the Blairs . . . to a duel," Goodwin, 389–93.

"Jesse demanded . . . Lincoln refused," Lincoln to Mrs. John C. Fremont, September 12, 1861, in *CW*, IV, 519–20.

"Jesse returned . . . for insubordination," Heidler, 786.

"When Lincoln . . . any military trial," Goodwin, 393.

SEP 30 "Lincoln, on . . . 'against the Government,'" Miers, 69.

"Maryland was . . . morre determined," McPherson, 289.

"In later summer . . . three congressmen," Neely, 15–6.

"editor of the . . . night of September 12," John A. Dix to Simon Cameron, September 13, 1861 (Arrests made in Baltimore), in *ALP*.

"Still more . . . in Frederick," short notice in the *New York Times*, September 18, 1861 found in *Times* archive, http://www.nytimes.com/ref/membercenter/nyarchive.html (November 26, 2008).

"These political . . . November 1862," McPherson, 289.

SB20 "This was due . . . was arrested," in ibid., 284–9.

"Secessionist newspapers . . . newspaper owners," "Abraham Lincoln and Maryland," article posted on *Abraham Lincoln's Classroom*, a website sponsored by the Lincoln Institute and the Lehman's Institute, http://www.abrahamlincolnsclassroom.org/Library/newsletter.asp?ID=108&CRLI=156 (September 17, 2007).

OCT 8 "The Lincolns . . . artillery units," Miers, 71.

"While the actual . . . conducted in the field," see ibid., 38–45, 47–9, 51–2, 58–9, 62, 64–5, 67–8, 71, 78, 81, 84, 87, 110, 114, 122, 142–3, 146, 151, 178, 220, 254, 267, 283, 291, 322–3, 326 for the recorded reviews.

"General Ulysses . . . 'has been universal,'" Goodwin, 452, 629–30.

"As one sargeant . . . 'palmiest days,'" Perret, 348.

OCT 19 "on this day . . . John Dahlgren," Miers, 41, 72.

"Lincoln was so with the experiment," Perret, 147.

"he returned . . . during the war," ordnance test dates, May 1, May 30, June 11, July 24, 1861; May 3, August 7, November 15, 1862; May 29, July 14, 1863; June 25, 1864. See Miers, 41, 45, 47, 50, 109, 132, 150, 187, 197, 268.

"The president also . . . 'from politicians,'" Perret, 147.

"On November 15 . . . unscathed," Miers, 150.

"Seven months earlier . . . to safety," Perret, 154.

"It was at the . . . *Merrimack*," Miers, 99.

"And on the last . . . on the *Montauk*," Kunhardt, *Twenty Days*, 19, 181.

OCT 20 "On this Sunday . . . his congratulations," Lincoln to Frank Fuller, October 20, 1861, in *CW*, IV, 558.

"The Civil War . . . Virginia, siege," Wagner, 353–5.

"Both sides developed . . . during the war," Eicher, 300.

"While telegraphs . . . 'Atlantic States,'" James Gamble, "Wiring a Continent: The Making of the U.S. Transcontinental Telegraph Line," originally published in *The Californian*, 1881 and on the Internet at http://www.telegraph-history.org/transcontinental-telegraph/index.html (October 30, 2007).

OCT 21 "By October . . . 'and dancing,'" Donald, *Lincoln*, 318.

"Finally, McClellan . . . the attack," Perret, 93.

"Lincoln and . . . son after Baker," Kunhardt, *Lincoln*, 160.

"Baker spent his . . . 'and abandon,'" Goodwin, 381.

"The next day . . . fifty Confederates," Eicher, 126–7.

"Lincoln received . . . into the street," Goodwin, 381.

OCT 27 "In the three . . . Fremont's dismissal," Goodwin, 389–95.

"On this day . . . October 25," Dennett, 32.

SB21 "Lincoln's delay . . . Lincoln's actions," Goodwin, 394–5.

"Fremont was extremely . . . nominee," Warner, 161.

"darling of Radical . . . 'into my lines?'" Goodwin, 393–6.

NOV 1 "While the seventy–five . . . the field," Warner, 429–30

"What was more . . . McClellan responded," Perret, 76–7, 92–3, 97–9.

"The next morning . . . 'see him off'" Goodwin, 382.

"The truth . . . to Scott," Perret, 99.

SB22 "Scott, known . . . mount a horse," Heidler, 1,717–8. For a listing of some of the Civil War generals who served under Scott in Mexico, see John C. Waugh, *The Class of 1846: From West Point to Appomattox: Stonewall Jackson, George McClellan and their Brothers* (New York: Ballantine Books, 1994), ix–xvi.

"Still, Lincoln . . . 'that is in the way,'" Goodwin, 378–9.

"In August 1861 . . . 'orders,' Scott said," Perret, 77–8, 92–3.

"He told Secretary . . . 'of the Union,'" Goodwin, 379.

NOV 13 "McClellan's headquarters . . . the White House," Richard M. Lee, *Mr. Lincoln's City: An Illustrated Guide to the Civil War Sites of Washington* (McLean, VA: EPM Publications, 1981), 132, 138.

"Lincoln visited . . . bring a victory," Goodwin, 379, 383.

"Then on this . . . 'gone to bed,'" Dennett, 34–5.

NOV 15 "In March 1861 . . . of nationhood," Foote, I, 134–8.

"By then . . . just off Havana," Perret, 102.

"At noon on . . . wired Washington," Heidler, 1972.

"Lincoln—along . . . at the news," Goodwin, 397.

"but asked his . . . action was legal," Perret, 103.

SB23 "When the South . . . India and Egypt," Wagner, 201–4.

"Nevertheless, it's clear . . . Lincoln said," McPherson, 546, 554–5.

"In July 1862 . . . Britain refused," Heidler, 1453.

NOV 16 "Lincoln, on this . . . [his] Regiment," Lincoln to Lorenzo Thomas, November 16, 1861, in *CW*, V, 25.

"In 1861 . . . 'of some of them,'" Benjamin B. French to Lincoln, October 15, 1861 (White House employees), in *ALP*.

"There was another . . . never made," Goodwin, 401.

"Watt, for instance . . . was provided," Michael Burlingame, *The Inner World of Abraham Lincoln* (Chicago: University of Illinois Press, 1997), 302.

"Worse, Watt . . . duties herself," Packard, 88.

"In exchange . . . enlisted as a private," Burlingame, *Inner World*, 303, 341.

SB24 "In the waning . . . was inadequate," Donald, *Lincoln*, 312.

"She asked . . . military spending bill," Goodwin, 401–2.

NOV 28 "Lincoln spent . . . and his wife," Miers, 79.

"Thanksgiving is a . . . days of the year," *New Standard Encyclopedia* Vol. 17 (Chicago: Standard Education Corporation, 1993), 211–2.

"For instance . . . November 29," Miers, Vol. II, 299 and Vol. III, 79.

"But until the Civil . . . was ratified," *New Standard Encyclopedia*, Vol. 17, 212.

"Hale was an accomplished . . . from 1836–77)," in ibid., Vol. 8, 16a–b.

"As editor of . . . Lincoln wrote," Proclamation of Thanksgiving, October 3, 1863, in *CW*, 496–7.

"Thanksgiving was usually . . . of the month," New Standard Encyclopedia, Vol. 17, 212.

NOV 29 "Lincoln, on this . . . to Congress," Miers, 79.

"In her first . . . Blue Room," Goodwin, 384.

"Her guests . . . 'influence over her,'" Henry Villard, *Memoirs of Henry Villard: Journalist and Financier 1835–1900* (New York: Houghton Mifflin and Company, 1904), 156–7.

"One such flatterer . . . lavish spending," Packard, 87.

"When the *Herald* . . . the leak," Donald, *Lincoln*, 324–5.

"confirmed Wikoff's . . . 'and Wikoff liberated,'" Ben Perley Poore, *Perley's Reminiscences of Sixty Years in the National Metropolis*, vol. 2 (Philadelphia: Hubbard Brothers, Publishers, 1886), 143.

"In February, 1862 . . . 'Mansion [White House] that night,'" Burlingame, *Inner World*, 305–6.

DEC 3 "On this Tuesday . . . 'well as regiments,'" Annual Message to Congress, December 3, 1861, in *CW*, V, 35–53.

"At the start . . . regimental elections," Wagner, 438.

"Sometime in September . . . on the subject," see Form Letter to Chaplains, December 3, 1861; Lincoln to F. M. Magrath, October 30, 1861; Lincoln to John J. Hughes, October 21, 1861, all in *CW*, the latter in Vol. IV and the other two in Vol. V, 53–54, 8–9, and 559–60 respectively.

"On May 20 . . . 600 at one time)," Wagner, 439–40.

"Almost all of them . . . African American chaplain," Heidler, 402–3, 1070.

"But at least . . . to let her serve," Wagner, 438–40.

DEC 26 "Lincoln, along with . . . in November," Miers, 85.

"Mason and . . . to Canada," Heidler, 1972–3.

"Secretary of State . . . told Seward," Goodwin, 398–400.

"The commissioners . . . the Confederacy," Heidler, 1973–4.

1862

JAN 6 "On this . . . be fired," Miers, 87.

"The previous month . . . earlier," Donald, *Lincoln*, 326–7.

"There is . . . refused," ibid., 329.

JAN 10 "Lincoln began . . . Confederacy," Donald, *Lincoln*, 328–30.

JAN 13 "Cameron was corrupt . . . admitted," Goodwin, 401–2

"But even . . . refused," Donald, *Lincoln*, 325.

"The final straw . . . the report," Goodwin, 404–5.

"When Lincoln . . . new post," Donald, *Lincoln*, 326.

"Lincoln then . . . 'be stopped,'" Kunhardt, *Lincoln*, 172.

SB25 "For one . . . gouging," McPherson, 324.

"The War Department spent . . . shoes," Oates, 299.

"Half wool blankets . . . blankets," Donald, *Lincoln*, 325.

"Textile contractors . . . quality," McPherson, 324.

JAN 26 "Flag Officer . . . 'brimstone,'" Current, 178.

"The manufacture . . . production," Miers, 92.

"Lincoln later . . . 'presented to him,'" Current, 178–81.

JAN 27 "Still waiting . . . Lincoln's strategy," Perret, 122–3.

"With the help . . . single massive battle," Archer Jones, *Civil War Command and Strategy: The Process of Victory and Defeat* (New York: Free Press, 1992), 99–101.

"In response . . . south," Perret, 123–4.

FEB 2 "At the White . . . Waldo Emerson," Miers, 93.

"Lincoln pointed . . . his honor," in ibid., Vol. II, 91. See also Gay Wilson Allen, *Waldo Emerson: A Biography* (New York: Viking Press, 1981), 606.

"He was also . . . 'their bowels,'" from a speech Emerson delivered titled "War" and delivered in March, 1838 in Boston, Massachusetts, in *CWRE*, XI (Miscellanies), 151–76.

"That same war . . . Smithsonian Institute," Allen, 597, 611–3.

"he found . . . 'cheerfulness'," Linda Allardt, David W. Hill, Ruth H. Bennett, eds., *The Journals and Miscellaneous Notebooks of Ralph Waldo Emerson*, Volume XV, 1860–1866 (Cambridge, MA, The Belknap Press of Harvard University Press, 1982), 187.

SB26 "'He has been . . . success,'" speech titled "Emancipation Proclamation" delivered in Boston, Massachusetts September, 1862, in *CWRE*, XI, 313–26.

"'Then, what . . . tongue,'" speech titled "Abraham Lincoln, Remarks at the Funeral Services Held in Concord [Massachusetts], April 19, 1865," in *CWRE*, XI, 327–38.

FEB 4 "While the United . . . sentence of death," Anne Farrow, Joel Lang, and Jennifer Frank, *Complicity: How the North Promoted, Prolonged, and Profited from Slavery* (New York: Ballantine Books, 2005), 121–4.

"Some 250,000 . . . and 1860," James Haskins and Kathleen Benson, *Bound for America: The Forced Migration of Africans to the New World* (New York: Lothrop, Lee & Shepard Books, 1999), 46.

"Gordon appealed . . . 'all men,'" Stay of Execution for Nathaniel Gordon, February 4, 1862, in *CW*, V, 128–9. The record indicates that Lincoln did consider commuting Gordon's sentence even after he granted a temporary stay of execution. Lincoln received several petitions for clemency and apparently had Attorney General Edward Bates look over the evidence. Bates wrote Lincoln that the evidence against Gordon was strong and that Gordon had a fair trial. Bates recommended that Lincoln not interfere with the execution. Lincoln followed his advice. See Edward Bates to Lincoln, February 17, 1862 (Case of Nathaniel Gordon) and February 19, 1862 (Case of Nathaniel Gordon), both in *ALP*.

"Gordon attempted . . . strychnine," Farrow, 124.

FEB 5 "In the first . . . 'and dancing'," Packard, 115–6.

"First ever in the White House," Goodwin, 415.

"During the . . . their guests," Packard, 114–5.

"'He [Lincoln] . . . failure,'" Sandburg, 290.

"Mary left . . . own pocket," Packard, 114–8.

FEB 12 "South of . . . of 1862," Brownstein, 53–4.

"the Lincolns . . . 'right in,'" Goodwin, 420.

"Willie had . . . Wales room," Kunhardt, *Lincoln*, 291.

"Mary was . . . his side," Goodwin, 419.

"The president . . . eleven–year–old," Oates, 314.

SB27 "William Wallace . . . brother–in–law," Kunhardt, *Lincoln*, 91.

"who had . . . his father," Donald, *Lincoln*, 154.

"Willie had a . . . people's feelings," Sandburg, 290.

"Willie memorized . . . two cities," Goodwin, 332.

"as he watched . . . 'results,'" Donald, *Lincoln*, 159.

"Julia Taft . . . 'gentle-mannered,'" Bayne, 3.

"Mary's cousin . . . 'was handsome'," Goodwin, 332.

FEB 16 "At daybreak . . . 'of the Confederacy,'" Eicher, 178–80.

"In Washington . . . 'Surrender' Grant," Peret, 135–6.

FEB 20 "At five . . . 'him die'," Packard, 120.

"'My poor boy . . . him so,'" Oate*s*, 314.

"'Great sobs . . . child,'" Packard, 120.

"'I did not . . . so moved,'" Goodwin, 419.

"Lincoln then . . . to cry," Oates, 314.

FEB 24 "At noon . . . last time," Packard, 121.

"As he lay . . . coffin," Kunhardt, *Twenty Days*, 136.

"Willie was . . . little hands," Sandburg, 290.

"During the . . . official Washington," Packard, 121.

"It was the first . . . House," Kunhardt, *Lincoln*, 175.

"Afterward . . . the storm," Packard, 122.

"Willie was . . . dead son," Kunhardt, *Lincoln*, 291.

FEB 25 "Before the war . . . Southern planters," Gary Walton and Ross M. Robertson, *History of the American Economy* (New York: Harcourt, Brace and Jovanovich, 1983), 168.

"When Andrew Jackson . . . bankrupt banks," Karen Flamme, *1995 Annual Report: A Brief History of Our Nation's Paper Money* (The Federal Reserve Bank of San Francisco, 1995 Annual Report) found at http://www.frbsf.org/publications/federalreserve/annual/1995/history.html (June 6, 2008).

"By the end . . . and public debt," Heidler, 1167.

"Lincoln signed . . . system of banks," Miers, 96, 171.

FEB 28 "McClellan had . . . acquiesced," Goodwin, 426–7.

"To placate . . . 'to do anything,'" Perret, 126.

MAR 6 "Early . . . part with it," Donald, *Lincoln*, 346.

"In his message . . . without compensation," Message to Congress, March 6, 1862, in *CW*, V, 144–6.

"There was . . . 'a ruler,'" Donald, *Lincoln*, 347.

SB28 "The border states' . . . Lincoln asked," Lincoln to James A. McDougal, March 14, 1862, in *CW*, V, 160–1.

"The more likely . . . '[of slavery],'" Appeal to Border State Representatives to Favor Compensated Emancipation, July 12, 1862, in *CW*, V, 317–9.

"West Virginia . . . nationwide," E. B. Long, Barbara Long, *The Civil War Day By Day: An Almanac 1861–1865* (New York: Da Capo Press, 1971), 332, 583, 633, 637, 692.

MAR 9 "At 2:00 PM . . . aground," Eicher, 195–6.

"'A terrapin . . . back'," Foote, Vol. I, 255.

"When Lincoln . . . engaged the *Virginia*," Perret, 161–2.

"The *Monitor* . . . withdrew," Foote, Vol. I, 259–60.

"The next . . . uncontrollably," Kunhardt, *Lincoln*, 177.

MAR 11 "On March 9 . . . 'outsat the other'," Foote, Volume I, 263–4.

"Worse, when . . . fielded," McPherson, 424.

"And some of . . . cannons," Perret, 128–9.

"On this day . . . 'retrieve his errors,'" Dennett, 37.

"McClellan wrote . . . was bitter," Foote, Vol. I, 266.

MAR 13 "McClellan wanted to ferry . . . 'through handsomely,'" Foote, Vol. I, 267–9.

MAR 14 "On the day after . . . Havana, Cuba," Lincoln to the Senate and the House of Representatives, March 14, 1862, in *CW*, V, 162.

"The U.S. invoked . . . could be seized," Lance E. Davis, Stanley L. Engerman, *Naval Blockades in Peace and War: An Economic History Since 1750* (New York: Cambridge University Press, 2006), 9.

"In the case . . . April 25," Lincoln to the Senate and the House of Representatives, March 14, 1862, in *CW*, V, 162.

APR 9 "General George . . . to move his army," Eicher, 215–7.

"A frustrated . . . "'stationary" engine,'" Goodwin, 431.

APR 10 "Lincoln, on this . . . 'naval forces,'" Proclamation of Thanksgiving for Victories, April 10, 1862, in *CW*, V, 185–6.

"General Ulysses . . . Confederates to retreat," McPherson, 406–12.

"Total casualties . . . Mexican War," casualties for the battle on both sides exceeded 20,000, ibid., 413.

"'I saw an open' . . . 'he fights,'" Eicher, 231.

APR 16 "As early as . . . of its voters," Protest in Illinois Legislature on Slavery, in *CW*, I, 74–6.

"As a congressman . . . in the country," Donald, *Lincoln*, 135–7, 346–8.

MAY 5 "At dusk on . . . his campaign there," Miers, 109.

"During almost the . . . back toward Richmond," Eicher, 215–7, 268.

"'I was much' . . . wrote his wife," Donald, *Lincoln*, 350.

"'Yorktown is in' . . . on May 5," George B. McClellan to Edwin M. Stanton, May 4, 1862 (Reporting Capture of Yorktown), in *ALP.*

"He later telegraphed . . . 'to the wall,'" George B. McClellan to Edwin M. Stanton, May 4, 1862 (Regarding Military Affairs), in *ALP*.

MAY 7 "After the fall . . . 'to imitate him'," Goodwin, 436–7.

"The *Miami* . . . Confederates had burned," Miers, 109–10.

MAY 9 "When Lincoln arrived . . . *Merrimack)*," Goodwin, 437–8.

"Lincoln ordered . . . stayed behind," Perret, 165–6. Perret has a typo on page 166 claiming the attack was on "March 11." The attack, according to Miers (111) and Long (210) was on May 10, 1862.

SB29 "Before Lincoln . . . into war," Perret, xiii–xv.

"'The Provision . . . Kingly oppressions,'" Lincoln to William H. Herndon, February 15, 1848, in *CW*, I, 451–2.

"So pervasive . . . directly under him," Perret, xiv–xv.

MAY 11 "On May 10 . . . 'Norfolk is ours!'" Perret, 167–8.

"Secretary of War . . . off the floor," Goodwin, 439.

"Five hours later . . . captured city," Miers, 111.

"'So has ended' . . . 'of my movements,'" Goodwin, 439.

MAY 15 "Lincoln, the son . . . his breaks," Kunhardt, *Lincoln*, 39.

"giving the false . . . working a farm," Miller, 29–31.

"In Lincoln's . . . population working as farmers," McPherson, 9.

"In his December . . . 'given,' Lincoln added," Annual Message to Congress, December 3, 1861, in *CW*, V, 35–53.

"He was referring . . . of the Interior," Wikipedia, "United States Department of Agriculture," at http://en.wikipedia.org/wiki/United_States_Department_of_Agriculture (December 3, 2008).

"Congress followed . . . Agriculture (USDA)," Miers, 112.

"Lincoln named Isaac . . . first Commisioner," To Whom It May Concern, March 4, 1862, in *CW*, V, 143–4.

"His staff included . . . president's cabinet," Wikipedia, "United States Department of Agriculture, see above.

MAY 16 "On this day . . . out the problem," Miers, 112.

"On March 8 . . . 'pamper' his favorite generals," Lincoln to George B. McClellan, May 9, 1862 (Reorganization of army), in *ALP*.

"After the Battle . . . 'themselves incompetent,'" Lincoln to George B. McClellan, May 9, 1862, in *CW*, V, 208–9.

"He neglected . . . sat idly by," Charles S. Hamilton to Samuel Beck, March 20, 1864 (Narrative of Hamilton's Civil War Service), in *ALP*.

"Lincoln allowed . . . corps organization," Lincoln to George B. McClellan, May 9, 1862, in *CW*, V, 207–8.

"Indeed, after Lincoln . . . to his command," Lincoln to George B. McClellan, May 21, 1862, in *CW*, V, 227.

"The next day . . . 'back to this Army," George B. McClellan to Lincoln, May 23, 1862 (Regarding General Hamilton), in *ALP*.

"Hamilton was sent . . . of a corps," Warner, 198, 379.

SB30 "George McClellan knew . . . 'that is in the way,'" McPherson, 359–60.

"He once wrote . . . 'state of affairs,'" Stephen Sears, ed., *Civil War Papers of George B. McClellan: Selected Correspondence 1860–1865* (New York: Da Capo Press, 1992), 85–6.

MAY 17 "On May 14 . . . for reinforcements," George B. McClellan, May 14, 1862 (Regarding Military Affairs), in *ALP*.

"(in actuality . . . Confederate's strength)," Eicher, 273.

"'If he [McClellan] . . . got himself into,'" Perret, 174.

"Lincoln ordered General . . . 'are to Judge,'" Lincoln to Irvin McDowell, May 17, 1862, in *CW*, V, 219–20.

"McDowell's movements . . . Valley exposed," Perret, 175.

MAY 19 "After Union forces . . . South Carolina," Goodwin, 435.

"Hunter—an abolitionist . . . 'forever free'," Proclamation Revoking General Hunter's Order of Military Emancipation of May 9, 1862, May 19, 1862, in *CW*, V, 222–4.

"The order was . . . of the West," Oates, 280, 284.

"As for Hunter's . . . 'my responsibility,'" Goodwin, 435.

"Lincoln declared . . . 'maintenance of the government,'" Proclamation Revoking . . . , May 19, 1862, in *CW*, V, 222–4.

SB31 "Just over a month . . . own proclamation," Matthew Pinsker, *Lincoln's Sanctuary: Abraham Lincoln and the Soldiers' Home* (New York: Oxford University Press, 2003), 25. For a discussion as to the reliability of the account that Hannibal Hamlin read an early draft of the Emancipation Proclamation, 27–8.

"The reason, in part . . . 'upon the colored element,'" Lincoln to Albert Hodges, April 4, 1864, in *CW*, VII, 281–3.

"Lincoln also . . . 'my responsibility,'" Goodwin, 390, 435.

MAY 20 "Shorn of . . . (creating paper money)," in ibid., 461–2.

"In America's early . . . Buchanan vetoed it," National Archives and Records Administration website, http://www.archives.gov/education/lessons/homestead-act.html (August 5, 2008).

"The Act that . . . sold to individuals," National Park Service's website for the Homestead National Monument, http://www.nps.gov/home/historyculture/abouthomesteadactlaw.html (August 5, 2008).

"The first plot . . . mid–1980s," on National Park Service websites, http://www.nps.gov/home/historyculture/firsthomesteader.html and http://www.nps.gov/home/historyculture/lasthomesteader.html (August 5, 2008).

MAY 23 "After Lincoln ordered . . . Friday in 1862," Miers, 114.

"As Lincoln relaxed . . . was canceled," Goodwin, 441–2.

MAY 25 "Lincoln had been . . . 'fast as I can,'" Eicher, 260–2.

"On consecutive days . . . to his generals," David Homer Bates, *Lincoln in the Telegraph Office: Recollections of the United States Military Telegraph Corps During the Civil War* (Lincoln, NE: University of Nebraska Press, 1995), 123.

"He wired McClellan . . . 'in their rear,'" Lincoln to George B. McClellan, May 24, 1862, in *CW*, V.

"Lincoln was also . . . 'utterly helpless,'" Lincoln to George B. McClellan, May 25, 1862, in *CW*, V, 236–7.

"Still later . . . 'of Washington,'" Lincoln to George B. McClellan, May 25, 1862, in *CW*, V, 235–6.

MAY 26 "Lincoln had been reluctant . . . 'to public service,'" Goodwin, 290, 403, 413.

"On this day . . . he added," Lincoln to the Senate and House of Representatives, May 26, 1862, in *CW*, V, 240–3.

"(from March to . . . 700,000)," McPherson, 313, 322.

"From the Russian . . . 'personal friends,'" Goodwin, 413.

SB32 "One trait of . . . 'would his friend,'" Miller, 406–7.

"Lincoln's first Secretary . . . of the presidency," Kunhardt, 172, 299, 304.

"Then there was Edwin . . . secretary of war," Miller, 410–8, 425–6.

MAY 28 "He received word . . . wrote Lincoln," John C. Fremont to Lincoln, May 28, 1862 (Regarding military affairs), in *ALP*.

"Unhappy, Lincoln wired . . . McDowell responded," Lincoln to Irvin McDowell, May 28, 1862, in *CW*, V, 246.

"Late in the afternoon . . . 'front of Richmond,'" Lincoln to George B. McClellan, May 28, 1862, in *CW*, V, 244.

"'That the whole' . . . crossed it out," Lincoln to George B. McClellan, May 28, 1862, in *CW*, V, 244–5.

JUN 1 "By the end . . . four miles of Richmond," Goodwin, 443.

"so close that . . . could be heard," McPherson, 454.

"Arrayed east and . . . 75,000 men," Heidler, 674–5.

"As news reached . . . Manassas to Richmond," Lincoln sent three telegrams (9:30 AM; 1:15 PM; 5:00 PM) all Lincoln to George B. McClellan, June 1, 1862, in *CW*, V, 255–6.

"Had Johnston's . . . Northern Virginia," Heidler, 675–6.

JUN 7 "On this Saturday . . . would be suspended," Miers, 120.

"For three weeks . . . was embalmed," Donald, *Lincoln*, 337.

"The annual . . . already been canceled," Goodwin, 433.

"Lincoln's secretary . . . 'but Willie,'" Pinsker, 21, 30.

JUN 14 "Before the war . . . north of E Street," Lee, 13, 28, 31, 39, 84.

"a Maine . . . 'have been still,'" Editors of Time–Life Books, *Soldier Life* (New York: Barnes & Noble, 2007), 70.

"Lincoln, however . . . Bates complied," Lincoln to Edward Bates, June 14, 1862, in *CW*, V, 270.

JUN 15 "Lincoln's plan . . . John Fremont," Perret, 176

"After Jackson . . . valley altogether," McPherson, 457–60.

"During Jackson's . . . in Washington," Foote, Vol. I, 464.

"Afterward, Fremont . . . substantially reinforced," see two messages, John C. Fremont to Lincoln, one June 12, 1862, the other June 13, 1862, both regarding military affairs, both in *ALP*.

"Lincoln, on . . . 'amounts to,'" Lincoln to John C. Fremont, June 15, 1862, in *CW*, V, 270–2.

SB33 "Lincoln claimed . . . Jackson's army," Donald, *Lincoln*, 355.

"behind a ring . . . sixty-eight forts," Lee, 165.

"What Lincoln really . . . a solid plan," For a detailed discussion of the pros and cons of Lincoln's plan see Current, 142–151. See also McPherson, 460.

JUN 19 "Almost from . . . and Nebraska," Wagner, 92, 106–113.

"In 1854 . . . semi–retirement from politics," Holzer, *Cooper* Union, 29.

"Lincoln answered . . . [the territories],'" Lincoln to Joshua Speed, August 24, 1855, in *CW*, II, 320–3.

"Six years later . . . 'a necessity,'" Holzer, *Cooper* Union, 267.

"Lincoln believed . . . indefinitely," Donald, *Lincoln*, 134.

"When Lincoln . . . territorial slaves," Miers, 122.

"according to the 1860 . . . territories," Wagner, 71.

JUN 20 "Despite a busy . . . persuade them," Donald, *Lincoln*, 391.

"In early June . . . 'may cease,'" Religious Society of Progressive Friends to Lincoln, June 7, 1862 (Memorial requesting abolition of slavery), in *ALP*.

"As the *New* . . . force of arms," Remarks to a Delegation of Progressive Friends, June 20, 1862, in *CW*, V, 278–9.

SB34 "From the beginning of . . . to act on it," Donald, *Lincoln*, 362–4. See also Goodwin, 459–63; Current, 223–5; Perret, 196–200, 202–6. For discussions on Hamlin seeing an early draft of the preliminary Emancipation Proclamation, see Brownstein, 115–7 and Pinsker, 26–8.

JUN 23 "Scott had been . . . the North," Donald, *Lincoln*, 357.

"When Lincoln boarded . . . for Richmond?," Perret, 177–8.

"Eleven hours later . . . John Pope," Miers, 122–3.

"Scott was convinced . . . 'the rebellion,'" Perret, 177–8.

"Scott recommended . . . its commander," Donald, *Lincoln*, 357–8.

JUN 25 "Confederate general . . . Seven Days Campaign," McPherson, 462, 464.

"That evening . . . 'if I could,'" Lincoln to George B. McClellan, June 26, 1862, in *CW*, V, 286–7.

"The next day . . . to head it," Miers, 123.

"Lee attacked . . . Gaines' Mill)," McPherson, 464–8.

"As McClellan began . . . to Lincoln," Donald, *Lincoln*, 358.

JUL 2 "For seven . . . the James River," McPherson, 464–9.

"His corps . . . and Lee's army," Perret, 179–80.

"Instead McClellan . . . 'simply absurd,'" Lincoln to George B. McClellan, July 2, 1862, in *CW*, V, 301–2.

"Nevertheless, Lincoln . . . more enlistments," Call for 300,000 Volunteers, July 1, 1862, in *CW*, V, 296–7.

JUL 9 "In the aftermath . . . nor sleeping," Donald, *Lincoln*, 358.

"Lincoln arrived . . . Lincoln's policies," Perret, 180.

"In particular . . . Lincoln's title)," George B. McClellan to Lincoln, July 7, 1862 (Thoughts on political and military affairs), in *ALP*.

"Lincoln finished . . . from the soldiers," Goodwin, 452.

"McClellan claimed . . . 'it very feebly,'" Donald, *Lincoln*, 359.

"On this day . . . with McClellan," Miers, 126.

"refused to even mention the letter," Goodwin, 451.

JUL 12 "Special awards . . . were executed," Heidler, 53–4, 1301–2.

"This was in . . . reinstated her medal," Wagner, 435, 481–2, 655–6.

JUL 17 "Lincoln surprised . . . Confiscation Act," Miers, 128.

"In the final . . . unenforceable," Goodwin, 460–1.

"Nor did Lincoln . . . commander in chief," Donald, *Lincoln*, 364–5.

JUL 22 "With his generals . . . legal document," Donald, *Lincoln*, 314–7, 362–5.

"But he ended . . . 'be free'," Emancipation Proclamation—First Draft, July 22, 1862, in *CW*, V, 336–8.

"While this . . . Lincoln agreed," Goodwin, 464–5, 468.

JUL 28 "Not long after . . . one loyalist," Jacob Barker to Lincoln and Reverdy Johnson to Lincoln, both July 16, 1862 (Situation in New Orleans), both in *ALP*.

"Lincoln, irritated . . . 'enemies stab me,'" Lincoln to Reverdy Johnson, July 26, 1862, in *ALP*.

"In response to another . . . 'means applied?'," Lincoln to Cuthbert Bullitt, July 28, 1862, in *ALP*.

"Despite Lincoln's . . . Phelps resigned," Warner, 368–9.

AUG 4 "Two weeks . . . he insisted," Donald, *Lincoln*, 367, 430.

"When Lincoln met . . . 'that were for us,'" Remarks to Deputation of Western Gentlemen, August 4, 1862, in *CW*, V, 356–7.

"When the men . . . Hamlin try it,'" Michael Burlingame, *Inner World*, 177.

SB35 "was skeptical that they would fight," Perret, 199.

"Lincoln later claimed . . . 'progressing'," Goodwin, 502.

"During the late . . . and Indiana," Donald, *Lincoln*, 430.

"By October . . . *New York Times*," Wagner, 428, 432.

"By March . . . military governor," Donald, *Lincoln*, 431.

AUG 14 " On this Thursday . . . Latin America," Goodwin, 469–70.

"Lincoln believed . . . de Fleurville," Donald, *Lincoln*, 166–7.

"former slave . . . 'objects of aversion,'" Goodwin, 470.

"Colonizationists . . . Granada (Panama)," Donald, 344.

"On this day . . . White House," Miers, 133.

"'We have between' . . . Chiriqui Lagoon," Address on Colonization to a Deputation of Negroes, August 14, 1863, in *CW*, V, 370–5.

"Free blacks responded . . . 'of the country,'" Goodwin, 469.

SB36 "As early . . . advocated colonization," Donald, *Lincoln*, 343.

"'Coming generations' . . . Henry Clay," Eulogy to Henry Clay, July 6, 1852, in *CW*, II, 121–32.

"But he acknowledged . . . during the Civil War," Donald, *Lincoln*, 166–7, 344.

"Frederick Douglass . . . 'stronger than iron,'" Goodwin, 407.

"As Lincoln considered . . . lubricated with colonization," Goodwin, 469.

"Congress appropriated . . . rescue them," McPherson, 509.

"By the winter . . . promoted assimilation," Oates, 358–9, 370–1.

AUG 22 "Lincoln's draft . . . victory," Donald, *Lincoln*, 369.

"Meanwhile . . . lambasting Lincoln," Perret, 204–5.

"'We complain . . . that,' he wrote," Lincoln to Horace Greeley, August 22, 1862, in *CW*, V, 388–9.

AUG 29 "After he decided . . . he was reinforced," Goodwin, 473–4.

"Lee sent . . . Manassas battlefield," Eicher, 319–26.

"On this day . . . roar of cannon," Perret, 209.

"According to a . . . from the west," Goodwin, 474.

"Lincoln spent . . . for information," Donald, *Lincoln*, 370.

"'What news' . . . he asked," Lincoln to Herman Haupt, August 29, 1862, in *CW*, V, 399.

AUG 30 "When McClellan . . . demoralize his troops," Perret, 182.

"When that failed . . . to stay," Goodwin, 474.

"'I am almost . . . what I wish,'" Donald, *Lincoln*, 370.

"Finally, on August . . . Pope to lose," Goodwin, 474–5.

"'Well, John . . . 'whipped again,'" Donald, *Lincoln*, 370.

SEP 1 "General in Chief . . . the capital," Goodwin, 475–8.

"'I must have' . . . Lincoln said," Donald, *Lincoln*, 371.

"Lincoln met with . . . of Virginia," Miers, 137.

"'I only consent' . . . 'have,' he said," Donald, *Lincoln*, 371–2.

SB37 "Lincoln's September . . . were stunned," Goodwin, 475–9.

"McClellan's command . . . 'of the army,'" Perret, 210–1

"Secretary of the . . . in a cabinet meeting," Goodwin, 479.

"But Lincoln persisted . . . 'hang himself'," Donald, *Lincoln*, 372.

SEP 5 "On this day . . . security detail," George B. McClellan to Lincoln, September 5, 1862 (Guard for Soldiers' Home), in *ALP*.

"In response . . . to the Soldiers' Home," Pinsker, 56–7.

"Still unaware . . . 'as my bodyguard,'" Brownstein, 171.

"Afterward, Lincoln . . . his presidency," Pinsker, 57–8.

SB38 "According to . . . 'President,' See said," Brownstein, 98–9, 181.

"Lincoln's youngest . . . antics again," Pinsker, 78, 82.

SEP 12 "Flush with victory . . . *Richmond Dispatch*," Eicher, 336–9.

"Lincoln saw . . . 'and Philadelphia,' he said," Lincoln to Samuel Treat, November 19, 1862, in *CW*, V, 501–2.

"Pennsylvania governor . . . Lincoln responded," Lincoln to Andrew G. Curtin, September 12, 1862, in *CW*, V, 417.

"'The emergency' . . . not in danger," Alexander Henry to Lincoln, September 12, 1862 (Telegram concerning affairs in Philadelphia), in *ALP*.

SEP 13 "The visitors . . . 'will I will do,'" Reply to Emancipation Memorial Presented by Chicago Christians of All Denominations, September 13, 1862, in *CW*, V, 421–5.

SEP 15 "After the debacle . . . 'me even now,'" Goodwin, 480.

"As Lincoln hoped . . . within days," McPherson, 534.

"Then came an . . . back the rebel forces," Eicher, 340–7.

"Lincoln wired . . . 'if possible,'" Lincoln to George B. McClellan, September 15, 1862, in *CW*, V, 426.

SEP 17 "The battle . . . held in reserve," Eicher, 340–1, 347–63.

"Lincoln was elated . . . 'so completely,'" Goodwin, 481.

"On September 18 . . . wasn't beaten," Eicher, 363.

"The next day . . . had escaped," Perret, 216.

"On this day . . . Home cottage," Miers, 140.

SEP 22 "Lincoln spent . . . to issue it," Perret, 217.

"'September 17 . . . *New York Times*," Goodwin, 481.

"Wishing to . . . wax figures," Perret, 217.

"After he closed . . . 'Maker,' he said," Goodwin, 481–2.

"Unused to Lincoln . . . 'of Maryland,'" Perret, 217–8.

"He then read . . . made public," Goodwin, 482.

"Postmaster General . . . (it didn't)," Oates, 346.

"and affect the . . . (it did)," Donald, *Lincoln*, 376.

SB39 "He kept his . . . 'would die,'" Joshua Wolf Shenk's *Lincoln's Melancholy* (New York: Houghton Mifflin Co., 2005), 181–2.

"His secretary . . . 'little conceits,'" Dennett, 179.

"While humor could . . . 'genial mood,'" Shenk, 119, 181.

SEP 24 "Two days after . . . their writ suspended," Neely, 52–65.

"Later this day . . . 'made no mistake,'" Miers, 141.

SB40 "Lincoln suspended . . . July 5, 1864)," Neely, 4–11, 14, 37, 51–65, 68–74, 90–2.

SEP 26 "A week after . . . 'save slavery,'" Lincoln to John J. Key, September 26, 1862 (Allegations against Key), in *ALP*.

"The next day . . . Lincoln's office," Miers, 142.

"When Turner . . . 'that supposed class,'" Lincoln to John J. Key, November 24 1862, in *ALP*.

"It didn't help . . . Southern sympathizer," Perret, 220.

SEP 28 "'God bless you . . . hold a jubilee,'" W. B. Lowry, H. Catlin, and J. F. Downing to Lincoln, September 23, 1862 (Emancipation Proclamation), in *ALP*.

"The great orator . . . 'righteous decree,'" Goodwin, 483.

"The Democratic . . . 'impossible,'" Donald, *Lincoln*, 380.

"The *Richmond* . . . 'generous thrill,'" Goodwin, 482–3.

"After Lincoln . . . 'kills no rebels,'" Lincoln to Hannibal Hamlin, September 28, 1862, in *CW*, V, 444.

OCT 2 "'The boys think . . . is accomplished,'" Eicher, 255.

"Admiral Andrew . . . his spirits," Goodwin, 483–4, 504.

"'I am stronger . . . the situation,'" Donald, *Lincoln*, 388.

OCT 3 "After the battle . . . at Harpers Ferry," Goodwin, 481, 484.

"On the same . . . after another," Perret, 218–9.

"On October 1 . . . at noon," Miers, 143.

"Lincoln rode . . . 'like a baboon,'" Donald, *Lincoln*, 387.

"In conference . . . 'advance in Virginia,'" Goodwin, 484.

"Early on this . . . 'McClellan's bodyguard,'" Perret, 220.

"When Lincoln returned . . . 'are good,'" Goodwin, 485.

SB41 "An incident while . . . 'to the singing,'" Memorandum Concerning Ward H. Lamon and the Antietam Episode, September 12, 1864, in *CW*, VII, 548–50.

OCT 4 "On this Saturday . . . near Antietam," Miers, 143–4.

"By October . . . to the south," Lee, 22.

"On this morning . . . 'extended his hand,'" Kunhardt, *Lincoln*, 191.

"On April 8 . . . Confederate wounded," Perret, 403–4.

SB42 "Six years after . . . letters for them," Goodwin, 457–9.

"Often Lincoln . . . 'are shot off,'" Perret, 347.

OCT 7 "On October 6 . . . 'remove him,'" Goodwin, 485.

"A McClellan subordinate . . . message to McClellan," Donald, *Lincoln*, 386.

"The general . . . were prohibited," George B. McClellan to Lincoln, October 7, 1862 (Telegram concerning Emancipation Proclamation), in *ALP*.

"As for moving . . . 'here at Washington,'" Lincoln to George B. McClellan, October 7, 1862, in *CW*, V, 452.

OCT 12 "In August . . . Lexington," McPherson, 515–7.

"On September . . . 'you tie me,'" Perret, 190.

"In mid-September . . . retreated," Perret, 190–1.

"despite outnumbering . . . two to one," McPherson, 515, 518.

"Lincoln on this . . . 'you anything?'," Miers, 145.

"Buell was content . . . hundred miles," Perret, 191.

OCT 14 "Lincoln, on this . . . 'himself with,'" Miers, 145.

"He owned . . . ability to function," Packard, 77.

"put his friends . . . 'nigger yet,'" Bayne, 32, 55, 57–9

"Tad pestered . . . minature cannon," Lincoln to John A. Dahlgren, October 14, 1862, in *CW*, V, 463.

SB43 "The president loved . . . 'see the shooting,'" Stoddard, 21–3.

OCT 17 "On this Friday . . . 'Commodore' Nutt," Miers, 145.

"Barnum had made . . . historical figures," Neil Harris, *Humbug: The Art of P.T. Barnum* (Boston: Little, Brown and Company, 1973), 21, 40, 43, 49–53.

"Then in December . . . best man," Phineas T. Barnum, *Struggles and Triumphs, or Forty Years of Recollections of P.T. Barnum* (Buffalo, NY: Warren, Johnson & Co., 1873), 567–8, 572–3, 584–6, 602–4.

"All three came . . . of puns," Harris, 162–3.

OCT 24 "Buell was a career . . . Corinth, Tennessee," Warner, 51–2.

"Unfortunately . . . Buell's job," Donald, *Lincoln*, 384–5.

"And he was strongly . . . emancipation," Perret, 190.

"But to Lincoln's . . . to follow him," McPherson, 520–2.

"'If we are beaten' . . . wrote Lincoln," Horace White to Lincoln, October 22, 1862 (Illinois politics), in *ALP*.

"Ohio Congressman . . . 'removal of Buell,'" Samuel Shellabarger to Lincoln, October 22, 1862 (Recommends removal of General Buell), in *ALP*.

"On this day . . . from command," Donald, *Lincoln*, 389.

"and on October 30 . . . command again," Warner, 52.

OCT 25 "It had been . . . his inaction," Donald, *Lincoln*, 387–8.

"'Are you not . . . Harpers Ferry,'" Lincoln to George B. McClellan, October 13, 1862, in *ALP*.

"'Our war on . . . specimen after all,'" Goodwin, 485.

"Lincoln's secretary . . . returned unscathed," Donald, *Lincoln*, 388–9.

"Early on this . . . 'fatigue anything?'" Lincoln to George B. McClellan, October 25, 1862, in *CW*, V, 474–5.

"Lincoln later pointed . . . Lincoln wrote," Lincoln to George B. McClellan, October 27, 1862, in *ALP*.

OCT 26 "As a young . . . 'how we will,'" Donald, *Lincoln*, 15.

"As president . . . 'of Providence,'" Current, 72.

"Sometime while . . . 'of either party,'" Shenk, 198.

"When Gurney . . . 'unknown to us,'" Reply to Eliza P. Gurney, October 26, 1862, in *CW*, V, 478.

"Toward the end . . . 'with the sword,'" Shenk, 207.

NOV 5 "Just a few . . . 'tough fighting,'" Perret, 271.

"The press . . . after the November midkrm elections," Donald, *Lincoln*, 389–90.

"'By direction . . . of that Army,'" Lincoln to Henry W. Halleck, November 5, 1862, in *CW*, V, 485–6.

"Burnside had twice . . . orders of dismissal," Perret, 224.

"'Poor Burn[side] . . . on my face,'" Goodwin, 485.

NOV 7 "Charles Ellet, a civil . . . Memphis Tennessee," Gary D. Joiner, *Mr. Lincoln's Brown Water Navy: The Mississippi Squadron* (Lanham, MD: Rowman & Littlefield Publishers, 2007), 67–71.

"Eight makeshift . . . of Ellet's rams," Long, 223.

"Ellet, however . . . commissioned a general," Joiner, 71.

"That fall Congress . . . join the navy," Order to Alfred W. Ellet, November 7, 1862, in *CW*, V, 490.

"They were also . . . Vicksburg, Mississippi," Joiner, 84–5.

NOV 14 "Lincoln claimed . . . Burnside and Richmond," Perret, 224–5.

"Burnside's plan . . . fifty miles away," Eicher, 396.

"On this day . . . 'otherwise not,'" Perret, 226.

"Halleck forgot . . . Fredericksburg as well," Eicher, 396–8.

NOV 22 "The fall of 1862 . . . and McClellan," Donald, *Lincoln*, 382–3, 389–90.

"Another general . . . bottom of them," Eicher, 241–2.

"On November 9 . . . from his cabinet," Perret, 194.

"asked Banks to set . . . 'is not abandoned,'" Lincoln to Nathaniel P. Banks, November 22, 1862, in *CW*, V, 505–6.

"Banks replied . . . be underway," Nathaniel P. Banks to Lincoln, November 24, 1862 (Telegram responding to Lincoln's letter of Nov. 22), in *ALP*.

"On December 14 . . . from Butler," Perret, 194–5.

NOV 26 "An opportunity . . . before it began," Perret, 226–7.

DEC 1 "The Santee Dakota . . . to hang," Heidler, 1,791–3.

"Lincoln had the . . . any pardons himself," Lincoln to Joseph Holt, December 1, 1862, in *CW*, V, 537–8.

DEC 6 "For three weeks . . . and the army," Arlene Hirschfelder, *Native Americans* (New York: Dorling Kindersley Publishing, 2000), 64–6.

"Over the objections . . . and/or rape," Donald, *Lincoln*, 394.

"To avoid mistakes . . . 'unlawful violence,'" Lincoln to Henry H. Sibley, December 6, 1862, in *CW*, V, 542–3.

"Despite precautions . . . family from harm," John G. Nicolay to Henry H. Sibley, December 9, 1862 (Case of Robert Hopkins), in *ALP*.

"A Dakota chief . . . in U.S. history," Hirschfelder, 64–6.

SB44 "Some 20,000 . . . House, Virginia," in ibid., 62–3.

"During the war . . . John Usher," Kunhardt, *Lincoln*, 301.

"At age . . . could kill him," Donald, *Lincoln*, 45.

"In the first . . . 'red brethren,'" Kunhardt, *Lincoln*, 207.

DEC 11 "Starvation prompted . . . to hang," Hirschfelder, 64–6.

"During Lincoln's . . . to furnish it," see Lincoln to Senate, March 26, 1861 (IV, 299), July 11, 1861 (IV, 447), December 14, 1861 (V, 70) and Lincoln to House of Representatives, July 27, 1861 (IV, 461–2), February 29, 1864 (VII, 214), and Lincoln to Senate and House of Representatives, May 26, 1862 (V, 240–3), all in *CW*.

"On December 5 . . . were hanged," Lincoln to Senate, December 11, 1862, in *CW*, V, 550–1.

"In April 1864 . . . the uprising," Lincoln, April 30, 1864 (List of Sioux Indians pardoned by Lincoln), in *ALP*.

DEC 12 "While New York . . . end to the war," Heidler, 2,146–7.

"He wasted no . . . 'general amnesty,'" Lincoln to Fernando Wood, December 12, 1862, in *CW*, V, 553–4.

"In late 1863 . . . cease-fire," Heidler, 2,147.

DEC 14 "Before the battle . . . 'fond of it'," Eicher, 396–7, 399–405.

"For a full . . . Curtin responded," Perret, 228–30.

DEC 17 "On this Wednesday . . . William Seward," Miers, 156.

"In the aftermath . . . informal caucus," Goodwin, 486–7.

"They knew . . . 'cabinet ministers,'" Donald, *Lincoln*, 399.

"The senators perceived . . . December 18," Goodwin, 487–9.

SB45 "What came to . . . 'in name,'" Donald, *Lincoln*, 402.

"Chase claimed . . . next evening," Goodwin, 489–90.

"Much to the consternation . . . in the cabinet," Donald, *Lincoln*, 403–4.

DEC 20 "The cabinet crisis . . . '[saddle]bag,'" Goodwin, 486–94.

DEC 29 "Looking for a . . . executive branch," Goodwin, 486–92.

"Supposedly the . . . prelimary Emancipation Proclamation," Donald, *Lincoln*, 400.

"On this day . . . the proclamation," Miers, 159.

DEC 30 "Lincoln, on this . . . 'letting me know,'" Lincoln to Ambrose E. Burnside, December 30, 1862, in *CW*, VI, 22–3.

"After the Battle . . . 'Gen. Halleck,'" Donald, *Lincoln*, 409–10.

DEC 31 "Lincoln, on this . . . Proclamation," Miers, 159.

"When Lincoln . . . that victory," Goodwin, 463–8, 481–2.

"The proclamation had grown . . . 'of Almighty God,'" compare Emancipation Proclamation—First Draft, July 22, 1862 (336) with Preliminary Emancipation Proclamation, September 2, 1862 (433) and Preliminary Draft of Final Emancipation Proclamation, December 30, 1862 (23–5), all in *CW*, the two former are V, the latter one VI.

1863

JAN 1 "'That fatal first,'" Donald, *"We Are Lincoln Men"*, 43.

"It was in or around . . . nearly a year," Donald, *Lincoln*, 86–7. Historians had long assumed that Lincoln's reference to "that fatal first" referred to the actual date of January 1, 1841 when Lincoln supposedly broke off his engagement with Mary Todd. Together with Joshua Speed's partnership in his Springfield store officially dissolving that day leaving him free to return to Kentucky, the romantic breakup supposedly sent Lincoln into a deep depression. In Joshua Wolf Shenk's *Lincoln's Melancholy*, he makes a strong argument that the break between Lincoln and Todd probably occurred before the holidays and Mary may not have even been in Springfield on New Year's Day. Shenk believes we may never know exactly what sparked Lincoln's depression or what Lincoln referred to in his now famous quote. See Shenk, 51–7. See also Douglas L. Wilson, *Lincoln Before Washington: New Perspectives on the Illinois Years* (Urbana, IL: Illinois University Press, 2006), 99–133.

"'done nothing . . . lived,'" Donald, *"We Are Lincoln Men"*, 44.

"Lincoln rose . . . 'is in it'," Goodwin, 497–99.

"'Now, this . . . some compunctions,'" Donald, *Lincoln*, 407.

"'I believe . . . realized,'" Donald, *"We Are Lincoln Men"*, 62.

JAN 4 "But cotton . . . from Tennessee," McPherson, 622–3.

"'The President . . . in our ranks,'" Kunhardt, *Lincoln*, 203.

JAN 5 "'God Bless . . . courage,'" Lincoln to William Rosecrans, January 5, 1863, in *CW*, VI, 39.

"The battle . . . strategic victory," McPherson, 579–82.

"'I can never . . . over,'" Lincoln to William Rosecrans, August 31, 1863, in *CW*, VI, 424–5.

JAN 8 "On this . . . 'commission,'" Lincoln to Ambrose Burnside, January 8, 1863, in *CW*, VI, 46–8.

"Just two . . . Chancellorsville," for more detailed account of the battle of Fredericksburg, see McPherson, 571–4 and the "Mud March" in ibid., 584.

"'The whole . . . bed,'" Foote, Vol. II, 129.

SB46 For accounts of resignations, see also January 13, January 25, February 29, Sidebar #22, May 29, June 15, June 27, June 30, Sidebar #43, July 14, September 23, November 1, December 17, December 20, December 30.

JAN 14 "Two weeks . . . command," Lincoln to John A. Dix, January 14, 1863, in *CW*, VI, 56.

"The next day . . . 'importance,'" John Dix to Lincoln, January 15, 1863 (Opinion on garrisoning Fort Monroe and Yorktown with black troops), in *ALP*.

"Lincoln, himself . . . 'rebellion,'" Donald, *Lincoln*, 367.

"At another . . . 'rebels,'" Perret, 206.

"By war's . . . combat," Walker, 427.

JAN 18 "On this . . . 'Society,'" Miers, 163.

"Early in life . . . religion," Miller, 42–3.

"Even after . . . church," Current, 62–3.

"As president . . . hospital," Lee, 133–4, 136.

"Lincoln never . . . 'my heart,'" Current, 65.

JAN 19 "On this . . . White House," Miers, 164.

"Lincoln loved . . . wrote it," Donald, *Lincoln*, 47–8.

"When he wrote . . . mortality," Shenk, 122.

"One of the poems . . . actual events," Miers, 164.

"William Scott . . . Lee's Mills," Sandburg, 590–1. See also the following found in *ALP*, Anne C. King to Lincoln, September 8, 1861 (Pardon for William Scott); Francis De Haes

Janvier to Lincoln, March 4, 1863 (Sends Copy of "Sleeping Sentinel"); Pachal P. Ripley to Lincoln, January 9, 1865 (Dying words of the "Sleeping Sentinel").

For text of Janvier's poem, Nathaniel K. Richardson, *One Hundred Choice Selections in Poetry and Prose: Both New and Old* (Philadelphia: P. Gerrett & Co., 1866), 13–6. In *GBS*.

SB47 Full text of Lincoln's poem "My Childhood–Home I See Again" in *CW*, I, 367–70.

JAN 21 "Porter, part . . . of Pope," Warner, 378–9.

"Porter reported . . . 'carried out,'" Eicher, 327–8.

"When Pope . . . this day," Warner, 379–80.

JAN 22 "'It seems' . . . wrote," Brooks D. Simpson, "Lincoln and His Political Generals," *Journal of the Abraham Lincoln Association*, Winter 2000, 63–76 and found on Association's website, http://www.historycooperative.org/journals/jala/21.1/simpson.htm (May 12, 2008).

"In many ways . . . Democrats," Warner, 293.

"In the fall . . . West Pointers)," McPherson, 577.

"and accused . . . 'functions,'" John A. McClernand to Lincoln, January 7, 1863 (Charges against General Halleck), in *ALP*.

"Lincoln, however . . . 'work'," Lincoln to John McClernand, January 22, 1863, in *CW*, VI, 70–1.

JAN 25 "General Ambrose . . . commanders," Miers, 165.

"Burnside's . . . existence," Donald, *Lincoln*, 411.

"Mindful . . . 'us victories,'" Lincoln to Joseph Hooker, January 26, 1863, in *CW*, VI, 78–9.

FEB 13 "Nearly a year . . . Lavinia," Kunhardt, *Lincoln*, 205.

"Stratton was . . . toured with him," Harris, 43, 63, 283.

"By the time . . . Warren," David Wallechinsky and Irving Wallace, *The People's Almanac* (Garden City, NY: Doubleday & Co., 1975), 109–10.

"The newlyweds . . . 'breaking it,'" Kunhardt, *Lincoln*, 205.

FEB 18 "The U.S. Congress . . . transporting slaves," Farrow, 124–5.

"In April of . . . Domingo," Lincoln to the Senate of the United States, February 18, 1863, in *CW*, VI, 110.

MAR 3 "Lincoln stayed . . . session," Miers, 172.

"By the spring . . . fighting strength," McPherson, 600.

"But state . . . presidential career," Neely, 68–9.

MAR 15 "On this Sunday . . . Confederate Navy," Miers, 173.

"The Confederacy . . . as pirates," McPherson, 315–6.

"As the war . . . were captured," Heidler, 1,396–7.

"By the summer . . . 'prizes,' respectively," Wagner, 563–5.

"These raiders . . . never delivered)," Heidler, 1,396–7.

MAR 20 "Lincoln, on . . . William Sherman," Miers, 175.

"Sherman had an . . . him insane," Heidler, 1,766.

"When Sherman set . . . 'is, Never,'" To Whom It May Concern, March 20, 1863, in *CW*, VI, 142–3.

"He lost 1,800 . . . Confederate's 200," McPherson, 579.

APR 7 "It was quiet . . . *Carrie Martin*," Goodwin, 513.

"After arriving . . . (April 6–10)," Miers, 178.

"During one review . . . 'their backs [in battle]," Goodwin, 516.

"The head of . . . to kiss him," Perret, 241.

"The journalist . . . 'kiss the President,'" Noah Brooks, *Washington in Lincoln's Time* (New York: Rinehart & Co., 1958), 70.

APR 20 "Despite the fact . . . for statehood," McPherson, 297–9.

"Lincoln was dubious . . . new government," Donald, *Lincoln*, 301.

"Nevertheless, he. . . the Union," Proclamation Admitting West Virginia into the Union, April 20, 1863, VI, 181.

APR 23 "During the 1860s . . . after the war," Brownstein, 78–9.

"Elizabeth Keckly . . . through a medium," Packard, 143.

"Mary hosted . . . the White House," Donald, *Lincoln*, 427.

"on this Thursday . . . beard," Kunhardt, *Lincoln*, 209.

"Lincoln's involvement . . . muscles," Goodwin, 509.

"Famous medium . . . a séance," Packard, 143–4.

"There was another . . . Proclamation," Nettie Colburn Maynard, *Was Abraham Lincoln a Spiritualist? Or Curious Revelations From the Life of a Trance Medium* (Philadelphia: Rufus C. Hartranft, 1891), 70–2. In *GBS*.

SB48 "Nettie Colburn . . . 'his understanding,'" in ibid., 82–91.

"Her story is supported . . . at the séance," Goodwin, 508.

APR 28 "On April 27 . . . Lee's left flank," Eicher, 474–5.

"Despite the fact . . . 'look now?'" Lincoln to Joseph Hooker, April 27, 1863, in *CW*, VI, 188.

"'I can perceive . . . Gideon Welles," Goodwin, 519.

"Hooker wired . . . Hooker wrote," Joseph Hooker to Lincoln, April 27, 1863 (Military plans), in *ALP*.

"Lincoln was worried . . . 'Mr. Capen,'" Memorandum Concerning Francis L. Capen's Weather Forecast, April 28, 1863, in *CW*, VI, 190–1.

MAY 3 "When Lincoln received . . . 'is Stoneman?'" Lincoln to Daniel Butterfied, May 3, 1863, in *CW*, VI, 196.

"General John Sedgwick . . . counter offensive," Eicher, 475–80.

"Late this afternoon . . . 'been heard from,'" Daniel Butterfield to Lincoln, May 3, 1863 (Reporting battle at Chancellorsville), in *ALP*.

"Butterfield had worse . . . peppered with shrapnel," Daniel Butterfield to Lincoln, May 3, 1863 (Reporting wounding of General Hooker), in *ALP*.

"When Hooker . . . 'success to us,'" Joseph Hooker to Lincoln, May 3, 1863 (reporting battle at Chancellorsville), in *ALP*.

"Lincoln spent . . . Lincoln's secretaries," Miers, 182.

MAY 6 "In the days . . . received the news," Donald, *Lincoln*, 435.

"When Hooker . . . against the Rappahannock," Eicher, 477–486.

"On this day . . . was retreating," Daniel Butterfield to Lincoln, May 6, 1863 (Concerning Dispatches to General Hooker), in *ALP*.

"When Lincoln . . . 'the country say !'" Donald, *Lincoln*, 435–6.

"Within the hour . . . with Hooker," Miers, 183.

SB49 "Lincoln went almost . . . Home cottage)," Gary, 341.

"According to . . . 'no further,'" Don Edward Fehrenbacher, Virginia Fehrenbacher, eds., *Recollected Words of Abraham Lincoln* (Stanford, CA: Stanford University Press, 1996), 26.

"Lincoln felt more . . . he quipped," Sandburg, 392–3.

MAY 12 "On this Thursday . . . was dead," Meirs, 184.

"At Chancellorsville . . . his fault," Donald, *Lincoln*, 438.

"Lincoln, however . . . said bitterly," Perret, 246.

"Three other generals . . . than any other," Eicher, 488.

"Jackson, a graduate . . . before dying," Heidler, 1,058–65.

MAY 13 "In the conservative . . . for treason," Donald, *Lincoln*, 416–7.

"A leading . . . 'of the whites,'" McPherson, 596.

"Vallandigham declared . . . 'his throne,'" Goodwin, 522.

"Lincoln was unhappy . . . the writ anyway," Neely, 65–6.

MAY 14 "General Joseph Hooker . . . 'brother officer,'" Lincoln to Joseph Hooker, January 26, 1863, in *CW*, VI, 78–9.

"The loss at . . . 'try it again,'" Donald, *Lincoln*, 438–40.

"The president declared . . . 'chance more,'" Perret, 246.

"Meanwhile, Lincoln . . . 'of another movement,'" Lincoln to Joseph Hooker, May 13, 1863, in *CW*, VI, 201.

"When he refused . . . 'superiors' in numbers," Perret, 247.

"In Lincoln's written . . . 'ruinous, if true,'" Lincoln to Joseph Hooker, May 14, 1863, in *CW*, VI, 217–8.

MAY 22 "For more . . . much less attack," Wagner, 269, 279–80.

"As time . . . leading an army," Oates, 373–4.

"He suggested . . . waited for news," Donald, *Lincoln*, 435, 445.

"Then, on this . . . the telegraph," Lincoln to Stephen A. Hurlbut, May 22, 1863, in *CW*, VI, 226.

"After crossing . . . audacious operation," Eicher, 457–69.

"'His [Grant's] . . . in the world,'" Donald, *Lincoln*, 445.

MAY 29 "On this day . . . 'service requires it,'" Ambrose E. Burnside to Lincoln, May 29, 1863 (Telegram Informing Lincoln to relieve him if his Conduct is not approved), in *ALP*.

"Burnside's actions . . . offer to resign," Donald, *Lincoln*, 419–21.

"Lincoln wired . . . 'through with it,'" Lincoln to Ambrose E. Burnside, May 29, 1863, in *CW*, VI, 237.

JUN 2 "Lincoln rarely . . . laying a siege," Donald, *Lincoln*, 445.

"On this day . . . break the siege," Miers, 187.

"If Grant wouldn't . . . 'to you . . . ?,'" Lincoln to Ulysses S. Grant, June 2, 1863, in *CW*, VI, 243.

"A week later . . . 'days,' he added," Nathaniel P. Banks to Ulysses S. Grant, June 4, 1863 (Military affairs), in *ALP*.

JUN 4 "When General Ambrose . . . 'in bloody anarchy,'" Donald, *Lincoln*, 419–21.

"On June 1 . . . 'which sustains us,'" Illinois Legislature, June 4, 1863 (Resolutions concerning suppression of the *Chicago Times*), in *ALP*.

"What convinced . . . against Burnside's order," Isaac N. Arnold and Lyman Trumbull to Lincoln, June 3, 1863 (Telegram protesting suppression of the *Chicago Times*), in *ALP*.

"On this day . . . lifted that ban," Lincoln to Edwin Stanton, June 4, 1863, in *CW*, VI, 248.

"Lincoln later . . . 'Press on the other,'" Lincoln to Isaac N. Arnold, May 25, 1864 (Arnold's role in the suppression of the *Chicago Times*), in *ALP*.

SB50 "One of the . . . their critical views," DiLorenzo, 145–7.

"On July 13 . . . implored Schofield," Lincoln to John M. Schofield, July 13, 1863, in *CW*, VI, 326–7.

JUN 5 "Lincoln was still . . . Chancellorsville," Lincoln to Joseph Hooker, May 13, 1863, in *CW*, VI, 201.

"In the wake . . . Shenandoah Valley," Eicher, 490–1.

"Hooker's cavalry . . . River at Fredericksburg," Joseph Hooker to Lincoln, June 5, 1863 (Concerning movement of the Confederate Army), in *ALP*.

"Lincoln advised . . . 'other,' Lincoln wrote," Lincoln to Joseph Hooker, June 5, 1863, in *CW*, VI, 249–51.

"A week later . . . 'true objective point,'" Lincoln to Joseph Hooker, June 10, 1863, in *CW*, VI, 257–8

JUN 9 "Lincoln was plagued . . . or literally," Shenk, 209.

"His wife, Mary . . . still there," Donald, *Lincoln*, 572.

"At three in the . . . in Philadelphia," Miers, 188.

"Prior to leaving . . . 'or powder,'" Donald, *Lincoln*, 446.

"After Lincoln returned . . . 'about him,'" Goodwin, 530.

SB51 "In the mid–1850s . . . 'rang,'" Donald, *Lincoln*, 163–4.

"As president . . . his assassination," Goodwin, 731.

"The night before . . . death and war," Oates, 360.

"The most famous . . . 'by an assassin!'" Goodwin, 728–9. Many historians are uncomfortable with Lamon's account, finding it too "pat" and "made-up" (see Current, 70). In fact Lincoln's words as Lamon relates them seem very un-Lincolnian. But Lamon admitted that his recollection of Lincoln's exact words was imperfect but was nevertheless based on notes he made immediately after Lincoln spoke them. Don Fehrenbacher makes a good argument that Lamon's recollection of when Lincoln related the dream (not long before his death) is wrong, making the entire story questionable (see Fehrenbacher, 292–3). On the other hand, there is nothing uncharacteristic about Lincoln relating dreams to his friends. And, in Lamon's testimony, when Lincoln downplays the dream's depressing prophecy, this is entirely characteristic of Lincoln ("Hill, your apprehension of harm to me from some hidden enemy is downright foolishness . . . . Don't you see how it will turn out? In this dream it was not me, but some other fellow, that was killed. It seems that this ghostly assassin tried his hand on some one else," Lincoln allegedly said. See Kunhardt, *Lincoln*, 334).

"He told Lamon . . . 'ever since,'" Kunhardt, *Lincoln*, 334.

JUN 12 "On May 16 . . . the resolutions to Lincoln," Lincoln to Erastus Corning, May 28, 1863, in *CW*, VI, 235.

"On this Friday . . . 'caprice' was wrong," Lincoln to Erastus Corning and Others, June 12, 1863, VI, 260–9.

JUN 16 "'If the head' . . . June 14," Lincoln to Joseph Hooker, June 14, 1863, in *CW*, VI, 273.

"Earlier that same . . . 'help them?'" Lincoln to Joseph Hooker, June 14, 1863, in *CW*, VI, 273.

"Hooker responded . . . continue as before," Joseph Hooker to Lincoln, June 14, 1863 (Telegram inquiring if there is news from Winchester), in *ALP*.

"Lincoln preferred . . . the other," Donald, *Lincoln*, 439.

"'If you and he' . . . wrote to Hooker," Lincoln to Joseph Hooker, June 16, 1863, in *CW*, VI, 281–2.

"By this day . . . 'to obey them,'" Lincoln to Joseph Hooker, June 16, 1863, in *CW*, VI, 282.

JUN 26 "In late June . . . left for bed," Pinsker, 100–2.

JUN 27 "During the month . . . Henry Halleck," Donald, *Lincoln*, 439–40, 444.

"The feud came . . . of the war," Perret, 275.

"On June 27 . . . 'once be relieved,'" Joseph Hooker to Henry W. Halleck, June 27, 1863 (Telegram requesting to be relieved of command), in *ALP*.

"It is likely . . . accepted it," Donald, *Lincoln*, 444–5.

"The next day . . . 'own dunghill,'" Kunhardt, *Lincoln*, 212.

JUL 3 "On this Friday . . . 'by her fall,'" Miers, 194.

"On the morning . . . wrote a subordinate," Pinsker, 102–4.

"When the carriage was examined . . . first family," Donald, *Lincoln*, 448.

"Instead of attending . . . at Gettysburg," Goodwin, 535.

"It wasn't until . . . legitimate danger," Packard, 162.

"Lincoln wired . . . 'more of you?'" Miers, 196–7.

"It took Mary . . . instability," Donald, *Lincoln*, 448.

SB52 "For instance . . . Lincolns' carriage," Kunhardt, *Twenty Days*, 5.

"A more credible . . . matter quiet," Pinsker, 163.

"Many threats . . . on his shirt," Brownstein, 84.

"Lincoln saw . . . 'used to things,'" Donald, *Lincoln*, 547.

JUL 4 "Confederate general Robert . . . frontal attack," McPherson, 647, 652–63.

"For all three . . . third of his army," Goodwin, 532–3.

JUL 5 "Stephens appeared . . . prisoner exchanges," Samuel P. Lee to Gideon Welles, July 4, 1863 (Telegram reporting the arrival of Alexander Stephens at Fortress Monroe), in *ALP*.

"Lincoln curtly . . . 'Confederate States,'" Lincoln to Samuel P. Lee, July 4, 1863 (Alexander Stephens' Request to pass military lines), in *ALP*.

"Stephens had been . . . offensive into the North," McPherson, 650, 664, 694–5.

"But when Lincoln . . . on this day," Miers, 195.

"The next day . . . 'pretended Confederate States,'" William H. Seward, July 6, 1863 (Draft of message in response to Alexander Stephens), in *ALP*.

JUL 6 "In the aftermath . . . to attack him," McPherson, 666–7.

"On July 4 . . . 'please look to it,'" Lincoln to Henry W. Halleck, July 6, 1863, in *CW*, VI, 318.

"When Lincoln read . . . 'is our soil,'" Donald, *Lincoln*, 446.

"The next day . . . 'rebellion will be over,'" Lincoln to Henry W. Halleck, July 7, 1863, in *CW*, VI, 319.

JUL 7 "Lincoln, on this . . . was finally over," Miers, 195.

"For forty-six . . . eighty-six years," Eicher, 468–9, 555–8.

"Word of the surrender . . . 'up his hat'," Goodwin, 533.

"A week later . . . 'I was wrong,'" Lincoln to Ulysses S. Grant, July 13, 1863 (Congratulations on capture of Vicksburg), in *ALP*.

JUL 13 "On this Monday . . . in American history," Miers, 196.

"Shortages of men . . . for a substitute," Perret, 288–9.

"While Lincoln . . . 'provocation or not,'" Goodwin, 536–7.

"*Harper's Weekly* . . . high as one thousand," Eicher, 554–5.

JUL 14 "After Lee's loss . . . 'harvest it,'" Goodwin, 535–6.

"That afternoon . . . accept Meade's resignation," Lincoln to George G. Meade, July 14, 1863, in *CW*, VI, 327–8.

SB53 "Lincoln certainly . . . 'might run away,'" Goodwin, 536.

"But was it even . . . Campaign of 1864?" for discussions on Meade's capability to destroy Lee, see Donald, *Lincoln*, 447; McPherson, 667; Eicher, 550–2; Jones, 169.

"But even if . . . April 1865," for discussion of the importance of the western theater of operation, see Perret, 56–7; Jones, 130–1, 136–7.

JUL 15 "He and his eldest . . . later wrote," Goodwin, 541.

"Lincoln was so . . . Gettysburg victory," Miers, 197.

"As the week . . . 'sack Phil–del,'" Donald, *Lincoln*, 447–8.

SB54 "Lincoln's oldest . . . than the Lincolns," Packard, 67–8.

"What's more . . . 'tyranny,' Lincoln said," Donald, *Lincoln*, 108–9.

"Robert took this . . . died with him," Packard, 150–1, 263–4.

JUL 18 "Lincoln's sour . . . 'to shoot them,'" Dennett, 68.

"Private Michael . . . Lincoln wrote," Lincoln to Joseph Holt, July 18, 1863, in *CW*, VI, 335.

"'He [Lincoln]' . . . Hay noted," Dennett, 68.

"Apparently this . . . for drunkenness," Lincoln to Joseph Holt, July 18, 1863, in *CW*, VI, 336.

"When Lincoln reviewed . . . six-hour marathon," Goodwin, 539.

"Lincoln's mood . . . wrote the next day," Dennett, 69.

"Lincoln derived . . . 'happy tonight,'" Current, 164.

SB55 "During the war . . . said forlornly," Perret, 352–3.

"He told Eaton . . . 'the battle begins,'" Goodwin, 539.

"One evening while . . . 'away with him?'" Current, 165–6.

JUL 24 "By the 1850s . . . work after marriage," McPherson, 33.

"But as the war . . . twenty years," Wagner, 705–7.

"Lincoln even considered . . . Illinois postmistress," Lincoln to John T. Stuart, March 30, 1861, in *CW*, IV, 303.

"On July 23 . . . a permanent position," Lincoln to Montgomery Blair, July 24, 1863, in *CW*, VI, 346.

JUL 25 "On this Saturday . . . 'gamblers & harlots,'" Dennett, 72.

"One of Lincoln's . . . and prostitution," Lee, 74, 83–4.

"The area north . . . *Tribune* reported," Pinsker, 37.

"Another of Lincoln's . . . lived on Vermont," Lee, 140.

"saw Lincoln . . . 'ago is needed,'" Pinsker, flyleaf.

JUL 29 "Meade's Army . . . 'disaster of the war,'" Perret, 279–82.

"Meade decided to . . . Lincoln's message to Meade," Lincoln to Henry W. Halleck, July 29, 1863, in *CW*, VI, 354.

"who did not attack . . . of the fall," Perret, 312.

JUL 30 "The South was . . . were summarily executed," McPherson, 565–6, 792–3.

"Lincoln did not respond . . . for the black soldier," Goodwin, 550–2.

"Finally, on this . . . in a prison camp," Order of Retaliation, July 30, 1863, in *CW*, VI, 357.

"Lincoln, however . . . officially enforced," McPherson, 794.

SB56 "Unofficially, Confederate . . . congressional investigation," Wagner, 298–9, 435.

"Lincoln devoted two . . . a recourse," Miers, 256.

"Lincoln decided . . . 'act for revenge,'" see Lincoln to Cabinet Members and Lincoln to Edwin M. Stanton, both in *CW*, VII, 328–9 and 345–6 respectively.

"Many black units . . . bayoneted," Wagner, 435–6.

"In April 1864 . . . 'of the Rebels,'" McPherson, 793.

AUG 1 "Lincoln, on this . . . the incident," Miers, 200.

"Winchester, which . . . bounty on his head," Jonathan A. Noyalas, "The Most Hated Man in Winchester," *America's Civil War Times*, March 2004, Vol. 17, 30–6.

"When Confederate . . . advancing on him," Perret, 274.

"Orders for him . . . sent to Lincoln," see Robert H. Milroy to Lincoln, July 13 and July 20, 1863 (both titled Defends his Conduct at Winchester) and John B. Klunk, et al, to John P. Usher, July 27, 1863 (Send Petition on behalf of General Milroy) all in *ALP*. See also Opinion on the Loss of Robert H. Milroy's Division, October 27, 1863, in *CW*, VI, 541–2.

"Even after . . . another command," Noyalas, 36.

"'I was deprived' . . . Milroy complained," Robert H. Milroy to Lincoln, October 2, 1863 (Facts pertaining to his case), in *ALP*.

"'You have just . . . is upon you,'" Lincoln to Robert H. Milroy, June 29, 1863, in *CW*, VI, 308–9.

AUG 7 "On July 4 . . . 'as by a government,'" McPherson, 609.

"A week . . . 'resist the government,'" Goodwin, 536–8.

"When the New York . . . were investigated," Horatio Seymour to Lincol, August 3, 1863 (Conscription in New York), in *ALP*.

"Lincoln, on this . . . 'in the field,'" Lincoln to Horatio Seymour, August 7, 1863, in *CW*, VI, 369–70.

AUG 9 "The summer of . . . busy and productive," Goodwin, 540.

"On August 7 . . . the new dome," Dennett, 76–7, 79, 82.

"On this day . . . stack of books," Kunhardt, *Lincoln*, 216.

"'He [Lincoln} . . . old bearings,'" Dennett, 77.

SB57 "While Lincoln was . . . 'gray eyes,'" Current, 2.

"Four years of . . . 'sea running,'" Kunhardt, *Lincoln*, 321.

"His ex–law . . . 'to his walk,'" Current, 3.

"Lincoln's back . . . a writer," Kunhardt, *Lincoln*, 321.

"Most of his . . . 'from his head,'" Donald, *Lincoln*, 115–6.

AUG 10 "On this Monday . . . Frederick Douglass," Miers, 201.

"Douglass was a . . . for abolition," Heidler, 614–5.

"During the war . . . 'gentleman receive another,'" Goodwin, 550–2.

AUG 11 "With the New York . . . district quotas," Lincoln to Horatio Seymour, August 11, 1863 (Conscription in New York), in *ALP*.

"Lincoln's relationship . . . his patriotism," Wagner, 191–3, 197–201.

"In early August . . . constitutionality of conscription," Horatio Seymour to Lincoln, August 3, 1863 (Conscription in New York), in *ALP*.

"Lincoln refused . . . Union Army," Lincoln to Horatio Seymour, August 7, 1863, in *CW*, VI, 369–70.

"Seymour fired . . . perversion[s] of law," Horatio Seymour to Lincoln, August 8, 1863 (Response to Lincoln's letter of August 7 concerning conscription in New York), in *ALP*.

"Lincoln's . . . 'nervous excitment,'" Dennett, 71.

"Lincoln responded . . . make them fairer," Lincoln to Seymour, August 11, 1863 (see above).

"He also sent . . . without incident,'" Donald, *Lincoln*, 450.

AUG 13 "By 1850 . . . from the old dome," from The Architect of the Capitol websites, http://www.aoc.gov/cc/capitol/ capitol_construction.cfm?RenderForPrint=1 and http://www.aoc.gov/cc/capitol/dome.cfm?RenderForPrint=1 (June 22, 2007).

"At the outbreak . . . 'shall go on,'" Perret, 342.

"On this day he wrote . . .," Dennett, 79.

"He was probably . . . completed in 1866," from The Architect of the Capitol websites, http://www.aoc.gov/cc/art/pediments/prog_sen.cfm?RenderForPrint=1 and http://www.aoc.gov/cc/capitol/c_const_seq.cfm?RenderForPrint=1 (June 22, 2007).

AUG 20 "Lincoln walked to the . . . *Birds of America*," Bates, 39.

"one from a governor . . . disloyal soldier," Oliver P. Morton to Lincoln, August 20, 1863 (Telegram concerning Case of Caldwell), in *ALP*.

"from a general passing . . . to Richmond," Lincoln to Edwin M. Stanton, August 20, 1863, in *CW*, VI, 399–400.

"It was in that . . . meaning emerges," Bates, xi, 115, 144, 146

AUG 26 "The Republican . . . in his stead," Donald, *Lincoln*, 456.

"'There are those . . . this great consummation,'" Lincoln to James C. Conklin, August 26, 1863, in *CW*, VI, 406–10.

AUG 27 "Despite prevalent . . . another bounty," Heidler, 256–7.

"On August 26 . . . on August 29," Lincoln to George G. Meade, August 27, 1863, in *CW*, VI, 414–5.

SEP 14 "Before the war . . . never happened," Neely, 69–73.

SEP 18 "When a young . . . wiry Lincoln," Donald, *Lincoln*, 40.

"As friend . . . Hannah recalled," Wilson, *Herndon's Informants*, 73–4, 525.

"When, in 1857 . . . star witness," Donald, *Lincoln*, 150–1.

"Then in 1863 . . . 'Ky,'" Lincoln to Mrs. Hannah Armstrong, September 18, 1863, in *CW*, VI, 462.

"Eight months . . . 'present time'," Hannah Armstrong to Lincoln, May 19, 1864 (Discharge of Louis Ishmael), in *ALP*.

SB58 "The trial that . . . possessed the weapon," Scott W. Johnson and John H. Hinderaker, "A Genius for Friendship," on the Claremont Institute website, http://www.claremont.org/publications/pub_print.asp?pubid=168 (October 1, 2008). See also Wilson, *Herndon's Informants*, 22, 316, 332–4, 526.

"Lincoln's masterstroke . . . nearly set," Donald, *Lincoln*, 151.

"In his closing . . . William Walker," Wilson, *Herndon's Informants*, 22–3, 316.

SEP 21 "In early September . . . Ben Helm," Eicher, 577–92.

"On September 19 . . . 'Burnside joins you,'" Lincoln to William S. Rosecrans, September 21, 1863, in *CW*, VI, 472–3.

"Lincoln then wired . . . 'moment delay,'" Lincoln to Ambrose E. Burnside, September 21, 1863, in *CW*, VI, 469–70.

"By the next . . . disaster," Miers, 209.

SEP 25 "From the beginning . . . on September 19," Perret, 312–4, 318–9.

"Lincoln tried . . . reinforce Rosecrans," Lincoln to Ambrose E. Burnside, September 21, 1863, in *CW*, VI, 470.

"On September 21 . . . 'Jonesboro,'" Bates, 201–2.

"Then Lincoln . . . 'without delay,'" Lincoln to Ambrose E. Burnside, September 21, 1863, in *CW*, VI, 469–70.

"'Yours of . . . filed it away," Lincoln to Ambrose E. Burnside, September 25, 1863, in *CW*, VI, 480–1.

SEP 27 "On this Sunday . . . under siege," Miers, 210.

"After Rosecrans' rout . . . Lincoln said," Perret, 319.

"But because . . . supply himself," McPherson, 675.

"Shortly after . . . twilight meeting," Perret, 319.

"As Lincoln got . . . 'sent for him,'" Goodwin, 557.

"Once at the . . . in a week," Eicher, 593.

"'I bet you . . . were nationalized," Perret, 320.

"Once a route . . . September 25," Goodwin, 558–9.

"arrived seven days . . . miles away," Eicher, 594.

SEP 29 "Lincoln, on this . . . evils of alcohol," Dennett, 96.

"Lincoln was not . . . Sarah said," Miller, 32.

"Even on the . . . instead served," Donald, *Lincoln*, 251.

"Lincoln's temperance . . . 'rye straw,'" Temperance Address, February 22, 1842, in *CW*, I, 271–9.

"When the temperance . . . 'green apples,'" Dennett, 96.

OCT 5 "Radicals—dubbed . . . favored secession," Donald, *Lincoln*, 452–3.

"'They are nearer' . . . Lincoln said," Goodwin, 567.

"Then on August . . . 50 civilians," McPherson, 786.

"When Missourians . . . District, refused," Heidler, 1712.

"On September 30 . . . 'for an instant,'" Dennett, 97.

"The president . . . 'retaliation follow,'" Lincoln to Charles D. Drake and Others, October 5, 1863, in *CW*, VI, 499–504.

"The Radicals . . . 'in Missouri,'" Donald, *Lincoln*, 454.

OCT 6 "On this Tuesday . . . National Theater," Miers, 211.

"Grover's, located . . . National Theater," Lee, 85.

"Was frequented . . . *Der Freischutz*," see Miers, 170–1, 175, 210–1, 235, 241–5, 250–1, 263, 296, 299, 306, 320–1, for the listing of "two dozen" shows Lincoln attended (including those named) and Goodwin, 609, for reference to a "hundred" attendances.

"When Lincoln went . . . 'I am here,'" Donald, *Lincoln*, 570.

"Tad sometimes . . . as an extra," Goodwin, 614.

"Tad was attending . . . 'in agony,'" in ibid., 741–2.

OCT 9 "Over 674,000 . . . 26,000 in those of the Union)," Wagner, 583, 591, 601–4.

"Mrs. Thomas . . . 'for her to go,'" Lincoln to Edwin M. Stanton, October 9, 1863, in *CW*, VI, 507–8.

OCT 16 "After the Battle . . . meager supplies," McPherson, 675–6.

"One witness . . . 'watering place,'" Eicher, 600.

"What was more . . . described the general," McPherson, 675.

"A change . . . 'of the Mississippi,'" Goodwin, 559.

"overseeing . . . eastern Louisiana)," Eicher, 595.

"The second . . . Chattanooga," Goodwin, 559.

"'The great thing . . . of purpose,'" Perret, 321.

"Grant quickly . . . 'rations, boys!,'" Eicher, 602–3.

OCT 18 "The 1863 fall . . . Massachusetts," Donald, *Lincoln*, 454.

"One Republican . . . 'better off,'" Dennett, 99.

"Chase wrote hundreds . . . 'we have not,'" Goodwin, 564.

"When Hay told . . . 'differently,' Lincoln said," Dennett, 100.

"Lincoln told Hay . . . 'department go,'" Goodwin, 565.

SB59 "Lincoln nurtured this . . . 'done in politics,'" Current, 210.

"Lincoln's friend . . . 'he could find,'" Goodwin, 565–6.

"For one thing . . . of the treasury," Heidler, 408–10.

"Chase was also . . . governor's race," Donald, *Lincoln*, 455.

"What was more . . . Fessenden," Goodwin, 635–6.

"Lincoln also knew . . . of them," for examples of this see Dennett, 99–100.

OCT 23 "In August 1863 . . . children to leave," see website "Camp Stanton—Training Post for USCT Marker," at http://www.hmdb.org/Marker.asp?Marker=4063 (December 16, 2007).

"The day after . . . complaining," Lincoln to Robert C. Schenck, October 21, 1863, in *CW*, VI, 530.

"The next day . . . discuss the matter," Lincoln to Robert C. Schenck, October 22, 1863, in *CW*, VI, 532.

"After the meeting . . . 'for its own sake,'" Dennett, 105.

"In March 1864 . . . and slaves," E. M. Sothoron to Lincoln, March 7, 1864 (Complains of treatment by military authorities), in *ALP*.

"Lincoln brought . . . War Department," Lincoln to Edwin M. Stanton, March 18, 1864 (Prisoners of War), in *ALP*.

"Her husband . . . was rejected," USCT marker at Camp Stanton website (see above).

OCT 28 "On this Wednesday . . . 'arming the disloyal,'" Miers, 216.

"Guerrilla warfare . . . of Missouri," Heidler, 1341.

"Faced with . . . to law enforcement," see notes of Lincoln to John M. Schofield, October 28, 1863, in *CW*, VI, 543–5.

"This practice . . . Schofield's removal," Benjamin F. Loan to Lincoln, October 3, 1863 (Report on military affairs in Missouri), in *ALP*.

"When Lincoln . . . used by Schofield," Lincoln to Schofield, October 28, 1863, see above.

"'If it is the . . . borders of the state,'" Benjamin F. Loan to Edwin M. Stanton, October 13, 1863, in *ALP*.

"On this day . . . Schofield wrote," Lincoln to Schofield, October 28, 1863, see above.

OCT 30 "On this Friday . . . *the Cricket*," Miers, 216.

"Lincoln frequented . . . at Grover's," see Miers, 116, 170–1, 175, 210–1, 216, 218, 227–8, 235, 241–5, 250–2, 263, 266, 296, 299, 302, 306, 320–1, 329 for listing of dates Lincoln attended Ford's and Grover's theaters.

"One reason for . . . that year," Gary, 359.

"When Lincoln . . . 'to the Chief,'" Donald, *Lincoln*, 595.

"At Grover's . . . unnoticed," Goodwin, 609.

"As he did at Grover's . . . heckler was expelled," article called "Ford's Theater" on "Mr. Lincoln's White House" website. An author was not listed. http://www.mrlincolnswhite-house.org/content_inside.asp?ID=188&subjectID=4 (November 11 2007).

NOV 2 "Lincoln, on this . . . *Henry IV*," Miers, 173, 217.

"On March 20 . . . 'by personal friends,'" Lincoln to James H. Hackett, August 17, 1863, in *CW*, 392–3.

"Hackett printed . . . classical literature," Donald, *Lincoln*, 569.

"On October 22 . . . 'am used to it,'" Lincoln to James H. Hackett, November 2, 1863, in *CW*, 558–9.

NOV 9 "On this Monday . . . Wilkes Booth," Miers, 218.

"One of his guests . . . 'doesn't he?'" Katherine Helm, *The True Story of Mary, Wife of Lincoln: Containing the Recollections of Mary's Sister Emilie (Mrs. Ben Helm), Extracts from Her War-Time Diary, Numerous Letters and Other Documents* (New York: Harper and Brothers, 1928), 243. In *GBS*.

"With a father . . . footlight life," Edward Steers Jr., *Blood on the Moon: The Assassination of Abraham Lincoln* (Lexington, KY: University of Kentucky, 2001), 27.

"One of the dramatic . . . kill Lincoln," Michael W. Kaufman, *American Brutus: John Wilkes Booth and the Lincoln Conspiracies* (New York: Random House, 2004), 99–100, 142, 188, 212. In *GBS*.

"Even in the North . . . always to tyrants," Donald, *Lincoln*, 549, 597.

NOV 12 "Perhaps the biggest . . . noted one observer," Goodwin, 308–9, 339, 433–5, 579, 581–2.

NOV 17 "After the massive . . . famous address," Garry Wills, *Lincoln at Gettysburg: Words that Remade America* (New York: Touchstone, 1992), 20–2, 24–6.

"On this evening . . . was pleased," Perret, 306–7.

NOV 18 "Of his 1,502 . . . in the field," Kunhardt, *Lincoln*, 308.

"One exception . . . not to leave," Miers, 220.

"A few witnesses . . . 'half of his speech,'" Goodwin, 583.

"The train arrived . . . returning to his address," Wills, 30–1.

NOV 19 "Around eleven . . . heroic battle," in ibid., 32–3.

"'He gave us' . . . or 'scour' off," Goodwin, 585–6.

"The public saw . . . *Chronicle* reporter," Donald, *Lincoln*, 465.

NOV 23 "On this Monday . . . William Seward," Lincoln to William H. Seward, November 23, 1863, in *CW*, VII, 29.

"In March 1863 . . . erupted," Eicher, 590–3, 613–4.

"'Nothing but the' . . . wrote Longstreet," McPherson, 676.

"Partly because . . . December 4," Eicher, 614–6.

NOV 25 "Lincoln, on this . . . previous days," Lincoln to Ulysses S. Grant, November 25, 1863, in *CW*, VII, 30–1.

"Chattanooga sat . . . Missionary Ridge," McPherson, 675–7.

"But when the . . . Ridge to Thomas," Eicher, 604–13.

"'I believe I' . . . Washington," Ulysees S. Grant to Henry W. Halleck, November 25, 1863 (Telegram reporting military victory in Tennessee), in *ALP*.

NOV 27 "On this Tuesday . . . official business," Miers, 223.

"After delivering . . . highly contagious," Packard, 169.

"'Yes, it is . . . everybody that calls,'" Goodwin, 588.

"Lincoln was ill . . . three weeks," Donald, *Lincoln*, 467.

"He was so sick . . . November 25," Miers, 223.

"His son Tad . . . November 18)," Packard, 167.

"Much of the . . . 'practical statemanship,'" Donald, *Lincoln*, 467.

SB60 "For instance . . . extended periods," Packard, 155.

"From testimony . . . 'phases of grief'," Shenk, 108–9.

"It was because . . . relieved his depression," Packard, 155.

"Some historians . . . months to live," Michael Woods, "Lincoln's Health Draws Scrutiny," July 25, 2000, *Post-Gazette* National Bureau, Bar Harbor, Maine. On website, http://www.post-gazette.com/headlines/20000725lincoln8.asp (November 14, 2008).

DEC 4 "On this Friday . . . White House," Lincoln to Stephen C. Massett, December 4, 1863, in *CW*, in VII, 34.

"Carpenter would gain . . . 'subsequent performances,'" Carpenter, v–vi, 160–1.

"still hangs in the Senate," Senate website, http://www.senate.gov/artandhistory/art/artifact/Painting_33_00005.htm (January 11, 2008).

DEC 8 "By late 1863 . . .'and freedmen,'" Donald, *Lincoln*, 469–70.

"Lincoln took a . . . by Congress," Proclamation of Amnesty and Reconstruction, December 8, 1863, in *CW*, VII, 53–6.

"The proclamation . . . floor of the House of Representations," Goodwin, 588.

DEC 9 "Lincoln, on this . . . by Congress," Miers, 226.

"The Constitution . . . 'Union' address," on the White House website, http://www.whitehouse.gov/stateoftheunion/print/history.html (January 15, 2008).

"The message . . . with the president," Donald, *Lincoln*, 471–3.

"'[Lincoln] is . . . [Salmon] Chase,'" Dennett, 132, 134.

DEC 13 "One exception . . . '[the Confederacy],'" Dennett, 139.

"After Ben Helm's . . . 'in Kentucky,'" Lincoln to Lyman B. Todd, October 15, 1863, in *CW*, VI, 517.

"The president . . . 'brother Alec[k],'" Packard, 164–5.

DEC 16 "On this Wednesday . . . in the North," Miers, 227.

"The week before . . . left within days," Goodwin, 592–3.

DEC 19 "During the Civil . . . industrial infrastructure," Heidler, 1687–8.

"'All this I did . . . industrial development,'" Konstantin George, "The US–Russian Entente That Saved the Union," *Executive Intelligence Review*, 1992 (reprinted from article in *The Campaigner*, 1978) and on the web, http://members.tripod.com/~american_almanac/risscwar.html (February 12, 2008).

"In the fall of 1862 . . . anchoring off Washington," Heidler, 1689–90.

SB61 "There is little . . . [with Western Europe]," George, see above.

DEC 22 "In at least . . . for the president," Bayne, 12–4.

"Rev. J. R. . . . for the president," Neely, 28.

"In December 1862 . . . from the state," Samuel B. McPheeters to Edward Bates, December 23, 1862 (Seeks assistance in resisting interference from military authorities in Missouri), in *ALP*.

"Lincoln first . . . 'run the churches'," Lincoln to Samuel R. Curtis, December 27, 1862 and January 2, 1863, both in *CW*, VI, 20 and 32 respectively.

"A year went . . . 'decline that also,'" Lincoln to Oliver D. Filley, December 22, 1863, in *CW*, VII, 85–6.

DEC 23 "On this day . . . many stories," Dennett, 143.

"'From his father . . . heartier than his,'" Benjamin P. Thomas, "Lincoln's Humor: An Analysis," *Journal of Abraham Lincoln Association*, Vol. 3, 1981, 28–47 and found on website, http://www.historycooperative.org/journals/jala/3/thomas.html (February 21, 2008).

"Sometimes he'd slap . . . with laughter," Kunhardt, *Lincoln*, 325.

"'His stories . . . perished with Lincoln,'" Thomas.

SB62 "Often he used . . . 'way,' Lincoln said," in ibid.

"To illustrate . . . 'a little'," Kunhardt, *Lincoln*, 325.

"Lincoln used . . . 'lugging him over?'" Thomas.

"By far the . . . 'me,' Lincoln said," Shenk, 116.

"One of his favorites . . . 'General Washington,'" Donald, *Lincoln*, 39–40.

DEC 28 "While at the White . . . his Father," Donald, 180–6. See also Stoddard, xi.

"On December 27 . . . do the same," Dennett, 145, 148–52, 154–62.

1864

JAN 7 "On this . . . 'lately,'" Endorsement Concerning Henry Andrews, January 7, 1864, in *CW*, VII, 111–2.

"'Black Friday,'" Kundhardt, *Lincoln*, 330.

"'No man . . . President,'" Current, 168–9.

"General Sherman . . . 'first,'" in ibid., 169.

"One day . . . lamented," Perret, 353.

"Attorney General . . . 'prevail,'" Current, 169.

SB63 "Speaker of the House . . . 'Methuselah,'" Allen Thorndike Rice, editor, *Reminiscences of Abraham Lincoln by Distinguished Men of His Time* (New York: North American Review, 1888), 343–5. In *GBS*.

JAN 16 "On this Saturday . . . met Lincoln," Kunhardt, *Lincoln*, 233.

"Called 'America's' . . . obscurity," J. Matthew Gallman, *America's Joan of Arc: The Life of Anna Elizabeth Dickinson* (New York: Oxford University Press, 2006), 9, 19, 24–30, 36–7, 40, 42, 81, 161, 205.

JAN 20 "Lincoln believed . . . swore the oath," Donald, *Lincoln*, 471–2, 561.

"Among the first . . . yet," Donald, *Lincoln*, 484. See also Nathan Kimball to Lincoln, April 11, 1864 (Telegram reporting on affairs in Arkansas), and Lincoln to Frederick Steele, January 30, 1864 (Political affairs in Arkansas), both in *ALP*.

"On this day . . . government," Lincoln to Fredericks Steele, January 20, 1864, in *CW*, VII, 141–2.

JAN 23 "With the war . . . starve," Kunhardt, *Lincoln*, 232.

"Radical Republicans . . . families," Donald, *Lincoln*, 470.

"On this day . . . Arkansas," Lincoln to Alpheus Lewis, January 23, 1864, in *CW*, VII, 145–6.

"He gave . . . rebellion," Oates, 410.

"'Such' . . . Lincoln wrote," Lincoln to Alpheus Lewis, January 23, 1864, in *CW*, VII, 145.

"Radical Republicans pushed . . . once did," Wagner, 775–6.

JAN 29 "Out of . . . capital," Kunhardt, *Lincoln*, 308.

"General Sickles . . . the battle," Heidler, 1784–6.

"At Gettysburg . . . Arkansas government," Lincoln to Daniel Sickles, January 29, 1864, VII, 160.

"Sickles agreed . . . Orleans," see To Whom It May Concern, March 15, 1864, in *CW*, VII, 250; Lincoln to Daniel Sickles, February 15, 1864, in *CW*, VII, 185; Daniel Sickles to Lincoln, May 16, 1864 (Telegram reporting progress of Sherman's campaign in Georgia), in *ALP*; Daniel Sickles to Lincoln, May 31, 1864 (Trade restrictions in the Border States), in *ALP*.

FEB 9 "Lincoln was . . . 'really handsome,'" Current, 1, 4–5.

"Two photos . . . photographed with," Kunhardt, *Lincoln*, 231, 234.

FEB 10 "Young children . . . sides," Donald, *Lincoln*, 309.

"It was while . . . 1862," Packard, 114–5.

"That night . . . 'be saved,'" Kunhardt, *Lincoln*, 235.

"Among the animals . . . Willie," Packard, 190.

SB64 "According to . . . 'hour at a time,'" Elizabeth Keckley, *Behind the Scenes of Thirty Years as a Slave, and Four Years in the White House* (New York: G. W. Carleton & Co., 1868), 179. In *GBS*.

"Lincoln was particularly . . . progress," Donald, *Lincoln*, 309.

"Jack the . . . 'killed,'" Louis Warren, *Lincoln's Youth: Indiana Years, Seven to Twenty-one 1816–1830*, (Indianapolis, IN: Historical Society, 2002), 225.

"Noah Brooks . . . not of 'age,'" Brooks, 196.

FEB 19 "On this . . . title role," Miers, 241.

"For Booth . . . playing Hamlet)," Eleanor Ruggles, *Prince of Players: Edwin Booth* (Westport, CT: Greenwood Press, 1972), 41–2, 44, 166–71, 205.

"This was . . . acting ability," Lincoln saw Edwin Booth on February 25, 26, March 2, 4, 7, and 10, all in 1864 (Miers, *Lincoln Day By Day*, III, 242–5). Lincoln saw John Wilkes Booth on November 9, 1863 in ibid., 218.

"'He makes . . . thrill,'" Kunhardt, *Lincoln*, 342.

"Perhaps the . . . Edwin Booth," John S. Goff, *Robert Todd Lincoln: A Man in His Own Right* (Norman, OK: University of Oklahoma Press, 1969), 70–1. See also Ruth Painter Randall, *Lincoln's Sons* (Boston: Little Brown and Co., 1955), 152.

FEB 22 "But by January . . . been won," Donald, *Lincoln*, 474–5, 477, 481.

"A second . . . Lincoln wrote Chase," Goodwin, 606–7.

FEB 29 "he couldn't . . . of the House," Donald, *Lincoln*, 482–3.

"on this day . . . 'a change,'" Lincoln to Salmon Chase, February 29, 1864, in *CW*, VII, 212–3.

MAR 1 "On this . . . Lieutenant General," Miers, 243.

"Previously . . . with him," Goodwin, 614.

"Grant's record . . . in the war," Warner, 184–5.

"At midnight . . . And he did," Eicher, 229–30.

"Grant would . . . 'and act,'" Kunhardt, *Lincoln*, 236.

MAR 2 "Lincoln, as a . . . 'by heart,'" in ibid., 36–7, 39, 42.

"In one book . . . remarkable memory," Miller, 50–1.

"Lincoln was posing . . . for Carpenter," F. B. Carpenter, *The Inner Life of Abraham Lincoln: Six Months at the White House* (Lincoln, NE: University of Nebraska Press, 1995), 49–51.

"King Claudius's . . . three hundred words long," Howard Staunton, ed., *The Globe Illustrated Shakespeare: The Complete Works Annotated* (New York: Gramercy Books, 1979), 1894.

MAR 7 "In January . . . of his men," Eicher, 642–3.

"On March . . . was alive," Miers, 244.

"To Lincoln's . . . was dead," Lincoln to Benjamin Butler, March 7, 1864, in *CW*, VII, 226.

"When Dahlgren's . . . a mystery," Eicher, 643.

MAR 8 "On this . . . 'Galena, Illinois,'" Goodwin, 614.

"Lincoln had . . . an hour," Donald, *Lincoln*, 490–1.

"The next . . . with Washington," Eicher, 624, 641–2.

MAR 21 "On this Monday . . . thirty-sixth State," Miers, 248.

"Lincoln believed . . . thirty-five states," Donald, *Lincoln*, 543, 676.

"One result of . . . and the war," McPherson, 47, 51–2.

"Nevada did ratify . . . for ratification," Long, 639.

SB65 "For one thing . . . 'upon us,'" Lincoln to William Herndon, February 15, 1848, in *CW*, I, 451–2.

"At the outbreak . . . foreign power," Donald, *Lincoln*, 303.

"When Polk argued . . . 'than it is,'" Speech in United States House of Representatives on Internal Improvements, June 20, 1848, in *CW*, I, 480–90.

"Most embarrassing of all . . . 'most sacred right,'" Speech in United States House of Representatives, The War with Mexico, January 12, 1848, in *CW*, 431–42.

MAR 24 "Under Lincoln's . . . readmission," Donald, *Lincoln*, 483–4.

"In February . . . the North," John Hay to Lincoln, February 8, 1864 (Affairs in Florida), in *ALP*.

"After the Union . . . 'falsehoods,'" Dennett, 165–7.

MAR 25 "Lincoln was deeply . . . twang," Donald, *Lincoln*, 47.

"He preferred . . . 'be Proud?'" Kunhardt, *Lincoln*, 237.

"Lincoln first . . . 'think that is,'" Shenk, 120–1.

"The poem was . . . 'from anxiety,'" Current, 8.

"His two . . . 'mortal be proud?'" Shenk, 121.

MAR 28 "When Lincoln . . . and a doorkeeper," Packard, 10.

"'The President' . . . Stoddard," Stoddard, 160, "White House Sketches No. VI," *New York Citizen*, September 22, 1866, 1.

"'Any assassin . . . him back,'" Ronald D. Rietveld, "The Lincoln White House Community," *Journal of the Abraham Lincoln Association* Summer 1999, 17–47. On journals website, http://www.historycooperative.org/journals/jala/20.2/rietveld.html.

"'I long ago . . . should be killed,'" Wayne Whipple, *The Story-Life of Lincoln: A Biography Composed of Five Hundred True Stories Told by Abraham Lincoln and His Friends* (Philadelphia: Johns C. Winston Company, 1908), 506. In *GBS*.

"At another time . . . 'losing his,'" *New York Times*, June 25, 1922, Special Features Section, Page XXI.

"'As to crazy . . . my chances,'" Fehrenbacher, 194.

"Early on this . . . elected in 1856," Miers, 249.

APR 3 "On March 26 . . . 'alone can claim it,'" Lincoln to Albert G. Hodges, April 4, 1864, in *CW*, VII, 281–3.

"Lincoln showed to . . . in 1864," Miers, 251.

SB66 "As a youth . . . 'of Providence,'" Current, 71–2.

"'Doesn't it strike' . . . Daniel Voorhees,'" Donald, *Lincoln*, 514.

"In his second . . . 'righteous altogether,'" Kunhardt, *Lincoln*, 267.

APR 18 "The U.S. Sanitary . . . Union troops," Wagner, 661–2.

"On this Monday . . . years before," Miers, 253.

"'Nearly a third . . . enter his city," McPherson, 285.

"In his Sanitary . . . 'and gratifying,'" Address to Sanitary Fair, April 18, 1864, in *CW*, VII, 301–3.

APR 22 "Lincoln signed, on . . . all paper money as well," On the Department of the Treasury website, "Fact Sheets, Currency & Coins; History of 'In God We Trust,'" http://www.ustreas.gov/education/fact-sheets/currency/in-god-we-trust.shtml and http://www.ustreas.gov/education/fact-sheets/currency/lincoln-cent.shtml (July 23, 2008).

APR 26 "On this Tuesday . . . his office," Kunhardt, *Lincoln*, 281.

"Lincoln's office . . . Bedroom," Gary, 335.

"Its two windows faced . . . star patterns," Kunhardt, *Lincoln*, 278–81.

"Gas lights . . . September 9, 1864,'" "Let There Be Light," *Response: The Seattle Pacific University Magazine*, Summer 2006, Features Section. Displayed on Seattle Pacific University website, http://www.spu.edu/depts/us/response/summer2k6/features/light.asp (July 24, 2008).

APR 30 "On this Saturday . . . meet the president," Miers, 255.

"Stanton was on . . . against the amendments," Geoffrey C. Ward and Ken Burns, *Not For Ourselves Alone: The Story of Elizabeth Cady Stanton and Susan B. Anthony* (New York: Alfred A. Knopf, 1999), 6, 28–30, 38–9, 49, 102–4, 112–7, 199–203.

"Stanton did not think . . . 'of his reelection,'" Jean H. Baker, *Votes for Women: The Struggle for Suffrage Revisited* (New York: Oxford University Press, 2002), 70.

MAY 2 "According to his . . . provider of the family," Mary Sheffield (Affidavit concerning her husband), April 28, 1864, in *ALP*.

"Lincoln pardoned . . . serve in the army," Order Concerning Alonzo Sheffield, May 2, 1864, in *CW*, VII.,

"Unbeknownst to Lincoln . . . 'final action is taken,'" Daniel T. Van Buren to John A. Dix, May 16, 1864 (Case of Alonzo Sheffield), in *ALP*.

MAY 8 "Grant's 1864 push . . . were thus cremated," Eicher, 662–71.

"So anxious . . . 'Executive Chamber,'" Miers, 257.

"To another . . . promised Lincoln," Kunhardt, 240.

"Instead of . . . 'kind of soldier,'" Eicher, 671.

"Lincoln remarked . . . 'that wins,'" Kunhardt, 240.

MAY 10 "Lincoln's official . . . 'by my authority,'" Lincoln to Oliver D. Filley, December 22, 1863, in *CW*, VII, 85–6.

"General Lew Wallace . . . had not read," Lewis Wallace to Lincoln, May 11, 1864 (Reply to Lincoln's May 10 telegram concerning Francis L. Hawks), in *ALP*

"on this day . . . explanation," Lincoln to Lewis Wallace, May 10, 1864, in *CW*, VII, 335–6.

"When Wallace . . . 'in the matter,'" Lincoln to Lewis Wallace, May 13, 1864, in *CW*, VII, 339–40.

MAY 18 "By 1864 . . . shot up 10 percent," Donald, *Lincoln*, 501.

"Lincoln responded . . . 'treasonable nature,'" Lincoln to John Dix, May 18, 1864, in *CW*, VII, 347–50. According to Lincoln's secretaries John Hay and John Nicolay, Secretary of War Edwin Stanton sent the order to suppress the two New York newspapers without consulting Lincoln (see Sandburg, 511). But according to the editors of *Collected Works*, the telegram was dated and signed in Lincoln's handwriting, indicating at least an awareness of it (*CW*, VII, 348). Whoever was responsible, Lincoln had an opportunity to disavow the order and blame subordinates but refused (Donald, *Lincoln*, 502).

"The next day . . . fist on a table," Donald, *Lincoln*, 502.

MAY 31 "As the 1864 . . . too soft," Goodwin, 624.

"'[Lincoln] looked' . . . Radical Democracy," Donald, *Lincoln*, 497, 502–3.

"had a platform . . . Reconstruction policy," Goodwin, 624.

"Attorney Solomon . . . 'destitute of enthusiasm,'" Solomon Newton Pettis to Lincoln, May 31, 1864 (Cleveland Convention), in *ALP*.

"The *New York* . . . 'hundred men,'" Donald, *Lincoln*, 503.

JUN 6 "On the eve . . . nomination unanimous," Goodwin, 624–5.

"A non-contentious . . . 'of the party,'" Dennett, 186.

"Enthusiasm . . . 7,000 casualties," Donald, *Lincoln*, 504.

"(compared to . . . in U.S. history," Eicher, 686.

"'I regret . . . Grant said," McPherson, 735.

"Many of the delegates . . . chose Johnson," Donald, *Lincoln*, 503, 505.

JUN 8 "On this second . . . awaiting results," Miers, 263.

"The certainity . . . sent to the White House," Goodwin, 623–4, 626.

"The next day . . . 'my present position,'" Reply to Committee Notifying Lincoln of His Nomination, June 9, 1864, in *CW*, VII, 380–4.

"When a Union . . . congratulate Lincoln," Donald, *Lincoln*, 506–7.

"He said, 'I am' . . . 'like to die of,'" Goodwin, 626.

JUN 10 "Before his secretary . . . 'especially worth regarding,'" Dennett, 187–9, 192–4.

JUN 11 "Many writers . . . until Lincoln's death)," Pratt, 124, 127–30.

JUN 21 "Worried about . . . an aide observed," Goodwin, 629.

"Despite an upset . . . 'Jeff Davis,'" Miers, 267.

"together they rode . . . 'I will go in,'" Goodwin, 629–30.

SB67 "For seven weeks . . . three years," McPherson, 741–2.

"'The immense' . . . Gideon Welles," Kunhardt, *Lincoln*, 240.

"Back in Washington . . . said of Grant," Donald, *Lincoln*, 513, 515.

"Lincoln told . . . "is dreadful,'" Kunhardt, *Lincoln*, 240.

"Lincoln was described . . . 'under his eyes,'" Donald, *Lincoln*, 500, 513.

"'Did I ever . . . to Bobby Lee,'" Perret, 364.

JUN 24 "Nineteen months . . . June 15, 1864," Wagner, 428, 436.

"On this Friday . . . the legislation," Lincoln to Edward Bates, June 24, 1864, in *CW*, VII, 404–6.

"During the . . . accept their pay," Wagner, 429, 432.

"'As men who' . . . James Gooding," Noah Andre Trudeau, *Like Men of War: Black Troops in the Civil War 1862–1865* (Boston: Back Pay Books, 1999), 92–3.

"Despite the . . . all black soldiers," Wagner, 434–6.

SB68 "Many black . . . accept any pay," in ibid., 430–2.

"Despite Douglass's . . . their combat deaths," Heidler, 2003.

"For the rest . . . blacks became officers," Wagner, 637, 429–30.

"'We want black . . . understand us,'" Trudeau, 373.

JUN 28 "In 1793 . . . lives in freedom," Wagner, 99.

"Between 1780 . . . slave-catchers," Heidler, 1494.

"It is an irony . . . chief grievances," McPherson, 78–88, 120, 237.

"Before the war . . . Section 2)," Oates, 126.

"In the early . . . slave owners," Wagner, 148.

"but on this . . . Lincoln's signature," Miers, 268.

JUN 30 "Lincoln had, for . . . useful to Chase," Goodwin, 631–2.

"Chase was . . . with Morgan," Lincoln to Salmon P. Chase, June 28, 1864, in *CW*, VII, 412–3.

"Chase penned . . . ended the issue," Lincoln to Salmon P. Chase, June 28, 1864 (different from letter above), in *CW*, VII, 413–4

"But Chase submitted . . . Lincoln wrote," Lincoln to Salmon P. Chase, June 30, 1864, in *CW*, VII, 419.

SB69 "Lincoln later . . . 'it,' Lincoln stated," Goodwin, 632–3.

"The president explained . . . 'elected to do so,'" Dennett, 199.

JUL 1 "Early on June 30 . . . considering another nominee," Goodwin, 633–6.

"He settled on . . . July 4," Donald, *Lincoln*, 509.

JUL 8 "As the presidential . . . unseat Lincoln," Donald, *Lincoln*, 510.

"Conspirators . . . reentering the Union," Goodwin, 639–40.

"Congress passed . . . strict guidelines)," Donald, *Lincoln*, 510–2.

JUL 10 "With General Ulysses . . . the Potomac," Goodwin, 641.

"Threats to . . . before withdrawing," Eicher, 715–7.

"On this day . . . 'keep cool,'" Lincoln to Thomas Swann and Others, July 10, 1864, in *CW*, VII, 437–8.

"Despite the fact . . . of Early's forces," Donald, *Lincoln*, 518.

"'Retain your . . . this vicinity,'" Lincoln to Ulysses S. Grant, July 10, 1864, in *CW*, VII, 437.

"That evening . . . Wright to Washington," Lincoln to Ulysses S. Grant, July 11, 1864, in *CW*, VII, 438.

"At ten that . . . White House," Miers, 271.

JUL 11 "Confederate general . . . the White House," Goodwin, 641–3.

"Lincoln was on . . . vacate the parapet," Donald, *Lincoln*, 519.

"Lincoln left . . . Lincoln to leave," Perret, 367.

"Lincoln instead . . . 'you fool!'" Goodwin, 643.

"Wright again . . . finally departed," Perret, 368.

JUL 16 "On this Saturday . . . end to the war," Lincoln to John Hay, July 16, 1864, in *CW*, VII, 443.

"When, in July . . . in November," Donald, *Lincoln*, 456.

"On July 7 . . . 'doing great harm,'" Horace Greeley to Lincoln, July 7, 1864 (Negotiations at Niagara Falls), in *ALP*.

"Lincoln knew . . . peace efforts dead," Donald, *Lincoln*, 521–3.

"Lincoln, on this . . . to Washington," Miers, 273.

JUL 19 "On this . . . relatives of the president," Miers, 273.

"Lincoln never lived . . . both acquitted," Charles H. Coleman and Paul H. Spence, "The Charleston Riot: March 28, 1864," *Journal of the Illinois State Historical Society*, March, 1940, Volume XXXIII, 1. Reprinted in *Eastern Illinois University Bulletin* April 12, 1961 (No. 234) and July 1, 1965 (No. 257) and found on the Internet, http://homepages.rootsweb.ancestry.com/~ktohair/Documents/CharlestonRiot.pdf (August 29, 2008).

"According to Lincoln's . . . (Young Winkler)," Dennis F. Hanks to Lincoln, April 5, 1864 (Family affairs), in *ALP*.

JUL 26 "On this Tuesday . . . to do just that," Pinsker, 146.

"Early's previous . . . quipped bitterly," Donald, *Lincoln*, 519.

"Mary echoed . . . 'shall be dismissed,'" Goodwin, 644.

"At the end . . . done about Early," Donald, *Lincoln*, 520.

JUL 31 "After Grant . . . gunpowder into the shaft," Heidler, 515.

"On July 30 . . . themselves trapped," Eicher, 721–3.

"The Union suffered . . . Confederate's 1,000," Heidler, 517.

"'It was the . . . assigned him,'" Goodwin, 646.

"Lincoln was on . . . the next morning," Miers, 275–6.

"Grant's confident . . . 'sleep at night'," Perret, 388.

AUG 8 "The Lincolns had . . . bitter tongue," Goodwin, 350–1, 590–3.

"When she decided . . . refused the oath," Lincoln, December 14, 1863 (Amnesty to Emily Todd Helm), in *ALP*.

"On this day . . . 'States authorities,'" Lincoln to Stephen G. Burbridge, August 8, 1863, in *CW*, VII, 484–5.

SB70 "Mary was the fourth . . . start of the Civil War," see Mary Lincoln's genealogy website titled "Donna McCreary as Mary Lincoln/Todd Family Genealogy Information, The Family of Mary Lincoln," found at, http://members.aolcom/beaufait/biography/geneology.htm (June 8, 2007).

"and more than . . . in rebel smuggling," see Kentucky, Lincoln Bicentennial website titled "Lincoln's Rebel Kin, The Todds of Kentucky," http://www.kylincoln.org/lincoln/rebel.htm (September 12, 2008).

"Later, however, she . . . 'mourn his death,'" Jean H. Baker, *Mary Todd Lincoln: A Biography* (New York: W.W. Norton & Company, 1989), 223.

"At another . . . 'destroy our government,'" Packard, 163–4.

AUG 12 "Two things . . . 'make laws,'" Donald, *Lincoln*, 523–4.

"With Radical . . . 'impossibility,'" Miers, 278.

"What was more . . . 'if they can,'" Donald, *Lincoln*, 524–6.

AUG 18 "On this day . . . his nomination," Miers, 279

"General Ulysses . . . Petersburg, Virginia," Wagner, 304.

"Together with . . . 'both in time,'" Goodwin, 646.

"Grant's horrendous . . . 'is a failure,'" Donald, *Lincoln*, 528.

"Swett, on this . . . 'could possibly do,'" Goodwin, 647–8.

AUG 19 "On August 16 . . . 'would have to be found,'" see Charles D. Robinson to Lincoln, August 7, 1864 (Lincoln's military policy) and Lincoln to Charles D. Robinson, August 17, 1864 (Reply to Robinson's letter of August 7), both in *ALP*.

"When Lincoln met . . . Robinson letter," Goodwin, 650–2.

SB71 "The two meetings . . . 'age,' Mills wrote," in ibid., 649–1.

"Lincoln was just . . . revised Robinson letter," Lincoln to Charles D. Robinson, August 1864, in *ALP*.

AUG 21 "On this Sunday . . . 'United States service,'" Order for Testing Wrought Iron Cannon, August 21, 1864, in *CW*, VII, 510. There is some question as to whether this order was written on August 20 or 21. It is dated for August 21 but the War Department records contain a summary of an "Order from Executive Mansion dated August 20th, 1864" that appears to be of the same order. Without further evidence, however, the author stays with the date written on the order.

"Horatio Ames . . . three hundred pounds," Robert V. Bruce, *Lincoln and the Tools of War* (Chicago: University of Illinois Press, 1989), 233.

"Before the war . . . for locomotives," Robert B. Gordon and Patrick Malone, *The Texture of Industry: An Archeological View of the Industrialization of North America* (New York: Oxford University Press, 1994), 104. In *GBS*.

"at the outbreak . . . for stronger cannon," Bruce, 233–4.

"Ames was so confident . . . it was fired," Gordon, 104.

"That April . . . damage to the forts," Eicher, 454–5.

"Lincoln began to . . . foundry and fortune," Bruce, 233, 245–6, 279–81.

AUG 23 "The day . . . to the Democrats," Donald, *Lincoln*, 529.

"Lincoln concurred . . . Lincoln responded," Perret, 391.

"On this day . . . unexplained," Miers, 279–80.

"as Lincoln later . . . 'my own conscience,'" Donald, *Lincoln*, 530.

AUG 25 "Lincoln, on this . . . still possible," Miers, 280.

"On August 22 . . . 'inevitable necessities,'" Henry J. Raymond to Lincoln, August 22, 1864 (Political affairs), in *ALP*.

"Lincoln seriously . . . 'peaceful modes,'" Lincoln to Henry J. Raymond, August 24, 1864, in *CW*, VII, 517–8.

"In the end . . . 'will be reelected,'" Goodwin, 652–3.

"'You think I . . . badly beaten,'" Donald, *Lincoln*, 529.

AUG 28 "At midnight . . . apologized the next day," Pinsker, 38–9, 52–3, 100–2, 165.

SB72 "Lincoln spent thirteen . . . acres to the government," Brownstein, 2–3, 13–15.

"which then named it . . . retreat to Lincoln," Pinsker, 2–3.

"The hilltop . . . left open," Brownstein, 56.

"The first summer . . . grounds with them," Pinsker, 3–4, 169.

"Lincoln received at . . . in the evening," Brownstein, 17.

"'How dearly' . . . husband's death," Pinsker, 5.

SEP 3 "The first news . . . 'fairly won,'" Eicher, 712–4, 726–8, 840.

"Lincoln responded . . . September 11)," Miers, 281–2.

"He also ordered . . . his thanks," Goodwin, 655.

"who had just . . . 'years of failure,'" Donald, *Lincoln*, 530–1.

SB73 "It's tempting . . . later capitulate," Kunhardt, *Lincoln*, 254, 264, 267–8.

"He did not like . . . rejected the platform," Goodwin, 654, 656.

SEP 4 "A number of . . . 'our own country,'" Wagner, 465, 696–7.

"In the fall . . . 'could and can,'" Lincoln to Eliza Gurney, September 4, 1864, in *CW*, VII, 535–6.

SEP 6 "Lincoln, on this . . . she was wounded," Miers, 282.

"During the war . . . in the hospital," Elizabeth D. Leonard, *All the Daring of the Soldier: Women in the Civil War Armies* (New York: Penguin Books, 2001), 165, 170–9, 191–7, 209–10, 212.

"She came to see . . . own pocket," Miers, 282.

SEP 7 "Lincoln, in his . . . 'and better man,'" Current, 58, 62–5.

"On this day . . . presented Lincoln," Miers, 282.

"pulpit–size Bible . . . slave's shackles," Carpenter, 197.

"'This Great . . . portrayed in it,'" Reply to Loyal Colored People of Baltimore upon Presentation of a Bible, September 7, 1864, in *CW*, VII, 542–3.

SB74 "Speculation . . . 'to call Christian,'" Current, 51–5, 58–9, 62–5.

SEP 8 "In August 1864 . . . Vermont," Goodwin, 652.

"On this day . . . total strangers," Lincoln to Mary Lincoln, September 8, 1864, in *CW*, VII, 544.

"Mary acknowledged . . . 'writing' to her," Goodwin, 540.

"Once, while . . . at another time," Donald, *Lincoln*, 130–1.

"During the summer . . . 'to see you,'" Lincoln to Mary Lincoln, September 21 and 22, 1863, both in *CW*, VI, 471–2 and 474 respectively.

SEP 19 "Lincoln, on this . . . state elections," Miers, 284.

"Many thought . . . both elections," Goodwin, 661, 664.

"By then nineteen . . . their districts," McPherson, 804.

"Democrats were . . . 'it,' Lincoln said," Goodwin, 663–4.

"What's more . . . 'died in vain,'" Wagner, 223.

"Lincoln, on this . . . home to vote," Lincoln to William T. Sherman, September 19, 1864, in *CW*, VIII, 11–2.

"As a result . . . congressional seats," Goodwin, 662

"In November . . . for McClellan," Wagner, 224.

SEP 20 "On this day . . . 'officers and men,'" Lincoln to Philip H. Sheridan, September 20, 1864, in *CW*, VIII, 13.

"fertile breadbasket . . . his troops," Heidler, 1747.

"During his Overland . . . down the valley," McPherson, 722, 724, 737–9, 758.

"'Sheridan and . . . to 'strike,'" Lincoln to Ulysses S. Grant, September 12, 1864 (Reinforcements for General Sheridan), in *ALP*.

"A week later . . . Shenandoah harvest," see McPherson, 777 and Perret, 389.

"Confederate Mary . . . 'me, forever,'" Eicher, 748.

SEP 23 "The powerful Blair . . . orders for soldiers," Heidler, 237, 240.

"The Blairs, however . . . to replace him," Goodwin, 658–9.

OCT 1 "Lincoln, on this . . . of the war," Miers, 286.

"On June 26 . . . in their place," W. Emerson Reck, "President Lincoln's 'Substitute,'" *Lincoln Herald*, Fall 1978, Volume 80, Number 3, 137–9. On website, http://www.lincolnherald.com/1970articleSUBSTITUTE.html (September 21, 2007).

"It was meant . . . pay $300," Perret, 370–1.

"In September . . . approached by Fry," Reck, 137–9.

"When Staples . . . Longfellow," Perret, 371–2.

OCT 10 "Out of nearly 92,000 . . . abolishing slavery," Heidler, 1258–60.

"Lincoln was invited . . . Lincoln wrote," Lincoln to Henry W. Hoffman, October 10, 1864 (Maryland Constitution), in *ALP*.

"On October 12 . . . constitution," Heidler, 1,260.

"'I had rather . . . applied to Maryland,'" Goodwin, 663.

"Then in the November . . . 40,000," Heidler, 1260.

OCT 11 "'At eight . . . for siege,'" Dennett, 227.

"The October elections . . . slight edge," Goodwin, 661–2.

OCT 13 "With news that . . . 'resuming his writing,'" Goodwin, 662.

"Lincoln predicted . . . 114 electoral votes," Estimated Electoral Vote, October 13, 1864, in *CW*, VIII, 46.

"Even if Lincoln . . . 'greatly impaired,'" Goodwin, 662.

OCT 15 "Lincoln, on this . . . Roger Taney," Miers, 289.

"Taney, whose . . . Dred Scott case," Heidler, 1,919–21.

"Supreme Court . . . 'self-inflicted wounds,'" Goodwin, 189.

"The case, incorrectly . . . Supreme Court," Heidler, 1,715–6.

"'The question is . . . become a citizen?'" Wagner, 114.

"Taney himself . . . around 1,660," Heidler, 1,919–20.

"Ignoring the fact . . . the Constitution," McPherson, 175.

"'[blacks] are' . . . election as president," Wagner, 114–5.

OCT 22 "In late September . . . Phil said," McPherson, 777–8.

"General Early . . . the battlefield," Eicher, 749–51.

"'With great' . . . on this day," Lincoln to Philip H. Sheridan, October 22, 1864, in *CW*, VIII, 73–4.

"Congress, too . . . a promotion," Warner, 439.

OCT 29 "Lincoln, on this . . . of her time," Miers, 292.

"Truth was born . . . black regiments," Heidler, 1,977.

"And moved . . . city's streetcars," Wagner, 135–6.

"When Truth met . . . 'to see you,'" Sandburg, 595.

"Truth later . . . 'cordiality,'" Donald, *Lincoln*, 541.

"Truth asked . . . 'A. Lincoln,'" Sandburg, 596.

"The old woman . . . 'his cause,'" Donald, *Lincoln*, 541.

SB75 "Modern ears . . . 'superior position,'" DiLorenzo, 11.

"Lincoln supported . . . were not racist," Miller, 356–7.

"He was, for . . . racist country," Goodwin, 469, 551–3. See also Packard, 212–3 and Sandburg, 595–6.

"Lincoln's Springfield . . . of the procession," Kunhardt, *Twenty Days*, 275.

OCT 31 "Lincoln, on this . . . thirty-sixth state," Miers, 292.

"Under the 1848 . . . and Wyoming," Wagner, 108.

"Nevada was still . . . now Virginia City," *New Standard Encyclopedia*, Volume 12 (Chicago: Standard Education Corporation, 1993), 160.

"There is a myth . . . government was formed," see the Nevada State Library and Archives website written by Nevada State Archivist Guy Rocha, http://dmla.clan.lib.nv.us/docs/nsla/archives/myth/myth121.html, http://dmla.clan.lib.nv.us/docs/nsla/archives/myth/myth12.html (November 12, 2007).

NOV 3 "On this Thursday . . . transportation for him," Miers, 293.

"Presidential . . . for themselves," Donald, *Lincoln*, 480.

"Just a week . . . 'political speech,'" Speech at Hotel Continential, Philadelphia, Pennsylvania, June 16, 1864, in *CW*, VII, 398.

"But Lincoln was . . . fracture the party," Donald, *Lincoln*, 538–9.

"Lincoln also worked . . . Dana wrote," Goodwin, 663–4.

"Three out of . . . their vote," Perret, 392.

"Lincoln, however . . . 'and ruined us,'" Donald, *Lincoln*, 539.

NOV 4 "The transcontinental railroad had . . . vacated Congress," McPherson, 108, 193–4, 451.

"On July 1 . . . in June 1863," David Bain, *Empire Express: Building the First Transcontinental Railroad* (New York: Viking Penguin, 1999), 115, 118, 158, 160–1.

"Lincoln gave Council . . . on this day," Approval of First Hundred Miles of Union Pacific Railroad, November 4, 1864, in *CW*, VIII, 89.

"Dodge was present . . . Summit, Utah," Bain, 661–2.

NOV 8 "'The [White] house . . . the President,'" Dennett, 232–3.

"Lincoln himself . . . out-of-state voting," Goodwin, 664.

"At seven . . . the president said," Dennett, 233–4.

"By the time . . . Delaware and Kentucky," Goodwin, 665–6.

"The next day . . . 'uncomfortable had happened,'" Brooks, 199.

SB76 "By election day . . . in today's dollars," Packard, 177.

"'Mr. Lincoln has . . . run in debt,'" Goodwin, 682.

"Mary was . . . 'would know all,'" Donald, *Lincoln*, 540.

"'The people . . . of kid gloves,'" Goodwin, 682–3.

"What was more . . . limit her debts," Oates, 58, 70–1.

"Her habit continued . . . with clothes," Kunhardt, *Lincoln*, 394–7.

NOV 11 "'The election demonstrated . . . common country?'" Donald, *Lincoln*, 546.

"When a friend . . . 'past against him,'" Goodwin, 665.

"Lincoln revealed . . . 'it afterwards,'" Dennett, 237–8.

NOV 21 "When a Boston . . . contact the president," Michael Burlingame, "The Trouble with the Bixby Letter," *American Heritage Magazine*, July/August 1999, Vol. 50, Issue 4. On the magazine's website, http://www.americanheritage.com/articls/magazine/ah/1999/4/1999_4_64_print.shtml (December 14, 2007).

"The result was . . . 'altar of freedom,'" Lincoln to Lydia Bixby, November 21, 1864, in *CW*, VIII, 116–7.

"Bixby did not . . . remains unresolved," Burlingame, "Trouble," see above.

"Two of her sons . . . deserted the army," Lincoln to Lydia Bixby, November 21, 1864, see above.

NOV 24 "Born of Virginia . . . former masters," Heidler, 189–90.

"He did, however . . . as Bate's replacement," Goodwin, 673–6.

DEC 2 "The exchange of . . . and starvation," Wagner, 585.

"Lincoln, hoping . . . Lincoln recommended," Lincoln to Edwin M. Stanton, March 18, 1864, in *CW*, VII, 254–7.

"For three days . . . 'Shortest and Best Speech,'" Story Written for Noah Brooks, December 6, 1864, VIII, 154–5.

SB77 "The Confederate military . . . malnutrition," Heidler, 48.

"Overall, Union . . . as their prisoners," Wagner, 583–5, 607.

"Initially, captured . . . sending supplies," Perret, 377–8.

"Five months later . . . even more," Heidler, 1571.

"There are no . . . 'men like that,'" Perret, 377–8.

DEC 7 "On this Wednesday . . . Supreme Court," Miers, 300.

"Lincoln had already . . . Roger Taney," Donald, *Lincoln*, 551.

"The president's . . . 'nomination or office,'" Goodwin, 676–80.

"That was not . . . in 1868," Heidler, 410.

"Nor was Lincoln . . . 'appointment I make,'" Donald, *Lincoln*, 552.

SB78 "When Lincoln became . . . fill the seat," Silver, 1–3, 8–10, 58, 64, 74, 86–8.

"Lincoln knew . . . abolitionists," Donald, *Lincoln*, 551–2.

"Indeed, the court . . . *vs. Griswold*," Heidler, 1907–8.

DEC 10 "There is little . . . knew him intimately," Donald, "*We are*", xiii–xvi, 65–6.

"The early death . . . close relationships," Shenk, 13–14.

"Lincoln's law . . . 'communicated nothing,'" Current, 12–3.

"Lamon submitted . . . without protection," Miers, 301.

"Lincoln was escorted . . . Lamon chided," Donald, *Lincoln*, 548.

SB79 "Speculation about . . . to share beds," Donald, "*We are*," 35–6, 140–6.

"During the Gettysburg . . . with two women," Wills, 30.

"Despite the fact . . . 'night-shirts,'" Donald, "*We are*," 36–9, 142–3.

DEC 15 "After General William . . . stubborn to quit," McPherson, 807–13.

"Washington viewed . . . Hood's army," Perret, 394. Perret incorrectly states that the December 15 battle was at "Franklin, Tennessee." The battle of Franklin was on November 30, Nashville on December 15–16.

"Meanwhile Grant . . . his thanks," Miers, 301.

DEC 21 "War Democrats hailed . . . hunt for glory," Heidler, 2,059–60, 329–31.

"As military administrator . . . 'incorrectly informed,'" Lincoln to Benjamin F. Butler, December 21, 1864, in *CW*, VIII, 174.

"Lincoln prickly . . . misinformed," Lincoln to Benjamin F. Butler, December 28, 1864, in *CW*, VIII, 186.

"Many War Democrats . . . that alliance," Heidler, 2,060.

DEC 25 "Lincoln, on this . . . 'bales of cotton,'" Perret, 395.

"Sherman's 'March . . . less relentless,'" Eicher, 761–3.

"His 62,000 . . . worth of damage," Heidler, 1,769–70.

"On December 20 . . . to Lincoln," Eicher, 768.

"The message arrived . . . 'But what next?'" Lincoln to William T. Sherman, December 26, 1864 (Acknowledges Sherman's Christmas gift—the capture of Savannah), in *ALP*.

"Sherman was already . . . Sherman wrote," Eicher, 768.

1865

JAN 2 "Because New Year's . . . decided to go in," Packard, 212–3.

"'For two hours . . . Abraham Lincoln,'" Sandburg, 643.

JAN 9 "The Lincolns . . . 'served him,'" Margarita Spalding Gerry, ed., *Through Five Administrations: Reminiscences of Colonel William Crook* (New York: Harper & Brothers Publishers, 1910), 5, 8–9. In *GBS*.

"The War Department . . . House," Perret, 65.

JAN 15 "On this Sunday . . . 'Illinois,'" Kunhardt, *Lincoln*, 262, 326–8.

"But inventions . . . the NAS," in National Academy of Sciences website, http://www7.nationalacademies.org/archives/nasfounding.html, http,//www7.nationalacademies.org/archives/founding.html (May 6, 2008). See also, Edward Lurie, *Louis Agassiz: A Life in Science* (Chicago: University of Chicago Press, 1960), 333.

"Agassiz was . . . evolution," Lurie, 254–5.

"Instead of . . . 'things are,'" Kunhardt, *Lincoln*, 262.

JAN 17 "One of the Union's . . . war," Wagner, 334, 543, 547.

"On this day . . . fight," Miers, 308.

"Confederate general . . . 'war,'" McPherson, 820–1.

"Confederate admiral . . . 'around us,'" Eicher, 797.

JAN 30 "This peace . . . 'one common country,'" Heidler, 919.

"Davis ignored . . . that stipulation," Lincoln to House of Representatives, February 10, 1865 (Draft of Message Concerning Hampton Roads Conference), in *ALP*.

FEB 1 "His three-year-old . . . tuberculosis," Kunhardt, *Lincoln*, 90.

"Lincoln finally . . . after the war," Donald, *Lincoln*, 553–4.

"'A question . . . evils,'" Goodwin, 686.

"Lincoln was . . . ratify it," Kunhardt, *Lincoln*, 264.

"More than . . . amendment," Long, 696.

"'If the people . . . have,'" Oates, 441.

FEB 3 "Lincoln, initially . . . the fortress," Goodwin, 692.

"There, he met . . . 'his head,'" Donald, *Lincoln*, 557–8.

"His nephew . . . next day," Miers, 311.

FEB 7 "Lincoln received . . . a pony," see the following in *ALP*, Charles Sumner to Lincoln, January 14, 1863 (Sends pears); E. Willard to Lincoln, February 11, 1864 (Sends venison); Ischar Zachario to Lincoln, February 13, 1864 (Sends barrel of hominy); Perkins Stern & Co. to Lincoln, December 16, 1864 (Sends wine from California); W. C. Cattell to Lincoln, June 23, 1864 (Sends fruit cake); Sara Phelps to Lincoln, January 1865 (Sends socks); Ethelbert P. Oliphant to Lincoln, December 1860 (Sends eagle quill); S. Shreckengaust to Lincoln, April 2, 1861 (Sends slippers and political advice); Benjamin Butler to Lincoln, July 1, 1862 (Sends captured swords); Lincoln to Shakers, August 8, 1864 (Acknowledges chair); D. M. Jenkins to Lincoln, June 10, 1862 (Sends eagle); James J. Lewis to Lincoln, February 18, 1865 (Sends sheep).

"On this Tuesday . . . 'generous gift,'" Lincoln to William Lloyd Garrison, February 7, 1865, in *CW*, VIII, 265–6.

"The 'Watch' . . . Proclamation," in White House official website, http://www.whitehouse.gov/history/art/presart-2.html (May 22, 2008).

FEB 17 "'During my' . . . later lamented," Current, 48.

"During Lincoln's . . . again," Kunhardt, *Lincoln*, 90, 288.

"Once the war . . . 'back to us,'" Donald, *Lincoln*, 571.

"Mary finally . . . boy safe," Packard, 214.

"Then on . . . a captain," Miers, 314.

FEB 26 "Lincoln was . . . write it," Miller, 14.

"In the case . . . was not," Donald, *Lincoln*, 465.

"But on . . . Carpenter," Miers, 316.

"It was the shortest . . . 'I suspect,'" Donald, *Lincoln*, 566, 568.

MAR 4 "Lincoln's first . . . 'outside,'" Donald, *Lincoln*, 565.

"Lincoln moved . . . 'nation's wounds,'" Kunhardt, *Lincoln*, 266–7.

SB80 "On that sunny . . . to speak," Donald, *Lincoln*, 282–3.

"He first . . . sixteenth president," Kunhardt, *Lincoln*, 26–8.

MAR 17 "On this Friday . . . to Richmond," Steers, 85.

"Booth hated . . . Baltimore and Washington," Donald, *Lincoln*, 586–7.

"When he heard . . . soon dispersed," Steers, 86–8, 306.

SB81 "Investigation into . . . never showed," Alan Axelrod, *The Complete Idiot's Guide to the Civil War* (New York: Alpha Books, 2003), 339. In *GBS*.

"Booth waited . . . leaving town," Steers, 83–88.

MAR 22 "In February . . . return to duty," Warner, 103.

"General in Chief Ulysses . . . send Crook to General Grant," Lincoln to Winfield S. Hancock, March 22, 1865, in *CW*, VIII, 370–1.

"Crook commanded . . . of the war," Warner, 103.

MAR 23 "For the first . . . a family reunion," Goodwin, 707–8.

"At 1:00 PM . . . the James River," Miers, 322.

"Tad's curiousity . . . the trip," Donald, *Lincoln*, 571–2.

"The ship . . . 'entirely recovered,'" Miers, 322.

"It was the start . . . as president," Goodwin, 707.

MAR 26 "On March 25 . . . 'don't you?'" Sandburg, 674, 676–7.

"When Lincoln . . . shouted at him,'" Oates, 455.

"At dinner . . . was ill," Goodwin, 712.

SB82 "Even before . . . 'walk off,'" Donald, *Lincoln*, 158–9.

"She did have . . . 'would break,'" Shenk, 102.

"Headaches . . . her eyes," Kunhardt, *Lincoln*, 396–7.

"Mary was also . . . mood swings," Brownstein, 225.

"Yet another . . . firewood," Donald, *Lincoln*, 108.

MAR 27 "On this Monday . . . conference," Miers, 323.

"Lincoln first . . . not happen," Donald, *Lincoln*, 573.

"The next day . . . 'to him,'" Foote, Volume III, 855–6.

MAR 31 "By March . . . escape route," Eicher, 804–6.

"On March 29 . . . 'present movement,'" Goodwin, 714.

"On this morning . . . forwarded to Washington," Lincoln to Edwin Stanton, March 31, 1865, in *CW*, VIII, 378–9.

"To meet Grant's . . . not rail," Eicher, 809, 811.

"Lincoln decided . . . next day," Miers, 324.

APR 2 "On April 1 . . . from the South," Eicher, 808–9.

"Grant sent . . . 'is victory,'" Foote, Vol. III, 893.

"Mary Lincoln . . . 'short scabbard,'" Goodwin, 715.

"Grant began . . . to Washington," Lincoln sent three telegrams to Secretary of War Edwin Stanton on April 2, 1865 forwarding news from the battle. See Lincoln to Edwin M. Stanton, April 2, 1865 (11 AM; 2 PM; 8,30PM), all in *CW*, VIII, 382–4.

"Twelve hours . . . 'I will do,'" Lincoln to Mary Todd Lincoln, April 2, 1865, in *CW*, VIII, 384.

"A weary Lincoln . . . 'foot sideways,'" Goodwin, 715.

"Lincoln received . . . his government," Lincoln to Edwin M. Stanton, April 3, 1865, in *CW*, VIII, 384–5.

APR 4 "Secretary of . . . 'to yourself?'" Edwin M. Stanton to Lincoln, April 3, 1865 (Telegram urging Lincoln to exercise caution), in *ALP*.

"When he wired . . . 'there tomorrow,'" Lincoln to Edwin M. Stanton, April 3, 1865, in *CW*, VIII, 385.

"On this day . . . 'to see Richmond,'" Kunhardt, *Lincoln*, 91, 268.

APR 8 "By the time . . . 'been disolved?'" Foote, Vol. III, 909, 917.

"On April 7 . . . 'be pressed,'" Long, 668–9.

"On this day . . . 'touch him further,'" Goodwin, 722–3.

"While Lincoln . . . capitulated," Miers, 327.

APR 11 "Washington . . . began reading," Donald, *Lincoln*, 581–2.

"'The speech was' . . . said Brooks," Goodwin, 727.

"Instead of delivering . . . he asked," Last Public Address, April 11, 1865, in *CW*, VIII, 399–406.

"In the audience . . . 'him through,'" Donald, *Lincoln*, 588.

SB83 "There were claims . . . in today's money," Steers, 60–1, 71, 73.

"While Booth . . . help the South," Donald, *Lincoln*, 585–6.

"He wrote after . . . 'punishment,'" Kunhardt, *Lincoln*, 355.

APR 14 "This Good . . . Union victories," Goodwin, 731.

"At three . . . to travel," Donald, *Lincoln*, 593.

"'During the drive . . . to a close,'" Goodwin, 733.

"At the Navy . . . be performed," Kunhardt, *Twenty Days*, 18, 80–1.

SB84 "It had been . . . 'about it,'" Donald, *Lincoln*, 593–5.

"At twelve after ten," Goodwin, 738.

"Booth presented . . . from the stage," Steers, 116–8.

"Most of . . . 'shot the President,'" Goodwin, 739.

APR 15 "John Wilkes . . . behind both eyes," Kunhardt, *Twenty Days*, 93–5.

"When Dr. Charles . . . 'became discolored,'" Steers, 121–4, 127.

"Stanton moved . . . telegraph was not," in ibid., 127, 129. Conspiracy theories about Lincoln's death form a virtual cottage industry and more than a few writers have made a living rehashing so-called evidence supporting the belief that either the Confederate government or Lincoln's own administration conspired to kill him. It would be generous to call their evidence flimsy. Edwin Stanton has been particularly vilified by such proponents. Stanton had plenty of faults but he certainly does not deserve to have his reputation smeared. For a more detailed debunking of such theories, see William Hatchett, *The Lincoln Murder Conspiracies* (Chicago: University of Illinois Press, 1986), 195–208.

"At seven . . . Stanton said," Kunhardt, *Lincoln*, 359.

Afterword-II

"After Lincoln's . . . previous fall," from the American Memory From the Library of Congress website, http://memory.loc.gov/cgi–bin/query/h?ammem/scsmbib:@field(DOCID+@lit(scsm001049)).html (June 22, 2009).

"When Daniel J. Boorstin . . . 'humanize him,'" "Lincoln's Pocket Contents at Time of Death Shown," *The Ledger* (Lakeland, FL), April 1, 1976, 4C, at website, http://news.goggle.com/newspapers?dat=19760401&id=nCeVAAAAIBAJ&sjid=9voDAAAA.html (June 24, 2009).

"There was no chance . . . back in 1914," "Federal Reserve Sends Out New $5 Bills," *Atlanta Business Journal*, March 13, 2008, on website, http://atlanta.bizjournals.com/atlanta/stories/2008/03/10/daily39.html (June 24, 2009).

"According to Boorstin . . . it in 1976," *The Ledger*, April 1, 1976, see above.

"After his death... 'mantle of Caesar'" David H. Donald, *Lincoln Reconsidered* (New York: Vintage Books, 1961), 4–5.

"It's no wonder . . . lock on the presidency," *New Standard Encyclopedia*, Vol. 13, 554.

"Franklin Roosevelt . . . Andrew Jackson," Donald, *Reconsidered*, 14.

"To others... a socialist," in ibid., 17.

"Twisting Lincoln's . . . Ku Klux Klan," Stephen B. Oates, *Abraham Lincoln: The Man Behind the Myths* (New York: Harper & Row, 1984), 21.

"After his death . . . 'died for his country,'" in ibid., 4.

"Dozens of stories . . . a Spiritualist," Donald, *Reconsidered*, 152-3.

"There was Josiah . . . democratic ideals," Oates, *Myths*, 5-10.

"After his death . . . 'A. Lincoln,'" Donald, *Reconsidered*, 147-8.

"Another bit . . . Home in Springfield," Beth Py-Lieberman, "Lincoln's Pocket Watch Reveals Long-Hidden Message," Smithsonian.com (March 11, 2009). Found at http://www.smithsonianmag.com/history-archaeology/Lincolns-Pocket-Watch-Reveals-Long-Hidden-Message.html.

Bibliography

Allardt, Linda, David W. Hill, and Ruth H. Bennett, eds. *The Journals and Miscellaneous Notebooks of Ralph Waldo Emerson*, Volume XV 1860-1866. Cambridge, MA: The Belknap Press of Harvard University Press, 1982.

Allen, Gay Wilson. *Waldo Emerson: A Biography*. New York: Viking Press, 1981.

Axelrod, Alan. *The Complete Idiot's Guide to the Civil War*. New York: Alpha Books, 2003.

Bain, David Haward. *Empire Express: Building the First Transcontinental Railroad*. New York: Viking Penguin, 1999.

Baker, Jean H. *Mary Todd Lincoln: A Biography*. New York: W.W. Norton & Company, 1989.

———. *Votes for Women: The Struggle for Suffrage Revisited*. New York: Oxford University Press, 2002.

Barnum, Phineas T. *Struggles and Triumphs: Or, Forty Years of Recollections of P. T. Barnum*. Buffalo, NY: Warren, Johnson & Co., 1873.

Bates, David Homer. *Lincoln in the Telegraph Office: Recollections of the United States Military Telegraph Corps During the Civil War*. Lincoln, NE: University of Nebraska Press, 1995.

Bayne, Julia Taft. *Tad Lincoln's Father*. Lincoln, NE: University of Nebraska Press, 2001.

Beran, Michael Knox. *Forge of Empires, 1861-1871: Three Revolutionary Statesmen and the World They Made*. New York: Free Press, 2007.

Brewer, John. *A Sentimental Murder: Love and Madness in the Eighteenth Century*. New York: Farrar, Straus and Giroux, 2004.

Brooks, Noah. *Washington in Lincoln's Time*. New York: Rinehart & Co., 1958.

Brownstein, Elizabeth Smith. *Lincoln's Other White House: The Untold Story of the Man and His Presidency*. Hoboken, NJ: John Wiley and Sons, 2005.

Bruce, Robert V. *Lincoln and the Tools of War*. Chicago: University of Illinois Press, 1989.

Buchanan, James. "Fourth Annual Message to Congress on the State of the Union." In "The American Presidency Project," edited by John T. Woolley and Gerhard Peters. Found at http://www.presidency.ucsb.edu/ws/print.php?pid=29501.

Burlingame, Michael. *The Inner World of Abraham Lincoln*. Chicago: University of Illinois Press, 1997.

———, ed. "The Trouble with the Bixby Letter." *American Heritage Magazine* 50, no. 4 (July/August 1999). Found at http://www.americanheritage.com/articls/magazine/ah/1999/4/1999_4_64_print.shtml (December 14, 2007).

———, ed. *Lincoln Observed: Civil War Dispatches of Noah Brooks*. Baltimore: The Johns Hopkins University Press, 1998.

Carpenter, F. B. *The Inner Life of Abraham Lincoln: Six Months at the White House*. Lincoln, NE: University of Nebraska Press, 1995.

Chapman, Ervin S. *Latest Light on Abraham Lincoln and War-Time Memories: Including Many Heretofore Unpublished Incidents and Historical Facts Concerning His Ancestry, Boyhood, Family, Religion, Public Life, Trials and Triumphs*. New York: Fleming H. Revell Company, 1917.

Coleman, Charles H. and Paul H. Spence. "The Charleston Riot, March 28, 1864." *Journal of the Illinois State Historical Society* 33, no. 1 (March, 1940). Reprinted in *Eastern Illinois University Bulletin* 234 (April 12, 1961) and 257 (July 1, 1965). Found at http://homepages.rootsweb.ancestry.com/~ktohair/Documents/CharlestonRiot.pdf (August 29, 2008).

Current, Richard N. *The Lincoln Nobody Knows*. New York: Hill and Wang, 1963.

Davis, Lance E. Stanley L. Engerman. *Naval Blockades in Peace and War: An Economic History Since 1750*. New York: Cambridge University Press, 2006.

Dennett, Tyler, ed. *Lincoln and the Civil War in the Diaries and Letters of John Hay*. New York: Da Capo Press, 1988.

Detzer, David. *Allegiance: Fort Sumter, Charleston, and the Beginning of the Civil War*. New York: Harcourt Inc., 2001.

DiLorenzo, Thomas J. *The Real Lincoln: A New Look at Abraham Lincoln, His Agenda, and an Unnecessary War*. New York: Three Rivers Press, 2003.

Donald, David H. *Lincoln*. London: Jonathan Cape, 1995.

———. *Lincoln Reconsidered*. New York: Vintage Books, 1961.

———. *"We Are Lincoln Men": Abraham Lincoln and His Friends*. New York: Simon & Schuster, 2003.

Eicher, David. *The Longest Night: A Military History of the Civil War*. New York: Simon & Schuster, 2001.

Farrow, Anne, Joel Lang, and Jennifer Frank. *Complicity: How the North Promoted, Prolonged and Profited from Slavery*. New York: Ballantine Books, 2005.

Fehrenbacher, Don Edward and Virginia Fehrenbacher, eds. *Recollected Words of Abraham Lincoln*. Stanford: Stanford University Press, 1996.

"Federal Reserve Sends Out New $5 Bills," *Atlanta Business Journal*, March 13, 2008. Found at http://atlanta.bizjournals.com/atlanta/stories/2008/03/10/daily39.html (June 24, 2009).

Flamme, Karen. *1995 Annual Report: A Brief History of Our Nation's Paper Money*. The Federal Reserve Bank of San Francisco, 1995 Annual Report. Found at http://www.frbsf.org/publications/federalreserve/annual/1995/history.html.

Foote, Shelby. *The Civil War, A Narrative*. 3 vols. New York: Random House, 1958, 1963, 1974.

Gallman, Matthew. *America's Joan of Arc: The Life of Anna Elizabeth Dickinson*. New York: Oxford University Press, 2006.

Gamble, James. "Wiring a Continent: The Making of the U.S. Transcontinental Telegraph Line." *The Californian*, 1881. Found at http://www.telegraph-history.org/transcontinental-telegraph/index.html (October 30, 2007).

Gary, Ralph. *Following in Lincoln's Footsteps: A Complete Annotated Reference to Hundreds of Historical Sites Visited by Abraham Lincoln*. New York: Carroll & Graf Publishers, 2001.

George, Konstantin. "The U.S.–Russian Entente That Saved the Union." *Executive Intelligence Review* (1992). Reprinted from *The Campaigner* (1978) and found at http://members.tripod.com/~american_almanac/risscwar.html (February 12, 2008).

Gerry, Margarita Spalding, ed. *Through Five Administrations: Reminiscences of Colonel William Crook*. New York: Harper & Brothers Publishers, 1910.

Goff, John S. *Robert Todd Lincoln: A Man in His Own Right*. Norman, OK: University of Oklahoma Press, 1969.

Goodwin, Doris Kearns. *Team of Rivals: The Political Genius of Abraham Lincoln*. New York: Simon & Schuster, 2005.

Gordon, Robert B. and Patrick Malone, *The Texture of Industry: An Archeological View of the Industrialization of North America*. New York: Oxford University Press, 1994.

Harris, Neil. *Humbug: The Art of P. T. Barnum*. Boston: Little, Brown and Company, 1973.

Haskins, James and Kathleen Benson. *Bound for America: The Forced Migration of Africans to the New World*. New York: Lothrop, Lee & Shepard Books, 1999.

Hatchett, William. *The Lincoln Murder Conspiracies*. Chicago: University of Illinois Press, 1986.

Heidler, David S. and Jeanne T. Heidler, ed. *Encyclopedia of the American Civil War: A Political, Social and Military History*. New York: W.W. Norton & Co., 2000.

Helm, Katherine. *The True Story of Mary, Wife of Lincoln: Containing the Recollections of Mary's Sister Emilie (Mrs. Ben Helm), Extracts from her War-Time Diary, Numerous Letters and Other Documents*. New York: Harper and Brothers, 1928.

Hirschfelder, Arlene. *Native Americans*. New York: Dorling Kindersley Publishing, 2000.

Holzer, Harold. *Lincoln at Cooper Union: The Speech That Made Abraham Lincoln President*. New York: Simon & Schuster, 2004.

———. "The Many Images of Lincoln." *Antique Trader* (April, 1995). Found at http://www/abrahamlincolnartgallery.com/referenceholzerpg1.html (February 29, 2008).

Johnson, Scott W. and John H. Hinderaker. "A Genius for Friendship." Found at http://www.claremont.org/publications/pub_print.asp?pubid=168 (October 1, 2008).

Joiner, Gary D. *Mr. Lincoln's Brown Water Navy: The Mississippi Squadron*. Lanham, MD: Rowman & Littlefield Publishers, 2007.

Jones, Archer. *Civil War Command and Strategy: The Process of Victory and Defeat*. New York: Free Press, 1992.

Kaufman, Michael W. *American Brutus: John Wilkes Booth and the Lincoln Conspiracies*. New York: Random House, 2004.

Keckley, Elizabeth Keckley. *Behind the Scenes, or, Thirty Years as a Slave, and Four Years in the White House*. New York: G.W. Carleton & Co., 1868.

Keyes, Erasus Darwin. *Fifty Years' Observations of Men and Events, Civil and Military*. New York: C. Scribner's Sons, 1884.

Kunhardt, Phillip B. Jr., Phillip B. Kunhardt III, and Peter Kunhardt. *Lincoln: An Illustrated Biography*. New York: Alfred A. Knopf, 1992.

Kunhardt, Dorothy Meserve and Philip B. Kunhardt Jr. *Twenty Days: A Narrative in Text and Pictures of the Assassination of Abraham Lincoln and the Twenty Days and Nights That Followed—The Nation in Mourning, the Long Trip Home to Springfield*. Secaucus, NJ: Castle Books, 1965.

Lee, Richard M. *Mr. Lincoln's City: An Illustrated Guide to the Civil War Sites of Washington*. McLean, VA: EPM Publications, 1981.

Leonard, Elizabeth D. *All the Daring of the Soldier: Women in the Civil War Armies*. New York: Penguin Books, 2001.

"Lincoln's Pocket Contents at Time of Death Shown." *The Ledger* (Lakeland, FL) (April 1, 1976): 4C. Found at http://news.goggle.com/newspapers?dat=19760401&id=nCeVAAAAIBAJ&sjid=9voDAAAA.html (June 24, 2009).

"Let There Be Light." *Response; The Seattle Pacific University Magazine* (Summer 2006). Found at http://www.spu.edu/depts/us/response/summer2k6/features/light.asp (July 24, 2008).

Long, E. B. and Barbara Long. *The Civil War Day By Day: An Almanac, 1861-1865*. New York: Da Capo Press, 1971.

Lurie, Edward. *Louis Agassiz: A Life in Science*. Chicago: University of Chicago Press, 1960.

Maynard, Nettie Colburn. *Was Abraham Lincoln a Spiritualist? Or Curious Revelations From the Life of a Trance Medium*. Philadelphia: Rufus C. Hartranft, 1891.

McPherson, James M. *Battle Cry of Freedom: The Civil War Era*. New York: Ballantine Books, 1988.

Miers, Earl Schenck. *Lincoln Day by Day: A Chronology, 1809- 1865*. Dayton, OH: Morningside, 1991.

Miller, William Lee. *Lincoln's Virtues: An Ethical Biography*. New York: Vintage Books, 2002.

Neely, Mark E. Jr. *The Fate of Liberty: Abraham Lincoln and Civil Liberty*. New York: Oxford University Press, 1991.

Nelson, James L. *Reign of Iron: The Story of the First Battling Ironclads, the Monitor and the Merrimack*. New York: HarperCollins Publishers, 2004.

New Standard Encyclopedia. Chicago: Standard Education Corporation, 1993.

Noyalas, Jonathan A. "The Most Hated Man in Winchester." *America's Civil War Times* 17 (March 2004): 30–6.

Oates, Stephen B. *Abraham Lincoln: The Man Behind the Myths*. New York: Harper & Row, 1984.

———. *With Malice Toward None: The Life of Abraham Lincoln*. New York: Mentor Books 1977.

Packard, Jerrold. *The Lincolns in the White House: Four Years that Shattered a Family*. New York: St. Martin's Press, 2005.

Perret, Geoffrey. *Lincoln's War: The Untold Story of America's Greatest President as Commander in Chief*. New York: Random House, 2004.

Pinsker, Matthew. *Lincoln's Sanctuary: Abraham Lincoln and the Soldiers' Home*. New York: Oxford Press, 2003.

Poore, Ben Perley. *Perley's Reminiscences of Sixty Years in the National Metropolis*. Vol. 2. Philadelphia: Hubbard Brothers, Publishers, 1886.

Pratt, Harry E. *The Personal Finances of Abraham Lincoln*. Springfield, IL: The Abraham Lincoln Association, 1943.

Phillips, Mark Salber. *Society and Sentiment: Genres of Historical Writing in Britain, 1740–1820*, Princeton, NJ: Princeton University Press, 2000.

Py-Lieberman, Beth. "Lincoln's Pocket Watch Reveals Long-Hidden Message." Smithsonian.com (March 11, 2009). Found at http://www.smithsonianmag.com/history-archaeology/Lincolns-Pocket-Watch-Reveals-Long-Hidden-Message.html.

Randall, Ruth Painter. *Lincoln's Sons*. Boston: Little Brown and Co., 1955.

Reck, W. Emerson. "President Lincoln's 'Substitute.'" *Lincoln Herald* 80, no. 3 (Fall 1978): 137–9.

Rice, Allen Thorndike, ed. *Reminiscences of Abraham Lincoln by Distinguished Men of His Time*. New York: North American Review, 1888.

Richardson, Nathaniel K. *One Hundred Choice Selections in Poetry and Prose: Both New and Old*. Philadelphia: P. Gerrett & Co., 1866.

Rietveld, Ronald D. "The Lincoln White House Community." *Journal of the Abraham Lincoln Association* (Summer 1999). Found at http://www.historycooperative.org/journals/jala/20.2/rietveld.html.

Ruggles, Eleanor. *Prince of Players: Edwin Booth*. Westport, CT: Greenwood Press, 1972.

Sandburg, Carl. *Abraham Lincoln: The Prairie Years & The War Years*. New York: Harcourt, Brace, 1954.

Sears, Stephen, ed. *Civil War Papers of George B. McClellan: Selected Correspondence 1860-1865*. New York: Da Capo Press, 1992.

Shenk, Joshua Wolf. *Lincoln's Melancholy*. New York: Houghton Mifflin Co., 2005.

Silver, David M. *Lincoln's Supreme Court*. Urbana, IL: University of Illinois Press, 1956.

Simpson, Brooks D. "Lincoln and His Political Generals." *Journal of the Abraham Lincoln Association* (Winter 2000).

Soldier Life. NewYork: Barnes & Noble, 2007.

Staunton, Howard, ed. *The Globe Illustrated Shakespeare: The Complete Works Annotated.* New York: Gramercy Books, 1979.

Steers, Edward Jr. *Blood on the Moon: The Assassination of Abraham Lincoln*. Lexington, KY: University of Kentucky, 2001.

Stern, Phillip Van Doren. *Prologue to Sumter: The Beginnings of the Civil War from the John Brown Raid to the Surrender of Fort Sumter*. Greenwich, CT: Fawcett Publications, 1961.

Stoddard, William. *Inside the White House in War Times: Memoirs and Reports of Lincoln's Secretary*. Lincoln, NE: University of Nebraska Press, 2000.

Seward, Frederick. *Reminiscences of a War-Time Statesman and Diplomat, 1830-1915*. New York: G. P. Putnam's Sons, 1916.

Thomas, Benjamin P. "Lincoln's Humor, An Analysis." *Journal of Abraham Lincoln Association* 3 (1981): 28–47. Found at http://www.historycooperative.org/journals/jala/3/thomas/html (February 21, 2008).

Trudeau, Noah Andre. *Like Men of War: Black Troops in the Civil War, 1862-1865*. Boston: Back Bay Books, 1999.

Villard, Henry. *Memoirs of Henry Villard: Journalist and Financier, 1835-1900*. New York: Houghton Mifflin and Company, 1904.

Wagner, Margaret E., Gary W. Gallagher, and Paul Finkelman, eds. *Civil War Desk Reference*. New York: Simon & Schuster, 2002.

———. *The Library of Congress Civil War Desk Reference*. New York: Simon & Schuster, 2002.

Wallechinsky, David and Irving Wallace. *The People's Almanac*. Garden City, NY: Doubleday & Co., 1975.

Walton, Gary and Ross M. Robertson. *History of the American Economy*. New York: Harcourt, Brace and Jovanovich, 1983.

Ward, Geoffrey C. and Ken Burns. *Not For Ourselves Alone: The Story of Elizabeth Cady Stanton and Susan B. Anthony*. New York: Alfred A. Knopf, 1999.

Warner, Ezra J. Warner. *Generals in Blue: Lives of the Union Commanders*. Baton Rouge: Louisiana State University Press, 1999.

Warren, Louis. *Lincoln's Youth: Indiana Years, Seven to Twenty-one, 1816-1830*. Indianapolis: Historical Society, 2002.

Waugh, John C. *The Class of 1846: From West Point to Appomattox: Stonewall Jackson, George McClellan, and their Brothers*. New York: Ballantine Books, 1994.

Whipple, Wayne. *The Story-Life of Lincoln: A Biography Composed of Five Hundred True Stories Told by Abraham Lincoln and His Friends*. Philadelphia: Johns C. Winston Company, 1908.

Whitney, Henry C. *Life on the Circuit with Lincoln, with Sketches of Generals Grant, Sherman, and McClellan, Judge Davis, Leonard Swett, and Other Contemporaries*. Boston: Estes and Lauriat, 1892.

Wills, Garry. *Lincoln at Gettysburg: Words that Remade America*. New York: Touchstone, 1992.

Wilson, Douglas L. and Rodney O. Davis, ed. *Herndon's Informants: Letters, Interviews, and Statements about Abraham Lincoln*. Urbana, IL: University of Illinois, 1998.

———. *Lincoln Before Washington: New Perspective on the Illinois Years*. Urbana, IL: Illinois University Press, 2006.

Woods, Michael. "Lincoln's Health Draws Scrutiny," *Post-Gazette National Bureau*, July 25, 2000.

Index

C

D

E

F

G

H

I

M

N

O

P

Q

R

S

X

Y